T0371749

Project Management Theory and Practice

Project Management Theory and Practice

Third Edition

Gary L. Richardson and Brad M. Jackson

CRC Press
Taylor & Francis Group
Boca Raton London New York

CRC Press is an imprint of the
Taylor & Francis Group, an **informa** business
AN AUERBACH BOOK

CRC Press
Taylor & Francis Group
6000 Broken Sound Parkway NW, Suite 300
Boca Raton, FL 33487-2742

Printed on acid-free paper

International Standard Book Number-13: 978-0-8153-6071-1 (Hardback)

Library of Congress Cataloging-in-Publication Data

Names: Richardson, Gary L., author. | Jackson, Brad M., author.
Title: Project management theory and practice/Gary L. Richardson, Brad M. Jackson.
Description: Third edition. | Boca Raton, FL : CRC Press, [2019]
Identifiers: LCCN 2018013784 | ISBN 9780815360711 (hb : alk. paper)
Subjects: LCSH: Project management.
Classification: LCC HD69.P75 R5225 2018 | DDC 658.4/04--dc23
LC record available at https://lccn.loc.gov/2018013784

Visit the Taylor & Francis Web site at
http://www.taylorandfrancis.com

and the CRC Press Web site at
http://www.crcpress.com

Contents

SECTION II FOUNDATION PROCESSES

SECTION IV SUPPORT PROCESSES

SECTION VI PROJECT EXECUTING, MONITORING, AND CONTROL

Preface

The roots of this effort go back many years in our collective attempts to install standard project development methodologies into large organizations. Also, through all those years we have been involved with projects of one kind or another. Around 2003, the roots of this effort began when one of the authors joined the University of Houston to teach project management thinking that it would be an easy subject given previous experience. However, it soon became obvious that this subject was not well documented in a student readable or model-type format. As a result, students struggled to get an understandable broad real flavor of the topic. Most of the textbooks on the market were either too sterilely academic, too narrow of an industry view, or too much real world "silver bullet" quick fix advice types. Based on that assessment, the vision of correcting that shortcoming began to take shape. After four years of thrashing around with the topic, the first edition of this text resulted. Over the next 10 years, two more iterations of this effort were produced, this being the third edition. The project model term for this type of evolution is "progressive elaboration." In plain language, that really means it can be done better and that is what this latest version has as its goal.

One major content target is to stay faithful to the Project Management Institute (PMI) Project Management Body of Knowledge (PMBOK®) Guide, which is considered to be the de facto standard for project management description. Beyond that, the goal is to make the verbiage readable and understandable. You as the reader will have to decide how well this effort matched these goals.

The academic program at the University of Houston is heavily based on the Project Management Institute's (PMI) model and curriculum guidelines. That bias formed the foundation for the text, but not the complete final table of contents. As packaged here, the core chapters not only stay reasonably close to the PMI model, but also attempt to show how this model fits a real-world project. In this regard, the material in the text is viewed as a companion to the technical model guide and should be of help to someone studying for various project management certifications.

There are several project-related sub-model frameworks sponsored by PMI today and many of these are covered in dedicated chapters of the text. Specifically, the following six major sub-model topics are discussed in some detail:

- Work Breakdown Structures (WBS)
- Earned Value Management (EVM)
- Enterprise project management (PMO)
- Portfolio management (PPM)
- Professional responsibility and ethics
- Agile life cycle

In addition, there are multiple chapters related to various other associated contemporary topics that are currently emerging in the industry.

Deciding how to define the final table of contents was more difficult than first envisioned. The introduction background section (Chapters 1–9) contains material outside of the model structure, but necessary to level set the reader background. Much of the middle text portions are drawn heavily from the 10 standard model knowledge areas (i.e., Chapters 10–25). Finally, other supplementary sections were added in Chapters 26–38 to make the overall package more complete. Specifically, discussions of advanced planning models and the project external environmental sections are all external to the core model detail.

Even though interest in the topic of project management is growing and maturing, this subject area is still in a relative neophyte maturity stage. In support of this writing effort, many industry experts have willingly shared their work and thoughts in their areas of expertise to help explain specific items. This input has been incorporated with credit and hopefully the resulting material shown does not distort the originator's intent. Based on the logic outlined above we believe the resulting package represents a legitimate overview of the project management environment today, but also recognizes that there is more left to evolve.

Some chapters of the text clearly push beyond the basic model view and some extrapolate beyond current practice. Please accept these few ventures as an attempt to broaden the current perspectives and offer a potential future pathway for the overall topic. These jumps in faith were carefully taken and directionally seem appropriate. At least they should stimulate thinking beyond the pragmatic view. Any professional working in this field needs to both understand the current model views and also be prepared to evolve those over time. In all the topics covered here one must note that time and technology have the potential to change the way a particular item may be properly handled.

The writing style used is not meant to be overly formal in the hope that it would create a more willing reader. Reading a dull project management text can be much like going to the dentist for a root canal. The authors originally proposed the new title to be *50 Shades of Project Management* in the hopes that the reader population would be more eager to pursue the material, but some in the publishing world felt that to be too excessive.

One way to gain a better perspective about project management is to observe the outside world—for example, road and building construction, IT projects, bad customer processes, and generally poor project execution in an organization. Realize that the basic role of a project is to change the current state and do that effectively. That process is not as easy as one might believe. Bon voyage.

Gary L. Richardson
University of Houston

Brad M. Jackson
cordin8

Acknowledgements

No effort of this scope and complexity could have been accomplished by one person in any reasonable time frame. This text is no exception to that rule. During the early incubation period (circa 2002), several colleagues provided stimulus for this effort. The first influence came from Walter Viali who is a 30-year professional associate who convinced us that the PMBOK® Guide and PMI were the right thought leaders to provide the foundation structure for the university academic program. That has proven to be a successful core strategic decision for the university program, as well as for this text. Rudy Hirschheim, Blake Ives, and Dennis Adams were instrumental in helping start the academic side of this venture. Later, Michael Gibson provided the final push and support to allow time to complete the first edition draft material. Ron Smith (PMP and CSPM) provided several of his published worksheets and helped customize these for use as end of chapter examples. And thanks to Teri Butler who taught me about chip theory and a lot of other soft skill things.

Industry gurus Watts Humphrey, Walt Lipke, Tom Mocal, Max Wideman, Frank Patrick, Lawrence Leach, and Don James contributed ideas, reviews, or material in their respective areas of expertise. Other sources such as PMI, The Standish Group, QPR, QSM, and the Software Engineering Institute shared their Intellectual Property.

Jerry Evans, Dan Cassler, and Ron Hopkins, my University of Houston office mates, continually provided an environment of friendly warmth and fun that may well be the most important support of all. Last but not least, Bob Fitzsimmons continued our 60-year friendship with frequent moral support and he became the volunteer chief graphics artist along the way.

Over the past several years, we have been blessed with having captive project management graduate students digging through this material and helping to make it more readable. The resulting text material is a compendium of intellectual thoughts and ideas from all the sources mentioned above, plus my own experiences. I have tried to credit the sources that were used and if any were missed it was unintentional.

Finally, my wife Shawn's tolerance through what seemed like endless nights and weekends in the Man Cave study upstairs must be recognized. Without her support this effort could not have been finished.

Gary L. Richardson

At the beginning of my career, I had the opportunity to explore emerging technologies, specifically, the application of collaborative technologies, in Texaco's Technology Planning, Assessment, and Research group headed by Gary L. Richardson. He also served on my Master's degree thesis committee. His philosophy of getting out of the way and letting the teams drive the work was empowering and produced innovative results. It was truly an honor when Gary asked me to work on the 3rd edition of his already successful project management textbook.

Over the years, my interests have formed around the intersection of organizations, teams, processes, and technology. At Texaco, Ed McDonald provided sponsorship for my research initiatives centered around technology-enabled, team-based organizations. Through those projects, I had the opportunity to work with great thought leaders on collaborative work systems, including Gerry DeSanctis, Scott Poole, Gary Dickson, Bob Johansen, Lynda Applegate, and Jay Nunamaker.

After leaving Texaco, I embarked on an initiative to develop a software platform, cordin8, with my business partner and collaborator, Andy Kalish, to deliver on a vision of an "organizational operating system." At the heart of this system are project teams. The framework that provides the structure for these teams is based on the PMBOK® Guide. Through engagements and prototype reviews, I've had the opportunity to work with so many knowledgeable practitioners all of whom helped form the development of the feature set in cordin8, including Rod Sipe, Chris Bragg, Tom Mochal, Mohamed Sherif, Ken Fitzgerald, Ben Lanius, and Walter Viali.

As an organizational technologist, I view project management as the language to manage the knowledge work component of an organization (e.g., research, engineering, development, marketing). While the technology platform has a heavy computational role in project management, I believe a much more valuable role resides in its communication capacity. For communications to be effective and efficient, there must be an agreed upon framework that everyone understands. That is why I believe anyone interested in management needs a foundation in project management.

Lastly, my utmost appreciation to my wife Alexis for her incredible support throughout all these years. She is truly a remarkable woman.

Brad M. Jackson

Authors

Gary L. Richardson is currently the PMI Houston Endowed Professor of Project Management at the University of Houston, College of Technology graduate level project management program. This program serves both the internal and external community and is focused on teaching the theory and practice of project management. Gary comes from a broad professional background including industry, consulting, government, and academia.

After graduating from college with a basketball scholarship, he served as an officer in the U.S. Air Force, leaving after four years of service with the rank of Captain. He followed this as a manufacturing engineer at Texas Instruments in the Government Products Division. Later non-academic experience involved various consulting-oriented jobs in Washington DC for the Defense Communications Agency, Department of Labor, and the U.S. Air Force (Pentagon). A large segment of his later professional career was spent in Houston, Texas with Texaco, Star Enterprise (Texaco/Aramco joint venture), and Service Corporation International in various senior IT and CIO level management positions. Interspersed through these industry stints he was a tenured professor at Texas A&M and the University of South Florida, along with adjunct professor stints at two other universities prior to arriving at the University of Houston in 2003. Through these various job experiences, he has held professional credentials as PhD, PMP, Professional Engineer, and Earned Value Management. He has previously published seven computer and management-related textbooks and numerous technical articles.

Gary earned his BS in Mechanical Engineering from the Louisiana Tech, an AFIT post-graduate program in Meteorology at the University of Texas, a MS in Engineering Management from the University of Alaska, and a PhD in Business Administration from the University of North Texas. He currently teaches various project management courses at the University of Houston, plus PMP and project management external education courses.

His broad experience in over 100 significant-sized projects of various types through his career has provided a wealth of background in this area as he observed project outcomes and various management techniques that have occurred over this time.

Brad M. Jackson is co-founder and CEO of cordin8, who are the developers of a software platform that facilitates enterprise-wide team work in key management processes, including: strategy execution, cyber risk management, PMO, program management teams, account management teams, quality improvement teams, and leadership teams. In this endeavor, he has worked with over 100 organizations across multiple sectors and geographical locations to improve their organizational performance.

He began his career as a systems analyst at Texaco, which included a stint in the Technology, Planning and Research group of the corporate IT department. He was later appointed as Assistant to the CIO supporting the coordination of global IT management and standards. He has served as an adjust professor and as a research affiliate with a non-profit technology forecasting organization. Mr. Jackson holds a BS from the University of Arkansas and an MS from the University of Houston, both in computer science.

CONCEPTUAL OVERVIEW OF THE PROJECT ENVIRONMENT

I

This initial section is designed to level set the reader with various basic concepts from the project management field. Upon completion of this section, the following concepts should be understood:

1. Definition of a project and its general characteristics
2. Basic history of project management
3. An understanding of the typical challenges facing project managers
4. Benefits of the project management process
5. An introductory overview of the Project Management Institute's project model
6. Some of the contemporary trends that are changing the view of project management
7. Basic project scope, time, and budget mechanics
8. Key project vocabulary that is needed to understand the more detailed sections that follow later in the text
9. A statistical overview of project success factors

Chapter 1

Introduction

The term *project* occupies the central theme of this text and it is a frequently used descriptor; however, there are many different perspectives regarding what the term means. A collection of key words from various sources and individuals will typically include the following terms in their definitions:

1. Team
2. Plan
3. Resources
4. Extend capability
5. Temporary
6. Chaos
7. Unique
8. Create
9. State transition

From these diverse views it would be difficult to construct a universal definition that neatly included all the terms, but collectively they do say a lot about a project's composition. The Project Management Institute (PMI) defines a project as:

> *A temporary endeavor undertaken to create a unique product, service, or result.*
>
> *(PMI, 2017, p.715)*

One key thesis of this text is that all projects fit the same conceptual model with only degrees of variation across the elements. That view has now become reasonably accepted as users begin to understand the concept of variability. Some projects have very high risk and others less so. Same is true for high versus low use of third-party vendors, etc. The common key in all these is that a team of skilled workers is collected to produce a defined outcome, hopefully within a planned schedule and budget. The management model outlined here fits this description and there is no intent to focus on IT, construction, manufacturing, or any other area of endeavor. It is important to understand that the model is universal. It fits lawsuits and medical research. Similarly, thinking the

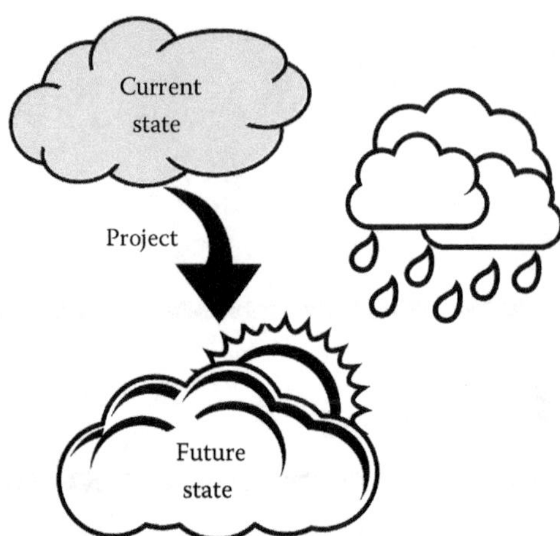

Figure 1.1 Project state transition process.

same way, one's personal life is a project and all of these same variables are at play in that context as well. So, let your mind stay open and test the concept. In the modern organization, the project model is used to accomplish many of their planning goals, that is, moving the organization from state A to state B (state transition). For these endeavors, resources are allocated to the target, and through a series of work activities the project team attempts to produce the defined goal. Typical goals for this type of activity involve the creation of a new product, service, process, or any other activity that requires a fixed-time resource focus.

Figure 1.1 is a visual metaphor to illustrate what a project is attempting to accomplish. The two fuzzy clouds depict an organization moving from a current state to a future state. The arrow represents the project team driving this movement. From an abstract point of view, the role of a project is to create that movement, whether that represents an organizational process, new product development, or some other desired deliverable.

Projects should be envisioned as formal undertakings, guided by explicit management charters and focused on enterprise goals. Practically speaking, this is not always the case, but given the nature of this text we need to reject projects that are not focused on improving the goal status for the organization and those that do not have the explicit support of management. Any other initiatives are not examples of a project, but rather contribute to "ad hoc chaos."

1.1 Project Management

The management of a project consists of many interrelated management pieces and parts. PMI defines this term as follows:

> *The application of knowledge, skills, tools, and techniques to project activities to meet the project requirements.*
>
> *(PMI, 2017, p. 716)*

One of the first management issues is to define the scope, schedule, budget, and resources required to produce the required output. These parameters are fundamental to all projects.

Closely related to this set is the concept of quality, which relates to both the project target and the work processes used to achieve that target. Collectively, these items represent some of the more visible components involved in project management. Supporting this activity group is another collection of items related more to "how" the goal will be accomplished. This second grouping of management focus activities involves more aspects of human resources, plus issues related to procurement, communications, and risk. During the course of the project, all of these topic areas interact with each other and therein lays the management complexity related to this topic.

1.2 Role of the Project Manager

Essentially, the role of a project manager (PM) is to "make it happen." This does not mean that he is the best engineer, programmer, or business process technician. It does mean that he has the necessary skills to acquire, develop, and manage a team of individuals who are capable of producing the desired product. Every project has unique characteristics and therefore the roles required change accordingly. The current state of understanding for this role has defined the basic knowledge areas (KAs) involved in this activity, but the operational techniques for creating productive project teams is still a fragile art form.

Many project success and failure studies have documented the basic factors leading to these conclusions. As projects have become more complex there is growing recognition that a skilled PM is the glue that brings these elements together. This involves the more mechanical management elements, but probably more important is the use of softer management skills for team motivation, conflict resolution, user communications, and general negotiation. We must not forget that project management involves humans and will never be reduced to a mechanical exercise. Nevertheless, the mechanical aspects are an important part of the overall management process in identifying what actions are required to influence changes. For example, to know that a project schedule is overrunning requires a complex set of decision processes, but does not in itself do anything about resolving the issues. Conceptualize the mechanical side of the management role as a meter—if your car's gas gauge is near empty this will stimulate the driver to seek out a gas station. Similarly, if the project schedule is not going according to the plan, the mechanical management processes help identify where and why. Recognize that other management action is also influenced by the status meter readings.

1.3 PM Skills

We are tempted to say that the ideal PM skills are the ability to "leap tall buildings with a single bound, faster than a speeding bullet, and more powerful than a locomotive," but that statement might be a little excessive (that comes from an old memory somewhere). However, it is accurate to say that this individual needs to understand how to deal with the various KAs involved, with additional high skills in both personal and organizational areas. Project dynamics create an amazing array of daily issues to resolve. If one cannot organize this activity into some workable process the project will stagnate. Through all this, it is the PM's goal to achieve the plan. Industry project failure statistics indicate that this is more difficult than is understood by most.

At the highest level, the PM needs to bring structure and organization to his project team. One senior PM once described this problem as "putting a lot of mush in a small bucket." A significant aspect of this is formalizing the roles and relationships of the various players in regard to their functions in the life cycle.

A second PM-level skill view is that he needs to be recognized as a leader of the effort. This does not mean that he is out front shouting "follow me," but he has to ensure that the team continues to move toward the required target. During early project phases, the target is not well defined, so the leadership role at that point is to bring the proper players together and help resolve various conflicts that typically emerge.

The third critical skill involves dealing with the various human resources related to the project. The most noticeable group will be the project team who ultimately will be the "builders." They collectively have the skills to execute the plan, but there are many human relationship issues that can get in the way of that effort. Project team members must be managed and nurtured through the life cycle. To properly do this, the PM needs to be an operational psychologist who understands individual and group needs. Project teams are a cauldron of human emotions. Kept at the right temperature they can produce amazing results; however, when allowed to boil the conflict can destroy the process. Finally, during this process, an additional role of the PM is to improve the skills of the team members and ensure that they are properly relocated at the end of the project.

In addition to the internal project team, there will be other human interactions with external groups such as users, management, and various organization entities. Each of these has a different perspective regarding the project and all their views must be dealt with. In each these cases, the PM is never given enough formal power to edict solutions even if he knew what the solution was. These human relationships require a more open communication and a more motivational style with the approach being to build partnerships. Each of the human interface groups holds a piece of the project success and the PM must extract that piece from each. This aggregation of project participants is called *stakeholders*. The formal PMI definition for this group is "An Individual, group, or organization that may affect, be affected by, or perceive itself to be affected by a decision, activity, or outcome of a project, process, or portfolio" (PMI 2017, p.723).

1.3.1 Success Management

The first step in success management is to understand the factors that lead to that conclusion. The basic management model outlined in this text offers a reasonably clear set of processes to achieve that goal. However, the organizational environment in which a project exists may contain factors that still make success unlikely. In some cases, a PM is assigned Project Titanic (i.e., a good ship may still sink because of other external circumstances). When this happens, it is important to realize that evidence now indicates decisions made by the crew of the Titanic actually caused it to sink faster than it would have if left on the iceberg. Of course, the best decision was to stay away from the iceberg in the first place. Therefore, in both situations a catastrophe could have been mitigated with the right management decisions. Here we see that a bad management decision can make a complex situation disastrous. The same conclusion is valid for the project environment. A good PM certainly has if they can find the right pathway through the project icebergs.

So, success management requires a series of strategies and related decisions. First, understand where success (or failure) comes from and mitigate as many of the problem factors as possible. Second, through the course of the project, the PM role is to influence the right set of actions to correct deviations that threaten to become a major problem. Third, when a threat surfaces take quick action using all the management skills at hand. Finally, if the boat is in fact sinking, you also have the role of communicating status and recommendations to all participants regarding how to handle the situation. Management will have been informed of status and forecasts along the way. In all of these modes, the PM must be both a leader and an *honest broker of information*.

One might ask "If we follow all these prescriptions, will every project be successful?" Probably not! There are too many uncontrollable variables to expect that, but proper use of the tools and techniques described here should significantly improve the outcome. If we continue to look at what went wrong with the last project and try to ensure that the previous item does not recur, the next project should progress better. Experience from the Japanese quality programs has taught the world how continuous improvement actions over a long period can take a country from a crude tool maker to the Toyota/Lexus manufacturer in slightly over 60 years. Likewise, we must realize that project management is not a short-term band-aid event; it is a process. Organizations must strategically focus on it and individuals must study it in order to achieve the desired results.

1.4 Text Content and Organization

This text looks at the project experience from the view of a PM. Material covered in the text has been selected from a personal database of "things I wished that I had known more about" at one point or another along the way. Also, in recent years the PMI has documented a great deal of professional project experience into the published archives on this topic and their documentation suite is respected internationally. Over the past several years, the authors have been heavily involved in teaching this topic after many years in industry attempting to master it. Those two diverse experiences lead to the amalgamation found here. The text content is a mixture of the PMI model view and comparable views of various practitioners. Attempts to translate this material to university and industry groups have supported the belief that a proper realistic source document with a reasonable dose of theory, vocabulary, and practice would help someone desiring to understand the breadth of this topic. This was the initial goal that started this effort.

The text material makes a reasonable attempt to stay consistent with the *Project Management Body of Knowledge* (PMBOK® Guide) which is considered to be the defining model document from the PMI (2017). In addition to this treatise on the topic, PMI publishes other supporting project related standards such as OPM3, Work Breakdown Structure (WBS), Professional Ethics, and others (each of these will be discussed later).

The resulting collection of material contained here is a compilation of project management models, concepts, vocabulary, and trends. Through all these elements, the goal is to make each item fit into the big picture and more importantly keep the discussion on an understandable level. If the reader wades through this material to the end, we will even share the secret PM handshake (this is probably the only joke in the text so it needs to be tagged).

Another stimulus for this effort has been the emergence of a formal educational curriculum accreditation process for PMs. This initiative is titled by PMI as the Global Accreditation Curriculum (GAC) (PMI 2001) and it offers more specific guidance regarding the role of a PM. Prior to this, individuals seeking project management certification studied various reference sources and then pursued a formal certification exam hoping that they had been exposed to the right material. In an attempt to ensure that the material covered in the text fit the PMI accreditation structure that document was used to cross-reference section material content. Learning objectives for each section map to this formal curriculum. This is intended to give the text legitimacy in regard to that section's topic menu.

1.4.1 Text Structure

The text material is partitioned into eight major sections that are essentially envisioned as "peeling the onion" away to open up increasingly complex levels of the total picture. Each major section represents a designed layer and each successive one opens up a new more complex layer related to the overall topic. In the first nine chapters there is no assumption made as to the reader's background. These chapters represent the foundation material. Recognize that this material has been previously tested on university and outside consulting groups over several years. The one important disclaimer regards whether the material can be viewed as a tutorial for the PMI certification exams. The answer to that question is clearly no! This text covers the same material found in the PMI standard sources, but is not meant to prep a person for one of the certification exams. However, it does give the reader a background that will make that preparation much easier and helps in the conceptual understanding of project management and the PMI model.

The summary below outlines the goal of each major section:

Part I. Conceptual overview. This section consists of nine chapters that collectively lay the foundation for the rest of the text. Basic vocabulary and concepts are covered here.

Part II. Foundation processes. This section describes the core deliverable activities of project management—scope, schedule, cost, and quality. This set of processes represents only a starting point for the PM, but there is sufficient theoretical material to justify its focus. This topic area is isolated from other more complex concepts related to the execution and control delivery mechanics.

Part III. Soft skills processes. Increasingly over time there has been realization that project success is driven by a complex interaction of human resources more than simple mechanics. For that reason, this collection of soft skills occupies a focus section describing human resources, communications, stakeholders, and team management.

Part IV. Support processes. In addition to the core management activities, the PM must also understand the role of other support KAs. This section finishes the discussion of KAs with procurement, risk, and integration. Each of these topics represents critical management decision area for the PM and they collectively must be dealt with along with the other items from Sections II and III to produce a viable project plan. Upon completion of this section, the reader has been introduced to the full set of knowledge processes recognized in the basic model.

Part V. Advanced scheduling models. This section is designed to highlight the idea that the model can have alternative ways to view the life cycle. The terms adaptive, simulation, and critical chain are used to illustrate sample methods for this more advanced view.

Part VI. Project execution, monitoring, and control. At this point, the text material has covered processes to produce a viable project plan that has been approved by appropriate management. The effort now moves into execution and the management challenge here is to produce the planned output as defined and approved. Unfortunately, the management process becomes muddier at this stage. There is more human conflict emerging, as well as more change dynamics and what some describe as raw chaos. If these dynamics did not exist, the management role in execution would simply be "task checker." A better metaphor for this stage is to compare it to an airplane pilot in rough weather with various mechanical and environmental problems to deal with. Most of the material described here is still model driven, but an attempt is made to give the model more of a reality flavor.

There are many control-oriented aspects in the project life cycle. Various related techniques are separated here for discussion. Each of these represents an important control knowledge component that the PM needs to understand.

Part VII. Project Environmental Support. One metaphor for this section is that the project is a seed in the organizational flower pot. What this translates to is recognition that various organizational process and culture impact the project from external sources. One of the key culture factors that occur both internal and external to the project team is professional responsibility or ethics. One only needs to read the daily news to see why this topic is worthy of inclusion. PMI has issued a code of conduct for the PM and the tenets of this code must be understood. In addition, some text scenario examples are used to show that it is not only a real topic, but one that is often hard to decide how to deal with.

Appendices. Three additional background topics are included in the text package:

A. Financial analysis mechanics
B. Project templates—reusable tools
C. Document repository—project data base.

In each of these supplementary sections, the material shown is considered as valuable technical background for an item the working PM should understand and use as part of his tool kit.

References

PMI Accreditation, 2001. *Accreditation of Degree Programs in Project Management.* Newtown Square, PA: Project Management Institute.

PMI, 2017. *A Guide to the Project Management Body of Knowledge (PMBOK® Guide)*, 6th ed. Newtown Square, PA: Project Management Institute.

Chapter 2

Evolution of Project Management

2.1 Introduction

Project management is an increasingly important topic of discussion today because all organizations have encountered problems in implementing a new business process, product, service, or other initiative. When we examine how organizations pursue changes, invariably it involves organizing a team of people with chosen skills to do the job. Management of the activities to complete this class of task is what project management is about.

We are indeed living in interesting times in regard to the project topic. On the one hand, it is now generally recognized that a disciplined approach to managing projects yields positive value in the resulting cost, schedule, and functionality. However, there remains great conflict over exactly what discipline is to be used in this process. In addition to this philosophical discord, technology itself continues to bring new challenges to the organization such that it is often difficult to replicate a successful approach multiple times. Managing a project the same way may well produce different outcomes based on the subtle complex relationships inherent in the process. Also, new tools, techniques, and products continue to enter the marketplace making even five-year-old project management strategies look dated. Therefore, the challenge in navigating this mine-strewn environment is to explore the subject and distill nuggets of information that have stood the test of time and then attempt to pave a pathway that can survive the next wave of technical discontinuity. In order to understand how the current situation got to its present state let us take a quick look at some of the not too distant evolutionary stages that the approach to project management has moved through. History offers subtle insights into broad-scale phenomenon such as this. The stages outlined below are somewhat arbitrarily grouped, but are designed to highlight the more obvious driving factors that have changed the approach to managing high-technology projects.

By scanning any library or bookstore today, you will find shelves stocked with volumes of books explaining in varying detail methods useful for successful completion of projects. Each author has their own *guaranteed* project management strategy designed to ensure a triumphant conclusion; yet real-world statistics still show marginal results for most projects. This section does not intend to attempt to trace all the historic trodden paths related to this topic, but does attempt to look back at the people and concepts in history that have formed the foundations of project management on which modern day approaches are based.

2.2 Early History of Project Management

The basic principles related to the science of project management have evolved over many decades. This body of knowledge mostly evolved since the early 1900s and accelerated after the 1950s. Some very early projects were quite impressive in their scale, but these did not follow what we would call the modern project management style or organizational culture. Incubation of the modern thought process can be traced to the industrial age during the latter 1880s, which provided much of the catalyst for the application of a more scientific approach to the management of project and manufacturing processes. Studies and experiments conducted by pioneers in the field during the early part of the twentieth century further paved the way for the understanding of project management as it is known today.

One has to look only at the historical structures and monuments left behind in past centuries to conclude that some form of managing a project was in place at that time. It is unfathomable to imagine that the Great Pyramid of Giza, Great Wall of China, or any of the ancient Greek or Roman projects could have been completed without some type of project management that basically guided the work process and managed the variables involved. Each of these undertakings was constructed with nothing more than simple tools and manpower, often slave labor. The early project managers (PMs) were technicians or engineers, generally multi-skilled generalists who could deal with many situations (Kozak-Holland, 2007). The manager in these endeavors was most likely the architect/designer of the project who understood how it needed to be constructed and they were given the authority for allocating sufficient resources to that goal. This style of the multi-skilled technical generalist overseeing projects was the norm throughout the early period.

2.3 Application of Analytical Science

As organizational processes became more complex, many underlying aspects of getting work accomplished began to change. Most noticeably, the manufacturing process moved out of the craftsman's homes into formal factory settings where the products could be mass produced. This necessitated a tighter coupling of work processes and more refined versions of them. Toward the end of the nineteenth century, new technologies using electricity and internal combustion brought a further expansion of manufacturing complexity. Suddenly, employee (non-owner) managers found themselves faced with the daunting task of organizing the manual labor of thousands of workers related to the manufacture and assembly of unprecedented quantities of raw material (Sisk, n.d.). This phase basically marked the beginning point for the application of analytical science to the workplace. If one could point to a birth date for modern project management, it would likely be in the two initial decades of the twentieth century and the names summarized in the next section made the subject more visible to the masses.

2.4 Frederick Taylor and Scientific Management

Frederick Taylor is called the father of Scientific Management and his influence can be traced through much of the early evolution of project management thought. Taylor came from what was considered a privileged background, but entered into employment with the Midvale Steel Company of Philadelphia as a common laborer in the late nineteenth century. The prevailing wage system in place at the time was called piece work. That is, employees were compensated based on their production rate; more production meant more pay. One common practice for management was to monitor the payroll and as soon as workers began earning "too much," they would cut the piece rate to try to entice the workers to do more for less. In reaction to this, employees scaled back their output to keep the quota lower. This practice was called "soldiering" (Gabor, 1999, p. 13). Years later, this concept would be called peer pressure and became added to the behavior theory of management. Taylor saw this practice and even participated. Sometime later, he was promoted to gang boss at the mill and became determined to stop the soldiering. Being an engineer, his method of doing this was to find a way to define "scientifically" what a fair pay-for-performance formula would be. In order to do that, he had to research the best method for the job. This would be called process re-engineering in modern terms.

Taylor's application of systematic studies for various jobs and the time required to complete each task represented the roots of project management theory circa 1910. He conducted time studies of various jobs using a stopwatch. This later became a common activity in manufacturing organizations under the title Time and Motion study (Gabor, 1999, p. 17). By standardizing the work processes and understanding the needed times to complete tasks within those processes, Taylor was able to increase the output at the steel company.

Taylor was recruited to Bethlehem Steel Works, where he conducted what is his most famous experiment, based on the loading of pig iron (NetMBA, n.d.). The impetus for the experiment was a rise in price for pig iron caused by an increased demand for the product. Using his knowledge of work process and time studies, Taylor set about to increase the productivity of pig iron loading. This task required backbreaking labor, but over the course of time trained workers with the proper skills were put in place. The initial average daily load of pig iron per worker was 13 tons. By conducting time and motion experiments to determine the proper timing of lifting and resting the workers could increase the production to 47.5 tons per day (NetMBA, n.d.). What is not so readily defined in history is that the workers did not readily adopt Taylor's method, even though he showed that it was more productive. It took several more years before the concept of group behavior was better understood. As is the case with most improvements in management thought, each small step forward leaves behind other unanswered questions. In this case, why would the workers not want to produce more if they did not have to work harder (even with the inticement for more wages)?

Taylor became famous after testifying before the U.S. Congress on ways in which the U.S. railway system could be made more productive. This testimony was published in the New York Times describing how utilizing his theory would save the railroads one million dollars per day. One could argue that this was the first of the management "silver bullet" ideas that represented all you needed to know to solve basically any problem. Many of the historians we examine were not afraid to tout their solutions in this way. Taylor left his mark on the industry with his 1911 publication of *The Principles of Scientific Management*. The four key Taylor management principles were (Ivancevich et al., 2008, p. 143):

1. Develop a science for each element of a man's work that replaces the old rule-of-thumb method.
2. Scientifically select and then train, teach, and develop the workman. In the past he trained himself as best as he could.
3. Heartily cooperate with the men so as to ensure that all the work is done in accordance with the principles of the science that has been developed.

4. There is almost an equal division of the work and the responsibility between management and workmen. Management takes over all work for which it is better fitted than workmen, while in the past almost all of the work and the greater part of the responsibility were placed on the workmen.

These early foundation concepts provided the framework from which modern project management evolution can be traced today.

2.5 Frank and Lillian Gilbreth

The fun trivia fact about these two individuals is that they were the subject of a classic 1950 movie titled "Cheaper by the Dozen." Clifton Webb and Myrna Loy were parents with 12 children and this was in reality the story of the Gilbreths. To suggest that they were experts in time and motion study would be obviously true. Frank Gilbreth and Frederick Taylor first met in 1907, which resulted in Frank becoming one of Taylor's most devoted advocates. As a result of this influence Frank and Lillian developed what the world came to know as time and motion studies (IW/SI News, 1968, p. 37). They collected numerous timing data on small human motions and cataloged the timings so that a trained analyst could construct "synthetic" time standards without having to measure an actual worker. These small time units were called "Therbligs," which is essentially Gilbreth spelled backward.

Through this pioneering research the Gilbreths contributed greatly to the knowledge of work measurement. Lillian was one of the first female working professionals with a PhD. Her focus was on the worker and she attempted to show how scientific management would benefit the individual worker as well as the organization (IW/SI News, 1968, p. 37). Frank utilized technology, including clocks, lights, and cameras to study work processes. The effort and intensity with which the Gilbreths pursued their chosen field of scientific study is most notably showcased in their time and motion study of bricklayers. In this study the Gilbreths observed the processes needed for a group of bricklayers to complete the installation of a wall. As stated in their biography printed in the September 1968 issue of the *International Work Simplification Institute* newsletter, the Gilbreths were able to reduce the number of basic motions needed for laying a brick from 18 to 4.5 (Gilbreth Network, n.d.). This scientific method was used to show how improved processes would make workers more productive and efficient. During this period there was an expanding recognition that the workers themselves had something to do with productivity, but for now, close supervision was the solution.

2.6 Henry Gantt

No discussion on the beginnings of project management would be complete without mentioning the contribution to the field by Henry Gantt. Gantt himself was an associate of Frederick Taylor in the late 1890s and he first documented the idea that work could be envisioned as a defined series of smaller tasks. Gantt was influenced in his view through involvement in Navy ship construction during World War I. A concise explanation of Gantt's contribution comes from the Gantt Group's document "*Who was Henry Gantt?*" (Gantt Group, 2003). It states, "He broke down all the tasks in the ship construction process and diagrammed them using the now familiar grid, bars and milestones." This familiar time grid is now called the *Gantt chart.* It remains today the most used planning and control document in industry after more than 100 years (see Figure 2.1).

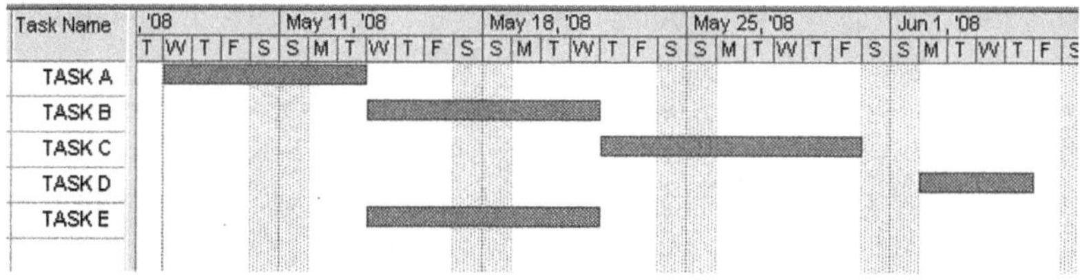

Figure 2.1 Sample Gantt chart.

Note that the Gantt chart defines tasks and times through the use of horizontal bars. The completed chart provides an overall view of the timeline and tasks needed to complete the project. The appearance and use of this format chart has many variants, but the basic idea has changed little since its conception. We will see more of this chart later in a modern context.

2.7 Mary Parker Follett

With the increased study of work processes and methodologies, industries began looking more at how to do the work than who was doing the work. Mary Parker Follett stepped out from behind scientific management theory and changed the focus more on the human element. She opposed Taylor's lack of specific attention to human needs and relationships in the work place (Ivancevich et al., 2008, p. 13). From this action, Follett takes the honor for spawning the behavioral side of management and was one of the first management theorists to take this view.

Follett focused on the divisions between management and workers: more specifically, the role of management instructing workers on what was to be done and how it was to be done. Follett believed that each worker had something to contribute and the amount of knowledge held by workers was not being tapped. She believed that it would benefit the workplace and all of society if instead of working as individuals or separate groups that these groups or individuals worked as a whole, so the modern view of teams was now part of the equation, although without an operational theory to support it.

Treating workers as something other than a means to get the task done was a concept that was counter to the Taylor school of thought. Gabor in her book *The Capitalist Philosophers* states that Follett's ideas came to be embraced by the most forward-looking management thinkers of her time, many of them also admirers of scientific management. Ironically, Follett's views of focusing on the worker would be accidentally validated in the future from the classic scientific management-oriented Hawthorne experiment.

2.8 Elton Mayo

The evolution of scientific management principles continued into the mid-1920s, following the concepts laid down by Taylor and his disciples. This area of study had attracted its share of detractors, such as Mary Parker Follett, but the visible quantification related to the scientific approach also attracted many to that school of thought. The *Taylorites* saw the factory as a complex set of processes that needed to be optimized and taught to the worker. Eldon Mayo and his research team followed that general principle in believing that one of the keys to improving productivity lay in improving the physiological environment of the worker. Looking back, we see elements from both the Taylor and Follett schools of thought in this view. At any rate, this premise led to what is known as the famous Hawthorne experiments (Gabor, 1999, p. 85).

The Hawthorne experiments were conducted by Mayo and his team from around 1927 to 1932 in Cicero, Illinois at the Western Electric Hawthorne Works. These experiments were designed to examine physical and environmental influences (e.g., brightness of lights, humidity, etc.) on worker productivity. Later versions of this effort moved into the more psychological aspects to include work breaks, group pressure, working hours, and managerial leadership (Envison, n.d.). The initial studies focused on the effect that changing light intensity might have on productivity. The results of this experiment were initially very confusing to the cause-and-effect-oriented researchers. They observed that an increase in light intensity corresponded to an increase in worker output; however, as the lighting decreased, productivity continued to show an increase. The puzzled researchers wondered what outside variables had not been considered and set about laying out a second cause-and-effect experiment in the relay assembly process.

The relay assembly control test room was set up to measure the productivity of workers under a myriad of changing conditions. Despite varying worker environmental conditions regarding work break durations and length of the work day, output continued to rise regardless of the change. This simply did not fit the Scientific Management principles of cause and effect. Eventually, analysis of this set of experiments would open the door wide in understanding some initial concepts related to worker motivation. In these experiments, essentially none of the chosen test variables were responsible for the worker behavior. It took more analysis before a cause-and-effect relationship was determined and this changed the field of modern management.

In the aftermath of the Hawthorne experiments, interviews were held with the test subjects. The results showed that the participants had formed their own social network that was different from the norm on the factory floor. Later analysis concluded that the test subjects felt as though they belonged to something special by being a part of the experiments. They were special because someone was paying attention to them. As a result of this new feeling, they wanted to produce like special workers should. In actuality, the group was purposefully randomly selected and was no more special than the hundreds of other workers outside of the control room. The conclusion now known as the *Hawthorne Effect* is described in the article "The Hawthorne Effect—Mayo Studies Motivation" (Envison, n.d.). The results of these studies formed the basis for the foundation of what is the modern-day behavior school of management.

2.9 Phases of Project Management Evolution

Intermingled with the basic management thought evolution was a corresponding evolution of project management thought. Description of this phase is somewhat arbitrarily started in the mid-1940s when large, time-critical projects exploded on the scene as a result of World War II.

Stage I: The first major epoch of modern project management came in the mid-1940s with the atomic bomb Manhattan project, plus other complex military programs that added much insight into methods for completing this class of complex endeavor. In the period following World War II, these methods were translated into more formalized and documented approaches, which became known as project methodologies. Military projects continued to push the technology envelope into the 1960s and this further increased pressure to improve technical project management. Many credit the activities surrounding the successful design and implementation of the highly complex contractor-developed Polaris nuclear submarine project in the 1960s as the beginning of broad non-military acceptance of a model-driven approach to project management. This ushered in the popularization of classic network management methods such as Program Evaluation and Review Technique (PERT) and Critical Path Method (CPM), which proliferated into all industries after this time. These early planning and control models were initially able to be used only in large organizations because high-priced computing resources were required to manipulate the network models. Further proliferation of these tools had to wait until low-cost and robust computer processing technology emerged in the 1970s.

Stage II: The 1970s and 1980s brought tremendous expansion in hardware and software technology offerings. Proliferation of minicomputers broke the cost barrier for operational modeling and this opened the door for improving planning and tracking of project status. General knowledge of the CPM-type network model existed, but there was still minimal understanding of the underlying management processes required to effectively utilize the model. Also, during this period, vendors sold "canned" methodologies claiming that they would universally solve the project management problem, but they seldom did. By the 1980s, the United States was in an economic boom and the key requirement for organizations was more toward speed of delivery than efficiency or quality. Improving the management approach to projects was low on the priority list.

A second constraining factor during this period was the organizational rethinking of the central IT department that up until that time had held the keys to accessing computing power. The 1970s ushered in smaller computing devices (minis and personal devices) and that trend further expanded user-based computation needed to make some of the project management tools available for general use. Over the 1980s and into the 1990s there was a deluge of new software produced for this environment and from this stimulus the project management maturity rate increased significantly. However, for one living through this era it seemed that little conceptual project management theory progress was made as organizations were moving from the highly controlled central mainframe computers controlled by a single department to a more distributed hardware environment with a "do whatever you want by yourself" mentality. Software maturity was outrunning the infrastructure necessary to support it with usable data. During this period, academic organizations and consultants published concepts, theories, and management strategies that would have moved the project discipline further along, but the general project audience was not yet convinced that a better approach to project management added value to the result. Many looked at available software and other defined documentation as requiring too much overhead and some still feel to this day that the current models add little value to the process. The favored development model during this period was one based on speed of product delivery and purchasing software from third parties. The latter strategy was thought to take away many of the needs for project management since "the code was already written," or that was the problem for the subcontractor to solve. Subsequent massive system development failures with attempts to install these "pre-written" systems uncovered yet another perspective. That is, there is more to successfully executing a project than loading code into a computer or buying some vendor's management methodology. Therefore, by the end of the 1980s, there was a new level of project management understanding. "Silver bullet" magic solutions continued to emerge, but none solved the issue of poor project outcome results as documented by ongoing surveys.

Stage III: As history evolved past the 1990s, so too did the availability and thought process related to the project management environment. Organizations such as the Project Management Institute (PMI) began to have an international presence and this brought increased interest and understanding in the topic. In this spirit, the 1990s are viewed as a period of maturation and proliferation of information tools, techniques, and user literacy. Small and powerful desktop devices solved the hardware processing availability issue and the emergence of the Internet solved many of the information distribution constraints. However, neither maturity, technology, nor visibility did much to improve the organizational discipline regarding the management of projects.

User-oriented desktop tools such as Microsoft's Word, Excel, Powerpoint, and Access turned millions of users into what looked like programmers and the project world become flooded with small pockets of disorganized data stores. These new capabilities improved the look of project documentation, but the underlying management processes or tools were not appreciably improved.

Another evolutionary thread emerged during this period in the form of improved software packages. During this wave, major mission critical systems were being replaced by suites of integrated commercial software packages as a strategy to cut computer expenditures. Names such as SAP, PeopleSoft, Oracle, J.D. Edwards, Lawson, and others became familiar terms. In many cases these "silver bullet" solutions often failed to accomplish their stated goals. In some cases, the results of these projects sometimes bordered on catastrophic for the organization. Once again, the primary reason for many of these failures was not the lack of purchased product quality, but the underlying process for selection and management of the process—this level of project complexity clearly showed the need for better understanding of the related management principles and process. Also, because these projects represented such a large resource commitment, there was an attempt to manage them in a professional way and yet they still failed to meet expectations of budgets, schedules, and functionality. Something was clearly not working right! The one item of good news coming from these failed initiatives was that the projects involved large segments of the organization and this uncovered another one of the missing issues in project management—that is, communications.

Because of these early experiences, the use of formal reporting processes and metrics related to project execution began to be recognized as a requirement and senior management became more interested in this aspect. Prior to this, the prevailing lack of computer literacy by management and the lack of appropriate project status metrics allowed projects to run under the radar of management scrutiny until the project was completely out of control. During the period of 2000 and beyond, there was a growing awareness that some type of prerequisite management process must be in place prior to embracing a complex highly technical undertaking, whether that be hardware, process, or software. Organizations that failed to understand this continued to believe that project management was simply an overhead and an added cost for no benefit. At this point organizations began to catalog the high cost of projects and recognize the failures. This stimulated more concern about management and the enterprise selection process for projects. Two major process initiatives spawned out of this. The first was a formalization of business cases to justify approval of a project. Second, there was a recognition that the organization might have hundreds or even thousands of projects either in work or proposed. Clearly, the process of initiating organizational projects was out of control and some formalization process was needed. The term *business case* became common as a formal technique to document the value of a project prior to approval. Second, data formalization of the organization portfolio of projects became known as *Project Portfolio Management (PPM)*. Also, project costs were being better captured with new financial systems and were now recognized as a major component of the enterprise capital budget. Expansion of this class of tools and procedures was stimulated as organizations strived to get control of the project runaway train. As the magnitude of the management problem began to be better understood the requirement for more rigorous project justification was further formalized and controlled.

During the 1990s, formal data collection and research began to uncover traits of project success and failure. As data on various project disasters began to be published, it highlighted that poor project performance was a general phenomenon and not one limited to local initiatives. As an example, the popular press chronicled a one-billion-dollar overrun for the new Denver airport that was essentially linked to a project management error; i.e., ineffective testing of the critical baggage handling system prior to installation. Also, various other large projects such as the FBI Terrorist Tracking System, multiple DoD weapons systems cost overruns, and Boston's Big Dig tunnel had similar results. Once broadly recognized, these outcomes became common fare for news reporting. The public was now in tune with the concept that much of this was a management problem. These daily news articles opened the door to increased sensitivity regarding the need to deal with the problem.

During the period from the 1960s through the 1990s, organizations attempted various management strategies to improve project results. Looking back on these efforts, they were lab experiments quite similar to the Hawthorne research—all essentially looking in the wrong place for the answer. Engineering-oriented professionals looked at the problem as a mechanical one, with little human influence. Some described this period as "finding a better mousetrap." Many root causes for failure were identified, but true fixes did not quickly emerge on a broad scale. Around this time organizations such as PMI became involved as an independent entity searching for solution techniques and through this effort pioneered the concept of a general project management model, which became known as the Project Management Body of Knowledge® Guide, or more commonly the PMBOK. Also, the Y2K (Year 2000) software bug phenomenon became widely discussed around 1998 and prognosticators predicted doom if all computer software was not repaired by the end of the decade. For the first time, global technical projects were perceived to require completion of their mission on time and within scope. For these reasons, the latter 1990s ushered in a worldwide recognition of project management. The technical and maturation events described here provided a broad view of what project management is and what it can contribute. We would be naïve to suggest that the problem is now ready for solution, but it is widely documented and discussed by industry and academia. So, we then enter what is defined here as Stage IV, the current trend view of topic.

Stage IV: The key philosophical question at this point is to forecast where the current trends will take the topic and in what time period. One view is that the current identified trends will continue to broaden across all organizations in essentially unaltered state. That is, new products, hardware, software, and telecommunications technology all driving the same processes but using the new tools and advanced technology for process, storage, and distribution. Also, it seems reasonable to predict that the global population in general will become more literate in the use of these tools and technologies. At the same time, the project environment will continue down the trail of increasing complexity and its methodologies will likely become more embedded in the fabric of everyday organizational work processes.

Certainly, one contemporary theme through this period is the dynamic nature of international organizations involvement in domestic projects. Just as the single organization project management model began to synthesize a workable set of tools and concepts for the organization, the operational model was transforming into a global model of loosely connected entities working on complex initiatives. Specifically, the globalization of organizational processes is now a reality and is being stimulated by the existence of low-cost foreign labor sources. This, in turn, has led to increased outsourcing to third parties. These initial outsourcing initiatives involved relatively simple organizational processes and they were marginally successful during the 1990s, but the trend continues to grow with some new approaches and a better understanding of how to manage such ventures. One of the major positive contributors to this is the increase in functionality and lower cost of international Internet telecommunications, which has in turn opened-up new vendor opportunities for distributing knowledge work. This has allowed the emergence of smaller niche vendors who do one function very well. In some cases, these niche vendors are often able to take over an entire business process at less cost than performing it internally. Each of these niche solutions changes the internal process of the organization and potentially changes the project management protocols related to those vendors. The number and scope of such activities is forecast to continue to increase.

Recent experience indicates that both local and international niche vendors can be successful in the marketplace because of their specialized skill level and lower cost, but once again we also see a trend that requires more complex project management techniques as the business process becomes fragmented across multiple organizational groups. As a result of these outsourcing trends, critical operational activities are being performed external to the consuming organization. One potential risk issue raised by this trend is the impact of an external vendor failure. This was a much more controllable situation in the traditional structure, but it can now have a significant negative impact on the organization and the project. Because of the complexity and loss of internal skills, a reverse migration of these processes becomes quite difficult. For this reason, risk management in such an environment takes on increased importance. A further risk extension of the contemporary trend for outsourced vendors is that they often reside in another country—an uncommon practice prior to the 1990s. Today, a full complement of technical service providers exists in locations such as India, Pacific Rim, China, South America, Russia, and others. These new technical entities continue to increasingly extract work from local U.S. organizations and this essentially changes the project management landscape.

With industry trends partially outlined above, there is an increasing need for more formalized and effective project management across the collaborative partner domain. Any new management processes hosted in this way must be compatible with the evolving business requirements of a global work force. As a result, planning, control, communication, and team collaboration are more critical processes in the contemporary environment. Experience has shown that the road to project success involves more than manipulating technology and tools. Success is clearly driven by proper management of the human element and the subsequent implementation of the output created by the project. In some ways, the project management tools are morphing into more of an operational management concept.

To support these contemporary organizational needs, a strong project management orientation is needed, and it will have to be sensitive to producing value for the organization and not just installing new products and processes. Organizations have now become sensitive to the issue of selecting the right project to start with. That often adds another layer of management to the traditional project view. Also, these organizations are demanding quicker cycle times from initiation to delivery, along with more complex visions. To gain respect, the project management function has to be seen by enterprise management as delivering value. One threat in such an environment is for the sponsoring entity to say, "if project management can't deliver this when I want it, I'll find another way."

History has shown that time pressure can cause planning to be ignored (i.e., planning is considered wasted overhead). Project management theory is built on the basic concepts of planning and control; therefore, it is going to be up to the profession to show value in a formal planning-oriented model. The dilemma with this is how to go fast and not make costly mistakes versus going slower and more successfully accomplishing the technical goals. Management wants to know how much formalization will cost and how much value it brings. That is difficult if you do not measure the process and learn from that along the way. Resolving this conundrum remains one of the toughest challenges of this period. To support this goal, there is a growing interest in new approaches to development now going under titles such as agile, Scrum, extreme, lean, spiral, critical chain, and other names. These new schools of thought focus on speed of delivery and customer satisfaction; less on initial planning and documentation. To date, many traditional managers have resisted most of these methods because they focus more on moving forward before a firm vision, cost, or schedule of the final deliverable is defined. One view of this approach is that lack of initial planning increases the future level of scope change and in turn makes the project cost more and may in fact then take longer to complete. The other school believes that user active involvement is the key, more than the formal planning process. There is insufficient proof for either side of this debate, but both appear to have positive and negative value positions. The result of this may be to conclude that each option focuses on different goal sets (e.g., schedule, customer satisfaction, cost, etc.). One of the more obvious potential benefits of the lower initial planning approach is customer satisfaction; however, the negative issues of management visibility and control are left to be dealt with. The key to future success in this arena is to find a proper blend of predefinition versus the increased customer satisfaction from a better match to their requirements. In the current traditional environment, most management groups will not approve a project without some reasonable view regarding the future project's functionality, resource commitment, cost, and schedule. This suggests at least some degree of planning to satisfy these requirements. Regardless of the final outcome, this is the methodology battleground for the next several years.

Each of the contemporary trends in project environment will bring new challenges to this arena. Certainly, the combination of business pressure for increased speed of delivery, increased use of purchased services, along with use of commercial off the shelf (COTS) packages, outsourced service providers, and use of offshore vendors impacts many aspects of the traditional project management model. This new environment will require an improved set of tools and strategies to navigate these initiatives successfully. Because of these dynamics, the subject of project management will remain under great conceptual stress, but will also be more recognized as a key requirement to success. Obviously, the management skill requirements for this class of project will be greater than those found in most organizations today. Because of these broad trends, one should not plan on a status quo approach to this subject over time. The new generation of PMs must evolve as the organizational environment evolves. Goals such as quicker and less cost will be the frequent drivers for the new model. More silver bullets will be introduced to accomplish this (i.e., less planning, less documentation, more technology, etc.).

2.10 Project Management Challenges

The upcoming challenges for PMs in the field involve how to deal with activities defined in a development life cycle and manage the associated technical resources. The following statistics provided by Successful Strategies International offer some insight into the current status of these two goals (SSI, n.d.):

- Twenty-four percent of organizations now cite inconsistent management approaches to their projects.
- Forty-six percent of the organizations cite management issues in the areas of task estimating and benchmarking.

On the positive front, development of project management capabilities integrated with the application of collaborative technologies has the potential ability to support a new level of globally efficient project management practices. As a result of this new capability, operational proficiency across functional management teams, organizations, and their business partners can concurrently view and interact with the same updated project information in real time, including project schedules, technical discussions, and other relevant communication activities. This capability becomes a prerequisite to move forward effectively with the underlying management processes.

2.11 Project Management Benefits

2.11.1 At the Macro Level

Senior management often has great interest and motivation in implementing processes that will help them evaluate status of projects. Previous goals for this were methods that focused on increasing status visibility, improving cycle times, delivering defined results on schedule, and meeting defined budgets. Based on the data available at this point the importance of senior management in project success is recognized, but remains a tough item to resolve.

2.11.2 At the Micro Level

At lower levels in the organization, there is frequent resistance to the discipline inherent in a formal project management approach because it is viewed as inhibiting personal flexibility. When pressured to conform, the local PM would likely describe his role as follows:

1. Customizing the project work to fit the operational style of the project teams and respective team members.
2. Proactively informing executive management of project status on a real-time basis.
3. Ensuring that project team members share accurate, meaningful, and timely project documents.
4. Ensuring that critical task deadlines are met.

The reality in accomplishing these goals is to understand that creating a mature project management environment is very difficult and even if successful does not assure project success. On the reverse side, doing nothing in this direction invites chaos.

So, what is the conclusion regarding the value of formalized project management? Some consultants would state that good project management techniques can produce up to a 25% savings for the project. If this could be proven to everyone's satisfaction, the only question would be "how fast can we start doing this?" Some would argue that every such historic attempt to implement increased project process formalization has been less than a success. Many top managers would more likely say that the organization has to do more because lack of process discipline is wasting money and they are in the dark as to status. Many on the technical side say that increasing process discipline is the cause of the efficiency problem. It is probably best to leave this question on the table and let the material in the text sell itself, or fail. So, as you the reader go through the following chapters try to ask yourself if the chapter set of concepts or techniques described seems reasonable compared to other approaches you may be familiar with.

References

Envison, n.d. The Hawthorne Effect—Mayo Studies Motivation. www.envisionsoftware.com/articles/Hawthorne_Effect.html (accessed August 14, 2008).

Gabor, A., 1999. *The Capitalist Philosophers*. New York: Times Business.

Gantt Group, 2003. Who was Henry Gantt? http://208.139.207.108/html/RGC-KO-04.htm (accessed March 28, 2008).

Gilbreth Network, n.d. Frank and Lillian Gilbreth Biographies. http://gilbrethnetwork.tripod.com/bio.html (accessed August 14, 2008).

International Work Simplification Institute, Inc. (IWSI), 1968. Pioneers in improvement and our modern standard of living. *International Work Simplification Institute News*, 18.

Ivancevich, J.M., R. Konopaske, and M. Matteson, 2008. *Organizational Behavior and Management*. New York: McGraw-Hill.

Kozak-Holland, M., 2007. History of Project Management. www.lessons-from-History.com/Level%202/History_of_PM_page.html (accessed March 27, 2008).

NetMBA, n.d. Fredrick Taylor and Scientific Management. www.netmba.com/mgmt/scientific (accessed March 27, 2008).

Sisk, T., n.d. The History of Project Management. www2.sims.berkeley.edu/courses/is208/s02/History-of-PM.htm (accessed March 28, 2008).

Successful Strategies International (SSI), n.d. How to Attain Project Success. www.ssi-learn.com/Downloads/Presentation%20-%20Attaining%20Project%20Success.pdf (accessed August 14, 2008).

Chapter 3

Project Management Model

3.1 Introduction

As indicated previously, the profession of project management has matured greatly over the past two decades and a large part of that has been a result of conceptualizing the project experience into an understandable model. Much of this recognition has come from efforts of organizations such as the Project Management Institute (PMI) and other similar international organizations. Through these collective efforts the topic of project management has become much more visible to an international audience and from this PMI is now recognized as de facto definer of the accepted model description; however there are other similar models defined. Two major competitor definitional models are PRINCE2, Projects IN Controlled Environments, from the UK and the Association of Project Management (APM), a Royal Chartered organization also in the UK. PRINCE2 approaches the project model view from the desired output, while the PMI model is more process and task oriented. APM focuses more on the training and professional interest groups than by sponsoring a custom model. Two other visible model sponsors are Australian Institute of Project Management (AIPM) in Australia and the International Standards Organization (ISO); however, in 2012 ISO adopted the PMI model. Based on international acceptance the material in this book follows the PMI model more specifically than the others mentioned.

3.2 Evolution of the PMI Model

PMI was founded in 1969 by a group of industry professionals who believed that a professional focus on project management processes was the right strategic answer for improving the management of projects. That view was further defined in 1975 with their goal statement to

> foster recognition of the need for professionalism in project management; provide a forum for the free exchange of project management problems, solutions and applications; coordinate industrial and academic research efforts; develop common terminology and techniques to improve communications; provide interface between users and

suppliers of hardware and software systems; and to provide guidelines for instruction and career development in the field of project management.

(Chumas)

Over time, PMI continued to formalize their view of the management process. By the 1990s it had grown to 90,000 members and the need to provide more standard definition to their message led to the 1996 issuance of a document called the Project Management Body of Knowledge, *PMBOK® Guide*, which is known in the industry today as the PMBOK. Over the next 20 years, six editions of this specification document have been released, with the sixth edition in late 2017. Each version expanded the view of project management in a term that PMI calls *progressive elaboration*. This is meant to imply that the topic is ongoing and admittedly has not reached what one would view as equivalent to an engineering discipline.

The evolution of PMI as an organization continued after the first PMBOK edition. In 1984, a credentialing effort was announced to formally recognize a project management skill level. This credential is called Project Management Professional (PMP) and is judged to be the gold standard in the industry today. The number of worldwide PMPs has grown exponentially over the 20-year time period. During this same period PMI continued to introduce various other certifications within the project management domain. The interested reader can trace further details on this aspect of the organizational evolution through www.pmi.org.

Through its 20 years of evolution the PMBOK became viewed as somewhat of a bible defining project management. Each iteration recognized some additional subtlety in the overall process and the size of the specification grew. In order to keep the material current, new editions of the PMBOK are planned for every four years. In its present state, this reference describes models and defines the project management life cycle processes and activities that should be evaluated and utilized in executing a project. The structure of this model is the guiding architecture for much of this text. Throughout these text chapters the goal is not to duplicate the technical material in the PMBOK, rather to show how it actually represents real-world type activities. Realize that the text material follows this model structure in sufficient detail to illustrate how it works in a real-world project environment, but should be considered a supplement to the full technical descriptions contained in the PMBOK.

The advent of a formalized view of project management has created an organized, intelligent, and analytical approach toward not only tackling large projects but the associated human and organizational issues as well. Since its inception, the guide has grown to become a standard that is recognized worldwide in terms of the knowledge, skills, tools, and techniques that collectively relate to the management and oversight of projects. The *PMBOK® Guide* (pronounced *pimbok*) is defined by PMI as

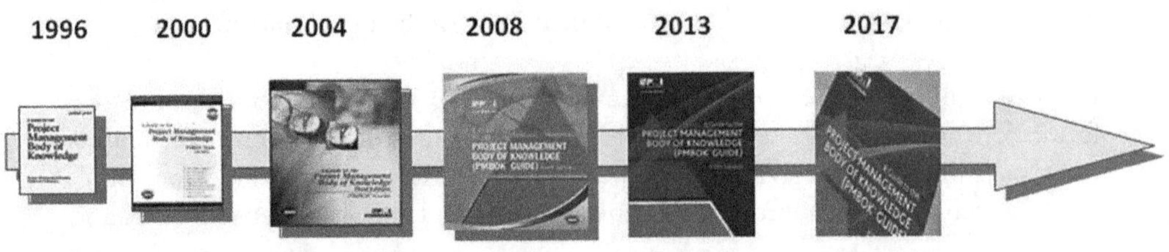

Figure 3.1 Evolution of the *PMBOK® Guide*.

> ...a term that describes the knowledge within the profession of project management. The project management body of knowledge includes proven traditional practices that are widely applied as well as innovative practices that are emerging in the profession.
>
> *(PMI 2017, p. 1)*

This model defines relevant project management processes and activities that should be utilized in executing a project. The text follows this model structure in sufficient detail to illustrate its management role in a real-world project environment. Those who wish to see the full PMI model processes and activity detailed descriptions can purchase the *PMBOK® Guide* through www.pmi.org, or other commercial sources.

3.3 Ancillary Standards and Certifications

PMI continues to provide knowledge and leadership in the standards and certification of project management principles. Beyond the PMP certification these are various other focus areas and certifications sponsored by PMI and all are internationally recognized. Details on these initiatives can be found at www.pmi.org. Each of the professional certification initiatives impinge on some aspect of the project world in some form. Chapter material related to technical background is given for several of the options. Each of these certifications would be considered a niche skill within the overall PMBOK.

- Agile Practitioner: See Chapter 25 for adaptive life cycles.
- *OPM3:* See Chapter 34; relates to organizational processes that support the project.
- *Certified Associate Project Manager (CAPM) Certification:* Similar to PMP certification for less experienced professionals.
- *Program Manager Certification (PMgP):* A senior manager certification for individuals who have a high level of experience and manage collections of large projects.
- *Risk Management Professional (PMP*): See Chapter 22.
- *Portfolio Management Professional*: See Chapter 35.
- Scheduling Professional (SP).
- *Professional in Business Analysis* (*PMI*-PBA): Designed for the individual who will be working on requirements and scope segments of the project.
- *Professional Responsibility Code:* See Chapter 38; a published set of code of conduct and ethics and responsibilities for the PM.
- *Work Breakdown Structure (WBS)*: See Chapter 12.
- *Earned Value:* See Chapter 31.

3.4 Structure of the *PMBOK® Guide* Model

Figure 3.2 shows a high-level view of the five major life cycle process groups defined by the *PMBOK® Guide*. The high-level groupings are as follows:

Initiating
Planning

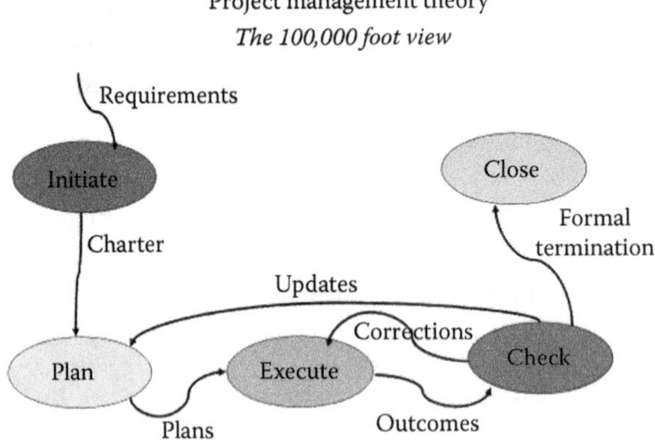

Figure 3.2 PMBOK process groups.

Executing
Monitoring and controlling
Closing

The flow arrows in Figure 3.2 imply that the five major phases are executed somewhat serially; however, the actual workflow is more iterative and complex than represented by this high-level diagram. In operation the planning cycle is iterative until a final agreed upon version is approved. During execution the theme is "work the plan," however the plan is also iterating through a change control process managed inside the Monitoring and Control (M&C) process. Also, the M&C process is designed to surround the four core work activity groups as a formal control shell. In this role it is designed to ensure that the project goals are being met through each of the stages. Embedded within these higher-level groups are 49 defined processes that represent fundamental management elements required to execute the project.

The role of each process (stage) group is summarized as follows:

Initiating: Outlines the activities required to develop the initial view and authorize the project or a project phase.

Planning: Attempts to outline the activities required to produce a formal project plan containing objectives, scope, budget, schedule, and other relevant information useful in guiding the ongoing effort.

Executing: Uses the project work plan as a guiding reference to integrate human and other resources in carrying out project objectives.

Monitoring and controlling: This process group of activities measures and monitors progress to identify plan variances and take appropriate corrective action.

Closing: Includes a group of activities required to formally shut down the project and document acceptance of the result.

The life cycle process described in the *PMBOK® Guide* requires that the proposed project be formally evaluated on its business merits, approved by management, formally initiated, and then undergo a detailed planning cycle prior to commencing execution. Within each life cycle step there is a coordinated management process designed to ensure that the project produces the planned results. Once the appropriate stakeholders and management have approved the project plan, the subsequent execution phase would focus on doing what the plan defines (nothing more and nothing less). Overseeing the execution phase and all other phases is an active monitoring and control process designed to periodically review actual status and take appropriate action to correct identified deviations. After all the defined project requirements are produced, the closing process finalizes all remaining project documentation and captures relevant lessons learned that are used to improve future efforts. When examined from this high-level perspective, the project model is a deceptively simple structure, but be aware that this simple view hides significant real-world challenges in executing the defined processes.

Scattered through the five process groups are 10 knowledge areas (KAs) and 49 associated defined management processes. The 10 KAs are summarized below with a brief description for each (PMI, 2017, pp. 22–23):

1. *Scope*—includes the activities necessary to produce a description of the work required to complete the project successfully.
2. *Schedule*—includes the processes related to manage timely completion of the project.
3. *Cost*—includes the processes related to plan, estimate, budget, fund, manage, and control costs.
4. *Quality*—includes the processes required to assure that the project will satisfy the operational objectives for which it was formed and within the organization's policy goals. This includes processes for quality planning, quality assurance, and quality control.
5. *Resources*—include the processes to identify, acquire, and manage resources needed for the project.
6. *Communications*—includes the processes related to ensure timely and appropriate timely information distribution and management related to the project.
7. *Risk*—includes the processes related to identifying and managing various risk aspects of the project.
8. *Procurement*—includes the processes required to purchase products and services for external sources.
9. *Stakeholders*—includes the processes required to identify and manage the individuals, groups, or organizations that can impact the project.
10. *Integration*—includes the processes and activities needed to integrate all of the other nine KAs into a cohesive and unified plan that is supported by the project stakeholders.

Embedded in each of the KAs lower-level process descriptions are the related inputs, tools and techniques, and outputs that drive each process. From this overall set of process specifications, the PMBOK provides a good high-level definitional roadmap for project management. However, this is not designed to be a cook book prescription to carry the project manager (PM) through all the somewhat abstractly defined steps. Rather it is a general knowledge model structure to provide guidance from which a specific project model can be constructed to fit unique project requirements. Experience and training are required to turn this standard model view into a specific operational project management tool and process.

3.4.1 Initiation

This process group is involved with the activities required to define and authorize the project or a phase. One of the most important aspects of the Initiation process is the evaluation of the vision from a goal alignment perspective. In other words, how does the vision support organizational goals? The decision to approve a project must also consider it in competition with other such proposals based on factors such as resource constraints, risks, technical capabilities, and so on. After consideration of these factors by management, formal approval to move the project into a more detailed and formal planning phase is signaled by the issuance of a formal Charter. This step outlines the basic approval of the project and the constraints under which it is to be governed. The model defines that a PM is formally named at this point to move the effort forward. Project Charters represent the formal authorization step and it formally signifies that management is behind the project.

3.4.2 Planning

This process group relates to the activities required to produce a formal project plan containing specified deliverable objectives, budget, schedule, and other relevant information to guide the subsequent ongoing effort. The principal goal of the Planning phase is to produce an accurate, measurable, and workable project plan that has considered the impact of all KAs. This particular phase consumes the second highest amount of resources in the life cycle and its goal is to lay out a path for execution that can be reasonably achieved. The key output from this phase is a formal project plan outlining not only the scope, schedule, and budget for the project but also how the project will deal with Integrating the other areas of Quality, Human Resources, Communications, Risks, and Procurement.

A great deal of formal documentation is produced in the various planning activities. First, each of the nine operational KAs would be defined in a related management plan outlining how that aspect of the project was to be managed. The most well-known examples of this would be the scope, cost, and schedule management plans; however, there would be similar plans for all of the KAs. Through an iterative process, each of the KA plans would be meshed (integrated) with the others until they are compatible with each other (i.e., HR, cost, schedule, risk, procurement, quality, etc.). The formal term for this is an Integrated Project Plan and the resulting planning documentation includes all the respective KA views for the project. This integrated plan would then be presented to management for approval. If approved, it establishes a baseline plan used to compare project status going forward. As changes in any of the KA elements occur the related artifacts would be updated so that the project plan remains a living document throughout the life cycle. This is an important concept—a static plan is considered wall covering.

3.4.3 Execution

This process group uses the project plan as a guiding reference to integrate all work activities into production of the project objectives. The actual project deliverables are produced in the execution phase. During this cycle, the PM has responsibilities including coordination of resources, team management, quality assurance, and project plan oversight. The initially approved project plan seldom, if ever, goes exactly according to the original vision. For this reason, it will be necessary to deal with unplanned variances, along with new work created by change requests that are approved by the project board. Another important activity is to communicate actual project results called work performance data. The ultimate execution goal is to deliver the desired result within the planned time and budget.

Formal management documents produced during this activity group relate heavily to performance data related to quality assurance, human resources, procurement, schedule and cost tracking. The project management mantra for execution is to "work the plan" and influence results. This means to use management skill to influence a successful completion to the effort as defined by the plan. Formal management documents produced during this activity group relate heavily to status information regarding quality assurance, human resources, procurement, schedule and cost tracking, and formal information distribution to stakeholders.

3.4.4 Monitoring and Controlling

As suggested by the title of this activity, there is a strong orientation toward control based on project performance results compared to the approved baseline plan values. From these measurement activities, corrective actions are defined. In addition to this, there are formal activities related to scope verification from the customer viewpoint and operation of an integrated change control process designed to ensure that changes to the plan are handled.

Monitoring and Control transcends the full project life cycle and has the goal of proactively guiding the project toward successful completion. As unplanned changes occur to schedule, scope, quality, or cost, the M&C processes work to determine how to react to the observed variance and move the effort back toward the approved targets. Much of this activity is driven by performance reporting, issues (deliverable variances or process issues), and the formal change management process. In addition, one of the most critical aspects of this phase is the risk monitoring process that involves monitoring various aspects of project risks including technical, quality, performance, management, organizational, and external events.

3.4.5 Closing

Formal project closing involves a group of activities required to formally shut down the project and document acceptance of the result. Also, this step completes the capture of lessons learned for use in future initiatives. It is widely noted that the closing phase gets the least attention; however, the guide model requires that all projects formally close out the activity, including both administrative and third-party relationship elements. The basic role of this phase is to leave the project administratively "clean" and to capture important lessons learned from the effort that can be shared with other projects. In regard to third-party agreements, it is necessary to view formal contractual closing as vital. Failure to execute final vendor status for the project can open-up future liability for the organization if a supplier later makes claims for nonperformance. If this occurs at some later time, the project organization would then have to scramble to rebuild the status with old records (often poorly organized) and missing team members. Similarly, documentation of lessons learned during the project has been found to provide valuable insights for future projects.

Finally, a close-out meeting or team social event is important in order for the team to review the experience and hopefully see the positives in their experiences. Too often, a project team just walks away from the effort without receiving any feedback. This can leave the individual feeling that the effort was a waste of time and this negative attitude can carry over to the next project assignment.

3.5 KAs

The 10 model KAs were introduced above. These represent a set of competency skills and processes that should be properly utilized by the project team throughout the life cycle. Processes contained in these KAs interact throughout the five high-level life cycle Process Groups. Basic roles for each of the KAs will be summarized below and more details about their interworking will appear in various formats throughout the book. The goal at this point is to briefly introduce them as key components of the life cycle model. These represent fundamental vocabulary concepts and are important ideas in the overall management framework.

3.5.1 Scope Management

In its simplest form, scope management involves the work efforts required to ensure that all defined requirements are properly produced based on the elaborated requirements statement. The processes in this KA take a high-level project vision and decompose that into a lower-level work breakdown view. During the detailed planning phase, this activity involves translation of a formal statement of requirements, while later activities deal with control of the requirements change process and verification that the ongoing results will meet customer expectations. The primary scope output for the planning cycle is a WBS that provides subsequent guidance for various follow-up project activities. Chapter 12 will cover this topic in more detail.

3.5.2 Schedule Management

This process deals with the mechanics and management requirements for translating the defined scope into work unit activities and then linking those activities into a project schedule. Chapters 13 and 14 will cover this topic in more detail.

3.5.3 Cost Management

This KA includes various activities and processes that create a project budget, then establish a control function to monitor ongoing results. Basically, the process of generating a project budget involves estimates of human resources (quantity and skills) and material costs for each defined work unit. The values that are determined from this process help the project team develop a Cost Budget which includes not only the direct work cost estimates, but also various other cost components needed to support the overall project activity. Cost budgeting organizes the values and estimates from the various sources and produces a cost baseline that is used to measure project performance. More details on the mechanics of this process will be described in Chapter 15.

3.5.4 Quality Management

This KA focuses on all aspects of both the product and project quality processes. The Quality Planning process is designed to focus the team on organizational or industry-related quality standards to be achieved for the project deliverables. Once the appropriate quality standards have been established and documented in the Quality Management Plan, the remaining processes focus on the appropriate activities needed to operationally satisfy the respective quality goals. The quality assurance process reviews the state of the project from its ability to deliver the required result, while the quality control process covers the tactical procedures to measure quality of the output. More details on this KA will be seen in Chapter 16.

3.5.5 Resource Management

This KA focuses on actions related to the human element of the project. Process activities in this area deal primarily with acquiring, developing, and managing the project team. In a matrix-type project organization, resources are typically not dedicated to one project, but are leveraged across multiple projects and sourced from various departments in the organization. This complicates the resource allocation mechanics for the PM and makes the acquisition step more complex than one might anticipate. Once a project is underway, the process of team development starts and continues through the life cycle. This includes both individual and team training with the goal being to improve the overall skill of the team members even after the project is completed. Part III of the book focuses on a collection of soft skill process, with resource management being the topic for Chapter 17.

3.5.6 Communications Management

Communication problems are now recognized as one of the most causal reasons for project failure. Project communications management activities are designed to support the information needs of the various project stakeholders. One of the key aspects involved in these processes is to identify who the targets are for communications, then explicitly plan how communications will flow during project execution. This area has been increasingly recognized as a critical aspect of project success. More is found on this topic in Chapter 18.

3.5.7 Risk Management

Many regard the current techniques for defining project risk as immature, or even impossible to do. Nevertheless, failure to deal with this aspect of the effort can be catastrophic to the final result. The primary focus of project risk management is minimizing the probability of negative events impacting the outcome and maximizing any opportunities that exist for positive events. The management of this class of activity is complex in that a risk event will not have yet occurred during the planning cycle, but if it does occur later, the earlier plan will be potentially affected. Identification of such events is a complex undertaking and represents a critical success factor. It is possible to do an excellent job of managing the defined effort only to find that some unspecified event, internal or external to the project, wipes out the entire value of the effort. For this reason, it is important for project teams to understand risks areas of vulnerability and have plans in place to deal with them. Risk Management will be discussed in greater detail later in Chapter 22.

3.5.8 Procurement Management

There are many situations that lead the project team to decide to procure material or human resources from third parties. The Procurement Management processes are utilized to manage the acquisition of these items. This area of project management has historically been considered very mature, but in recent years, the increase in outsourcing has made this a troublesome area for the PM as his project resources have become scattered across wide geographic areas. The procurement planning process lays the policy groundwork to guide how project material and external human resource needs will be externally acquired. This activity area often involves the organization's procurement function and legal department. The work activity in this KA involves selecting vendors and entering into contractual or formal relationships for the supply of goods or services. More specifics on this area will be found in Chapter 21.

3.5.9 Stakeholder Management

This KA represents the latest addition to the model and is a result of what some term "success/failure." What this means is that a project can finish according to defined requirements and be judged a success, only to be judged later as a failure in the light of unrecognized stakeholder expectations. The focus of this area is involved with identifying who the stakeholders are and then keeping them in the communications channel throughout the life cycle. Chapter 19 will describe these processes in greater detail.

3.5.10 Integration Management

The model describes Integration Management as the first KA; however, it is hard to explain this process until one has a better understanding of the other nine KAs and their embedded processes. It is these elements that need to be integrated into a working and viable whole. Integration is defined as including "...the processes and activities to identify, define, combine, unify, and coordinate the various processes and project management activities within the Project Management Process Groups" (PMI, 2017, p. 69). There are many examples that can be offered to illustrate this activity, but one should suffice for basic illustration now. Let us assume that a major change request representing a change in scope has been approved for the project. From this, it would seem reasonable to suggest that this scope change event might well bring with it changes in schedule (time) and cost. Also, related to this could be changes in staffing or procurement or risk, and so on. The key idea of process integration is that changes in one KA process often spawn changes in others. From a high-level viewpoint, project management is Integration Management. More examples of this activity will be found throughout the book.

3.6 Overall Process View

Figure 3.3 shows a physical distribution of the 49 processes across the major life cycle process domain groups.

In this view, note how the various KA processes are distributed across the project life cycle groups. The process box numbers reflect the *PMBOK® Guide* KA chapter number and reference number sequence. For example, the process box labeled 5.4 *Create WBS* would be described in the guide Chapter 5 as the fourth reference process. A more detailed technical discussion related to the Process Groups and KAs described above can be found in the *PMBOK® Guide.*

In summary, there are 49 lower-level process descriptions embedded in each of the guide's 10 KAs, and further embedded in the five major project stages. Recognize that the PMBOK content provides a good high-level roadmap for project management and it represents an internationally accepted standard. However, also recognize that it is not designed to be a project management *How To* cookbook. Rather, it is a general knowledge base to provide guidance from which a specific project approach can be constructed. Experience and training are required to manipulate this model template view into workable customized project management tool and process.

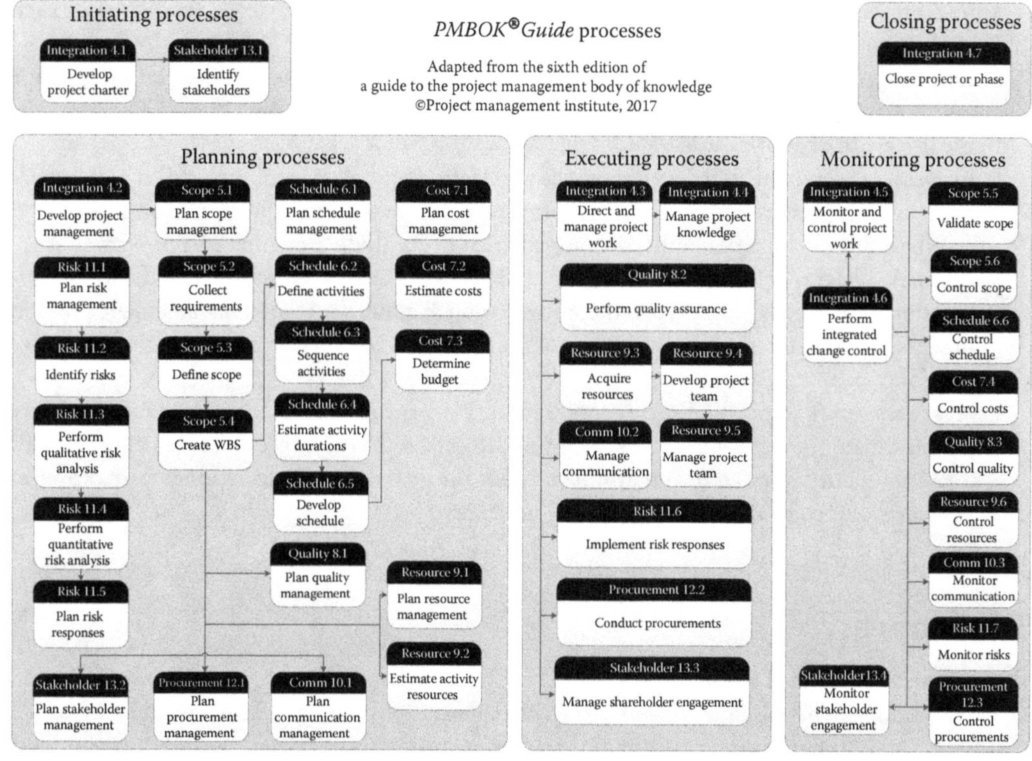

Figure 3.3 PMBOK processes.

3.7 Introductory Vocabulary Terms

One of the values of defining a standard project life cycle model is the consistency of approach and vocabulary that it brings to the organization. There are many vocabulary terms that are important in communicating project management concepts and these will be seen frequently as we navigate through the various text topics. At this stage, 10 terms have been selected to include here as being "fundamental" to the model vocabulary. The following terms and their related concepts are summarized here and future chapters will amplify how they fit into the overall model scheme:

PM: The person assigned by management to oversee the ongoing activities of the project in pursuit of its goals. This individual coordinates life cycle activities with senior management, project sponsor, users, and stakeholders.

Sponsor: This is a senior level individual who provides general vision, guidance, and funding for the project.

Stakeholders: The collection of individuals and organizations who are involved or affected by the project. Some stakeholders exert influence over the direction of the project, while others are impacted by the outcome of the project deliverables.

User: The individuals or organizational groups that utilize the project's output product. This group is often called the "customer" for the project.

Progressive elaboration: This term is important to understand in that it describes how details related to project requirements and other aspects of the management process can evolve in increments or steps as more is known. The planning stage can be viewed as a series of such elaborations leading to the desired final plan.

Project life cycle: Project evolution is divided into a series of phases that are designed to provide better management control of the overall project. The defined phases collectively constitute the life cycle.

Project management: This term represents the application of tools, techniques, skills, and knowledge to the project domain. Also, the term may also be used to represent a formalized and standardized organizational methodology which helps guide execution of a project.

Portfolio: A collection of projects or programs. This term is often used to describe the total organizational package of proposed and approved project efforts. A related management decision process should attempt to optimize the organizational value based on selection of the active portfolio members (see Chapter 35).

Project Management Office (PMO): A contemporary organizational unit assigned responsibility to coordinate the selection and oversight of projects within the enterprise. Specific roles for a PMO function vary across organizations, but the general goal is to support formal project selection, approval, and execution (see Chapter 36).

3.8 Summary

This chapter has provided a brief overview of the PMI project management model as described in the 2017 edition of the *PMBOK® Guide.* The concepts and philosophy of this model are reflected and supported in the structure and topics throughout this text. Individuals serious about project management as a profession should seek certification from PMI as either a PMP or a CAPM, or one of the other more specialized topic areas. PMP certification requires more work experience than the CAPM, but both are respected professional credentials and they add increased marketability for the holder. Many organizations now use this certification as a prerequisite for hiring or job assignment as a PM. Further specifics on various PMI certification and standards programs can be found at www.pmi.org.

References

Chumas, S.J (ed.). (1975) *Directory of United States Standardization Activities.* NIST Publication 288, p. 147.

PMI, 2017. *A Guide to the Project Management Body of Knowledge (PMBOK® Guide)*, 6th ed. Newtown Square, PA: Project Management Institute.

Chapter 4

Industry Trends in Project Management

4.1 Standardizing Project Management

One of the secrets of success for companies such as Apple, Disney, Nokia, Johnson & Johnson, Vodafone, and Virgin Air is that they have produced phenomenal customer products spawned from innovative ideas and then followed that up with project/development methodologies that facilitated their innovativeness to deliver their projects to market more quickly than their competitors. Experience has shown that the use of a standard project methodology is often an effective strategy for developing projects in the IT, energy, aeronautical, social, government, construction, financial, or consulting sectors. A project methodology contains processes designed to maximize the project's value to the organization (Charvat, 2003). In its operational form, a methodology must accommodate a company's changing focus or direction. Over time, it becomes part of the organizational culture and embedded in the way projects are executed. To be effective over a long term, a methodology must fit the perception of activities required to execute the project. This perception involves both technical and personal views. For that reason, individual managers often resist using someone else's methodology. This statement suggests that project management contains both scientific and artistic aspects, as well as specific organizational cultural factors.

4.2 Enterprise Project Management

Enterprise Project Management (EPM) and Portfolio Management are two of the newer management practices shaping the view of project management in action today. Project Portfolio Management (PPM) is an organizational level methodology that caters to the enterprise-wide collection of projects, while EPM is less well described, but essentially deals more with the overall organizational processes utilized in executing projects. EPM enables organizations to manage projects as a collective portfolio of activities, rather than as separate, isolated initiatives with no overlap (QAI, 2005). EPM provides a big-picture perspective for all project assets, such as enterprise goals, staff, equipment, and budget; it allows projects to be aligned across departmental boundaries and containing key strategic organizational initiatives. This approach is designed to provide visibility to all project stakeholders so that overall project initiatives remain in alignment with organizational objectives, and required status information is properly communicated.

Portfolio level views offer multiple perspectives. One perspective is a software tool that helps plan and implement all projects in an organizational unit. Another view is that it is a management process to support selection, planning, control, and implementation from a central location. A formal definition of either organizational portfolio management or the enterprise level is as follows:

> An enterprise view of the Project Management activities. It is a strategic decision process that aims at linking the organization's mission, vision, goal, objectives and strategies in a hierarchical fashion to ensure that the resources are allocated to the right projects at the right time.
>
> *(Ireland, 2004, p. 1)*

In operational form, EPM represents the process model showing to incorporate the art and science of project management in a new way to do business. It focuses on consolidating project selection and approval across the entire organization, with the goal of optimizing organizational value for the chosen ventures. Companies such as American Express, ABB, Citibank, and IBM are acknowledged as business pioneers pursuing this approach and each has now taken substantial steps toward applying EPM principles on an enterprise level (Morris, 2000). EPM is a methodology that combines standardized project management processes and support tools to better meet an organization's project or program management goals (Landman, 2008).

One of the major distinctions of EPM versus project management or portfolio management is the implied high-level integration process throughout the organization. In the EPM structure, project teams would no longer feel like they were on an isolated island. Rather, various formalized organizational processes would be actively involved in formal support of the project effort.

Figure 4.1 symbolizes how the various components integrate and align the project process life cycle into the organizational goals. A brief description of each component is presented below.

Project Portfolio Management: The normal industry acronym designator for this function is PPM. Various other titles could be used for this activity, but its primary role is to establish some form of high-level portfolio view of the organizational project and process environments. This entails defining operational details regarding what projects are being worked on and data related to proposed projects. In some cases, the portfolio will also include the status of existing processes and products, indicating what work needs to be done to upgrade them. Out of the portfolio view would be derived engineered proposals that would collectively produce the greatest positive impact

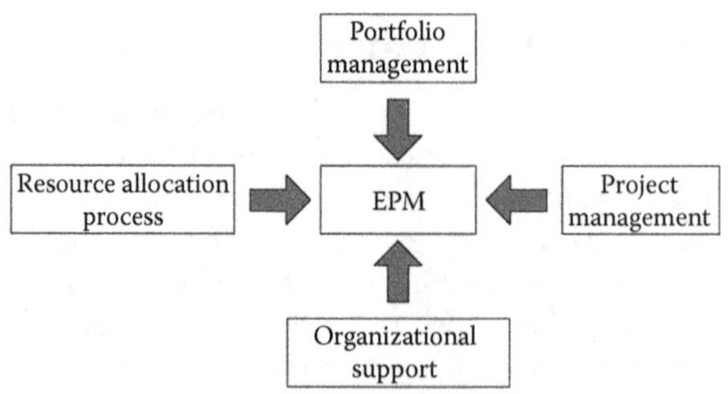

Figure 4.1 EPM architectural components.

on organizations, regarding improvement toward its defined goals. Think of this activity as a very complex analysis of current state versus desired state. In this mode the role of a project would be to move that segment of the organization toward the desired state. This activity implies a strong role for senior management in the goal setting and project selection process. Chapters 35 and 36 will pursue this topic in greater detail. Our goal at this point is to recognize how portfolio management differs from project management.

Simply stated *project management* involves delivering the defined results that were specified in the portfolio process. One central theme within this area is to recognize that the goal of a project is to support and align with organizational goals. Therefore, the portfolio function essentially links the organization to the project through its selection logic. However, it is important to recognize that this involves more than just defining those processes. There is still great resistance by many in believing that such rigor is required to produce successful outcomes. Hence, an EPM organization would require a mature organizational culture in this regard. There is mounting evidence that ad hoc practices of project management are not successful and that improved rigor does help improve the resulting outcomes (Thomas and Mullaly, 2008). Nevertheless, recognize that project management involves more than the definition of mechanical steps.

Organizational support environment: This term implies that projects cannot successfully exist without the support of their host organization. This support comes in various ways:

- Senior management for general support and high-level decision-making
- Users who help with requirements definition
- Functional managers who own the critical resources
- Organizational support processes that are needed by the project team
- Capital resources that must be supplied by the organization in competition with other groups

Each of these provides valuable support to the project team in various ways throughout the project life cycle.

Resource allocation process: The typical project organization is staffed as a matrix, which means that required project team human resources are supplied by various functional organizations or external vendors through some form of planned relationship. Of all the project critical success factors, access to appropriate technical and business knowledgeable resources is the most significant variable assuming that the proper target has been selected. Failure to garner those resources in the needed time periods will yield less than desired results in time, cost, or technical outcome. Exacerbating this issue is the dynamics of the project world and the multitasking approach that is often used for the resources. Competing demands across multiple projects for scarce resources means that the resource allocation process becomes a vital component in the overall EPM process. There are other views for the EPM process and it certainly is more complex in operation than described here, but this is the essence of the model.This discussion level simply provides the necessary foundation for the material that follows.

4.3 EPM in Operation

The various EPM functional decision processes collectively serve as a basis for selecting projects that have a high degree of both strategic and operational fit to the enterprise goals. From a top-down view, the model provides both general and organizational guidance to project-specific implementation. Each of the decision process nodes are linked in a way to ensure consistency of purpose and predictable outcomes (Ireland, 2004).

4.4 Implementation and Advantages of EPM

It is the responsibility of senior management to determine whether sufficient benefits exist for moving to an enterprise level project management organization. Step one of the decision process would be an analysis of existing projects to determine whether the project selection process is adequate and whether the existing project state is less than optimal in terms of size, risk, profitability, and strategic fit compared to the organizational goals. If a decision is made to switch to an enterprise level focus, it is necessary to design a transition strategy away from the current method. In this transition, it is important for senior management to be the leader and make sure that all stakeholders understand the rationale for the change and the associated benefits. The potential benefits for EPM would include the following:

- Greater management visibility into project status in terms of profit and alignment to organizational strategies.
- A disciplined approach toward allocation of resources to the projects.
- Resources allocated to right projects result in more timely delivery of the project deliverables (Ireland, 2004).

4.5 Other Trends Impacting Project Management

Organizational maturity: There is a growing recognition that the maturity of the organization is supportive to project success. Recognition of this basic concept has spawned a growing interest in defining what a mature organization looks like and does. One aspect of maturity is to grade just how much support the organization supplies to the project, meaning that the project does not have to invent all its necessary processes, but can simply attach itself to the organization and move forward with minimal process overhead. There is a great deal of evidence to support the notion that moving the organization up the maturity scale can improve project success rates and operational productivity; thus, this is a potential goal for the project manager (PM).

As described earlier, the EPM model involves both organization and project level processes. The concept of maturity is embedded in both of these levels. Most maturity grading scales are based on a numerical value ranging from 1 to 5, with 1 basically indicating no formal process and 5 indicating an optimal level of maturity. The basic unanswered question at this point is "Maturity of what?" The Project Management Institute (PMI) model as described in Chapter 3 helps in answering this question in its definition of the 10 project knowledge areas and specifications for their related processes (PMI, 2017). From these two perspectives, one could envision a two-dimensional model of five maturity grades mapped against the knowledge areas as a method of portraying an organization's status from the project view (Grant and Pennypacker, 2006). The intersection of these two dimensions, knowledge area and maturity level, can then be further decomposed into various lower-level knowledge area process components to produce a measure of operational maturity at a fairly low level of granularity. One could then envision this result as a three-dimensional view of the overall project maturity—that is, maturity measure by knowledge area and by knowledge process. The key point for this discussion is to recognize that both projects and the organization have operational maturity that helps support effectiveness of the project activity. This view of maturity can be assessed for organizational, departmental, and project levels. Our focus is to primarily deal with the project level, but it is hard to isolate that from the surrounding organizational components.

Contemporary trends: Brief samples of trends that are impacting the current working environment of a PM are as follows:

- Increasing use of technology within the daily operational processes including project modeling, computer-based document management, web-based tools, enterprise-level resource databases, and sophisticated collaboration tools.
- Increasing trend of customer-driven projects. (both internal and external to the organization)
- Geographically dispersed teams. The trend of working in a virtual environment has resulted in project management across multiple time zones where communication becomes more long distance and impacted by cultural and language diversity.
- Moving from stand-alone project management to portfolio model perspectives increases the complexity of the overall process and requires the PM to become more focused on broader organizational goals.
- Implementation of PMOs that adds a layer of centralized control above the project level. This has the potential to increase bureaucracy and inhibits the speed of decision-making. Many PMs (and some sponsors and clients) will not like this added layer of "help" for their projects.

PM skills: In order to survive in this highly dynamic world of today, the PM must enhance their interpersonal behavioral skills and work habits in order to keep proficient in dealing with the changing trends as outlined in this section. This essentially means that the modern PM must do the following:

1. Keep abreast of current best management and technical practices.
2. Develop skills in customer-centric communication.
3. Learn to coexist in the more politically charged EPM-type organizational environment.
4. Develop soft skills regarding team motivation, diversity, and corporate culture.
5. Improve emotional intelligence. (feeling and thinking)
6. Improve management skills in developing high-productivity teams while using less formal authority mechanisms.

4.6 Project Management Perspective

Project management should be viewed as a set of techniques, theories, and tools that collectively help organizations effectively execute designated projects. However, it is also important to recognize that the use of these mechanical methods does not automatically guarantee project success. Over the last 50 or so years modern project management has developed into an applied science (albeit still a pseudo one), which has proven helpful in the achievement of the project goals. However, the current set of methods and tools are quite young by management standards; hence, there is every expectation that the operational mechanics and theories for managing projects will continue to evolve. Topics such as risk management, organizational maturity models, virtual team management, and project value analysis are likely to be at the forefront of this evolution.

At the tactical project level, there is now growing acceptance of operational approaches to project management, but resistance remains as to the value of project management in the success of the project. Despite this resistance, management continues to press for more success in this arena. Project management as described here is the general model being pursued by growing numbers of organizations (Barnes, 2002).

To improve knowledge regarding project management value, PMI chartered a three-year research study in 2005. The results of this study published in 2008 concluded that project management added value, but also showed that understanding that value was more complex than using simple financial measures (Thomas and Mullaly, 2008). The interested reader is encouraged to review this groundbreaking research to get a better idea of how projects bring value to the organization. Other studies have shown that projects do in fact produce value, but often not in the way originally predicted. The goal of this text is to understand the fundamental mechanics of producing successful project outcomes and some key external organizational factors that support the process.

Discussion Questions

1. Why would the existence of standardized project management procedures help achieve higher rates of project success?
2. If it makes such logical rationale for organizations to properly select their portfolios of projects, why is this activity not well practiced?
3. Using the high-level description of EPM, describe some of the implementation issues that you see for the organization pursuing this goal.

References

Barnes, M., 2002. *A Long Term View of Project Management—Its Past and Its Likely Future.* Presented at 16th World Congress on Project Management. Berlin.

Charvat, J., 2003. *Project Management Methodologies: Selecting, Implementing, and Supporting Methodologies and Processes for Projects.* New York: Wiley.

Grant, K.P. and J.S. Pennypacker, 2006. Project management maturity: an assessment of project management capabilities among and between selected industries. *IEEE Transactions on Engineering Management,* 53, 1, 59–68.

Ireland, L., 2004. Enterprise Project Management—A Strategic View. www.asapm.org/resources/a_epm_ireland.pdf (accessed January 30, 2009).

Landman, H., 2008. *Enterprise Project Management Using Microsoft Office Project Server.* Ft. Lauderdale, FL: J. Ross Publishing.

Morris, H.W., 2000. Winning in business with enterprise project management. *Project Management Journal,* 32.

PMI, 2017. *A Guide to the Project Management Body of Knowledge (PMBOK® Guide),* 6th ed. Newtown Square, PA: Project Management Institute.

QAI, 2005. International Conference on Project Management Leadership. www.qaiindia.com/Conferences/pm05/papers_15.htm (accessed May 13, 2005).

Thomas, J. and M. Mullaly, 2008. *Researching the Value of Project Management.* Newtown Square, PA: Project Management Institute.

Chapter 5

Project Types

In earlier discussions, we theorized that all projects have more similarity than most understand, but the additional question is "how much similarity?" To explore that idea further we need a starting point. Archibald studied the question regarding where projects exist and for what purpose. His research identified projects in the following 20 industry areas (Archibald, 2004):

1. Aerospace/defense
2. Automation
3. Automotive
4. E-business
5. Environmental
6. Financial services
7. Government
8. Healthcare
9. Hospitality events
10. Information systems
11. Information
12. Technology/telecom
13. International development
14. Manufacturing
15. New product development
16. Oil/gas/petrochemical
17. Pharmaceutical
18. Retail
19. Service and outsourcing
20. Utility industry.

Obviously, each of these industries has unique technical characteristics in their projects; however, the key point is that all have a somewhat similar life cycle and management process. Recognize that there will be differences in the underlying technology, formality of documentation/ communication, risk, human skills required, and a host of other subtleties, but fundamentally there is a strongly consistent management view appropriate for all.

Archibald and Voropaev compiled project data to classify projects into a smaller and more coherent classification grouping by characteristics. The hypothesis of this effort was that a classification scheme could begin to help in better understanding various life cycle methodology variations based on the features and processes found in a particular group. From a categorization model theory, there is a belief that each group could have more specifically defined processes, tools, and methodologies that fit their needs and the potential for reusable components that would save development time and effort. Success from such a definition would be at least one level deeper than that defined in the Project Management Body of Knowledge (PMBOK), which tends to be more of a single level view. Even though a formal industry-based customization effort has yet to reach maturity, it is still worth examining. Table 5.1 shows the model draft of 11 project categories. Collectively, this list provides a good overview of a global industry project environment and scope.

Table 5.1 Project Categories

Project Categories[*]	*Examples*
1. Aerospace/Defense Projects 1.1 Defense systems 1.2 Space 1.3 Military operations	New weapon system; major system upgrade. Satellite development/launch: space station mode. Taskforce invasion.
2. Business & Organization Change Projects 2.1 Acquisition/Merger 2.2 Management process improvement 2.3 New business venture 2.4 Organization re-structuring 2.5 Legal proceeding	Acquire and integrate competing company. Major improvement in project management. Form and launch new company. Consolidate divisions and downsize company. Major litigation case.
3. Communication Systems Projects 3.1 Network communications systems 3.2 Switching communications systems	Microwave communications network. Third-generation wireless communication system.
4. Event Projects 4.1 International events 4.2 National events	2004 Summer Olympics; 2006 World Cup Match. 2005 U.S. Super Bowl; 2004 Political Conventions.
5. Facilities Projects 5.1 Facility decommissioning 5.2 Facility demolition 5.3 Facility maintenance and modification 5.4 Facility design/procurement/ construction Civil Energy Environmental High rise Industrial Commercial Residential Ships	Closure of nuclear power station. Demolition of high rise building. Process plant maintenance turnaround. Conversion of plant for new products/ markets. Flood control dam; highway interchange. New gas-fired power generation plant; pipeline. Chemical waste cleanup. Forty-story office building. New manufacturing plant. New shopping center; office building. New housing sub-division. New tanker, container, or passenger ship.

(Continued)

Table 5.1 (*Continued*) Project Categories

*Project Categories**	*Examples*
6. Information Systems (Software) Projects	New project management information system. (Information system hardware is considered to be in the product development category.)
7. International Development Projects 7.1 Agriculture/rural development 7.2 Education 7.3 Health 7.4 Nutrition 7.5 Population 7.6 Small-scale enterprise 7.7 **Infrastructure**: energy (oil, gas, coal, power generation and distribution, industrial, telecommunications, transportation, urbanization, water supply and sewage, irrigation)	**People and process Intensive projects** in developing countries funded by The World Bank, regional development banks, U.S. AID, UNIDO, other UN, and government agencies; and **Capital/civil works-intensive projects** often somewhat different from 5. Facility Projects as they may include, as part of the project, creating an organizational entity to operate and maintain the facility, and lending agencies impose their project life cycle and reporting requirements.
8. Media & Entertainment Projects 8.1 Motion picture 8.2 TV segment 8.2 Live play or music event	New motion picture (film or digital). New TV episode. New opera premiere.
9. Product and Service Development Projects 9.1 Information technology hardware 9.2 Industrial product/process 9.3 Consumer product/process 9.4 Pharmaceutical product/process 9.5 Service (financial, other)	New desk-top computer. New earth-moving machine. New automobile, new food product. New cholesterol-lowering drug. New life insurance/annuity offering.
10. Research and Development Projects 10.1 Environmental 10.2 Industrial 10.3 Economic development 10.4 Medical 10.5 Scientific	Measure changes in the ozone layer. How to reduce pollutant emission. Determine best crop for sub-Sahara Africa. Test new treatment for breast cancer. Determine the possibility of life on Mars.
11. Other Categories?	

Source: Russell Archibald.

* Each having similar life cycle phases and a unique project management process.

Within the standard project model, there are nine basic knowledge areas (plus one more for integration). Each of the project types categorized in Table 5.1 represents unique management issues for these areas. The challenge for the project manager is to identify the critical success characteristics for his project category and then use that knowledge to develop an appropriate management process that best leads to success. Each of these project types has varying priorities for achieving their schedule, budget, technical requirements (scope), and quality. Many would say that all of these views are required in every case, but given the characteristics of each environment, there must be a priority order defined to facilitate future goal tradeoffs. For example, in the commercial aerospace environment, quality (safety) would be paramount. Beneath that highest goal, there likely would need to be design tradeoffs for other project goals (i.e., fuel economy, maintenance costs, speed, etc.). The point here is that all design objectives cannot always be met. When that situation exists, a key part of the project management process is to trade-off lower priority items to salvage maximum value for the overall effort. The traditional view of this is to manage planned technical requirements, cost, and schedule based on their respective priority rankings.

To carry this theme further, some projects involve high inherent risk. In this situation, the project manager typically pursues strategies to minimize risk exposure, but in some cases, this cannot be avoided based on the goal of the project. To illustrate, building a manned spaceship for a trip to Mars is a radical example of this. Even though there is extensive effort to mitigate risk, the fact remains that the project goal has significant embedded risk that cannot be completely avoided. There are similar issues in more traditional projects but they are probably less obvious. Whenever an organization decides to pursue a new technical product and establishes a project team to develop that product, there are varying degrees of associated risk involved. The technology may not work; the market may not want the product as produced, along with many other outcomes. In these situations, an organization must decide whether to pursue a risky effort in order to gain a competitive advantage. Achieving this goal may bring a competitive advantage to the organization, but failure is another possible outcome. Hence, it is important to recognize that managing high-risk projects is quite different from constructing a standard building, although there have been examples in the past where the wrong technical decisions have been made even here (i.e., failure to let concrete dry before removing forms causing the entire building to fall).

One memorable risk management example was observed recently from a deep-sea multibillion dollar drilling rig project where various quality tests were cut for the sake of saving time and money. As the completed rig was being floated out to sea, it sank and was a complete loss. One could easily argue that this was a management trade-off decision, but even if the budget and schedule were met, the ultimate result was a project failure.

Therefore, it is important to recognize that during a project it is normal to have to deal with trading-off project goals owing to the dynamics of the process. When this situation arises, the PM must make intelligent decisions to juggle the output targets to achieve the best result possible. To do this, there should be an understanding of the relative importance of each management parameter and knowledge area involved. Understanding the idiosyncrasies of the various project categories may well be the first step in making a more coherent management process part of the proper operational base theory. Until then, it is up to the skills and intellect of the PM to wade through this minefield.

Reference

Archibald, R.D. and V. Voropaev, 2004. Project Categories and Life Cycle Models: Report on the 2003 IPMA Global Survey. www.ipma-usa.org/articles/RussPaper.pdf (accessed October 26, 2017).

Chapter 6

Project Organization Concepts

Previous discussions have outlined the general life cycle of projects and the basic types of activities that must be accomplished in that life cycle. In this section, the focus moves to the technical and process skills to support getting the job accomplished. The first item to recognize is that for projects of any size, the combination of knowledge and skills will not reside in a single organizational functional group through the full life cycle. During the early phases, the requirement focuses more on WHAT is to be done and this evolves later into HOW the various work activities will be performed. To accomplish this, various skills are required at different times through this process. Therefore, we must recognize that it will normally not be the most efficient use of human resources to allocate a fixed complement of individuals to the project for the duration. This may be feasible for a core portion of the team, but not for the total resource picture. The point being made here is to recognize that the typical project has a complex operational problem associated with moving appropriate resources into and out of the effort according to some approved plan. Also, these resources will be used in other project initiatives, so that there is also a broader organizational perspective to the resource allocation problem.

6.1 PM Role

Within the structure of the team, there are other organizational issues to resolve as well. According to the PMBOK, a companion decision defined in the originating Charter document is the assignment of a PM. That then becomes the first organizational decision. Is this person allocated to this task full-time or part with other duties? That decision has a cascading effect on other organizational issues. In the formal vernacular there are three titles that the model defines for PM roles.

1. Project Manager (PM)—the person formally assigned to lead the team and charged with achieving project goals. He provides management oversight for a complex set of interactions between sponsor, team, and stakeholders. This person is the main management focus in managing the scope, schedule, cost, and quality of the defined deliverables.
2. Project coordinator—a person who often works for the project sponsor or some other management level person who is given responsibility to keep track of project status, but

has little else in the way of formal responsibility. This approach should be used only for small, low-priority efforts.

3. Project expeditor—this person is assigned to help the technical team participants and collect data, but they have essentially zero responsibility for the effort. Think of them as information distributors. This form also does not fit the requirements for a project of any size.

For projects of any size, the desired approach is to formally assign a full-time PM. Also, the goal is to provide that individual with appropriate levels of authority and a clear vertical reporting relationship.

6.2 Reporting Relationships

A model project structure would report to a project sponsor who is the executive level person who *owns* the project and oversees its overall success. In addition to this, a *Project Board* should be established to serve as the operational agent of the sponsor. This board will have authority to make change decisions and other ongoing management decisions within the Charter constraints or the later approved project plan. Membership on the board should minimally be a sponsor representative, a technical representative, and possibly the PM. Other members could come from the future user community or other appropriate organizational elements that have an interest in the project. One of the key roles of the board is to approve changes and generally aid in helping resolve any issues that cannot be handled by the PM.

One possible modification of a reporting structure would be to have a project created as part of a larger collection of related projects called a *program*. In this case, the sponsor's role would be served by the program manager and the board structure would work essentially the same, but in this case, it may be more interlocked across multiple projects. This linkage issue would be required because the various projects would have to fit together for the whole program to work as envisioned. NASA space projects are the best-known examples of large programs with critical project interrelationships; however, this same pattern emerges as organizations begin to recognize that high level initiatives have all the characteristics of a program and need the same type of management structure.

6.3 Team Resources

The issue of resource ownership is one of the most contentious management decisions in project organizational design. We have already described the project technical requirement that requires a broad array of various skills that need to be dynamically allocated through the life cycle; however, this still leaves the question of *ownership* of that resource while they are involved in the project. Can the PM select those employees he wants on the team? Does he handle their formal performance appraisal and other HR items such as raises and bonuses? Can he fire them for lack of performance? In most organizations, the answer to all these questions is no!

The personnel ownership issue is clearly one of the PM's Achilles heels. In the formal organizational model, functional managers maintain formal ownership of their resources and allocate them to the project, hopefully on the agreed schedule (another potential issue). This leaves the PM with little formal control to select and allocate specific resources for his project team. Low performers can be given back to their home organization, but dealing with the performance issue is left to the functional manager. This relationship description should give insight into some of the key skills needed by a PM. In this situation, he must be able to negotiate with the functional manager and motivate the team without a high degree of formal power. Managers who need formal authority will be frustrated by this model.

There are some project types in which the skills are not so varied, and the core team will stay intact through the life cycle. In this case, many of the resource allocation issues are lessened. Regardless of the staffing profile, the PM needs to be very sensitive to the management style that fits his model. Beyond the source and ownership aspects of the resource, there are many other people-related issues that affect the project organizational structure. Part III of the book covers this area in more detail.

6.4 Team Productivity and Size

Putnam and others have performed research on team size and the results of this effort have concluded that maximum productivity occurs in team sizes in the range of 5–7 (Putnam, 1997). There are many behavioral and communication reasons affecting why this might be the norm, but it is a common observation. Certainly, one of the most obvious reasons for issues to emerge as team sizes grow is the complexity of the communication channels about this number. Unfortunately, some project teams need to be larger than this. When this is the case the best strategy may well be to break the larger group team into sub-teams with focused sub-goals. Here, the team organization strategy needs to be collections of relatively small, focused groups such that the overall team remains connected and productive. The idea is sound, but once again the management process is more complex, and communication processes must be more formalized.

One possible approach to achieving a cohesive team goal is to envision the project as a collection of work units in which the team members participate in defining. As these work units are defined, it will help the individuals understand how they fit into the broader scheme. Later, as specific individuals are assigned responsibility for a work unit, it will be easier to gain buy-in to the resulting work definition and should lessen communication needs since the team was involved earlier. Achieving this measure of goal responsibility and recognition are major factors in achieving overall team productivity.

As team size grows beyond the optimum, the management processes for team coordination and work responsibilities also grows. Communication issues rise in importance and process formality becomes more of a requirement.

6.5 Team's Physical Location Issues

Physical housing locations for the project team are a common issue in a matrix-type structure. Recall that the team members permanently belong to various functional groups and have assigned space there. Hence, the question often arises as why allocate duplicate space? The simple answer to this is to facilitate team communication and improve the social team culture. This is especially important in the formulation stages of the project where requirements are being defined and technical issues discussed. The initial core project planning team forms the foundation for the future work requirements and mistakes made at this point are compounded if not discovered early. During this period, the core team is working to translate the Charter vision issued by the sponsor into a viable set of work activities. Representatives from various skill groups are required for this effort as they translate the business vision into technical work units. This formulation period is an important element for success and the key players should have full access to each other and strive to develop good working relationships. Projects formed with unresolved requirements will spawn conflict and changes later that will likely decrease the changes of a successful completion. Team building in a common work area is an important early space consideration and from this early camaraderie the participants will better be able to negotiate future conflicts.

One of the best methods to facilitate communication and productivity is to place the team in a *co-located* space. Beginning with the post-Charter initiation phase and following later into the formal planning phase there is a great deal of decision volatility and potential conflict between organizational and technical members as the requirements are being translated into a project plan. During this period, the team should be physically close and have every opportunity to develop personal ties with other members. Relationships built during this period will be vital later in the life cycle when unanticipated issues must be resolved and will involve complex tradeoffs.

Private offices are often status symbols in organizations, but that is not the right layout solution for the early project phase. A large open workspace called a *war room* has been found to be conducive to more open communication and team building. In this mode, draft documents can be hung on the walls for review and discussion. There should also be space for planned visitors to come in for consultation (i.e., future users, vendors, management, etc.). Once the planning cycle is complete and an approved project plan is produced, it is then more feasible for the various work teams to exist in more private facilities. As the team size grows using an open space layout becomes less attractive; however, there is still value in a small core team staying in close proximity for coordination purposes.

Studies performed at IBM during the 1980s compared productivity of knowledge workers in different physical environments. Two factors surfaced from this analysis. First, a closed office environment was conducive to better concentration. Second, proper tools are important. In the case of a project team, this means that some form of quiet office space is appropriate when work is isolated to a single individual. Surprisingly, many companies today use open cubicles as a layout strategy and workers often complain about noise and interruptions. Also, lack of access to an outside window view is also a common complaint. The cubicle layout format suggests that organizations are focused on the cost of housing a worker, but may not have given the same level of attention to a productive environment for that worker.

A second factor emerges as the team becomes more physically separated. Where physical closeness resolved the internal collaboration requirements during the early phase, the team is now more separated, and the communication process must adapt to that. Modern collaboration tools are available to improve the ability of team members to communicate and have appropriate virtual access to technical and management artifacts being created and used by the members. Actually, the process of capturing and distributing project information is important regardless of physical location. Modern document content storage and retrieval technology available through Internet links and "cloud" storage offers a viable way to accomplish this information access goal. Various topics throughout the text will describe examples of project management artifacts that need to be accessible to team stakeholders.

Since projects are often viewed as temporary organizational activities, the assignment of appropriate physical space for the team is often not given proper consideration. Normally, this creates the obvious problem with team members scattered about. However, several years ago, the author experienced a team location event that was educational and went against the theory. In this example, there was a lack of office space in the main building, so the project team was moved out of the building to an old deserted 1940s Quonset building with only scrap furniture. On the surface, this was the worst space decision one could imagine. The building had only open space inside (no walled offices). Surprisingly, this move turned out to be a great location for the team. Our team was *stuck* out behind the main building complex for over a year, and the old Quonset hut became our home. Surprisingly, this isolation from other organizational units made the group very cohesive. Internal communications were great, and the group learned to respect each other's opinions. As a result, this very fuzzy, abstract, and political project delivered a result that most likely would not have happened if the players had stayed in their original offices and communicated only at planned meeting times. The key for the PM is to find a way to create this type of environment regardless of the physical location for the team.

6.6 Team Dynamics

Projects represent one of the best-known organizational breeding grounds for conflict given their complex interrelationships among the organizational groups. Early conflict can occur over the interpretation of exactly what the project is meant to accomplish, the desired time schedule, or whether the stated vision is technically achievable. Later, that conflict can evolve into one of resources or technical options. Regardless of the source, one way to decrease this is to have good communication processes among the various groups. Communication theory suggests that up to 90% of conflicts are the result of misunderstanding between the parties. Much of this can be better dealt with if the individuals or groups have good relationships and can discuss the issues in an open manner. During the early project phases this can be best accomplished by recognizing the role that physical space can have in the conflict equation. The greater the separation of the members, the more difficult these interrelationships become.

6.7 Virtual Organizations

A clear definition regarding what constitutes a virtual organization is still in the formulation stage and therefore varied. Some of the common characteristics of such organizations are that they are geographically distributed and likely linked together via some form of technology-based collaboration tools (often just email). The members in such an organization might have different employers, yet collectively their goal is to operate as a single organizational entity. Customer call centers today are an example of a virtual organization in that they are very mechanically efficient from both a process and technical perspective at handling calls (note we did not say that the customer likes this approach, but it is cost efficient). If you are the customer who is calling organization XYZ you will get organization ABC's call center representative who will answer as "Hello this is organization XYZ." That individual might well be on another continent, but modern Internet or telephone technology makes the geography transparent. This type of organizational virtual fragmentation occurs across many skill and service lines.

As a similar example, a software development project for organization XYZ might employ software programmers in organization ABC located halfway around the world, or even XYZ employees at that location. Similar allocations could occur for a wide variety of virtual work activities needed by the project. One form of a virtual organization involves employees from the same organization scattered across wide geographic regions. A second form involves employees from multiple employers combining to accomplish a project goal. In this second case, the relationship formality must be somewhat more rigorous. In these situations, formal work specification and competitive bidding-type actions are generally required. When the project team members are from the same organization but geographically dispersed, the required formality of the relationship is somewhat less, but the basic management issues are quite similar.

A third hybrid model of a virtual organization is the geographical division of work by time zone, often called "chasing the work around the sun." What this means is that three geographically dispersed teams would ship their work at the end of each day to the next location to the West. Hence, the work might migrate every eight hours from Texas then to China and then on to Russia and back to Texas for the start of the next day. In a highly linked virtual environment such as this, there is tremendous productivity potential since the same unit of work is being processed for 24 hours, rather than the typical eight. This is a doable model in some cases, but obviously a very difficult work coordination process. Work models defined this way have been information technology projects doing design, coding, testing, and user acceptance. Each geographic group serves one of the roles in this linkage, so small items are routed through the chain each day as the local unit closes.

Virtual organizational relationships are on the rise as companies continue to find ways to partner for common good. In each case, the management and collaboration issues resulting from these arrangements are challenging to the PM.

6.8 Organizational Culture

Essentially, every project is linked to some host organization and the project work environment is impacted by that external culture. Ideally, the project team needs support from the organization. However, in many cases, the team feels that they are on a lost island alone, trying to survive. Hence, organizational cultures can be either supportive or restrictive to the project. Productivity will be improved if the organization provides needed support. The most obvious examples are skilled resources and space, but there are various other ways that may help the project without having to invent processes for themselves. The services of the host organization should be made available as needed. Also, various stakeholder and management groups should strive to support the project effort.

Most organizations are structured according to skill specialties such as—engineering, manufacturing, information technology, marketing, legal, and so on. This structural form is defined as a functional organization and some would say that this structure is dysfunctional for the project. In such structures, the functional roles are so inbred over time that they become micro-organizations of their own and take a very independent view of their internal resources, goals, and so on. A name given to this culture is *stovepipe*, meaning that each functional entity tends to live in its own space. Another popular metaphor is to describe this as a *fiefdom* with its leader being a *Tribal Chief*. Obviously, these connotations indicate more of a closed relationship, but are good memory devices to highlight the potential issues.

Project processes basically need to work horizontally through the functional organization structure to acquire the needed diverse set of resources. This requires the functional culture to be supportive. The most noticeable collaborative example between the function and the project is the flow of resources. Failure to achieve a reasonable timely allocation of quality and quantity of resources for the needed functions will almost certainly sabotage the project. Such support can either come voluntarily or through some formal authority relationship at a higher level. One of the cultural challenges is to find a way for the functional organization to view the project as a partner in the effort.

The concept of culture is also a relevant term for the overall organization. Ideally, the operational mode for top management is to be a supporter of the project and not a control overseer, but that is often a difficult tightrope to walk. If project is no longer fulfilling its need, then top management has the obligation to shut it down. However, if the project is struggling and needs help with priorities, resources, or refereeing then top management should be prepared to step in and save the project. We will see in upcoming discussion that lack of senior management involvement is one of the major success factors for projects. That role is yet another part of the cultural need.

Organization culture is also like family. It can be harmonious or combative. The more organizational maturity that the organization has, the more likely it is to produce a positive environment for the project. Chapter 34 discusses various contemporary strategies for producing a mature organization that is supportive of the project role.

6.9 Summary

Organizations are complex collections of human beings. The project organization is normally housed inside of its host enterprise envelope and draws much of its energy and resource from that mother organization. Within this structure, the project's physical team organization structure is important, but the physical organization is not the entire picture. Other related factors, such as, formal authority processes to achieve timely decision-making, conflict resolution, resource allocation, and general skill availability also impact the project. In an ideal case, the PM wants to be able to have access to needed skills exactly when they are needed. These team members need to be motivated to accomplish the defined work as specified (scope, schedule, and budget). Similarly, timely decisions by the host organization are needed. Finally, in this ideal heaven, the project team wants everyone to rush to their aid when Murphy's Law comes calling (i.e., things going wrong at the worst possible time). That, then, is the ideal host organization that we need to engineer for success.

Reference

Putnam, D., 1997. "Team Size Can Be the Key to a Successful Project," QSM. www.qsm.com/process_improvement_01.html (accessed October 26, 2017).

Chapter 7

Project Life Cycle Management

7.1 Life Cycle Models

There are many project life cycle model designs based on the project's goal objective, complexity, and bias toward planning. Each one has some unique aspect of its structure and phasing. Small projects typically will combine project logical groups and exhibit a lesser level of planning detail and control. The Project Management Body of Knowledge (PMBOK) would suggest that the various KAs (risk, resource management, quality, etc.) always be reviewed before deciding to omit them from formal consideration. Large, high-technology projects such as those found in the military, NASA, or other government agencies often encompass technical state of the art issues to resolve before the project can move forward. In that type of situation there should be strong consideration to strictly following the full model phases and reviews. Also, in this situation the role of formal technical reviews related to requirements creation and evaluation has value.

Mega-projects spend a significant amount of planning and review time in the various life cycle stages because of related complexity, stakeholder interest, and the high level of resources involved. Alternatively, in the case of a lower technology effort such as that found in traditional building construction there would be much formality in the risk, communication, and HR planning aspects of the project so long as standard components were defined in the design. Also, construction and other industries profit from having well-defined quality standards that can be easily specified in their requirements definition and subsequently implemented based on existing standards documentation. The value of this degree of standardization is a lesson all industries need to adopt more.

7.2 Overview of Project Methodologies

Formalized project management methodologies used today are varied in form and discipline. Recognize that this is a general term, and there can be a methodology to operate a lathe in the machine shop, or to execute a specific type of project. The term is prescriptive in nature, and in the project management domain implies something akin to a standard that is formally supported by management. In fact, a methodology without this level of support is generally worthless. Some commercial products have a reasonable life cycle view, but often document excessive structure to cover all situations. Taken without customization, these tend to fall into disuse. In these situations, use of a predefined methodology is resisted and the team reverts to personal preferences.

In today's environment there is a proliferation of approaches to organize project work, with no one technique broadly accepted as being better than another. Like so many items in the project world, individual beliefs as to the best approach take on religious forms with little real substance to back up one's beliefs.

There are many ways that one can approach selection or definition of a project methodology. One very mature model guidance overview can be found in ANSI-EIA 748. This industry standard offers 32 guideline processes that should be included in the project management architecture. The breadth of this model would certainly be a challenge to tactically implement, but does offer full life cycle tested concepts to review. At the very least it would provide a mechanism for "gap" analysis to evaluate current missing processes. Dwelling deeper into the specific details of this set of guidelines is beyond the scope of this section, but does represent a good technical research target for the organization to commence its review. Therefore, what is this project management methodology? Essentially, it is a *set of guidelines or principles that can be tailored and applied to a specific situation*. In a project environment, these guidelines might be a list of things to do, or general processes to be followed. A methodology could also be a specific approach with defined templates, forms, and even checklists used over the project life cycle (Charvat, 2003, p. 3).

The increased complexity of current projects requires much tighter organizational integration and innovativeness than ever before. This is not to say that everything described in the PMBOK model is the absolute correct answer, but one should carefully question moving away from tested techniques such as those found in the PMBOK. One of the factors driving contemporary project management is the push to improve completion speed. Several methodologies being offered today use that banner to attract attention. Certainly, one way to achieve a faster result is to adopt newer, swifter, and "lighter" project methodologies. On the counter side of this argument, projects are becoming more complex, which brings with it the need for careful time-consuming planning. The dilemma with this conflicting dual goal conundrum is how to cut cycle times while maintaining quality and visibility. Whatever one's answer to the standardization question, it should consider how best to make this trade-off.

We have stated earlier that all projects have similarities in process, so can a specific methodology be applied to an industry, or customized to reflect a specific project environment within a single organization? The answer to this is yes, but the question is to what degree. The secret to success for any methodology is that it contains defined processes that serve as the foundation for a successful project initiative, supported by sufficient documentation. Attributes of a successful methodology approach include:

- Defines best practices,
- Supports consistency of results,
- Defines work required, and
- Internal logic leads to quicker results.

In addition to these attributes, the following process design ideas can speed up even a traditional methodology:

- Maintaining a library of historic artifacts that can help other follow on projects (i.e., lessons learned, templates, etc.)

- Improving the team communication technology, particularly for virtual teams (i.e., video conferencing)
- Focused training programs to educate team members on both technical and management processes (see Chapter 20)
- Improved management related tools to help the methodology process steps flow faster (i.e., scheduling, planning, tracking, reporting, etc.)
- Improved resource allocation process to deliver team resources in a more timely and efficient manner
- Improved plan scheduling ideas to improve cycle times (see Part V of the book for several ideas on this)
- Design a nimbler methodology, or find ways to produce required documentation more efficiently (i.e., workflow automation, etc.)
- Organizational support process that can help the project to be more efficient (see Part VII of the book for ideas here)

When organizations describe their methodology, they are implying that there has been some formal thought regarding the technical and management approach to be used by their projects. There is a well-known comment that emerges in the technology project world that goes something like this: "the nice thing about our standards is that we have so many to pick from." Pause for a second and think about that statement (a variety of *standards*?). This same view often applies to methodologies and unfortunately raises a question about following any one of these, since another "silver bullet" solution is soon to follow.

Realize that the various defined activities in a methodology are intended to help create specific artifacts related to management activities in the project life cycle. A well-designed methodology can increase operational productivity through a common set of vocabulary which is used for communication among the various participants. A third element of the methodology that aids productivity is the use of a template library of tested life cycle artifacts, work processes, and sample documentation (see Appendix B). Having these items in place represents a critical element in a mature project infrastructure.

It is important to recognize that a one size fits all methodology may well not be the best approach. As an example, one very mature organization customized its methodology into three separate project types—small, medium, and large. In this fashion the specifications better fit their environment and the project teams had less customization required to fit their specific project needs. Also, as project teams are trained to utilize these standard materials there is less thrashing around designing similar items. As a result, a standard methodology-based project should progress with less stress than typically found in other less mature structures. The point to recognize here is that a methodology does not bring value unless it fits the environment and a standard commercial package may not be the best fit.

Commercial methodology models are offered by various vendors. A good starting place to pursue implementation of an off the shelf model would be to review industry-specific project models from sources such as trade associations and web search engines. Also, organizations such as PMI, TenStep (www.tenstep.com), and other industry organizations have models and data related to their products. In addition, several large consulting firms offer models and services in this area. Other published methodologies are often associated with industry or consulting organizations and fit their general class of projects, organizational culture, and other such factors. For many industry types, very robust methodologies exist; however, buying a commercial methodology and installing it unaltered in an organization will typically result in minimal or nil value. We now know that project management is more than a mechanical set of steps.

The important item to realize regarding project methodologies is that they can dramatically impact the culture of an organization both positively and negatively; therefore, installation represents more than dumping the documentation and expecting the participants to change behavior. In fact, changing human behavior is the most difficult part of this process. Though project methodologies offer many benefits, they have potential shortcomings too. It is equally important to understand where methodologies can possibly go wrong. Many users characterize shortcomings in traditional project methodologies as follows:

- Too abstract and high level to be translated into workable processes
- Does not address crucial areas such as quality, risk, communications, and so on
- Ignores current industry standards and best practices
- Looks impressive but lacks real integration with the business
- Uses nonstandard project conventions and terminology
- Does not have appropriate performance metrics
- Takes too long to execute because of embedded bureaucracy and administration
- Too hard to learn

At a high-level, the PMBOK is a project management methodology model that has stood the test of time regarding its structure and general content. However, this model is not a canned methodology with how to sample documentation and templates. Nevertheless, it would be useful as a guide in a customization exercise. To be successful with any methodology implementation, there is a required stakeholder buy-in and some customization required to fit the environment. Customization helps gain organizational buy-in and generally increases the odds of success. The caution here is that an organization cannot just create a methodology and send out the documentation for team members to read. Motivation and selling are needed, as well as proper training. The final result has to make sense to the project teams who will use it. A project team member once described his required methodology as "feeding a dinosaur." The implication was that it required a lot of feeding and did not bring added value. If that is the perception, it will be hard to sell the process. Project team members are under too much time stress to want to do something that does not appear to help them produce a desired output. This same criticism is common for project management in general and educational efforts are important to show why doing activities that appear to be wasted overhead do in fact add value. There is a fine line between good project management and excessive overhead. Only enlightened professionals can judge the proper balance.

Part of the evolutionary process for a successful process is to document past experiences (good and bad) and continually redesign them in an attempt to optimize the next iteration. Projects have both a technical process component and an intertwined management layer. The technical components are represented by the task sequence necessary to produce a defined deliverable, while the associated management tasks add needed visibility and control related to the technical group.

As an organization matures in their methodology usage, they will tend to add selective processes related to the various knowledge areas (KAs) represented by the PMBOK model. For example, the maturation process will highlight the value of formal management activity related to areas such as risk, communications, and quality that might not have been a major part of the initial implementation. This statement is particularly true related to risk management activities. Earlier discussion outlined a general set of activities relevant to the project life cycle. Many organizations have taken this type of view to describe their methodology around a customized standard time-phased task list. In this view, the tasks cascade through the life cycle. Models of this type have even been given the name *waterfall* to describe how the various tasks progress (cascade) in more or less serial fashion. There is similarity in this view across most methodologies.

Given the definition of a project, all methodologies should define a formal starting point (initiating) and a closing process regardless of how the internal work processes are connected. The middle of the life cycle will contain activities related to planning, execution, and control in some form. Logically, some level of initial planning is required, and the execution phase represents the core product delivery activity, so much of the technical work sequence would be defined there. Monitoring and control strategies are more philosophical in nature in that there are varying opinions as to how much of this should be done; however, some form is required in the basic workflow. Very few projects can exist without a formal status reporting activity. The PMBOK is rigorous in this area, more so than most organizations follow. In addition to these broad process groupings, the concept of defined phases is fundamental to the management control process. Even in a low technology project, such as, a house construction project, there is a need for some defined phase management review. In this example, the phases may need to be established simply to confirm that the foundation meets specifications, or that the wiring and plumbing are installed properly before allowing the process to move forward. For more complex projects, the phase reviews become much more rigorous and include the complete gamut of project status parameters. In this complex project class, the phase review often deals with the decision to kill the project, rather than just being sure that the previous step was done properly. Note in these two diverse examples, the management role is to properly approve what needs to be done for successful completion and then monitor that definition and status through the life cycle. In building a house, the primary issue is to execute the technical sequence using industry standards, while in a high-technology effort the control focus might be more concerned with status tracking and various management concerns.

For all the reasons outlined here, one should look at a methodology as more than a single cook book of instructions. There is great commonality in the concepts but also subtle differences across the spectrum of project types. Organizations should work toward finding some reasonable level of standardization across their project suite. As employees are transferred across this domain, the level of learning required is greatly reduced if similarity of process and vocabulary exists. The most obvious value is the savings related by not having to reinvent a basic technical and management sequence for each project. It is much easier to tweak a standard tested model and use most of it rather than having to think through a complete project design process each time. The standard model will have been tested for general validity, and the workforce should be knowledgeable regarding its processes and vocabulary. In addition, management will have approved the defined control processes. Personal experience suggests that this form of project execution can provide significant productivity benefits. All underlying rationale related to the role of methodology standardization is important to the PM and he needs to understand its value, as well as its limitations. The challenge is to motivate the project team and organization to follow something akin to a standardized approach. If the organization views the project team to be process mavericks, they will be judged as poor team players. This is not the attribute that one wants to exhibit.

Realize that this topic involves more than simply defining a process. There are additional complexities related to the associated organizational and human culture side. Internal technical and philosophical discussions on this topic can go on forever as each side pushes for their answer. At some point senior management is going to have to decide the level of standardization that they require. Doing nothing and leaving the organization to drift is the worst answer, so some degree of standardization is the typical approach chosen. At that point, an organization may enter into an internal customization effort which may help with the acceptance aspect, but this also does

Table 7.1 Benefits Offered by Project Methodologies

No.	*Focus Areas*	*Supports Project By*
1	Effective processes	Defining key processes required
2	Reusability	Using key artifacts from project to project
3	Integrated metrics support	Provides techniques to evaluate project performance
4	Quality focus	Ensures proper consideration for quality management
5	Managing complexity	Provides techniques to help sort out root cause issues
6	Project documentation	Provides templates and aid in producing required documentation
7	Standard approach	Provides a mechanism for cross-project comparisons and simplifies team training
8	Consistency	Pursues projects using a similar approach
9	Project planning	Provides project planning techniques
10	Team management	Guides the project team to completion by defined phases
11	Elimination of crises management	By establishing an improved structure, future crises situations are avoided
12	Training	Supports team training through its formal process documentation
13	Knowledge	Supports lessons learned to improve future projects

involve some design efforts. Some organizations will believe that it is easier and cheaper to just buy a solution. Regardless of the direction chosen the following list contains what would be considered significant components of a management methodology whether it be internal or externally defined:

- It defines project phases and decision milestones used to control major activity groupings.
- It defines techniques and variables used to measure progress.
- It defines techniques to take corrective actions based on identified variances from the approved plan.
- It defines the resource management process.

There is sufficient evidence in the industry to support the notion that an effective methodology offers many benefits to the project and organization. Even though a methodology is custom tailored to an organization or a specific project type, it should be recognized that there are well-established best practice management principles that should be examined for inclusion. In other words, customization is more than packaging a set of activities (Charvat, 2003). Table 7.1 outlines many additional benefits offered by a project methodology and it also summarizes what the related project support value is.

The final point to be made here is that methodologies by themselves are not the sole solution to project management problems. They do have the potential of helping guide a project through its life cycle, but there are many other factors involved. An organization must look at its overall strategy before trying to define or implement a standard or custom methodology. Also, the project participants must believe that such a technique will help them achieve their goal and not just be overhead to suffer through.

7.3 Methodology Vocabulary

There is some common language used in most project methodologies and understanding these terms is important for both the model view used in this book as well as other methodologies that one might encounter elsewhere. This section will introduce a sample set of project management life cycle vocabulary that is prevalent in the project environment.

One of the values of a standard methodology is that it uses a defined vocabulary. In the absence of this, communication among the team participants is more difficult as they struggle for terms to represent various project issues and processes. The selected vocabulary items below are frequently used and need to be understood in their context.

7.3.1 Feasibility Review

Most projects have some formal examination review steps regarding technical, political, resource, or economic aspects of the project. In the early stages, these are feasibility-oriented; while later in the life cycle such reviews would be more of a check on that aspect of the project. These planned events are important to have because they collectively decide and dictate the future direction of the project. In the early stages, these events deal with the Business Case vision—i.e., what is the value and reality in pursuing this vision? Once the potential organizational position is dealt with, follow-on steps are needed to evaluate technical, political, and economic feasibility. For example, can the vision be executed technically and at what cost, time, and risk? The concept of feasibility also occurs in other steps of the life cycle as the project moves forward. Each of the feasibility milestone reviews is looked at as a gate through which the project adjusts and then either stops, changes direction, or moves forward. It is important to keep testing the question "is this project still feasible?"

7.3.2 Project Plan

A project plan is like a road map used for a driving trip. There is a defined goal and a defined path to reach that goal. It is recognized that unplanned road outages may occur somewhere along the way and efforts are discussed to deal with such events. However, the key point of the plan is that the goal is defined, along with the time and cost to achieve the goal. The same attributes are true for the project. Every project should proceed under the control of a plan customized in formality level related to its size and complexity. One analogy for this is that one would not consider building a house without a plan, yet multimillion dollar projects are pursued with only rudiments of a plan. An appropriate plan must contain more than a technical goal and more than time and budget projections. It must also describe how the work will be performed and other aspects of the various KAs defined previously.

A key management question for every project is to resolve how much planning is appropriate and how detailed should the plan be. A well-formed project plan should contain sub-plans based on the nine KAs—i.e., quality, risk, procurement, communication, resources, and stakeholders. However, there may be pressure to move into execution before a coherent plan is completed. This move creates added risk and impacts the ability to control the project. On the other side of this coin, there is always the question as to when a plan is sufficient to proceed. At the extreme level, there is a concept called "analysis paralysis" which means the problem was over-analyzed. The underlying theory of planning is that you can't control something that has not been planned. Project plans represent one of the most fundamental artifacts of the management process.

7.3.3 Monitor and Control Process

This activity essentially lies across all the life cycle phases and its role is to measure status and take corrective action as needed to influence the results of the project in the proper direction. Much more on this topic will be described in Part VI of the book.

7.3.4 Project Status

There are several formats and audiences related to this project activity. In some cases, the goal is to periodically distribute formal status results as regular stakeholder communication. A second format is a more rigorous process, typically a formal presentation that verbally describes status. This audience would be focused on examining results and might be charged with assisting in analyzing and resolving deviations from the plan. The third status format involves project future value projections. When is the project forecast to finish? How many more dollars are required until completion? What is the anticipated performance data for the item?

Regardless of the audience or goal, there is a common theme of needing to share project status for one purpose or another. Different audiences will have varying levels of interest and topics in these sessions. One should be able to see from this description that one of the major management activities is collecting status information on a wide variety of items. Chapters 30–33 describe many aspects of the status and tracking side of this topic. The project manager will be constantly challenged to use status data to explain where the project is currently, how it will finish, and evaluate root-cause issues related to ongoing variances.

One of the key management artifacts for this activity is a communications management plan that describes the who, how, what, when, and where targets for ongoing project communications. Failure to execute this part of the management process well is a major causal source of project failure.

7.3.5 Milestone and Stage Gate Reviews

Beyond the major review points outlined above, projects have some additional requirement for a more formal face-to-face technical, user, management, or other group reviews. These may occur at key budget cycle points, with visiting dignitaries, or at key points in the life cycle. One example of a milestone review would be the demonstration of some key technology or pilot prototype performance. As an example of this, during the early design stage for the Dreamliner commercial airplane Boeing engineers were charged with demonstrating that the new carbon fiber wing design was safe. Their approach to a status report was to build a physical mockup of the wing and bend it until it broke. This somewhat unusual status report was meant to ensure all (including the future riders) that the design was safe. One could call this a technical milestone review, but it was also filmed and externally distributed to others, so in fact had a dual role. This is not the typical method to show status, but in this case, it was very effective as consumer concerns over the new material died down. Regardless of the delivery mode, the role of these key control events is to communicate status and obtain feedback.

7.3.6 Logical Versus Physical Design

During early stages of the project life cycle there are various techniques to define the future view of the desired product or process prior to actual work being performed to produce that output. In the case of a physical product, prototypes or scale models are often used (e.g., houses, commercial buildings, airplanes, cars, refineries, software). These examples would be called physical designs since they each represent the output in a somewhat physical form, but do so without actually building the item. In some industries, this process is very mature, whereas in others it is less used. Regardless, physical images of the future items are appealing to non-technical audiences.

In the situation where the project goal is less tangible, the requirements may be translated into what is called a logical design. This format represents an abstraction from the real product. A CAD drawing for a house would be a logical design. Likewise, a flowchart or data model for a computer program would be a logical view.

Regardless of the method used, there will be some effort undertaken to document the design concept for the deliverable. This process helps both future users and technical participants examine the project goal. In similar fashion, it will later help define and estimate the required time to accomplish that goal. Regardless of the method used to document the future project goal, some process of requirements elaboration and evaluation should be undertaken with both technical and user stakeholders prior to moving very far into the life cycle. At this early stage, the concern is more on "what" is going to be done and less initial focus on "how" it would be accomplished.

7.3.7 Quality Control and Assurance

These two quality activities are focused on processes related to delivering the item specified (product or process). Formal review points in the life cycle are used to evaluate the technical process or functional aspects of the output goal. Prior to a physical product being delivered, the technical quality specialist reviews the planned general approach, tool selection, or any other issues related to the ability to deliver the defined output. This process review activity is technically called quality assurance (QA). Its goal is to evaluate the project processes ability to deliver the outputs.

As physical output becomes available, the quality control (QC) function "measures" that output per the plan and defines whether it meets the defined objective. There are many ways in which QC occurs in the organization. In the modern organization there may no longer be an assigned person titled QC inspector. The product evaluation function may come from users and peers who take that role, either formally or informally. Regardless of the individual performing the QC function, the goal is to assess how the output compares to the design specifications. In the case of software, one of the stage evaluations would be code modules that are unit tested and compared to defined requirements. In similar fashion, tangible products would have their subsystems tested based on defined specifications. In all cases, the end-product would be evaluated by internal and external sources as to specification match.

7.3.8 Project Close

All projects should enforce a formal closing process. At this point, appropriate stakeholders and the project team should review final status of the project to evaluate both good and bad results.

This activity includes the deliverable itself, artifacts created during the project, procurement documents, and the orderly release of the team members. The closing process should focus on cleaning-up the shutdown of the project and documenting items that will help future projects (i.e., lessons learned). Capturing lessons learned has been proven to be a viable aid for organizations to improve their internal processes. An often-neglected aspect of the project shutdown is recognizing the team efforts. The goal should be to hold a celebration, regardless of the actual state of the project. It is poor management to just shuffle the players off to the next project with no formal positive recognition of their work efforts.

7.3.9 Templates

Organizations typically develop reusable templates for various types of project documentation and these provide a good starting point for laying out a reasonable process approach to a new project. There is no universal set of templates that will fit all projects, but the use of this strategy can save a great deal of documentation time in the various documentation requirements for the project (See Appendix B for further template discussion and examples). Note that across all projects, there is much more similarity of processes than most recognize. The argument that a particular project is unique is often a lack of understanding of basic project management principles. This point is one of the most important items to take away from this section. The technical sequence of tasks required is certainly different, but the basic life cycle management processes are fundamental. That thesis is stressed throughout the book, but not always accepted by some practitioners.

7.3.10 Project Communication Processes

Various project communications activities will be focused on a variety of organizational entities (typically project team, future users, sponsor, or management). These communication processes often take of the form of paper distribution, web sites, individual conversations, and face-to-face meetings. Communications and related problem solving are some of the most difficult goals for the project team to accomplish. Specifically, excessive use of face-to-face group meetings for this purpose is very costly and represents one of the time and productivity robbers that must be recognized. On the other hand, lack of communications is frequently mentioned as the root cause of project failure.

During project execution, one of the key communication roles is to provide confidence that the project is moving forward in an appropriate manner, or conversely to communicate actual status and reveal what corrective action is being pursued. From a management control viewpoint, continuation of a project that has fallen below its value threshold should be shut down and the communication process is a major part of that decision activity. Runaway projects consume resources that could better be spent on other options. Phase reviews are key life cycle points for formal communication regarding project status.

7.3.11 Baseline

This term refers to some approved project metric parameter. A baseline value can be defined at any stage and for any project parameter. In the ideal case, baseline values would be established after the planning cycle when a well thought out project plan has been approved by stakeholders and appropriate management. At this point, baseline values would be defined for at least schedule and budget, but additional targets could be set for other project attributes such as quality (defects)or performance values (i.e., how fast, etc.). When a baseline parameter is defined, a suffix modifier will be added (e.g., cost baseline, schedule baseline, performance measurement baseline, speed baseline, etc.). One strategy for baselines is to use them for comparative analysis of project performance based on the defined values. In this case, the baseline values would be kept constant and compared to dynamic values for the ongoing project. Another option for baseline definition is to define it consistent with approved changes. So, if formal changes are approved during execution then conceptually that work would be added to the original baseline value. In practice this dynamic view is not the norm.

A third option for handling baselines is to modify the value when the current project is judged to be no longer valid as originally defined. This variance could be caused by internal project issues or external. For example, a period of bad weather could significantly affect the project schedule. Rather than showing the project behind the original baseline owing to external factors, it might be better to change the schedule baseline and track status from that modified value. Philosophically, a baseline is meant to help evaluate project status.

Regardless of the mechanics used, baseline values represent formal targets that are used for comparison and control. Some organizations require that the original baseline be maintained, even if other baselines are defined. This restrictive option clearly shows the amount of variance that has occurred since the initial approved plan.

7.4 Key Project Management Artifacts

Loosely defined, an artifact is an output created in the project work process. Note that this also includes various technical and management documents created as part of the overall life cycle process. This collection of work product is designed to support the management and technical processes as they evolve through the life cycle. The list of items described below is not a complete summary, but provides a good general overview of the basic project management artifacts and processes occurring in the life cycle. Examples are:

- Project plans
- Status reports
- Technical papers
- Change requests
- Meeting notes
- Internal and external communication documents
- Test results
- Project prime deliverables (widget)

More specific examples of these will appear throughout the text in their respective discussion areas.

7.5 Summary Points

The potential operational value of a standard methodology has been outlined here. An effective project management methodology is not just about focusing on life cycles, but also about shortening a company's strategic goal delivery life cycle. No matter how efficient a company is, it needs to adapt constantly to maintain a successful market share. In today's format, project management is struggling with the compromise of trading-off risk for time. For this reason, one should not have a fixed view as to how they will need to proceed toward project success. There clearly is a point that some projects fall into "analysis paralysis" with excessive management rigor. This means that the project studies the effort to death without ever moving into execution. In this case, the effort consumes time and resources without delivering a usable product. On the other side of this argument, a project that performs ineffective planning can fail for myriad of reasons that a good plan might have uncovered. If done properly, planning supports successful delivery. Knowing when to move to the next step is an art form for the PM. Management and users will typically be pushing to move too quickly. Keep these trade-off concepts in mind as you struggle with the question of methodology and level of planning detail.

A final point to leave this discussion-- do recognize that a well-tested standard model has the advantage of supplying an extensive pedagogical and documentation base from which to evolve. Regardless of the process chosen, organizations need to consider making ongoing investments in improving their standardized process methodology. This continuous improvement concept is the essence of a learning organization.

References

Charvat, J., 2003. *Project Management Methodologies: Selecting, Implementing, and Supporting Methodologies and Processes for Projects.* New York: Wiley.

PMI, 2017. *A Guide to the Project Management Body of Knowledge (PMBOK® Guide)*, 6th ed. Newtown Square, PA: Project Management Institute.

Chapter 8

Role of Projects in the Organization

Each organization will have a somewhat unique role for projects based on their business type and level of maturity. This issue can be looked at in two parts. One part involves how a project's value is defined and the second part deals with how project targets are created and pursued by the organization. Both views have undergone significant evolution over the past several years. Regardless of the underlying mechanics, formalization of project roles in the enterprise has been increasing over the past several years. Most organizations now look at the project model as the preferred operational approach to pursue changes in organizational products or processes.

8.1 Project Valuation Models

The process for selecting project targets within the organization remains quite diverse across various industries. Traditionally, these decisions were driven within localized business entities; however, more recent trends have moved toward a more centralized view of project selection and management (Chapters 35 and 36 will discuss these trends in more detail).

While it is obvious that projects are significant features in the landscape of most organizations, the rationale for creating them is not so obvious. It would seem reasonable to conclude that a project is created to pursue some credible organizational goal, but what goal? In reviewing the typical stated benefits for a project, it is common to hear such attributes as follows:

- Achieve competitive market advantage
- Cut operational costs
- Satisfy compliance requirements
- Achieve a strategic objective (that may not be financially quantified)
- Improve an operational process
- Evaluate a new technology (R&D)

A project is often chartered to improve an existing process. For example, automating a payroll system might be justified by cutting labor cost, improving preparation cycle time, or cutting processing errors. In many such early cases, an attempt would be made to justify the project by showing how it produced some tangible benefit over its projected life cycle. Technology-based projects often have the characteristics shown for the payroll example—cost, cycle time, and lower processing errors. Justification for such projects is often based on a schematic cost-benefit view as exemplified in Figure 8.1.

Using this valuation model, the initial costs would be represented by a down arrow, while upward arrows would represent the future benefits. Monetary values would then be estimated for all cost and benefit flows over a reasonable projected life of the product. From this view, various financial metrics could then be produced to show a value parameter. Typical evaluation metrics used are:

- Payback—how long it took to pay back the investment,
- Net present value (NPV)—using the time value of money is the investment justified,
- Internal rate of return (IRR)—a more sophisticated analysis of the actual percentage return from the investment, or
- Benefit-cost ratio (BCR)—a modified metric to show benefits divided by cost.

Appendix A offers more details on the calculation mechanics for these metrics. In the case of projects designed to replace human labor, the financially driven methods are reasonable, but as the breadth and complexity of project goals increased, it became obvious that a valuation model was much more complex than described above.

A second evolution of the project valuation model added consideration of intangible benefits to the structure, although these less quantitative considerations are evolving it is still common to keep some form of quantitative justification. The basic problem with intangibles is that various stakeholders might value or rate them differently and this complicates comparative analysis across projects. Financial types are more sensitive to quantification, while operational types might be more sensitive to softer items such as morale, ease of operations, and so on. In any case, recognition of intangibles opened the door to a more complete view of project value. Projects that would have been rejected using tangible criteria might now be accepted for less financial reasons.

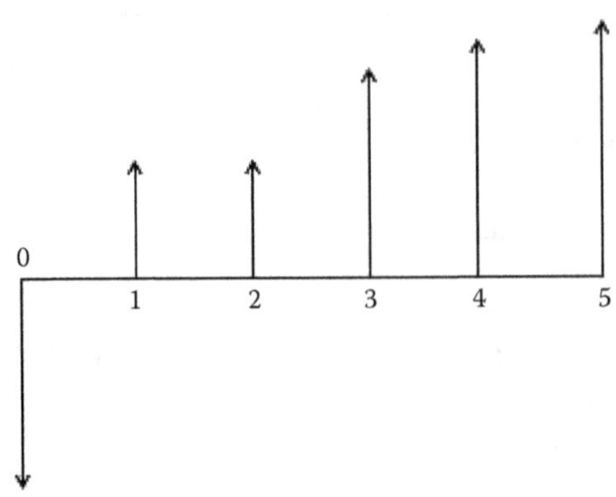

Figure 8.1 Project cost-benefit forecast.

As the valuation process continued to evolve, various other factors were added to the equation. Intangibles could be included for items such as customer or employee factors. In this mode, an automated customer response system might be rated lower based on a less desirable intangible factor (i.e., customer desires for a live person). If the automated system chases the customer away, is this project still considered a successful option? Cost effective for sure, but it does not help the organizational goal set. This example shows that intangibles are often subtle, but clearly should be considered in the valuation process. Some projects have little technical or customer risk, but when one of those considerations is present it highlights yet another dimension of the evaluation. If risk was considered in the early evaluations, it was more on the delivery side. As the processes matured it became obvious that failure to consider the downside of risk on the user side could wipe out a project that otherwise showed a great tangible financial benefit.

A third stage of project valuation perspective recognized yet another role of projects in the organization. This view hits at the core of the organizational goal structure. That is, projects should be created to support organizational goals and these goals can be very diverse in nature. Whereas the traditional view of a project was more local in scope, the third evolutionary wave moved that view toward a more top-level perspective. It now became necessary to deal more with linking organizational goals to projects than just evaluating the project itself. This view highlighted that some projects might be undertaken with no tangible estimation of future value. Management might decide that some initiative should be undertaken to evaluate the potential of a technology or market. From this view, they would charter something akin to an R&D pursuit. Some government regulatory-oriented projects have a similar lack of tangible benefit. Historically, high-tech organizations have derived values from projects in quite unexpected ways. The perceived reason to pursue an initiative was not at all where the future benefits were eventually recognized. This new view of projects seeks to encompass tactical versus strategic initiatives, along with environmental, stockholder, and other perspectives. Clearly, the new generation of evaluation metrics must include both soft and hard financial justification, with organizational goal perspectives linked to the project objectives.

The concept of linking project roles to organizational goals remains a fundamental aspect of project value measurement; however, the enterprise view of value measurement continues to mature in its perspective as we will see shortly. Expanding the view of project value to include multiple attributes minimizes the idea that some quantifiable metric can be used to compare one project with another. In reality, the valuation activity has long been political in nature and that situation has grown as the cost of projects increased and the level of review expanded more toward top management. Today, project overview remains extremely political, risky, and technically complex. It certainly should not be thought of as simply defining the cost versus benefits with the decision made obvious from that calculation. Defining multidimensional project valuation criteria compounds the complexity model in regard to comparing dissimilar proposals. Many different techniques are described for this in the literature. Merkhofer describes multiple types of metrics useful for allocating resources. This includes the following (Merkhofer, 2003):

- Opportunity cost analysis
- Sensitivity analysis (variable estimates)
- Multi-period planning

This level of model sophistication remains beyond the capability of the typical organization, but it does reveal some of the analysis issues that are relevant in the discussion. Concepts are related to missed opportunities, variation in estimates (risk), resource availability constraints, multi-period views and project grouping, and so on. In this environment, the process of project selection has risen to a new plane of sophistication, but remains an ongoing challenge for organizations.

The fourth evolutionary wave brings the project valuation story to the current time period. During the latter 1990s, proliferation of project activity in organizations made it clear that some type of centralized control was needed for project selection and resource allocation. Multiple studies of project selection indicated that organizations were not getting full value from their allocation of resources. Merkhofer reported that only about 60% of the value was realized (Merkhofer, 2003). Recognition of this phenomenon spurred industry interest in two directions: better project selection techniques and better project management to deliver the defined results. This fourth wave is described as a portfolio view of projects. No longer were projects reviewed on a stand-alone basis with local benefits. Now, projects were viewed at the enterprise level and focused on organizational goals and comparison with other proposals in the portfolio. The analogy used here is similar to a capital allocation model. So, the primary selection goal is to select and complete a slate of projects that optimize organization goal achievement. Unfortunately, we are still left with the basic question regarding how to do this mechanically in terms of a valuation metric. Chapters 35 and 36 will explore the operational project portfolio mechanics in greater detail. For the remainder of this discussion, we will focus on basic organizational strategies that are used to develop project candidates.

8.2 Project Selection Strategies

Hirschheim and Sabherwal envision a project role consistent with the business personality. In concert with this, they describe a framework consisting of three project selection strategies: Defenders, Prospectors, and Analyzers (Hirschheim and Sabherwal, 2001, p. 215). In this structure, the primary role of the project is one of the following:

- Defender—defends a stable and predictable but narrow niche in its industry.
- Prospector—seeks new opportunities and creates change in the market.
- Analyzer—seeks to simultaneously minimize risk while maximizing opportunities for growth.

This view is insightful in that it shows how an organization should approach the project selection process to be in philosophical alignment with what the broad company mission and goals. This view also dictates other decision strategies such as project organization structure, resource acquisition sources, and the target change level to the business.

A Defender-type organization tends to work toward maximum operational efficiency and the likelihood is that the organization does not have high growth objectives. On the other extreme, the Prospector organizational culture seeks out targets of opportunity and the project selection bias should follow that path. This would result in higher project expenditures and more aggressive use of new technologies.

Unfortunately, some organizations do not define clearly what they really are trying to be and in fact are schizophrenic in their project selection behavior. Both traits can cause a mismatch in project selections and a less effective alignment with organizational goals. One example of this occurs when the organization selects a high-risk strategic goal, while leaving many other project selections in the Defender mode. Another mismatch situation occurs when the timing of one proposal does not match with another, even if both are appropriate technical choices. Beyond these examples, there are also many other situations that create internal misalignment and cause the selection process to be out of synchronization. To better identify these issues, it is necessary to have a common valuation process that matches the organizational goal structure.

The project selection process represents the demand side of the equation, while monetary and human resources are related key supply side considerations. In most cases, it is the supply side represents the critical constraints that most impact what projects can be undertaken. Second, organizations are also constrained by the level of tolerance they have for levels of change created by excessive project initiatives and this represents a subtle constraint that is often overlooked. All organizations have change absorption limitations, but the operational question is at what point do you curtail spending and where do you allocate scarce resources.

Benefit timing is yet another aspect of the resource allocation issue. It is much easier to envision the value for short-term opportunities and often deemed much riskier to pursue strategic targets with a long-term payback. Based on this, many organizations focus only on the short-term initiatives, which in turn will limit their market position over the longer term. To maintain the organization over the longer time period, some mix of tactical and strategic options must be pursued. Imagine the buggy whip company that acted in the Defender mode and continued to refine that business model by being the most efficient in the industry only to wake up one day to find out that no one needed buggy whips any longer. Clearly, some consideration should have been given to the changing market view at the expense of operational efficiency.

All organizations need to stay positioned for strategic change and their project slate should support that evolution. As an example, Apple computers saw that they were not being competitive in their traditional computer industry and modified the project slate to significantly change their business model with iPod and iPhones. These were nontraditional, high-risk projects that moved the company to a new market and beat the competition. Failure for the host organization to invest in these initiatives would have left Apple as a minority computer company. Imagine what this business decision must have looked like with a planner going to a senior organizational manager saying something like "boss, I want to start making a small device to play music." Most Defender organizations would have responded to this by saying "we don't do music, we do computers. You need to understand our goals." Conversely, Prospector organizations must have a management culture that is willing to look at new perspectives. Several years ago, Digital Equipment was the leading producer of minicomputers. When the proposal for producing personal computers was made to the founder, his response was that no one wants a computer in their home. Digital no longer exists in the market and that is the penalty for being dogmatic in regard to project selection criteria.

Regardless of one's belief about the correct way to allocate resources, it is clear that there needs to be a formal project decision-making mechanism that adds a degree of high-level management and control to the process, whether this is at the departmental or enterprise level. The chosen allocation slate should be consistent with the organizational goals. This suggests that the way to obtain maximum value is to centralize the allocation of these resources and focus them on management approved target areas. Some would argue that centralized planning adds a level of bureaucracy that in turn takes away the agility of the organization to react quickly to business changes. The challenge for centralized management of this activity is to not let the process get bogged down in bureaucracy, yet keep a nimble approach to project selection based on competitive factors. A historical review of organizational decisions by Apple, Digital and more recently Toyota Prius would help reinforce these ideas.

In 2003, BMC undertook a survey of approximately 240 respondents to quantify the state of alignment maturity in medium to large organizations (BMC, 2003, p. 3). The results of this survey provide a good discussion structure for the topic and some analytical data to show how organizations do the project selection process. The survey grouped 45 alignment practices into four broad areas: Plan, Model, Manage, and Measure. The level of operational maturity was categorized into five groups (BMC, 2003, p. 4):

- Chaos—no standard process.
- Reactive—multiple processes/procedures in place; little standardization.
- Proactive—standards and documentation exist; minimal compliance assurance.
- Service—processes are standardized, and compliance is managed; some automated tools.
- Value creation—processes have been matured to best practices; continuous improvement and benchmarking in place.

Based on this maturity grading scale, there were six qualitative conclusions drawn that were very interesting, (BMC, 2003, p. 5):

1. There is a strong relationship between business alignment maturity level and the participants' assessment of overall efficiency and alignment.
2. Organizations that rated highly on item one also showed positive assessments in managing change.
3. Existence of a strong management organization was linked to item one.
4. Integrated metrics and scorecards by mature participants provided consistent management data across all functions.
5. Top performers in the study based on maturity scores were also viewed as top in the qualitative assessments.
6. Overall, the study population did not rate highly in the alignment area, although there were a few who were very mature in this area.

Within the model groupings, there was more process maturity observed in measurement than in modeling capability. The average score was halfway between reactive and proactive, with 70% of the respondents below the proactive state. Large organizations fared better than middle-sized ones in terms of maturity across the model groups. Quantitative studies of this type add improved understanding of the value resulting from proper goal alignment and ultimately how to accomplish the goal. Another key point derived from this study is that organizations have not yet achieved mature decision processes in the alignment arena and more management focus is needed in this area to improve the project selection process.

8.3 Conclusion

Maintaining a project's goal alignment with its host organization is a fundamental management activity that lies above the project management domain. There is a familiar adage that "garbage in results in garbage out." This is certainly true in the case where a poor project approval decision process can lead to nothing but a bad outcome, no matter how well the effort is managed. We have also seen evidence that there is much to be gained in regard to added business value and improved perceptions when this activity is properly carried out. Industry surveys and other research indicate that most organizations can use improvement in this process. In any case, selecting the right portfolio of projects to pursue is a fundamental activity in the global view of project management.

Discussion Questions

1. What key project-type decision led Amazon to beat competitors in the Internet marketing game? Name some of the internal synergies that collectively helped win this competition.
2. What kind of project selection decision should Apple follow to maintain their competitive position in the electronic tool market? How can a competitor displace Apple?

References

BMC Software, 2003. Business Service Management Benchmarking Study Stage II. Routes to Value: An Actionable Approach to Business Service Management (A White Paper). www.bmc.com (accessed January 26, 2005).

Hirschheim, R. and R. Sabherwal, 2001. Detours in the path toward strategic information systems alignment. *California Management Review*, 44, 1, 87–108.

Merkhofer, L., 2003. Choosing the Wrong Portfolio of Projects: And What Your Organization Can Do About It (A Six Part Series). www.prioritysystem.com/reasonscomplete.pdf (accessed October 26, 2017).

Chapter 9

Project Success Factors

9.1 Which Factors to Consider?

If one were to search the Internet for titles such as *project success factors*, or *project failure statistics*, a myriad of responses will emerge. After sampling a few of these studies one comes to the conclusion that there are many factors mentioned and the studies often conclude different rank severity. Even the definition of success or failure is varied across the list. One almost has to admit defeat on this topic from the beginning. One way out of this is to just suggest that most of the chapter titles in this book represent success/failure root causes. In other words, perform each one of these well and the results will be better. The fact is, there is research evidence suggesting if all projects were executed using all of the principles in this book the success rate would be higher than average. Contrarily, we are not saying that doing this would result in 100% success either.

Projects have both internal and external variables at play that can overwhelm even the best of management processes. Many of the external issues are very hard to control and even one of these may be sufficient to cause failure—one example of this is frequent changes in requirements coming from organization goal changes. Also, there are factors in the internal project environment that will also contribute to failure regardless of the management or process skills used. What is more important at this stage is to understand that projects are complex and they do suffer significant failure rates. In some cases the failures can bankrupt the organization, but in any case the overall global cost of U.S. project failure is billions of dollars annually. Here is another interesting point to consider. There is not a lot written about the projects that are successful, but the typical focus is on projects that did not do well. Many assume that if you reverse the failure variables, success will result. There is probably some truth to that, but this still avoids the best overall approach.

9.2 Standish Surveys

The Standish Group has been tracking criteria for project success and failure for several years, and these surveys offer great insight into issues that are important to success (Lynch, 2015). Since their inception during the 1990s, these annual survey results have surprisingly varied very little in regard to the top 10 items linked to success/failure. Given this relatively static perspective, it

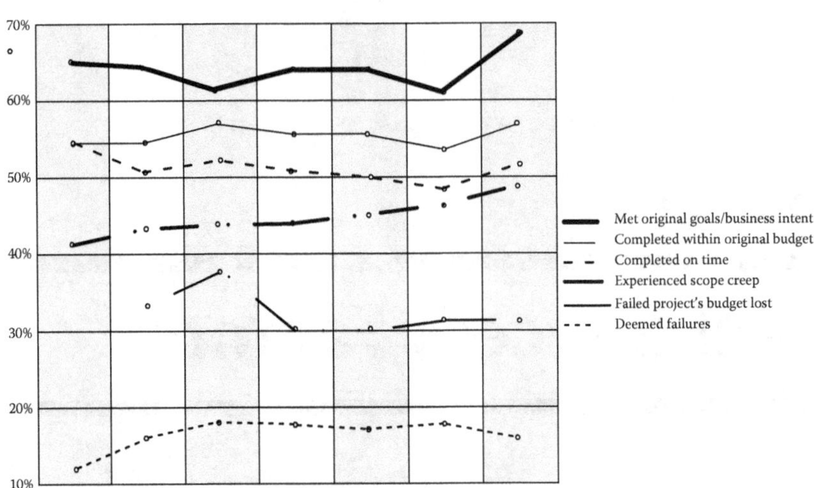

Figure 9.1 Project performance history. (Standish Group. With permisson.)

seems prudent to review these and other similar factors as a first look at the project environmental factors. Figure 9.1 contains industry project performance trends from 2011 to 2015.

Project performance also varies by the size of the effort. Traditionally, success was defined by how well the project finished in regard to function, schedule, and cost. As time has gone by this metric has become more complex and now has added factors. We'll see more of that definitional issue later, but at this point you have a clue that the definition of success is not a simple quantitative calculation.

9.3 Project Performance Trends

Table 9.1 shows various project performance trends over the period of 2011–2017.

Three notable results can be seen from this data:

- Projects hit the major business target 60–70% range—this does not mean it succeeded, but was focused on the right target
- Projects on average fail in the teens (approx. 18%)
- Projects finish on schedule and budget in the lower 50% range

Table 9.1 Project Performance Metrics 2011–2017

	2011 (%)	*2012 (%)*	*2013 (%)*	*2014 (%)*	*2015 (%)*
Successful	29	27	31	28	29
Challenged	49	56	50	55	52
Failed	22	17	19	17	19

Source: PMI Pulse (2017, p. 5).

Table 9.2 Project Factors by Size

	Successful (%)	*Challenged (%)*	*Failed (%)*
Grand	2	7	17
Large	6	17	24
Medium	9	27	31
Moderate	21	33	17
Small	62	16	11
Total	100	100	100

Source: Standish Group (with permission).

More importantly, note that these trends are not showing much improvement over time. Does this mean that organizations are not learning how to manage their projects better, or is there some factor hidden below this level that inhibits improvement? The answer to that question is much more complex than a yes or no.

9.4 Project Performance by Size

One of the first clues regarding performance variability is answered in the results shown in Table 9.2. There are clear performance differences in large versus small projects. Some often-stated reasons for this are:

- Easier to define requirements (smaller scope)
- Quicker to produce results (less time to need changes)
- Smaller team size makes communications easier
- Often times has a smaller set of users to deal with

Although not a surprising revelation, it is important to recognize that larger initiatives are more complex in many ways and the results reflect that. What is not so obvious is the degree to which this statement is true. Note the success rate of small versus large projects is (62% versus 2%) in favor of small. The failed category is not so significantly different, but the extreme differences on the success side must be kept in mind.

9.5 Standish Factors of Success

The next view of success factors is what Standish defines as attributes or elements correlated to success. Table 9.3 ranks the top 10 factors that are attributed to success, along with a point value to indicate level of correlation.

Historically, the most frequent top three items have been Senior Management, User Support, and Clear Objectives (requirements). The 2015 survey results inserted Emotional Maturity into the second slot and replaced Clear Objectives which moved down to the 10th position. Notice, if the "point" value for first five items on this list was added, the total factor impact would be 71%.

Table 9.3 Standish Factors of Success

Factors of Success	*Points*
Executive sponsorship	15
Emotional maturity	15
User involvement	15
Optimization	15
Skilled resources	20
Standard architecture	8
Agile process	7
Modest execution	6
Project management expertise	5
Clear business objective	4

Source: Standish Group (with permission).

This implies that if these five items were eliminated a major improvement in success would be anticipated. And the corollary is that failure would be decreased.

Once again it is important to point out that 20 years of results have shown very little improvement in the 10 factors related to project success. This is an almost unbelievable statistic and one that the industry has been slow to deal with. If these are truly the factors, would it not make sense to actively pursue how to engineer these processes more effectively? On the surface all the items seem like they can be addressed. The alternative conclusion is that these are constant factors that cannot be improved. The author's bias is that the truth is more of the former. There is survey data to suggest that serious pursuits of project management initiatives are not favorite topics for many organizations, at least not on the level described in this text. Rather, there is a visible survey trend indicating that the more popular focus is on speeding up the project life cycle, which may in fact worsen some of the other existing factors. The speed-up trend can be seen in Table 9.3 for the Agile and Modest Execution (size) items. Item eight does mention Project Management Expertise, but that does not show specifically what the improved expertise strategy is.

One interesting survey result occurs in line 10 for Clear Business Objectives. This item has been much higher ranked in the past, so there is some evidence of a rational reaction to improve this area. However, the main question about general stability of the major factors remains unexplained. Why are the top factors not declining each year as efforts are made to improve? Our task here is not to answer that question, but to point out the targets and suggest that they would make good initiatives for improvement. Every organization and project should be reviewed keeping these characteristics in mind. The sections below will offer some further discussion on selected items from the factor list in Table 9.3.

9.5.1 Executive Management Support

Support from senior management is the long-term winner for the number one item on the Standish list and is a similar ranking on many other surveys. On one hand, it is not obvious why someone outside of the project team can have such an impact on the final results. It would appear that a well-structured project team with appropriate business and technical participants could execute the requirements without significant senior management involvement. This might in fact be the case if requirements were completely and accurately defined at the initial stage, cost estimates were accurate, schedules accurately defined, and all other extraneous organizational events insignificant. Unfortunately, few of these positives exist in the typical project. Requirements evolve and grow as more is defined in the course of the project life cycle. Various stakeholders surface with differing views on scope and direction for the team. Unplanned technical issues often surface that lead to adverse issues for the plan (i.e., time, cost, etc.). To top all this, the organizational priorities may change over time in such a way as to cause corresponding changes needed in the project goal set. For these reasons and many more, the proper role for senior management in these situations is to be an engaged supporter and help to keep the team focused on the right targets.

In model theory, senior management formally approves a project Charter, which formalizes the project and implicitly says that management will support the effort. Later, from periodic status reports and timely communications senior management must understand enough of the ongoing situation to judge how to support the effort from the enterprise viewpoint. This does not always mean to continue funding a project, but it does mean that they have a role in deciding when and how to support the effort. If senior management is not involved at a reasonable level they cannot properly help or make these difficult decisions. In the final analysis, the project is their ultimate responsibility. The sponsor, project manager, and the team should all feel like they own the project. If the effort goes well, the reward should be left with the team. If it begins to erode, the ownership issues creep up the organizational ladder until all are left with the responsibility. This is a subtle point, but an important management concept.

9.5.2 Emotional Maturity

This second ranked term is a somewhat catch all description related to the soft skill capability of the team to execute the project goal. Project teams are a caldron for potential conflict and failure to have this level of maturity can destroy the team's ability to function. An environment with low emotional maturity (EM) will struggle with conflicts and group decision-making. Also, proper communication, collaboration, and team building are other factors that fit this category. What has been recognized over the last few years are the differences in team productivity. Even though this is a difficult factor to measure, the result on project performance is observable.

9.5.3 User Involvement

Item number three on the success factor list is easy to relate in regard to impact on success. Omission of this group from the equation leaves the project team to guess at requirements for one thing. As the project unfolds, needed changes in the required deliverables would be missed. Intuitively, this factor seems even more important than the senior management role, but both make sense as key factors. During the early project period, scope of the effort must be clearly defined. This comes from the user side, so missing that element would lead directly to poor requirements. In many cases, the non-technical human component believes that their involvement is complete when the project is approved. History suggests that is not the case.

In order to be successful, a project team must build an ongoing close partnership with the business sponsor, key subject matter experts (SMEs), and the project team who will execute the requirements. A gap results when users do not understand that technical work is translated from the defined functionality, which in turn comes from the user side. This linkage needs to stay intact through the life cycle to ensure ongoing alignment. There is one subtlety here. The users actually define ultimate success and not the sponsor, project manager, or team. This does not necessarily mean that the project will have been finished on time or on schedule.

Regardless of time and cost overruns, only the users can effectively judge the final resultant value of the effort. Failure to keep them involved can mean that the functionality gap is not found until the end when changes can't reasonably be made. Omission of close user support leaves the technical team to interpret requirements to fill the gaps. Leaving success definition to the project team would default to them trying to interpret the initial defined requirements (good or bad). From that base the only other variables for them to deal with are the initial schedule, and budget. This support gap can actually create excessive scope creep once the requirements gap is recognized later in the life cycle. Continuous communication is required to ensure that the right business problem is being solved, even if it is not the one originally understood. A well-run project producing the wrong output is still a failure.

To counter the lack of user involvement factor, many organizations believe that the project team should be managed by a business person in order to ensure close participation between the business and technical sides. There are pros and cons for such a strategy. On one hand, this increases the linkage to the business side of the effort, but placing a business person in charge of a technical team can lead to flawed technical decisions that in turn lead to equally bad project results. Hence, there is no clear answer as to the best way to deal with project team management. Regardless of the option chosen, there must be clear communication input from both the business view and the technical side. The concept of a partnership is often used to describe the proper arrangement. Roles of both parties need to be understood and managed. The business side should view their primary responsibility as the "what" of the project, while the technical participants should be held responsible for the detailed "how." Project team organization roles and responsibilities should be created to support this view. Regardless of the structure selected, failure to achieve user involvement through the life cycle will almost surely doom the effort to less than desirable results.

9.5.4 Optimization

This term is one of the more difficult factors to define, but the essence of this lies in the way in which the project is managed in terms of a business focus, as well as the internal processes used to achieve the goal.

Previous discussion has described the role and structure of a formalized methodology for project execution. If properly applied, this form of standardization can be productive because of the underlying processes that are familiar to the various stakeholders. Properly done, the result will improve productivity and speed through reusable components such as templates, operational processes, lessons learned, and a common vocabulary. There is research evidence from William Ibbs and others that this type of organizational maturity has a positive impact on project success (Ibbs and Young, 2000). The sensitive issue here is to ensure that the methodology is flexible enough to handle different project types and sizes. One approach does not fit all situations. The issue of increased risk management has come up in other discussions. In this case, the risk element is related to management oversight and documentation specified in a methodology. Improperly employed it will in effect sabotage team productivity. More control and oversight should be applied to larger and mission critical projects; less for smaller and noncritical projects. One size methodology is not the correct approach. Project teams left to their own devices often choose to do little documentation or status communication. Obviously, this is not a desirable outcome for most efforts, so it is necessary to think through the control and management activities for each effort and obtain agreement regarding how much is appropriate and then specify this as part of the formal project plan.

9.5.5 Skilled Resources

Of all the factors on the success list this one is the most obvious. How can you execute a complex technical undertaking without skilled human resources that understand how to execute the task? The fact that this item is not number one of the list likely means that it is widely recognized and already focused on as part of a success strategy. It surely does not mean that it is number five in importance. Every manager recognizes that skill levels are variable across different workers, so their impact on budget and schedule are clear in this regard. Also, there may be some aspects of the project that can only be accomplished by a highly skilled individual. We will see implications resulting from skill variability in many future discussions. As a side note, this is one of the hazards of looking at the factor side of the issue. Dropping concern for this item would quickly pop it back up in importance later.

9.5.6 Standard Architectures

One way to think of a project architecture is to envision the project existing inside a larger organization. That host provides a lot of the elements needed for the project to execute—facilities, systems, resources, functional support, etc. A well-run organization nurtures the project with these variables. Conversely, lack of this support means that the project has to essentially deal with supplying these items and not really being prepared to do much of this (i.e., legal, procurement, resource skills). By having a good host organization, the project can focus on doing the technical work and utilizing standard processes from the host by just plugging into a defined and well-managed foundation. Too often, a new project will have to create its own tools and processes that have to be created as part of the project technical work. Having to create this support processes is essentially nonproductive to the end requirement and consumes valuable resources. If excessive, such activity will negatively impact the project capability to deliver. Using the host organizations standard management components and processes should be stressed whenever possible for this reason.

9.5.7 Agile Processes

There is a growing school of thought among project cultures that the classic waterfall model outlined in Chapter 7, Project Life Cycle Management, does not work well since users do not really know what they want until they see some piece of the output. In some project types the Agile approach is not feasible, but the concept of finding methods to show functionality early is increasing. Use of quick prototypes has long been a technique in many industries and can be useful to illustrate a requirement to a future user. The prototype can be quickly changed if it was not correct. In this fashion, the project would be more quickly executed by managing creation of these small "chunks" of capability. This methodology school of thought is most often called Agile, Extreme, Scrum, or more recently Lean (among other names). In using this approach, the user would work closely with the technical team to produce quick and small instances (chunks) of the solution. In some cases, these would be called iterative prototypes. The goal of this approach is to quickly generate user value and to validate requirements through more of a visual approach, rather than abstract drawings. One clear advantage of the iterative methodology is that project deliverables are seen by the user earlier than would be found in the traditional "big bang" serial waterfall life cycle implementation. Conversely, some would argue that this "blow and go" approach could lead to extensive rework and therefore additional cost. Chapter 25 will describe this topic in more detail as it is one of the growing approaches with recognized positive outcomes when done properly. It is important for the contemporary PM to be versed in all life cycle models and understand which option best fits in a particular requirement.

Before we oversell the value of prototyping realize that in some cases a schematic or graphical design is adequate. Regardless of one's conceptual view of the best project life cycle methodology, there is general agreement that defining accurate requirements is fundamental. It seems clear that one of the needed improvements in the management model is to find some strategy to identify requirements more effectively. From that high-level goal perspective, either the iterative or the traditional (or both together) approach could be pursued to improve the requirements definition role. The cartoon shown in Figure 9.2 illustrating how a requirement can become distorted as it passes through the life cycle is hard to believe, but more true than one might want to believe.

Regardless of one's conceptual development methodology model, there is general agreement that defining accurate requirements is fundamental. How to accomplish this goal remains a challenge for all projects. Cartoons similar to Figure 9.2 have draped walls in almost every protect team area for many years. When first seeing this example, people laugh. However, after being in the job of a few years, all better understand its message. Communicating accurate requirements is hard work and often not done well. This classic cartoon describes a not too far out scenario showing how requirements get garbled through the organizational layers. Hopefully, this view will serve as a memory device to watch out for what might be described as *requirements bleeding*. Constant feedback and communication must be done to keep this item under control. This is yet another view showing why active user engagement is needed.

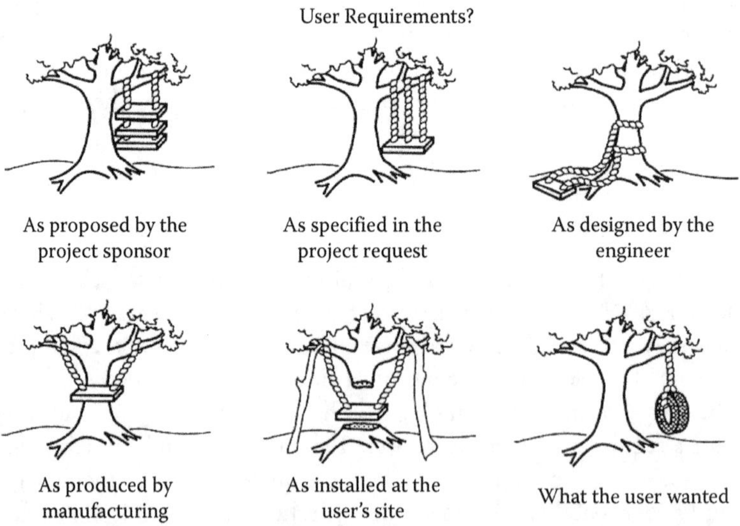

Figure 9.2 Development cartoon.

9.5.8 Project Management Expertise

Logically, it would seem that the effect of the project manager would be highly ranked in the success factor list, maybe number one or no less than number two. As in a couple of the other factors the relatively low rank shown may in fact represent a good trend in that the topic is being addressed. Efforts of organizations such as the Standish Group, Project Management Institute (PMI), Software Engineering Institute (SEI), PRINCE (UK and Australia), and other such management research-oriented organizations have been instrumental in model development, education, and communication of theory and approach. This has certainly made the topic more visible and hopefully contributed to better success rates. The author's bias suggests that individuals who are trained in this art/science are beginning to distinguish themselves through their positive project results. In other words, project management is a learnable skill and process that can help produce more successful outcomes. That does not mean that everyone who is trained the same way will be an equally good PM, but it does say that they should be better than before they were trained.

One view of the term "expertise" is that it describes someone who has studied the art and science of a topic and is sensitive to the type of issues being described here. Historically, a PM was often selected from the ranks of technicians. Being good at one job would get them promoted to the leader role (a halo effect), only to find out that the required new skill set was quite different in dealing with human relations, communications, politics, budgets, and the like. Experience shows that selecting a good technician for this role does not necessarily translate into a good manager. Managing people and work processes bears a different skill and mindset than being good at doing technical work.

PMI's annual Pulse surveys agree with many of the factors in the Standish surveys, plus both surveys outline differences across organizations performing the same task. Here is an example from a recent Pulse survey:

> *Over the years, analysis of our Pulse data shows that high-performing organizations have focused more on proven project, program, and portfolio management practices. As a result, their projects meet original goals two-and-a-half times more often (89 percent versus 34 percent) and waste 13 times less money.*
>
> *(PMI Pulse, 2016, p. 8)*

From all of the factors discussed here the term "expertise" is still a weakly defined item. Part of project expertise is to know where to look for problem areas and what processes to focus on. Survey data as described in this chapter represents a window into the key problem areas to deal with, but certainly there are many more subtle areas lurking in the maze. During the early days of attempting to model a successful project methodology the focus was on defined processes. That focus remains, however, there is growing evidence that the key to project success lies strongly in the soft side of decision- making, leadership, and communications. The following quote supports this statement:

> *Without a doubt, good project management drives more success, lowers the risk, and increases the chance of success for delivering the economic value of the project.*
>
> Bill Seliger, PMP
> *Director, Supply Chain and Project Management*
> *Fortune 500 manufacturing company*

Recent editions of the Project Management Body of Knowledge (PMBOK) have added more soft management processes than any other knowledge area.

9.5.9 Clear Business Objectives

One might argue that creating clear objectives is simply a restatement of the user involvement factor listed above. The key point to understand here is that users have a strong linkage to objectives. In order to accomplish this goal, it is necessary to involve an appropriate collection of users to produce a consensus-based view—that is, user involvement on a broad scale. Conversely, one can have a sufficient quantitative level of user involvement that never is able to agree on the objectives. Hence, this factor is more than the involvement aspect. Failure of users to not be able to accomplish a consensus will surely leave the technical team in a quandary. Given this latter view, we need to recognize that there must be a viable process that translates the original objectives into usable project requirements and not just a collection of user wish lists. There is an "objectives" problem even if all the users agreed that the project requirement was to build a widget that "leaped tall buildings with a single bound." From the Clear Objective view this would not be a sufficient scope statement for the team, but might sound adequate to the user side.

Accurate requirements generation remains one of the weakest technical areas of project methodology, and the effectiveness of the approach taken in dealing with this situation affects the project outcome. The individuals who are used by the project team to define requirements are often called *domain experts,* business analyst, or more pragmatically SMEs. These classes of individuals often represent the core members of the organization for defining requirements. Historically, a common process to collect requirements was to personally interview various business sources to document their views on the project requirement. At the end of this interview cycle, the analyst would combine these views into a requirement statement that would then be circulated to the various stakeholder entities for comment. This serial process suffers in its lack of internal collaboration of ideas, so the resulting requirements were often flawed. To be effective, the participants need to have the opportunity to give and take ideas concurrently. Also, a second fundamental problem with the serial process is that it takes too long to execute, gain consensus, and obtain approval. The net conclusion is that traditional requirements definition processes are not the best or most efficient. Recognition of this shortcoming has led project teams to seek out methods to improve the data gathering activity.

A popular requirements gathering technique, titled *facilitated workshops* or Joint Application Development (JAD), is often employed. In this model, key SMEs are brought together at the same time to work out a combined view of the project. This model is intense and interactive and results in a more consensus view because the process allows ideas to flow back and forth dynamically. Disagreements are worked on in the session. Also, the participants are moved away from daily work conflicts and in two or three days most projects can produce a reasonable consensus list of requirements. This semi-structured process is led by a trained person who guides the group through a series of steps designed to produce a draft requirement definition document. Note that the key points outlined here are speed and collaboration improvement. Less paper documentation is involved and a faster process.

9.6 Managing for Success

One way of looking at the Standish type results is through that old comedic skit:

> *[Patient] Doctor, doctor my arm hurts!*
> *[Doctor] When does it hurt?*

> *[Patient] When I do this!*
> *[Doctor] Then don't do that then!*

Trying to figure out how to achieve project success has some of these same characteristics. If something causes the project to hurt, don't do those things. One approach to improve an organizational process is to do a gap analysis of best versus current practice in selected areas and then define an improvement approach to close that gap. If the items selected are in fact causal, the future results should improve. One could start with the Standish factors and work outward from that point.

Beyond the obvious gap management strategy and going after focused targets, there are other less obvious items found in various surveys that support success. Most of these would be categorized as less specific and certainly more difficult to address. As an example, PMI suggests that:

> *...organizations are searching for ways to be more* ***agile, customer focused, and competitive.*** *A large majority of organizations report greater agility over the last five years. More than half attribute the improvement to critical change factors, such as the need to innovate, a leadership mandate, and shifting customer demands. Nearly half also credit their greater agility to the* ***enhanced skills and experience of project managers.***
>
> *(PMI Pulse, 2017, p. 13)*

This form of directive guidance given in a survey statement is certainly difficult to transform into action items but does offer a directional view.

9.6.1 Analyzing Industry Tool and Process Trends

A third form of survey analysis data reveals industry usage trends with various tools and techniques. These items are not necessarily linked to success causal factors as defined by the Standish data, but they do indicate industry trends for such items. The implication with this group of techniques is that positive trends indicate perceived value in that process, while a negative trend may require analysis to interpret. As with all raw data the logic behind the number may be difficult to translate, but trend views do give a target management area to review. In some measure this is like a potential best practice analysis.

A 2012 PMI Pulse survey tracked trends usage frequency in 11 key process areas. The list below is adapted from this set of data to use as a working gap analysis approach. The items shown below represent the highest organizational interest areas for common processes. This list is organized in high to low interest. Each of the positive trends correlate with various model process areas discussed in more detail throughout the book. The positive trend process areas are:

- Change Management*
- Risk Management*
- Having a PMO
- Using Program Management*
- Standardized Project Management**
- Process to Mature Portfolio Management—declining trend
- Process to develop Project Manager Competency—declining trend
- Using Earned Value*
- Use of agile model methods*
- Use of Extreme model methods*

The items with one asterisk (*) indicate that it is used always or often, while the one item with two asterisks (**) indicates that it is used often or always across all departments. PMO and Portfolio Management show high interest, but declining.

From this type of survey data, it is possible to infer prevalent industry process practices and trends for each. The top five areas are instructive in that they suggest a strong focus on managing change, risk management, and a couple of strategies related to high-level enterprise project management focus. The double asterisk for standardized project management is a clear direction that is easy to judge for gap measurement. There are two declining trend areas that need further analysis. The use of portfolio management is slightly declining, but there is high frequency of having a Project Management Office (PMO). More research is needed to explain this dichotomy. Chapters 35 and 36 will shed more light on why such a dichotomy of goals might exist. The significant decline in building PM competency is clearly a warning light. Often times HR training programs are the first to be cut in tight times, but this is a short-term strategy that needs to be watched. From data of this type it is possible to examine the internal environment to see how it matches. There are other industry best practice process models that also can be used in this format. See PMO, ANSI, SEI, and others for more details on related offerings.

Our goal here is not to show an answer to this question. All organizations are different. The theme of this chapter is to provide some insights regarding why projects are not successful and reflect on how an organization can begin work on a solution that fits their needs. Learning organizations should always be on the lookout for ways to improve.

9.6.2 Communications

One of the most difficult factors to measure in project management is the communications process. When one distils the job of a PM down to its essence, it is communicating. The model theory says that a PM should spend approximately 90% of their time communicating with various stakeholder groups (Mulcahy, 2013, Chapter 9). This activity is vital in resolving conflicts, work issues, and coordinating the various project activities. Failure to perform this function adequately has major adverse implications. Often times, a technically oriented manager will hold the belief that his primary goal is to produce a technical product and that will make the users happy. History shows that this is not the case. This statement is not to suggest that a PM does not have to be technically literate or uninvolved in technical activities within the team, but even that role becomes one of communicating. PMI and other research organizations state that lack of effective communications is the root cause of project failure. Note that this item did not appear on any of the success factor lists, yet it pervades all of the areas. We will see more on topic in Chapter 18.

9.6.3 Organization maturity Implications

PMI's Pulse of the Profession survey divides respondents into Champions and Underperformers to evaluate their differences in performance. One of the metrics collected is waste (inefficiency) and it is estimated to be 12% of the total budget on average. The Champions level wasted 1/28th as much as the Underperformer group. In addition, they enjoyed more successful business outcomes and fared better at other measures of project completion as well (PMI Pulse, 2012).

9.6.4 *Talent Triangle®*

One of the key Standish success factors was project team skill. This term seems obvious in its value, yet the management question becomes how to create, measure, and execute this aspect of the overall resource management role. Note the decline trend mentioned earlier showed that organizations were decreasing focus on this item. Many organizations assume that learning on the job through work experience is adequate; however, the PMI Champions group performed better by prioritizing the formal development of technical skills (76% versus only 19% for underperformers), leadership skills (76% versus 16% for underperformers), and strategic and business management skills (65% versus 14% for underperformers)—these are all critical areas illustrated in the PMI Talent Triangle®. These statistics seem to indicate that this aspect of the management equation is worth keeping in consideration. In support of this a key management strategy is to have human resource development as a defined part of the organizational resource plan.

9.6.5 *Building the Right Mousetrap*

If you want to catch a mouse, you need a good mousetrap. If you want a successful project you need the right support structure. One important definitional source for this is the PMBOK knowledge areas (KAs) and processes. Likewise, organizations such as American National Standards Institute (ANSI) also offer a management guidelines package defined as ANSI-EIA 748 (NDIA). The UK sponsors a similar model approach with their PRINCE2 and P3M3 guidelines (Turley). These and other lesser known sources are offering insights into their version of "how to build the mousetrap." In many ways, the messages are similar. Each of these sources is attempting to design an environment to improve project success. A browse through any of the major models will reveal a story very similar to the one outlined in this chapter and the previous introductory material.

Therefore, how do you start moving toward an improvement in internal project management. Clearly, the first step is for management to essentially sign a formal Charter indicating what goal they seek. This should then create a small study team to manage the following steps:

1. Review existing theoretical models—PMBOK, ANSI, PRINCE2, etc.
2. Perform an internal analysis of management practices to see how the organization y compares to the models—gap analysis.
3. Define the major gaps and decide on a tactical and strategic approach for closing the selected gaps.
4. Document the plan and review it with key organizational units—seek buy in.
5. Review the plan with appropriate management. Outline the scope, schedule, and budget for the effort, along with expected benefits—seek approval to move forward.
6. Ask management to formally announce the plan to move in this direction.

Defining steps for an organizational change is easy. Getting that organization to follow the defined steps is very hard. One does not change an organization in a few days. Executive management support is a major key to success for this project (now you should see why it is number one on the factor list). Also, did you get the subtle message for this activity? Yes, this is a project too!

9.7 Defining Success

It has become clearer over time that the definition of a successful project is now broader than the traditional measures based solely on scope, time and cost performance. Even in this simplistic state there is some question as to how close to targets to consider that parameter as successful. Is it 90% or does it have to be 100%? Hence, there are now rumblings in the industry about this idea of success. One strategy that would help this statistic is to not allow any changes and focus entirely on the initially approved baseline values, but that defeats other aspects of the project goal. Much has been defined in this chapter regarding the problem of initially achieving accurate requirements. Given this situation, one can see that requirements change is a tough to control reality, but is not the favorite topic for the project team. Even with the best of involvement and change efforts there is evidence that the project requirements are often still not exactly correct at the time of implementation.

Several years ago, the author was involved in an early email implementation. At that early technology point it was difficult to obtain management approval for this new tool because the benefits were not clear. Eventually the first version was installed without formal approval and as they say, the rest is history. After this, there were multiple new versions as the user community began to understand what this tool could do. Three years later an internal portfolio study ranked email as the most important application, but now the problem was how to compress the number of such systems to one standard. The point of all this is to suggest that early requirements, project performance, and long-term business benefits may well be three different events with different answers at different time periods. This does not answer the question of how to measure project success, but does suggest that some expansion of the definition is needed.

Lynch describes how Standish has defined an expanded success metric. Rather than the traditional three factors, there are now six. These are as follows: on Time, on Budget, on Target, on Goal, Value, and User Satisfaction (Lynch). Even with this version there are questions remaining in regard to exactly how to measure and when can one measure success—end of the project and three years later, respectively, in production. This ambiguity leaves the project team in somewhat of a dilemma regarding how to pursue end-of-project target values. When it is all said and done, success lies with the organization and the user community. If the result has more value than the project cost and the user feels that it was successful, then it was successful; just one more conundrum in the complex nature of project management. What this conclusion strongly suggests is that the PM must involve both the management and user elements to provide guidance as the performance variables begin to drift away from the initial approved plan.

9.8 Empirical Forecasting

Table 9.4 provides a sample technique to illustrate how to perform a quick success assessment of a high-technology project. Local experience will be required to supply appropriate comparative results in your environment and this customization will require tweaking of individual parameter weights to achieve better outcome prediction. The sample worksheet is intended to illustrate how the evaluation of certain key success parameters can lead to a quantitative measure for project success. Previous use of this model suggested that any score less than 75% indicated the project could be headed for a troubled outcome—scope, time, or budget. Worksheets of this type can be customized to fit local conditions by adding appropriate items and weights to the model. Also, usage experience will supply information to allow tweaking individual weights to better predict outcomes.

Use the worksheet to fill in your own numbers under the “Your Project” column and perform the indicated calculations.

Table 9.4 Project Success Worksheet

	A	B	C	D	E
		Example		*Your Project*	
Questions to Ask About Your Project:	*Success Weight*[a] *High = 5* *Medium = 3* *Low = 1*	*Answer* *Yes = 1* *No = 0*	*Success Value* *A · B*	*Answer* *Yes = 1* *No = 0*	*Success Value* *A · D*
1. Project is part of the execution of the business strategy	1	1	1		
2. There is a project sponsor	3	1	3		
3. You have full backing of project sponsor	3	1	3		
4. Project does not have multiple sponsors	3	1	3		
5. Has real requirements	5	1	5		
6. Has realistic deadlines	5	0	0		
7. Uses current technology	5	0	0		
8. Everyone knows the "big" picture	1	0	0		
9. Project processes (e.g., solution design/ delivery) are defined	5	1	5		
10. Project processes are understood	3	1	3		
11. Project processes are accepted	1	1	1		
12. Project plan is defined by participants and affected people	5	1	5		
13. Doing some small experiments to validate project	3	0	0		
14. Overdue project plan tasks elicit immediate response	3	0	0		

(*Continued*)

Table 9.4 (*Continued*) Project Success Worksheet

	A	B	C	D	E
		Example		*Your Project*	
Questions to Ask About Your Project:	*Success Weight*[a] *High = 5 Medium = 3 Low = 1*	*Answer Yes = 1 No = 0*	*Success Value A · B*	*Answer Yes = 1 No = 0*	*Success Value A · D*
15. Issues are converted to tasks in project plan	3	0	0		
16. You do not have a great dependency on a few key resources	3	0	0		
17. Enforced change control process	5	1	5		
18. Risks are correctly quantified	3	0	0		
19. There is project discipline	5	1	5		
20. PM is not the final arbiter of disputes	3	1	3		
21. There is a communications plan	5	1	5		
22. There are weekly status meetings	5	1	5		
23. There is a one-page project-tracking dashboard	3	1	3		
24. All project documentation is stored on shared database	1	0	0		
25. Lessons learned are adopted to improve project processes	3	0	0		
Totals = sum of 1–25	85	15	55		
Probability of success	C total ÷ A total = 64.7%			E total ÷ A total =	

Source: This worksheet is adapted from a similar version published in *Baseline*, May 2006. The version shown here is approved by the author Ron Smith (with permission).

[a] Assumes weight is constant.

[b] Probability of success less than 75% suggests you need action plan to change key "no" answers to "yes."

Filling in the values:

1. Fill in your project assessment values (0–5) under "RISK SCALE." The higher the number, the greater the risk.
2. Multiply your risk number by its corresponding "SUCCESS VALUE" and enter the "SCORE" results for each item.
3. Add up the scores to get your project's TOTAL SCORE.
4. Values at the bottom of the table translate risk level for this project. Future experience can be used to adjust these values accordingly for local data.

To illustrate the variation in evaluation criteria, a second worksheet is shown in Table 9.5. In this version, the project type is higher technology, which raises the risk index. These two variations show how weighted criteria can be part of the initial project evaluation process.

Table 9.5 Project Success Worksheet—Technology Projects

Tool: Project Success Assessment Table		*Example: Oracle Upgrade*		*Your Project*	
	Success Value	*Risk Scale*	*Score*	*Risk Scale*	*Score*
Top 10 Reasons Projects Fail	*Total—100%*	*0—Minor 5—Major*	*Value · Risk*	*0—Minor 5—Major*	*Value · Risk*
1. Incomplete and/or changing requirements	25	5	125		
2. Low end-user involvement	15	3	45		
3. Low resource availability	10	1	10		
4. Unrealistic expectations	10	2	20		
5. Little executive support	10	1	10		
6. Little IT management support	5	3	15		
7. Lack of planning	5	4	20		
8. System/application no longer needed	5	1	5		
9. Bleeding-edge technology	5	2	10		
10. Other/miscellaneous	10	0	0		
Total score			260		

Source: This worksheet is adapted from a similar version published in *Baseline*, June 2008. The version shown here is approved for use by the author Ron Smith (with permission).

What your total score means: 0–125 = high probability of success. Review week areas if any; 126–250 = low probability of success. Work one week areas; 251–500 = cancel project it will most likely fail.

9.9 Conclusion

This chapter has outlined some of the major factors involved in project success and failure. Each of the factors described needs to be understood by the PM and project team as they move through the life cycle. Business goals and technology change rapidly—with significant events occurring every 6–12 months. A project's success ultimately depends on people, not technology or tools. This statement holds true across all industries, from manufacturing to information technology. Thus, the role of project planning requires both the science of compiling appropriate estimates and the art of manipulating these on the fly as the project requirement unfolds.

Much of the material in this section falls into the category of *traitism*, meaning that the items identified do not necessarily cause failure or success, but they do correlate to it. In some cases a measured trait is really a reflection of some other unidentified item. For example, why are requirements not accomplished well? One reason for this could be lack of interest from stakeholders, bad management, poor processes used, etc. There is every reason to believe that the items outlined here are valid target areas for results improvement, but the answer for how best to actually identify the causal underlying element in order to improve it remains a creativity exercise.

We are now some 50 or more years into what one would consider the evolution of modern project management. The models outlined here are not mature in comparison to say chemical engineering theory, but they are now quite usable to improve the current state. The final point for this chapter is to suggest using the type of survey data described here and use it to find ways to improve the current processes.

References

Ibbs, C.W. and H.K. Young, 2000. Calculating project management return on investment. *Project Management Journal*, 31, 2, 38–47.

Lynch, J., 2015. Standish Group 2015 Chaos Report—Q&A with Jennifer Lynch, October 4, 2015. www.infoq.com/articles/standish-chaos-2015 (accessed November 4, 2017).

Mulcahy, R., 2013. *PMP Exam Prep*, 8th ed. Minnetonka: RMC Publications, Inc.

NDIA, 2014. *Earned Value Management Systems ANSI/EIA-748-C Intent Guide*. Arlington, VA: National Defense Industrial Association.

PMI, 2017. *A Guide to the Project Management Body of Knowledge (PMBOK® Guide)*, 6th ed. Newtown Square, PA: Project Management Institute.

PMI Pulse, 2012. *Pulse of the Profession*. Newtown Square, PA: Project Management Institute.

PMI Pulse, 2016. *Pulse of the Profession*. Newtown Square, PA: Project Management Institute.

PMI Pulse, 2017. *Pulse of the Profession*. Newtown Square, PA: Project Management Institute.

Turley, F., 2010. *The PRINCE2® Foundation Training Manual, Ver 1.0, MgmtPlaza*. Hengelo: Trans-Atlantic Consulting Group. www.mgmtplaza.com (accessed November 15, 2017).

FOUNDATION PROCESSES

The initial two chapters in this section focus on the role of projects in the organization and the planning process from the project vision and management-approved project plan. In the early conceptualization stage the two main learning objectives are:

Role of Projects in the Organization

1. Understand the role that projects play in organizations.
2. Understand the concept of selecting project targets from a portfolio of project initiatives based on value alignment with enterprise goals.

Project Formulation and Planning

Projects often emerge from vague visions. This segment of the text traces the key process from the early vision through the basic steps to create a formal plan for execution.

1. Understand the steps required to move the visioning stage to a requirements description adequate for management to approve moving forward for more detailed planning.
2. Understand the basic process to document project goals in order to elaborate the organizational value for pursuing the initiative.
3. Understand the basic process to document project goals in order to elaborate the organizational value for pursuing the initiative.
4. Understand the management mechanics related to the initiation phase, specifically steps related to the Business Case, Project Charter, and creation of the formal planning team.
5. Identify, estimate, and document key resource requirements required to support the project plan.
6. Understand the project management process related to the initiation phase.
7. Understand how to identify and document the project schedule, budget, resource, quality, and other constraints through coordination with stakeholders.
8. Understand how to construct a viable project plan from the derived requirements that includes planning assumptions and constraints.

9. Understand how to define an appropriate development project strategy by evaluating alternative approaches in order to meet stakeholder requirements, specifications, and/or expectations.
10. Understand the role that defined performance metrics has in the control of future results.
11. Understand how to define and document the project budget and schedule by determining time and cost estimates.

After completion of the format initiation review process, a solidified project vision emerges with the belief that the defined target worthy of pursuing and has positive promise for the organization. Through this stage, the project formal planning cycle process performs activities to move the initial vision through a series of managerial and technical elaboration and definition steps. This activity has a basic goal to formalize the vision into a clearer work-oriented definition that further verifies that the project can be executed according to the constraints defined by the earlier Charter.

As the project moves through the formal planning stage four major output deliverables are focused on. These are scope, schedule, budget and quality. Upon completion of the planning stage the following goals should be realized:

1. Identify, analyze, refine, and document project requirements, assumptions, and constraints through communication with stakeholders and/or by reviewing project documents to baseline the scope of work and enable development of the plan to produce the desired result.
2. Develop the Work Breakdown Structure (WBS) using the Scope Statement, Statement of Work (SOW), and other project specification documents. From this definition, decomposition techniques are used to facilitate detailed project planning, which is then used in the executing, monitoring and controlling, and closing processes.
3. Analyze and refine project time and cost estimates by applying estimating tools and techniques to all WBS tasks in order to determine and define the project baseline, schedule, and budget.
4. Understand how to develop the resource management plan required to complete all project activities and then match planned resources to those available from internal, external, and procured sources.

The primary planning stage deliverable is a project plan that represents a formal forecast of the future product or process state (i.e., scope, schedule, budget, and quality). This artifact will define the deliverables, required work processes, schedule, budget, and other information relevant to the project. Core variables dealt with in the plan are scope, time and cost; however, other supporting management areas will also be included. There is wide diversity of views regarding what constitutes the appropriate level of project planning. The real world often defines this as publishing a budget and schedule. At the next maturity level, other groups might suggest that project planning involves a broad scope statement along with the budget and schedule. A fully expanded planning level would involve an integrated more robust view of all knowledge areas as defined by the PMBOK® Guide's definition. Along with an expanded level of review, the PMBOK defines the resulting project plan as an artifact describing "... how the project will be executed, monitored and controlled, and closed. It integrates and consolidates all of the subsidiary management plans and baselines, and other information necessary to manage the project. The needs of the project determine which components should be included in the project management plan are needed" (PMI, 2017, p. 86). In this model-based view, the mention of "subsidiary plans" implies that other decision considerations are required in the planning process beyond more skeleton views mentioned above. Specifically, the model guide implies that planning involves the knowledge areas described earlier as:

- Scope
- Schedule
- Cost
- Quality
- Procurement
- Risk
- Communication
- HR
- Stakeholders
- Integration

More details on other planning subsidiary area processes will be described in later sections of the text. Eventually, all the supporting areas will need to be integrated into a coherent whole in order to achieve a viable project plan. For example, the available budget is appropriate to achieve the defined scope, quality, and schedule.

At this point, recognize that a good plan is not the only condition for project success. It is a road map, but there will almost always be unexpected unplanned roadblocks found along the way. In order to make this part easier to understand some simplifying assumptions are used to help focus on the fundamental mechanics. These assumptions will be released in future parts of the text as more reality is introduced.

Reference

PMI, 2017. *A Guide to the Project Management Body of Knowledge (PMBOK® Guide)*, 6th ed. Newtown Square, PA: Project Management Institute.

Chapter 10

Project Initiation

10.1 Introduction

The basic goal of the initiation stage is to evaluate the merits of a vague project proposal vision that is intended to improve some aspect of the organization. It should not be a surprise to recognize that the conversion from a business vision to the related project definition of work required is a complex human communication process. Project ideas can be spawned from a variety of sources, but one needs to recognize that a lot of work is left to be done in the time span from the original vision to a completed project deliverable, or even a clear understanding of the organizational value of the proposal.

The steps associated with the initiation phase are designed to translate a fuzzy vision to a definitional point where management can assess its business value and is willing to sponsor moving the proposal forward into a more detailed planning phase. If approved, at the end of this cycle a Charter signed by the management sponsor will officially recognize that it is to move forward and under what conditions. A second goal for this stage is to develop approaches involving stakeholders who are interested in the venture.

10.1.1 Expanding the Project Vision

At inception, an organizational entity spawns a project idea or proposal dealing with some product or process change (this is the WHAT side of the process). From this, the role of the technical project side is to translate that vision-type statement into technical work units (HOW to do it).

One common analogy to help explain a key element of the initiation process is to envision a project requirement statement for a widget to "leap tall buildings with a single bound." That definition may be somewhat sufficient for the user, but is hopelessly inadequate for the technical side who are charged with producing the widget. Before this high-level vision specification can move forward there are several detailed questions that need to be resolved. This elaboration step may be executed prior to the project being approved, or may be delayed until early in the follow-on detailed planning stage. For this example, let's assume that the project is approved to move into the planning phase with rough estimates. In this case, the follow-on enhancement step will occur in the early planning stage. One term to describe the artifact from this elaboration step is a Preliminary Scope Statement.

The role of the Preliminary Scope Statement is to document the elaborated requirements in more quantitative or descriptive terms. In the tall building widget example, one elaboration to some specification as to the maximum height of the building and also add other operational goals that a technical designer would need. This important translation step helps to move the abstract vision toward a technical specification by adding quantification to that vision. Technical designers can only guess at the goal for such parameters unless they are defined as part of the requirements. Gaps of this type create change requests later in the project.

PMdocs offer the following sample Table of Contents template for the Preliminary Scope Statement (PMdocs):

Scope Statement Table of Contents

I. Project and product objectives
II. Product or service requirements and characteristics
III. Product acceptance criteria
IV. Project boundaries
V. Project requirements and deliverables
VI. Project assumptions
VII. Initial project organization
VIII. Initial defined risks
IX. Schedule milestones
X. Initial WBS (high level)
XI. Order of magnitude cost estimate
XII. Project configuration management requirements

This template shows similar information that might have been included in the Business Case, but now is being elaborated toward a more technical format. Examples like this show up later in line items for project organization, initial Work Breakdown Structure (WBS), and configuration management. Also, items II and III indicate more specification than initially documented in the typical Business Case.

Based on this, the goal is to select those project portfolio targets that best align with the goals of the organization within the resource constraints. A support role for this stage is to identify stakeholders who need to be involved in subsequent activities related to the project activities.

The role of formal project initiation is important for many reasons. Ad hoc projects that might be spawned throughout the organization without this level of analysis and approval drain away critical resources that would be better spent focused on higher-level organizational goals. Mature organizations have well-developed processes to develop this part of the life cycle and as a result projects do not emerge in isolation without a formal management review and approval.

One of the cardinal goals for organizational projects is that they align with the enterprise goals and have acceptable value. Stated another way, the goal is to pursue initiatives that optimize the allocation of assets to the betterment of the enterprise. The ideal approach is to link all project goals to organizational tactical and strategic plans. In order for the formulation process to function as described, the complete slate of proposed and existing projects should be analyzed on a consistent basis using some standardized review format (e.g., a standard business case template for new initiatives, or a standard status reporting format for ongoing projects). The normal analysis approach for evaluating a project vision is to include both quantitative and qualitative estimates. Regardless of the approval process used, the key for project selection should be guided by a formal management review activity. Ultimately, senior management is responsible for the use of enterprise resources and the selected project results arising from that allocation. Large projects should also be managed even more carefully through the life cycle stages given their higher probability of failure and likely high business value.

10.2 Project Initiation

Project initiatives philosophically should have characteristics of improving current business processes, growing the business, or transforming the business. Consideration of a specific project proposal involves analysis of the investment level, goal alignment, and organizational capability to accomplish the initiative, inherent risk, competitive needs, and return on the investment, among others. Beyond the activity of evaluating how the new vision will impact the organization, management considerations in approving the project to move forward involve the following:

1. How well does this proposal mesh with enterprise goals?
2. How long will the effort require?
3. What is the cost of the initiative?
4. What is the related resource requirement and from which sources?

It is important to recognize that the initiation stage is "fuzzy" in regard to the accuracy of data quantification that can be produced. Resource estimates at this stage often contain errors of 100% or more and the estimates regarding project time and cost can be equally inaccurate. Certainly, the goal of this first-phase process is to do the best job possible in decreasing these predictive errors and from that point make the best decision possible in selecting the right projects to approve and move forward into a more rigorous planning effort.

Steps in the Project Approval Process

1. Project Vision—what does the output look like or do?
2. Develop Business Case
3. Organizational review
4. Management review
5. Charter signed
6. Preliminary scope statement

10.2.1 Project Origins

From a theoretical view, a project's role is to move the organization from one operational stage to a second more desirable one. Think of this as one enterprise capability point to another. As an example, a project vision might state the need to improve customer relations or financial reporting capability. This form of statement is the initial seed to start the initiation process.

A second possible initiation path can come from internal ideas generated within the organization. Grassroots ideas of this type can be submitted through a formal system, or through some other less formalized collection method. The key difference in these two approaches lies primarily in the origin of the vision. The grassroots method starts within the organization business levels and from this point one must find some level of management support sufficient to support development of a formal business case for that idea. In this scenario, the initial idea driver is often an aggressive employee who is seeking to solve a local problem. The challenge inherent in this method lies in the fact that the ideas tend to be local and not necessarily best fit for high-level organizational goals. Some call these "stovepipe" projects because of their local focus. Regardless of the vision seed origin, both need to move that initial idea to business case, so the next step is to move the process to where they can be approved to move forward.

10.2.2 Business Case-Documentation of the Vision

Early in the development of a project vision it is common to produce a document called a Business Case. A business case document is typically used to translate the initial view into an analysis of tangible and intangible value for the initiative. The business case provides necessary financial estimates, risk assessment, and goal justification for approving the expenditure of resources in competition with other project initiatives that are also being considered. In all project situations, the availability of resources constrains the level of project activity that can be supported by the enterprise.

Major sections of this document typically contain data related to

- Project objective
- Problem/Opportunity statement
- Potential solution strategy
- Organizational goal fit
- Strategic goal fit
- Key assumptions
- Competitive analysis
- Benefits (tangible and Intangible)
- Cost estimates (Initial and life cycle)
- Competition
- Recommendation

Audience for the Business Case can be varied and depends upon the scope of the effort. If the proposal is coming from the bottom of the organization the next step would be to some higher-level manager who might support the idea. Other visions come from senior management and the analysis will be sponsored by them. If the organization has a Project Management Office (PMO) structure, all proposals would go through them for review and grading. Absent that structure, the decision point would come from the management entity that was interested in the concept and had a budget to support it, or they would at least be the person fronting the effort with even higher-level management. Regardless of the local process, the goal for the Business Case step is to obtain management support for a formal planning stage where the various requirements and management details can be further refined.

The business case format would describe the value of pursuing the initiative, then describe solution alternatives and present recommendations to the sponsor. Using this core data, there would be further review based on local processes.

10.3 Organizational Review

The level of review after the Business Case created can vary widely. If the project vision is large and involves a major strategic change the review could be very formal and involve the enterprise Board of Directors. Alternatively, major department heads and senior management are often targets for review. As with all project activities, communications with future stakeholders and users can add improved insights into the organizational value and risk. Later in this process, a formal management review will be held to add further input to the process. This review may be with a PMO function as one exists, or otherwise with some other management entity. The format of formal management reviews varies depending on the size and impact of the proposed initiative. Another management review model involves a standardized presentation format that would then be held with a central screening committee in many organizations. Here, the defined alternatives would be translated into a standardized presentation format that would then be reviewed. Ideally, the goal at this point is to rank this initiative in terms of other proposals. Some organizations will handle the actual approval process annually, which facilitates the ranking. Regardless of the local review process, the result of the effort is to decide whether this Business Case is worthy of support. If approved, the next step is to seek formal signoff by the sponsoring manager.

There is one alternative process that can add time to the approval process. Some visions encounter conflicts and disagreement among the various players. This is not a rejection attitude, but disagreement of scope, approach, value, etc. This lack of a consistent view makes it necessary to attempt to homogenize the perspective and get key players on the same page as to the project goals. Without some agreement as to the future target, it is impossible to produce a valid decision document. If this conflict cannot be resolved, the initiation phase begins to take on more of an analysis of alternatives view, which multiples the work required in producing multiple decision options and parameters.

10.4 Management Review

Assuming that the items contained in the Business Case and the following internal review process has been favorable, the next step is to obtain formal approval to move forward. Assuming the PMO model, this might be an annual portfolio session to rank all the projects and select those to go forward. The stand-alone model would have a management sponsor who had sufficient budget to approve the effort. Regardless of the process leading up to approval the key model artifact signifying that the project is to move forward is called a Charter. This document becomes an important element in the long-term support of the project as it will be key to providing guidance for the effort throughout the entire life cycle. Its primary role is to protect the project and help with issues that can't be resolved with normal processes.

The sponsor Go/NoGo decision should be based on the data supplied from the Business Case and other information emerging from the follow-up reviews.

10.5 Formal Charter Signed

The role of the Charter is to formally approve the project and establish necessary guidance and assistance to move the project forward into a formal planning cycle. An important management concept behind issuance of a Charter document is that this explicitly authorizes the existence of a project and the subtle impact of formal chartering is to limit ad hoc project from springing up. Since the chartering process follows a rigorous review process it helps to focus resource expenditures on those visions that have been judged to best align with the organization goal structure.

A project Charter contains various authorizations and guidance information designed to help follow-on planning activities. The following data should be included in the documentation (PMI, 2017, p. 194):

- Project objectives approved based on Business Case details and related organization discussions
- High-level requirements, boundaries, and deliverables description

- Summary milestone schedule
- Authority given to acquire resources and expend funds
- Define organizational resources that can be used
- Define constraints that must be met
- Define next management review step
- Key stakeholder list
- Project manager named

At a high level, the project charter provides sufficient specification for the planning function to commence and signifies that formal support has been explicitly given by the management signature

10.6 Preliminary Scope Statement

Adding another layer of requirements documentation may seem redundant after the Charter has been approved; however, there is a valid explanation for doing just that. At the beginning of a formal planning process the definition of the project requirement is essentially a vision statement based on little real technical analysis. The level of specification is primarily a vision statement and not so much on the mechanics or feasibility of achieving that output. As we move up the process into a more detailed planning step, it is important to clarify the requirements in terms more amenable to technical specification of the deliverables and related work definition. Also, there are some future project management implications that need to be resolved at this stage. The PMBOK classifies the results of this elaboration as a *Scope Statement*. This document describes the deliverables in sufficient detail to guide the design process. Its role is to take the high-level description offered by the Charter specification and translate this into a more clear and quantitative specification that will support planning the technical work aspects of the project. Four expanded scope items defined by the model are (PMBOK, 2017, p.193):

- Elaboration of the Charter output characteristics
- Expansion of deliverables specification
- Acceptance criteria for final deliverable
- Exclusions to the defined scope

We earlier saw a scope statement template that would help guide this elaboration process. A more model-driven format for this is summarized below:

1. Project and product objectives
2. Product or service requirements and characteristics
3. Product acceptance criteria
4. Project boundaries
5. Project requirements and deliverables
6. Project constraints
7. Project assumptions
8. Initial project organization
9. Initial defined risks
10. Schedule milestones

11. Initial WBS
12. Order of magnitude cost estimate
13. Project configuration management requirements

For the items listed here, the documentation goal is essentially a review and edit of the original specification into terms that are more specific and understandable by the project team. Using the previous "to leap tall buildings with a single bound" specification, this might be clarified by adding it "must be able to jump a four-story building in a single attempt 95% of the time." The original specification performance requirement would obviously have to be technically resolved later and would remain a point of design confusion for the technical side. In this manner, the preliminary scope document attempts to clear up as many such definitional issues as possible while the initial user-created requirement goals are fresh. The scope statement should be written in clear language consistent with the terms of the Charter. Clearing up such requirements early helps resolve future confusion and wasted efforts.

In addition to the technical clean-up process, the scope statement should also include some specification regarding various management procedural activities for the new project. Typical of these would be as follows:

1. Initial project organization
2. Project board—management steering process
3. Project configuration management requirement
4. Change control process to be used

Upon completion of the approval and scope specification documents, the project is ready to move into the work specifics related to these requirements.

An approved project Charter and follow-on Preliminary Scope Statement represents two key formal initiation documents that will be used to guide future planning decisions. Given these two artifacts, a high-level vision of the project objective and its value is documented, along with rough estimates for budget, schedule, and other related decision factors. The subsequent challenge for the PM is to refine these still crude statements into a detailed formal project plan that will once again need to be approved by appropriate management. Often times, a project will be approved subject to refinement or rationalization of the initial project parameter estimates (i.e., cost, schedule, and functionality). Seldom is management willing to approve the entire project based on the business case unless many similar projects have been handled prior to this.

Once a project is underway, it is important to recognize that the Charter needs to be re-evaluated minimally at each formal review point to reaffirm the ongoing project scope and direction of effort. As changes are approved in the project life cycle, the plan will need to be adjusted and reissued as necessary; however, the Charter document can only be changed at the source of approval—typically at a senior management level.

References

PMdocs, 2017. Project Preliminary Scope Statement Template, Project Management Docs. www.ProjectManagementDocs.com (accessed November 6, 2017).

PMI. 2017. *A Guide to the Project Management Body of Knowledge (PMBOK® Guide)*, Sixth Edition. Newtown Square, PA: Project Management Institute.

Chapter 11

Project Plan Development

Approval of the project Charter moves the project process into a more formal plan development stage. During the earlier concept-visioning period the project was likely supported by a small number of individuals who philosophically believed in the endeavor and may have even been passionate about it. The planning process now moves the issue beyond this sponsor's emotional point into steps designed to translate the original vision into a workable technical approach to achieve that vision. The goal now becomes one of defining the path and work elements required to achieve the vision.

In order to achieve future project success, the appropriate planning process should open up a more logical and technically driven analysis of the required work effort. Planning stage participants now include a wider variety of organizational and technical skill backgrounds and these new participants tend to view the proposed effort with less bias than the original visionaries. The primary goal of this second stage activity is to collectively resolve the ambiguities remaining from the original definition and produce a work plan that will guide the project to completion. First, the process has to define in greater detail the WHAT (requirements) and then work toward architecting HOW the effort can be accomplished. This evolutionary activity will uncover a breadth of diverse opinions regarding the merits and technical approach required. This activity will likely produce political, organizational, and technical conflicts that the project manager (PM) will be challenged to resolve. Through all this, it is the role of the PM to work toward a common positive team spirit regarding successful completion of the project as compromises are sought. The planning participants must look at this stage as an attempt to find a workable integrated solution to the problem, while at the same time attempting to deal with the various internal and external issues that can negatively impact the outcome.

It should be recognized that the real-world PM will often be required to take many shortcuts in developing the project plan, and personal experience suggests that few real-world projects follow the complete rigor as described in this text. Many project teams do not do it because they fail to recognize the value in this level of analysis, while others do not do it because they believe that their environment does not fit the model, or is either too dynamic or uncertain to plan.

There are multiple reasons to explain why these past quick-fix solutions failed. Certainly, one common scenario is the tendency for senior management and key users to prod the project to move into execution before a reasonable planning cycle is complete. In many of these cases, formal planning is not respected as having value. This rationale is often justified by saying that something different would happen anyway, so why waste time creating a document that does not map to reality. Regardless of the reason for taking planning shortcuts, realize that the views regarding project planning are controversial in organizations. It is also important to realize that many projects fail because these issues were not properly considered.

One example to illustrate the operational nature of a project plan involves work elements dealing with fragile technology. It is true that the impact of a yet unknown risk event cannot be included in the base plan because it has not happened yet; however, we must recognize that it might occur and find a way to manage the potential events in this category. The project plan defines work units as they are expected to occur, but when the risk events actually occur later, the operational plan will have to be adjusted accordingly. An approved project plan is a documented view of the anticipated project, hence changes during the planning or execution stages need to be continually updated in the operational plan.

Another characteristic of the planning process is its iterative nature. One should not expect to plow through the process in sequential work unit order and end up with an approved result. A more realistic vision is to view planning like "peeling an onion." As one layer is uncovered another layer of issues becomes visible and better defined. Maybe the vision of fear should be kept with this analogy as this is another emotion one might have as the project complexity is recognized. One example of this layering view is that uncovering project scope details will help understand the related time and cost requirement. A less obvious situation occurs when the defined plan resources do not match available capacity. This situation will require replanning to match the available resources. Therefore, not only is the idea of a dynamic project expectation part of this evolution, but the iterative nature of the process is also part of the understanding. Once project constraints in schedule, cost, resources, etc. are encountered it will be necessary to replan what was already planned to deal with those constraints. Failure to do this will invalidate the previous work. All too often the constraints are not properly taken into account, only to find later that the project will not work as defined. Ideally, a plan should be a future roadmap for the project and it should work just as a roadmap works for an auto trip. It should recognize where detours might exist and define ways to deal with such events. This is a risk-oriented view of the process. One does not just view the future path as clear roads and sunny skies. If you have a good roadmap and then receive information that the road ahead is under construction it will be possible to look at the map and take an alternative route. The project plan should have these same characteristics. Hence, when you think about planning keep the roadmap vision in mind. Also, note in this scenario the concepts of iteration, contingency, and status information.

11.1 Planning Philosophy Arguments

All project teams are typically pressed to move on into execution quicker than they would prefer. Management and other stakeholder groups push the team to move forward and start getting visible items accomplished. Users feel like they have defined the requirements with the original business case or vision statement and the planning process is not adding anything to the process other than time.

To achieve success planning should not be viewed as a waste of time. If a reasonably well-defined target can be derived the underlying technical steps necessary to achieve that target are better understood. The Achilles heel in this design logic is that user requirements are typically not well defined or understood even by the user much less than the project team. Also, project team members often have diverse views regarding how to produce the item. Given these fuzzy issues, there are perspectives that favor the development of a less thorough initial planning process with some form of ongoing iteration in developing the output. In other words, let the users see something working and then define the next step, iteratively marching toward some completion point. From a management viewpoint, the lack of an initially defined schedule, budget, and some definition of the final goal makes this approach hard to sell. One counter to this argument is based on the view and belief that iteration can waste resources. There is truth in both positions and thus a source of conflict in work approach. The sections below summarize a few of the common rationale supporting a more focused planning process.

11.1.1 Conflicting Expectations

A project vision is often spawned in one segment of the organization and for that reason it is common to focus the solution on that isolated segment. As the scope and impact of the project is better understood, there will likely be conflicting views regarding how best to orient the requirements for the benefit of the overall organization. What might be very productive for one segment of the organization could well create chaos elsewhere? Failure to define and review the broader requirements will often leave issues to be uncovered later when they are costly to correct. Even when the issues are relatively minor, stakeholder's frustrations are often caused by his lack of understanding of the project directions—derived scope, technical direction, resource issues, and so on. The classic example of this would be to produce a costly product successfully according to the original requirements only to have the user population say "we can't use this," or to find a better product already in the marketplace.

One of the major purposes of the planning process is to evaluate the various views of the vision and work toward one that the overall organization understands and agrees to support. Everyone may not agree with the result, but they should agree to work positively toward that agreed upon goal and to understand why that particular choice is either appropriate or approved. Failure to go through a planning process would omit this negotiation process and resulting buy-in.

11.1.2 Overlooking the Real Solution

Often times, a new technology looks promising and brings hope of some breakthrough solution to a perceived problem. Moving too fast towards the use of a new technology can result in similar negative outcomes as described above. In this case, the new technology could require changes in organizational processes, structure, governance, or reward systems (Henry, 2004). In other situations, a narrow perspective of the project goal might completely miss the proper target. A valid solution at one point in time could be absolutely wrong at a future time given dynamics in the organization or the external marketplace.

11.1.3 Competing Solutions

In the organizational environment, multiple project proposals and active projects are likely to start at any one point in time. As efforts continue to define the technical approach or scope of direction for a particular project, different solutions can emerge elsewhere. Experience indicates that the initial approach is often not the best strategic approach. Unfortunately, zeal of the various parties can turn the selection process into a battleground of egos and parochial positions. It is up to the project governance structure to ensure that reasonable options are viewed and explored without turning the process into an "analysis paralysis" activity with no productive direction. Certainly, one of the reverse side risks of planning is overplanning. Finding the right balance between spending too much time and not enough is a critical management skill.

11.1.4 Misaligned Goals

One of the cardinal tenants of project management is to seek organizational alignment of projects pursued to organizational goals. As obvious as this point might be, it is one that is often difficult to achieve in the operational environment. This is yet another reason why management needs to stay involved with this process throughout the life cycle.

11.1.5 Quality Solutions

Even in the situation where the target project vision is properly developed, there is still a need to a produce a quality output. In order to achieve that goal the resulting plan must find an appropriate balance between the vision (scope), cost, schedule, risk, and quality. Very few projects are worth pursuing without regard to balancing these variables. Likewise, few projects can afford to produce the highest possible quality. Therefore, the planning and execution functions must find the correct balance between these competing goals. The best way to evaluate these parameters is to carry out a reasonable level of planning.

11.1.6 Project Monitoring and Control

One of the classic rules of management is that you can only control what has been planned. This means that the omission of a coherent plan also means that you are missing significant ability to control the project given that there is no approved baseline for results comparison. From a management perspective, the plan becomes the baseline on which to measure performance status through the life cycle.

In order to create an effective plan that properly deals with the issues outlined above, there are five items that must be resolved:

1. A combination of scope, technical approach, resource, and process considerations must be dealt with
2. Diverse stakeholder expectations must be negotiated and documented
3. A proper balance between tactical and strategic needs must be reviewed and resolved
4. A solid review of the approved business case must be completed and matched with the subsequent requirements developed during planning
5. The organizational goal alignment requirement needs to be verified.

11.2 Plan process and Components

There is wide diversity in organizational views regarding what constitutes a project plan. Certainly, the real world often defines this simply as a budget and a schedule with high-level statements of objectives. In order to be the type of roadmap outlined here, it must be recognized that a viable plan consists of many interrelated components involving the 10 knowledge areas (KAs) (risk, communications, HR, etc.). In an overall planning model-based view, there are essentially primary and supporting sets of activities required to create a plan. In this view, the final plan will contain a collection of related subcomponents.

The primary plan components are often summarized for presentation to senior management and this view highlights various key issues that are relevant for the project (i.e., cost, schedule, risk, etc.). Some project plans need to emphasize risk and time, whereas others might focus heavily on quality, time, or availability of critical resources. In any case, the total project plan should produce a broad vision of expectations and issues that are relevant to the activity and its stakeholders. The KAs form the organizational structure from which to view plan components.

11.3 Plan Artifacts

It is important to recognize that the planning process is initially triggered by an approved project Charter signed by appropriate management. This formal initiation step includes a preliminary scope definition blessed by the sponsoring source. Both of these early artifacts are preliminary in nature in that they do not provide sufficient guidance to complete the project or the required visibility to measure its general technical or organizational viability. A second-stage basic planning question involves resolution of these broader views. There are many possible decision support artifacts that need to be produced as part of the planning process. The following list provides typical samples of planning artifacts that have high probability of being included in the final project plan documentation:

1. Approved scope definition—an expanded human language statement outlining the required project deliverables. This list will be reviewed by a broader group of stakeholders than the preliminary version.
2. A Work Breakdown Structure (WBS) that decomposes the project into work units necessary to produce the defined output.
3. Assumptions and constraints made as part of the planning process.
4. Work unit time and material estimates.
5. Work unit relationships (sequence).
6. Time-phased resource allocation plan (human and capital).
7. Major review points—technical, stakeholder, and management.
8. Documentation requirements for subsequent phases.
9. Testing and user acceptance plans.
10. Project team training plan—skill requirement definition.
11. Status reporting metrics and delivery process.
12. Communications management plan.
13. Risk management plan.
14. Stakeholder management plan.

Items 1–7 will be described in Chapters 12–15, while the remaining items will be generally dealt with in various other parts of the text. This summary list of artifacts is not meant to be comprehensive, but more to show that planning involves a broader perspective than is understood by most.

The degree to which the various output artifacts are utilized in a particular project depends on many factors. The following list summarizes some key decision variables to judge the proper planning level and approach:

1. Large or costly projects often have sufficient impact on the organization to require a thorough plan in both scope and depth.

2. Projects involving new technology need a heavy focus on risk management and work definition.
3. Projects involving a new-type target or skill should be approached carefully with adequate planning.
4. Smaller commodity-type projects can be pursued with less complex planning.
5. Projects involving a common theme might require much less detail in their plans, or might be able to use templates from earlier similar efforts.

The point of each example type is that projects have a lot of similar structural characteristics, but also have significant differences in their internal emphasis characteristics. It is important for the PM to decide on appropriate levels of detail for each KA in each project. Some organizations require a mandatory core set of activities and a supplementary collection of optional items.

11.4 Conclusion

It would not be appropriate to leave this section without a comment regarding the real-world view of project planning. Do not be surprised to find that few real-world projects follow the rigorous planning definition described in these sections. Many do not do it because they do not recognize the value in this level of analysis. Many others do not do it because they do not believe that you can plan accurately, therefore, a waste of time. Hence, the effort would be wasted in documenting something that will not come to pass. Regardless of the reason, realize that the views regarding project planning are controversial. It is also important to realize that many projects fail because these issues were not properly considered. As an example, risk management is one of the newly emphasized topics and many organizations are now recognizing that failure to respect this area can create significant problems if not dealt with properly in the planning phase. Our mission here is not to take sides on the ideal level of initial planning, but rather to show why each of the KAs has an important planning perspective that must be considered in the management process.

The key point to recognize in this overview is that the project plan should attempt to evaluate each of the processes for each KA and deal with these areas to the degree required for a particular project. In some cases, a KA is not of critical concern and can be minimized in the plan. However, the 10 KAs have been identified by very seasoned PMs and their associated processes are defined in the formal model. From this, one might suspect that each of them is relevant to some degree in every project plan.

The next chapter will review the process of transforming the approved Charter project vision into an understandable deliverable and work view.

Figure 11.1 illustrates a high-level schematic way of looking at the aggregate planning process. In this view, the basic output is represented by four project output components, while five other KAs are more involved in driving the work to generate those outputs. Note that the Integration KA sits in the middle and tweaks the various items to influence the best outcome possible. This overall view is not a perfect characterization, but conceptually puts the right focus on the overall management view.

In the final plan, all KAs should be integrated such that each is viable and consistent to support the resulting plan outputs. As a simple example of this integration process the final plan can

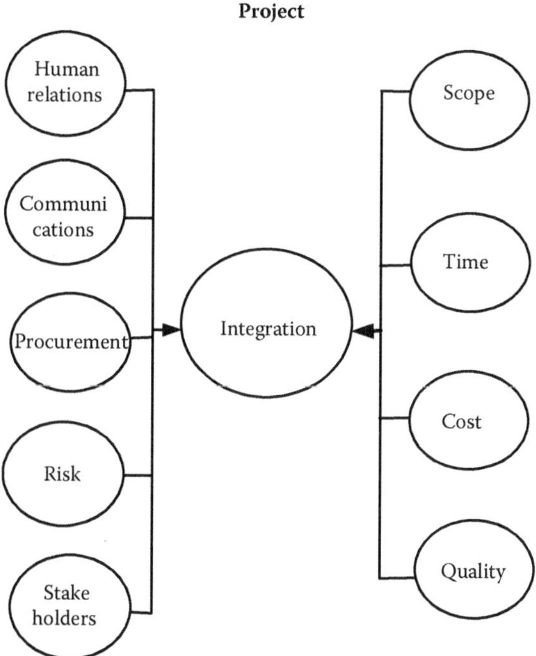

Figure 11.1 Knowledge area overview.

not specify HR requirements that are not actually available. A similar evaluation is made for all of the other variables.

Reference

Henry, G., 2004. *Best-Laid Plans*. www.projectmanagement.com/searchResult.cfm?searchstring=Best%20Laid%20Plans (accessed September 29, 2017).

Chapter 12

Scope Management

12.1 Introduction

The first planning step involves the process of creating a common view of a desired deliverable and the related work. This process unfolds in a series of increasingly detailed steps. Typically, the first stage of this process is a vague user statement of requirements. However, it is important that this preliminary attempt to document the project objectives only serves as a starting point for the project team in technical work definition. The initial project view typically focuses on the logical requirement, but offers little focus in regard to the associated technical work requirements to achieve those goals. In order to structure the project work it is also necessary to translate the output requirements into work units required to produce those deliverables. Also, the initial verbiage outlining the project requirements is not rigorous enough to support a detailed work planning process or to give other decision makers enough information to approve the initiative. The defined goal for this activity is to identify "the sum of the products, services, and results to be provided as a project" (PMI, 2017, p. 722). This activity has elements related to both an output goal and the project work related to that goal.

To ensure that these criteria are met, both the users and the technical producers must have the same understanding of the required deliverables. The process of gathering these dispersed specifications is called scope definition and the result of this is often translated into a deliverables-oriented Work Breakdown Structure (WBS).

The formal project planning phase commences with various scope definitional activities designed to produce a clearer understanding of the project work units, deliverables, assumptions, and constraints. This activity leads to the development of a detailed work outline that represents the primary scope definition artifact for the project. Essentially, scope analysis must provide definition for the following:

1. Definition of stakeholder *needs, wants, and expectations* translated into prioritized requirements.
2. Definition of *project boundaries*, outlining what is included in the project scope and what is not included.
3. Definition of the project *deliverables* including not only the primary product or service, but all interim results as well. This includes items such as documentation and management artifacts.

4. Definition of the *acceptance process* to be used in accepting the products produced.
5. Lists and defines project *constraints* that must be observed by the project.
6. Lists and defines project *assumptions* and the impact on the project if those assumptions are not met during the course of the life cycle.

Italicized items above highlight the key resolution points that are essential elements needed for a clear specification. The *PMBOK® Guide* outlines the following six sequential steps for scope determination and control (PMI, 2017, p. 129):

Plan Scope Management: This initial step is designed to formulate the approach for definition, validation, and control of scope through the life cycle. This is essentially an overall management guidance document.

Collect Requirements. This activity is an extension of the preliminary scope statement produced during the initiation phase. The earlier effort was designed to provide a general view of scope, while this second iteration will be more rigorous in its structure and will include inputs from a broader group of stakeholders. The goal for this stage is to produce refined definitional statements related to definitional areas summarized above. The resulting set of specifications is documented in the updated Scope Management Plan.

Define Scope. This step involves packaging the requirements into a more technically detailed description. Exclusions are defined here as well as a detailed description of the project and product. The primary artifact produced is a formal project scope statement.

Create WBS. The WBS is a hierarchical representation outlining the structure of work for the project. This process decomposes the project into layers of smaller and smaller groups of work until the lowest level represents manageable work packages (WPs). The WBS is a fundamental core document for the team and drives many of the subsequent phase activities.

Validate Scope. This step formalizes the acceptance of the produce or process.

Control Scope. Monitors the ongoing status of this process group through the life cycle and managing the change control activity.

12.2 Defining Project Work Units

Envision for a moment a "package" of work has been defined as a component of the project. This could involve tasks such as installing piping, testing software, or producing a software module. For now, view this simply as a defined set of work activities associated with a larger project effort. The vocabulary for the lower-level work units is a WP. One metaphor for a WP is to view it as a box, such as the one shown in Figure 12.1, with the three dimensions representing time, cost, and scope (of work). The sequencing of WPs will be discussed in Chapter 14.

In order to develop a project plan to execute the contents of this box we must first make certain technical decisions regarding the work necessary to produce the desired product. This section will discuss some of the basic processes required, then derive an initial schedule and budget for this project. As a starting point let us define a WP as "...the work defined at the lowest level of the WBS for which cost and duration can be estimated and managed" (PMI, 2017, p. 726). These elemental work units become the major control points through the life cycle.

At this point, we have not yet illustrated how a WP fits into the full project structure, but the key point for now is to recognize that it represents a defined work deliverable component of

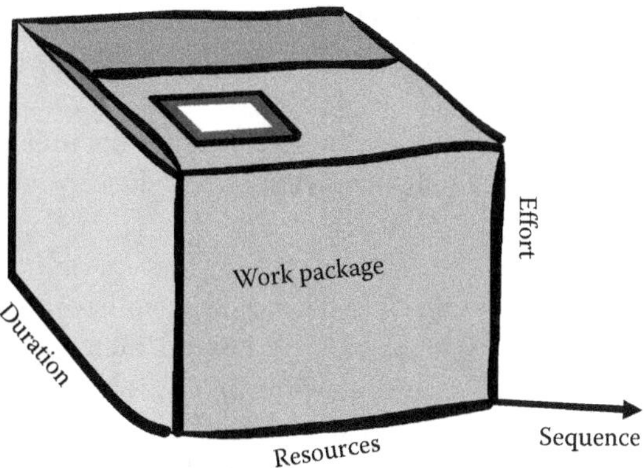

Figure 12.1 WP dimensions.

the overall project that requires work to accomplish. The collection of these WPs then represents the complete project scope definition.

One common rule of thumb is that a WP should be defined and sized to represent approximately 80 hours of effort and/or two weeks of work; however, that definition might not be appropriate for some project types. The key point is that this work unit definition becomes a management focus point for the entire life cycle of the project. A WP will be defined and managed by its estimated requirements for human and material resources, support equipment, and other parameters related to the work. From these input parameters the WP will produce some defined output. From these specifications it is possible to estimate how long it will take to do that work and how much the effort would cost. In essence, this is an important foundation concept of a project plan.

12.3 WP Planning Variables

Effective project WP planning requires many items of information related to the activity in order to assess the content of the work and integrate it into the rest of the project. Conceptually, it is desirable to capture this information into a single data repository. Such a repository may not be visible by that name in real-world projects, but the type of data described below will need to exist somewhere in the project records. In order to estimate and track the project activities, it is necessary to define the following types of definitional parameters for each WP:

1. ID reference—this is a code used to identify where the WP fits into the overall scheme of work
2. Labor allocation for the task (e.g., number and skills of workers)
3. Estimated duration for the task, given the planned worker allocation
4. Materials associated with the activity and their cost
5. Name of individual responsible for managing the activity
6. Organizational unit assigned to do the work
7. Defined constraints (e.g., activity must be finished by…)
8. Key assumptions made in the course of the planning activity

9. Predecessors—linkages of this activity to other project work units
10. Risk level for the activity—more work will be needed on this aspect later; for now, a general measure of risk could be defined as H, M, or L
11. Work description—this defines the output objectives for the unit
12. General comments—free-form statements that help understand the technical aspects of the work required

In addition to these core definition items, it is also necessary to have sufficient management oversight into the estimated values derived. In order to control these values, it is common to have additional approval fields in the WP record showing approvals by the performing organizational group and the project manager (PM). With this set of information completed, the intent is to be adequate for the performing organization to produce the defined outputs.

12.4 Multiple WPs

Moving one step up the food chain in our Scope theory, let us review what information can be derived from this low level set of specification. This example assumes that two WPs are related, meaning these two sequential steps are required to produce some desired outcome. This view is technically called a Finish–Start (FS) relationship. Metaphorically, we are stacking our two boxes end to end as shown in Figure 12.2.

For this example, let us assume that all workers involved have the same skill levels and can do all tasks required. They are also paid the same. These handy assumptions allow us to avoid many messy issues in the schedule calculation process, but they help simplify the focus on basic raw mechanics of scheduling and budgeting. We will see more of these terms in Chapter 13 and beyond.

12.5 Developing the Total Project View

Up to this point, we have looked at low-level components of the project and this helps to understand the management model for that level. Unfortunately, a project consists of hundreds or thousands of such elements. In a large project, it is necessary to group boxes into higher levels called summary packages. These help group work into more manageable work views; however, the fundamental scope building block elements consisting of WPs will stay essentially intact. The key conceptual additions from this point are WP interactions with each other and the linkage to the support organization. If all WPs could be accurately estimated as described thus far the process of developing schedules, budgets, and the overall management process would be relatively simple. However, the fact that most organizations do not experience project success rates much above 50% (many lower than that) suggests that other factors somehow get introduced into this process.

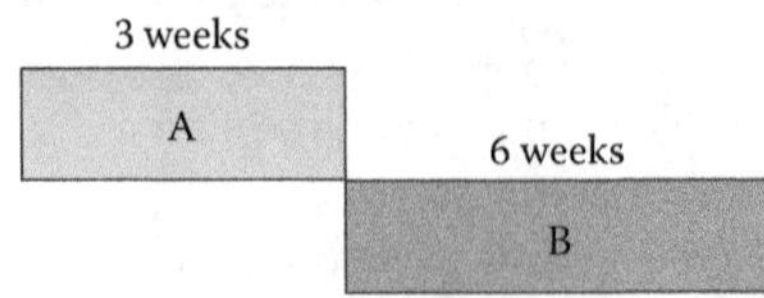

Figure 12.2 Multiple WPs in sequence.

Nevertheless, building a solid WP level management foundation is a key step in dealing with the vagaries of the external world. Regardless of where or how we start the planning process, the goal is to produce this level of work definition granularity.

12.6 Developing Project WBS

It is always difficult to suggest that any one activity is the most significant one to support the management and work control process, but there is heavy evidence from industry researchers that indicates failure to properly define project scope creates an array of problems later and often leads to decreased success rates. One proven technique that has been found to be of broad value in the project planning and control process is the WBS. Our bias is that a properly created WBS is the most important planning and control artifact and it has broad impact across the various project management processes. A well-developed WBS is the best tool available to define and communicate various aspects of scope and status for the project. In latter sections of this chapter, we will review some of the key concepts and mechanics related to this activity.

As the project scope definition moves from a high-level vision-oriented definition of requirements toward the technical work required there is a need to translate the original plain language specification verbiage into something more akin to a structured technical work definition. This requirement-to-work translation process is the fundamental role of the WBS. The value of this approach is that the result serves as a good communication tool between user plain language requirements and the technical work required to produce those requirements. Both technical and nontechnical groups can understand the result, and it provides a communications bridge to confirm that the stated requirements are being produced by the defined project work units.

Before jumping too deeply into this topic let us illustrate a WBS with a simple example. Figure 12.3 shows what a defined project structure for a house might look like. The nine WPs are meant to identify major skill and work areas necessary to complete the project. The role of each component is to deliver a defined portion of the overall project requirement. Collectively, these combined boxes represent the total scope of the project. Also, note that a box dedicated to project management is included in the scope definition since it is a required work activity and consumes resources.

Various reference sources describe their approach for the WBS construction process. As an example, Project Management Institute (PMI)'s *Practice Standard for Work Breakdown Structures*

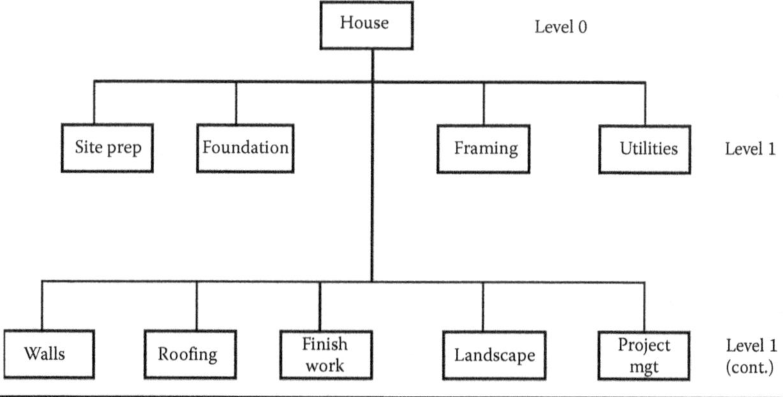

Figure 12.3 Basic WBS Structure.

provides guidance and sample templates for various types of projects (PMI WBS, 2006). An accepted approach shows the top WBS box with a short name of the project or program that is being defined. The second level would contain high level groups. Examples of this are subsystems, project phase, or processes depending on the type and scope of the project. The third level continues the scope decomposition and by this point, the structure should begin to reflect the major work groups and/or key deliverables. According to the Department of Energy (DOE) methodology, the first three levels of a WBS are:

Level 1: Major project-end objectives
Level 2: Major product segments or subsections of the end objective. Major segments are often defined by location or by the purpose served
Level 3: Definable components, subsystems, or subsets, of the Level 2 major segments (DOE, 1997)

Even though standard construction rules have logical value for future project comparison and potential reusability, there is no one right answer for constructing a WBS. Its primary role in the process is to describe the work structure from the eyes of those responsible for delivering the output. In essence, a WBS is variable depending on project size, technical approach to the effort, and the organization mix doing the work. The list below shows several optional ways to construct a proper WBS structure:

1. Using standard templates from similar recurring project types
2. Modifying the structure from a similar effort
3. Defining the major work organization groups and then decomposing the structure from the top-down level
4. Start with lower-level defined work elements and aggregate them upward into a logically defined hierarchical structure
5. Package the structure using the required deliverables as guidance (Schwalbe, 2006, p. 163)

Regardless of the method used or resulting structure, the final WBS view should eventually contain a set of reasonably small WPs at the lowest level. These collections of defined work effort represent the total scope of the project. In other words, project requirements should be mapped to specific WPs to ensure that all user-approved requirements have been defined in the technical work structure. Envision a WP as a defined and managed unit of work. As a memory metaphor, think of the boxes as molecules in the chemical compound; it might also be worthwhile to expand this analogy to include the view that the human and material resources assigned to these molecules are then the atoms.

For operational reasons, a WP should normally be linked to a single organizational work group, or at least have a single manager assigned responsibility for the effort. What is not obvious at this point is that the WP will be a basic item used for detailed planning, execution, and control. In order to construct the project plan, it is necessary to define the related work content, resource requirement, schedule, and budget, plus other requirements relevant to the individual WP. As the project progresses, actual status will be collected for these items.

All WBS summary aggregations above the WP level are simply groupings of their lower level items. From the descriptions outlined thus far be sure that you have a clear understanding of the WP concepts introduced. These items are the basic technical and management building blocks for the project and they are the items that must be in place to help drive the project to successful completion.

12.6.1 WBS Dictionary

In addition to the visible project activities related to product delivery, there are other supporting activities that should be captured in the WBS data repository, which is now named the WBS Dictionary. A sample of these follows:

1. Define product approval processes with the future user
2. Define recurring planned meetings (team and external)
3. Define Team/management/customer interfaces activities
4. Define Quality inspections and defect repair processes
5. Show Training activities (team and users)
6. Define project formal communication requirements (status reporting and presentation preparation)
7. Additional project-related management processes that need to be developed (i.e., change control, quality assurance, etc.)
8. Document project startup activities
9. Store and advertise planned deployment of the project output and ongoing support
10. Draft and store operational service level agreements with outside support groups
11. Project closeout details
12. Define stakeholders involved with the WP

Many of these items represent key life cycle management decisions more than work unit specification; however, if issues such as this are not accounted for the required staffing level will be inaccurate. What this means is that the WBS must also include various environmental work activities that on the surface do not look like requirements, but in fact represents additional work requirements that are put in place to improve the probability of success. As an example, project management must be shown in the project scope as it consumes resources.

A WBS is a great tool for showing the basic work and deliverables organization of the defined effort, but it is weak on work specification. To supply these needed details the WBS Dictionary is used (Table 12.1). The primary purpose of this document is to provide needed descriptive

Table 12.1 Data dictionary format

<table>
<tr><td colspan="3">Project</td><td colspan="4">WBS Task no.</td><td colspan="2">Person responsible</td></tr>
<tr><td colspan="9">Total authorized description</td></tr>
<tr><td colspan="9">Task deliverable</td></tr>
<tr><td colspan="9">Acceptance criteria</td></tr>
<tr><td>Duration (days)</td><td>Total costs $</td><td colspan="3">Direct costs $</td><td>Material costs $</td><td>Misc. costs $</td><td colspan="2">Deliverables</td></tr>
<tr><td>Due date</td><td colspan="4">Preceding activity</td><td colspan="2">Team member assigned</td><td>Succeeding activity</td><td>Team member assigned</td></tr>
<tr><td colspan="9">Resource assigned purchasing</td></tr>
<tr><td colspan="4">Approved by PM</td><td colspan="3">WP owner</td><td colspan="2">Date</td></tr>
</table>

detail for each WBS component. PMI lists the following types of data for the dictionary (PMI, 2017, p. 162):

1. Statement of work (SOW) description
2. Codes to support tracking of organizational resources and project financial details (i.e., WBS or organizational accounting codes)
3. Deliverables
4. Acceptance criteria
5. Associated activities/tasks (predecessors and successors)
6. Milestones
7. Responsible organization for the work
8. Resource estimates
9. Start and stop schedules (this may be kept in the project plan)
10. Quality requirements and metrics
11. Technical references
12. Contract information
13. Constraints and assumptions
14. Risk level (high level indicators)

Because of the data-intensive nature of the dictionary items defined above, many organizations do not employ a single repository strategy. It is possible to avoid having a single data source of project data, but for future ease of access a single repository makes sense. If the project supporting data is documented in a formal computer-based repository, the internal project team can have ready access to needed work items. Searching for data can be a very wasteful activity for team members. Details related to items such as schedule, budget details, resources, organizational assignments, and task relationships should all be contained in the formal project repository. The modern class of document management software makes this consideration mandatory.

Development of a good WBS structure is not an easy task and the guiding principle is that its design should help both the project team and external stakeholders understand how the project is structured. In order to be of maximum value, the project plan structure should map to the WBS, therefore, one approach to developing the WBS structure would be to align it around the development methodology being used.

12.7 WBS Mechanics

Recognize that a WBS will not always be fully decomposed to the WP level during the planning phase. Prior to completion the decision could be made that the requirements are sufficiently defined and then leave further elaboration for the execution phase. This means that some segments of the WBS would contain work units at a higher level of definition than described thus far. This also means that there is a higher potential error in the resulting plan values. These higher-level work units are called *planning packages and their accuracy is often titled Rough Order of Magnitude (ROM)*, meaning that their related error rates can be ±100%. These units have the same general definitional needs as a WP and will need to be mechanically dealt with prior to their execution. This form of plan evolution is called the *rolling wave* approach.

Regardless of the work unit level reflected in the planning phase of WBS, each box in the structure should be linked to some specified organizational entity and a defined manager. The list below offers some basic decomposition alternative steps to consider:

1. Identify the top-level view that represents how the project will be defined within the program, phase, or component structure.
2. Identify the goals of the entire project. Consider each primary objective as a possible top-level element in the WBS hierarchy. Review the SOW and project scope documents to aid in this decision.
3. Identify each phase or component needed to deliver the objectives in step one. This will become second-level elements in the WBS.
4. Break down each phase into the component activities necessary to deliver the above levels. This will become third-level WBS elements.
5. Continue to break down the activities in step three—these tasks may require further decomposition.

This process should continue downward until the work units are identified to a single organizational unit owner. Where possible, the defined work units fit into the size definition supported by the organization. If this is not feasible at this stage the unit should be labeled a planning package and marked accordingly. It is a management decision regarding further decomposition of the larger packages, but scheduling accuracy and future control granularity will be lessened if large work unit packages remain.

The theory and concepts for a WBS are easy to understand; however, a basic question remains regarding how to identify the correct WBS structure for a particular project. The list below contains items that may help decide on the proper packaging design:

1. Are there logical partitions or major phases in the project?
2. Are there milestones that could represent key groupings?
3. Are there business cycles that need to be considered (e.g., tax period, production, downtime schedule, etc.)?
4. Are there financial constraints that might dictate phases?
5. What external company life cycles might impact the structure?
6. What development methodology process will be used? Does it help define a logical grouping?
7. Are there risk areas that need to be recognized (e.g., technical, organizational, political, ethical, user, legal, etc.)?

Project team active involvement is imperative for moving the WBS through the development stage. In this planning cycle team members should discuss proposed views and draft possible package names on sticky notes or white boards that allow proposed boxes to be moved around. The result of this activity is a draft WBS hierarchy tree structure, as shown in Figure 12.4.

Through subsequent discussions various items will be moved around on the board until a particular work organization is agreed upon. This process should normally work from a top-down view of the project scope. Once a particular WBS level is defined, it may be possible for a portion of the structure to be allocated to a team subgroup for more detailed discussion and decomposition. Later, each subgroup would make their presentation to the whole team to ensure that other "horizontal across-the-tree" editing is not needed. This should generally occur on a level-by-level

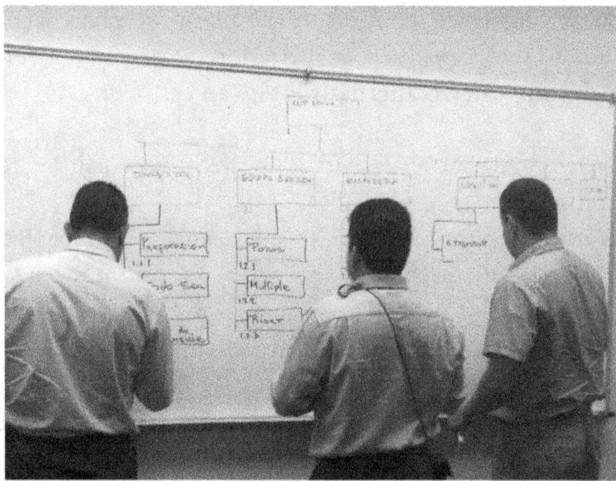

Figure 12.4 Developing the WBS on a white board.

basis through at least the planning package definitions. As the process moves downward the level of interaction across the structure should decline as the work begins to align itself into more isolated organizational units. When the draft process is complete, a final project team review of the overall structure is required. At this point, the team must buy into the structure and its represented work. This design process benefits the project team, as they will gain a deeper understanding of the project scope, roles and responsibilities, potential risk areas, and critical assumptions. In addition, this overview stimulates team communication and a spirit of collaboration. Sessions of this type can complete a draft WBS structure in fairly short time periods, assuming the project scope is familiar. However, if the project involves high complexity or a new-type venture, then this process might be iterative and require multiple sessions to resolve. Regardless, the process of decomposition and review remains the same.

In this model, some boxes have been labeled as a deliverable rather than a summary package. The focus point of this view is that defined deliverables were part of the discussion and the team wished to ensure that the structure contained the specified requirements. In any case, it is important to review the final structure to ensure that the work defined will produce the required deliverables and that should be included in the quality management aspects of the scope development. In other words, if work unit 1.3.1 is to produce a specified deliverable, that should be part of a future quality check on completion of that activity (Figure 12.5).

Keep in mind that the number of levels in a WBS depends on the size and complexity of a project. Another stylistic consideration is to use nouns as titles in the structure, rather than verbs. This helps focus on what is to be done and not how it will be produced. *Remember, a WBS is defined as a deliverables-oriented structure, but the lower layers are work focused to produce the project deliverables!*

12.7.1 WBS Numbering Scheme

There are various schemes used to label the boxes in the WBS structure; however, in most of these a decimal point approach is used to reflect the hierarchical layers. Mature project management organizations such as the Departments of Energy and Defense have standardized schemes for box numbering. One common method is to label the top box "1," then the layer below would be 1.1,

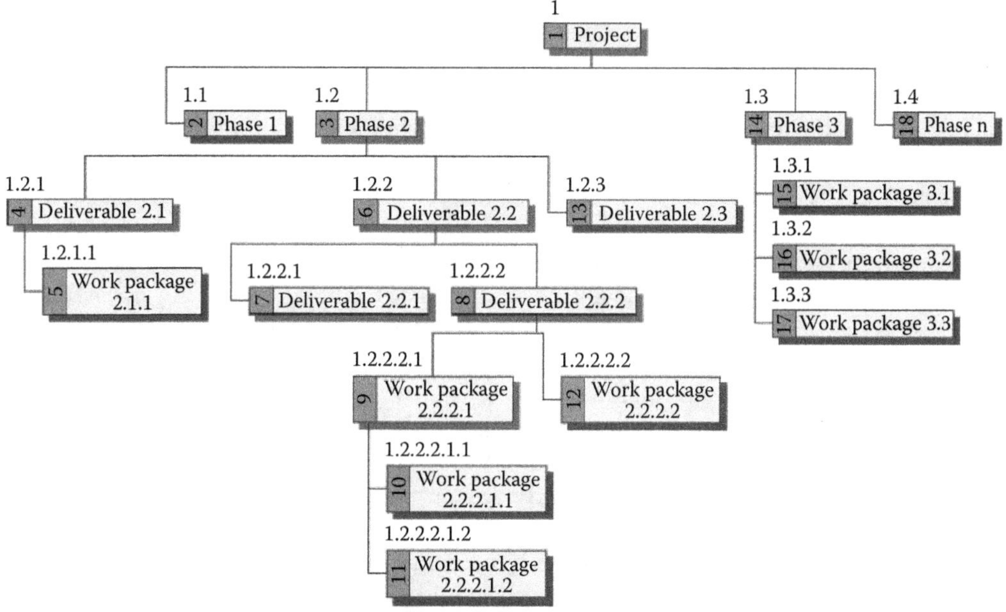

Figure 12.5 Sample draft WBS with deliverables identified.

1.2, 1.3, and so on. However, if the top layer is labeled "0," then the layer below would be defined as 1, 2, 3, and 4. Regardless of the scheme chosen, the layers below generally attach a decimal-type notation to reflect linkage to the layer above. Figure 12.6 shows a skeleton sample WBS with typical numbering notation.

It is given that scope changes will occur during the life cycle and will affect the geometry of the WBS. For this reason, it is advisable to use some form on non-sequential ID numbers to leave open codes for future changes and additions to the scope. This could be done by using increments of 10 in the numbering sequence. In any case, recognize that future changes will likely add work units to the structure, so the numbering can get messy and disorganized without space to add new boxes. As a final point on the schematic mechanics, realize that these numbers will be linked to other project processes for cost and schedule tracking, risk, communications, HR, contracting, and others. This coding system provides an excellent method to communicate understanding of the overall process.

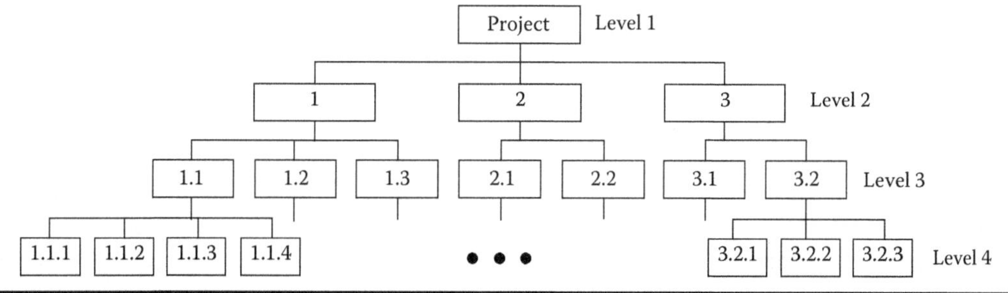

Figure 12.6 Sample WBS numbering scheme.

12.7.2 Other WBS Views

The concept of structuring work has many operational benefits to the project management process. In order to support different control or analysis needs, it is typical to sort the basic WBS data into other views. The most common restructuring occurs in the case of third-party vendors being involved in some subset of the project. In this situation, the element of the WBS that is contracted will generally not be under the control of the internal project team. Assuming that is the case, then the contracted "branch" of the structure would essentially be extracted from view and allocated to the contractor for management. In some cases, the contractor would need little added specification for their activity, while in more complex situations they might have to be fully involved in the decomposition process to the WP level just as though they were internal members of the team. If the contractual arrangement is fixed price, that substructure of the plan might be shown on the WBS as a single summary box. However, other reporting needs or contractual options might necessitate further WBS detail be displayed, but most likely not to the vendor's internal WP level. This substructure is called the Contract WBS (CWBS). It is connected to the master WBS, but generally stays under control of the third-party vendor to manage without specific details being visible to the buyer.

A second presentation form for the WBS is organizational centric, meaning that it is sorted into collections of work by organizational group. This view is called an Organizational Breakdown Structure (OBS). Similar to this view is a time-phased sort by resource categories used to show total skill requirements represented by the WBS. This view is called a Resource Breakdown Structure (RBS). Therefore, if we were attempting to capture product costs or levels by resource type, it is possible to define that level of detail in the WP and sort the data accordingly.

Once the final WBS is approved by appropriate user, technical and management entities that version is frozen and used later to compare actual results. This view is called the *Scope Baseline.* As projects evolve, changes invariably creep into the requirements set. These often occur because more is now understood about the target and if the changes are properly managed this can be a reasonable process. As part of the change control process management has to agree that the change proposal is positive and a desirable choice. This typically means that the budget will increase because something extra has been added. When this occurs, it is possible to reset the project plan baseline. This would be called the *revised baseline* and the process is called *rebaselining.* It is important to understand what each of these baseline points represents. As an example, it is not appropriate for the PM to be blamed for a budget overrun if management has approved a 20% increment in the project requirements through various changes. In this case, a 20% growth in actual costs over the original baseline may be reasonable. On the other hand, comparing end of project costs to the original baseline does show how much the project expanded since the plan was approved. Analysis of these comparisons can provide important lessons learned for future projects, and for that reason the role of various baselines is an important control concept.

12.7.3 Tracking Status of the Project

In order to compare project status, it is necessary to establish a linkage mechanism between the WBS and related accounting data, which is typically located in a formal enterprise resource system. Developing a translation key between the enterprise resource system and the project WBS detail is needed for tracking purposes. In this process, the financial system codes (chart of accounts) are mapped to corresponding WBS code of account boxes. These common WBS mapping points are called *Control Account Packages* (CAPs) and they can be arbitrarily linked to low-level WBS boxes, or summary level activities. The level of visibility into actual resource usage dictates the desired location for CAPs. It is theoretically desirable to have actual cost data captured at the WP level, but in many cases the extra administrative work to do this is not justified. Hence, location of the various CAPs in the WBS hierarchy is a management decision. In operational mode, actual status would be collected for the appropriate CAP, which in turn would allow for plan versus actual comparisons to be made at that level.

For the examples used in the rest of the book simple WBS coding schemes will be used, but keep in mind that large organizations would have to deal with a more complex code structure, or a mapping algorithm to link the simple internal project scheme to the enterprise financial system.

12.8 WBS Construction Checklist

At this stage in the project planning process, the goal is to translate the logical requirements into a technical structure that will produce the defined deliverables. The six steps outlined below are intended to provide some guidance in regard to how to look at the requirements and translate them into a technical work structure for the project. The guiding design principle is that the resulting structure will map to the way in which the project is envisioned to be executed. A sample development checklist to evaluate this process follows:

1. *Identify the top box structure.* Group this level using one of the following structuring approaches:
   a. Major project phases (i.e., phase I, phase II, etc.)
   b. Major projects under a larger program
   c. Methodology life cycle phases
   d. Major deliverables
   e. Organizational responsibility
   f. Geographical location
   g. Process sequence
   h. A hybrid of the above structures.

   **Regardless of the WBS structure chosen, it should reflect the way in which the project will be managed and executed.
2. Decompose the structure until manageable size WPs result in the lower tiers. Ensure that adequate definition exists for each WP
3. Use organizational defined coding structures, assign a unique identifier to each WBS activity based on its hierarchical level (see Figure 12.7).
4. Assign management owners to all boxes. Each WBS box entity requires assignment of a responsible manager who is charged with overseeing that aspect of the work. Activity owners assist in planning their activities and are later responsible for ensuring that the work gets done to specifications and within agreed schedule and resource constraints. When no owner is explicitly assigned to a work unit the ownership role defaults to the responsibility of the PM.
5. Define completion criteria. Documentation of project WBS activities is an important planning requirement. The purpose of this is to provide a measurable mechanism to judge future status of the activity. These requirements should provide guidelines to evaluate completeness. A possible test script statement could say "Complete six error-free runs of the approved

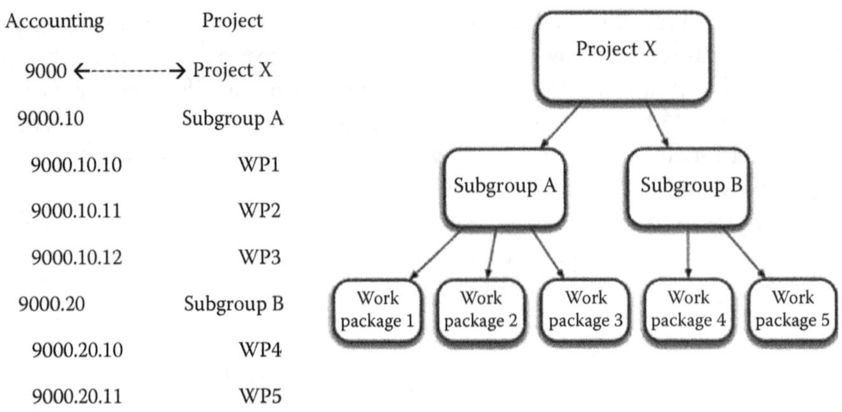

Figure 12.7 WBS to accounting cross-coding.

test script against the integrated code produced by the WP and document the results in the project test database."

6. Support area review and further analysis. The last step involves reviewing the work defined with the various performing organizations. The theme of this review is to ensure that all of the relevant knowledge area issues are identified. For each performing entity the following knowledge perspectives should be reviewed:
   a. Human relations (skill availability, capacity, and organization)
   b. Quality plans (test plans, quality processes)
   c. Risk assessment and response plans (general risk management)
   d. Communication plans
   e. Project organization and staffing plans
   f. Procurement plans (third-party human resources and material)
   g. Project management.
   h. Key stakeholders identified

   Limitations in any of the knowledge areas outlined above can in turn cause changes in the project work scope. For example, the decision to outsource a portion of the scope would impact defined work units related to that activity. In similar fashion, decisions on risk mitigation or transfer would likely impact other aspects of the project. Decisions from these related areas must be integrated into the WBS plan since they impact the resulting scope, schedule, or budget. Once this review cycle is complete the next step is to move forward to begin estimating task durations and resource allocation to WPs.
7. *Management approval of the scope.* Once the WBS is considered to be complete it needs to be formally approved by management and appropriate stakeholders. With that action completed the scope baseline is set and the process begins to move forward toward scheduling activities.

12.9 Requirements "ibilities"

On the surface, the requirements definition concept seems pretty simple—to identify what the customer wants and then engineer the technical details necessary to construct it. The general scope discussion to this point has had that flavor. However, there are a set of not so obvious issues that often fall into the crack of the requirements definition. We call these the basic nine "ibilities":

1. Traceability
2. Affordability
3. Feasibility
4. Usability
5. Producibility
6. Maintainability
7. Simplicity
8. Operability
9. Sustainability.

Each "ibility" represents a work unit attribute to be considered in the requirements definition. We must recognize that the project goal is not just trying to produce a stated deliverable. It must also consider a broader technical look at the attributes of the result. In order to do this it is necessary to review the approach taken and adjust the scope statement according to each of the nine *ibility* attributes to ensure that the approach chosen appropriately matches the real requirement. In many cases, a particular solution will involve a trade-off of one or more of these attributes based on time, quality, functionality, or cost constraints. These decision alternatives will present themselves along the following general lines:

1. Present versus future time aspects
2. Ease of use versus cost or time
3. Quality versus time or cost
4. Risk of approach
5. Use of new strategic technology versus a more familiar tactical approach, etc.

As the project moves through its life cycle processes of scope definition, physical design, and execution each of these considerations should be reviewed. All too often one or more of the *ibilities* is ignored or overlooked and the result is downstream frustration by someone in the chain of users or supporters of the item. The section below will offer a brief definition and consideration review for each of the *ibility* items:

Traceability relates to the ability to follow a requirement's life span, in a forward and backward direction (i.e., from origin, development, and specification, its subsequent deployment and use, and periods of ongoing refinement and iteration in any of these phases). Envision traceability this way. If a design element or WP specification is changed, the configuration management process will document this and be able to ensure that the proper version is used.

Affordability relates to a match of the design approach to the budget. There is always pressure to cut costs through the design, but many of those decisions cause some adverse impact on other *ibilities*.

Feasibility can wear many hats in the project environment. The most obvious of these is the technical feasibility of the approach. Often times, stretching to achieve some performance goal will go beyond the existing technical capabilities and create additional risk. In similar fashion, the lack of critical skills availability can adversely affect the outcome. Think of feasibility as anything that can get in the way of success, whether that be technical, organizational, political, resource, or otherwise.

Usability is similar in concept to operability, except that in this case it more involves the resulting value generated by the output. It is what the process or product does in the hands of the future user. This can be either reality or perception based, but is certainly a concern for the project team to deal with.

Producibility is an attribute associated with how the actual item will be created. In many cases, there is a gap between the designer and the builder, so the key at this stage is to be sure that the building entities are represented in the design and probably even in the initial requirements process. Think of this as a "chain" of events that need to be linked together and not just thrown over the wall to the next group. Each component in the life cycle needs to consider this attribute.

Maintainability deals with the item in production. The consideration here is how much effort is involved in keeping the device ready for operations. In the case of high-performance devices there is often a significant downtime for maintenance. Having a device capable of "jumping tall buildings with a single bound" sounds good, but what about if it can only do that about 10% of time, with the remaining period being down for some type of maintenance. There is clearly a trade-off consideration here. The design trade-off in this case is to design a way to perform the maintenance quicker, cheaper, or with less downtime. Certainly, the best choice is not to ignore the issue.

Simplicity is an overarching concept. Complex is the natural state. The goal here is to find ways to achieve the required output as simply as possible. This is a motherhood statement, but a real requirement to keep in perspective.

Operability involves the future user's ability to easily and safely use the product or device. Many years ago, aircraft designers found that the location of gauges, switches, and knobs had a lot to do with the safe operation of the airplane. Every device has characteristics similar to this. Think of this attribute as not changing the requirement, but rather making the functionality easier to use and safer. Automobile designers in recent years have found this to be an issue with some of the new dash functions being installed in the modern car (i.e., how do I turn on the radio?).

Sustainability is likely the least understood of the *ibilities*. This goes beyond all other attributes in that it evaluates the ability of the process or product to exist for a long term. Will the underlying technology survive? Will the design last as long as required? In high-technology projects this can be one of the most difficult factors to deal with given low predictably of the next new technology. Maybe "predictability" is in fact the tenth *ibility*. If the project team had an accurate view of the technical and organizational future this goal could be better achieved. All too often, an underlying technology is used in the design only to find much too soon that some better technology has been introduced to make the current approach obsolete.

The final word on the *ibilities* set is that they are important to both short- and long-term success of the project. One of the keys in both requirements and design reviews is to go through the nine *ibilities* list and resolve the trade-offs outlined here. This process may well be equally important to getting the user requirements correct because if the correct choices are not made here the user will still feel that the requirements were not met.

12.10 Moving Forward

This chapter has illustrated how scope definition is the functional jumping off point for project planning. At this stage, the important point to understand is that planning decisions made in other areas can impact various aspects of the plan including scope. We have touched on the interactive characteristics that KAs can have on each other. A more detailed discussion related to that idea will be deferred for now, but is the main topic of a complete chapter later.

The next chapter will focus on schedule management as the core planning activity that follows from scope definition. Essentially, this involves an evolution of scope definition through the time required to produce defined work units. As illustrated earlier the linkage of WPs is a key aspect in producing a schedule. Likewise, the resource information collected is also fundamental to the budgeting process.

References

Department of Energy, 1997. *Cost Codes and the Work Breakdown Structure.* Department of Energy. www.directives.doe.gov/pdfs/doe/doetext/neword/430/g4301-1chp5.pdf (accessed October 15, 2008).

PMI, 2017. *A Guide to the Project Management Body of Knowledge (PMBOK® Guide),* 6th ed. Newtown Square, PA: Project Management Institute.

PMI WBS, 2006. *Practice Standard for Work Breakdown Structures,* 2nd ed. Newtown Square, PA: Project Management Institute.

Schwalbe, K., 2006. *Information Technology Project Management.* Boston, MA: Course Technology.

Chapter 13

Quick Start Example

13.1 Introduction

It is important at this stage to demonstrate how a somewhat abstract graphical Work Breakdown Structure (WBS) can help to develop a schedule and cost plan for the project. As we will see, scope is actually the foundation for the project because it starts the technical and work definition, outlining what needs to be produced and what units of work are required. This specification process leads directly to the time and cost aspects of the work defined. For this Quick Start demonstration, the focus is on illustrating how the WBS leads mechanically to the creation of a first cut schedule and budget. Understanding how these pieces play together is a critical learning step in that many view project management simply as scope, schedule, and budget. We will see more complexity in this process as the text discussions evolve the topic. However, illustrating this fundamental linkage is a valuable metaphor for understanding this part of the model story.

13.2 Project Management Work Packages

The vocabulary term introduced in Chapter 12 for defined work units is a work package (WP) and the tool for linking these together is the Work Breakdown Structure (WBS).

In order to combine these two concepts into something meaningful it will be instructive to show how these two artifacts lead to a plan for schedule and cost. The example developed here will demonstrate some of the basic mechanical inputs needed to derive an initial schedule and budget from the WBS view.

We previously described how WPs were the building blocks to form the project WBS and through these the overall project work and deliverable scope is defined. From a work definition perspective, the WP becomes a management focus point for both planning and control activities. The most visible outcome of examining the internals of a defined WP is to see that it initially contains estimates for the required resources to execute the work, estimated duration, cost, and linkages to other work tasks. From these specifications a model first iteration schedule and cost can derived. Embedded in this will be not only the project schedule and budget, plus can include a summary of the planned resources as well. Collectively, the results of this process would represent a first cut schedule and cost estimate that can be aggregated through the WBS to reflect the total direct cost for the project. The concept of "first cut" implies that more details will need to be added before this process is finished, but this simple example provides a good introduction to this fundamental activity

13.3 Multiple WPs

Chapter 12 discussed the concept of linked WPs. These linkages (predecessors) indicate the order in which work units will be executed. Moving one step up the food chain in our WP theory, we can now see what happens when we admit that there are two WPs. A larger work view to define the whole project can be represented in the same manner regardless of the number of WPs. To offer a simple example of two related WPS assume that task A involves pouring concrete and task B involves smoothing the finish. This structure can be modeled by showing the two boxes stacked end-to-end. This serial form is called a finish–start (FS) relationship. Metaphorically, we are stacking the two boxes as shown in Figure 13.1.

For the schematic outlined above the project duration would be calculated by adding the two individual task durations. Hence, if WP A has duration of three weeks and WP B has duration of six weeks, the calculated duration for the set would be nine weeks. Simple, huh? One should always be wary of such simplistic arithmetic. First, there is a difference in the meaning of duration and elapsed time. Let's say that the normal work schedule is 40 hours per week and five days each week. Weekends would count on the elapsed time calendar, but not part of the duration count since the workers are not on scene at this time. This brings up our first convoluted definitional problem to resolve. There are three views of time that need to be understood. These are:

Effort/work—the amount of total effort required to execute the defined scope.

Duration—the amount of working time required to execute the work; multiple resources can be used to cut calendar time (i.e., two workers executing a job may cut the original estimate by 50%).

Elapsed time—the calendar time required executing the work. Work schedules typically are five-day weeks, so weekends would be lost time in the schedule.

The three variables outlined above represent potential confusion. For example, the WP time estimate might be 80 hours, but with two resources allocated the duration is 40 hours. Then, if the job starts on a Wednesday it will not finish until seven days later (i.e., two weekend days off).

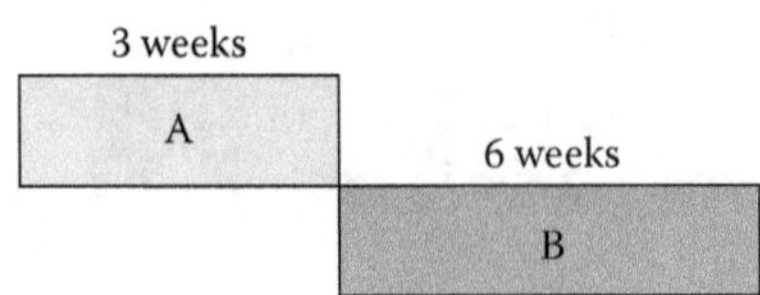

Figure 13.1 Two box model.

13.4 Example: Pool Project Mechanics

It is now time to show the mechanics related to this process. Installation of a swimming pool will be used as the reasonably well understood example to make the plan development process more visible. Since this is a small project, it is possible to elaborate the whole activity set in a single WBS layer as shown in Figure 13.2. The staggered layers in the figure are required to fit the visual inside the page space.

The first step in the translation process is to flatten the WBS into a columnar format as previously described in Chapter 12. Table 13.1 shows the equivalent table, plus it adds duration and sequencing (predecessor) information to the various WPs. This is required to move this data into a schedule format.

Two of the data elements come directly from the WBS. That is, WBS code and Activity title. Three additional data elements are needed to finish the table. The three variables needed to finish the required data are: duration, predecessor, and cost estimate.

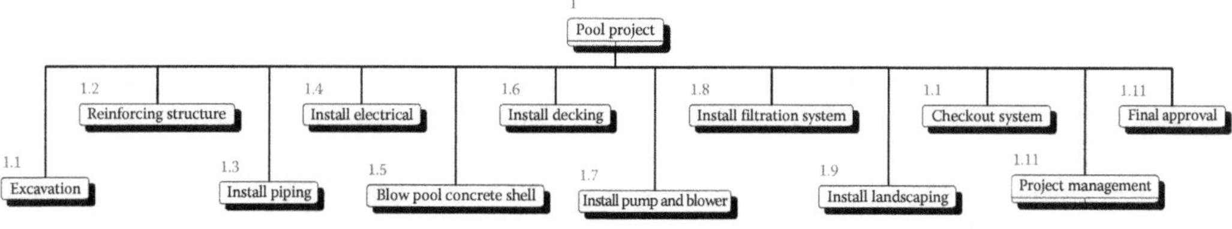

Figure 13.2 Pool project WBS.

Table 13.1 Pool Activity Listing

No.	*WBS*	*Activity/Task*	*Duration (days)*	*Cost ($)*	*Predecessor*
1	1	Pool project	37		
2	1.1	Excavation	5	6,000	
3	1.2	Reinforcing structure	3	5,900	2
4	1.3	Install piping	4	3,800	3
5	1.4	Install electrical	3	3,900	3
6	1.5	Blow pool concrete shell	5	13,500	5, 4
7	1.6	Install decking	5	6,000	6 FS + 5 days
8	1.7	Install pumps and blower	4	4,200	7
9	1.8	Install filtration system	2	3,600	7
10	1.9	Install landscaping	5	6,000	9, 8
11	1.10	Checkout system	1	600	10
12	1.11	Final approval	0	0	11

FS, finish–start.

The WP cost estimate is derived from planned allocations of the human resource cost, material cost, and other. Note in the table data that the task linkage specifications are defined by line numbers. For example, line 6 task cannot be started until tasks on lines 4 and 5 have completed. Unless stated otherwise, all of the tasks relationships are finish–start (FS). The one exception is line 7. Note that this task specifies that it follows line 6 which is a concrete install task; however, the concrete needs time to dry, so there is a five-day lag (wait) specified (i.e., 6 FS + 5 days).

The table WBS column can be viewed as a mailbox code and used for reference purposes. In this case, lines 2–12 are subordinate to line 1, meaning the entire project consists of lines 2–12. Also, note that line 12 shows a zero duration. This is called a milestone. Milestone tasks are used to show timing for technical, user, or management type reviews and can be placed wherever needed.

Data from Table 13.1 can be fed directly into a scheduling utility such as Microsoft Project or Oracle's Primavera. A sample Microsoft Project output for this is shown in Figure 13.3.

Note that the software utility scheduled the defined work tasks according to the predecessor codes and durations. Also, note that the total pool project duration and cost has been summarized from the individual WP values. The real value of the software comes from seeing its ability to schedule this work based on the defined work calendar. In other words, it recognizes weekend and other non-work times. Finally, the resource (worker) schedule is known to the utility and it will move schedules to fit the defined resources capacity limits. That aspect is not relevant here, but certainly is in the real project. In this case, the only time gap is weekends. The project schedule output is shown in both table and Gantt graphical format (Figure 13.4). Also, realize that more status data can be displayed given space available (i.e. start date, finish date). If all of the tasks are executed according to the plan this project would require 37 work days (more elapsed time) and a direct cost of $53,500. In other words, this view replicates the estimated WP parameters into schedule and cost equivalents. Very simple, but a powerful start to the modeling idea.

From this simple example we see the data elements required to build a mechanical schedule and cost plan. The only new idea added here is the recognition of sequence relationships for work units. These are called *predecessor relationships*. Basically, the values shown in this column simply define how the various activities link to each other. There are other predecessor relationship coding options that can be used, but more on this will come later. From a structural model view, all projects would use this same set of variables to produce a schedule and budget. Real-world WBSs would certainly be much larger than this and have more layers and the predecessor relationships would be more complex, but the mechanics would be identical to this example.

Before feeling too confident and starting to feel too good about this nice looking plan, remember that Murphy's Law dictates that things will go wrong and at the most inopportune time.

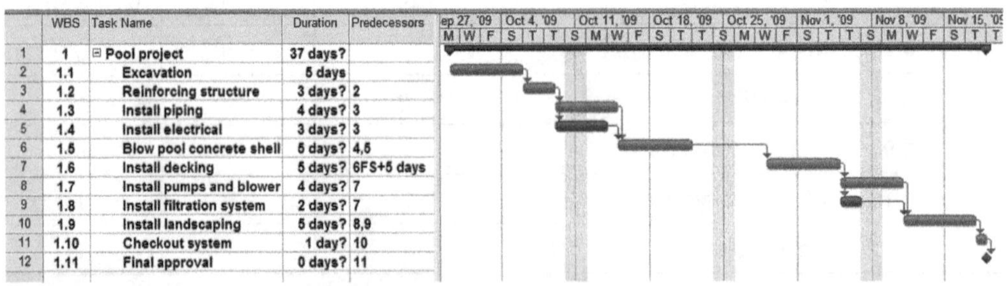

	WBS	Task Name	Duration	Predecessors
1	1	⊟ Pool project	37 days?	
2	1.1	Excavation	5 days	
3	1.2	Reinforcing structure	3 days?	2
4	1.3	Install piping	4 days?	3
5	1.4	Install electrical	3 days?	3
6	1.5	Blow pool concrete shell	5 days?	4,5
7	1.6	Install decking	5 days?	6FS+5 days
8	1.7	Install pumps and blower	4 days?	7
9	1.8	Install filtration system	2 days?	7
10	1.9	Install landscaping	5 days?	8,9
11	1.10	Checkout system	1 day?	10
12	1.11	Final approval	0 days?	11

Figure 13.3 Pool project first cut plan.

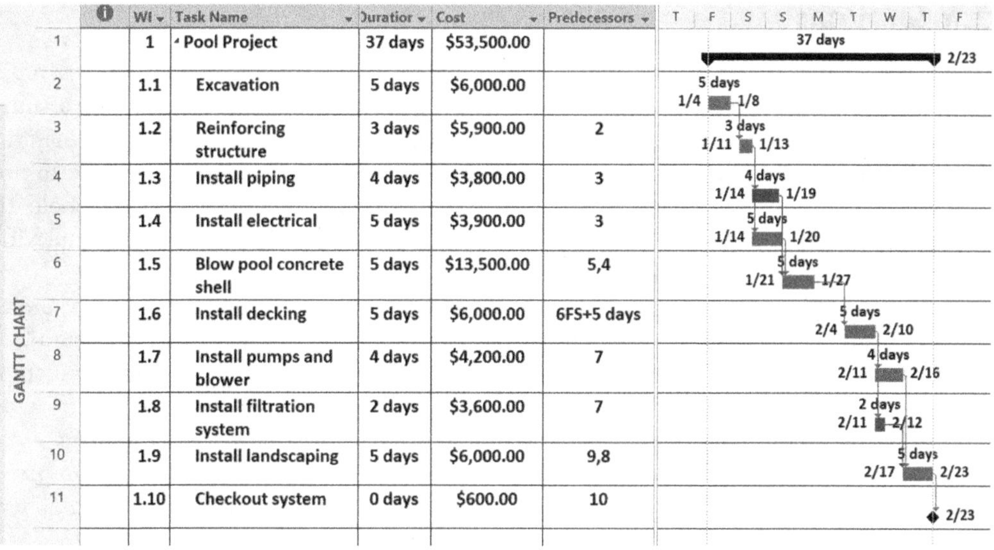

GANTT CHART

	WI	Task Name	Duration	Cost	Predecessors	T F S S M T W T F
1	1	Pool Project	37 days	$53,500.00		37 days 2/23
2	1.1	Excavation	5 days	$6,000.00		5 days 1/4 1/8
3	1.2	Reinforcing structure	3 days	$5,900.00	2	3 days 1/11 1/13
4	1.3	Install piping	4 days	$3,800.00	3	4 days 1/14 1/19
5	1.4	Install electrical	5 days	$3,900.00	3	5 days 1/14 1/20
6	1.5	Blow pool concrete shell	5 days	$13,500.00	5,4	5 days 1/21 1/27
7	1.6	Install decking	5 days	$6,000.00	6FS+5 days	5 days 2/4 2/10
8	1.7	Install pumps and blower	4 days	$4,200.00	7	4 days 2/11 2/16
9	1.8	Install filtration system	2 days	$3,600.00	7	2 days 2/11 2/12
10	1.9	Install landscaping	5 days	$6,000.00	9,8	5 days 2/17 2/23
11	1.10	Checkout system	0 days	$600.00	10	2/23

Figure 13.4 MSP Chart.

Nevertheless, if the PM can keep the defined WP variables in line this set of mechanics is an important project management step and represents an important artifact that serves as a useful tool to communicate goals and status among the various project stakeholders.

13.5 Vocabulary Summary

Important introductory vocabulary and concepts have been introduced here and these concepts are useful throughout the remainder of the book. It is important that the reader not get lost in the details of the lower-level discussions and forget what the overall goal is—*to influence the desired outcome that mirrors the defined plan, which minimally involves deliverables, schedule and cost. All this supporting organizational objectives as approved by management.*

The vocabulary terms shown below represent key pieces in this discussion. If any one of these terms are not clear at this point, mark that term and either go back to review or watch for further explanation of it in subsequent discussions. The quick start vocabulary list follows:

1. Activity
2. Work package
3. WBS
4. WBS dictionary
5. Predecessor
6. Duration
7. Elapsed time
8. Baseline
9. Scope
10. WBS code
11. Gantt chart
12. Microsoft Project

13.6 Summary

This quick start overview has attempted to demonstrate how a few key planning variables can produce what appears to be a coherent plan. That is in fact a valid statement given a risk-free assumption. In reviewing this process, several simplifying assumptions were made to focus on generating a complete first cut schedule and to summarize the general process for moving from scope to time to budget. More on this elaboration process will appear in various other sections of the book. The simple pool example does portray the general process, but it does not illustrate all the complexities that a robust example would need to deal with.

At this stage, we have introduced a reasonable mechanical overview outlining how a project goes from the fuzzy vision stage to defined tangible activities and then on to a schedule and budget. Recognize that projects have significant structural similarity, regardless of the industry or type—*essentially that means allocation of defined resources to defined work to accomplish a defined goal*. The model described in this book is meant to portray all projects, even if some of the internals are small (e.g., such as procurement). There may well be some disagreement regarding how best to move a project through its life cycle, but little disagreement about the underlying list of high level KAs involved in that process.

Throughout the book chapters there will be many references to projects that failed at near catastrophic levels. The key question in each of these examples should be to examine why that occurred given the well-documented root causal factors available from previous research. Realize that no textbook model will make a poorly conceived project successful. The modern PM must use every trick in his tool kit to overcome the myriad of negative issues that can exist to create failure. It is important to understand that the model view outlined here is a core knowledge requirement to begin this process.

Discussion Questions

1. What is the difference in effort, duration, and elapsed time? What would happen to these three parameters if the allocated resources were cut in half?
2. If a WP represents an item that has to be completed in order to execute the project, why would the total project schedule not be the sum of all WP durations?
3. Define the five basic items necessary to generate a schedule.
4. Name some reasons why a WP estimate might be wrong.
5. How does procrastination affect a schedule?
6. What does Murphy's law have to do with project plan schedules?

Chapter 14

Schedule Management

14.1 Introduction

The process of creating a project schedule follows directly from the scope definition process and builds from the Work Breakdown Structure (WBS). The interface point for this process is the work package (WP) definition from the approved WBS. From this starting point the goal is to create a task sequence and cycle time (duration) for each of the activities in the project, then meld these together to create a schedule. The sections that follow will construct the schedule in the following steps (PMI, 2017, p.173):

1. *Plan Schedule Management:* As in all the 10 knowledge areas (KAs) a management plan signifies how that area will be executed. In this case, the plan focuses on the necessary processes to plan, execute, and control the project schedule.
2. *Define Activities:* This segment will translate the WBS scope baseline and translate these into work tasks to show in the project plan. Each of the defined items will have the schedule variable demonstrated in the Chapter 13 Quick Start example.
3. *Sequence Activities:* This step establishes the desired order for the activities to be processed. This is called defining the predecessor–successor relationships. Sequencing decisions can be a combination of technical and management factors.
4. *Estimate Activity Resources:* This activity reviews the general availability of various resource quantities and skills needed to complete the project.
5. *Estimate Activity Durations:* This step focuses on defining the amount of work required to accomplish the activity, then allocating specific resources to each activity in order to estimate the working time for each. This estimate may either be a single deterministic time unit or a probabilistic (three-point) one. For this segment of the text we will assume a single-time estimate.
6. *Develop Schedule:* This step combines all the elements above into a network structure. From this view a final first cut schedule can be created. More iterations of this process will be required to deal with various other technical and management actions faced during the planning process (i.e., risk, resource availability, vendor issues, etc.).
7. *Control Schedule:* This activity involves supplying status information to appropriate decision makers in aid in moving the project back into plan alignment.

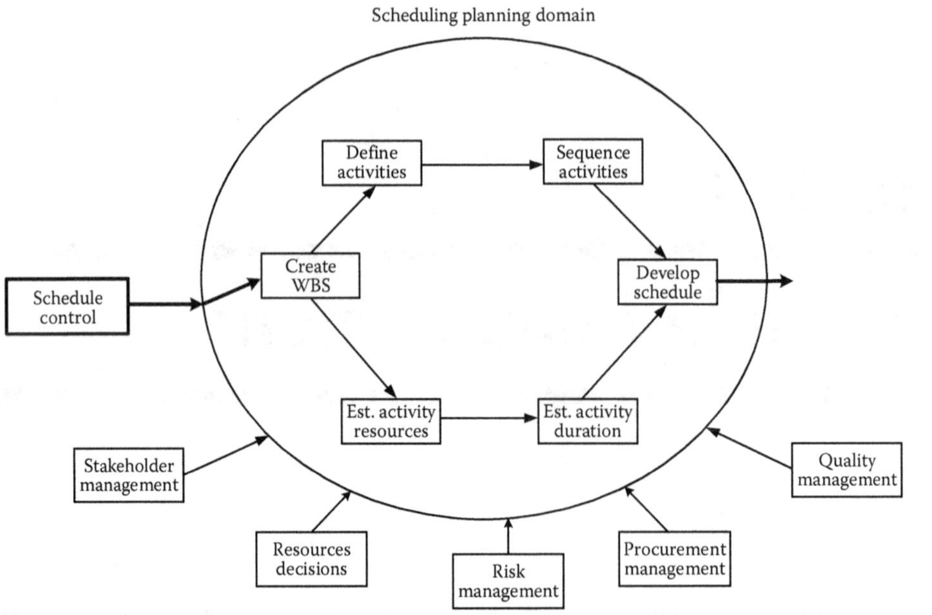

Figure 14.1 Plan overview.

Figure 14.1 shows the model logical flow linkage of time-related processes, moving from the WBS scope-approved baseline creation step described in Chapter 12. Note that this process shows two essentially parallel paths to the schedule. The three logical groupings of this process are:

1. One subpath defines the task list and from this generates a task-linked network view of the schedule.
2. A second subpath generates task durations based on work estimates and resource allocation to those tasks.
3. Using the results from the two subpaths above a network sequence with task durations can be computed to generate the project critical path and slack data.

Figure 14.2 illustrates the logical flow of the basic schedule process; it would be instructive to compare the description above with this graphic view.

The completed project plan will pass through scrutiny from various KAs, stakeholders, and management. Eventually, the initial plan will be modified from this process and approved. From the approved version a baselined version will be used for future control comparisons. As the project moves through the life cycle tasks may be added and duration times will vary. This dynamic version will be used to supply needed schedule data to appropriate stakeholders.

14.1.1 Defining Project Activities

Defined work units minimally need the following planning data defined in order to support further project plan creation:

1. Work unit name
2. Time estimate

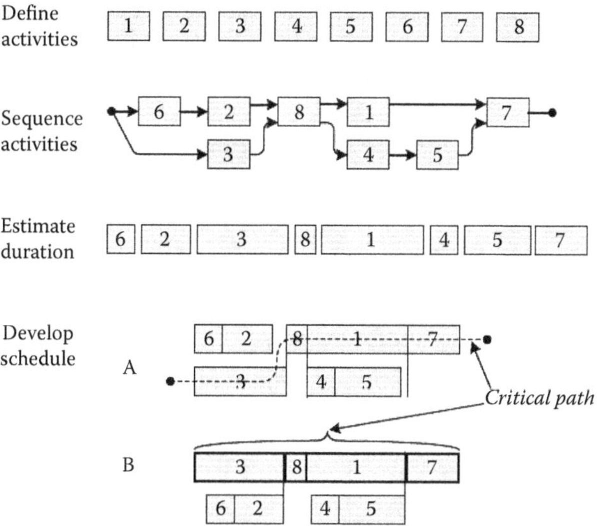

Figure 14.2 Layered view of process.

3. Cost estimate
4. Individual(s) responsible to execute the task
5. Material resources required to execute the task
6. Any operational constraints (required completion, start, etc.)
7. Associated technical details (predecessors, assumptions, etc.)

All information related to the work unit details should be kept in a WBS Dictionary, or an equivalent formal repository, for future reference purposes. One of the key roles of activity definition is to map the technical deliverables into defined WPs. Second, resource estimates required to deliver those WPs are estimated. At this point in the project, an increased level of control is needed over who can load or change these data values in the project repository. The manager in charge of the individual work unit is primarily responsible for the estimate, but the project manager (PM) should have final control over the number being used in the resulting plan.

In this section, we will use the term "activities" to represent work units. This term can represent WPs, planning packages, summary activities, milestones, or tasks. The next process question now becomes how to define the sequence of activities into the project plan.

14.1.2 Activity Sequencing

There are two important management considerations for sequencing. First, is the notion of *technical sequence*, which is based on the technology of the activity. For example, the technical sequence required to build a building would define that the foundation would have to be in place before constructing the walls. Likewise, a software system would have to be constructed before it could be tested. All project activities have some sequence that is generally dictated by their underlying technology or purpose.

A second consideration of sequencing falls beyond the technical issues. That is, many activities can be performed at management discretion, different from the technical view. In these cases, the PM may sequence the activities to accommodate availability of resources, weather, or other factors. In both the technical and discretionary sequencing situations, it is incumbent on the skills of the project team to make the appropriate activity sequencing decision. However, it is important to recognize that these decisions do impact the schedule results, so sequencing considerations are often an iterative activity until the plan is fixed. Regardless of how the sequencing decision is made, a schedule will result by linking the WPs in the order prescribed. This is the essence of the sequencing process.

14.1.3 Estimating Activity Resources

This process estimates the quality and quantity of skills required to execute a WP. From that assessment valuable data is collected that will lead to a cost estimate of the WP. This is also a fundamental data source that has major impact on time and cost calculations. Note that this allocation process essentially defines the direct cost of that WP and in similar fashion aggregates to the total direct project cost. It also starts the quantification process for compiling a total aggregate resource view.

14.1.4 Activity Duration Estimating

One of the most difficult time management activities involves estimating the time required to produce a defined work unit or the entire project. There are many techniques and factors involved in producing such estimates. Creating a duration estimate is both science and art. It is a science because the estimator is often utilizing historical data, mathematical formulae, and statistics to determine the estimate for a work unit. Also, it involves art because each situation is somewhat different and the ability to customize the value requires skill that is obtained through study, observation, and experience with projects (Baca, 2007, p. 135). Later, more details on various estimating techniques will be summarized. Regardless of the technique used duration estimates become basic building blocks to create the project schedule and budget.

14.2 Tips for Accurate Estimating

One of the goals of activity estimation is to create the most accurate duration, budget, and resource requirement possible. If an estimate is too low, the project will likely not finish on plan, exceed its budget, or suffer from inadequate resources. As a result of this, the project will have a higher potential for cancellation as senior management loses confidence in the project. Conversely, if estimates are too high excessive budgets and human resources will be dedicated to a project where they are not needed. Also, the projected value of the project will be defined at a lower point than it deserves, which then may make the initiative look undesirable. Recognize that estimates are used to not only evaluate a project's initial merit, but also formulate the schedule and budget for the execution cycle. Estimation errors can work negatively in both directions. Low estimates can cause a negative view later when the plan overrun the baseline values, whereas high estimates may make the project look nonviable because of high cost and bloated schedule estimate. Both situations are damaging from a management viewpoint.

There are several potential reasons why it is difficult to make accurate estimations. One basic reason lies in the fact that every project has unique variables that are difficult to anticipate. It is impossible to incorporate every possible scenario into the estimate. The more complex the project, the tougher it will be to make accurate estimates. Size, technology complexity, and newness of the project target are the most difficult factors to deal with. In response to this project team members often pad estimates to ensure that they do not overrun the target. In other cases, the result is to estimate what management wants to hear, or simply to be overly optimistic (Soomers, n.d.). Estimates can also be inaccurate because the specifications for the project are poorly defined (Verzuh, 2005, p. 168). The worst case scenario results when optimistic estimates are used in order to get the project approved. As indicated above, all of these situations lead to future management issues when reality surfaces later.

While it is impossible to have estimates that are 100% accurate all the time, there are tips that can be followed before, during, and after estimating to ensure that the estimates are as accurate as possible. These tips include the following (Soomers, n.d.):

1. Create and maintain a database that records the actual time, cost, and resources spent on each task in your project. This data can then be used to make estimations on future projects.
2. Create standard planning documents such as specifications and project plan templates that are used consistently for all projects.
3. Carry out a detailed requirements analysis of the project's work requirements.
4. Compare the new estimate to a former project to determine if it is more or less complex, then adjust based on size, technology, the number of groups involved, or other factors.
5. Apply multiple estimating techniques to arrive at the final estimate. Recognize the potential variability of the estimate and decide if a single-time estimate is prudent.
6. When making an estimate, identify the assumptions, constraints, and caveats that were used to produce the value. Monitor these factors throughout the project to ensure that the environment has not changed.
7. In situations where the estimated budget or duration does not appear adequate to complete the project, propose an upward or downward adjustment to the design criteria (scope). These criteria can include factors such as quality, risk, functionality, schedule, and cost.
8. When planning the project, consider simpler and more efficient ways to do the work. The simpler the tasks, the easier it is to make an estimate.
9. To avoid a chaotic scramble of the project rollout at the end, start planning and estimating the project rollout from the very beginning. This is a key part of the overall plan.
10. When estimating a project characterized by limited information, consider a phase-based approach. In the first phase, the focus should be on refining scope.
11. Categorize the project's deliverables into the "must-have" and the "nice-to-haves." This will help the PM to create contingency plans if overruns occur.
12. Create a lessons-learned database for assistance in future projects. Use this database from past projects to create best practices to apply to the estimating technique.
13. Make sure that the estimator has experience with the type of work being reviewed and that they understand the estimating technique. The estimator should also consider skill of the individuals who will be performing the work (Verzuh, 2005, p. 169).

14.2.1 Types of Estimates

Different organizations have different methods to describe levels of accuracy. Two terms that are common are rough order of magnitude (ROM) and budget. ROM estimates indicate a low confidence level with variance up to +/–100%, while budget level variance is more like +/–10%. Beyond these two views the real question on estimate accuracy comes from the level of variability that an organization will give to the project. If the budget or time overruns more than 10% what is the response. A mature organization probably would negatively view variances higher than 10%. The PM really needs to know how the organization views such variances and be sensitive to that cultural view.

14.3 Estimating Techniques

There are several estimating techniques used in differ scenarios. Some of the more common examples are:

- Expert judgment
- Analogous
- Bottom-up
- Heuristic
- Parametric
- Phased
- Effort distribution (top-down)
- Monte Carlo techniques
- Delphi

No one of these techniques is optimal for every case and in most situations multiple approaches should be used to confirm the derived value. In order to produce accurate estimates successfully one has to have a good understanding of the capabilities of each technique. Beyond the creation of a work required for the effort the second half of the equation involves an understanding of the skill of the workers involved. Historical involvement with both of these variables helps with the resulting accuracy. This section describes several common estimating techniques and the environment where each is most effective.

14.3.1 Expert Judgment

Expert judgment is a very popular technique for making both high and work unit level estimations. According to a software industry study, 62% of cost estimators in this industry use the expert judgment technique (Snell, 1997a). An estimator using this approach relies on his expertise and is often guided by historical information and experience with similar projects. For improved accuracy, expert judgment is often used in combination with other estimating techniques. As an example, imagine that you wanted to provide an estimate to repair the transmission in an automobile. One option could be to say that a standard repair of this type is 100 hours; however, given extensive history with this brand you might lower that initial value. Lack of experience with that brand product would likely lead to a contingency increase in the estimate.

There are three main advantages for using expert judgment as an estimating technique. First, it requires little data collection and simply uses experience from past projects. Second, it has sufficient flexibility to be adapted to the conditions of the current project. Finally, it provides a quick assessment because the expert will have a large knowledge set from which to derive the estimate (Snell, 1997a).

There are also drawbacks to consider when using the expert judgment technique. First, the estimate provided by the expert will not be any better than the objectivity and expertise of the expert (Snell, 1997a). An accurate estimate requires that the estimator have extensive experience dealing with the type of task or project being estimated. Second, estimates made by experts can be biased, which will produce a number with no easy way to verify the logic of creation. Finally, since the expert is often basing his or her estimate from personal memory, but that may not fit the current target.

14.3.2 Analogous Estimating

Analogous estimating has similar traits to expert estimating in that it is based on prior experiences. However, in this case, the comparison is based more on data from the previous method. This process would typically produce an order of magnitude estimate unless the new project is very similar to the comparison one. This estimating technique often uses measures of scale such as size, weight, and complexity from a past situation in order to make the estimate (Callahan, n.d.). When using analogous estimating, the estimator needs to factor in any differences between the new work being estimated versus the previous effort being used for comparison. Examples of complexity factors include new technology that is now being utilized or any changes in the complexity of the task or project (Callahan, n.d.).

Analogous estimating is best used in the early phases of a project before significant details are visible. This method provides quick and easy estimates for projects or tasks that are not very complicated; however, the main drawback is that the results are often not very accurate (Baca, 2007, p. 136). To make sure the estimate is as accurate as possible, use past projects that are very similar in fact and not just in appearance. There is also an element of estimator expertise involved in this method (PMI WBS, 2001).

A simple example of an analogous estimate would be to determine how long it would take to unload a ship and move it back to its home port. Past experience with this same size ship and cargo offers the base comparison value. From this, a review of variable differences such as resource availability, weather, and any other such factors would need to be considered. Based on this type of analysis the estimator should be able to derive a reasonable work or elapsed time estimate.

14.3.3 Bottom-Up Estimating

This technique is considered by experts to be the most accurate of all the techniques described here. However, in order to be utilized a fully decomposed WBS to the WP level is required. In this view, the total project consists of relatively small work units that can be estimated reasonably well by the performing work groups. In most cases, the estimating method used for the low level units would be expert judgment, given that the individuals who will actually be doing the work would provide the values. Once the full collection of individual WP estimates is complete, they are rolled up in the WBS structure to generate higher-level aggregations. From a statistical point of view, each of these estimates would be subject to typical estimating errors; however, over the full WBS range the errors should compensate. In this case, the resulting estimate would be based on real views of the work to be done and the errors made in estimating should be less than other methods reviewed. The main constraint to this technique is the requirement for detailed WP information. Failing that, it will be necessary to seek another option.

The main advantage of using the bottom-up technique is the accuracy that it should provide. It also better involves the individuals who will be performing the work, so actual content review is better, as well as producing an increased commitment to the resulting values. It is not hard to imagine the feeling that a work group might have when an estimator brings a value to the group and says "this is how long it should take you," compared to the work group coming up with the same value. The concept of commitment is clearly on the side of the latter.

The main disadvantage of this method is that it takes more time to create and involves larger organizational involvement. Another subtle problem that often comes with this process is excessive padding of the value by the work groups. External estimators do not have this motive, but internal groups do. One reason that the internal estimates are often padded is to take into consideration risks that are perceived for that activity (Johnson, 2007, p. 224).

The goal of work unit estimating is to derive estimates that do not have excessive padding, but represent reasonable values for the activity. In order to ensure this, some cross-checking by the PM is required. Readers interested in the psychology of this phenomenon should review the Theory of Constraints (Critical Chain) discussion in Chapter 19.

14.3.4 Heuristic Estimating

When using heuristic estimating, the estimate is based on a "rule of thumb." This process is based on parameters derived from past experiences. In that sense, heuristic estimating has flavors of both expert judgment and analogous except in this case the estimate is translated into a mathematical-type expression. Also, realize that expert judgment estimating has to be performed by the expert, whereas heuristics estimating can be transferred to others who are capable of manipulating the defined relationships (Mind Tools, 2008). Imagine the situation where you need an estimate for a new roof on your house. The person that comes to provide this has never seen your house or possibly never even done roofing. What he has is the heuristic estimating formula. Assuming that the roof type is specified and relevant to the model an estimate is derived by plugging in the defined parameters. In this case, the calculation could be as simple as multiplying the measured square footage by a constant. A list of add-on increments would finish the estimate. Expansion of the formula could be required if the roof does not fit the profile for which the model was derived. This class of estimating would typically be found in situations where the same type project is performed repeatedly such that the relationships are well established—roofing, suburban house construction, installation of a water heater, auto repair, and so on. Whether the vendor is willing to make this a firm fixed price or not is based on the potential variability of the task. The house construction bid might have several caveats and be only noncommittal rough order of magnitude estimate, whereas the roofer might feel comfortable making his bid a fixed price.

The benefit of using heuristics is that they are easy to use and do not require a lot of detailed research. If multiple estimators were used to make bids it would be necessary to formalize the estimating parameters so the estimates will be consistent. In many situations, the heuristic estimate is not expected to be highly accurate and they should only be used in situations where the inherent risks are acceptable (Mind Tools, 2008). As an offhand conceptual example, if one was using the average 25 MPG for his car as a forecasting heuristic to decide whether to drive 100 miles across an isolated area, would it make sense to do this with an estimated four gallons in the gas tank? What if you were flying an airplane across a water route with similar variables to consider? Do you see the risk elements in these two examples?

14.3.5 Parametric Estimating

Parametric estimating is a technique that uses statistical relationships between historical data and resulting work levels (PMI, 2017, p. 213). Parameters based on size, footage, or other scope-related values can be used to produce time and cost estimates for the related work. Given the mathematical sophistication of the parametric estimating model, the process of creating a formal parametric model involves collecting data from thousands of past projects and from this produce a regression-type model with multiple variables (more sophisticated and complex than the heuristic models). Parametric techniques are most useful in the early stages of a project when only aggregate data is available. These estimates are considered order of magnitude in accuracy because they may lack requirements precision (Kwak and Watson, 2005). As used, the difference in parametric versus heuristics is the sophistication of the mathematical relationship used.

Parametric techniques were first developed by the U.S. Department of Defense (DoD) during World War II to estimate high-technology projects such as weapons systems and space exploration. The technique is most commonly used now in the construction and auto repair industry. Other applications include, but are not limited to, determining the conversion costs associated with new technologies in electronics manufacturing, or estimating the cost of developing intellectual property such as engineering designs. The technique can be applied to any situation in which sufficient historical data are available.

The parametric estimating technique needs to take into consideration the type of development methodology that was used in its data collection because it could impact the calculated value. Some of the methodologies variances include the waterfall method, incremental development, spiral development, and prototyping. For example, when developing software using the waterfall method, the cost of documenting the requirements prior to coding needs to be considered because this is a common practice in this method but less so in the other options.

The main drawback of the parametric estimating technique is the accuracy of the estimate it provides. According to one researcher, estimates that are based on the final project design will be roughly in the range of +10% to −5% accurate. If the estimate is based on project designs that are from 1% to 15% complete, the estimates accuracy will range from +30% to −25% (Kwak and Watson, 2005). Accuracy can also be affected by such factors as the experience of the individual making the estimate, changes in scope, design specifications, and other incorrect assumptions. Accuracy is especially problematic for construction companies that use parametric estimating to produce bids for projects. They will not win the project if the bid is too high, and the project will not be as profitable if the bid is too low. Hence, high accuracy ranges make the provider vulnerable to adverse results. With the increased amount of historical information available in databases, innovations in statistical applications, and the availability of expert data over the Internet, the accuracy of parametric estimating techniques should improve over time.

14.3.6 Phased Estimating

Phased estimating is based on a life cycle-oriented rule of thumb and is most frequently used when there is not enough detail level supporting the overall estimate. Instead, the estimating process is broken up into a series of sequential decisions linked to project phases. At the defined decision points, called a phase gate, a management review process will determine whether it is appropriate to continue with the project, redefine its scope, or to terminate the project. According to Verzuh, the performance baseline should be considered reset at each phase gate and the project re-evaluated at that point. The following series of steps are used to create a phased estimate (Verzuh, 2005, p. 174):

1. Break the project life cycle into phases. Each of these phases will be considered a subproject.
2. For the first phase, detailed estimates are made for the cost and duration for this phase. At this point, the estimator should also create an order of magnitude planning estimate for the

entire product development life cycle. With this, the project is approved to move to the next phase.
3. When the first phase is completed, a decision must be made regarding whether to continue with the next phase. The review process must make specific decisions to re-evaluate the project direction and make changes to its scope or product requirements and specifications, or alternatively whether to cancel the project altogether.
4. If the project is approved to continue to the next gate, a detailed estimate is created for that phase and the order of magnitude estimate for all subsequent phases is updated based on current information.
5. The cycle of phased estimating continues until the project is either completed or terminated.

When using the phased estimating or *rolling wave* technique, it is important to understand what is required at each phase gate. There are three main components that each active cycle should contain. First, the phase must specify its required deliverables. Each gate will have a different deliverable or set of deliverables. Second, each gate should define a set of success criteria. These criteria are used to determine whether the project should proceed to the next phase or be terminated. The final component is the specific outputs. These outputs help answer the question "What is the purpose of the gate?" The number of phase gates that will be required depends on the size and complexity of the effort. When the project scope is well defined, fewer phase gates are required. Project teams should try to consistently use the same gates at consistent points for similar projects as this will help to improve the review process.

The main benefit of using the rolling wave estimating approach is that it allows the effort to move forward quicker and recognizes that early planning in an uncertain world may be a waste of time. However, this approach requires much more monitoring from management and the level of predictability is low in regard to future budget and resource requirements. This approach does not help greatly in comparing two options in that the decision metrics are known to have high ranges.

In this model, the amount of uncertainty regarding the project will be decreasing as the project progresses, so each subsequent phase estimate will be more accurate. Another subtle issue in this approach is that the project team has more potential to meet the short-term phase goals, whereas the longer-term full estimate approach could lead to situations where the team had no chance to be successful.

One of the main criticisms for the use of phased estimating is that many experts feel that the project team loses accountability. Their argument is that the team cannot be accountable when the baseline is reset after each phase gate. One method to hold the team more accountable is to require justification for the cost and schedule estimates. When estimates change, the project team should be able to justify these changes with evidence of changes in difficulty or scope (Verzuh, 2004, p. 4).

Organizations whose phase reviews perform in this matter are utilizing phased estimating in their estimation methodology. Those organizations that do not meet these criteria are more typically using milestone reviews instead of phase gates. This latter approach tends to hold the original baseline plan intact through the life cycle and measure variances from that point.

14.3.7 Effort Distribution Estimating (Top-Down)

This method basically looks at the project as a whole and apportions the total estimate into high-level groupings. An approach such as this may be necessary in the early stages of planning when sufficient details for lower level approaches are not yet available. Once the high-level value is derived a WBS is used to assign percentage values to main levels in the structure. Normally, this type of allocation would only go to one or two levels below the top of the structure. Historical data for similar past projects are typically used to determine the percentages for each phase and/or the summary activities within a phase (Horine, 2005).

This technique works reasonably well in organizations using a common methodology for similar type projects along with good historical data. This method also works well with the phased estimating technique in that the historical data provide reasonable estimates for future phases without extensive definition. For example, when a phase gate is completed, the actual amounts from the previous stage can be used to project future values.

One hazard in using this approach is that an aggregate estimating error for the project is proliferated through all segments by the apportioning method. Another drawback is that the technique uses historical data to define the apportioning formula (Verzuh, 2005, p. 176). If the projects are not technically similar, these values can provide erroneous results that are once again proliferated through the life cycle. For example, if the organization's projects do not have the same number of phases or the phases are different for every project, it will be difficult to apply a consistent apportioning formula to new projects.

To illustrate a top-down approach, imagine that a project goal is to design and deploy a new car model. The organization has defined five phases for this effort and an estimated overall budget of $250,000. These defined phases include initiation, planning, design, construction, and deployment. The construction phase is further decomposed into three activities—frame, exterior, and interior. Past projects indicate the following main phase resource cost distribution:

Initiation = 10%
Planning = 15%
Design = 15%
Construction = 40%
Deployment = 20%

Further, at a lower level the activities within the construction phase typically consume resources in the ratio:

Frame = 14%
Exterior = 13%
Interior = 13%

**Note that these add to the 40% value shown for construction level.

Using these allocation values, the construction phase would receive 40% of the estimated budget and that would compute to $100,000 (0.40 × $250,000). Similarly, within the construction phase the frame activity would be estimated to cost $35,000 (0.14 × $250,000). Assuming that the effort distribution technique was being applied along with the phased estimating technique, these estimates could be updated at each phase review point. The original allocation estimate for the initiation phase was $25,000 (0.10 × $250,000), but the actual cost was $30,000, which is 20% higher than the plan. From this result, the overall cost estimate would then be revised by 20% to $300,000, so the new estimate for the construction phase will increase from $100,000 to $120,000, and the estimate for building the frame will increase from $35,000 to $42,000. The key issue in these comparison methods is whether the project team can modify the planned values dynamically. Some organizations will allow this and others will hold the original value constant and pressure the project team to take corrective action elsewhere to stay on the plan. These are management philosophy issues beyond the basic estimating methods.

14.3.8 Monte Carlo Simulation

This technique's name is derived from similarities between its mechanics and roulette gambling popularized at Monte Carlo casinos. First, individual work estimates are recognized as having a range of values—no other technique discussed above specifically deals with this. To simulate a variable work activity, random numbers similar to the roulette wheel are used to represent the variable estimated time. From this, the project is "simulated" hundreds of times to see what the completion probability distribution looks like. Because of the volume of calculations related to this method, it is considered a computer-driven activity and there are models available to support this type of analysis.

In order to drive a simulation model, it is necessary to supply a probability distribution assumption (range of values) for each activity. For example, it is common to suggest that the probability distribution is triangular and estimates for the conditions surrounding the variable will determine the resulting probability distribution shape. The estimator now creates estimates for the minimum, most likely, and maximum values for each activity. A computer model will then select random values from this range (according to the probability distribution) and execute the plan, say 1000 times. Each of these passes will generate a discrete value and the total results will present a histogram-type presentation of likely outcomes. For this type of situation, it is then prudent to estimate the most likely completion date by recognizing variability defined by the model. Recognize that the type of analysis derived from simulation can be very important given the uncertainty related to all estimating techniques.

The Monte Carlo technique provides two main advantages when used for estimations. First, the technique provides a better understanding of the potential range of actual outcomes for the project than other techniques. A second advantage involves the capability of running "what if" analysis to evaluate various assumptions. In this mode, multiple complex scenarios can be defined and outcomes generated. This supports sophisticated analysis of possible outcomes. The main drawback of using simulation is the amount of time that it can take to set up and run the various scenarios and the cost associated with the activity. Another potential drawback is that it is easy for individuals who do not have experience with the technique to misuse the simulation because they are unfamiliar with the assumptions and restrictions of the technique (Johnson, 2007, p. 224).

Work activity estimation is a vital part of project management. It should be one of the fundamental building blocks in creating schedules and budgets for the project. Poor estimating plagues a project in many ways and the sophistication of simulation modeling adds great insights into potential outcomes. Recognize that the typical project estimate says that the project will be finished on June 4th. Would it not make more sense to simulate the variability of the outcome and say that the project has a 70% probability of finishing in the range of May 1st to July 4th, with a most likely (median) date of June 4th. This type of estimate would provide a much richer understanding than the traditional discrete value. The reader should review Chapter 18 to get a more detailed overview of this technique.

14.3.9 Delphi Technique

The Delphi technique is another variety of expert judgment. It is most effective when making top-down estimates in the early stages of projects where there are many unknowns and a single expert is not sufficient because of the breadth or uncertainly of the goal. A radical example of this is "How long will it take us to get to the Mars?" In complex situations, the Delphi approach gathers the estimates from a group of experts with expertise in the space industry (Snell, 1997b). This technique involves the following steps:

1. Experts are given the specifications of the project and an estimation form.
2. The group meets to discuss any estimation or product issues.
3. Each expert provides his or her individual estimate without collaboration with others.
4. Estimates are returned indicating the median group estimate and the individual's estimate.
5. The group meets again to discuss the results and individual logic for their estimate.
6. Each expert again provides his or her individual estimate.
7. Steps 3–6 will be repeated until the group of experts reaches a consensus (Snell, 1997a,b).

Table 14.1 shows a sample estimation form that can be used by the members of the Delphi panel to record their estimations. In this example, an estimate is given for each of the six tasks in the project and totaled at the bottom. Once the first iteration is complete, the panel meets to discuss the results; then estimators review their estimations in the Delta column. The Deltas are totaled and changes to the total estimation are made at the bottom. This process will continue until a consensus is reached.

Normally, the Delphi technique is used for highly complex estimates for which there is little historical background; however, the concept works in situations where a nonbiased estimate is needed. In the example illustrated in Table 14.1 the original time estimate was 56 days. After two iterations, the Delphi experts refined that as shown by D1 and D2. The first round was summarized as having the "expert" estimates at +18 above the original estimate. The second round shared the logic of D1 estimates and that total variance shows as +16. From this, a consensus estimate would be made as 72 days.

Because this technique seeks estimates from multiple participants, it tends to remove bias and politics that can occur when an estimate is based on only one expert's judgment. Group meetings also allow experts to discuss any issues or assumptions that may impact the estimate. One of the

Table 14.1 Delphi Technique Estimation Form

Job Name: Gary's New Mansion

Date: 6/30/2009 **Est. Units:** Days

WBS	*Task Name*	*Est. 0*	*Δ1*	*Δ2*	*Δ3*	...	*Key Notes*
1	Foundation	10	+3	+2			Question soil composition
2	Walls	15	+3	+2			Drawings not clear
3	Plumbing	5	+1	+1			
4	Electrical	5	+1	+1			
5	Landscape	9	+6	+5			
6	Ext. paving	12	+4	+4			Scope not defined well
	Est. Delta		**+18**	**+16**			
	Total	**56**	**74**	**72**			

main drawbacks for this type of technique is the significant amount of time it can take for the panel of experts to reach a consensus. Larger numbers of experts will increase the number of iterations required and therefore the time it takes to reach a final estimate. Another potential issue is the experience level of the panel. If the panel is made up of individuals that are not very experienced, the estimate will likely not be so accurate. It is also important to make sure that strong facilitators are available to guide the group and keep them focused on the topic. The central idea of the Delphi is to anonymously share the estimates made by others along with their basic rationale. The next iteration would allow the group to think about other views and possibly adjust their estimates. This is essentially a consensus building process.

14.4 Activity Sequencing

There are basically two ways to define and review the sequence of activities in preparation for a more analytical view. We can model the process using symbols such as circles or boxes to represent activities and sequence, or by using arrows or to represent activities. Let us look at these two classical sequencing options.

14.4.1 Activity on Arrow

The Activity on Arrow (AOA) network design approach constructs the project plan as a set of nodes connected by arrows to show how the various activities are sequenced. This depiction was introduced in the late 1950s as the Program Evaluation and Review Technique (PERT). This method ushered in the modern network view of project scheduling.

An AOA network can be high level or very detailed depending on the individual bias related to project control. This diagram structure shows an orderly, systematic series of actions that must be completed in the defined order (as directed by the arrows) to reach a specific definable objective. There are two primary elements of the AOA network diagram: arrows and events. Events are usually shown as circles or rectangles and are interconnected by a series of arrows indicating an activity. The activity is symbolic of a defined work unit, while an event is representative of a point in time that represents a completion of an activity and the start of the next one. In this view, it is important to understand that an activity (arrow) consumes time (Stires and Murphy, 1962). Without exception, every activity except for those that start and stop the project must have both a predecessor and successor event. Events can be classified into two parts: predecessors and successors. Predecessor events must occur before the following one in the network. This is called the predecessor/successor sequence. These paired relationships provide the specifications necessary to draw the network diagram. Once it is satisfactorily drawn, the pertinent information is available to be able to begin schedule calculations.

The diagram shown in Figure 14.3 illustrates the AOA model. In this example, the activities are indicated by arrows and letters to identify the activity along with an optional time estimate for each activity. Node values represent terminators for the activities and indicate how the project activities would be constrained.

14.4.2 Activity on Node Model

The Activity on Node (AON) approach surfaced independently at roughly the time period as the Project Evaluation and Review Technique (PERT) AOA model. This technique is known as CPM

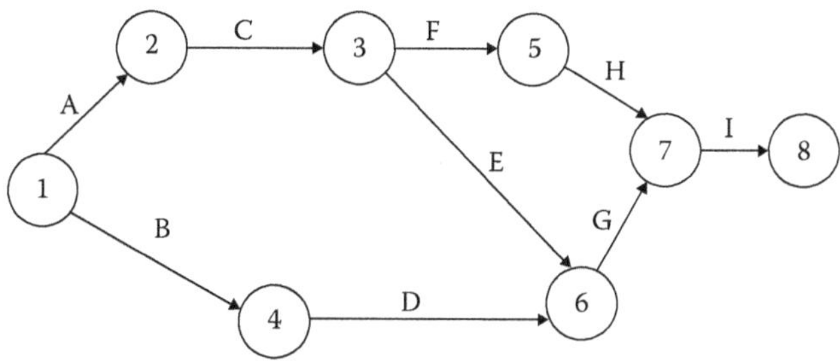

Figure 14.3 AOA network.

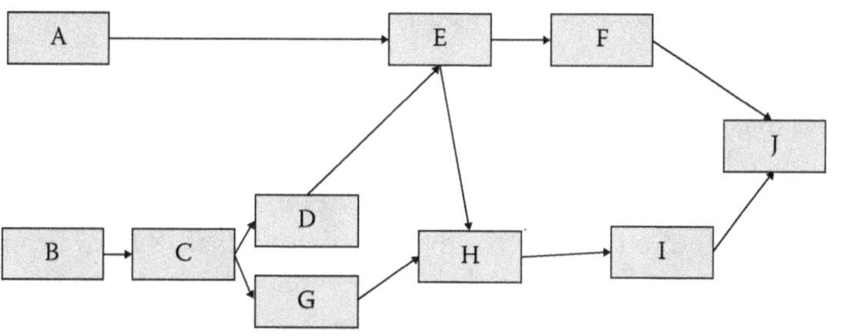

Figure 14.4 AON network.

(Critical Path Method). Over the years the two methods have essentially morphed into one and are now often referred to as PERT/CPM. Few know or care about the original technical origin or internal assumptions. As described here these are simply two different ways to model a project schedule.

One significant difference in the two model techniques is the possible requirement in the AOA model to use zero time "dummy" tasks to enforce the predecessor specifications, whereas the AON structure does not require this (Kelley and Walker, 1989). However, in reality one's favorite format likely becomes the one they learned first as both can generate the same results. The AON format uses a rectangle to depict the activity and arrows between the boxes to show relationships.

A sample AON network is shown in Figure 14.4. Note in this example that activity C must be complete before activities D or G can begin. As in the AOA model, this structure is now set up for calculation of project times and other schedule parameters.

14.5 Time Calculation

Given either an AOA or AON network model specification it is possible to produce a mechanical project schedule showing task start and stop times, plus project completion. In either model the same specification variables are required (essentially task name, duration, and predecessor specification).

Once the work activities have been sequenced and durations estimated, a project schedule results. In the early days, this model was still found to be cumbersome to draw and maintain. It was not until the late 1970s that growth in smaller computing devices help move the planning world away from the 1917s era of raw Gantt charts and magnetic scheduling boards.

Even today, there is still a strong user bias to the look of a Gantt chart. Fortunately, this modern view now has the network logic embedded underneath to support linked time calculations. Microsoft Project and Primavera are two popular tools used in industry for this class of scheduling.

Recognize that if all work unit activity estimates were perfect, all resource skills available and equally productive, and all defined materials available as needed, a project schedule would become mechanically deterministic and clearly show the time and cost variables for the project. That should be reasonably obvious from the AOA or AON network views. That view is important from a model perspective; however, it is also important to recognize that all the risk-free simplifying assumptions are suspect. Fact is, real-world projects are very complex in both the initial estimates as well as the ongoing predictability of the task actual outcomes. Thus, the job of project time management becomes one of dynamically tweaking and guiding the variables involved to achieve the plan target schedules.

What we have seen to this point is a time calculation that is often called the *first cut view*. What this means is that there will be many other issues to consider in refining this view into a final project plan. For example, factors related to risk assessment, outsourcing, resource availability, and other such factors can either expand the required time or take time away. Also, as the level of work definition improves, it is quite common to find that the original estimates contained sufficient errors to require a major rework of the initial plan—both duration and sequencing. In addition to this, management factors can require that the initial plan be rejected as being too long. How can we shorten a plan given what we know at this point? All of these issues require that the time planning process be viewed as an iterative one until a final version is approved by management. Even during this refinement process we must keep in mind the trade-off potential between scope, time, and cost. If the current view of the plan exceeds the desired cost or time, it may be necessary to cut scope. Likewise, if scope expands with new insight into the effort, then schedule would likely also expand. Dynamics such as these dictate changes to the WBS structure and a recycle of the time planning process.

14.6 Estimating Checklist

The estimation process has been summarized. It is now time to review the results. An example checklist illustrates the type of questions that should be reviewed a final part of the process. This example illustrates how a formal list of items can help ensure a more standardized approach across various groups across the enterprise. In many cases, such items would have a formal signoff requirement for each to verify compliance. Review the list below to see if the logic for each item seems relevant to producing a good initial schedule:

1. Have you established a formal, documented data collection process for the project?
2. Do you have a complete and detailed WBS for the project, including management activity areas?
3. Do you have historical information, including costs, from previous similar projects?
4. Have you identified all sources of costs to your project (i.e., different types of labor, materials, supplies, equipment, etc.)?
5. Do you have justifiable reasons for selecting your estimating methods, models, guides, and software?

6. Have you considered risk issues in your plan?
7. Do your estimates cover all tasks in the WBS?
8. Do you understand your project's required and approved funding profiles (i.e., amounts and timing for each)?
9. What risks have been identified for funding?
10. Have you developed an integrated project plan that synchronizes scope, schedule, cost, and available resources?
11. Have you established adequate schedule flexibility in the baseline?
12. Do you have a plan/process for dealing with variances between actual performance and the baseline?
13. Do you have a process for keeping records of your project activity for future efforts?

14.7 Network Mechanics

This section will outline the basic mechanics required to generate a project schedule. Before jumping into this process, it is important to understand the related input and output variables. The following list of 10 basic terms involved in the input and output parameters of a project plan is important to understand:

1. Activity title—a short description of the work [Input]
2. Activity duration—number of working periods (days) [Input]
3. Predecessor—defining the order of execution [Input]
4. ES or T(E)—early start; earliest time the activity can commence [Output]
5. LS or T(L)—late start; latest time the activity can start and not affect project schedule [Output]
6. Slack—measure of idle time in the node or activity [Output]
7. EF—earliest time that an activity can finish [Output]
8. LF—latest time the activity can finish and not affect project schedule [Output]
9. Total float—the difference between the *earliest* date that the activity can start and the latest date the activity can start before delaying the completion date (LS—ES) [Output]
10. Free float—the amount of time an activity can be delayed before the successor activity will be delayed (EF—ES) [Output]

For this sample exercise, we will assume that all activity relationships are *Finish-Start* (FS), that is, each predecessor activity has to completely finish before the successor activity can commence. A schematic view of this type of relationship is shown in Figure 14.5.

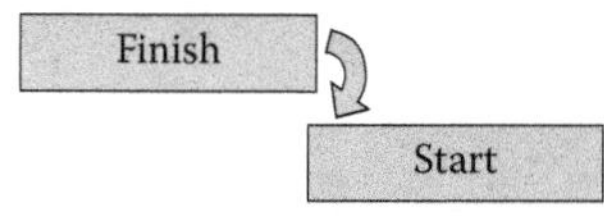

Figure 14.5 FS relationship.

14.8 Establishing the Project Activity Sequence

There are other task relationship types that can be defined, but for calculation simplification the FS option will be demonstrated here. In order to generate the base project schedule, the following three input items must be defined:

1. Work activities in the project (WPs and planning packages)
2. Duration estimates for the work and planning packages
3. Sequence relationships (predecessors)

Table 14.2 defines a sample project activity list that these three items defined.

14.8.1 Sample Project Definition

Review Table 14. 2 to be sure that you can decipher the task and schedule coding. Note that activities A and B can start at any time. All other activities are constrained by some predecessor activity—that is, activity C cannot start until activity A is complete. From this duration and sequencing description, the project schedule model can be sequenced using either an AOA or an AON network model format. The schematic shown in Figure 14.6 translates the project data using an AOA format. This

Table 14.2 Project Task List

Activity	Dur.	Pred.
A	3	--
B	4	--
C	4	A
D	6	B
E	5	C
F	2	C
G	4	D,E
H	3	F
I	5	G,H

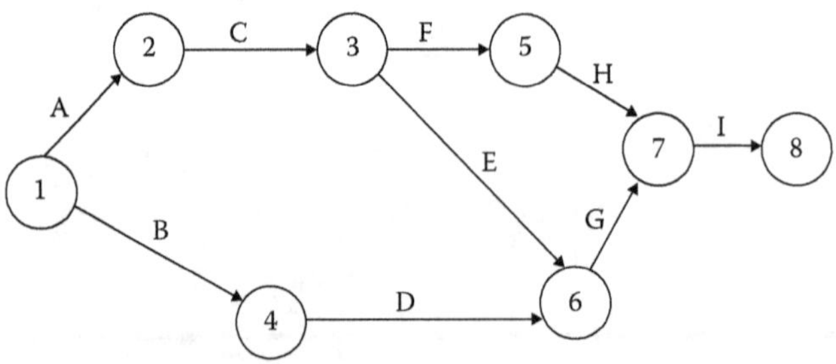

Figure 14.6 Sample project AOA network.

model obeys all the sequencing constraints identified in the project specification. Review this result to ensure that you understand what the sequencing step involves and how it is constructed. One common misunderstanding at this stage is the calculation of total project duration. Some would simply add the duration times in the table and define the project to be 36 time units or the sum of all durations. Since some activities occur in parallel, this is not a correct view as we see in Figure 14.6.

14.9 Forward Pass Calculation

From the initial network setup, step two of the mechanical plan formulation is to perform what is called a *forward pass*. This means that we need to calculate the time through the network while obeying the predecessors. These early start times are recorded on the nodes in the format of "T(E)/." Figure 14.7 shows the calculated T(E) values for each of the nodes. The note 8 calculation says that the project will take 21 time periods (work days).

The example calculations are quite straightforward except for two nodes—6 and 7. For node 6, two activity paths have to be considered for the parallel activities D and E. Node 4 has a T(E) value of 4 and a following activity D time of 6; therefore, the resulting value for node 6 would be 10. However, the other parallel path coming into node 6 starts at node 3 with a value of 7 and an activity E time of 5, so that the path value is 12. For forward path calculations, the highest value is selected for such parallel paths, thus we assign the value 12 for T(E) at node 6. This means that the earliest we can claim completion of project activities at this point is 12. The same type logic applies to node 7 where a value for T(E) of 16 is calculated. The key calculation mechanic for the forward pass is to remember to take the *highest* value for any multiple input paths. T(E) values at each node represents the earliest time that these points in the project can be reached. This calculation also shows that the final node (8) can be reached at time period 21. This defines that the project duration as 21, given this set of parameters. At this point, we have a crude schedule (Figure 14.7) resulting from the duration and sequencing parameters. However, there is more needed beyond just the total duration. We will get that out of the backward pass.

14.10 Backward Pass Calculation

Step three of the process involves performing a backward pass on the network model. The rationale for doing this is likely not clear as yet, but let us first describe the mechanics of the calculations before attempting to describe the function of these values. The backward pass generates a variable coming to the end of the network and moving back toward the front. These values are defined as

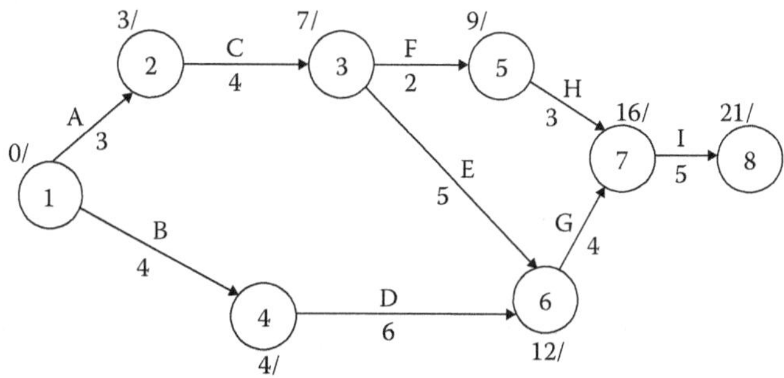

Figure 14.7 AOA network with T(E) calculations.

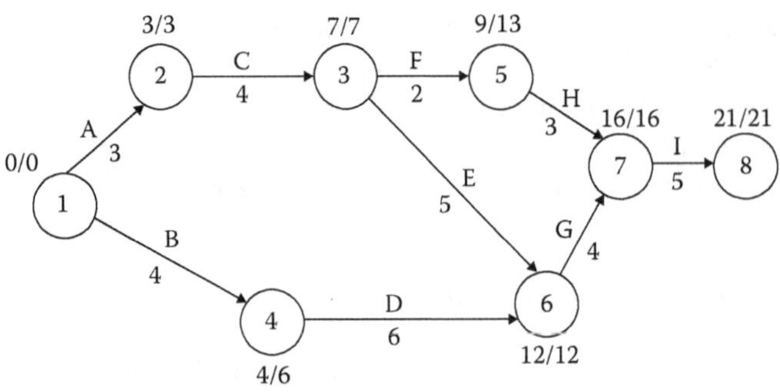

Figure 14.8 AOA network with backward pass calculations.

T(L) and it is formatted on the network nodes as "T(E)/T(L)." Note that the nodes in Figure 14.8 now show two such numeric values above each node.

For this basic network, the assumption is made that the planned time at termination is equal to the forward pass calculated time shown (e.g., 21 time units). Stated another way, we are saying that the forward plan specified that the project would take 21 time units and we are accepting that value for the backward pass.

In order to calculate T(L) values, we start at the completion node (8) and insert the same process used to calculate the forward pass. Therefore, we start at node #8 at 21 in the sample case. From this value, we work backward to the front of the network, one node at a time. For node 7, the T(L) value would be 21–5 (for activity I) yielding 16. Node 6 would be calculated as 16–4 (for activity G) or 12. As observed in the forward pass mechanics are straightforward until you encounter a converging path into the node. The same problem occurs in reverse going backwards. In this case, there would be multiple paths coming into the node. When that occurs calculate the T(L) value for each path and select the lowest (we selected the highest for the forward pass). In the sample network, the T(L) calculations would compare the two paths for activities F and E yielding a 13–2 or 11 for activity F, versus 12–5 or 7 for activity E. The calculation rule for the backward pass is to take the *lower* value of the two paths and record that as the nodal T(L) time. This same process would be required for node 1 and at that point the value should be zero since we started with 21/21 at node 8. Review the values shown in Figure 14.8 to be sure that you understand the basic idea of T(E) and T(L) mechanical values.

Once we have the values for T(E) and T(L), it is possible to analyze two important time management factors—the longest path through the network and slack time details. The simplest item to calculate is nodal slack time. This is simply the difference in T(L) and T(E). So, node 3 would have a slack value of zero (7–7), whereas node 5 has a slack value of 4 time units (13–9). Each of these values defines the amount of time that this node can stay idle without affecting project completion date. Also, note that the computed slack for the start and finish of the network will be zero using the assumption of 21/21—that is, we are happy with the original computed project duration. You might be thinking about what you would do if this was not the case. It just changes the arithmetic, but the mechanics are the same.

Three other slack-type status parameters can be derived from this view. These are total float, free float, and late finish. Each of these relates to activity views rather than node calculations, but can be derived from the node values. Total float relates to the amount of activity slack before project completion is impacted, while free float deals with the same view only for the successor activity. Late finish describes the latest time that the activity can be completed without impacting the schedule.

14.11 Defining Critical Path

Using the calculation assumptions outlined above, zero nodal slack time can be used to define the critical path which is the longest path through the project. In mechanical terms, this means that the earliest time to reach a node and the latest time to leave the node are the same—that is, no idle time. Zero slack nodes constrain the network time and thus defines *the longest path through the project plan*. Any activities that cause the zero slack at these nodes then cannot be delayed without delaying the project completion date.

In order to find specific critical path activities, the key mechanic involves checking any activity bounded between the zero slack nodes to see if in fact that path is a critical activity. In some more complex networks, parallel paths can both appear to be on the critical path, whereas only one actually is. In this sample case, the critical path definition is straight forward and is shown by bolded arrows in Figure 14.9.

Note that the critical path passes through nodes 1–2–3–6–7–8 and the critical path activities are A-C-E-G-I. Specifically, the critical path should be thought of as a vector containing both the activity list and the total duration, so it would be more proper to state the critical path as A-C-E-G-I, and 21 time units. To reiterate, this is the longest path through the network and represents a critical management issue for the PM (Brown, 2002).

Management importance of the critical path lies in the fact that any delay in these activities will delay project completion. Thus, it is important to focus management attention on this set of activities. Other activities that have slack generally require less rigorous monitoring since a minor slippage in these will not affect the completion date so long as slack remains. As an example, node calculations for the start of activity H indicate that it could start as early as period 9, or as late as period 13 without affecting the completion schedule. In similar fashion, activity F could start as early as period 7 or wait as late as period 11 with no adverse impact (this calculation is a little trickier, so it is worth looking at to ensure that you understand the meaning of the node values). This latter calculation is not as obvious as the previous one, but it is found by noting activity H could wait until period 13 (late start) and activity F only takes 2 time periods. Note that activity E must start at time period 7 in order to keep the project on schedule.

Understanding and interpreting slack values is vital in time management and requires that the PM keep these in mind as the project unfolds. Also, recognize that errors in duration estimate can cause these values to change during the project, so they are not static variables by any stretch. Understanding activity slack or float gives the PM flexibility in scheduling the start of a particular activity within the early start and late start time ranges (Uher, 2003). This also allows PMs to

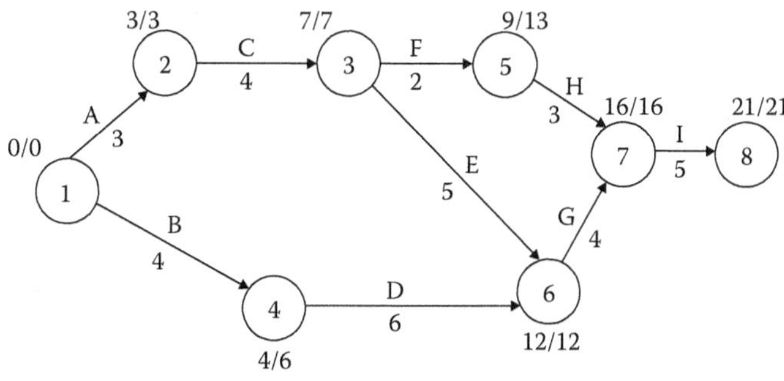

Figure 14.9 AOA network with critical path defined.

establish proper priorities for resources across the project plan. For example, if there are two activities occurring within the same time range, one critical and one noncritical, that are competing for the same resource, the PM can allocate the resource to the critical activity first and then use the float time to delay the start of the noncritical activity.

14.12 Manipulating the Schedule

If the project begins to fall behind schedule, the PM often undertakes various initiatives to recover the planned schedule. One approach to performing this is to allocate more resources to critical path activities in order to shorten the path and thereby move the project back toward the planned schedule. This option typically increases the project budget, but can shorten the resulting schedule. Alternatively, the predecessor relationships can often be changed in such a way as to shorten the schedule. In this option, no additional resources are allocated, but this may increase risk or cost if we assume that the original plan was already optimum. The vocabulary terms for these two management options are as follows:

Crashing—allocating extra resources to the critical path with the goal of shortening the schedule.

Fast tracking—rearranging the predecessor relationships to shorten the schedule.

In order to decide which of these options to pursue, it is necessary to evaluate the value of recovering time versus the cost. Also, consideration must be given to risk and other factors involved in the chosen approach.

14.12.1 Automated Calculation Tools

Fortunately, there is an increasingly available set of calculation tools available to handle the project time mechanics outlined above. To illustrate this, Figure 14.10 duplicates the sample project data in a Microsoft Project view format.

Note that the software converts the manual AOA model into a Gantt bar format; however, it also recognizes that the results are equivalent to those shown for the manual example above. The only two new items shown in the Gantt view are a summary bar for the entire project and the use of line numbers to specify the predecessor rather than using an activity name.

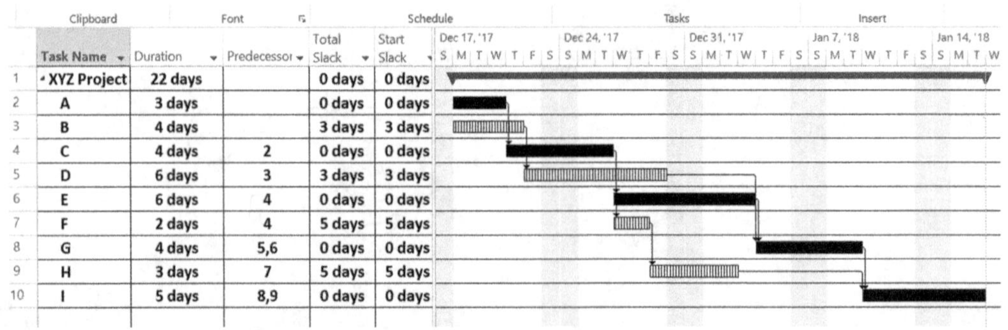

	Task Name	Duration	Predecessors	Total Slack	Start Slack
1	XYZ Project	22 days		0 days	0 days
2	A	3 days		0 days	0 days
3	B	4 days		3 days	3 days
4	C	4 days	2	0 days	0 days
5	D	6 days	3	3 days	3 days
6	E	6 days	4	0 days	0 days
7	F	2 days	4	5 days	5 days
8	G	4 days	5,6	0 days	0 days
9	H	3 days	7	5 days	5 days
10	I	5 days	8,9	0 days	0 days

Figure 14.10 MS project equivalent schedule calculation.

14.13 Formatting Activity Results

As stated earlier, there are different biases regarding which network model sequencing format is to be used—AOA or AON. The sample data here focused on the AOA view, which contains less information on the diagram than a corresponding AON model. If an AON model is used, the activities are represented by the nodes rather than an arrow. Standard formatting for this approach would require that more of the slack and float values be computed and shown on the model. Figure 14.11 shows a typical format for displaying the activity parameters in an AON box structure.

In this example, task name is used instead of activity, but recall the earlier warning that these terms are not standardized in industry. Either terminology is the same in the model mechanics.

Figure 14.12 shows what this formatting would look like in a full network with only 10 activities.

Personal bias says that this format tends to be more overwhelming than the AOA view and the multitude of data shown makes the analysis more difficult. At any rate, this should be shown in tabular format. Fortunately, use of automated software such as Microsoft Project can handle

Early start	Duration	Early finish
Task name		
Late start	Slack	Late finish

Figure 14.11 AON box notation.

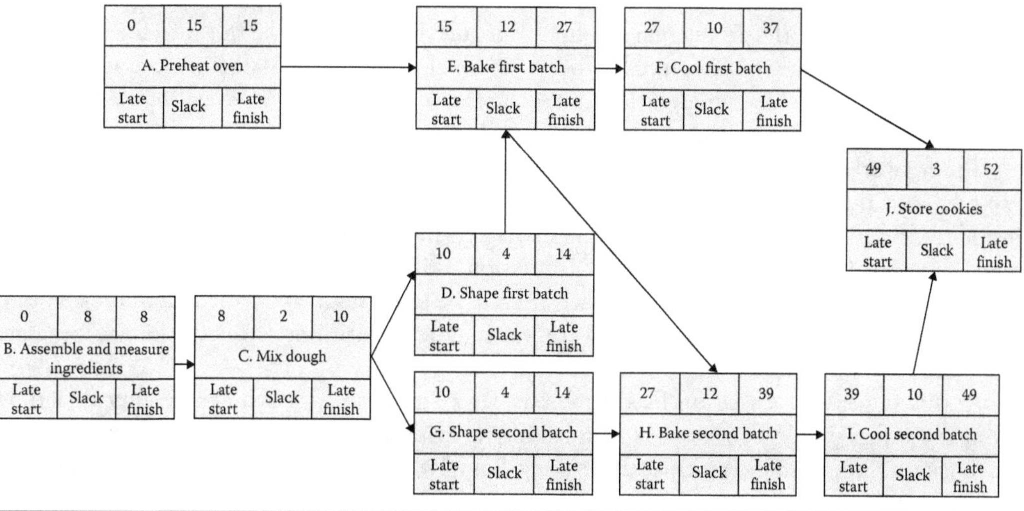

Figure 14.12 AON total network view.

these calculations and present the data in any format desired. The contemporary environment favors a Gantt bar format as the preferred method to display schedule results. Regardless of the approach used to create a project schedule, the key issue is to recognize that a PM must understand the network concepts. Different audiences will have varying needs for levels of nodal detail and the various network management software packages can format their output to fit these needs.

14.14 Which Diagram Format Wins?

As indicated earlier, the AOA model was created to be used with the PERT model assumptions and the AON with fixed time durations (underlying detailed mechanics of the PERT option is discussed in Chapter 24). The interesting trend for these two methods is that they have now morphed together to the degree that few remember the original reasons for either. It is instructive to browse the Internet using the search words "PERT" or "CPM." What you will find from this is that the outside world does not distinguish between these two terms or how they are diagrammed. Over the years, the original definitions that were outlined in this chapter have been scrambled. Networks today are drawn both ways and called by either name. The one remaining idea is that a network predecessor diagram is a good tool to reflect activity sequencing. However, in more recent times, the emergence of easy-to-use PC-based tools such as Microsoft Project has made the manual drawing of networks passé. Modern software tools typically generate their results in the Gantt chart format with connectors between the bars to make the result conceptually fit the network model. So, both of these approaches have somewhat lost out to the classical format first described by Henry Gantt in the early 1900s. But do recognize that the underlying computer calculations do obey the network mechanics described here.

14.15 Summary

This chapter described how time-related aspects of the project evolve from scope definition and are then translated into a first cut schedule for the project. There are many more management issues to deal with related to the production of a final schedule, but for now take this introductory deterministic model view as the conceptual process by which scope is translated into an activity list, and then that view evolves into duration and sequence specifications. We are calling this version a first cut plan, meaning that more massaging is needed before it is finished.

The network models illustrated here are not perfect for showing how the project will be executed, but they represent the underlying scheduling model and best illustrate the method to introduce the fundamental aspects of time management. Embedded in the network model is a quantification of the scope, work activities, duration estimates, sequencing, resource allocations, and budget. For this reason, network models need to be understood as a basic tool in the PM tool kit, even though modern computer software will handle the arithmetic calculations to generate this result.

At this stage, we focused on fixed time estimates and dealt little with the reality that time estimates in fact should be viewed as a probability distribution with ranges. Subsequent chapters will open up these limitations for further review. For now, let us move forward to the next chapter and see how project cost emerges from the schedule model.

Problems

1. Use the activity specifications outlined in the table below to generate a first cut project schedule.

WBS	*ID*	*Task*	*Duration*	*Predecessor*
1	1	Project summary task		
1.1	2	Design office complex		
1.1.1	3	Determine budget	13 days	
1.1.2	4	Determine the three best potential architects	4 days	3
1.1.3	5	Interview architects		4
1.1.3.1	6	Architect 1	1 day	
1.1.3.2	7	Architect 2	1 day	6
1.1.3.3	8	Architect 3	1 day	7
1.1.3.4	9	Select an architect	1 day	8
1.1.4	10	Prepare first draft plan	1 day	5, 9
1.1.5	11	Review the plan	0.5 days	10
1.1.6	12	Finalize the plan	0.5 days	11
1.1.7	13	Obtain construction permit	0 days	12
1.2	14	Plan office layout		2
1.2.1	15	Prepare layout plan	2 days	
1.2.2	16	Estimate costs	2 days	15
1.3	17	Buy materials		14
1.3.1	18	Rent tools and equipment	1 day	16
1.3.2	19	Purchase materials	1 day	16
1.4	20	Prepare the site		17
1.4.1	21	Excavate for foundation	8 days	
1.4.2	22	Build the foundation	12 days	21
1.5	23	Begin construction		20
1.5.1	24	Build the pillars	10 days	
1.5.2	25	Lay the roof	8 days	24
1.5.3	26	Build the walls	14 days	25
1.5.4	27	Flooring	14 days	25
1.6	28	Miscellaneous		27

(Continued)

WBS	*ID*	*Task*	*Duration*	*Predecessor*
1.6.1	29	Install plumbing fixtures	4 days	23
1.6.2	30	Install wires and cables	3 days	29
1.6.3	31	Plastering	4 days	30
1.6.4	32	Woodwork for doors and windows	3 days	31
1.6.5	33	Furnishing	2 days	32
1.6.6	34	Project close	2 days	33
1.7	35	Project completion	0 days	34

From these specifications, develop a network schedule and answer the following questions.

a. What is the project duration?
b. What type of activity is 1.6?
c. What type of activity is 1.7?

References

Baca, C.M., 2007. *Project Management for Mere Mortals.* Boston: Addison-Wesley.

Brown, K.L., 2002. Program Evaluation and Review Technique and Critical Path Method—Background. Reference for Business: http://www.referenceforbusiness.com/management/Pr-Sa/Program-Evaluation-and-Review-Technique-and-Critical-Path-Method.html (accessed March 17, 2008).

Callahan, S., Project Estimating—Fact or Fiction? http://www.performanceweb.org/CENTERS/PM/media/project-estimating.html (accessed April 9, 2008).

Horine, G., 2005. *Absolute Beginner's Guide to Project Management.* Toronto: Que Publishing.

Johnson, T., 2007. *PMP Exam Success Series: Certification Exam Manual.* Carrollton: Crosswind Project Management, Inc.

Kelley, J.E. and M.R. Walker, 1989. The origins of CPM—a personal history. *PM Network*, 3, 2, 7–22.

Kwak, Y. and R. Watson. 2005. Conceptual Estimating Tool for Technology-Driven Projects: Exploring Parametric Estimating Technique. http://home.gwu.edu/~kwak/Para_Est_Kwak_Watson.pdf (accessed April 10, 2008).

Mind Tools, 2008. Heuristic Methods: Using Rules of Thumb. http://www.mindtools.com/pages/article/newTMC_79.htm (accessed April 12, 2008).

PMI, 2017. *A Guide to the Project Management Body of Knowledge (PMBOK® Guide).* 6th ed. Newtown Square, PA: Project Management Institute.

PMI WBS, 2006. *Project Management Institute Practice Standard for Work Breakdown Structures.* 2nd ed. Newtown Square, PA: Project Management Institute.

Snell, D., 1997a. Expert Judgment. http://www.ecfc.u-net.com/cost/expert.htm (accessed April 10, 2008).

Snell, D., 1997b. Wideband Delphi Technique. http://www.ecfc.u-net.com/cost/delph.htm (accessed April 10, 2008).

Soomers, A., 12 Tips for Accurate Project Estimating. https://www.projectsmart.co.uk/12-tips-for-accurate-project-estimating.php (accessed April 24, 2018).

Stires, D.M. and M.M. Murphy, 1962. *PERT/CPM.* Boston: Materials Management Institute.

Uher, T.E. 2003. *Programming and Scheduling Techniques.* Sidney: University of New South Wales.

Verzuh, E., 2004. Phase Gate Development for Project Management—Part IV. http://findarticles.com/p/articles/mi_m0OBA/is_1_22/ai_n6134862/pg_1 (accessed April 11, 2008).

Verzuh, E., 2005. *The Fast Forward MBA in Project Management.* Hoboken, NJ: John Wiley.

Chapter 15

Cost Management

15.1 Introduction

The goal of this chapter is to describe the activities related to project cost management in the planning phase. From this process, the desired result would a viable project budget that can be approved by management. This chapter will outline the planning processes and Part VII of the book will focus on various aspects of the Monitoring and Control processes that are also a later part of the cost management processes. Figure 15.1 illustrates the key steps in this process.

In essence, the costing process involves allocating human and material resources to work units and then dollarizing those allocations. Also, there is the need to recognize reserve allocations for future events such as risk and other unplanned overruns.

When one thinks about project cost it is most often the view of how much money in a particular currency—dollars, euros, pounds, etc. One budgetary view could be to define the project cost as $100,000 and that would satisfy some. Others might want to know how this was divided into various resource types—$65,000 for personnel and $35,000 for material. Most of this type of information can be derived from the WBS Dictionary data in somewhat the same fashion that was used to generate the time schedule. The previous three chapters have laid out the basic techniques to define and schedule work units so that the monetization process should now be reasonably straightforward. It is not uncommon for the local finance type to drop by with a dazzling array of questions related to things called assets, overhead rates, depreciation schedules, chart of account data, *ad nauseam*. Hence, our simple total dollar view is now gone. This signals that there is more yet to deal with in the cost side of the equation.

As in so many of our project management discussions, the answer to the cost question is both simple and complex. Yes, we can calculate the direct work package (WP) resource costs for the project using reasonably straightforward techniques, but that simple view is not adequate for all concerned, or even the project itself. For example, accountants look at money for the enterprise in much more complex ways than the layperson. The project manager (PM) must understand these views as well as those needed to manage the project. Likewise, he has to deal with various other cost-related considerations in order to fulfill his role in the organization. Previous discussions have taken a *peal the onion* view to the management process and that seems even more appropriate here. Let us start off with a simple approach to understand the basics of resource management, and then

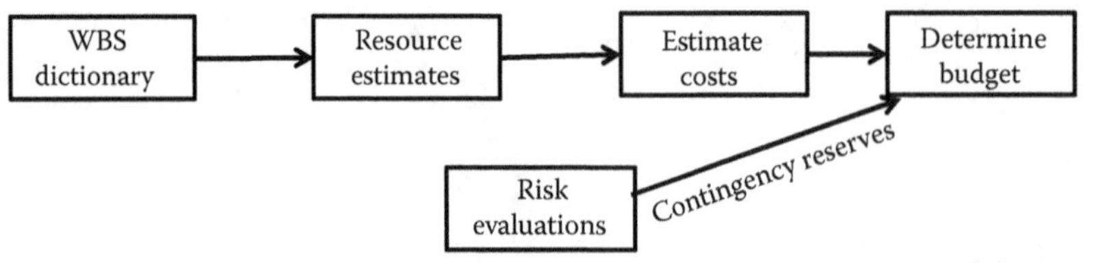

Figure 15.1 Cost management processes.

work on expanding into a more reasonable view after that. For the first segment, we will focus on defining the direct cost estimates for the Work Breakdown Structure (WBS) boxes.

15.2 Project Cost Planning Basics

There are three basic project planning cost-related activities. These are (PMI, 2017, p. 231):

Plan cost management—defines the process to be used for defining how the costs will be estimated, budgeted, managed, and then controlled.
Estimate costs—the process related to approximating the required monetary resources needed to complete the defined project activities.
Determine budget—the process of aggregating the estimated costs in order to produce an authorized baseline, including appropriate reserves.

This is the point where the previous fundamental groundwork definition begins to payoff. Recall that the WBS Dictionary has defined data related to all work units—both work and planning packages. The key items required in generating a raw direct cost for those work units would be the amount of work estimated for the unit multiplied by the associated resource rate. Hence, if the WP is estimated to require 100 hours of work by a particular skill group, the direct cost for that effort can be calculated by multiplying work hours times the allocated resource rate. Since the specific name of a resource is typically not known at planning time the typical costing process is to use average rates for that skill group. This same assumption was made by the estimator who derived the work time for the task. Both of these assumptions will remain one of the potential significant error sources for time and cost estimates.

If a work unit was estimated to require 100 hours of effort and the generic rate of the allocated resource was $25 per hour, the direct labor estimate for the activity would be $2500. Additionally, if the material estimate for this work unit was $1000, then the total estimated direct work unit cost would be $3500. Now, assume that we do this for all WBS work units and add all those costs. Is that not the aggregate project cost? Why not? Certainly it is a rough estimate of the direct project costs as defined by the WBS scope definition, but it is not a cost number that represents a realistic total actual project budget.

15.3 Cost Planning

From a raw mechanics viewpoint, if there were no future changes anticipated to the project, we might take the calculated direct cost number and use the network plan to lay out a time-phased

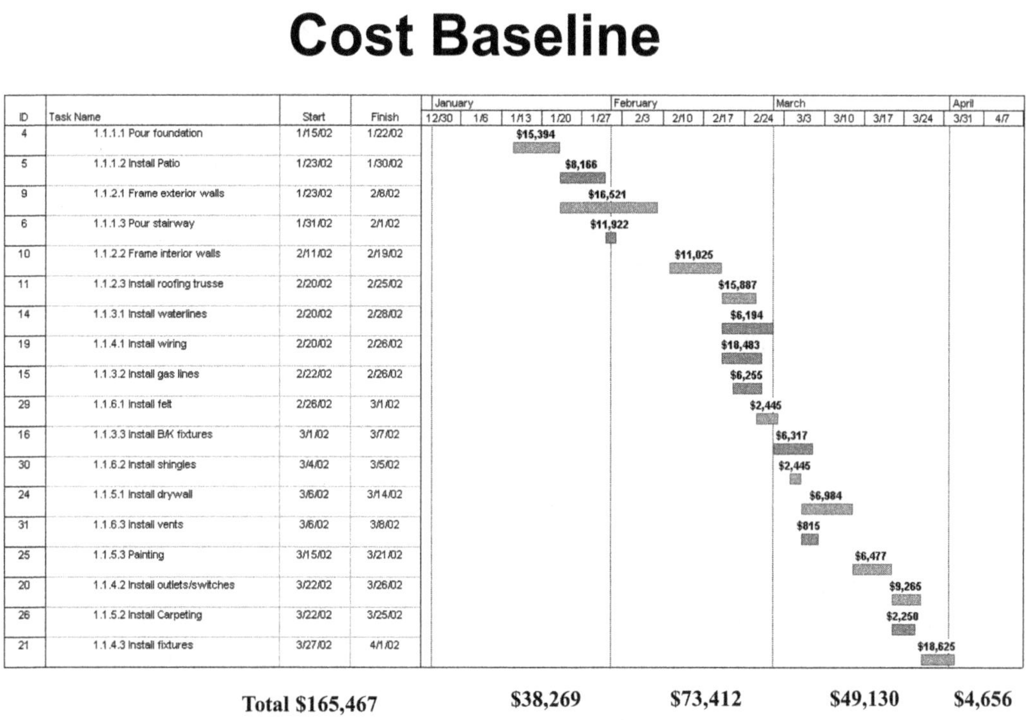

Cost Baseline

ID	Task Name	Start	Finish	Cost
4	1.1.1.1 Pour foundation	1/15/02	1/22/02	$15,394
5	1.1.1.2 Install Patio	1/23/02	1/30/02	$8,166
9	1.1.2.1 Frame exterior walls	1/23/02	2/8/02	$16,521
6	1.1.1.3 Pour stairway	1/31/02	2/1/02	$11,922
10	1.1.2.2 Frame interior walls	2/11/02	2/19/02	$11,025
11	1.1.2.3 Install roofing trusse	2/20/02	2/25/02	$15,887
14	1.1.3.1 Install waterlines	2/20/02	2/28/02	$6,194
19	1.1.4.1 Install wiring	2/20/02	2/26/02	$18,483
15	1.1.3.2 Install gas lines	2/22/02	2/26/02	$6,255
29	1.1.6.1 Install felt	2/26/02	3/1/02	$2,445
16	1.1.3.3 Install B/K fixtures	3/1/02	3/7/02	$6,317
30	1.1.6.2 Install shingles	3/4/02	3/5/02	$2,445
24	1.1.5.1 Install drywall	3/6/02	3/14/02	$6,984
31	1.1.6.3 Install vents	3/6/02	3/8/02	$815
25	1.1.5.3 Painting	3/15/02	3/21/02	$6,477
20	1.1.4.2 Install outlets/switches	3/22/02	3/26/02	$9,265
26	1.1.5.2 Install Carpeting	3/22/02	3/25/02	$2,250
21	1.1.4.3 Install fixtures	3/27/02	4/1/02	$18,625

Total $165,467 — January **$38,269** — February **$73,412** — March **$49,130** — April **$4,656**

Figure 15.2 Basic cash flow diagram.

view to show how those costs would occur over time. Figure 15.2 illustrates how dollars and time can be integrated. The typical assumption is that the planned cost is spread linearly over the work package activity time. This data would yield both a project direct cost and a time-phased distribution of those costs.

In addition to the direct cost items, assumptions are necessary as to how other cost items will impact the schedule. For instance, material items are often purchased in advance of the work unit and this would actually create a budget flow earlier than indicated from the direct cost calculation. Activity variability will also affect the magnitude of the actual resource flow and this can create cash forecasting issues as well. Finally, other project dynamics related to changes, risk, and other unknown events make the process of creating an accurate budget complex. The sections that follow from this point will each describe a unique characteristic that impacts the budget process. Collectively, all these have to be incorporated into the final budget view.

15.4 Cost Accuracy

Project budget accuracy is an often-misunderstood concept. Too often an early initiation phase rough estimate gets carried into an approved project budget before detailed planning takes place. In any case, budgeting cost accuracy changes over the life cycle as more specifics regarding the project are known. Mature organizations realize this and make their decisions accordingly. For instance, it needs to be recognized that budget estimates at initiation can easily be ±100% for a

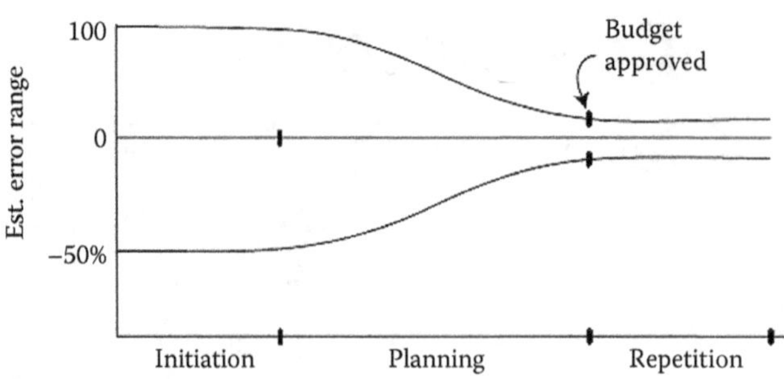

Figure 15.3 Planning cost accuracy.

large, complex project (maybe higher). For smaller repetitive projects, this range would be much smaller. Regardless, in general terms, the cost accuracy estimates evolve through three basic stages:

1. Rough order of magnitude (ROM): An estimate based on general knowledge of the requirement, but little knowledge available regarding specific detailed requirements (+/−100%).
2. First cut: An estimate based on reasonable requirements resulting from an approved WBS, but incomplete analysis related to such areas as risk and resource capacity (+/−25%).
3. Baseline approval (budget): The normal goal for a project budget formulated at the completion of a formal planning phase should strive for an accuracy level within ±5–10%.

Figure 15.3 shows this in schematic format. In a mature organization, this notion would be more the norm and is an important concept to stress. For example, one very mature organization color coded their estimation documents. Hence, an estimate presented on red paper fits the ROM category, while a yellow one would be assumed in the definitive range. Finally, the formal budget would be called a green estimate. This approach let everyone know how to adjust their view of the data. More typically, only one value will be used and it is often not clear at what stage of analysis the data represents. Project budget discussions need to have this graded management view of accuracy.

15.5 Organizational Overhead

The term *overhead* is often used with a negative connotation. It is common to have certain overhead charges allocated to a project on a percentage basis with no real explanation. For example, 100% of direct costs might be added to all direct labor estimates, 5% to all material purchases, and another 50% to the total project for corporate overhead. Obviously, numbers like this will significantly increase the stated cost of a project, yet they are organizational reality that must be dealt with along with the direct cost items. Oftentimes, the PM does not know how these allocations are derived, nor does he have any real control over their inclusion in his budget. In many cases, the only defense is to finish the project as quickly and efficiently as possible since some administrative overhead fees are time based. The necessary management strategy for this cost category is to understand the various allocations and be sure that they are included in the planning budget. If not included, the actual allocations coming later would represent a budget overrun in that the value would not have been in the plan.

15.6 Scope, Time, and Cost Alignment

Before the planning cycle is overwork, it is not uncommon to find that the project requirements cannot be produced in the time and cost approved in the project Charter. At this point the project is unworkable. One choice is to go back to the management approval authority to ask for more time or budget and possibly the project is so worthy that neither time nor cost are of great concern. Good luck on that one! The more typical situation is to attempt to cut scope in such a way that the schedule and budget are in line with constraints. In any case, the final planning view must balance these three variables.

15.6.1 Scope Replanning

During the course of scope development, we described prioritizing requirements as must have, needed, and some as nice to have. The nice to have category often become the first to go in the scope replanning process. Hopefully, this tactic would resolve the problem and the required schedule and budget constraints would now be met. Failure to do that necessitates a second alignment strategy.

15.6.2 Fast Tracking

If the alignment problem is more time than cost related, it is possible to look at fast-tracking the schedule. This was mentioned previously in Chapter 14. Basically, we look for ways to resequence the plan in order to make the activities fit into the required time frame. This strategy may in fact have other adverse implications in cost or risk, but if done carefully can decrease the schedule without significant increase in cost.

15.6.3 Schedule Crashing

This strategy emerges in the situation where the required schedule is not met, but more budget funds are available—a time-constrained schedule with money available. This process involves more complexity than the previous two options. Crashing involves the trade-off of budget resources for time. There are various situations in which this option is relevant to the PM. If budget is available and scope is required, then budget can be traded for time through the crashing process. In similar fashion, a contractor may want to crash a project when there are financial incentives to finish the project ahead of schedule. In order to decide whether to crash an activity, one must compare the cost of crashing the activity with the value gained by the reduction in schedule. Another less obvious reason to crash the project is to decrease indirect costs that are more time based. Direct costs are considered to be labor, materials, and equipment associated with a particular project, while indirect or overhead costs cannot be identified and charged specifically to one project. Examples of indirect costs are facilities, utilities, basic infrastructure items, level of effort activities for the project, and so on (Uher, 2003). Some of these are charged to the project monthly, regardless of status, and their effect on the project budget is tangible. Shortening the project time would decrease this class of cost.

In order to perform the crashing process, two time and cost estimates are required for each activity in the network—*normal* and *crash*. These cost estimates only use the direct cost component since that is the only real component to minimize. The normal estimate is considered to be the optimum time and cost for that work unit. A crash estimate is considered to be the

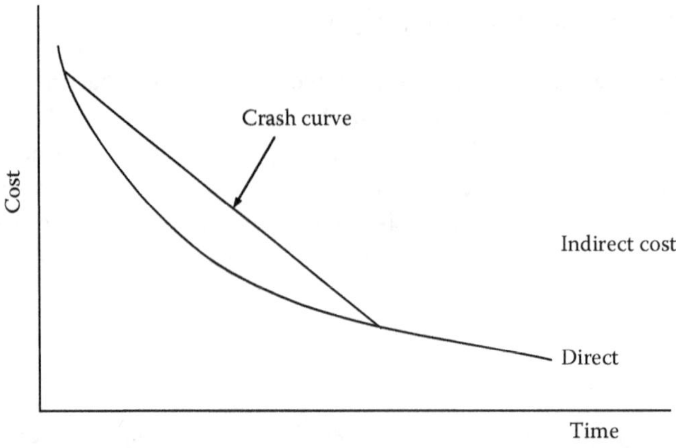

Figure 15.4 Time–cost curve.

"absolute minimum time required for the job and the cost per each time unit from that optimum point" (Stires and Murphy, 1962). Primary concern in the crash estimate is the incremental cost to decrease the activity time. The crash relationship for activity is shown in Figure 15.4 as a time–cost trade-off curve.

A linear approximation of the incremental unit time (per day) crash cost can be determined by the formula:

$$\text{Cost to expedite} = \frac{(\text{Crash cost} - \text{Normal cost})}{(\text{Normal time} - \text{Crash time})}$$

Another way of expressing this is to say that Crash Cost is equal to $\Delta\$/\Delta\text{Time}$. This formula assumes a linear relationship through the crash time range, which once again introduces an estimating error (see Figure 15.4). However, the management benefits obtained usually justifies the shortcut. If necessary, a more rigorous estimate can be derived for each unit time increment. The graph shows that each increment of time increases the project cost and eventually crashing will result in diminishing returns. At that point it does not make sense to try to shorten the project any further. Once this data is derived for each activity, we have the fundamental parameters necessary to execute the process. In order to arrive at the optimum total project investment curve, the following five-step crashing plan is required (Stires and Murphy, 1962):

1. Develop a first cut schedule using normal time and cost estimates for each activity.
2. Develop crashing information for each activity. This should include lowest crash point and crash cost per time unit.
3. Select the lowest crash cost on the critical path and reduce that activity time by one time unit. Recompute the critical path for the new time.
4. Repeat steps 3 and 4 until the desired project duration is reached, or available budget is depleted.

Data to illustrate the mechanics for crashing are provided by Figures 15.5 and 15.6 and the corresponding crashing data are presented in Table 15.1. These three items represent the starting point for the process. The goal for this example is to illustrate the crashing steps with a reasonable-sized activity set.

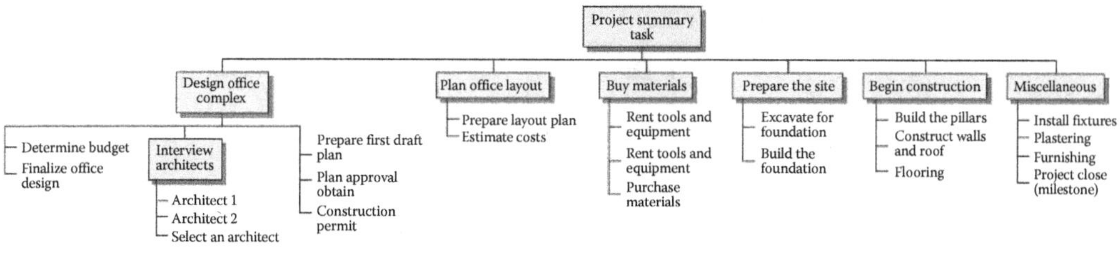

Figure 15.5 WBS for crashing.

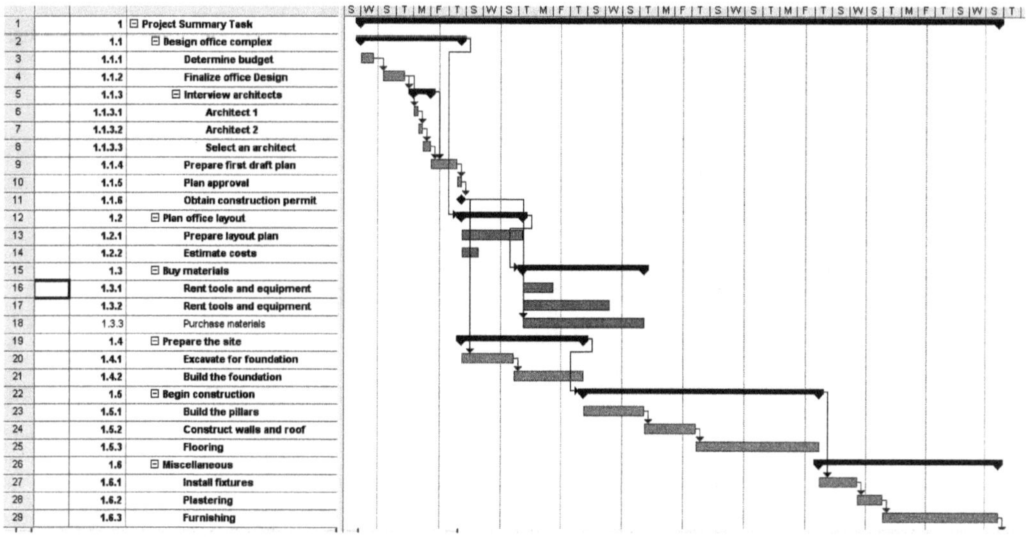

Figure 15.6 Project Schedule.

Table 15.1 Crashing Parameters

WBS	*Activity*	*Duration (days)*	*Predecessor*	*Minimum Crash (days)*	*Crash $/D ($000s)*
1	Project summary task	105		–	–
1.1	Design office complex	17		–	–
1.1.1	Determine budget	3		3	2
1.1.2	Finalize office Design	5	3	4	3
1.1.3	Interview architects	4	4	–	–
1.1.3.1	Architect 1	1	4	–	–
1.1.3.2	Architect 2	1	6	–	–
1.1.3.3	Select an architect	2	7	–	–

(Continued)

Table 15.1 (*Continued*) Crashing Parameters

WBS	*Activity*	*Duration (days)*	*Predecessor*	*Minimum Crash (days)*	*Crash $/D ($000s)*
1.1.4	Prepare first draft plan	4	5, 8	3	4
1.1.5	Plan approval	1	9	—	—
1.1.6	Obtain construction permit	0	10	—	—
1.2	Plan office layout	10	2	—	—
1.2.1	Prepare layout plan	10		4	5
1.2.2	Estimate costs	2	13	1	3
1.3	Buy materials	20	12	—	—
1.3.1	Rent tools and equipment	5		11	
1.3.2	Rent tools and equipment	14		12	4
1.3.3	Purchase materials	20	11	2	3
1.4	Prepare the site	20		—	—
1.4.1	Excavate for foundation	8	18	6	10
1.4.2	Build the foundation	12	20	9	20
1.5	Begin construction	38	19	—	—
1.5.1	Build the pillars	10		9	19
1.5.2	Construct walls and roof	8	23	7	18
1.5.3	Flooring	20	24	13	17
1.6	Miscellaneous	30		—	—
1.6.1	Install fixtures	7	22	—	—
1.6.2	Plastering	4	27	—	—
1.6.3	Furnishing	19	28	10	3
1.6.4	Project close (milestone)	0	29	—	—

The first step in the crashing process is to identify the lowest crash cost on the critical path. Inspection of Table 15.1 data shows this to be activity 1.1.1 with a cost of $2,000 per day. Figure 15.6 total slack column (zero value) shows that this task is on the critical path. Hence, crashing these tasks will shorten the project duration. No more days can be taken out of 1.1.1 since it is now at the minimum duration (e.g., Minimum Crash Time).

For the second iteration, Table 15.1 identifies four activities 1.1.2, 1.2.2, 1.3.3, and 1.6.3 at the next lowest crash cost ($3,000). Figure 15.6 shows that activities 1.2.2 and 1.3.3 are not on the critical path; therefore, shortening these two activities would not shorten the project. So, activity 1.1.2 is selected and the duration decreases one time unit to 100 days. The activity cannot be shortened further. We can see from inspection of the Gantt chart that the critical path will stay the same.

Step 3 selects critical path activity 1.6.3 from the options shown above. This will add another $3000 per day to the project budget; however, in this case, the activity can be crashed three time periods for $3000 each day. Taking that option adds $9000 to the budget and reduces the project duration to 97 days.

It will be left as a reader exercise to crash this plan further. As each subsequent step is executed the incremental crash cost will increase. Also, in larger plans, it is common for multiple critical paths to emerge. The mechanics as described here will work for any network, but obviously the complexity of the setup increases. Also, it will be necessary in these situations to actually recompute the critical path for each iteration. Crashing mechanics are not a simple process, but an important tool for the PM.

15.7 Indirect Costs

Many project cost components occur through allocations or time-based charges. Facilities overhead, level of effort support charges, and other cost categories contribute to increased cost regardless of the actual project work activity. These charges can occur at both the activity and the project level. Figure 15.7 illustrates how indirect costs help justify activity crashing.

Figure 15.8 adds the two cost elements to show the total time–cost tradeoff and the optimum point. An understanding of these views can help establish an optimal strategy for project duration. Once again, we see logic for understanding the fast-tracking and crashing logic.

15.8 Resource Alignment

It is one thing to tweak the plan until it fits certain scope, time, or cost constraints, but it is quite another to match this against resource availability. The initial cost estimates were based on a generic cost for each skill. We are now recognizing that the quantity or quality of those required skills may not be available at the time specified by the plan. Figure 15.9 shows this situation.

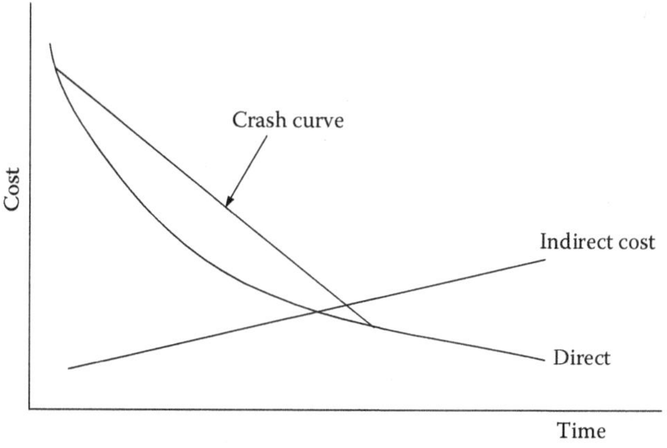

Figure 15.7 Direct/indirect curve.

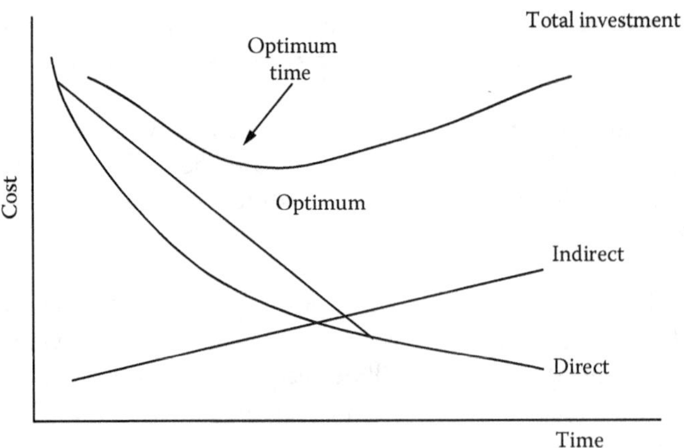

Figure 15.8 Total project investment curve.

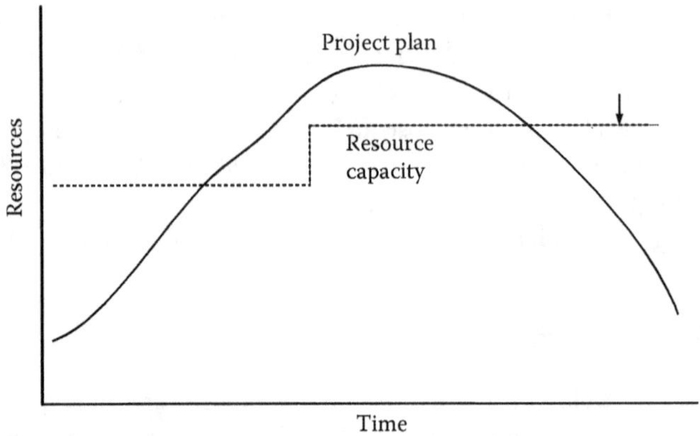

Figure 15.9 Resource capacity leveling.

In this view, the y-axis can represent either the number of resources or the cost. The situation shown indicates that the plan requires more than available, so we have a resource capacity issue. Basically, the plan is of no value in this situation because it will indicate a schedule that cannot be met and possibly a false budget as well. In order to have a viable plan, the required resources must match the allocation shown in the plan. Experience indicates that this situation is a common management issue and the cause of many projects failing to meet their plans, even with all other factors under control.

The following are two basic options for dealing with lack of timely resources to fit the plan:

1. Increase the capacity of resources available to meet the plan through reallocation, hiring, or outsourcing.
2. Lag the plan work units until the capacity matches the requirement. Increasing capacity can be achieved by reallocating internal resources from other projects to this one, hiring new employees, or contracting needed resources from third parties. Technically, each of these choices could work if properly managed.

Either decreasing the allocation of resources to various work units that will cause the activity to increase in duration or simply moving the activity to a later time when resources are available can accomplish a decrease in the resource requirement. If this is done to slack activities the action will not affect the critical path; however, moving critical path activities will also move the completion date.

Recognize that this class of problem is not solved overnight since it often involves multiple-level organizational decisions. For this reason, resource capacity issues need to be defined as far in advance as possible to allow various solution options to be resolved. In order to do this, a formal project resource plan created along the lines outlined here is a prerequisite. Beyond the project plan view there must be a workable organization-level resource management system that can identify aggregate capacity and then link available capacity to the project. During the planning phase we do not have to know that Joe Smith is going to be allocated to our project for some planned period, but we must know that someone with the appropriate skills will be. Failure to accomplish this basic linkage means that the project schedule slips and corresponding budgets likely slip as well. If there is one operational Achilles heel in most organizations, it is the one described here. Recognize that multiple departmental groups typically staff matrix format organization projects. The various internal resource suppliers must be able to have visibility into the portfolio of projects planned in the organization, and in order to do this, enterprise-level information systems are needed to support this process.

15.9 Budget Reserves

Up to this point, we have attempted to view the budget environment using basically deterministic assumptions—that is, nothing will happen outside of the original planned scope and time estimates. As a modern-day Wizard of Oz might say "Dude, this ain't Kansas." Fact is, a project exists in a very dynamic environment with things changing all the time. Any deviation from the plan has the potential to impact scope, time, or cost estimates. Some feel that these dynamics are so radical that planning is a waste of time. This is not the case, but clearly the plan has to recognize the dynamics. The key question is how to incorporate unplanned contingencies in a reasonable manner. Figure 15.10 shows the three major areas of dynamics that have to be dealt with in the final plan.

15.9.1 Plan Dynamics

The most obvious dynamic is unplanned work resulting from requested and approved changes to the original project scope. Each of these actions will occupy the project team's attention and resources, thereby taking away productive time from the current plan. When a new work unit is approved, the WBS structure needs to be modified to reflect the new scope and all planning

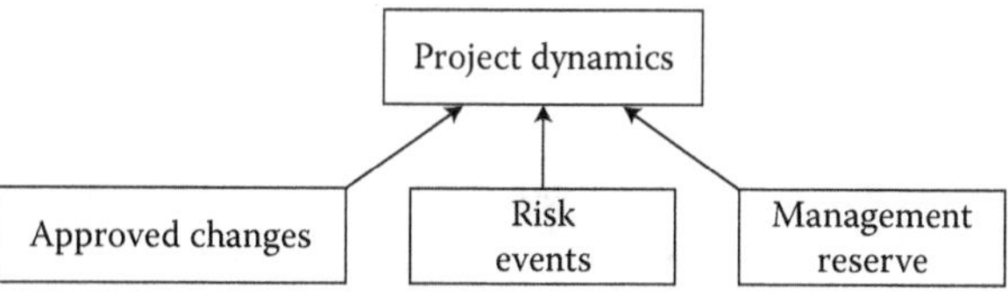

Figure 15.10 Major sources for project dynamics.

related to how the new work fits into the current plan represents additional project work activity. It is hard to estimate how much time this activity actually takes, but clearly it is a visible amount of time that should be recognized in the project budget. These work activities have an impact on schedule, budget, and required resources for the project. One possible method to show this in the plan is to allocate a level of effort work unit with some attached budget. All change requests work could be charged to this work unit and minor approved changes could be absorbed through this.

A broader management question involves how to physically incorporate an approved change request into the project work plan. If it results in additional work or new WBS WPs, the basic question is, do you allocate budget from the change pool into those packages or leave them empty from a budget point of view. This process can be handled via either the pool approach or by allocating the pool funds into defined WPs. Realize that leaving the funds in a pool will complicate the ability to track WP costs later. A more significant management issue emerges when the change request is large. A first consideration is to specifically identify such requests. For those designated in this category, the pool approach is not appropriate. In this situation, the approved plan needs to reflect the change in some manner. This could be handled by allocating some segment of the change pool for large changes and moving the funds out of this group into the project-approved plan just as though it were there in the beginning. Regardless of the funding process selected for this class of dynamic it is not fair to the project team to ignore these events and assume that they can be absorbed by the original budget. If this is in fact the local culture, the project team will pad their estimates and hide the activity, which camouflages the true costs. A key PM activity involves tracking what is going on at the WP level and not hiding behind padded estimates put in place to keep the budget intact.

15.9.2 Risk Events

A second dynamic occurs from risk-related events that occur through the life cycle. A more detailed discussion of the mechanics for dealing with risk will be discussed later in Chapter 22, but for now we need to recognize that some allowance for this class of activity is needed. A risk event is called a "known/unknown." This means that certain things that the project team is aware of may not go well, but these potential events may or may not occur. The project plan assumes that they will not occur, but must cover the recognition that some will. The traditional method for handling such events is to set aside a contingency allocation that has been estimated to cover anticipated events. This allocation will be held external to the working budget and used as a particular event occurs. Think of this as a phantom work unit that is not in the plan. When the event occurs, the related corrective work unit is moved into the plan and funds are taken out of the risk contingency pool to cover it. The goal is to have a contingency fund that just covers the future needs for this class of dynamic. As in most project estimating situations, this is a difficult number to derive, but the concept is to recognize that risk events fall outside the operational work units. We want the budget to reflect the work as planned, but have mechanisms to invoke to cover "bumps in the night." Scope changes and risk are two such items.

15.9.3 Management Reserve

A third dynamic is a class of issues falling into the category of "unknown unknowns." These are issues that occur, but were not planned or anticipated. This class of contingency is called a management reserve and it is designed to deal with unplanned, but required, changes that occur during the course of the project. Management practices to handle such events are not a standard industry practice item. As in other such dynamics, this class of events is often buried under padded estimates, which violates our management approach. Ideally, the PM would have a defined management reserve buffer set aside of these events and the process would simply be to record the unplanned event and allocate necessary funds from this source to cover the item overrun. Management reserves are typically assigned to some management entity to allocate to the project and are generally not part of the approved visible project budget.

Technically, a management reserve event is any work-related activity that does not meet the plan. In theory, this can be the result of a work unit that exceeded its planned amount, or any unanticipated work requirement. Project management theory says that reserve fund requirements and the allocations for all such events are under the control of a defined external project management entity. However, as a practical matter, this is not a reasonable operational approach. From a more practical viewpoint, this level of external control for overruns can be onerous and the PM needs to have some level of flexibility for minor additional funding events. For example, if a WP overruns by 5% should that overrun be taken from a general overrun buffer or a larger externally controlled management reserve account? A PM-controlled buffer approach would seem more logical. Likewise, the requirement to pay a minor bill to repair a piece of equipment should fall into the same category. However, if a major event occurs, or the project overall budget exceeds 10% that process it would seem worthy of more external oversight. In this second case, a higher level of funds is also required and allocation of these will most likely not be delegated to the PM. The budget management question in this case is about the proper source and control process for additional fund allocation. An allocation for larger-size management reserve funds needs to be recognized in the overall budget, but not necessarily shown in the public budget and not under the control of the PM. One operational way to handle this could be to have a management reserve fund similar to the risk fund, but under formal control of a group such as the project steering committee or the sponsor. In this review process, the management question would involve not only the fund allocation, but other correction actions such as whether the project should continue.

Hence, the recommendation for management reserve budgeting is to allow a small amount of funds to be left in the project-controlled portion of the budget to handle this class of dynamics. The main segment of management reserve would in an external fund held and controlled outside of the project manager's authority level. This fund may or may not be visible as part of the public budget, but will be part of the overall consideration for the project in terms of financial justification.

In this section, we have described three dynamic budgeting issues that have the potential to consume budget funds that were not defined in the original base plan. Each of these variance situations will occur to some degree during the project life cycle and some arrangement for handling each category needs to be part of the plan and somehow reflected in an overall budget view.

15.10 Resources have Different Colors

As stated earlier one view of a budget is simply the number of dollars or euros required in executing the project. This view can become muddled as the PM begins to deal with various types of resources. Budget monies are often allocated to many different categories and organizational unit groups. This means that the project budget has to be structured to fit these required categories. In some cases, budget funds may come from different sources at different time frames. So, managing the budget is not as simple as just keeping a single actual total spending level within the planned value. In many cases, it is keeping various cost groups within each of their bounds. Our goal here is not to understand the accounting theory related to this issue, but it is necessary to understand and be sensitive to the fact that the budget will have various resource categories and sources. Some of these groupings must be considered as part of the estimating process, but others will just require that the source be marked and managed individually as part of the control process. Industry professionals call this bean counting.

15.10.1 Budget Expense Categories

The following list of project cost elements provides an example to show how a budget may contain multiple fund categories within what would be called "the budget." The major categories of budget expenses are as follows (Lane, 2003):

Personnel
- Salaries and benefits (including hiring fees and bonuses)
- Training and education
- Travel
- Morale
- Staff-related depreciation
- Temporary help/consultants
- Miscellaneous (space, telecom, etc.)

Hardware
- Depreciation
- Maintenance
- Repairs
- Leases

Software
- Depreciation
- Maintenance
- Customer support
- Updates
- Repairs
- Leases

Services
- Leased lines
- Outsourced network services
- Security services
- Third-party service providers
- Miscellaneous (transport, courier, periodicals, etc.)

Other
- Local sources and terms

Beyond the categorization aspect of the funds another example is found in the depreciation item. This is an accounting entry based on the anticipated useful life of an item. In this case, the item might cost $100,000 with an estimated life of five years and the amount allocated to the project might be only $20,000 per year. This is the capital funds category. Without carrying this point further, realize that a budget will have to obey the organizational financial rules and your support financial person will be needed to ensure that these are obeyed. In order to comply with this level of cost management granularity, WP estimating detail will be more complex than outlined thus far. Organizational financial systems will dictate how the cost is categorized and ultimately reported in the budget format.

15.10.2 Assets versus Expenses

Expenses are cash budgetary outlays for project goods and services that are consumed during the course of the project life cycle. A capital expenditure is an accounting entry in cash units, but it is not equivalent to actual dollars as reported. Simply put, capital expenditures create assets that are then depreciated over scheduled periods of time, and these depreciation expenses will be charged according to some set of rules established by the financial organization, which attempts to match service value to expenditures. The cost allocation goal for this class of asset is to match cost to service life so that an asset cost is recognized over its useful life rather than as the expenditure occurs. The basic decision regarding whether to consider a purchase to be expense versus asset is its cost and useful life. Guidance on these issues is provided by the financial function and governmental regulations tend to be the guiding policy.

A capital expenditure is identified on the organization's asset schedule and some form of depreciation schedule is established for it. From this base a periodic depreciation value is entered on the project budget. This has the impact of initially showing the asset at a lesser value than the actual cost. This impact on the expense budget is important to recognize, as it can be significant. In some cases, there are favorable tax credits for some investment types, which have a further impact regarding how the organization views the decision.

As a side note, it is even becoming common to view large technology-based projects as enterprise capital assets. The implication of this would be that the total cost of the project is depreciated over time, so a $1 million project that is depreciated over five years (straight line) would show on the organizational financial statement as costing $200,000 per year even though the organization would have expended more funds than this. Depreciation of this class of project has the impact of improving the short-term accounting profitability of the organization, but diminishes that view in future years as the depreciation expense is recorded.

The PM needs to work carefully with the financial organization to deal with proper methods for handling all budget expenditures. Some of the decisions related to asset versus cash categorization are flexible based on internal situations. It is always possible to expense an asset and take the cost penalty up front. This has the impact of showing the organization making less profit in that time period, but possibly saving current taxes.

15.10.3 Budget Cost Components

Table 15.2 illustrates how budget cost components might be specified for a project. It may also be necessary to define in greater detail the types of skills required if this data would be needed by internal groups. Beyond this view, it is common to array cost and resource date into a time-phased plan. From that view the data could be divided into direct and indirect categories as shown in Table 15.2.

Table 15.2 Project Cost Components

Cost Category		*Cost*
Direct labor	Hours	$
Indirect labor	Hours	$
Total labor costs		$
Hardware acquisition		$
Materials acquisition		
Software acquisition		$
Total acquisition costs		$
Consulting or subcontracting		$
Travel or other employee or contractor expenses		$
Financing costs, such as interest on project capital funding		$
Total other costs		$
Contingency costs		$
Total project costs		$

15.11 Management Approval and Baselines

As the various budgeting iterations are resolved, a total project cost view becomes the final proposed project budget. As we have seen in this chapter, there are many embedded financial items to consider as part of this process and each project has somewhat different cost issues and characteristics. However, recognize that more organization segments are interested in budgets than any other project activity. In any case, the assumptions that have been made throughout the planning phase are now packaged into a formal cost document with funds categorized as dictated by the financial organization. From this, enterprise management will now make a go-no-go decision on the project based on their review of this document, along with the other planning artifacts.

Once management has approved the project budget data, a formal cost baseline is set. Because cost is both a total value and time phase-oriented management issue, the cost baseline will be presented in a *cash flow*-oriented manner. Basically, this involves "stamping" that version of the overall plan for use in future status comparative measurement. Regardless of what occurs after this, the original baseline data will be kept. Recognize that the term *baseline* can apply to more than just schedule and cost. There can be a performance baseline, a quality baseline, a staffing baseline, or any other measurable parameter that management wishes to monitor.

The cost baseline is a time-phased presentation by budget category that is used as a basis against what to measure, monitor, and control for the project. This view is created by summing estimated costs by category and period, then displaying them in either tabular or graphic form. Figure 15.11 shows a graphical view in which the approved baseline is set higher than the anticipated plan. In

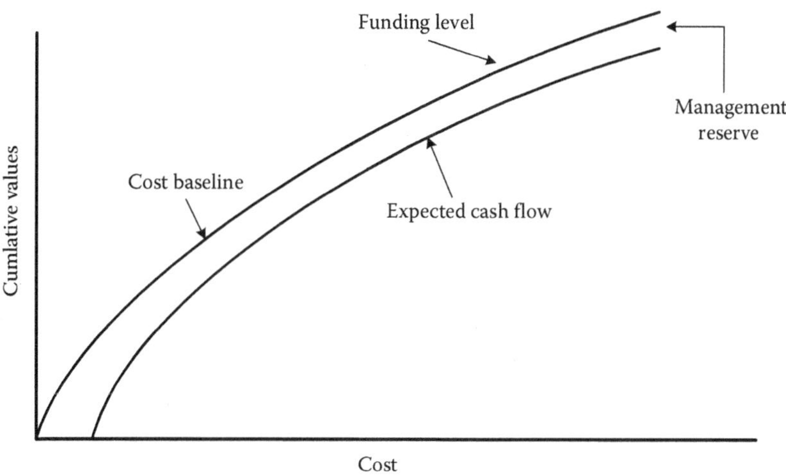

Figure 15.11 Cost baseline graph.

this example, the graph is showing the cost baseline versus planned cash expenditures and funding constraints. This type of presentation is a key item in the project management plan. Many projects, especially large ones, have multiple cost or resource baselines, as well as baselines related to consumable production items (e.g., cubic yards of dirt moved per day). In each case, these are used to measure different aspects of project performance. These various baseline comparisons may also be included in regular project status measurement.

15.12 Summary

The project budget is one of the most important planning artifacts and it has wide exposure across the stakeholder community. Basically, budgeting represents the cost component of the holy trilogy and is a major management consideration for any organization. It represents the primary metric benchmark for project monitoring and control.

A second theme of this chapter is to highlight the multidimensional view of funds that a budget has with various organizational stakeholders. In order for the PM to have internal organizational credibility, the formal budgeting rules and regulations must be understood.

References

Lane, D., ed., 2003. *CIO Wisdom: Best Practices from Silicon Valley*. Boston, MA: Pearson.

PMI, 2017. *A Guide to the Project Management Body of Knowledge (PMBOK® Guide)*. 6th ed. Newtown Square, PA: Project Management Institute.

Stires, D.M. and M.M. Murphy, 1962. *PERT/CPM*. Boston, MA: Materials Management Institute.

Uher, T.E., 2003. *Programming and Scheduling Techniques*. Sydney: University of New South Wales.

Chapter 16

Quality Management

16.1 Introduction

This chapter emphasizes the importance of and need for quality management through the project life cycle. Major Project Management Body of Knowledge (PMBOK®) Guide components of this knowledge area (KA) contain defined processes for quality planning, quality assurance (QA), and quality control (QC). Also included in the quality process is a suite of tools to support the analysis process.

The understanding of this topic evolved from the classic Japan roots in the mid-1940s and is now broadly visible across international industry today, including the current popularity of Six Sigma. All of the various conceptual threads of the quality movement have had a positive impact for those organizations that have been able to successfully implement them; however, the implementation process is often complex and unsuccessful. The key theme of this chapter is that quality management is a key attribute not only of the project, but the organization's ability to survive long term. However, this is not a quick fix topic and should be viewed as a process journey rather than a one-time event.

16.2 Evolution of Quality

Quality issues are observed in all aspects of society. We talk about quality art, products we use, customer experiences, and many other aspects of our lives. In its broadest sense quality is that which adds value and improves our lives. There is always a vague indefinable and somewhat immeasurable side to quality and all cultures view quality somewhat differently. There are visible examples of this in the Australian aborigines, nomadic tribes of Africa, Great Wall of China, Christian cathedrals of Europe, and various man-made monuments around the world. Each of these examples is viewed as having a unique form of quality, but each has its own cultural, social, and personal interpretative facets attached to it (i.e., size, beauty, function, etc.). Achieving high quality requires both art and engineering because we cannot completely separate the aesthetic, indefinable, irreproducible side of quality from the engineering side, which contains the technical, more definable, more measurable, and more reproducible side.

Table 16.1 Early Contributions to Quality Management

Year	*Person or Organization*	*Matching Idea/Achievement*
1755	John Smeaton	Applied the scientific method to engineering problems
1788	James Watt	First feedback device
Around 1850	U.S. military	Defined the first industry standard
1876	Thomas Alva Edison	R&D laboratory for new inventions and viable commercial versions of products
Early 1900s	Assembly lines	Inspection, followed by rework or discard
1911	Frederick W. Taylor	Scientific Management
1920s–1950s	Walter Shewhart	Statistical Quality Control
1920s–1980s	Walter Shewhart and Edwards Deming	Plan, Do, Check, Act model
1940s–1980s	Edwards Deming	Quality principles and management

Today, many companies improve their competitive position through an unplanned political process of new idea pursuits. Most organizations have a defined process for proposing an improvement, demonstrating that it has value and then putting it in place through a project-type initiative. Through the evolving stages of quality, we have seen that high quality is achieved by an understanding of certain universal, unchanging principles combined with a practical application of those principles to changing circumstances. Over the past 100 years, we have seen these concepts mature and evolve in various ways.

The key to understand quality management is to understand how organizations through time have slowly developed new ways to apply the scientific method to their situations. Initially, the scientific revolution (roughly 1600–1687) changed our perception of the universe. This was followed by the industrial revolution (roughly 1760–1830, and beyond), which brought a new generation of mechanical technology to our lives. During these periods the relationship between science and industry, particularly the relationship between the scientific method and business management, formed the conceptual foundation for modern quality management principles. This topic evolved as engineers, managers, and functional organizational groups responded to the problems of their day. Table 16.1 provides a list of the early quality pioneers who contributed classical perspectives that evolved into quality management as we know it today.

Organizations seek to solve problems related to effectiveness, efficiency, and quality. Through all of this history the theory has remained far ahead of practice. In fact, many of today's quality problems could be solved by proper application of Taylor's 1911 treatise on Scientific Management.

16.3 Definition of Quality

The definition of quality offered here is derived from a combination of four disciplines—Philosophy, Economics, Marketing, and Operations Management. Although such a diverse combination seems unrelated, combining their respective views provides a perspective that includes customer focus, consumer satisfaction, standards, and production efficiency. *Philosophy* offers the broad perspective of human variance. *Economics* looks at quality in terms of value and the fulfillment of needs. *Marketing* looks at customer value and the customer decision-making process to better understand how customers define quality and choose value. *Operations Management* views quality as conformance to specifications with a manufacturing view. Philip Crosby provided one of the classic definitions of quality as:

> Quality means conformance to requirements.
>
> *(Crosby, 1979)*

It does not matter whether or not the requirements are articulated or specified. If a product does not fully satisfy the customer, it lacks quality in some respect. This infers that quality lies in the eyes of the beholder.

Other common definitions of quality are the following:

- The degree of excellence of a product or service
- The degree to which a product or service satisfies the needs of a specific customer
- The degree to which a product or service conforms to a given requirement

Eight lesser used variants of a quality definition are added to this list above to show more on the breadth of this term. These definitions say that quality is:

1. The ongoing process of building and sustaining relationships by assessing, anticipating, and fulfilling stated and implied needs.
2. The customers' perception of the suppliers' work output value.
3. Nothing more or less than the perception that the customer has of you, your products, and your services.
4. The extent to which products, services, processes, and relationships are free from defects, constraints, and items, which do not add value for customers.
5. A perceived degree of excellence as defined by the customer.
6. Do what you have to do when you have to do it to satisfy your customer's needs and make your product or service do what it is supposed to do.
7. An ever-evolving perception by the customer of the value provided by a product. It is not a static perception that never changes but rather a fluid process that changes as a product matures (innovation) and other alternatives (competition) are made available for comparison.
8. It is the eyes of the beholder and in a business environment the beholder is always the customer or client. In other words, quality is whatever the customer says it is.

This collection of definitions illustrates that the view of quality is quite varied and that makes the theoretical discussion more difficult to structure. The following are the three basic concepts that exist in most quality definitions:

- Level of goodness
- Customer satisfaction
- Conformance to requirements

However, it is important to add to these points that if the original specification is not defined in a proper manner, meeting a non-specific specification with a quality process will not produce a quality result. One way to develop specifications that will satisfy the customer is to clearly identify the properties that are desired in the final product. In this sense, the term "property" might be thought of as a generic attribute such as strong, durable, or smooth; however, these properties must be translated into some more quantifiable characteristics that can then be engineered and tested to verify conformance. The term "quality characteristic" is used whenever reference is made to a value that is measured for either quality control process purposes or to assess product functional acceptability.

Quality for the customer means that, in selecting and buying the product or service the customer has a hassle-free experience, and in using the product or service it meets or exceeds expectations for as long as they want. If we are providing quality for customers, then at any moment during or after the process they would buy more from us or recommend us to others. Key issues include:

- Identifying the target market and the needs of that market.
- Establishing effective communication with customers or customer representatives to develop good requirements.
- Providing high-quality sales and customer service so that the customer likes doing business with the company and the interaction, as well as the product or service.
- The final result is viewed as value compared to cost.

Technical project groups can only deliver quality to the customer if the requirements are an accurate, complete, clear representation of the wants needs, and expectations of the targeted customers and all stakeholders. For the most part, attempting to delight the customer by meeting all of their needs, wants, and expectations in the product and providing a high-quality customer service experience is strategically beneficial for the company. But, as is the case with many business decisions, success requires balance. It is possible to become too customer focused. Fact is, the term *expectation* may represent something beyond reason. The operational focus needs to be on agreed result targets. The tough cultural issue with quality is to actually believe all of this extra effort is really worthwhile for both sides. The business side of the equation needs to make a profit to stay in business, while on the other side the customer must feel like they get something out of the arrangement or they won't return. Can a quality environment with "extra" processes really be free? If one never gets beyond this philosophy the move toward a quality culture will likely not occur.

16.4 Project Quality Management

The first view of this topic comes from the project side of this equation with the following operational definition: "The primary purpose of quality management in the project is to ensure that the project will satisfy the needs for which it was undertaken." To accomplish this, the project team must develop good relationships with key stakeholders and understand what quality means to them. This is certainly more than technical team members defining what they believe quality to be. It is through this relationship path that quality will be defined. Many technical projects fail because the project team focuses only on meeting the written requirements for the products originally specified and ignoring other stakeholder needs and expectations. For example, the project team should know what the value will be in customer terms if the item is delivered as specified.

Based on the perspectives outlined here, quality must be on an equal level of importance with project scope, time, and cost. That is the key rationale for bundling these four knowledge areas into one major text group. These are the four output parameters that represent status of the project.

16.5 Quality Perspective

Any organization that is serious about success must define its quality goals to be consistent with their core customers' needs and the strategic goals of the organization. These organizational goals then need to be decomposed into a set of standard quality requirements that then become an integral part, perhaps even the end goal, of the organizational or project quality plan. We will call this linkage organizational *alignment*.

For many organizations, minimum quality requirements or merchantability standards are established by a regulating body within the industry and/or government organizations. However, mature organizations in many industries understand that minimum requirements are not sufficient to meet the growing desires of customers in a competitive environment. On the other hand, an organization must be cautious in establishing quality requirements that are impossible to attain or cost prohibitive for the market in which they are competing. The project manager (PM) and the organization must ask what existing standards are in place for comparison and determine if they are reasonable to achieve. The project team must be familiar with the standard quality requirements that apply to the project and carefully assess how they align with the expectations of the customer for the particular project. Allocating time during the planning phase of the project to negotiate any gaps with the customer and then assessing the impact on the technical direction of the project are important for mutual understanding of expectations and for establishing a realistic scope, budget, and schedule. Some projects, such as those pertaining to the development of a new product or service, may have minimal input from the customer but are highly dependent on winning future business by properly anticipating the needs of these potential customers. The traditional approach of simply matching output to original specifications may not be sufficient or applicable, and therefore the project team must ask the following questions in establishing their project quality requirements:

What aspects of the project will be controlled?

- How will quality be defined and measured?
- What are the standards to be met?
- How are the output measures to be compared with the standard?
- How are deviations to be corrected?

These and other similar quality specifications are key planning steps and represent the quality plan activity. It is also incumbent upon the PM to ensure that the customer is also clear on the level of quality that has been agreed upon. Without this foundational agreement, the probability and impact of scope creep due to quality-related misunderstandings can escalate beyond the PM's control. Once agreement has been reached the requirements are baselined and managed through the formal change control process.

16.6 Implications for Project Planning

Quality planning involves identifying the products (deliverables) at the start of the project and deciding the best steps to verify and validate them so that they meet the standards. A second dimension of the planning process is to understand the broader organizational goals in regard to planning. Third, and equally important, every project should have the goal of improving the current state. This goal falls into the category of *continuous improvement* which is one of the main tenants of the quality model. Organizations and project processes that stay static are falling behind by definition.

Project quality process and deliverable quality are two different facets of project quality. The quality process side means to follow the correct project management practices and comply with the company objectives (QA), whereas deliverable quality refers to the correct product specifications or defined deliverables that meets user's needs (QC). A high project process quality may produce low deliverable quality, whereas a high deliverable quality may have low process quality. The PM must manage both aspects of the effort.

The organizational quality policy is used to philosophically guide the project in evaluating whether their defined level is appropriate in meeting the quality level specified by the customer. Feedback (lessons learned) from current or previous projects can add insight into existing quality levels and identify gaps in the current processes. If there is any doubt of meeting customer expectations, then the project management team must be aware of this and take steps toward improving the existing quality approach. This may require creating new procedures or necessitate adding more resources to improve the quality level. Embedded in this decision process are the associated cost and schedule impacts related to the quality level (cost of quality). An appropriate balance between quality and other performance variables needs to be carefully analyzed and communicated with senior management and the customer. From this, a formal agreement should be documented as trade-offs in some dimension are often required.

Project quality management processes help prevent recurring problems by organizing and managing resources to ensure that project deliverables are completed on time, within budget, and are of high user-perceived quality. The main philosophical drivers underlying project quality management are as follows:

Customer satisfaction: Defined by the customer and requires the understanding, evaluation, definition, and management of expectations so that appropriate requirements are established.

Prevention inspection: Prevention over inspection is the commonsense principle implying that the cost of preventing mistakes is generally much less than the cost of correcting them.

Management responsibility: Management's responsibility in quality management is to provide the resources needed to sustain success and protect the project team from environmental disruption. Quality is a management responsibility!

Continuous improvement: Continuous improvement implies that there is no such thing as absolute quality. Each day offers the opportunity to improve and each step is one more toward the goal.

The underlying support processes to accomplish this goal are quality planning, QA, and QC. These three terms will be discussed in more detail in the sections below.

16.7 Quality Planning

Quality planning plays a significant role in a variety of business processes. Each organization defines their view of quality in terms that deliver the greatest alignment with their unique business values. For this reason, it is difficult to create a single definition of quality that covers every aspect of every organization. Therefore, it is more appropriate to discuss the framework of quality planning by dividing the topic into two specific components: quality policy and quality objectives.

16.7.1 Quality Policy

The guiding principle behind organizational quality involves creating policies that support specific business values. These policies are produced through the use of defined processes that seek to deliver substantial benefits by improving the performance of an organization. *ProjectsAtWork* has defined a number of standard documented approaches for quality policies that could benefit a broad range of business processes (Microsoft, 2008).

A few of the more well-known quality management methodologies include Six Sigma, LEAN, Total Quality Management (TQM), ISO models, PMI's OPM3, SEI's CMMI, and Balanced Scorecard (BSC). Each of these methodologies or models provides a wealth of distinct and resource-rich information for their quality niche segments. The majority of these methodologies comprised procedures for defining and monitoring key business processes, performing record keeping, checking for output defects, reviewing individual processes, or facilitating continuous improvement. Many businesses combine standards and methodologies from these external sources with their own culture to create local quality polices that align with their own organizational goals. The advantage of using a commercial product as a base for this is that it has been extensively tested and provides quality specifications that are known to be competitive.

16.7.2 Quality Objectives

The first step in establishing quality objectives is to define the specific organizational objectives for quality. As a prerequisite, the organization has to be prepared to answer the following types of questions:

- What is our objective for quality?
- How do we assess the adequacy of internal processes to achieve desired quality?
- What do we need to do in terms of QC to achieve the quality goal?
- What is the procedure to obtain formal product approval from the customer?
- What quality management methodologies should be adopted to meet the customer needs and support the organization's quality goal?

Each of these questions should be dealt with and answered during the quality planning process. From this goal definition, specific operational procedures can be defined and implemented.

Customers seek quality as an important attribute in the product and service they receive. As a result, high-quality products or services are important competitive differentiators. One way of communicating these requirements in a quality business relationship is to create a "*Quality Level Agreement*" (QLA). This provides a formal method to match customer requirements with control level deliverables and takes the ambiguity out of that relationship (Table 16.2).

The two foundation components of the quality plan are the QA and QC plans. The former details "quality assurance procedures, defined quality control activities, and other technical activities that need to be implemented to ensure that the results of the work performed will satisfy the stated performance or acceptance criteria" (EPA, 2001).

Table 16.2 QLA Examples

Metric	*Standard for Final Acceptance*	*High Tolerance*
Design review to specs gap	Less than or equal to 10	More than 15
Earned value total	CPI = 1.0	CPI ≤ 1.2
	SPI = 1.0	SPI ≤ 1.2
Subsystem A defects	2	Fewer than 4
Subsystem B defects	2	Fewer than 4
Final acceptance test defects	7	Fewer than 10

The QC plan is "the overall system of technical activities that measure the attributes and performance of a process, item, or service against defined standards to verify that they meet the specifications established by the customer" (EPA, 2001).

The quality plan then combines the elements of assurance and control into an organization-specific quality management guideline for the project team. It documents the minimal quality requirements, data collection, measurement and analysis activities, QC procedures, and procedures for communicating and correcting quality defects. It also outlines roles and responsibilities for ensuring proper implementation. Each organization should have a standard quality plan that serves as a basic minimal starting point specific to the strategic goals of that organization, their industry, and the products and services that they offer. From this base, it is the project team's responsibility to identify and address any gaps between customer specifications and that of the standard quality plan.

There are a number of specific quality management methodologies that an organization may choose to shape the foundation of its quality plan. Documentation of quality objectives should be seen as an elaboration of quality management principles. These objectives establish the structure required to develop procedures and goals for QC, QA, and quality improvement. It is important to detail the differences between these elements in order to appreciate their relationship and impact on the organization.

16.8 Quality Management Components

From these somewhat abstract perspectives of quality, one can look at processes to define a simpler, more concrete framework for quality management at an enterprise-wide level. This overarching high-level model includes the following five stages—quality definition, quality planning, QC, QA, and quality delivery (customer delight). The *PMBOK® Guide* does not explicitly define the first and last stage, but its model concepts fit this life cycle view.

16.9 Quality Definition

The point has been made earlier that quality definition is customer oriented. In order for this to occur the first step in the process is to produce an understandable specification document that the customer agrees with. The list below summarizes some useful practices for obtaining requirements:

1. Define the goal clearly at the start in the project scope statement. From this, the project team must translate this into a technical deliverable goal in such a manner that meets the customer's product or service needs. The problem with this approach is textual language is easy to misinterpret, so this process must iterate until both parties agree on the translation.
2. Prototype models. Users learn more by being able to try out or play with a sample or prototype rather than verbalizing those requirements.
3. Use formal focus groups and requirements definition methods. This requires mature documentation methods.
4. Learn how to perform good user surveys. Good survey documents are harder to develop than one would think.
5. Study the results. Spend time analyzing the data for trends and variances in views.
6. Test your results. Bring customer or future users in for a review of the results (subsystem or final). Using a scale or working prototype that emulates the survey is one interesting approach. If that is not feasible a story-board walk-through can be effective.

Various industry organizations outline the characteristics of quality specifications in regard to documentation characteristics. A well-written quality specification should contain the general attributes summarized in Table 16.3.

Table 16.3 Characteristics of Quality Specifications

Characteristic	*Description*
Complete	Ensure that all attributes that deal with customer satisfaction are included, defined, and given measurable specifications.
Consistent	Should contain no internal contradictions across the various categories.
Feasible	Should deal with the technical and logistical feasibility of its development.
Modifiable	Organized in such a manner that it can be kept current over time.
Necessary	Each defined requirement should be assessed to ensure that it adds value to the customer.
Prioritized	Requirements are ranked based on value. Priority coding is recommended for this purpose.
Correct	Language of the specification accurately reflects customers' needs.
Testable	Each requirement must be defined in a way that allows for one or more tests of either process or product that will ensure conformance or detect an error.
Traceable	Each element is uniquely identified so that its origin and purpose can be traced through the life cycle to ensure that it is properly incorporated.
Unambiguous	Each requirement is not prone to multiple interpretations.

16.10 Implementing a Quality Plan

Quality planning includes the required work to be performed to organize and lay out a plan for all five process areas. Some of the planning work begins even before requirements definition is finalized. After the requirements specifications are approved by the project sponsor, future users, and the project team, it is then possible to complete the definition of quality management actions related to reviews, inspections, and tests. These definitions are focused on more than confirming product validity. They also are concerned with processes for rework, scrap, and process improvement.

The quality planning process does not end with the planning stage. As the product is developed and delivered any information obtained about gaps in quality being delivered is reviewed for inclusion in the plan. By making use of what is learned during the life cycle and feeding that knowledge into ongoing quality planning and then implementing those plans, we energize the continuous improvement cycle. The term "customer delight" used earlier may be a little too much hype, but it certainly has the flavor that a quality organization needs.

16.11 Quality Assurance

QA is defined as the *assessment process* related to a set of planned and systematic activities to ensure that a product or a service will satisfy the standards of quality established by the organization and those required by the project. QA covers all activities from design, development, production, installation, servicing, and documentation. This role represents a vital and important part of the overall quality management process. It is designed to ensure that the operational environment is capable of producing the desired outcome. The QA process utilizes various techniques and methods to ensure that the expected quality level will be achieved. Stated another way, it evaluates whether the process design or even the underlying development process is capable of producing the required quality. QA covers all activities starting from design, planning, development, production, and installation to ensure that the necessary quality elements are in place. It also deals with all levels of the organization, starting from upper management down to the lowest organizational level. QA's goal is to ensure that the organization's processes are appropriate to produce the defined deliverables. To support this, project quality plans are needed for all related functions and organizational levels to show what is required.

It is important to recognize that quality does not just occur, but requires a technical management activity. The QA function requires technical skills to examine all operational details regarding delivery of products and their services. QA processes use many methods and tools to accomplish this role. One of the most widely used models is the PDCA approach, also known as the Shewhart cycle. This is an iterative four-step problem-solving process first described by Walter Shewhart in the 1930s and popularized by Edwards Deming in the 1940s and beyond. The meaning of the PDCA acronym is explained as follows:

Plan—This phase establishes the methodologies, tools, objectives, and processes that are necessary to deliver the resultant product in accordance with the specifications given by the manufacturer.

Do—The execution processes required to implement the plan.

Check—The process that checks, monitors, and evaluates all the processes and their output results against the set of objectives and specifications. From these data, status is reported.

Act—This stage reviews the outputs from the other three stages (Plan–Do–Check) and defines modifications d in order to improve the process according to the set standards.

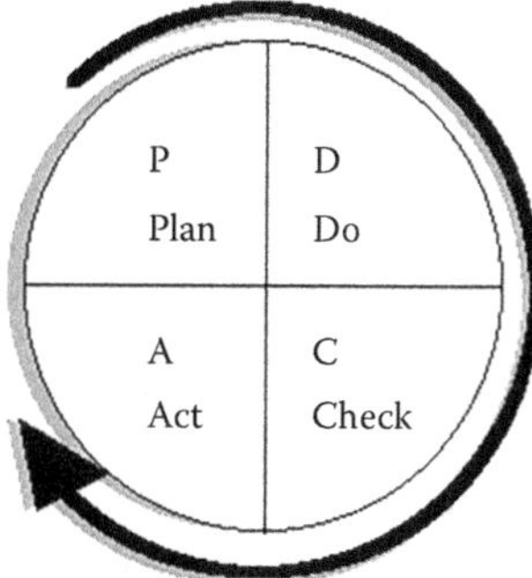

Figure 16.1 PDCA model.

The basic concept behind this method is to monitor all processes and continuously improve the quality standards of the organization. Interestingly, this same model was the foundation used to formulate the *PMBOK® Guide* and many other lesser-known project life cycles. Figure 16.1 shows the four steps as a recurring circle, meaning that the process continues forever.

QA may also include activities that investigate business processes to ensure that they adequately maintain a desired quality. Lastly, QA focuses on detailed process elements such as documentation and subsequent business processes that define the quality requirements specified by an organization.

16.12 Quality Control

In contrast to QA, QC comprises activities that *measure* the quality of a finished product, subassembly, or process. QC involves activities such as inspections, reviews, and tests that collectively ensure the quality of a product. From this measurement the QC team evaluates expected and unexpected variations of the finished product. The measurement procedures are designed to ensure that the project deliverables adhere to the defined specifications. The foundation of QC is a defined set of specifications and a procedure for evaluating them (for more detail on this, see http://www.qualityadvisor.com/sqc/start.htm).

16.13 QA versus QC Operational Roles

QC is a companion process to QA and the two are often labeled together as QA/QC. The basic delineation between these two activities is that QC focuses on the results of the work performed, whereas QA is concerned with the adequacy of the underlying processes, methodology, and standards in place to create the output. QC involves inspections, reviews, and tests to measure status (Mosaicinc, 2001). Some comparison examples are shown below:

- Many professional organizations design QA and QC template plans to provide an outline of specific review criteria to ensure that a process and companion product quality are consistent with desired outcomes. For example, the EPA defines a QA plan as a written document that describes the QA procedures, QC specifications, and other technical activities that must be implemented to ensure that the results of the project or task to be performed will meet project specifications (EPA, 2001). Basically, the purpose of these plans is to provide the organization with guidance for measurement and assessment of the quality system performance. In this role, it is important to detail the functional differences between QA and QC and their interrelationships. One interesting perspective on these two areas is:

- QA works to ensure that the organization is doing the right things in the right way, whereas
- QC helps to ensure that the results of the work performed meet approved specifications.

In both activities, the goal is to look for ways to improve the output of the process or product. Collectively, QA and QC functions are the operational arm of quality management.

16.14 Quality Gurus

Modern quality management can be traced back to the AT&T manufacturing organization in the latter 1920s where Walter Shewhart worked to develop a statistically based QC model based on sampling theory. This model eventually came to be known as Statistical Quality Control (SQC) and focused on process measurement and evaluation. SQC continues to be used in repetitive processes, but the real contribution from this tandem came from their classical analytical model called PDCA that formed the basis for quality management. Because of Shewhart's conceptual work in these two areas he is often called the Grandfather of Quality, leaving the title of Father of Quality to Edwards Deming who did much to proliferate the quality concepts.

16.14.1 Edwards Deming

Deming's role in the resurrection of Japan's manufacturing infrastructure after World War II was mentioned earlier in the text, but we now need to understand more about what he brought to the field of international quality management.

After WWII Japan's infrastructure and manufacturing capability was destroyed. Deming arrived there in the late 1940s and gained access to senior management who wanted to improve their organizations. From that exposure, and somewhat based on the Shewhart PDCA model, Deming began to guide Japan out of their war-related shambles. Looking at this scenario offers a stark reality to the impact that a long-term cultural quality focus can have. Fact is, Japan has done an amazing job of rebuilding itself from the mid-1940s until the present. Much of the internal management and technical process behind this effort could be called quality management as it is being described here. It is lessons such as this that should help sell what a quality culture can do for not only a country but for a single organization as well.

Because of Deming's success in selling what became known as quality management the world slowly began to understand what he was talking about. Although he was not a great writer anything he did write became gospel theory. One of the classic foundation documents was his 14 points of quality. This early list became an abbreviated view of how to do it. Some of these ideas look somewhat dated now, but are still considered classical views of quality from the master. Five of his original points have clearly stood the test of time and are briefly paraphrased as:

1. Management leadership required
2. Inspection does not create quality

3. Training is needed.
4. Team approach, rather than individual.
5. Elimination of work standards.

Another concept that Deming offered (but never proved) is that 85% of problems in quality are linked to either management or process. Only 15% is linked to the worker (training or morale type issues). Because of his credibility this statistic has never been refuted, nor has anyone offered another view. This was one more way of recognizing that strong leadership is important even if they may not be exactly correct.

It is important to recognize that these points are now more than 60 years old, and a modern comparison does not give due credit to the major impact these had when first introduced. The key point to understand is that these statements eventually changed the way organizations thought about quality. It was some period of time before the U.S. management groups embraced these ideas.

In any case, we credit Deming with being the Father of Quality. He was successful in eventually leading this movement into the rest of the world and much of what we see today in the quality arena can be traced back to his work and writings.

16.14.2 Joseph Juran

Dr. Joseph Juran was the second major thought leader who contributed to the Japan quality movement. His most visible contribution was the *Quality Handbook*, which is now in the fifth edition. Although this bible of quality is significant, his true lasting contribution was an extension of the Deming philosophical view of quality. Juran believed that there were four elements to quality: TQM, quality planning, QC, and quality improvement. Within this structure he saw different levels of the organization having different roles to play. In reviewing his various writings, we see an expansion of the Deming views and one that comes closer to a more contemporary set of notions. For example, the term *customer* is recognized as the driver for quality and he emphasized measurement. Both of these ideas remain in place. A third contribution credited to Juran was the incorporation of the human element into the quality equation. A couple of his other focus points were

- Use of the Pareto tool for identifying problem sources
- Defining quality as *fitness for use*

Many of his ideas evolved gradually over a period of years as he tried to implement the quality concepts in organizations, mostly in Japan. It is important to note that for both Juran and Deming there was a general lack of tools to perform the functions we see today. At this point quality was a somewhat a philosophical concept, but that was enough to get an initial start.

16.14.3 Philip Crosby

It seems as though every successful idea or product needs both a conceptual side and a marketing side. Crosby added the marketing side to the quality movement. Up until his point, the quality movement had been considered only understandable by *quality geeks*. Many believed that quality was overhead and you really could not afford to hire any more inspectors to improve output. Crosby developed his view of quality from previous experience at the Martin Company where he was QC manager for the Pershing Missile Program. In this role, he was credited with cutting the product rejection rate by 25% and scrap costs by 30% through an improved quality program. As a result of this experience he published his 1979 book titled *Quality is Free*. This book described and quantified an example showing how producing good quality actually repaid its cost in subsequent savings. At this point, the U.S. quality environment was recognized as not being up to international par, particularly with the Japanese who were really beginning to show progress in this area. Based on the marketing flavor of free quality the book was widely read and understandable by the masses. From this, U.S. audiences finally seemed to grasp the concept that good quality was necessary for competition and not just overhead. This development stimulated the quality movement takeoff on this side of world. Crosby's mantra for quality was labeled *Zero Defects* and several organizations embraced the idea with organizational programs designed to change the local culture

16.14.4 Kaoru Ishikawa

Ishikawa is not as well-known as the earlier guru group; however, his contributions are equally valuable. Many would recognize his *fishbone* diagram as a tool to analyze problems (see tool section later). What we see in Ishikawa is a man who wanted to measure quality and evaluate how to improve it. If we have to put a label on him it would be *toolsmith*, although he also coined some additional quality philosophies as well. Nevertheless, in Ishikawa we see a technician trying to identify problems and improve output. He led the effort to identify and teach the use of quality tools and documented use of tools as basic to the process (see 7QC in the quality tools section). Ishikawa inbred in his organization the concept that they had to get better every day and one way to do that is to not keep making the same mistakes. He used the fishbone diagram to evaluate problem areas in seeking solutions. This process is now called Root Cause Analysis (RCA) and remains a well-recognized problem-solving technique. The fishbone diagram along with the Pareto maldistribution chart became key tools in improving processes. More on this will be described later in this chapter.

There are many other operational contributions that Ishikawa brought to the quality movement, but he stayed below the international radar and does not get the literature credit that the U.S. trio received.

16.14.5 Genichi Taguchi

Taguchi is another guru whom the world generally knows little about, but many prosper from his contributions. In many ways, his contributions were similar to Ishikawa but in his manufacturing area the contributions have been very significant. For example, he is generally credited with the conceptual design of the Toyota Production System (TPS) that eventually led Toyota to world dominance in auto-manufacturing. His approach optimizes a customer-perceived value versus the design functionality. Another of his ideas is the Design of Experiments technique to evaluate early performance of processes and designs (see Tools section for more).

16.14.6 Armand Feigenbaum

Feigenbaum used statistical techniques at General Electric during World War II to evaluate early jet engine manufacturing. His techniques are titled Total Quality Control and generally fall into the category of an extension of Shewhart's methodologies. He is one of the quality gurus who added more mechanics to the philosophical theory.

16.14.7 Six Sigma

This quality methodology program has exploded on the U.S. quality scene based on high-level management support and great claims of success. It does have a similar history in that it started based on the needs of an organization. The Six Sigma program was launched by Motorola in 1987 with the initial goal being to improve chip manufacturing quality at the company. The Shewhart model called for three sigma (standard deviation) ranges and the new goal was to cut the variability to Six Sigma, thus the name. The engineer typically credited with the creation of this program is Bill Smith, but he died in 1993 before ever knowing the broad impact that this program would have. Therefore, the credit for popularity of the program goes to the host organization and two high-level managers who publicly touted it.

In the Six Sigma case, we have something more akin to an organizational guru than a single individual. Beyond the complex underlying theory and mechanics of this process analysis program, the popularity is often credited to organizational leaders Larry Bossidy of Allied Signal and Jack Welch of General Electric (iSixSigma, 2017). As a result of this high-level sponsorship and advertisement of high economic saving successes, some leading electronic companies such as IBM, DEC, and Texas Instruments launched Six Sigma initiatives in the early 1990s. However, it was not until 1995 when General Electric and Allied Signal launched Six Sigma as a more strategic initiative that a rapid dissemination took place in non-electronic industries all over the world. In early 1997, Samsung and LG Groups in Korea began to introduce Six Sigma within their companies. The primary maturity brought by this tool is its formalization of process and tool kit. We will see a more detailed discussion of this in the tool section later in the chapter.

16.14.8 Other Gurus

Each of the individuals and methodologies mentioned here contributed to moving the concepts of quality along through its reasonably short evolution. There were other pioneers in the quality era that are not credited here. Individuals such as James Harrington and Shigeo Shingo are examples, but our goal is to understand the evolution and the major ideas that have been captured in the classic concepts and how they most impact the project management arena.

16.15 Quality Management Programs

There are a number of well-known quality management methodologies that an organization may choose from in helping to shape the foundation of its internal quality initiatives. The following set of commonly recognized programs will be described here are: TQM, Zero Defects, Six Sigma, Lean methodology and ISO 9000. A brief over-view for each of these follows.

16.15.1 Total Quality Management

This program emphasizes a systematic and integrated organization-wide perspective involving everyone and everything, not just the end products. The heart of the TQM philosophy is the prevention of problems and an emphasis on quality in the design and development of products and processes. A formal quality planning process is integral to the TQM philosophy.

A TQM program strives for one basic aim: providing the best possible services and products to the customers. It also stresses both current quality and the continuous improvement of products and services directed at increasing business and reducing losses due to wasteful practices. The methodology aims at management and employees working together to achieve these goals. "TQM is a management approach for an organization, centered on quality, based on the participation of all its members and aiming at long-term success through customer satisfaction, and benefits to all members of the organization and to society" (ISO 8402:2000). The design focus of TQM is a customer-first orientation rather than focusing on internal activities and constraints (Sharma, 2007). In order to achieve these goals, there is a strong focus on process measurement and controls to identify means of achieving current quality and continuous improvement. The four integrated process component subsets of TQM are derived from Deming's original 14 quality points. Many feel that TQM was the first formal quality management methodology and had a significant international impact on quality perceptions and teaching. To balance this view, we need to recognize that the implementation history of TQM is not all bright. One survey reports that only 36% of organizations that undertook TQM were at least partially successful (John Stark Associates, 2008). This statistic is another way of saying that significantly more than half did NOT successfully implement the program. However, it is also significant to note that organizations that did successfully implement TQM were more successful in the marketplace than their competitors. One final lesson learned in the TQM experience is that these programs are not quick fixes and must be conceived as long-term organizational strategies.

16.15.2 Zero Defects

This concept was the first quality program known to most American organizations. It emerged from Philip Crosby's view that quality defects were not acceptable and everyone should "do things right the first time." Interest in this quality initiative emerged primarily during the period of 1970s.

Philip Crosby coined this phrase in his 1979 book titled "*Quality is Free*" (Crosby, 1979). There were two major contributions to the quality movement that resulted from this event. First, the book made American managers sensitive to the quality topic in recognizing that there was also a significant cost to bad quality. Crosby's view of quality also focused on the idea that errors were not inevitable and could be sorted out and improved. Second, quality output requires conscious work on the part of the organization, even though the idea of "zero defects" is not an achievable goal. We now look at this program as more of a philosophy than a methodology or even a program, but nevertheless it is an important step along the quality trail.

16.15.3 Six Sigma

This program is currently the most popular of the quality programs and encompasses much of what has been learned over the previous 60 years. Based on this, it receives the bulk of discussion here. The two key methodologies embedded in Six Sigma are described by the acronyms DMAIC and DMADV (defined further below). Both of these methods are inspired by Shewhart's PDCA model.

Based on the extremely low defect rate defined for Six Sigma it is a program aimed at the near elimination of defects from every product, process, and transaction. One commonly asked question is "where does this term come from?" Sigma (σ) is a letter in the Greek alphabet that has become the standard statistical symbol to signify variation in data (measure of dispersion). In quality terms sigma describes the variability of a quality measure as defects per unit, parts per million defectives, and variation of output. Classic QC from the original Shewhart era used a three-sigma (3σ) variation to imply a reasonable measure of variation in a process. This meant that 99.7% of the process variations are within this range, which equates to three outputs out of 1000 being outside of this range. When Six Sigma was defined, the allowed level of variation was shrunk to produce no more than 3.4 defects per million. This compares to 66,000 defectives that would have been allowed in the traditional model. Tightening the operational performance to this degree has drastic process quality implications. For this reason, Six Sigma is viewed as more than an incremental change in quality perspective.

Pursuit of the Six Sigma model implies three things: statistical measurement, management strategy, and a quality culture. In practice, it also requires a focused target established at a high level in the organization. In this mode, it is a new strategic process under the leadership of top-level management to create quality innovation and total customer satisfaction. It provides a means of doing things right the first time and working smarter by using data information.

In many organizations, the Six Sigma methodology is simply defined as a measure of quality that strives for near perfection. But the statistical implications of a Six Sigma program go well beyond the qualitative customer-perceptible defects. It is a methodology that is well rooted in mathematics and statistics. If the design goal is to produce no more than 3.4 defective parts-per-million, the process variation has a very narrow band between the upper and lower control points. Looking at variation in this way means that we are concerned with only six standard deviations of variance, hence, the name Six Sigma. This represents a great leap forward in terms of process management and the underlying quality culture of an organization.

As the sigma value increases the level of acceptable defects declines, reaching a point that essentially equates to *zero defects*. Certainly, the attitude of the organization culture must view it that way. Figure 16.2 shows the effect on allowable process variation changes from three-to-six Sigma.

There are several reasons for the international popularity of Six Sigma. First, Six Sigma is regarded as a fresh quality management strategy that incorporates the best of earlier programs such as TQC, TQM, and others. In a sense, we can view the high-level evolution towards of Six Sigma as shown in Figure 16.3.

The second driver for Six Sigma popularity comes from its view as having a more robust systematic, scientific, statistical, and smarter (called 4Ss) approach for management innovation that is better aligned for use in a knowledge-based information society.

Six Sigma methodology represents an integration of four elements—customer, process, manpower, and strategy—to provide managed innovation. The tools and methodology of Six

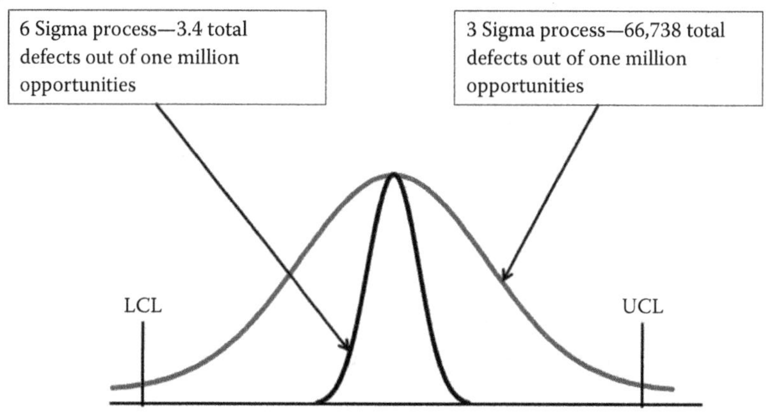

Figure 16.2 Statistical interpretation of Six Sigma.

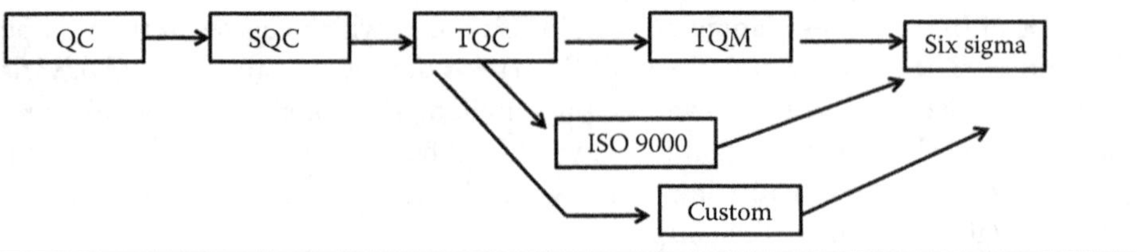

Figure 16.3 Six Sigma evolution.

Sigma provide a scientific and statistical basis for quality assessment and the underlying defined methods allow comparisons among all processes to describe the state of a process. Through this analysis it is possible to discern what path to follow to achieve process innovation and customer satisfaction.

Third, Six Sigma provides a formal training method that has been missing in previous programs. It employs a belt certification system in which the levels of mastery are classified as green belt, black belt, master black belt, and champion. As a person obtains certain training they will be recognized with a belt level. It is common to require at least a black belt level to lead a Six Sigma project team and several green belts would be mentored as part of that team.

Fourth, the many published Six Sigma success stories have been a major stimulus for organizations to learn more about the technique. Nothing spreads in organizations more than the claim of economic success with a new idea.

Lastly, Six Sigma is capable of embracing common problem elements facing organizations today. These are the 3Cs of *change, customer focus, and competition*. The pace of technological change during the last decade has been unprecedented, and the speed of change in the new millennium is perceived to be even faster. Most notably, economic power is now in the hands of an increasingly sophisticated customer who has access to more quality-related information than ever before. The producer-oriented monopolistic industrial society is over, and the customer-oriented information society is the new model. At this point, the customer has all the power to select competitive sources for order, evaluation, and purchase of their goods and services. This is especially obvious in the e-business domain. Ready availability of comparative information related to quality and price is ever-increasing through international Internet access. Second-rate quality goods and service cannot survive in such an environment. With all these trends Six Sigma is recognized as a popular tool for organizations to use in identifying and pursuing quality improvements. Six Sigma includes two key defined process methodologies called DMAIC and DMADV.

DMAIC is used to evaluate existing business processes, and DMADV is used to formulate new product or process designs for predictable, defect-free performance. The DMAIC methodology consists of the following five steps:

1. **D**efine the process improvement goals consistent with customer demands and enterprise strategy.
2. **M**easure the current process and collect relevant data for future comparison.
3. **A**nalyze to verify relationship and causality of factors, determine the key relationships, and ensure that all factors have been considered.
4. **I**mprove or optimize the process using techniques like Design of Experiments.
5. **C**ontrol to ensure that any variances are corrected before they result in defects. Set up pilot runs to establish process capability, transition to production, and thereafter continuously measure the process and institute control mechanisms.

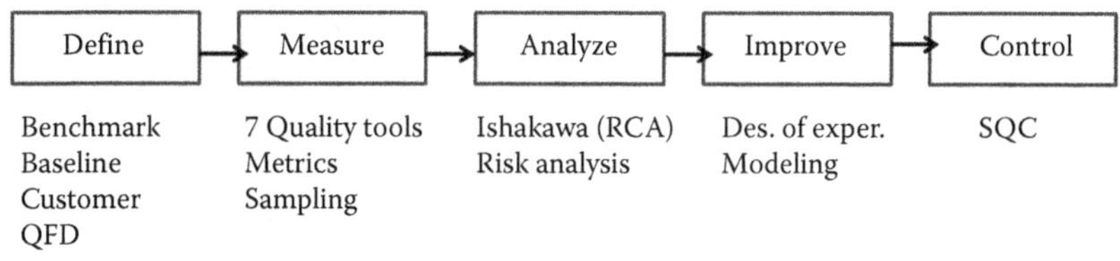

Figure 16.4 DMAIC framework.

Figure 16.4 expands this basic view by showing a sample of some of the tools and techniques that are employed in each of these steps.

The companion DMADV methodology has a set of steps similar to DMAIC.

1. **D**efine the goals of the design activity consistent with customer demands and enterprise strategy.
2. **M**easure and identify critical to quality (CTQ), product capabilities, production process capability, and risk assessments.
3. **A**nalyze to develop and design alternatives, create high-level design, and evaluate design capability to select the best design.
4. **D**esign details, optimize the design, and plan for design verification.
5. **V**erify the design, set up pilot runs, implement production process, and handover to process owners.

As far as a formal corporate program framework is concerned, Six Sigma embodies five elements that have been recognized in other quality initiatives. These are top-level management commitment, training schemes, project team activities, measurement systems, and stakeholder involvement.

The DMAIC process will be described in more detail here in order to obtain a better sense of what Six Sigma involves. This process was designed to deal with a problematic process related to a product and/or service in order to improve its cost, quality, and/or characteristics. Such fixes often include defect rates, failure areas, excess process steps, and deterioration. The five defined steps are Define, Measure, Analyze, Improve, and Control. This method is primarily based on the application of statistical process control, quality tools, and process capability analysis. It is not intended to be a product development methodology, although it can be used to help redesign any process. Let us briefly review each of the five steps, their requirements, and typical combinations of tool–task–deliverables.

The objectives of the *define* step (D) are twofold: to confirm the existence of a problem or opportunity and to define the improvement project boundaries and goals. Formal goals are identified in measurable terms. This is very similar to the initiation process outlined for a typical project. Just as in all projects, scope definition for this effort is critical to control the project. This step produces the following deliverables:

1. Identify and quantify the problem or opportunity.
2. Develop a high-level process map.
3. Gather business requirements.
4. Develop a communication plan.
5. Finalize the project charter.
6. Select a project sponsor and members.
7. Identify stakeholders.
8. Gain approval and necessary funding to conduct the DMAIC project.

The *measurement* step (M) gathers the necessary data to understand and measure the current state.

The *analyze* step (A) identifies the root cause of the problem, coming from the classical theory of Ishikawa. From this definition the team delves into the operational details in order to enhance its understanding of the problem. Analytical tools are used in this step to dissect the root cause of process variability and separate the *vital few inputs from the trivial many* (Pareto maldistribution).

The fourth implementation step (I) involves developing solutions targeted at confirmed causes and seeking an improvement strategy. The two primary objectives are to verify that the confirmed causes (or critical inputs) are statistically significant and to optimize the process or product/service with the defined improvements. Prioritization and validation are important components in selecting a recommended fix to the problem. The short list of tasks within this step includes the following:

1. Develop potential improvements or solutions for root causes.
2. Develop evaluation criteria.
3. Select and implement the improved process and metrics.
4. Measure results.
5. Evaluate whether improvements meet targets.
6. Evaluate risk.

The fifth and final step is to complete (C) the analysis and transition of the improved process to the process owner with procedures for maintaining the improvements as an ongoing operation. An essential part of this activity is to verify the ability to sustain the solution in the operations phase. A summary list of tasks to be completed within this step follows:

1. Document the new or improved process and measurements.
2. Validate collection systems along with repeatability and reproducibility of metrics in the new operational environment.
3. Define the control plan and its supporting plans.
4. Communications plan outlining the improvements and operational changes to the customers and stakeholders.
5. Implementation plan.
6. Risk management (and response) plan.
7. Cost/benefit plan.
8. Change management plan.
9. Train the operational stakeholders (process owner and players).
10. Establish the tracking procedure in an operational environment.
11. Monitor implementation.
12. Validate and stabilize performance gains.
13. Jointly audit the results and confirm financials.

Six Sigma methodologies have nurtured broad interest in improving both products and processes. In many ways, this quality program is an extension of previous ones. Park offers the following summarization of Six Sigma attributes (Park, 2003, p. 126):

- Bottom-line business results delivered
- Senior management leadership role defined in the process
- Disciplined approaches (DMAIC and DMADV)

- Rapid completion of target actions
- Clearly defined measures of success
- Defined roles for participants
- Clear focus on customers and processes
- Use of sound statistical tools

16.15.4 ISO 9000

The International Standards Organization (ISO) is chartered to manage a host of public standards. ISO 9000 is one of the most visible of these. This is an internationally known quality program that defines the organizational requirements for development and documentation of a quality program. This program is defined as:

"The ISO 9000 family addresses various aspects of quality management and contains some of ISO's most recognized standards. The standards provide guidance and tools for companies and organizations who want to ensure that their products and services consistently meet customer's requirements, and that quality is consistently improved" (ISO 9000).

16.16 *PMBOK® Guide* Quality Process Model

The Project Management Institute (PMI) model quality management knowledge area (KA) is philosophically aligned with the models and terminology described here. Three basic quality processes are outlined: quality planning, QA, and QC. Process specifications for each are consistent with the definitions described in the standard models, except that these processes are focused on the project level only. Hence, quality planning would address how the project would deal with specific quality standards for that specific project.

The guide's QA and QC processes require the same type of project customization as the high-level quality planning model. The only uniqueness of the guide's approach is in its level of specificity for the project. For example, each of the three-quality processes has defined inputs, tools and techniques, and outputs. Embedded in these are tangible management activities or artifacts such as

- A guiding management plan
- Quality metrics
- Quality reports
- Checklists
- Testing and evaluation documents
- Quality baseline
- Change management activities

16.17 An Evolving Quality Program

Evolving out of the Six Sigma and Toyota quality environments is a new perspective on quality titled *Lean*. This is an attractive sounding term and is now being attached to other quality ideas such as Six Sigma and manufacturing. Common themes are to achieve precise higher customer value—goods and services with higher quality and fewer defects—less human effort, less space, less capital, and less time than the traditional system of mass production (see www.lean.org for more details on this). At this point the term is more of a philosophy, but there are growing examples where it has been successfully utilized to improve a process. The Toyota Production System (TPS) is in concert with this idea, as are Just-In-Time (JIT) manufacturing processes. One of the more interesting views of this new term is to note the broad impact that the quality movement now has on all business environments regardless of the name attached to the initiative.

16.18 Evaluating Quality

There are several common techniques used to measure quality. Each of the three methods/techniques summarized below have a role in aiding organizations in their quest for quality. The following three items selected for this discussion:

- Benchmarking
- Continuous improvement
- Failure modes and effects analysis

16.18.1 Benchmarking

> (Def.)... benchmarking ... [is] ... "the process of identifying, understanding, and adapting outstanding practices and processes from organizations anywhere in the world to help your organization improve its performance."
>
> —*American Productivity & Quality Center*

16.18.1.1 Benchmarking Process

The process of benchmarking represents a strategic management process in which an organization evaluates its processes with respect to other competitors or industry standards. By doing this type of comparison the organization can evaluate areas in which they need to seek improvement for competitive purposes. Benchmarking techniques use both quantitative and qualitative standard measurements for comparison with other organizations in order to gain a perspective on organizational performance. Benchmarking can be performed by independent consumer-oriented organizations or within the organization. Obviously, obtaining valid data is the major issue with this type of analysis (Reh, 2017).

Benchmarking can provide qualitative and quantitative data to answer various process and product questions. Perhaps more important, benchmarking can offer guidance on how to achieve improved results. When performed across major competitors it provides an external reference and best practices on which to base evaluations and standards to design work processes.

> Benchmarking is the search for best practices, the ones that will lead to superior performance. Establishing operating targets based on the best possible industry practices is a critical component in the success of every organization.
>
> *(Camp, 1995, p. 4)*

Benchmarking is also a competitive analysis tool used to measure and compare the organization's internal processes or products in terms of cost, time, or quality against similar factors from another competitive or best-in-class organization. These results lead to the identification, understanding, and adaptation of product and process targets. Although benchmarking within the same industry is important since the enterprise should have a good understanding of its own business, it is even more essential to compare customer and external perceptions of products and services.

16.18.1.2 Types of Benchmarking

There are essentially three types of benchmarking: strategic, data-based, and process (ASQ, 2008). They differ depending on the type of information being gathered. Strategic benchmarking looks at the strategies that companies use to compete. A second goal is to focus on uncovering how well other companies perform in comparison with you and others, and how they achieve this performance. This requires an analysis of performance and process data (ASQ, 2008). Many business processes are common throughout industries. For example, NASA has the same basic HR requirements for hiring and developing employees as does American Express. Likewise, British Telecom has the same customer satisfaction survey process as Brooklyn Union Gas. Although completely different industries, all essentially have the same requirements, therefore, comparable benchmarking metrics are useful.

J. D. Power and Associates (www.jdpower.com) is a well-known commercial benchmarking organization that surveys various industries with the goal of comparing products. One of the most read of these is the automobile industry benchmark outlining the comparative "quality" of vehicles. This report documents defects, issues, and malfunctions experienced by owners during the first 90 days of vehicle ownership, and more. This report has an impact on purchasing and producer activity. In fact, the study shows that the automobile industry quality trend has been to improve quality metrics at a rate of about 6% per year on average. The J. D. Power 2017 auto study reports that new vehicle quality has improved significantly over the past three years. They also note that automobile problem counts drop by 50% every seven to eight years (J. D. Power, 2017). Further, in these benchmarking surveys one can see individual car rating in comparison to other manufacturers. Even though this is a highly specialized example, it does show what benchmarking can do to the quality requirements definition process. In this case, all auto manufacturers are chasing after industry leaders who continue to profit in the market because of their reputation.

16.19 Continuous Improvement

This term represents more of a philosophy than a set of tools or techniques. The key idea for quality culture of an organization is to sell the idea that today's quality is not good enough for the future. Therefore, the focus must be on continually and incrementally moving to new quality levels that "excite" the customer. This can be measured using resource or performance efficiency, in competitive functionality in the product. In order to accomplish this goal, processes and methods of production or service delivery are tested continuously and shortcomings removed, thus improving the process or product in a continuous manner.

16.20 Failure Mode and Effect Analysis

This procedure is used with physical products to analyze failure characteristics in the design. The results of these tests classify the impact of the failure and rationalize strategies to improve taking into account the quality goals versus the cost. Failure causes can result from any error or defect in the process, design, or execution (manufacture) of a product. Effect analysis refers to studying the consequences of those failures in regard to the customer experience with the product. This type of activity goes beyond the process and inspection-type components in that it uncovers the limits of the product design. Modern examples of this would be impacting passengers in a car crash test, or tests to evaluate mean time to failure for an item. The performance of a product is checked and tested under increasing stress until it fails to work. This exposes the weakest points of the product as it is vibrated, dropped, heated, or otherwise abused. From these tests, the quality management team can decide whether it is viable to improve the design or process in order to improve the resulting product. Sometimes small changes in a product or process can have significant impact on the resulting overall quality of the product.

16.21 Quality Tools

As the quality movement evolved from a more philosophical bent in the latter 1940s to a more analytical one later, the need for measurement and analysis support tools emerged. Around 1960, a group of Japanese quality professionals defined a core set of tools for general use. Over the years since then, many such visual, statistical, and descriptive tools have been developed and used. In more recent times, maturation of tool usage grew significantly in the various life cycle processes such as those defined by Six Sigma's DMAIC and DMADV structure. Within each of these stages various tools and techniques are used. A reasonable cross-section of quality-oriented tools will be described in this section. The first set of tools described here is classified as the core quality tool kit, which is represented by seven tools (a.k.a. 7QC). However, actually eight tools are shown in this list because some industries replace stratification (7A) with flowcharting (7B). Collectively, these tools are used to review various quality aspects; however, their primary role is in quality measurement and analysis activities. The core tool set is as follows:

1. Cause and effect
2. Check sheet
3. Control chart
4. Histogram
5. Pareto
6. Scatter

7A. Stratification
7B. Process flowchart (process mapping)

Sung Park offers an excellent overview of this area in *Six Sigma for Quality and Productivity Promotion* (Park, 2003).

1. *Cause-and-effect diagram.* The cause-and-effect diagram is an effective tool for use in the problem-solving process. It is also known as the Ishikawa or fishbone diagram. This problem-solving technique is useful to trigger ideas and promote a balanced approach in group brainstorming sessions where individuals list the perceived sources (causes) with respect to outcomes (effect). Figure 16.5 illustrates how this tool is used.

   In this example, the variance target is shown in the box on the right-hand side, and the potential causal areas are listed in boxes on the lines. Essentially, the box is the effect and

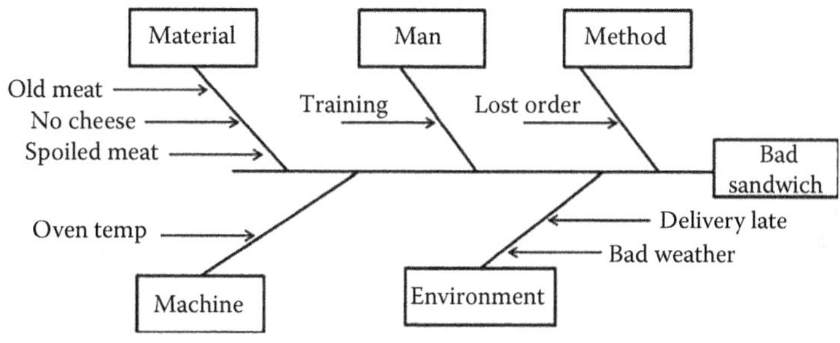

Figure 16.5 Example of fishbone diagram.

the notes on the various lines are meant to portray possible causal factors from that area (i.e., man, machine, etc.). When constructing a manufacturing-oriented diagram, it is often appropriate to consider six main causal areas that can contribute to an outcome response (effect). These are called the 5Ms (man, machine, material, method, and measurement), plus the environment.

In Figure 16.5, the sample diagram models the RCA of a hypothetical problem of producing a bad sandwich. In this case, potential causal factors are collected for each of the items and attached to the figure. Obviously, in this case the root cause would not be difficult to identify, but the example does show the process in understandable form.

2. *Check sheet.* A check sheet is a template used for data collection of any desired characteristics of a process or product. It is frequently used in the measurement phase of the DMAIC process.
3. *Control chart.* The control chart is a very important tool in the "AIC" phases of DMAIC. In the analysis phase, control charts are often used to judge whether the process output is in the predictable range. In the improve phase, it aids in providing evidence of special causes of variation so that they can be acted upon. In the control phase, it is used to verify that the performance of the process is under control. Recall that the original control chart was first described in the quality context proposed by Walter Shewhart in 1924 as a core component of his SQC model. Since that time the tool has been used extensively in industries to evaluate repetitive processes. These control charts offer an excellent means to study process variation. Observations failing outside of the control bands often give early identification of an unexplained or abnormal variation so that there can be timely corrective action before the process goes out of control and unusable products produced. Shewhart's control charts track processes by plotting data over time as shown in Figure 16.6.
4. *Histogram.* It is meaningful to present data in a form that visually illustrates the frequency of a value's occurrence. During the analysis phase, histograms are commonly applied to help understand the distribution of the data by value. The classic example of a histogram is a document of the values thrown by two dice over 200 observations. Each value would be shown on the x-axis (i.e., 1–12) and the corresponding number of times each value was thrown would be represented by a vertical bar (y-axis). If these dice were "honest" we would expect to see a bell curve for this experiment. The typical role of a histogram is to simply document the results with no conclusion.
5. *Pareto chart.* An Italian economist originally derived the Pareto chart in the later 1800s to describe the maldistribution of incomes across the population. Juran reintroduced it to the quality world in the 1940s as a way to distinguish the "vital few from the trivial many." It is

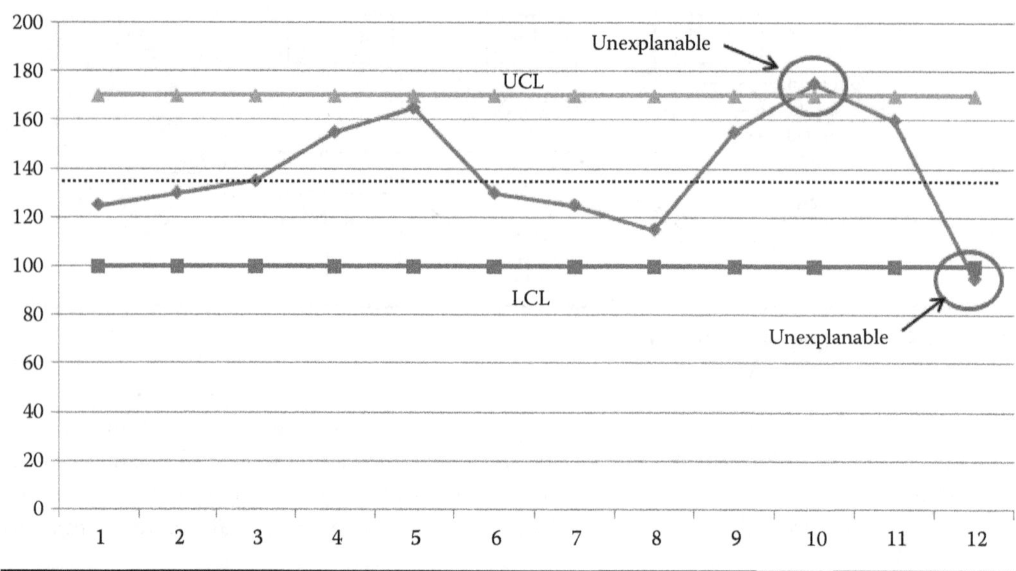

Figure 16.6 Statistical quality control chart.

now better known as the *80/20 rule*—80% of the problems stem from 20% of the causes. The Pareto chart has many implications both in the quality arena and elsewhere. One of its quality applications is for selecting appropriate improvement targets during the define phase. Figure 16.7 shows a sample format for this chart.

6. *Scatter diagram.* A scatter diagram is a useful way to show a display between two factors plotted on a *xy*-axis. An important feature of the scatter plot is its visualization of a relationship pattern. As part of the improve phase one often searches the collected data for *X* values that have a special influence on corresponding *Y* values. By examining the status of such relationships, it is possible to identify input variables that appear to have causal relationships.

7A. *Stratification. This* tool is used to split collected data into subgroups in order to determine if any contain special cause variation. Using this method, data from different sources in a process can be separated and analyzed individually. Stratification is mainly used in the analysis phase to organize data in the search for special cause variation.

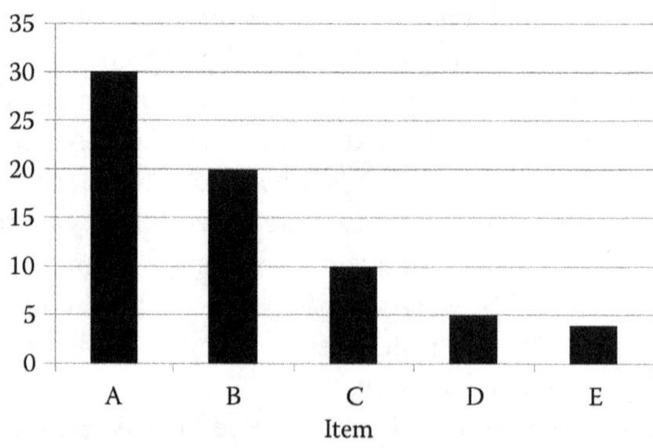

Figure 16.7 Sample Pareto chart.

7B. *Process flowchart and process mapping.* Some types of processes and structures can be better understood through visualization of flow patterns. A flowchart is a method used to provide a picture of the steps and relationships in a process. This technique would be considered one of the classical diagnostic tools used in areas such as information systems, quality management systems, and employee procedural handbooks. The flowchart can also be used in the measurement phase as a procedural aid, as well as in the analysis phase for identifying improvement potential compared to similar processes. It can be useful in the control phase to aid in describing new processes and would help guide those executing that process.

16.22 Other Quality Analysis Techniques

This final set of techniques has been developed to support various aspects of the quality process. Three additional quality technique analysis examples are notable in their use of tools and for that reason they need to be included in our discussion. These are design of experiments, quality function deployment (QFD), and quality auditing.

16.22.1 Design of Experiments

This is a quality planning technique that helps identify which variables have the most influence on the overall outcome of a process. Understanding which variables affect an outcome is a very important part of quality planning and product design. Quality planning involves communicating the correct actions for ensuring quality in a format that is understandable and complete. In quality planning for projects, it is important to describe important factors that directly contribute to meeting customer's requirements, such as:

- Organizational policies related to quality,
- Particular elements in a project's scope statement,
- Standards and regulations that are defined in the project requirements.

A second and even more specific use of design of experiments comes in the specification of untested or critical elements in the design. If a particular element is specified to perform in some way, but has been tested in that mode it makes sense to design some type of early test to confirm that it will perform Boeing 777 Dreamliner design engineers questioned the use of carbon fiber to build an airplane of that size given that no one had ever done this. To counter this, they designed a wing test and proceeded to test the strength of the wing before it was committed into the final design. That is a classic use of the technique and one that every technical project manager should be sensitive to.

16.22.2 Quality Function Deployment

QFD is a structured technique to ensure that customer requirements are included in the design of products and processes. In the Six Sigma methodology, QFD is mainly applied in improvement projects related to the redesign of products and processes (Park, 2003). Shigeru Mizuno and Yoji Akao originally developed this technique in Japan during the late 1960s. It was first applied in shipbuilding in 1972 and then migrated into the Japanese auto industry some years later. It eventually was used in U.S. manufacturing in the mid-1980s.

The QFD process is an important technique for use in product design. Its process relies heavily on a formal translation of customer requirements into product and process characteristics including specified target values. Basically, QFD can be divided into four phases:

Phase 1: A market analysis to establish knowledge about current customer requirements and the related translation into product characteristics.
Phase 2: Translation of critical product characteristics into component characteristics, that is, the product's parts.
Phase 3: Translation of critical component characteristics into process characteristics.
Phase 4: Translation of critical process characteristics into production characteristics, that is, instructions and measurements.

These four phases embody four standard units of analysis that evolve in the following order: customer requirements, product characteristics, component characteristics, and production.

Quality audits. This review technique is used to confirm that the system is working and producing output as required. The two forms of audit are classified as internal and external.
Internal audits. The goal of the internal audit program is to review the entire organizational quality system specific assessments and shall include at least one management review of the overall effectiveness of the quality system. These are typically conducted at scheduled intervals. The following areas should be reviewed as part of the project schedule.
Documentation audit. This will include a review of the quality manual, all control documents, and records.
Management responsibility audit. This includes a planning and management review to ensure that management is committed to the company's policies and values.
Resource management audit. This focuses on items such as employee turnover and competency of personnel. Outsourcing will also be included for areas that are subcontracted.
Product realization audit. This covers a wide array of business processes and customer-related processes such as customer communication and other related activities.
Design and development audit. This includes areas such as planning, inputs, outputs, design review, verification, and validation. This audit is one of the most important to review owing to the design changes that typically occur. Scope creep and budget issues usually impact these areas if the design changes are not conducted according to the outlined processes.
Purchasing audit. This focuses on the purchasing process and the verification of purchased products as outlined in the quality system. The company must be able to verify that the products purchased do not turn into scrap. Product and service provisions as well as the control of measuring devices are also included in this area.
General audit. This includes all remaining areas such as customer satisfaction and the monitoring and measuring of processes. The audit process will also identify the need for continuous improvement and will include both corrective actions and preventative actions to eliminate further discrepancies in the future.
External audits. This will be conducted on all external suppliers and vendors in order to evaluate whether the products delivered will meet company specifications. This is normally a graded level audit. For example, the more critical suppliers require a detailed audit classified by letter "A" and the less critical suppliers will be identified as a "B" supplier. This method may

also be used for service companies. All vendors graded of high importance will be required to have a quality system in place and must be able to demonstrate their effectiveness during the audit and should be able to meet many of the requirements of the internal audit criteria as mentioned above.

16.23 Organizational Roles and Responsibilities

The process of creating a quality organization would appear to be somewhat mechanical from the discussion thus far; however, experience shows that this is not the case. Installing a quality culture in an organization is difficult for many reasons. Probably the most obvious being that it takes time and the results may not show for some period. If management is not convinced that it is worthwhile they will lose interest and pull resources to other activities. If we assume that the goal is to produce such an organization there are clear steps in that process.

The first step in creating a quality organization is to convince senior management that it is a worthy goal. They must be the formal initiator and driver for the subsequent activities required. As with all major projects, a formal definition of goals is necessary. In this case, the goal definition involves approving a policy document that includes a statement or definition of the organization's quality objectives. This document should also address what will be done to comply with the standard after implementation (Besterfield et al., 1995). The intent of the quality program should be formally documented with a goal of making the quality objectives clear, precise, and easy to understand. In this regard, the formal quality policy is considered to be the foundation for a strategic roadmap of continuing quality improvement and business success. Included in the document are key processes needed for the quality management system and explanations showing how the overall system will be applied across the organization.

According to the ISO process, creation of the operational system first involves gathering all existing policies, procedures, work instructions, and forms that are presently in use. Every document should be reviewed and approved for use by the management and made to fit into one of the elements. As the new documents are produced, the implementation team becomes the review committee. As changes are necessary, suggestions are made and reviewed with the team (QSAE, 2008).

From an organizational structure point of view, some management representative should be placed formally in charge of shepherding the quality implementation process through the entire structure. Implementation of the quality system should involve everyone in the organization. Once the formal process definition has been communicated to the functional management groups, the next step is to develop a quality awareness program. This process will affect the day-to-day operations and the potential benefits (QSAE, 2008). After everyone has been informed of the organization's intentions to develop the quality system, an implementation team should be assembled, with members drawn from all levels and areas of the organization.

Successful implementation of a quality system requires full support of the organization from the top to the very lowest levels. It must be driven by a formally documented and approved system. Quality emphasis is placed on problem prevention, rather than detection (inspection), in all organizational areas from customer sales through installation and service after delivery. Appropriate responsibility and authority must be defined for all personnel affecting quality, and they must be given the freedom and authority to take the actions necessary to prevent proliferation of nonconforming products or services. This activity includes RCA and problem correction. Management review is required to ensure that the system remains effective and this process makes use of information from customers and internal audits, as well as process and product performance. From the results of these reviews, management can determine if a change is required in the organizational structure or the operations of the organization to improve the quality system.

16.24 Implementation Issues in Quality Management

The early quality process was strongly associated with two important aspects: measurement and inspection activity. However, the contemporary concept of quality management now is expanding into a broader perception. Today, it is associated with a wide variety of indicators to describe perfection, consistency, waste elimination, delivery time, policies, procedure compliance, and customer satisfaction, to name a few. All of these factors relate to the development of a product or service designed to be *fit for use* and to ensure that the execution process is meeting customer needs.

The modern purpose of quality management is to ensure that the product and services meet and even customer's expectations. This concept is finally consolidated during the execution phase of the process. Quality management is an important element of the planning phase since it provides the framework and direction for the execution of quality. However, it is during the execution phase of the project where the conceptual philosophy of project management is matched with the actual deliver of quality.

The perception of quality can be quite variable among stakeholders. Therefore, it is necessary to formalize a general understanding between these perceptions and some measurable criteria for control purposes. Quality management is implicitly associated with the parameters used to compare the product quality with these predetermined standards. There are several QC and QA techniques that are utilized in performing this activity is quality testing which is based on compliance with a standard. Therefore, effective quality measurement requires that the standard be accurate. When the measurement of the goods or service does not fit the standard, it creates a variance, which needs to be corrected or modified in order to meet customer expectations. There are several areas where these discrepancies can occur:

- *Misalignment of customer expectations and translated specifications.* The project team might believe that they understand the customer's perception of compliance, but in reality this might not be the case. As a result, all the subsequent deliverables would be flawed.
- *Mismatch between quality standards and defined specifications.* The resulting design does not properly translate the customer requirements.
- *Inconsistency between designed and actual specifications.* This implies that manufacturing and engineering designs must execute quality in a coalescent effort.
- *False expectations by customers.* Customers should only be promised what can realistically be produced based on the actual capacity of the quality of the deliverables.

All identified discrepancies should be exhaustively evaluated throughout the life cycle of the project. The goal in performing these reviews supports the organizational goals of delivering promised project performance that meets or exceeds customer's expectations. There is no known better visible example of the merits of building a quality organization than the culture created at Toyota.

16.24.1 Toyota Quality Perspective

The internationally recognized flagship quality organization is Toyota. This organization now reaps the economic benefits of a long-term quality culture and today stands at the top of the automobile manufacturing world as a result. Jeffrey Liker in his book *The Toyota Way* outlines their 14 quality principles (is this an accident that Deming had the same number?). In this review, Liker summarizes the following five main ideas that drive this culture:

- Base management decisions on a "philosophical sense of purpose."
- Use long-term planning.
- Have a formal problem-solving process.
- Develop employees.
- Recognize the value of continuous improvement.

Toyota has taken the classic ideas of quality and developed its own internal quality management program. The assembly line segment is known as TPS and represents a custom set of principles, philosophies, and business processes designed to enable the manufacture of quality products (Toyota, 2008). The input side of this equation involves utilizing the leanest manufacturing techniques (i.e., quality and value combined). Additionally, Toyota exercises business process management (BPM) to help identify opportunities for improvement throughout its business activities and then ensuring that appropriate actions are taken in order to benefit from those opportunities.

The origins of quality improvement in the Toyota Group date back to 1902, when founder Sakichi Toyoda invented a textile loom that monitored defective production by halting operation if snapped threads were detected. This helped prevent the creation of defective products and developed into a process known as *Jidoka*. In the 1930s, Toyota developed what is now known as the JIT supply chain system. This system allowed Toyota to draw its resources efficiently by only acquiring necessary inventory from suppliers at appropriate intervals rather than having unneeded supplies pushed onto them by other manufactures. Provided here are some examples of how Toyota applies these balanced quality and value principles today in their assembly line (Liker, 2004):

JIT. After new cars are painted, a computer-controlled system sends a production request to its seat manufacturers with details regarding color, materials, quantity, and other configuration options. The seat manufacturer then processes the requests thereby minimizing costs due to wasted materials.

Jidoka. Both humans and automated workers have the capability to stop a vehicle's progress at any stage of the assembly line if defects are detected. Action is taken to correct the issues and then production is continued. This prevents costly defects from occurring later in the life of the product and improves long-term customer satisfaction.

Kaizen. This is a tool originally used by Toyota to foster continued improvement within its TPS. It began as "Quality Circles," a means of factory shop floor employees to solve quality issues within a structured team framework, using specific new tools. It is now used around the world by many companies and has been adapted to suit their individual needs and customs. This system is directly related to the promotion of continuous improvement by eliminating waste from processes. For example, the layout of an assembly area may need to be reorganized so that a worker does not have to waste time and energy by excess motion around the assembly floor in order to finish working on their task. This promotes greater efficiency throughout the assembly line.

Muda. This deals with the concept of avoiding waste and is actually where the term Lean came from. According to the concept, the 10 forms of waste are:

1. Overproducing (making more just because the material is available, a machine or HR is available)
2. Waste of time (excessive lines—batch and queue mentality)
3. Waste from transporting (excessive movement of materials)
4. Waste from over-processing (process is too complex process or ineffective)
5. Excessive work in process inventory
6. Excess motion of operators and workers (lack of good job design)
7. Waste from scrap and rework
8. Human underutilization (poor resource allocation processes)
9. Improper use of technology
10. Wrong metrics

Andons. This process uses visual signals and controls to display the status of the assembly line. As a result, operators and supervisors are aware in real time the current status of all manufacturing processes. They can also display critical information about a faulty machine and the action required to keep the assembly running smoothly.

PokaYokes. This process utilizes a number of devices that help to prevent defects. Electronic sensors scan for predetermined movements and send out warning signals when appropriate. For example, these are used to remind the assembly workers to use all the components needed in the final assembly of a larger part.

Genchi Genbutsu. This process requires employees to investigate a problem directly, thereby promoting teamwork and collective action toward the resolution of an issue.

By promoting continuous quality improvement throughout its business processes, Toyota has learned to identify and manage the factors that are advantageous to its business processes and to take out the factors that impact the company negatively. Utilization of the TPS and BPM processes has yielded direct benefits such as increased customer satisfaction, lowered costs, and the production of reliable products. These benefits have moved the company into the number one brand position in their industry with internationally recognized quality and sales volumes. It is important to recognize that this has not been a short-term process, but one pursued consistently over many years. This is the nature of building a quality organization.

16.25 Future of Quality Management

This chapter has traced the evolution of quality management and concepts from the 1930s with Shewhart's process model to the currently in vogue Six Sigma version and organization examples of quality cultures. If we examine the basic focus of the various quality program targets through this period, a high-level perspective emerges. The key quality concepts discussed thus far can be generally summarized as follows:

- Defect filtering by sampling inspection models—Shewhart
- Creating a quality organization management culture—Deming
- Process improvement tools—Ishikawa (analyzing status)
- Customer focus—various sources
- Organizational improvement targets—Six Sigma

These summaries are oversimplified in that the human view is not specifically shown, nor is training requirements of the worker. One might conclude that we are still in the maturation process for the concept and more evolution will follow. The breadth of this topic defies simple definitions or projections to clearly predict what that evolution would look like. Up to this stage, we have seen quality management start with a philosophy (Deming) and work toward a broader integrated mechanics view (Six Sigma). It seems now that the latest stage has essentially combined the fragments of the past into a single view and matured the analytical processes. More subtly put, there is a broadening of the concept of quality, so projection of what the next iteration might entail becomes risky. One view would suggest that it would have to minimally incorporate customers, processes, training, measurement, analysis, products, and goals. But what might be added beyond that is vague. Given the lack of a crystal ball, projecting focus areas of the next quality wave is conjecture. Any other conversation should be taken simply as thought provoking. Only time will answer this question.

One reasonable projection is that the future quality domain should include a formalized decision process whereby organizations can improve selection of product targets that better fit consumer desires (the market view). This has the characteristic of how to develop the organizational product portfolio based on this analysis. In relation to this selection process, the organization would profit by having efficient work planning and management processes to produce those products (including efficient process design and implementation). Accomplishment of this goal requires an effective resource allocation process that is much more robust than what exists in most organizations today. Also, a second potential target is developing techniques to improve worker productivity through some form of formal skill improvement process similar in design to the Six Sigma "belt" certification methods. Third, the growing popularity of international virtual organization structures has highlighted weaknesses in overall management across the physically dispersed groups. A new organizational structure option would focus on building project teams from multiple organizations into a homogeneous view of processes and management. In this new model, the actual division of work may be more of a peer relationship among the players than a hierarchical buyer to contractor relationship. Fourth, the Six Sigma model has introduced formally trained layers of quality professionals to guide the organizational efforts. This formal process-mentoring approach would seem desirable in future projects or quality models.

So, which of these ideas will emerge in the next era beyond just the maturation of the current ideas outlined above? Regardless of the next wave we can expect it to be a complex undertaking and thus involve broad changes across the organization.

In the project arena there are two areas that have interesting promise. First, the current waterfall life cycle management methods by which project objectives are produced would seem the most suspect. Embedded in this change is the need to re-engineer the classic network management model along the lines of the critical chain (CC) model, as described in Chapter 27 of the book. This would then require more effective methods for task management to deal with the timely completion of projects. One of the more productive changes involves finding the secret method of producing high quality and motivated teams. It is actually the humans that produce the quality so this would seem to be the right place to start. Dealing with any of these area changes will impact how the concept of project quality will be viewed in the future.

The final and wildest conjecture of this quality future is the most abstract, but worthy of thought. This view deals with an analytic-based methodological approach to be used for allocating organizational resources to selected targets. As an example, IBM is currently exploring methods of quantifying human metrics of their workforce in regard to their skills and other variables. If successful, these metrics will support their ability to more effectively allocate team members based on cost, skill, and availability factors. The evolving technique called *numerate* is an advanced form of metrics capture and exotic analytical systems related to the work force analysis. Further discussion of this concept is beyond our scope here, but the essence of the idea is that a lot more employee information will be used in future decision-making. As a result of these metrics, a more effective job of allocating proper and cost-effective resources to specific task assignments can be achieved. Obviously, this level of change in human profiling will not happen in a short-time horizon; however, pragmatic approaches for more effective resource allocation and management procedures can be developed in reasonable time frames. A full analytic view will take significantly longer.

Can we categorize these new ideas into the realm of future quality programs? Maybe the future title for these will change to something more expansive. Note that the Six Sigma program does not have the term "quality" in it, so we might have already begun to drift away from the narrow view of the term. The more important consideration is what management implications need to be considered to make the organization more competitive and successful. This is the real meaning of quality. Many of the terms outlined throughout this book have this same flavor. So, regardless of the next installment, it is likely that all of the components listed here will be somehow involved in that future definition.

16.26 Quality Worksheet Exercise

Table 16.4 shows a demonstration worksheet to illustrate project QA reviews. There are three types of QA reviews: deliverable, compliance, and health. The role of each one is as follows:

1. *Deliverable:* This activity can range from an early client approval of the project plan to a later approval of a defined outcome product.
2. *Compliance:* Covers areas such as meeting the requirements of a project and complying with established standards and processes.
3. *Health:* Evaluates how well a project is doing; if it has run off the rails. The team can use this review to decide which actions to take to get the project back on track.

Besides serving as an external check-and-balance on the project's performance, the QA staff will ensure that a project and its related artifacts are being developed according to an acceptable process. Every project should have periodic or "mini," reviews to rate its progress against certain defined metrics such as staying within budget. The worksheet below combines these three types of project reviews into one mini review that can be used to determine whether the project is proceeding smoothly.

Table 16.4 Quality Analysis Worksheet

Item	*Metric*	*Example/Comments*	*Problem Weight: 0–5 0=Minor 5=Major*	*Your Project*
Deliverable				
A	Road map	The solution, or technical outline, is one week behind schedule, which means implementation will be delayed	3	
B	Milestones	There are two late milestones:	5	
		1. Approve project plan		
		2. Approve success criteria		
C	Resource changes	There has been some minor staff turnover; no additional staff changes are anticipated	1	
Compliance				
D	Workflow/ reasonability	The project plan has a good Work Breakdown Structure, which defines the organized elements needed to meet the projects scope and deliverables	0	
E	Critical path	There are a number of tasks on the critical path (i.e., a group of related tasks that have no slack time between them) that are delayed, on average, by one week	5	
F	Client processes	The client is slow in getting its field people to validate its requirements. PM will follow up	2	
Health				
G	Hours in project plan versus financial plan	For both plans, the actual hours are over by 150 hours; expected remaining hours are on track	3	
H	Earned value	The earned value or overall project performance, is below the target, see the above item	3	

(*Continued*)

Table 16.4 (*Continued*) Quality Analysis Worksheet

Item	*Metric*	*Example/Comments*	*Problem Weight: 0–5 0=Minor 5=Major*	*Your Project*
I	Risks and issue	The risk plan is up to date. Two issues—procurement and network response—remain open and need to be resolved	3	
J	Impact of changes	Two project change requests are awaiting the client sign-off. If approved, the project plan (schedule and/or cost) will need to be updated	2	

Instructions: Fill in your own numbers under your project, compute your total, and compare results with the ratings at the bottom. If your score is in the mid-1920s or higher—which is the case below—the project could be headed for trouble; the table uses potential trouble spots to generate the QA grade.

Interpretation: If the rating values are in the range of 1–19, the project is on track; between 20 and 39, it needs attention and values higher than 39 indicate that the project is headed for failure.

Source: This worksheet is adapted from a similar version published in *Baseline Magazine*, October 2006. The version shown here is approved for use by the author Ron Smith.

Discussion Questions

1. How would you describe a quality organization or project team?
2. What are some of the key components of quality management?
3. How does Juran's Quality Trilogy compare with Deming's 14 points?
4. Why did Crosby's book impact the U.S. quality movement?
5. Briefly describe the key methodologies of Six Sigma. How does Six Sigma differ from traditional quality ideas?
6. What is the ultimate goal of a quality program?
7. Why is it important for the PM to understand the differences between project-specific requirements and the quality policies of the organization?
8. What can be gained by involving personnel from all functions of the organization in the quality planning stage of a project?
9. When the organization does not consider the quality function to be important what would be the best way to emphasize why you were attempting to sell the idea to senior management?
10. What is the role of data collection and analysis in quality management?
11. How can you justify the overhead cost of a quality management program? What are some of the less noticeable quality-related costs?

References

American Society for Quality (ASQ), 2008. Benchmarking. www.asq.org/learn-about-quality/benchmarking/overview/overview.html (accessed January 9, 2009).

Besterfield, D.H., et al., 1995. *Total Quality Management.* Englewood Cliffs, NJ: Prentice Hall.

Camp, R., 1995. *Business Process Benchmarking: The ASQC Total Quality Management.* Milwaukee, WI: ASQC Quality Press.

Crosby, P.B., 1979. *Quality is Free.* New York: McGraw-Hill.

Environmental Protection Agency (EPA), 2001. EPA Requirements for Quality Assurance Project Plans (EPA QA/R-5). http://www.epa.gov/quality/qs-docs/r5-final.pdf (accessed December 15, 2008).

iSixSigma, 2017. The History of Six Sigma. https://www.isixsigma.com/new-to-six-sigma/history/history-six-sigma/ (accessed November 8, 2017).

ISO 8402. Quality Management and Quality Assurance (ISO 9000:2000). https://www.iso.org/standard/20115.html (accessed October 4, 2017).

ISO 9000. Quality Management. https://www.iso.org/iso-9001-quality-management.html (accessed October 4, 2017).

Power, J.S. 2018. New-Vehicle Initial Quality is Best Ever, 7. http://www.jdpower.com/press-releases/2017-us-initial-quality-study-iqs (access April 28, 2018).

John Stark Associates, 2008. The Ten Step Approach to PLM. www.johnstark.com/fwtqm.html (accessed December 15, 2008).

Liker, J.K., 2004. *The Toyota Way.* New York: McGraw-Hill.

Microsoft, 2008. Adopting Quality Management for Business Success. Projects at Work. http://www.projectsatwork.com/article.cfm?ID=242007 (accessed November 30, 2008).

Mosaicinc, 2001. What is the Difference between Quality Assurance, Quality Control, and Testing? Selected Risk Management Tip. http://www.mosaicinc.com/mosaicinc/rmThisMonth.asp (accessed November 30, 2008).

Park, S.H., 2003. *Six Sigma for Quality and Productivity Promotion.* Tokyo: Lean Sigma Institute, Asian Productivity Organization.

PMI, 2017. *A Guide to the Project Management Body of Knowledge (PMBOK® Guide)*, 6th ed. Newtown Square, PA: Project Management Institute.

Quality and Standards Authority of Ethiopia (QSAE), 2008. Implementing ISO 9000 Quality Management System. http://www.qsae.org/web_en/pdf/ISO9000ImpSteps.pdf (accessed January 9, 2009).

Reh, J.F. 2017. Benchmarking Overview, Practices and Approaches in Business, The Balance Careers, March 31, 2017 https://www.thebalance.com/overview-and-examples-of-benchmarking-in-business-2275114 (accessed April 28, 2018).

Sharma, S., 2007. Quality Management for Business Success. www.gantthead.com/article.cfm?ID=236228 (accessed December 15, 2008).

Toyota, 2008. Toyota Production System. http://www.toyota.co.jp/en/vision/production_system (accessed December 15, 2008).

Tudurov, B., 1996. *ISO 9000 required: Your Worldwide Passport to Customer Confidence.* Portland, OR: Productivity Press.

SOFT SKILL PROCESSES

Learning Objectives

Upon completion of this section the following concepts should be understood as to why they are required as part of project planning and execution:

1. Understand the role that resource management has on the planning and execution of the project
2. Understand the importance of planning project communications
3. Understand the value of engaging stakeholders
4. Understand an approach to team development

This section will expand the foundation processes with a focus on the soft skills knowledge areas. Part II essentially laid out the delivery goals of the project. This part starts from that defined basepoint and shows how planning and managing resources, communications, and stakeholders as well as team development are vital areas of the soft skills environment. The final chapter in this part will describe how each of these components must be integrated into a single working entity, called a team.

Previously, Part II made several simplifying assumptions in order to better facilitate building a firm foundation. At this point, we have a risk-free requirements model in place. We now need to begin taking the wraps off this and start looking closer at the real world of projects. This means that it is necessary to deal with implications of at least the following additional issues:

1. Resources are limited in both quantity and skill level.
2. Duration estimates are not accurate in many cases.
3. All team member motivations and skills are not equal.
4. Conflict is a frequent item with which to deal.
5. Expectations of external stakeholders are difficult to keep in synch with the ongoing plan changes.

These and many other situations cause the project manager to have to manipulate a series of management variables to achieve scope, schedule, cost, and quality objectives described in Part II. Building on these foundational processes, the next step is to identify resource requirements, communication needs, stakeholder implications, and team management. Each of these elements represents the glue that holds the project goal together. The last chapter in Part III focuses on techniques to produce high productivity in project teams. Much of this material is adapted from various SEI literature on Team Software Process (TSP) and Personal Software Process (PSP).

Chapter 17

Resource Management

Resource management involves the set of processes required to plan, acquire, and manage both team and physical resources. Team resources refer to human resources while physical resources include equipment, material, facilities, and infrastructure (PMI, 2017, p. 309). The basic goal of managing team resources is to execute the project by allocating the right individuals to the correct roles at the proper time to complete the plan successfully. A secondary goal of this area is to attract and maintain skilled employees and to manage them effectively (brij, 2007). This activity also includes dealing with the numerous team issues that arise during the life cycle of a project. The objective of physical resource management is to utilize materials and equipment in an efficient and effective way for the project.

The *Project Management Body of Knowledge (PMBOK®) Guide* defines six major processes for the Project Resource Management Knowledge Areas (KAs) (PMI, 2017, p. 307):

- *Plan Resource Management*—define how to estimate, acquire, and manage both physical and team resources
- *Estimate Resource Activities*—estimate all resource team resources, materials, equipment, and supplies (see Chapter 14)
- *Acquire project team*—obtain the defined HR to execute the project
- *Develop project team*—improve the "competencies team interaction, and the overall team environment to enhance project performance" (PMI, 2017, p. 307)
- *Manage project team*—"… tracking team member performance, resolving issues, managing changes to optimize project performance" (PMI, 2017, p. 307)
- *Control resources*—ensure physical resources are available as planned, monitoring performance, and making corrective action as needed

Projects primarily fail or succeed because of people. This makes the Project Resource Management Plan very important—not just in the planning phase of a project where the development of a good road map for the project work is defined, but also through the other life cycle phases as the project dynamics begin to unfold. Even with an accurate plan based on the original user specifications: "… requirements change so quickly these days that, unless the PM is fully aware of the issues at a business level, even a project that delivers the planned scope within time and cost may be deemed unsuccessful because its deliverables are no longer relevant to the business" (AST Group, 2001).

17.1 Resource Planning

In spite of the dynamic nature and highly technical work product, the planning phase is charged with the development of a reasonably detailed project plan complete with descriptive work units (i.e., work units and planning packages in the Work Breakdown Structure (WBS)). Details regarding the core planning mechanics were described earlier in Chapters 11–15. At this early stage, the team resource planning process was abstract in the sense that the future project team is usually not named at this point. The resource allocation process defined in Chapter 14 provided the information to quantify levels for various skill groups. From this data, a resource breakdown structure (RBS) for the project defines generic quantities and skills or each work unit. *Note*: Be aware that the RBS acronym is also used in risk management to show a similar outline for risk events, so this can be confusing.

The Resource Management Plan, which may be organized into two parts (*Team Management Plan, Physical Resource Management Plan*), may include the following items (PMI, 2017, pp. 318–319):

1. Identification of resources—methods for identifying and estimating physical and team resources
2. Acquiring resources—guidance on how to acquire team and physical resources
3. Roles and responsibilities
   - Role—the function assumed by, or assigned to, a person in the project.
   - Authority—the rights to apply project resources, make decisions, sign approvals, accept deliverables, and influence others to carry out work of the project.
   - Responsibility—the assigned duties and work that a project team member is expected to perform to complete the project's activities.
   - Competence—the skill and capacity required to complete assigned activities within the project constraints.
4. Project organization charts.
5. Project team resource management—guidance on how project team resources should be defined, staffed, managed, and eventually released.
6. Training needs—training strategies for team members.
7. Team development—methods for developing the project team.
8. Resource control—methods for ensuring adequate physical resources are available as required.
9. Recognition plan—which rewards and recognition will be given to team members and when.

If we could assume that all humans had equal skills and were available as the plan defined, the HR component of the planning process would not be overly complex. However, that is not the case.

17.2 Responsibility Assignment Matrix

A responsibility assignment matrix (RAM) is used in linking activities to resources in order to ensure that all work components are assigned to an individual or team. One format for this is to define four category roles in the responsibility assignment—Responsible, Accountable, Consult, and Inform. This is called a RACI chart, because it assigns those roles for each work unit.

Table 17.1 can be constructed either at a high level (major project groups) or at a detailed level (WPs). The coding schemes used in a RACI chart specify who is responsible for various functions

Table 17.1 Comparison of Beta SD and Triangular Formula Sample RACI chart

WBS ID	*Bill*	*Gary*	*Ron*	*Bob*	*Bud*	*Teri*
4.F	R	A	I	C	C	
6.A	I	A	C			R
2.A	R	A	I			C
2.B	R	A	I	C	C	C

related to a work unit. In some cases, these codes can be more than the four shown here; however, a brief translation of the basic codes is as follows:

R—the organizational unit or individual assigned to do the work.
A—designates the management level person or organizational unit responsible for the work.
C—designates the person or organization responsible for functionality of the work. This can be the subject matter experts for the effort.
I—designates those individuals or organizational units who will be informed regarding status of the work unit.

Other coding schemes can be used in the matrix, but the key point here is that a RACI format chart is useful as a communications specification tool to help ensure proper coordination and information distribution at the work unit level. Tools of this type are often ignored.

A RACI table is typically constructed with activities/work units on the vertical (i.e., WBS IDs) and resources on the horizontal (i.e., by name or organizational unit) plane. Not every resource will have an entry for every activity. Table 20.1 illustrates the format for a fragment of this type chart.

A second name for this class of chart is a linear responsibility chart (LRC) and it focuses more on naming who is responsible for specified work units at the lower levels of the WBS. In this model, each row could represent a WBS ID (all of them) and each column a person or a team name. The boxes could then be completed with the letters P (Prime support), S (Support), and N (Notify). This is like a RACI chart, but in this case, it shows more the degree of involvement than the multiple management-type roles of the classic RACI chart.

Regardless of the coding schemes used, RAM-type charts are useful to map the work of the project as described in the WBS to the individuals or groups responsible for performing that work. For smaller projects, it is best to simply assign WBS work units to individuals; for larger projects, it may be more effective to assign the work to organizational units or teams.

17.3 Resource Histograms

A resource histogram is a bar chart that shows the number of resources required or assigned over time to a project. In showing project staffing needs the vertical bars represent the number of people needed in each skill category and by stacking the columns, the total number of resources required for each time period can be represented. In some cases, this same view can be produced for each resource by name, type, or organizational unit. The resource histogram is a tool that is often used to produce a visual representation of resource requirements. This can show various views as well.

For example, one view might be planned versus available resources to show resource capacity shortages. This is a handy format to show various stakeholder groups resource views for the project.

17.4 Team Management Plan

The Team Management Plan is a subset of the Project Resource Management Plan, and it describes how the human resources requirements will be met. This document describes the types of people needed to work on the project, the numbers needed for each skill type by time period, and how these resources will be acquired, trained, rewarded, and then reassigned elsewhere after the project.

Development of a project-staffing plan also involves the process for selecting and assembling a project team. This definition builds on the high-level staffing needs roughly identified first in the Initiation Stage. When developing a staff plan, the focus includes specific roles and responsibilities for team members in the project and the specific staffing profiles across the project's life. This plan describes the approach and detailed "baseline" information regarding staffing and roles. It also describes the specific roles and responsibilities as they have been tailored for the project. These are not meant to be job descriptions, but rather a summary of the responsibilities for each role. Individual responsibilities are tailored based on the life cycle phase and actual project staffing.

A Team Management Plan describes the appropriate procedures used to manage staff on the project. It discusses mentoring, cross-training, primary/backup role assignments, training and development assignments, performance evaluations, performance recognitions, and promotions, as well as disciplinary actions and demotions. It states how a staff vacancy is to be handled, and what happens if it appears that the position will not be filled for a while, and what will happen if the vacancy cannot be addressed by a single person (given current skill sets available). Also, review of qualifications to ensure the replacement will be able to assume the work, addressing differences or discrepancies.

17.5 Training Programs

Team skill development can be nurtured through mentoring or various types of training programs. Mentoring is a good practice for emulating skills of more senior team members, but may also perpetuate old habits that you wish to change. Formal training programs can be used to transfer defined information or to build a defined cultural attitude. In any case, the process of skill development needs to be recognized and pursued. For projects that have specified skill requirements that do not exist in the incumbent team, the training needs to be dealt with prior to their arrival on the team, or soon thereafter. One approach to this is to create a skills assessment for the team members and from this decide how to pursue training and in what format.

One helpful approach is to categorize the training into three groups: environment, project, and miscellaneous, then prioritize specific training sessions into time blocks. Examples of these types of training sessions are summarized below.

Environment

- External organization and its goals?
- Basic HR requirements that all employees need to know (benefits, medical, security, etc.).
- Pay related.
- Employee selection and recruitment, promotion, planning, and management.

Project

- Work processes that the team need to know how to access and use (i.e., project plan, change control, technical documents, time keeping system, status reports, etc.).
- Methodology used for project life cycle management.
- Performance of management process.
- Skill issues required (this can be both informational and specific).

Miscellaneous other courses:

- Presentation skills training
- Business writing
- Being an effective team member
- Virtual teams training
- Decision analysis training
- Ethics training
- Various productivity tools used in the team

Organizations use different strategies to accomplish training, but one desirable approach is to establish a time allocation for this activity and then prioritize the training into that time. Very few organizations overdo the level of training. Once the skill gaps are defined and prioritized, an effective training program can be developed.

17.6 Team Charter

Another artifact created in this phase is the Team Charter, which is a set of ground rules for responsible team membership. It lays out expectations and responsibilities for team members. A team charter is an objective set of rules that govern team behavior. It may include some of the following elements (PMI, 2017, p. 319):

- Team values
- Communication guidelines
- Decision-making criteria and process
- Conflict resolution process
- Meeting guidelines, and
- Team agreements

17.7 HR in Execution

The project team resource management processes that are included in execution phase relate to the project team acquisition, development, and management. Developing the project team deals with improving competencies, such as team member interactions, overall team environment, and enhancing project performance. Managing the project team involves tracking team member performance, providing feedback, and resolving issues. Controlling resources involves monitoring resource expenditures.

The first step to executing a successful project is assembling the proper mix of resources as defined in the project plan. This process can be tricky because of the time variability that most experience and the linkage between activities makes the output of one work process become the input of another process. Some have described this as similar to managing a relay race. The management goal is to have a planned resource standing at the finish line waiting on the previous task to complete.

17.8 Acquire Project Team

Acquiring a project team involves identifying sources for consideration, negotiating with various management units to obtain the required resources, and getting them to the project on schedule. The project team acquisition process involves obtaining the specific people needed to accomplish all phases of the project. Within this structure, each team member brings specific qualifications and capabilities to the project team.

The PM oversees the team selection and negotiating for these individuals from their functional managers or other sources. Key attributes for this search are required skills, work experience, availability, personal characteristics, and personal professional interests. Team members can be specifically hired for the project or acquired as contractors from outside organizations. Some project activities might require special skills or knowledge and it may be necessary to look outside of the company for this skill. Consequently, it is important to take into consideration a staff member's prior experience before assigning him to a specific activity. Personal interests and characteristics also play an important role. If the candidate is not interested in the project, it is unlikely that he or she will perform at their best. We also must recognize that some employees do not work well with others. One solution for this issue is to separate those individuals who cannot get along well by assignments to different projects; however, in some cases, the employee who lacks people skills is the only person available who possesses a set of specific skills. In this situation, other management techniques will be required to maintain and keep team cohesiveness and performance. The final consideration is the availability of selected key team members, as the project can only function when these skills are in place.

Pre-assignment, negotiation, hiring, and virtual team plans are the typical sourcing issues during the process of staffing the project team. Although a Project Charter gives the PM formal authority to acquire resources, it does not give the ability to do that in any form he wishes. The project matrix resources will be owned by the various host functional managers and it requires negotiation with them to identify specific names who will be made available to the project. Pre-assignment of specific-named individuals occurs when they are included in the original proposal for the project. This often occurs when a project is being performed for an external entity and the defined names were a condition for accepting the project. When staff members are allocated as part of a project proposal, they should be identified in the Project Charter to minimize allocation issues later. Availability, competency levels, and personal characteristics of the staff members become key topics in the negotiation in almost the same manner that a professional athlete is drafted.

One other staffing condition that is worthy of comment involves the practice of splitting a resource into multiple pieces and allocating them to more than one project in a single time period. This is called *multitasking*. This is a common practice because technical resources are typically scarce and sometimes are not needed full time on a project. Nevertheless, the practice of splitting resources across multiple project assignments is found to create more severe scheduling issues for the PMs involved. More specifics on this multitasking issue can be found in Chapter 27. The short answer view is to avoid it if possible, because that is just one more place where allocation issues can occur.

The acquisition option implies hiring individuals or teams of people for certain project activities. This has the disadvantage of introducing new organizational members to the team and usually requires some start-up time before they can become fully productive. Only in the case of a long-term project or to resolve aggregate staff shortages would an organization hire a project.

Virtual teams are defined as project team subgroups that do not work in the same location, but share some aspect of the project goals, and have a role in the project. These can be individuals from the same organization or from third-party contracted organizations. The challenge with these types of teams is that communications are more complex and there may be cultural issues as well for teams located in other countries.

There is disagreement among project professionals regarding the type of person who should manage both the project and the sub-teams. One school of thought says that the leaders should be from the business area that the project impacts and the other view is that a business person makes a poor technical PM. There is probably merit in both views. Without attempting to take on that argument here, the essence is that whoever is put in charge needs to be sensitive to both the business and the underlying technology. This means active participation from both sides regardless of the organizational grouping. The better the team, the less important is the formal organizational structure or the skill type of the leader.

The final issue to consider before the team gets started is the need for training. Without proper skills, the work will not get done effectively, but the other side of this is the need to show the requirement in terms of specification by individual, along with associated adjustments for schedule and budget to accommodate the training schedule.

17.9 Orienting Team Members (Role Specifications)

Closely related to the resource acquisition process is the idea of role assignments for the team. Once the team staffing is generally defined, the next goal is to make sure that the team members understand their roles in the project. There are several things that can be done to help the team members understand the overall project and their particular role in it. At the highest level, the WBS offers a good tool to explain the overall scope and work activity, particularly for the work units that those team members will be responsible for. Also, the project plan contains documentation on the various KAs related to the project and describes each of these. This needs to be mandatory reading for the team members.

One way to start the definition of team member roles is to convene the team for that purpose. A formal kickoff meeting is one recommended method for this. Depending on the size and scope of the project, this meeting could be a multiple day exercise and involve not only the technical and management aspects of the project, but some socialization as well. This is a good time for the team members to get to know each other and develop some camaraderie. It is important for the team to believe that this project is worth doing. No one wants to be working on a project that is viewed as not worth doing.

Once the basic technical issues are understood by the team, the indoctrination process should move to team organization and roles. Once again, the size of the team will affect what level of formality will be used to define the role and responsibility structure. A general guideline for this is to keep sub-team sizes in the range of seven or less. If the project goals can be decomposed into work groups of this size, there is a better chance of building productive groups and simplifying communications. A decomposed team structure of this type then requires sub-team leaders who can create and manage an effective team and they become the key drivers for the project effort. Obviously, smaller projects would have only one or two such groups to deal with. Another organizational activity that should be going on at this point is bringing key stakeholders into the kickoff sessions and make sure the team knows who they are and the role they play.

The preparation of exact role specifications, usually in written form, was introduced during World War I, when staff officers compiled elaborate tables of organization for the infantry. Today, schematic organization charts are still used to show authority relationships, but they are less used than in the past primarily because of the complexity of contemporary organizations.

17.10 Project Organizations

Project organizations can exist in a wide variety of forms. The essential element is a collection of individuals formed for a temporary time period to execute a planned initiative. Most host organizations are structured along what is called functional lines. This means that major skill groups are housed together. Names such as engineering, manufacturing, marketing, accounting/finance, legal, and others are common departmental titles. This structure is called a *functional* organization (i.e., structured around functional groups). Projects formed inside of any one of these organization departments would be under the authority of that department and are often called silo projects. The downside of this project location is its ability to obtain the various skills needed to execute the variety of skilled tasks.

A second project organizational alternative model exists for very large projects such as those found at NASA. Resource levels in this class of project are huge and the internal view consists of multiple related projects under the overall control of a program manager. In this organizational model, called a *projectized* organization, the program manager is the central authority for the resources attached to the group.

A third organizational structure is the most common for project teams. In this case, the requirements call for a variety of technical skills to be drawn from various functions within the organization and possibly even external resources. Also, the project plan calls for these resources to move in and out of the organization and only work on assigned work tasks when they are needed. The remainder of the time these resources will be elsewhere and not charging the project for their time. For example, engineering might be heavily involved early, but less so later. Manufacturing might be the central resource for execution, but not heavily involved elsewhere. Marketing, legal, and finance requirements would be scattered through the life cycle. In this case, the resulting organization structure is called a *matrix* and is shown schematically in Figure 17.1.

There are disadvantages to this structure, but the significant advantage that makes a structure somewhat like this a requirement is as follows:

- Required resources can be managed moving into and out of the project team.
- Project cost is lessened because resources are only used as needed.
- There is an appropriate focus on the project objectives through a single PM.
- The overall enterprise utilization of resources is better handled in the mode.

The paradox of the matrix structure shown in Figure 17.1 is that it has advantages for the organization, but complicates the life of the PM. The one basic issue that plagues most projects structured

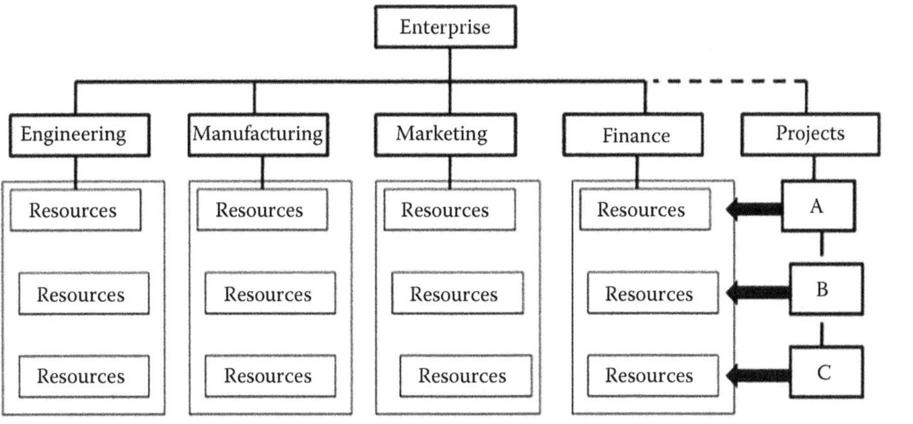

Figure 17.1 Matrix organization structure.

in this form is the weak level of control over the resources. It is up to the PM to negotiate needed resources from the owning functional departments and he must do this without any real authority to obtain the specific resources he wants. There is an obvious conflict built-in as there will be other projects attempting to also obtain the best people. If the project schedule shifts, as it often does, the individuals originally planned may not be available. From a project view, this means that the resource allocation aspect has become much more complicated than if the resources were "owned" by the project. In addition to this, the authority delegated to the PM in a classic matrix structure is weak, meaning that the functional manager is still the team member's boss and the project team member will feel like he has two bosses as a result. This watered-down authority level can be an issue if the assigned team member is not performing adequately. Because of this dual ownership view, there is often divided loyalty of the team member between the temporary project and his permanent professional home.

17.10.1 Dotted Lines

In many ways, the matrix project team is afloat in the organization in that the project team member may not be easy to show in a formal organization chart. In some cases, this is partially resolved by having an organization structure that looks much like a functional one with a senior manager as the defined authority, but dotted lines to other organizational groups. The dotted line relationship is yet another way in which the PM has more than one boss. Nevertheless, even in this case, there are many other management stakeholders that are not formally identified by the organization chart, but nevertheless are very interested in the outcome of the project. This means that the PM has multiple bosses regardless of the organization form used.

17.10.2 People Issues

Assembling team members together brings many issues that are discussed here and elsewhere in the book. Projects are breeding grounds for conflict of various types and it is not easy to keep a project team focused on a target. A.T. Kearney found in a survey that seven out of 10 teams failed to produce the desired results (Hall, 2008, pp. 23–34). The one major issue observed was in the dynamics related to moving dissimilar organizational types together and keeping their roles and relationships defined. If a distributed geography is added to this equation, the complexity of coordination grows even greater.

Therefore, the reality of project organizations is that they will be formed as a matrix and the second half of that reality is that this brings with it increased management challenges. Also, the issue of team collaboration (information sharing) remains one of the current focal points as team members are increasingly being dispersed.

17.11 Motivation Theory

As teams are formed, the job of motivating the team members to willingly take ownership of the project goals does not just happen. An understanding of the potential triggers to spur humans into production action is a complex undertaking; however, there are a few basic motivation concepts that can help start the process. Quite apart from the moral and altruistic views for treating colleagues as human beings and respecting human dignity, research has shown that well-motivated employees tend to be more productive and creative in the workplace. Unmotivated team members tend to be less productive and supportive of the project goals. Since the job of a PM is to get things done through his team, it is important to understand some of the key triggers for energizing those individuals and the team as a whole. Accomplishing this goal is the essence of the management task.

There are many motivation theories in existence, but matching these theories to real humans remains an art form. To understand motivation, one must understand human nature itself, and therein lies the problem! There are two project views for motivation. One is from the individual perspective and the second is a team (group) view. The management processes for each are somewhat different. We will first examine the individual theories and then look at how groups of humans react.

17.12 Individual Motivation Theories

Since the Hawthorne experiment in the latter 1920s attempted to show the impact of light intensity on worker productivity, the behavioral school of management has been hard at work to expand knowledge about human needs and motivation. The discussion below refers to four of the classic behavioral researchers and their core set of concepts regarding human behavior and motivation. These four researchers are the following:

1. Douglas McGregor (1906–1964): Theory X and Y
2. Abraham Maslow (1908–1970): Hierarchy of needs
3. David McClelland (1917–1998): Achievement Motivation theory
4. Frederick Herzsberg (1923–2000): Motivation/Maintenance theory

The individuals are listed in chronological order to emphasize to some degree the evolution of this research.

Douglas McGregor: His theory is based on the idea that there are two basic types of people: Theory X types, who do not want to work and must be directed closely and Theory Y types, who look at work as natural. The latter types will seek and accept responsibility while being self-directed. This theory opened the door for participative management rather than an authoritarian command and control form that was more prevalent at the time.

Abraham Maslow: Dr. Maslow developed his view of humans by studying Rhesus monkeys. From this base, he formed a five-stage hierarchy of needs as it applied to humans and documented this in his 1954 book titled *Motivation and Personality* (Maslow, 1954). He illustrated this by a pyramid to show how humans move up the need hierarchy as they fulfill lower-level requirements. Figure 17.2 shows the five major need levels.

The Maslow need hierarchy model describes individuals at level one as looking for the basic items that sustain life, notably food and sleep. This would be characteristic of someone who was basically nothing and was struggling for bare survival. As level 1 needs are met, the individual begins to look upward to what are described as safety needs. At level 2, the needs would include safety aspects of the job, financial and physical. So, a reasonable job that offered more than enough money to maintain level 1 needs would represent this need level. In addition, physical safety would remain a need regardless of the other items. At level 3, the individual is fed and is safe, so finding social outlets takes on importance. This can be exemplified by friends, belonging to a group, and love. Level 4 enters with the humans wanting a sense of belonging. Terms such as self-respect and achievement are often used to define this need level. Note that these terms would seem to have the most relevance to the knowledge worker and his potential motivation triggers, since he is earning enough to satisfy the lower need levels. Level 5 is the summit of the need hierarchy in which the humans are looking for something that allows them to reach their full potential as a person and this often is a non-work-related view of the world. Terms such as wisdom, justice, and truth are used to describe individuals at this level. Bill Gates giving away billions of dollars is an example of an individual at this level.

Maslow's implication was that the layers of the need hierarchy were motivators for individuals at that level, and essentially if you knew where the individual was located on the hierarchy, those items would serve as motivators—that is, money buys food, house, cars, and so on. Even though he did not specifically say this, the implication is that money was a motivator if it was linked to a need. A great deal of research has gone on with this model and much of it has been refuted in its simplicity; however, almost everyone can relate to it to some degree. We should also note that many professionals are clearly above level 2, and we see strong behavioral motivation correlations at levels 3 and 4. Occasionally, we even see somewhat successful professionals who leave good

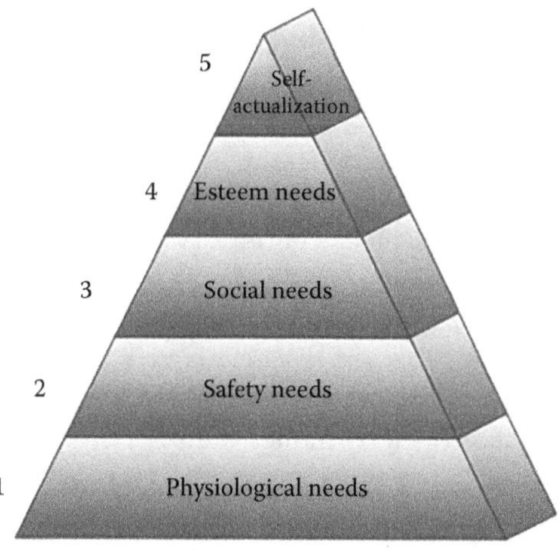

Figure 17.2 Maslow's need hierarchy.

paying jobs to go teach at universities and write textbooks. Hence, there is some reasonableness to the Maslow model and it offers an interesting structure to review for a starting place.

David McClelland: This behavioral model has some of the same concepts as Maslow's, but it begins to focus more on the motivational triggers rather than if human needs lead to motivation. McClelland hypothesized that motivation could be created by two sources: intrinsic and extrinsic. Intrinsic motivation comes from something satisfying that one enjoys. Extrinsic motivation occurs from some external factors. One of the long-term arguments among behaviorists has been whether money was in fact a motivator or not. McClelland classified money as both an intrinsic and an extrinsic motivational trigger. Intrinsic because it represents success (fancy car, big house, etc.), while the extrinsic view was that money would cause the individual to seek it out in return for some act. The acceptance of the value of money as a motivator remains controversial to many. McClelland believed that intrinsic forms of motivation were more effective.

In its basic form, the McClelland *Need Acquired Theory* (1965) described individuals as being motivated by one of the three general needs (McClelland, 1965):

Need for power—strong need to lead; increase personal status
Need for achievement—seeks advancement, feedback, and accomplishment
Need for affiliation—seeks relationships and human interactions

Each individual has varying degrees of these three needs and their ratio mix determines a great deal about their resulting style and motivation. From a work performance point of view, McClelland was most interested in the achievement characteristics because he believed they were the type of individuals who made things happen and got results; however, the downside of this was their potentially negative impact on those around them because of their excessive demands. As in the case of Maslow, we see these characteristics in project teams. Even if the theory is correct, we see that the key is to find the correct balance.

Frederick Herzsberg: The Motivation/Maintenance theory was published in 1959 and it was the first behavioral research to describe specific motivators by source (Herzsberg et al., 1959). It also had a second mirror-type view regarding what Herzsberg called dissatisfiers. These are factors that can cause one to be dissatisfied with the job, but do not necessarily become satisfiers or motivators if fully supplied. The basic idea of this two-pronged approach was that individuals might stay on the job because of certain factors, but would not be motivated unless an adequate level of satisfiers existed. Figure 17.3 provides a high-level aggregate summary of the Herzsberg research results. The decreasing curve denotes general strength of each satisfier (motivator) item, while the increasing curve shows the same for the dissatisfiers.

These data have been interpreted by the author from the original Herzsberg research data and this figure is intended to illustrate which items are generally strongest for each factor. In attempting to quantify the relative frequency of these two parameters, the author reviewed multiple reviews of the data from other sources. Some researchers disagreed with the methodology of the original research and refuted its conclusions, while many others discussed the conclusions. One of the issues found was that the different survey populations that tried to duplicate the Herzsberg data for engineers and accountants got different results. School teachers, for example, seemed to be more motivated by money than the original group. However, given the Herzsberg original survey population types the results may well match the technical project team factors reasonably well.

Attempting to quantify a human attribute with an "intensity" measure for satisfaction or dissatisfaction is not our goal here. Figure 17.3 attempts to show general relationships that have a

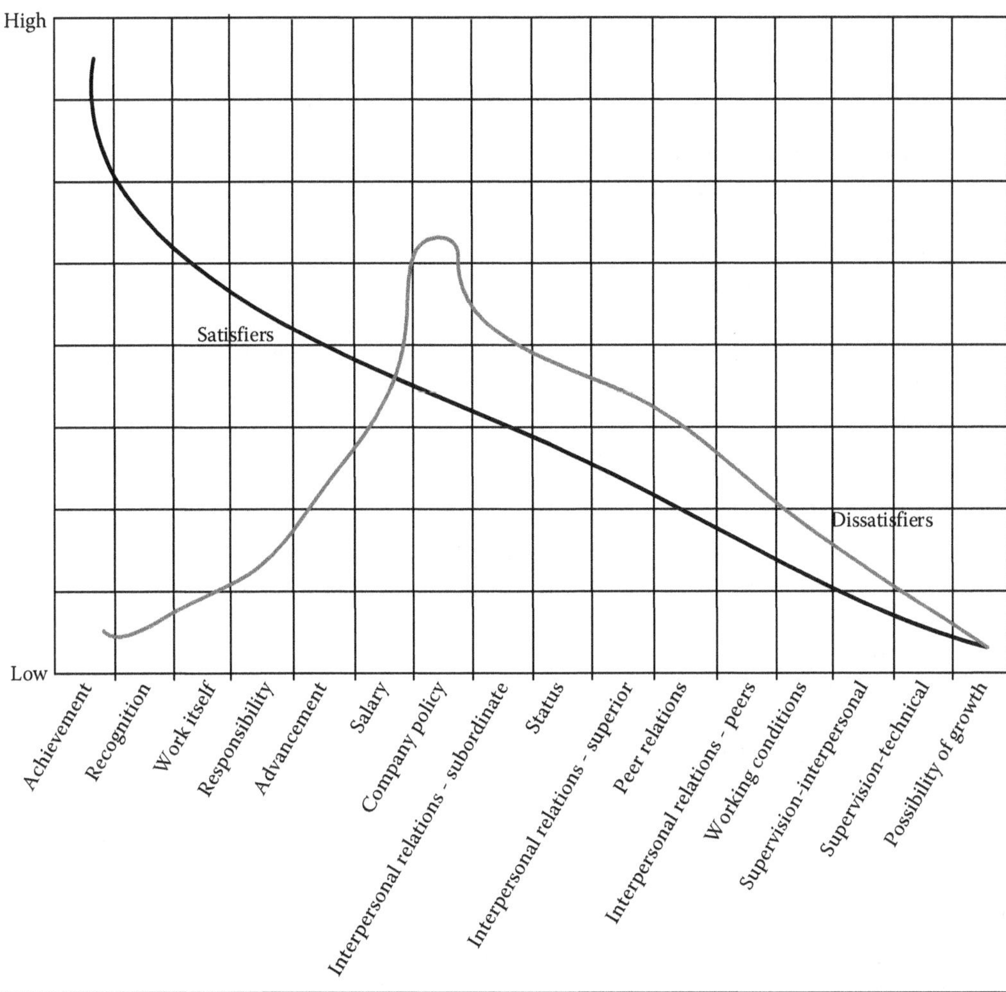

Figure 17.3 Herzberg chart.

varying probability for motivation, as well as those that have high potential for being dissatisfiers. There is general consistency with other researchers that achievement, recognition, and responsibility factors are high motivators and Herzsberg adds to this that they can also be dissatisfiers if not present in the job structure. Also, note from the figure that salary falls into the sixth position as satisfier, but is also a significant dissatisfier if not adequately supplied by the job. This translates to an interpretation that money is not a strong motivator, but can be a demotivator if it does not exist at a reasonable level. On the dissatisfier side, company policy and supervision win the potential dissatisfier awards. The PM must understand this list of factors and use the knowledge to minimize dissatisfiers and maximize the satisfiers.

17.13 Team Motivation

Motivating a team is obviously more challenging than motivating a single individual given that teams have both individual and interpersonal aspects to deal with. A management technique that might work with a single individual can well be wrong in a team setting. Bringing a group of diverse individuals together to work on a project does not necessarily yield a functioning unit even if all members are highly motivated and have high achievement needs as defined in the behavior theories.

The first critical aspect of team motivation is to establish a clear goal direction for the project. In the team organization, individuals must execute their individual roles, but should be willing to support team goals over their own. Assuming that the team has been staffed properly, each of the individual skills is important in completing the overall goal, but no one of them alone is sufficient for success. This diversity of member personalities and skills can be a positive force if each performer can be motivated to find a way to contribute their unique capabilities when and where needed. Team organizations can be very powerful mechanisms to produce spectacular results if the team leader can provide the proper management and operational climate. This is the essence of the project team goal.

Alignment of goals, purpose, and values between stakeholders, team members, and the external organization represents a complex set of management activities for the PM. Team goal alignment and a positive internal chemistry are key attributes of a productive group. When team members are not aligned with project directions, then motivation and productivity will likely be reduced. The role of team leaders (or team members in self-directed teams) is to achieve the following five motivational goals:

1. Foster mutual respect for the individual expertise of all team members.
2. Help weaker team members believe that their efforts are vital to the team.
3. Support a shared belief in the cooperative capabilities of the team.
4. Create individual team member accountability for their contributions to the team effort.
5. Direct the individual's competitive spirit toward the team and the organization; success is defined as team success.

These protocols and attitude goals do not mean that the team sings *Kumbaya* to start each day, but it does mean that the team leader and members have certain civil behavioral protocols toward each other.

17.14 Hygiene Dissatisfiers

The reverse side of motivation is the existence of dissatisfiers that take away from motivation. In this regard, it is also important to be aware of any adverse environmental hygiene factors that may exist. In many cases, these cannot be resolved quickly, but sensitivity to the issues can help. The Herzsberg model offers a list of these to review, but others may also exist. One of the management keys in team motivation is to first take away as many negative influences as possible and then focus on the positive factors inherent in the project work. In addition to the organizational and physical hygiene factors outlined by the Herzsberg model, there are three environmental prerequisites needed to position the individual or team member to be motivated (AMA, 2008).

1. A clear definition and ownership of their defined tasks.
2. Removal of external inhibitors that hinder the individual from accomplishing the required tasks.
3. Ensure that the individual has appropriate training and skills to execute the defined tasks.

The job of a PM in a motivated and productive team is to protect his team from external negatives, whatever they may be.

Techniques to create high-productivity teams are still not sufficiently understood to the degree that a mechanical checklist can be defined. Such a list would contain much of what has been described in this section, but it still takes management skill to produce the desired outcome. More details on the creation and management of high-performance teams are presented in Chapter 23. For this discussion, we stop at this theoretical point and recognize that a collection of humans formed into a project team structure brings a wide variety of motivational trigger mechanisms that are unique for each person.

17.15 Employee Satisfaction

Herzsberg has provided a good starting place to understand the basic drivers for employee satisfaction. His data indicate that effective people management is about more than traditional mechanical human resource management practices such as work allocation and training. We are now sensitive to the value of finding these motivational triggers for achieving team member satisfaction with both their current job and growth development for the future. Part of the satisfaction dimension comes from outside the project in the way the employee sees their company as a community, where there is a social environment. Research indicates that the more successful organizations are those in which a positive socialization climate exists. Some of the organizational characteristics that foster this attitude are a feeling of concern for employee welfare, lower status barriers, good communication, high-quality training, and overall respect for employees.

Research by the Gallup organization about Great Managers and Great Workplaces also suggests that measures linked with employee satisfaction, such as turnover correlate with profitability (Gallup, 2008). Researchers noticed that organizational excellence was driven by high-performing workgroups, rather than the organization as a whole. They found that a number of situational factors such as pay and parking, which are often elements of an organizational HR strategy, do not make significant difference to the most productive workgroups in the companies studied. If they exist, they are not dissatisfiers, but neither are they motivators. What did matter were a number of other work-related factors that are more firmly within the responsibility domain of team managers (i.e., interesting work, positive feedback, and friends at work). These factors also included employees having effective communication regarding what is expected of them through the setting of explicit expectations by their manager. However, individuals expressed the need to have some freedom in finding their own way of achieving these expectations if they are to feel ownership of their job.

PMs need to be able to define how to help each employee take responsibility and be able to maximize their productivity in an energized team. This does not mean working of the team for 60 hours a week. This strategy will yield the opposite result. The positive approach is to establish an environment for job satisfaction and assign work that makes the best use of individual talents. The new generation knowledge worker reacts very positively to recognition for good work and constructive feedback. Development of this team culture is a clear requirement for the PM.

17.16 Conflict Management

One of the fundamental precepts of conflict is that it is 90% misunderstanding among the parties. Whether one accepts that as fact or not, this is the required starting point for resolution—i.e., level set the group with the same facts. Conflict in the project team can come from various sources and involves some divergence of opinion. One conflict scenario involves two very rational team members who have a disagreement over some technical direction issue. Other scenarios are represented by disagreements over other aspects of the project—scope, schedule, budget, and so on. Each of these situations demands some resolution. In all cases, conflict must be seen as a problem to be solved rather than a war to be won. The key theme of conflict management is that it cannot be left to fester and increase. Confrontation is the PM mantra. He must be on the lookout for its existence and activate a strategy to deal with it. However, the strategies are situational, and therein lies the management art.

There are many different methods to handle conflict. In each case, a win–win approach is the goal (Fisher, 2008). Win–lose outcomes often create other conflict issues later. From the management view, there are three basic concepts involved in the resolution process:

Problem-solving approach—the first step should be to clearly and concisely identify the issue and its relevant points. It has been estimated that 90% of team conflict is created by a misunderstanding of the situation (Mulcahy, 2005). Once the problem is defined and all agree with the issue defined and the related facts, then try to develop various solutions to consider (without initial judgment as to each one's merit). Even if the parties agree quickly with one of the options developed, it is best to review that option thoroughly to ensure that it does not create another issue elsewhere. Once the issue is agreed on, the solution should be documented along with rationale for the choice.

Use patience and respect—realize that the existence of a conflict means that the parties have diverse opinions. These will not magically dissolve under the light of inspection and if they do that can also indicate a process problem—probably one of the parties has been intimidated by one of the players and backed out with no change in belief or attitude. So, the first step is to try to achieve an open conversation with as little emotion as possible. Every participant should have a respected opinion even if it is clearly wrong. The problem-solving process is as much a training process as a conflict resolution one. The fact is that team members must learn to discuss controversial issues and seek logical answers without a PM always stepping in to play referee. In many cases, the participants know more about the details of the conflict that the PM, so he adds little content in this case. When intelligent participants cannot arrive at some resolution, there likely are some goals or views that are not clearly understood. In this case, the PM has to step in and may need to establish some guidelines for the process. A more hands-off approach also helps to build healthy relationships between the parties involved. In addition, better solutions are produced through this type of dialogue so long as the players can focus on the task issue and not the individual's role in the opinion.

Construct an agreement that works—on reaching an agreed solution, the identified areas of the agreement should be clearly specified in writing along with the rationale for that option. In some cases, it is best to air the situation to other groups or individuals to see what feedback occurs from these sources before moving forward. The final goal is to not create another conflict with the solution to the current issue. The agreement should be evaluated on the following criteria:

- Enforcement—does agreement rely on others who were not present in the discussion? Have they commented on the solution?
- Realistic—do we have resources and expertise to implement the agreement?
- Future oriented—should we consider other similar issues for common solutions or relationship to this agreement being made?

17.16.1 Conflict Sources

There are four basic sources of conflict (ALS, 2008):

Value conflict—values are the beliefs that people use to give meaning to their lives. They explain individuals view as "good" or "bad," or "right" or "wrong," Disputes occur when an issue is viewed by two individuals with different value systems. There is no right or wrong answer to this category, because the individual value system will likely not change regardless of the discussion.

Data conflict—data conflicts occur when there are different data used to form opinions. This results in a conflict that can be resolved by supplying the same data to all parties (Fisher, 2008).

Interest conflict—interest conflict occurs when one party believes that, to satisfy their needs, a certain direction should be pursued that is opposed to other views. This class of conflicts can occur due to one of the following reasons:

- Money, time, and physical resources
- Method of solving the dispute aids one side
- Perception of fairness, trust, desire for participation, and respect.

Structural conflict—structural conflict occurs from forces external to the individuals in conflict. Important factors that can cause structural conflict include the following:

- Inadequate physical resources
- Geographic constraints
- Time to complete task.

Interest conflicts are the most difficult internal issues to deal with because the players are not looking at the team goals, but rather primarily their own. Structural conflicts have an interesting side effect on the team. When external forces create conflicts for the team, the team members often band together to "fight" that external source and in that process team cohesiveness is increased. From a PM viewpoint, the key issue with conflict is to recognize that it will occur, and it can either be a destructive or creative force. There are two extremes of team conflict. If team members do not have visible disagreements, they are performing like lemmings following the leader over the cliff, while visible excessive internal personal emotion of other team members' ideas can be disastrous in every sense. The team leader needs to mend his team toward embracing these events as work challenges, not dumb opinions. If individuals can learn to professionally negotiate their ideas to others, their value to the team increases greatly (Fisher, 2008).

17.17 Negotiation Skills

The negotiation process involves in dealing with another person or party to settle a matter. "In a successful negotiation, everyone wins. The objective should be agreement, not victory" (Wertheim, 2008). The key goal of team negotiation is to convert the situation to win–win in which both parties feel that they were heard, and the solution makes the most sense for the project. Negotiation should result in the settlement of an issue or argument for the benefit of all parties involved in the conflict. To achieve this goal, the communication process between the parties needs to be open and honest. Hidden agendas will cloud the result otherwise. Communication is obviously one of the important components required to negotiate an issue.

Before the negotiation process begins, it is important to clearly define what is being negotiated. This process should be done face-to-face given that a rich flow of information is needed. Relevant data to the issue should be collected and your view of the situation should be clearly formulated. The type of conflict should be evaluated from the list above to judge how strongly you feel about the situation and what a desirable outcome would be. It is also important to recognize that the other party has an opinion that is different from yours; so laying out the two positions is the beginning of the process. Two essential skills required for negotiation are influence and confidence. Influence comes from your ability to be stylistically persuasive in selling your view. Confidence comes from being able to define the issue in terms that the other party understands and show the merits or worth of your view. This approach may be couched in data terms, qualitative goals, technical parameters, timing, cost, customer expectations, or other approaches. In the end, the negotiation process should obey the 3Fs—Fair, Fast, and Firm. Some of the successful tactics that are used for negotiation are listed below:

1. Be firm yet polite when making a stand.
2. Emphasize advantages and disadvantages of your approach.
3. Put ego aside and concentrate on the matter at hand.
4. Aim for solutions that are interest based and not based only on what any individual desires.
5. Value time, schedules, and deadlines. Try to not waste time, but be sensitive to the other party's needs to discuss.

17.18 Techniques for Handling Conflict

In the earlier discussion, we have seen various categories and sources of conflict and a general strategy for negotiating resolutions. However, in real life these come in various forms and the PM needs to be sensitive as to his timing to jump into the fray. One long-term goal is to train team members to resolve their own conflicts and stay out of the way. However, that is only good when a reasonable and timely result occurs and unfortunately that is not always the case. Mulcahy reports that 20% of a PM's time is spent in conflict management, so this activity will be a significant time allocation (Mulcahy, 2005). Specific sources and topics for conflicts come from various aspects of the project and these vary stage by stage. Typical areas are schedule, resources, technical, scope, budget, change requests, and personalities. Thamhain and Wilemon rate these sources over the life cycle (Thamhain and Wilemon, 1975, p. 35). Their research shows that schedules and priorities are the most typical conflict topic, but all items mentioned are also recorded.

Let us see if we can outline how to deal with the mechanics of the conflict process. When a conflict issue emerges, the first step is to decide your reaction. Frankly, the natural reaction is to hope that it will go away and do nothing. Unfortunately, experience shows that this is the worst management approach. Hence, the first point is that conflicts will tend to get worse if left alone and the management mantra for this is to *confront* those events using some measured strategy. There are multiple options to invoke and they may be taken sequentially or iteratively.

1. Withdraw—stay away from the situation.
2. Compromise—get involved with the situation to seek out a solution whereby each of the two parties gets something that they are looking for.
3. Smooth—try to convince each party that some solutions really give each some measure of satisfaction and de-emphasize the negatives.

4. Force—basically, the PM becomes official referee in this case. A decision can be made by either listening to the facts and making a decision, or just making a decision (autocratically).
5. Problem solve—this is the rational mind model that will work assuming that the parties are not mind locked to their position and will react to a set of facts. In this situation, the negotiation process unfolds, using the negotiation rules outlined earlier.

The question remains as to which option to select and when. The preferred choice is to try to minimize team leader involvement in the beginning other than to visibly recognize that you are aware that the issue exists. Also, if necessary, define some resolution constraints such as timing when an answer is needed. If facts are missing, help supply those but then let the team members work on the problem up to the constraint point. When that point occurs, the leader has to move to a second strategy and become an active member. The next step involves selecting a negotiation strategy realizing the following likely outcomes for each:

1. *Compromising*—offers some short-term win for both parties, but long term is likely viewed by the participants as lose/lose since neither got what they wanted.
2. *Smoothing*—depending on the skill level of the leader he may be able to placate the parties, but once again, this has lose/lose potential for longer term.
3. *Withdrawing*—the issue likely does not resolve itself. One of the only logical reasons to do this is to allow time for fact collection and then be better prepared to select another option later.
4. *Forcing*—in this case, the leader uses his formal authority to make the decision in whatever form he wishes. From a management perspective, this is the worst choice of all and if used, time should be spent with the parties on damage control. There may be situations that make this option necessary—timing or executive edict being examples.
5. *Problem solving*—this is the desired option and should be attempted as the most desirable step. Attempts to follow the steps are outlined earlier by first defining the problem and then spending time motivating the individuals to solve the problem. This has the best potential to be long lasting and leaving the parties with a win–win attitude.

Working with the project team on conflict management techniques is a mandatory mentoring activity for the PM. Failing to create this culture in the team leaves the leader with excessive time doing the team's job of getting the work done. Also, recognize that the development of a good plan that properly balances the scope, time, and cost variables will help minimize conflicts later.

17.19 Conflict Management Scenario Case

Envision two team members arguing over a technology-based planning issue. Both members are viewed to be technically competent. One person's view is that option A will result in cost savings for the project, while the other view is that option B will result is a technically superior product. It is agreed that option A will in fact potentially produce a higher-performance product and option B will extend the schedule. With these brief facts, how would you approach the conflict resolution of this issue under the following scenarios?

1. For step one, what would you say to the two parties and what would be your involvement in the process?

2. As an alternative view, the two parties are very dogmatic in their views and tend to have a narrow focus that is reflected by their individual positions. Neither will change their perspective.
3. All problem-solving efforts have failed up until now. The parties have followed the negotiation process, collected extensive data on their position, and the facts stay as they were first defined with no compromise. Either option A or option B must be selected. An answer to this question is now on the critical path of the planning effort. How would you deal with this situation? This makes a good open discussion scenario.

17.20 Leader versus Manager?

The question often arises as to whether the PM should be a leader or a manager of the team. Warren Bennis once described a leader as one who knows which direction to go (vision), whereas a manager knows how to get there (mechanic). PMs require at various points in the life cycle some of both characteristics. During the early project stages, finding the right vision is a leadership challenge since there is no clear vision yet. In this situation, the manager needs to help supply that direction in concert with user input. Later, the challenge evolves to executing the plan and that involves getting defined work accomplished. This is more of a management activity; however, even in this latter case the role remains to add a leadership element to the team as they strive to reach the goals. Based on this dual perspective, we are not going to try to segment these two roles here. Instead, the term *style* will be used to reflect how the PM accomplishes the required goal through his team. In one case, he may be behaving as an orchestra leader waving his baton with great music flowing, whereas in other situations he may be more like a military leader saying "follow me over this dangerous hill. This is what needs to be done." In many cases, the appropriate manager/leadership style will vary depending on what type of situation and circumstances are present. To be an effective leader you must know when to cross from one style to another and choosing the correct style at the right time is an important determinant for team success. No one style will work for all situations. As in the case of handling conflicts, style selection is a key skill.

17.21 Attributes of a Leader

Embedded in the style of the leader are his attributes. These represent qualities and characteristics that collectively make up how he is perceived by the project team. What makes these attributes different from the ordinary is that they stand out in a crowd. These attributes come in different mixes, but include the following: vision, action orientation, attitude, communication skills, motivation, relationships, ethics, responsibility, and confidence. Former Secretary of State, General Collin Powell summarized this idea in a 1996 speech:

> The ripple effect of a leader's enthusiasm and optimism is awesome. So is the impact of cynicism and pessimism. Leaders who whine and blame engender those same behaviors among their colleagues. I am not talking about stoically accepting organizational stupidity and performance incompetence with a "What, me worry?" smile. I am talking about a gung-ho attitude that says, "We can change things here, we can achieve awesome goals, and we can be the best." Spare me the grim litany of the "realist;" give me the unrealistic aspirations of the optimist any day.
>
> *(Harari, 2007)*

Leaders/managers bring out these attributes in the team. Another attribute of a leader is their persuasiveness that influences groups to follow them, even to the wrong goals. We must recognize that not all leaders lead to the correct goals. Hitler was a great leader and we see other negative international leaders today who would fall into the same category. The PM must also work on finding the right direction to lead. Leaders can move their teams to great heights or low depths. Thus, the job of a PM is to realize that this is his fate.

Good leadership also involves responsibility for the welfare of the team, which means that some will not agree with your actions and decisions. This is an inevitable outcome. Trying to make everyone like you is a sign of mediocrity. To do that you will have to avoid such things as making the tough decisions, confronting the people who need to be confronted, or not offering differential rewards based on differential performance because some would get upset. Ironically, by procrastinating on difficult choices, by trying not to get anyone mad, and by treating everyone equally "nice" regardless of their contributions you will simply ensure that the only people you will wind up angering are the most creative and productive people in the organization (Harari, 2007). Effective leaders know that they cannot make everyone happy with every decision or action that is made. Leaders do not always like to engage in these types of actions but must do so because this sets the tone for other employees in recognizing that the overall team is more valuable than a single individual.

Another aspect of project leadership is taking responsibility for outcomes. When certain things go wrong, something or somebody else usually caused those events. The inclination is to find the source and make sure that everyone knows that it was not you—that is, human nature. Poor leaders want everyone to know that the problem was not caused by them. They do not want to take blame for things that go wrong or take responsibility for the welfare of the group. An effective leader must do both. Effective leaders take responsibility for bad issues and leave credit to others for the good things that happen.

Final point is that a leader may be a good manager, but a manager is not always a good leader (this goes both ways). The position of manager may be achieved through a formal job assignment by the organization. Leaders, on the other hand, unite followers with their vision and this can occur outside of formal organizational structures. Regardless, leadership traits as described here are needed in the PMs' skill set and they must use these qualities to their maximum potential to get the team headed in the right direction.

Good management skills complement leadership. Management is commonly defined as the process of getting work done through others. Leadership is the process of influencing people to give their energies, potential, determination, and to go beyond their comfort zones to accomplish goals. Management affects work; leadership affects people (Barr and Barr, 1989). These collective traits are the key to moving the HR toward the desired targets.

17.22 Summary

This chapter has provided a summary overview of the Team Management process in the project team. Managing team resources is a complex undertaking. Every PM needs to go through a self-assessment of his management style and this is a valid internal improvement process that all should undertake. It is important to get to know the project team members and understand their individual goals. Once this is done, you can do a much better job on roles and responsibilities, as well as work allocation.

References

Academic Leadership Support (ALS), 2008. Conflict Resolution Menu—Step 6. www.ohrd.wisc.edu/onlinetraining/resolution/step6.htm (accessed October 23, 2008).

American Management Association (AMA), 2008. Team Building. www.amanet.org/onsite/team-building/67715.htm (accessed October 23, 2008).

AST Group, July 12, 2001. The Top 10 Reasons Why Projects Fail. www.itweb.co.za/office/ast/0107120730.htm [Gijima AST Group Limited (GijimaAst)] (accessed October 24, 2008).

Barr, L. and N. Barr, 1989. *The Leadership Equation: Leadership, Management, and the Myers-Briggs: Balancing Style = Leadership Enhancement.* Austin, TX: Eakin Press.

brij, 2007. brij Technology Dictionary. www.brij.net/technology_dictionary.html (accessed November 2008).

Fisher, R., 2008. Sources of Conflict and Methods of Conflict Resolution. www.ohrd.wisc.edu/onlinetraining/resolution/step6.htm (accessed October 24, 2008).

Gallup, 2008. Conflict Management. http://gmj.gallup.com/content/532/How-Great-Managers-Define-Talent.aspx (accessed October 24, 2008).

Hall, K., January/February 2008. The Teamwork Myth. An Interview with Kevan Hall. www.humancapitalmanagement.org.

Herzsberg, F., B. Mausner, and B.B. Snyderman, 1959. *The Motivation to Work*, 2nd ed. New York: Wiley.

Harari, O., 2007. Quotations from Chairman Powell: A Leadership Primer. GovLeaders.org. 1996. April 10–24, 2007. www.govleaders.org/powell.htm (accessed October 24, 2008).

Maslow, A., 1954. *Motivation and Personality.* New York: Wiley.

McClelland, D., 1965. Toward a Theory of Motive Acquisition. *American Psychologist*, Vol 20(5), May 1965, 321–333.

Mulcahy, R., 2005. *PMP Exam Prep*, 5th ed. Minnetonka, MN: RMC Publications, Inc.

PMI, 2017. *A Guide to the Project Management Body of Knowledge (PMBOK® Guide)*, 6th ed. Newtown Square, PA: Project Management Institute.

Thamhain, H.H. and D.L. Wilemon, 1975. Conflict management in project life cycle. *Sloan Management Review*, 16(3): 31–50.

Wertheim, E., 2008. Negotiations and Resolving Conflicts: An Overview. http://web.cba.neu.edu/~ewertheim/interper/negot3.htm (accessed December 15, 2008).

Chapter 18

Project Communications

The problem with communication ... is the illusion that it has been accomplished.

—*George Bernard Shaw*

18.1 Introduction

Communication is the fuel that drives project success and the mishandling of this activity is one of the top reasons why projects struggle. Various authors claim that communication is the most important skill for a project manager (PM). Clearly, effective communication is required between the PM, the project team, management, and other stakeholders. An environment that achieves effective communication among this diverse group will find an improved outlook for project success. Some of the basic activities include interacting with diverse audiences, holding effective meetings, and facilitating communication among external parties involved in the project. This chapter will describe the model processes related to project communication and review basic concepts related to human-to-human relationships.

18.2 Engaging Employees: A Case Study

Before jumping into communications theory, it would be good to illustrate the impact of "engaging" the employee. The Gallup Management Journal (GMJ) surveyed U.S. employees to discover what effect engagement had on team-level innovation and customer service delivery (Gallup, 2006). The results of this survey indicate that employees who are engaged were more productive and this produced "powerful catalysts for creative thinking in regard to new management and business processes within the company" (Gallup, 2006). Sixty-one percent of those surveyed responded that they were inspired by the creativity of colleagues and an engagement process brought out the best of their creativity, whereas only 3% of those who felt disengaged strongly agreed. Engaged employees were also found to be more communicative with customers and the result of that was a greater sharing of ideas.

Other positive work performance attributes were noted regarding engaged employees having greater self-motivation, confidence to express new ideas, higher productivity, higher levels of customer service, reliability, less employee turnover, and lower absenteeism. The result of this positive impact on employee performance can be translated into finding hidden profits for the organization. On the negative side, the GMJ 2006 survey estimated that disengaged employees' costs the U.S. economy about $328 billion in lost productivity (Gallup, 2006). With this knowledge one might ask why organizations are not more visibly concerned with programs to improve these attributes in their employees.

The effect of good communications is hard to measure, but this case illustrates the positive motivational results from an effective program to make employees feel that they are engaged in the organizational processes. The same reaction occurs in project teams, which brings us to the topic of this section. Communications Management is a significant and tangible issue not only for projects, but for entire organizations.

18.3 Communications Management Processes

The knowledge areas (KAs) of Project Communications Management include the processes required to ensure timely and appropriate generation, collection, distribution, storage, retrieval, and ultimate disposition of project information. This topic involves processes and methods for transmission of information among the project team members and stakeholders. The *PMBOK® Guide* specifies three basic communications processes (PMI, 2017, p. 359):

1. Plan communications management
2. Manage communications
3. Monitor communications

As with all the guide, the first step for each is a plan to define the steps to be followed for the rest of the operational processes. This area follows that basic approach.

18.4 Plan Communications

A vital foundation component in the successful management and completion of a project is the creation and implementation of a communications plan at the start of a project. The purpose of this first step is to identify the information and communication needs of the stakeholder population (PMI, 2017, p. 359). As simple as this idea sounds, it is surprising to find that many projects never bother to formally identify their communication targets, timing, content, or receiver's preferred media for the information. One clear message that needs to be discussed in this chapter is that project communications tend to be lacking and effective implementation of this planning step is required to establish the base for improving that situation.

Recognition that communication is a crucial challenge that projects face enforces the motivation to pursue this area with the same diligence as other planning aspects of the project. The primary output of this planning step is a *communications management plan* that attempts to integrate the communication requirements needed to manage project scope definition, technology to be utilized for communications, and the underlying development process within the organizational culture (Richardson and Butler, 2006, p 293). The *Project Management Body of Knowledge (PMBOK®)*

Guide outlines in some detail the content recommendations for this plan (PMI, 2017, p. 377). This plan also addresses the technology to be utilized for communications and the underlying development process within the organizational culture (Richardson and Butler, 2006, p. 293). For our purposes, envision this document as a repository containing information about targets, templates, policies, methods, and individuals who are defined as project communications receivers.

Effective communications processes are required for stakeholders to deal with the human interaction required in achieving the project work. Communication techniques utilized in a project include various formal and informal methods. Examples of formal options include the following items:

- Periodic status reports
- Progress review meetings
- Kickoff meetings (project and stage)
- Executive reports
- Formal presentations to various stakeholder groups
- Project financial status reports
- Governmental (or external agency) reports
- Issue logs
- Risk logs
- Change request logs
- Role responsibility
- Project organization
- Milestone reports
- Deliverables status reports.

Each of these items represents a unique communication strategy for the selected stakeholder groups. One of the basic problems with project communications is that no one method will satisfy all constituents. Timing, media choice, and content requirements vary significantly by audience. Definition of the targets and these issues represent the fundamental planning challenge to resolve.

Once the targets have been identified and discussions are held with them regarding what and how they wish to receive project communications, the documentation step would include the following specifics:

Recipient: The individual or group that will receive the communication.
Who: Identifies the team member who is responsible for the delivery of the communication.
What: Defines the output content of the communication. This includes a defined format in the case of status-type reporting (i.e., monthly project status report).
Location: Defines where the item will be stored prior to distribution.
When: Defines the calendar time for delivery (i.e., monthly, daily, on demand, etc.).
Media: Identifies the media used for delivery (i.e., e-mail, web, paper, telephone, group briefing, verbal, video conference, etc.).
Focus: An indication of the stakeholder's particular communication focus (i.e., cost, schedule, technical status, subsystem, etc.). This section could also indicate the level of detail desired.

Collectively, this family of formal communication options is intended to keep the project team and its other stakeholders linked to project status and to help maintain proper priorities and guidance information for their respective efforts.

Informal communications tend to be more dynamic and less planned than the formal items outlined above. Many of these will be ad hoc and focused on a specific topic of the moment. The key in these is to attempt to create an open exchange of ideas between the parties and to generate a feeling of trust with the PM.

Beyond the project, internal team key organizational stakeholders are obvious audiences for project communications, but there are other less likely groups that need—or want—project information. Therefore, the search for communication targets needs to include both internal and external stakeholders. The project team is the core of the communication network. Team members work on the project every day and they require active communication. This group is both a heavy user of communication and a significant provider to others.

Management stakeholders are not involved so closely with the project on a daily basis, but they make key decisions about it and for that reason must not be ignored. Typical management groups consist of the project sponsor, project board, change management board, functional managers, future users, and others.

One example of a supporting group need for status information occurs when the project goal is to create a new commercial product for sale. In this case, the marketing department would want to be kept abreast of such things as product features, cost, and availability. The legal department is involved in procurement activities and could benefit from information regarding risk issues and vendor problems. Each supporting organization would have different information interest needs and that issue must be defined in the planning process.

An external communications audience is very diverse in their interests. For example, vendors, suppliers, partners, and their respective project counterparts are often extensions of the internal team in many ways. However, communications with external audiences will be generally in less detail. Investors and regulatory agencies (such as the Internal Revenue Service (IRS), Environmental Protection Agency (EPA), or a public utility commission) represent additional examples of external audiences. Governmental organizations may specify the format and schedule required submittals. Once the project communication requirements are defined, it is common to document these in a format called the project *communication matrix*. Table 18.1 is a mock-up of such a format.

The communication matrix helps manage the flow of formal documents out of the project and helps ensure the integrity of the process. In addition to the regular outflow of information,

Table 18.1 Communication Matrix

Audience	*Information Item*	*Media*	*Frequency*
Project team	WBS status report	Email	Weekly
Project team	Project newsletter	Email	Weekly
Project team	Risk review	Meeting	Bi-weekly
Sponsor	Monthly status report	On-line	Monthly
Project board	Change control status	On-line	Daily
Stakeholder A	Project overview status	Email	Monthly
Stakeholder B	Technical deliverables	Paper	Monthly
HR	Manpower report	Email	Monthly

there are various milestones or checkpoints that require additional reporting. These key points are identified in the project plan and are typically management (time and cost) or technically oriented.

Once the communications plan is complete it becomes one of the subsidiary plans compiled into the overall project plan.

18.5 Distribute Information

The physical process of moving needed information to project stakeholders in a timely manner is called *information distribution*. This includes the specific items outlined in the communications plan as well as various ad hoc requests for information. The distribution process requires consideration of methods to gather and store the information and related technology to transmit it to the recipients.

Within the project team, the distribution process deals more with intragroup- sharing-needed information related to the technical aspects of the project. This includes items such as product design architecture, technical drawings, and other information needed by the team to produce the product. Finally, two somewhat subtle aspects of the distribution process are lessons-learned documentation and understanding the behavioral aspects of communicating with internal and external project contacts. Both deal with the notion of strategic improvement in the communication process, mostly for future projects.

18.6 Report Performance

Much of the Information Distribution process is focused on reporting project status in one form or another. The general theme of reporting involves time, schedule, baselines, quality, risk, and technical aspects of the project sorted into user interest segments. Example for reporting items include the following:

1. Time and schedule variance (ideally with earned value [EV])
2. Work performance status
3. Quality related data
4. Change request data
5. Deliverables status
6. Project forecast metrics

In all reporting activities, the PM must maintain an ethical stance of honest reporting to all parties. In many situations, it is tempting to withhold bad information that might trigger an overly negative response with the rationale that this is a temporary problem that will be resolved. The reporting rule says that the facts must be presented along with an action plan to deal with any major issues.

18.7 Human Communications Model

The mechanical communication processes required for project management have been outlined above, but the real communication management issues occur at the human-to-human level. There is an art to effective communication and it is necessary to be sensitive to the general processes that

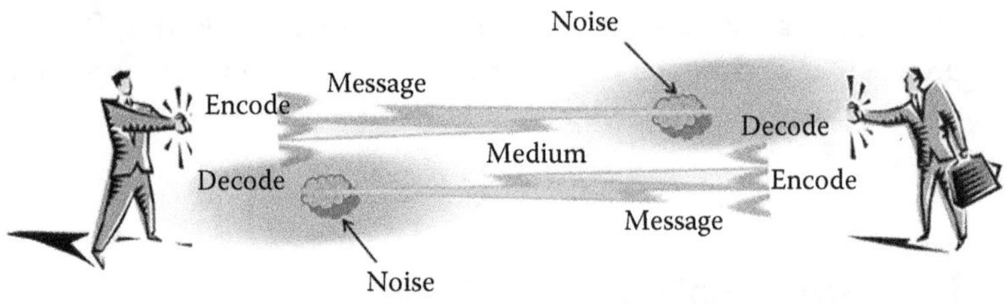

Figure 18.1 Basic communication model.

assist in this activity. This certainly involves more than just passing bits through some technical communications channels. All humans communicate with others on a daily basis, but we rarely step back and dissect what is actually happening and how is it received by others. Most technical PMs have never been taught or trained to analyze the communication process, so it is not surprising that it often creates unintended consequences between the parties.

It is relatively easy to learn a simple communications framework that will help to understand the process better and apply it to daily situations. Using this knowledge, we can better deal with many daily work-related issues that result in conflict, errors, or unintended emotions. It has been estimated that 90% of conflicts are created by misunderstandings caused by communications shortcomings (Mulcahy, 2005).

The first step in improving communications skills is to understand the basic communication model and think about its implications in daily information transfer. Figure 18.1 is a schematic view of the model components, and its basic building blocks are a sender, receiver, and transmission media.

In this model, the sender formulates a message and the receiver attempts to translate that message into understandable meaning. In order to successfully accomplish this, five elements have to be completed:

1. Encode—translating mental images or ideas into an effective format (language) understood by the receiver
2. Message—bits resulting from the encoding step
3. Medium—method used to transmit the message (verbal, visual, tactile, etc.)
4. Noise—anything that interferes with the transmission and understanding of the message
5. Decode—receiver processes the bits transmitted (minus noise) into meaningful thoughts or ideas

In addition to this, a feedback loop helps to ensure that the message was properly received. This can be accomplished in various ways, but is an important component of the process. If all goes well, the two parties end up after the process with exactly the same mental perceptions for the item being communicated. Unfortunately, there are many places where accuracy can be eroded.

It has been noted from personal experience that speaking plainly to a person who does not speak the same language as you is not very effective no matter how many times you repeat the transmission, or how loudly you speak. In this case, the model is working almost exactly as described, but the encoding step results in mental garbage for the receiver. Likewise, noise in the channel can be created by physical noise or other distortions of the message (i.e., speaking too fast, dialects, vocabulary used, and emotion). When any of these distortions occur, the model does not work, and the desired mental perception match fails to achieve its goal. In these and

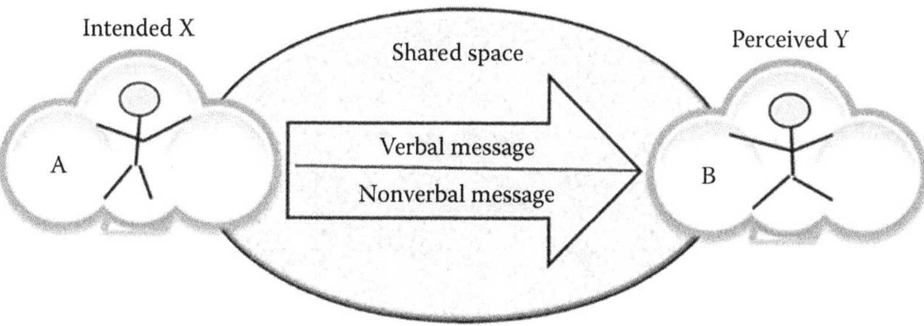

Figure 18.2 Actionable communications model.

other situations voluminous bits are flowing between the parties, but no real communication is occurring. Synchronization between the two has not occurred. Both parties must understand the transmission, whether they agree with the content or not.

For real communication to occur, five elements are needed. The process is only partially successful if it reaches the third state (understanding), and is progressively improved at the fourth (agreement) or fifth (action) steps. Figure 18.2 illustrates this process with a slightly expanded communications model.

For a successful communications event to be successful the following five steps must occur: transmission, reception, understanding, agreement, and useful action. Let us explore the communication implications of these steps in a little more detail.

1. *Transmission:* In transmitting a message via e-mail or voice mail, the intent is to remotely communicate with the receiver. However, this does not mean the receiver has read or will hear the message. It just means the message has been sent and is assumed to be encoded later. Current technology offers the opportunity to send great volumes of "communication" in this remote forward and store manner, but we often do not consider the other side of the equation. Obviously, the link is broken if the message is not received.
2. *Reception:* When someone finally checks their e-mail, voice mail, or signs for an overnight letter, the message is finally received. Once again, we still do not know whether the entire message was listened to, understood, or even opened. In each case, the recipient may not have the inclination to interpret or spend any time trying to properly encode the message. While confirmation receipts for the class of transmission indicate physical receipt, they confirm nothing else.
3. *Understanding:* Digesting and interpreting a message's information correctly represents a significant jump in communication compared to simply receiving the message. This step requires cognitive activity to understand the original intent. Depending on the message content, understanding might involve learning something new and it might require other researches on the topic. The message may be ambiguous without the ancillary research and when a question is involved both parties may seek clarification. In this situation, both sides are looking for the completion of a communication receipt and feedback. In some situations, the message may contain items that are not understood. For example, if the original transmission was "what do you think we need to do in order to correct problem X?" the receiver may not know there was a problem X. After some research, they can uncover the details about problem X and can then add more content to the next communications cycle. In this example case, a feedback communication loop leaves both parties with more knowledge

than they initially had. In project communications, it is common for the recipient to start the process asking for additional information. The understanding step does not occur until some improved level or response action occurs. Also, the research portion of this example can spawn other additional questions asked back to the original transmitter or other parties. In this form, the communications cycle is iterative with each cycle adding content to the initial ambiguous message. Moving from a raw bit transmission view of communications to achieving understanding requires more active involvement of the parties than is evident from the schematic model.

4. *Agreement:* Achieving understanding of the message does not necessarily mean that a person agrees with what was transmitted. Take, for example, the statement "you are an idiot!" This message might be quickly understood but would not yield instant agreement. Achieving agreement between two technically oriented, intelligent, and opinionated communicators can be a complex and time-consuming activity, especially if the "facts" related to the issue in question are philosophical or technically judgmental. This class of communications comes closer to what one finds in a complex project environment. When the PM finds himself embroiled in such team discussions the communications channels have already been filled with transmissions, but little agreement. In this situation, the challenge is often to first get emotions under control and then work to collect a common set of facts and observations. Until a common understanding of the issues is achieved the conflict and agreement levels will remain.
5. *Useful action:* When we look at the basic reason for project communication, it is to achieve an improved level of understanding and produce some desired action as a result. Team members need to understand what work is required to accomplish the desired goal and take actions because of that knowledge. Stakeholders need to use status information to make appropriate decisions regarding the project, even though that decision might result in a cancellation of the project. Failure to achieve an appropriate level of understanding in either case will yield the wrong action. At this level in the model, we need to recognize the true role of communications. We all have experienced an aged relative who wanted only to hear himself/herself talk. They were not interested in hearing what you had to say, but the communication process was almost like a brain dump for them. This approach does not work in a project team environment. Failure to successfully accomplish the communication process can contribute to the following undesirable effects:
   - Project team members will make wrong choices on work efforts
   - Conflict will be created among the project team by misunderstandings
   - Stakeholders have erroneous expectations regarding project status
   - External organizations not receiving the information they require can cause major issues with the project team or the resulting product
   - Senior management will not have appropriate information to use regarding the project
   - Team morale becomes eroded because of low "engagement" in what is going on inside the team.

Good communicators transmit information with the intent of it being understood and then producing appropriate action. Instead of just sending an e-mail, voice mail, or letter and seeing what happens, the effective communicator will carefully analyze each of the five steps described above. They select language, media, and examples that best fit the receiver instead of those most convenient for them. In addition, they follow-up to clarify what the likely points of confusion or argument are and identify what actions they want the recipient to take in response. Finally, follow-up occurs until the issue is concluded. Good communication occurs when there is a natural and open sequence of exchanges between the parties. Even when the topic is confrontational, being aware of the communication model framework helps identify where the process is breaking down.

18.8 Communication Channels

The communications models outlined earlier have focused on a process occurring simply between a single sender and a receiver. This is a micro-view of the process, but the more realistic macro-view involves multiple communications channels occurring simultaneously across the project. Therefore, the communication goal is not just to get a single individual involved, but to accomplish it with all stakeholders. As the size of the project stakeholder population grows, it gets harder to keep everyone "on the same page." Also, the communication flow process is not homogeneous since the various channels are different and each has unique characteristics. There are basically three channel types:

- Upward communication (vertically or diagonally)
- Downward communication (vertically or diagonally)
- Lateral communication (horizontally).

Not only is the approach and content of communication different across these three types, but collectively they represent a significant volume of channels to deal with. A mathematical formula for determining how many channels (C) exist within a population of N people is (Schwalbe, 2004, p. 361):

$$C = \frac{N * (N - 1)}{2}$$

Therefore, if four people are involved the number of communication channels would be

$$C = \frac{4 * (4 - 1)}{2}$$

If we increase that number to 10, the number grows to 45 channels. Figure 18.3 shows this schematically.

Figure 18.4 expands this view to show what the channel count would be for an even larger project group. Given the geometry of this relationship, it should be easy to see why experience shows that optimum project team size is less than approximately seven.

Communications breakdown is considered by many researchers to be the number one reason for project failure (Berkun, 2005). There are five primary causes for project communications breakdown: common language, communication mechanics, personal factors, communications style, and workplace factors.

Common language: Global projects often use English as the common language, though this may be a second language for many participants, particularly in an outsourcing situation. Because of this, understanding is decreased because of dialect, vocabulary, miscomprehension, or misunderstanding of words. Often, this situation is not resolved because one of the parties does not want to admit they do not understand the information given.

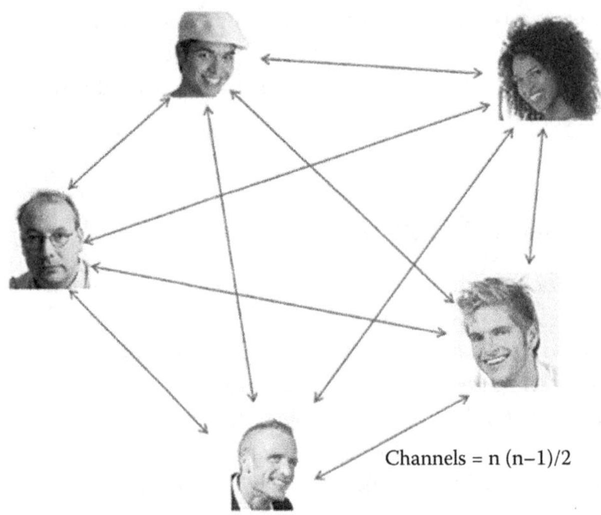

Figure 18.3 Channels of communication.

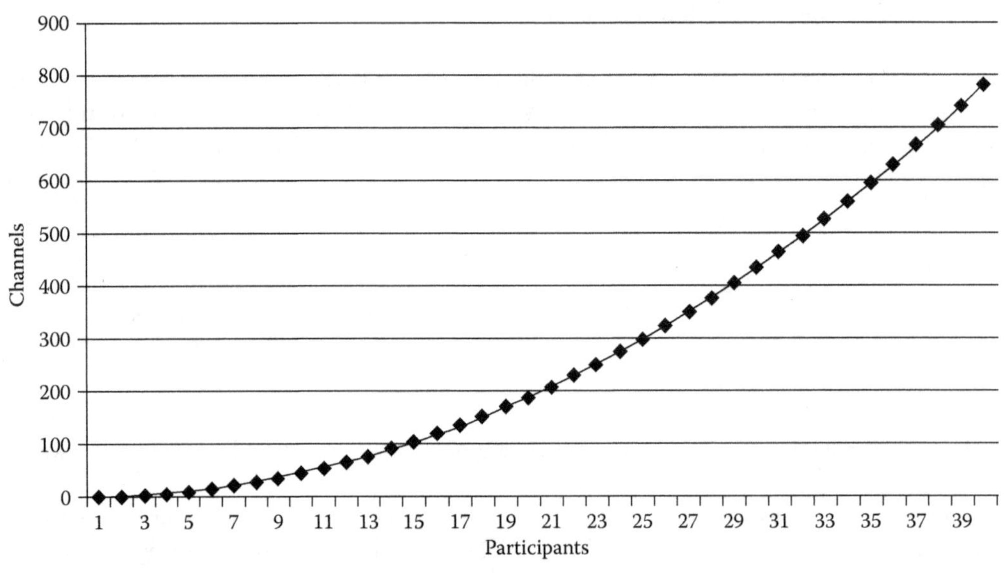

Figure 18.4 Communication growth versus team size.

Communication mechanics: The mechanics of effective communication involves not only passively passing messages, but to actively listen to the other person. This involves more of a dynamic interchange between the parties. Clarifying questions and other techniques help to ensure that the process will produce an accurate understanding of the message.

Personal factors: Workplace performance is affected by a wide variety of issues, but external job issues often impact performance on the job. Oftentimes, these issues get into the work communication and become negative noise.

Communication style: Some individuals are easier to talk to than others. The style aspects of the process deal primarily with the setting for the conversation and the way in which the presenters interact with each other.

Workplace factors: To successfully complete a project the deliverables must match the requirements. To produce this outcome, the PM is constantly dealing with decisions designed to keep the triple constraints within schedule and budget, while meeting the requirements. Balancing these variables has the potential to send the wrong signals to one or more stakeholder groups.

One strategy to mitigate this problem is to institute a program to sensitize the project team to the issues outlined here. Creating an improved understanding regarding how to produce effective communications is the core requirement. In addition to this review, the source and analysis of conflicts can help with project functioning. Sartor says, "In my 25-year career I have discovered that the most successful projects were the ones where respect for everyone's point of view enabled mature and open dialogue and trust building to work through the project challenges. Quality takes time. That's how great companies are built" (Berkun, 2005).

18.9 Communicating Information

Project status information is typically communicated often using tools and jargon-related terms such as WBS, Gantt, and Earned Value (EV), but the primary requirement is mainly about communicating with people. This requires that customers, stakeholders, and team members know what is required to do their jobs in language they understand. Other forms of communications involve negotiating with a broad array of stakeholders, defining team member's assignments, or working with a group to resolve an issue that is impacting the project. All these scenarios are designed to synchronize various parties' communications requirements regarding the project. For these processes to work effectively, the process requires good communications skills.

18.10 Improving the Effectiveness of Communication

Because PMs spend a significant amount of time communicating with individuals and groups, they inevitably carry a broader responsibility for effective communication than other individuals on the team. Success with these activities amplifies the effectiveness of everyone they encounter.

Being an effective communicator does not mean that the person necessarily be an extrovert game-show-host personality; nor does it demand a brilliant sense of humor or charismatic powers. Each of these might help, but the first requirement is to understand the important role that this process plays in a well-run project. From this initial step, there will be more sensitivity to the issue and from that will come an improved understanding of the process.

18.11 Effective Listening

One of the key attributes of a good communicator is to be an effective listener. The person who can do this successfully will develop a greater degree of mutual respect, rapport, and trust among project participants. Some of the techniques used to improve active communication involve effective listening and some techniques to increase the content of a conversation include the following:

- Asking questions to clarify and gather more focused information
- Paraphrasing what the speaker said to be sure that you understand his point
- Stopping at intervals to review what you have understood up to that point
- Asking the speaker for examples of a point being made
- Ascertaining the speaker's feelings and acknowledging them (e.g., "You seem angry")
- Showing interest by directing the speaker to the most appropriate person to help
- Using nonverbal listening techniques including:
  - Making eye contact
  - Being expressive and alert
  - Moving closer to the speaker
  - Listening for the meanings beyond the words used
  - Using body language to show emotion and agreement

18.12 Barriers to Effective Communication

There are many things that a communicator can do to inhibit effective communication. Simply breaking the rules outlined in the communications model is the most obvious. The most important item is to recognize that communications is a two-way process. Input is needed from both sides to improve content. The second major barrier is the physical environment where the communication takes place. Telephone or personal interruptions can negatively impact a conversation. Being in the boss's office versus a nice quiet restaurant can make a world of difference in the process. After the basic environmental issues are resolved, the success of the conversation moves to the topic itself. Two individuals talking about a sports contest can disagree and still enjoy the conversation, while two technicians arguing/discussing their diverse views on a technical issue may become more negative and become a negotiation or problem-solving challenge.

In addition to the mechanical and intellectual aspects of a communication process, the internals in play within the individuals can influence the outcome. For example, consider the following examples (Nokes et al., 2004):

- Judgment—lack of respect for the other's views
- Mind block—already made up your mind on the topic; no more information wanted
- Filtering—picking out some subset of the stream and focusing only on that
- Assumptions—misinterpreting elements of the conversation without confirming
- Side tracking—losing sight of the topic and digressing to others

Each of these inhibitors will decrease the effectiveness of the conversation. With a little practice each of these can be avoided to a great degree.

18.13 Communication Tension

Beyond the mechanics and attitudinal aspects of the communication process, there are also issues even for the experienced communicator regarding the philosophy behind how the message is created. These difficulties arise mainly from styles pulling in opposite directions, thus the term *tension* (Nokes et al., 2004). Table 18.2 summarizes six examples of this.

Table 18.2 Communication Tension

The need to communicate the complete story or situation	versus	The need to be brief
The need to tailor the message to the audience, and to simplify	versus	The duty to be open and honest
The need to treat all stakeholders fairly and equal	versus	Competing needs and expectations among stakeholders and the need to release some information over time
The need to listen	versus	Time constraints require a more one-way approach
Demand for the full story now along with all details	versus	The need to release some information over time
The value of being very specific in terms volumes of raw data to back a position	versus	The value of a quicker understanding of the fundamental issues, with details provided later. This requires some faith on the part of the receiver.

In some cases, these tension scenarios cannot be controlled or managed because of other environmental constraints. In these situations, the communicator must decide how to navigate through the conflicting options. Also, in many cases the receiver has a bias for one of the options and it is up to the communicator to sense this and react accordingly. These tensions occur frequently in the project environment because of time pressure, mixed skill types of the participants, and transient nature of matrix staff.

18.14 Communication Styles

Everyone has a unique communication style that fits their personality and environment. Some will approach the communications process in a friendly manner first and then drift into content, whereas others view it more as a data passing exercise with mostly content. There are basically four model communication styles that can be briefly described as follows:

Concrete-sequential: Fix-it. This style focuses communications on ideas and tasks. They see the project as a set of tasks that need to be completed and the conversation focuses primarily on that.

Abstract-sequential: Organizer. This style uses logical analysis and systematic planning to solve problems. This conversation works to collect data from other sources in order to seek a decision. Organizers are called people and task oriented, which makes them effective team builders.

Concrete-random: Explorer/Entrepreneur. This style relies on people and technology in a search for practical theories and models. Decisions are made after thorough analysis and evaluation. These individuals excel at facilitating planning sessions, discussions, and changes.

Abstract-random: Intuitive free thinker. This style sees situations from different perspectives. They also look at the big picture and the long-term view. Abstract-random communicators make good "brainstormers" because they can listen actively and enjoy the process of generating new ideas.

All models are abstractions of reality; however, a key point to observe is how an individual formulates his conversation, fact gathering, decision-making, socialization, and so on. Good communication requires that one party adapts to the other's preferred style. This is called *style flexing*. Once that style is identified, the conversation should be packaged into that form as much as possible.

18.15 Communications: The Impossible Goal?

With all these variables and contributing factors, can effective communications be possible? Hopefully, this discussion has highlighted the reasons why it is not easy and will require careful consideration. If it were possible to write a communications goal statement for the PM and the team, it would contain at least the following six communications attributes:

1. *Project goal:* Significant effort should be made to effectively communicate requirements to the entire project team and confirm that these have been translated into technical work units.
2. *Information distribution:* The project environment is data rich, but can be information poor if an appropriate distribution environment is not created. Enterprise information infrastructure is an important delivery aspect of maintaining effective communications.
3. *Team engagement:* By having a communications-rich environment, team members will be motivated to achieve project goals. In such an environment, the engaged project team will be capable of doing the right work the right way.
4. *Status:* Various stakeholders have different status needs. Formulate the communication processes accordingly and make sure that the channels are energized. Understandable communications of status will keep expectations in order and help team members focus on the proper targets.
5. *Cohesive team:* There is a selfish reason for the PM wanting a mature project communications environment. When effective communications can be achieved, and team members are engaged they do not have to ask questions or guess at the answer. This increases productivity and morale.
6. *Continuous improvement:* Every project needs to have the attitude of making the next project run better than the current one. The communication process does not stop at the end of a project. The lessons learned process is itself a communications process designed to help both the current and future projects run more effectively.

Achieving these six communication attributes should be the guiding focus of the PM. These communications-related goals can be successfully achieved if the project team can establish the correct attitudes and processes related to their environment.

18.16 Conclusion

This chapter has described the importance of effective communications in the project. The basic models for one-to-one communication and group equivalents were outlined. Research indicates that 90% of the PM's time should be spent in this activity, so failure to effectively accomplish this goal will have adverse implications on project performance. Various surveys grade the lack of effective communications as the number one reason for project failure. In a technical project, accurate results can only occur when there is a clear chain of communications from the initial user requirements through to final delivery. The human communication frailty along this process makes this KA a complex one to deal with.

Discussion Questions

1. Describe the basic role of project communications as it directly impacts project success.
2. Which method of communications is most effective for change requests?
3. Name some of the communications-oriented attributes a team should have for successful project execution.
4. What do you believe are the most important skills a PM must have to ensure effective team communications?
5. What are some key communications style attributes in dealing with a customer?
6. If you are responsible for coordinating various meetings related to your project during the execution phase, what would be an effective method of keeping track of the outcome of these meetings?
7. What are some of the basic approaches you would use to provide performance feedback to the project team? What communications issues would you predict for this process?
8. One of your subordinates has very good skills in her area of expertise, but for some reason she finds it difficult to perform well on your project. What would you do about this situation?
9. One of your friends is the PM for a large project and is finding it difficult to meet his schedules. What advice would you offer to help in this situation?
10. You are assigned a new responsibility for a project where there is a difficult negotiation going between your organization's management and the external customer. You are now involved in the negotiation process. What can you do to help resolve this situation?
11. You foresee an opportunity with your long-term customer to generate huge additional income through a new market that you are familiar with. As the relationship stands currently your organization will not profit from this suggestion. What will you do?

References

Berkun, S., 2005. *The Art of Project Management.* Ann Arbor: O'Reilly Media, Inc.

Gallup Study: Engaged Employees Inspire Company Innovation. *Gallup Management Journal,* http://gmj.gallup.com/content/466/Gallup-Study-Indicates-Actively-Disengaged-Workers-Cost-US-Hundreds.aspx (accessed October 12, 2006).

Mulcahy, R., 2005. *PMP Exam Prep,* 5th ed. Minnetonka: RMC Publications, Inc.

Nokes, S., I. Major, A. Greenwood, and M. Goodman, 2004. *The Definitive Guide to Project Management: Every Executives Fast-Track to Delivering on Time and on Budget.* Harlow: FT Press.

PMI, 2017. *A Guide to the Project Management Body of Knowledge (PMBOK® Guide),* 6th ed. Newtown Square, PA: Project Management Institute.

Richardson, G.L. and C.W. Butler, 2006. *Readings in Information Technology Management.* Newtown Square, PA: Course Technology.

Schwalbe, K., 2004. *Information Technology Project Management.* Newtown Square, PA: Course Technology.

Chapter 19

Project Stakeholder Management

19.1 Introduction

"Every project has stakeholders who are impacted by or can impact the project in a positive or negative way. Some stakeholders may have a limited ability to influence the project's work or outcomes; others may have significant influence on the project and its expected outcomes" (PMI, 2017, 504). In this chapter, we are focused solely on processes dealing with stakeholders outside the project team. Recognizing individuals external to the project team as being a major influence of project success is a somewhat new idea. One could feel that this topic has already been covered in the previous chapters on communications management and to some degree this feeling is justified. However, there are some different perspectives to deal with as we focus on this external interface segment. The role of this chapter is to highlight issues involved in managing stakeholder communication and is concerned more as viewed from their impact than in just general communication theory. In this view, the project manager (PM) must negotiate issues the stakeholder raises in such a manner to keep the internally defined project plan requirements aligned with this population's dynamic views. Therefore, with this perspective we now somewhat alter the management goal of the project team to one of delivering items that are dynamically aligned with this audience and not necessarily the existing project plan that has driven the process up until now. The results of this activity can yield yet another source of formal change requests that the project team seeks.

In the stakeholder scenario, we are recognizing these external groups as collections of entities interacting with the project primarily as either a funding source, higher-level decision maker, resource supplier, governance body, or future user. Each of these groups plays a subtle but important role in the success of a project. They collectively and dynamically define project success in a manner quite different from the original vision-driven scope definition that the project team is focused on in their daily work efforts, moving toward an output defined by the defined holy trilogy of scope, time, and cost as described in the existing project plan. We must recognize that much of the future evaluation of a project's success lies in the eyes of these beholders. There is growing evidence that failure to recognize this aspect of project management can be one of the leading causes of a project being graded as a success or failure, regardless of the actual completion status of the project output. In other words, a project may in fact complete with all of the defined requirements, on time, and on budget but then be judged as a failure because that was the wrong target as perceived by influential stakeholders. The project team must now see the project goal as accomplishing the defined target, but also marketing and negotiating perceptions of the stakeholders. This is an additional outbound communication effort on the part of the project team. This requires both a selling aspect, as well as a listening one.

19.2 Identifying Stakeholders

Surprisingly, it is not uncommon to have a new stakeholder surface late in the life cycle. They may have suddenly recognized that the project would impact them, but up to this point had been left out of the communication channels. Obviously, if this stakeholder has influence over project direction this will not be a friendly time for them to enter the scene. This suggests that an important early activity for the project team is to spend sufficient time identifying the stakeholder population and documenting their characteristics. Once defined, the data should be maintained in a formal repository officially called the *stakeholder register*. This artifact will be the prime documentation used to store related data and define the communication strategy for each stakeholder.

19.2.1 Communications Planning

If a project manager wants effective communication with relevant stakeholders it must be planned. The communication plan involves determining the relevant details and this document content was defined previously in Chapter 18. Essentially, the fundamental questions to answer is who needs what information, when will they need it, how will it be given to them, and by whom. In developing this plan, the project manager is now better prepared to identify external interests in the project and avoid potential barriers to communication. Factors to consider include: geographic location of the stakeholder, delivery style preferences, and cultural differences. From this information, the communication strategy can be tailored. One must understand that this is critical planning. It will not "just happen."

The key to effective stakeholder relations lies in the definition of items contained in the Communication Management Plan. We now look at this plan from the standpoint of not only communicating, but managing the linkage in both directions. This involves managing without authority, by the way, and this will require the highest level of PM skill to negotiate through the various views and opinions residing in the stakeholder community. Also, it is necessary to recognize degrees of granularity among this group, particularly considering power and influence factors related to project activities. In other words, not all stakeholders are equal and the communications strategy must deal with this. No simple organization chart will answer how these types of influences can come into the project. For example, third-party vendors and governmental bodies do not show up as internal entities, but they can have considerable impact on project outcomes. Not recognizing the role of a third-party vendor with financial trouble, or a government regulator's power can stall a project just as well as internal technical or financial issues. Likewise, a user need not recognized can influence future acceptance of the final product.

19.2.2 Stakeholder Composition

The following stakeholder group types need to be reviewed for communication needs (inbound and outbound):

- Sponsor—As the champion for the project this individual holds a key role in the communication process. It is necessary to closely manage communication flows here and he should be considered a partner to the project team. In most cases, this is the major communication target for the team and must be kept abreast of the current and any important developments. Surprises here can be catastrophic.
- Functional management—This is potentially a large and diverse group of individuals. Some segments of this population feed working resources to the project matrix organization and may be a major user of the final deliverable. These relationships must be understood and dealt with properly.
- Financial management—This group is generally mostly interested in the budgetary aspects of the project. In this role, they may require special views of project cost status and completion forecast.
- Customers—This group or individual is the future user of the deliverables. They are obviously very interested in functionality and schedule parameters. It is necessary to convince them that the delivered item has merit and they feel a part in defining its functionality. It is also important to note that customers can exist both internal and external to the team and each has unique communication requirements.
- Senior management—The ultimate success grade for a project comes from this group as they measure value across the organizational portfolio of projects. Every effort should be made to show the value of the project. Failure to do this can lead to an early demise for both the project and the PM.
- Third-party vendors—These sources serve the role of supporting the project with contractual items.
- External stakeholders—This group can come from a wide variety of sources: interested citizens worried about the environmental issues or governmental regulators concerned with compliance. Environmental issues are common characteristics of this category, as well as compliance with some formal regulation (i.e., construction, financial reporting, noise, etc.).

19.2.3 Communication Steps

The previous chapter described the basic model for project communications management and that model content is equally valid here. It is important to understand that simply sending an outbound message regardless of its format or mode is not truly communicating. The project manager must be sensitive to all five of the following active communication steps:

- Transmitted
- Received
- Understood
- Agreed with
- Useful action results

The last two items are of high interest in the stakeholder situation. Even if agreement is not achieved, it is important to make the rationale for a specific situation understood. Clearly with this diverse population, agreement on all aspects is a pipe dream, but surprises cannot be allowed.

19.2.4 Content Definition

Once an information content requirement is defined the next step is to answer the following questions regarding delivery of that information:

- The process to be used for gathering and storing the defined information.
- Defining specifically who should receive the information
- Defining the media technology for sharing the information
- A layout format to be used
- Schedules showing when each type of communication will be produced
- Definition of internal responsibilities for the various processes required to create, store, and manage the outbound activities

This is essentially the same process outlined for general communication, but now segmented by stakeholder needs.

Information format definition is one of the classic steps in project information distribution reporting and is a well understood requirement. What may not be so well understood is the need to customize this format to fit multiple stakeholder models and to find a way to receive feedback from those segments.

19.2.5 Delivery Media

Embedded in the communication decision is the media technology defined to move the data bits from sender to receiver. Every stakeholder has a preferred method for receiving data. It is important to recognize that the mode chosen will have both measures of efficient and effective delivery. Hence, selecting the mode is an important step in the process. Twenty years ago, the concept of stakeholder communication primarily was involved in what format the status report should be produced. The assumption for this was the stakeholder would be anxiously awaiting the report and would understand and agree with what was presented. The concept of a feedback loop was often distant in this view. There was no anticipation that these had a major role in the project and therefore did not need to react and hopefully would not. We see a quite different picture in the modern view. Not only do we want to communicate status effectively, but we want to know how that status is received. If certain stakeholders disagree with it, the desire is to either alter the direction of the project or negotiate with that stakeholder and obtain an agreeable result.

In recognition of an effective/efficient tradeoff the project team needs to consider the mode of information distribution. If a user is in the high power/influence group and wants to hear status directly from the project manager that is the way it should be delivered. In the email-centric world of today too much project status information is simply dropped into an email attachment and assumed to be effectively communicated. Obviously, this is an efficient method for the outbound route, but one must carefully measure whether it accomplishes the real goal. It is not a rich communication format and unless the reader spends time with the message it may do little to communicate. When one is receiving one hundred such messages a day it is easy to lose one of these or to not read it carefully. A quick look at the communication characteristics of the following eight common modes of information interchange seems worthy in our approach to defining how to communicate. One way to grade the richness of a communication to a stakeholder is to think about the list below in effectiveness descending order:

- *Face-to-Face*—This mode offers the full measure of active two-way communication, but suffers in time efficiency for the project team. Regardless, some measure of this form is needed, and every opportunity should be taken to talk personally to a stakeholder. The method that has grown most of the past several years is web access in which the stakeholder can retrieve data and drill down to whatever level they wish. Once again this is passive and assumes that the stakeholder will take time to do this. It still does not offer the feedback that a message was received or understood. That measure is important in the final analysis. If the pulse of the stakeholder is not understood, there is a risk of some hidden issue emerging too late to resolve.
- *Telephone/Conference Calls*—Some of the projects stakeholders or team members may be in different geographical locations in which case a conference or phone call maybe the most efficient means of communication. However, it is important to remember that when you communicate using the telephone it is impossible for the participants to pick up on any nonverbal communication that is taking place. This makes it more difficult to communicate effectively and increases the chances of miscommunication. Therefore, it is important that the participants keep the communication clear and concise and leave no room for interpretation.
- *Face-to-Face Group Meetings*—A face to face meeting with a focus group can be one of the most effective ways to provide rich active communication on both sides. This provides a method to not only provide rich feedback, but supports consensus-building within the group that is not easily obtained in other forms. Care needs to be taken, however, to ensure the meeting is focused and not just another rambling conversation. This mode requires prior planning, complex time management, and follow-up if it is to be useful. One should always evaluate the cost of such a format versus the value gained. This is a frequent model chosen, but one often misused from a value standpoint.
- *Ad-hoc Meetings*—Ad-hoc meetings are defined as unplanned chance encounters such as a quick chat in the hallway, a conversation over the water cooler, or a lunch discussion. Whatever the encounter form is, this is one of the most productive and effective communications opportunities available to project participants. The problem is how to schedule such encounters at the proper time. With this format, it is important to take the time to document the discussion and follow-up with the information obtained.
- *Formal Meetings*—This is certainly the form most would recognize, yet in many ways the greatest waste of organizational resources if not handled properly.
- Video Conferencing—Technology to link geographically dispersed groups for near face-to-face discussion can be created through this technology. Third-party vendors are bringing this capability to all-size organizations. At the high end of the spectrum, this class of technology can produce the feel of a formal meeting concurrently with many scattered stakeholders.
- *Website Access*—A project website is an excellent technical mode to provide both static and dynamic information to the project's stakeholders. However, care should be taken when relying on any type of technology that "automatically" provides information to stakeholders. Maintenance of such a communication vehicle is costly and time consuming for the project team. Also, one cannot be sure that the various stakeholders are getting what they

need from this source. This should not be the sole method of interface to the stakeholders for that reason.

- *Instant Messaging*—This form of communication can be a very quick and efficient way to communicate between individuals who have a familiarity and in which the questions are brief. Data volume is limited in this mode.
- *Email*—Email is the default global communication mode for most projects today. It is cheap and efficient for sending out reasonable-sized data groups to a wide audience. It can also be a reasonable individual method to interchange data informally. With this format care should be taken however, to ensure the information transmitted is clear and unambiguous, leaving no room for misunderstandings. As this technology grows it is reasonable to anticipate the addition of a video conference type functions to the email capability.

Once the various communication groups or individuals are identified the next step in the process is to gather further data regarding the expectations and level of influence for each. From this profile the ideal situation would be to define a communications strategy to make each stakeholder group a supporter of the project goal as defined. That likely is an overly idealistic goal, but should be the starting point. It is important to recognize that this planning process is not wholly an internal team activity, but requires some face-to-face interaction with stakeholders to identify their views regarding how they wish to be involved from a communication standpoint. In many ways one can look at this process very similar to the requirements definition problem associated with the project scope definition as outlined early in the text. In both cases the goal is to identify the work and related processes that will be put in place to resolve this set of communications requirements.

19.2.6 Success/Failure Syndrome

Projects have more stakeholders than first appears, and, in some cases, these are not recognized until it is too late to incorporate their input. These are absent groups or individuals who either need to be involved with defining the project, or need to be communicated with regarding the ongoing status. Stakeholders can reside either inside the host organization, or external to it. The key planning documentation artifacts related to this process are a stakeholder register and a stakeholder engagement plan (PMI, 2017, p. 504). One other added item of information that could prove useful later is the decision impact of defined stakeholders regarding the project (i.e., power, supporter, resistor, etc.).

Professor Ryan Nelson of the University of Virginia has been studying completed projects for several years and has identified some very interesting conclusions regarding project success. He is generally credited with coining the terms "success/failure" and "failure/success" described above. His primary contribution to this section is summarized in what he defines as the three major reasons for project failure as (Klein, 2006):

- Stakeholder management
- Poor estimation and scheduling
- Ineffective risk management

This is likely the first formal explicit research mention of stakeholder management as a primary project success topic. A second conclusion from this research was that success depends upon the people or process-related aspects of the project, not the underlying technology. This is consistent with the Standish research described in Chapter 9.

A third stakeholder success link comes in what Professor Nelson calls the Winner's Curse. This would be a procurement-oriented stakeholder area. In this situation, the procurement process selects the lowest cost bidder only to find out later that they have a difficult time meeting the requirement because they underbid to get the job. This has major implications in third-party relationships and the role of that process in project success. It may be better to define a win-win partnership with this stakeholder group rather than looking for lowest bid.

19.3 Stakeholder Classification

Another way to grade the communication needs of stakeholders is to evaluate the group or individual by intrinsic characteristics regarding their impact on the project. The vocabulary term for this type analysis metric is *salience*, which attempts to measure the ability of a stakeholder to impose their will on the project direction (PMI 2017, p. 513).

Not all stakeholders will receive the same level of data content or interaction with the project. To make this decision rationally the first question is to identify the interest profiles of this group and measure their potential impact on the outcome of a project. One can look at the stakeholder interest profile groups as follows (PMI 2017, p. 521):

- Unaware—not presently involved
- Resistant—not supportive of the project goal
- Neutral—aware of the project but not impacting it one way or the other
- Supportive—positive toward the project and involved
- Leading—actively involved in the project and supportive of the goal

As evident from this list, one of the key communication strategies is to understand who these players are and what their stance is toward the project. Table 19.1 is a useful tool to convey the current level of stakeholder engagement indicated by a "C" whereas "D" represents the desired level of engagement. The gap between the two indicates the level of communication that will be necessary to engage the stakeholder (PMI, 2017, p 522).

In the final analysis, communication is an integral part of any project and the key to whether a project will succeed or fail. The visible outcome of ineffective communication is unrealistic stakeholder expectations, incorrect work efforts by the project team, and ineffective decision-making regarding risk, schedule, budget, and resources. In the final analysis, communication is an integral

Table 19.1 Stakeholder Engagement Assessment Matrix

Stakeholder	*Unaware*	*Resistant*	*Neutral*	*Supportive*	*Leading*
Stakeholder 1	C			D	
Stakeholder 2			C	D	
Stakeholder 3				DC	

Source: Adapted from PMI (2017), p 522.

part of any project and the key to whether a project will succeed or fail. It is also a "soft" activity that is not amenable to easy definition or mechanics, so represents a particularly complex management issue.

Within the enterprise environment there are four basic classifications that help to segregate the stakeholder population communications strategy. These are:

- Power—formal authority to impact the project decision-making processes
- Influence—less formal authority but actively involved in the project
- Interest—groups who have an interest in the outcome, but less linked to day-to-day decision-making
- Impact—ability to impose their will on the project direction

One of the related analytical tools used to evaluate these factors is to matrix display showing pairs of characteristics such as power and influence in a matrix format (other pairs could be also shown this way). Figure 19.1 shows a sample matrix chart ranking power versus influence by stakeholder entity (identified by letters in the figure).

Note how the four quadrants can be used to indicate a communication measure of focus for the stakeholders graded this way. For example, a stakeholder labeled H would have an important status defined in the communication plan and every reasonable attempt would be made to ensure that they were on-board with the current project direction through the life cycle. At the other end of the scale, the stakeholder labeled J would be given less attention and placed in the standard "Monitor" category. Each of these quadrant groupings would have identified communication strategies commensurate with their ranking.

19.4 Managing Stakeholder Engagement

Remember that the term stakeholder means anyone involved with the project, or others who have a formal interest in the project. Therefore, when we speak about managing stakeholders

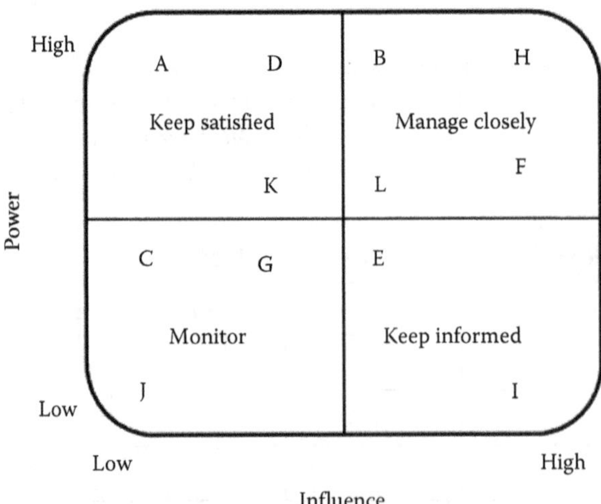

Figure 19.1 Power/influence grid. Adapted from Mitchell et al. (1997).

this can translate into a wide audience. Management of internal team members and involved subject matter experts (SMEs) is much more visible to the PM than anticipating what communication a senior manager, future user, or government official requires regarding the project. There are many examples in project management archives about projects that were completed only to find some significant hurdle waiting at implementation time that cratered the effort. Many of these issues could have been avoided with earlier recognition and problem-solving or negotiation time. There are also many issues that occur during the execution process that require much more complex communication skills than just sending out regular status reports. From the project team standpoint, the need is not only to understand the wishes and expectations of the stakeholder community, but to negotiate a supportive acceptance when those wishes cannot be met. Typically, issues that need to be addressed with the external stakeholder population are not those that can be dealt with by simply issuing a formal report, email, phone call, or letter. Many of these encounters will require more face-to-face back and forth negotiation. A sample of these activities is:

1. Negotiation with the project sponsor or senior management regarding the schedule, cost, and scope balance (i.e., insufficient resources approved to meet all three).
2. Negotiation with a functional manager over allocation of staff (timeliness, quantity, or skills).
3. Critical review of the project by senior management regarding viability of the current effort.
4. Disagreement with a customer over whether a requested change was part of the original contractual specifications.
5. Dealing with a powerful and influential stakeholder who has modified the baseline requirements in the middle of the execution phase.

If left isolated, many stakeholders would think that the initial project charter or early requirements represented the current project view, regardless of the changes that had been approved since then. As a project evolves, changes do occur that may have a subtle but important impact to a distant stakeholder who is not wired into the current status. For this basic reason, not defining who these groups are and dealing with them as part of the ongoing process is a recipe for future problems. It is important to reiterate here that the goal of stakeholder engagement is not to be an order taken from all defined groups. That is an impossible mission. The goal is to deal with these groups and negotiate solutions. If some aspect of the project plan does not meet a specific stakeholder wishes, then at least try to find some middle ground. The worst situation would be to not care and not work on communicating reasons for not doing what they want. It may well be necessary to have organizational groups simply recognize that the scope of this project is not focused on them. In many ways, this aspect of the management process is the most difficult because it is widespread across the organizational landscape, with equally widespread wishes and opinions. Formal authority links are also vague across this level.

If the project drifts away from a desired requirement, the management process becomes one of negotiating or informing that segment of the current status. Also, if the external organizational goal environment drifts, it is up to the project to capture those new expectations and decide how to move forward. Delivering the wrong set of requirements with all the right methodology remains the wrong project. Projects seldom have a static set of requirements through their life cycle and from this simply execute the initial plan to produce to a happy stakeholder group. A PM should assume just the opposite environment and that would be closer to reality.

19.5 Adoption and Organizational Change Management

Yet another aspect of the project life cycle occurs when the stakeholder conflict issue emerges during the integration of project deliverables into the operational environment. Many projects focus almost entirely on getting the product completed as though that is the mission. Contrarily, stakeholders view the mission as having a working version in their organization with trained users who are happy with the new outcome. Seldom does a new project outcome arrive in an organization and be received with open arms. At least half of a typical work group, if not more, does not embrace change well. This means that they must learn something new and often it is not perceived to their advantage. Skilled workers suddenly become process rookies again. If one understands this behavioral reaction it should not be hard to convince the project team that some degree of discussion with this future user group is required for success in their eyes. This is yet one more project layer in which the topic of change management is critical. Once the project deliverable is completed, it needs to be moved into an operational status in the user environment—this is the process state change that was discussed in Chapter 8 and represents the reason that the project was initiated in the first place. The deliverables can be a new software system or some new product widget. Regardless, in most cases this process upsets the status quo of that organization unit. The work group is now being asked to change the way they currently understand how to perform tasks and therein lays the basic project management change challenge.

Technical project teams often become convinced that the item they are delivering will be loved by all, only to find out later that this is not the case. These teams are also often not sensitive to the fact that the new user will not intuitively know how the new item works, even though the project team feels that it is intuitive (a popular term) because they created it. In this situation, the change process is not oriented toward analysis and approval; rather it is oriented more toward motivating and teaching the new user group to be successful in using the item. It is a worthwhile goal to convince them that the new system is an improvement. This is yet another aspect of stakeholder management.

The following story is a real-world example to illustrate the new system acceptance phenomenon. Several years ago the author was involved in implementing a word processing system into a government organization typing pool. Everyone today knows what such a system can do and it would probably not be resisted, but in the 1970s computers were relatively new tools for end users and the new word processing systems seemed pretty complicated to the traditional typist. The legacy system was essentially a stand-alone set of manual typewriters in a typing pool and there was near zero computer literacy in the group. Also, it was led by a senior person with almost 30 years of typing experience. As a relevant side note, this supervisor was not a particularly good typist and her documents were often filled with correction fluid (used to blot out typos). When the initial system was introduced to a small pilot group there was a lot of resistance to its "complexity." In particular, the typing pool supervisor said that it was too complicated to use, and her attitude impacted the acceptance of the system by others. Management pressure continued the group to work with the system until one day the supervisor found that she could make corrections to her document simply by backspacing. No more correction fluid was needed, and her document looked just as good as everyone else's. Her net typing speed was now almost normal. Magically, from that point onward the rest of the project moved smoothly into production. The "complexity" did not disappear, but suddenly the value of the new system became greater than the pain of learning how to use it. The message here is that if value is not obvious, there will be limited acceptance of new systems or product. Experiences like this sensitizes PMs to understand that the methods used to introduce new technology into the organization need to be user value based and finding a way to make the human user believe that they will benefit from the new process is a key element—another stakeholder management element. Once trained and productive, the user will once again become hesitant to move to the next new environment where they become a rookie user again. This same transitional reluctance to change phenomenon has been observed in the introduction of technical systems related to email, document repository systems, Enterprise Resource Planning (ERP), process control, budgeting, and a host of other applications where new processes, screen formats, and key stroking are part of the new requirement.

The stated original conceptual view of a project was that it was designed to move an organization from State A to improved State B. It is the role of the project team to produce the defined output, but that goal is not achieved until the new State B function is in operation. This last implementation step is part of the project and should be represented in the project plan and managed as a work activity much like the regular core work tasks. Project teams cannot throw the results over the wall and walk away as they often want to do.

19.6 Summary

This chapter described the need to focus attention on stakeholder views and how they can affect the perception and direction regarding a project. The major focus outlined here involves understanding the important role that stakeholder views have on project success. One might characterize this view of project management as saying effective communication is less about actual project status metrics and more about what your stakeholders perceive about the status. This summarizes the approach that the project team should have toward their stakeholders. In the final analysis, the goal of stakeholder management is simply one of achieving solid stakeholder linkage to the project throughout its life cycle. Building and maintaining positive project partners is the desired stakeholder management goal, but one very difficult to achieve.

References

Klein, K., 2006. Lessons Learned in the Rearview Mirror. www.gantthead.com (accessed November 15, 2006).

Mitchell, R.K., B.R. Agle, and D.J. Wood, 1997. Toward a theory of stakeholder identification and salience: Defining the principle of who and what really counts. *Academy of Management Review*, 22, 4, 853–888.

PMI, 2017. *A Guide to the Project Management Body of Knowledge (PMBOK® Guide)*, 6th ed. Newtown Square, PA: Project Management Institute.

Chapter 20

High Performance Teams

This chapter focuses on techniques to produce high productivity in project teams. Much of this material is adapted from various Software Engineering Institute (SEI) literature on Team Software Process (TSP) and Personal Software Process (PSP). SEI is a federally sponsored research center dedicated to improving quality of system development, primarily in the IT arena. Many of their findings now are being applied outside of IT. This chapter will approach the subject as a general purpose application that has merit for all project types.

To start this discussion, a base notation set is described here for TSP and then is translated into a more generic description that is amenable to all project types.

20.1 Background and Overview

Watts Humphrey was the research leader from the SEI team who originally described this process, and since that time a significant amount of research has occurred to expand and verify the process. The reader can refer to voluminous SEI research results and technical literature related to this topic for further background (www.sei.cum.edu).

Beyond describing the SEI TPS and PSP models, the basic goal of the chapter is to provide a more general mechanism for high team productivity beyond behavioral management techniques. The methods described are based on mechanics pioneered by SEI. This model approach was selected for inclusion because it has been tested in a variety of real projects and fits the operational theme of this book. The approach used here will translate the original TSP fundamental process into a general project team productivity model. Underpinning the mechanics of this approach are basic quality-oriented methods for improving productivity.

As we have demonstrated in Chapter 9, projects often fail for nontechnical reasons. The essence of the TSP model is that proper training of the project team will produce a higher-quality output regardless of other improvement strategies employed (Humphrey, 1998a). This idea has many similarities to the organizational maturity theme, but in this case, is focused primarily on the human element and the project team.

Over the past several years, various SEI projects explored various aspects of the project and organizational environment. Their most notable contribution has been in introducing the technical project world to the concept of organizational maturity (Chapter 34) with Capability Maturity

Model (CMM) and Capability Maturity Model Integration (CMMI) models. Both are now widely recognized, and their five-point maturity scales are used by various other researchers in their niche areas. Humphrey's work expanded this view downward into the project team structure with two operational models titled TSP and PSP. These techniques were stimulated as the researchers recognized the need for a coherent team organization prior to starting the project. In other words, throwing competent professions together without such as effort does not often yield a productive result.

The initial idea behind the development of better team management processes was to help software engineers use better process improvement principles in their development work and to find a workable method to put team members in charge of their work and to make them feel personally responsible for the quality of the products they produced (Humphrey, 1998b). This work led to the formulation of the PSP and TSP companion processes to guide project teams to consistently produce quality products on aggressive schedules and within cost constraints. The design objective of the TSP model was to create a highly productive, self-directed team environment. This chapter will focus on the team model mechanics required to produce that result.

Experience gained from the use of these project team management tools have shown them to be valid for all team environments and not just those dedicated to software. As we have stressed throughout the text, all projects have more similarity than is generally recognized. Based on that view, this discussion will explore these two model approaches from the view of managing high-performance teams in a general project environment regardless of output objective. To keep that objective clearer, the SEI acronyms will be modified to *PP for Personal Process* and *TP for Team Process* as the concepts are generalized. When the terms PSP and TSP are used here, they are referring to the SEI literature. All the basic concepts discussed map back to SEI research on the topic.

20.2 Introduction to TSP Concepts

SEI research results document that the TSP methodology helps to reduce defects, improve productivity, and reduce test time (Humphrey, 2000a). Use of CMM descriptions provides an overall *operational context* for effective project engineering, whereas the TSP process guides team member in doing the work. TSP is the process element focused on the project team activities.

One of the complex process issues within a project team is management of activities such as requirements management, enterprise goal alignment, management constraints, technical capability, and meeting customer expectations. To balance these often-conflicting forces, a project team must understand the complete context of technical and business issues in order to produce a consensus approach that minimizes the ongoing conflict. This means that the team must be familiar with and have the capability for dealing with the following attributes (Davis and Mullaney, 2003):

- Understand business and product goals.
- Produce their individual work plans to address those goals.
- Make personal work commitments.
- Direct their own tasks.
- Consistently use the methods and processes that they select.
- Manage output quality.

To achieve these capabilities, there must be a defined relationship among management, project team, and members. Figure 20.1 shows how these relationships are distributed in the PSP and TSP models.

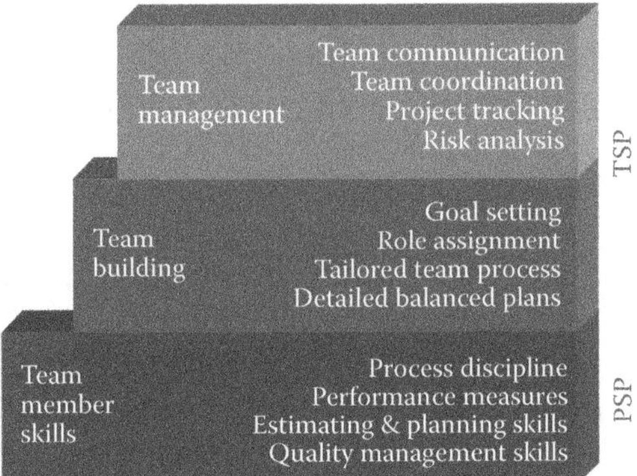

Figure 20.1 Elements of the PSP and the TSP. (From Davis, N. and J. Mullaney, 2003. *The Team Software Process TSP(sm) in Practice: A Summary of Recent Results Technical Report*: Pittsburgh: Software Engineering Institute. With Permission.)

Chick (2006), de Oca and Serrano (2002), and Serrano and de Oca (2004) have evaluated the use of PSP and TSP techniques in various types of multidiscipline projects. These experiences suggest that the same concepts can be used as the operational and management foundation for any project team. With this as the historical introduction, the rest of this section will introduce the key ideas of PSP and then focus on operationalizing the TSP concepts into a general project team environment. In this discussion, it will be assumed that the external organizational maturity is sufficient to support the ideas discussed here.

20.3 Personal Process Concepts

This section will translate the SEI PSP model into a general Personal Process (PP) model. This model's general principles are based on the following five basic planning and quality principles (Humphrey, 2000a):

1. Every team member is different; to be most effective each must plan their own work and base their plans on personal capabilities.
2. To consistently improve individual performance, actual results must be measured and then used as a guide for improvement.
3. To produce quality products, individual team members must feel personally responsible for the quality of their products. Superior products are not produced by accident, but through a conscious individual striving to do quality work.
4. A team culture must be created that it is more efficient to prevent defects than to find and fix them.
5. The team must clearly understand that the right way is always the fastest and cheapest way to do a job.

20.3.1 Personal Process Example

One of the primary tenets of the PP model is that team members must plan their work before committing to or starting on a job. In addition, they must use a defined process to plan that work.

To understand personal performance results, team members measure the time that they spend on each job step, the defects that they inject and remove, and the sizes (scope) of the products they produce. The goal of these steps is to consistently produce quality products, improve work planning skills, measure results, and track product quality throughout the project life cycle. Finally, the individual must analyze the results of each work activity and use these findings to improve their personal processes. If team members are not trained in these disciplines, the resulting culture will not advance. The management dilemma for this level involves methods to get teams to try to use disciplined methods, since most team members do not believe that this level of rigor is justified or efficient. The PP model addresses this by putting the team through a rigorous training course to learn the methods and see results in simulated case activities. From this experiential approach, the team members are more likely to buy into the method as they see visible results.

The PP training design structure is composed of several incremental components. Figure 20.2 outlines one example of this showing how the SEI PSP courses are introduced in six upwardly compatible steps titled PSP0 through PSP2.1 (Humphrey, 2000a). These courses are used to train software engineers in coding and quality control (QC), but a similar approach can be used for any project team. Note that the structure of the training fundamentally deals with techniques for scope definition, estimating based on requirements, and then design of work units. In this training mode, team members plan their work, produce a sample output, and then gather and analyze quantitative data from their work. From this process the team member is taught to analyze their results to improve the next iteration. If one examines this process, it is very similar to classic Deming quality management approach (i.e., PDCA).

PSP0 and PSP0.1—at this initial training stage, team members are taught and mentored techniques to develop three assignments using a standard methodology. The objective of this phase is for the members to learn how to follow a defined process and to gather basic size, time, and defect data for that class of work. In the more general case, this could involve techniques to collect requirements from users, Work Breakdown Structure (WBS) development, and collecting standard performance metrics as previously described in various sections of the book. From these focused training sessions, the team member is sensitized to a defined work process and performance data collection.

PSP1 and PSP1.1—once team members have learned to manipulate the standard work process and compile historical data, the focus moves to estimating and control. In this step, statistical

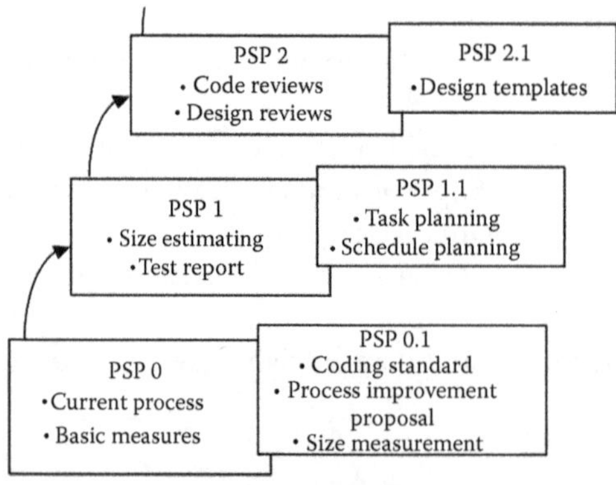

Figure 20.2 The PSP course structure. (From Davis, N. and J. Mullaney, 2003. *The Team Software Process(sm) in Practice: A Summary of Recent Results Technical Report.* Pittsburgh. Software Engineering Institute. With Permission.)

methods are taught and used to produce size and resource estimates for individual work units. Participants are taught to use earned value (EV) techniques for schedule planning and tracking.

PSP2 and PSP2.1—at the third stage, team members learn the basic model techniques for developing project plans and measuring output results. This stage focuses attention toward a more quality-centric management view. In this phase, team members are taught techniques to identify defects in design and perform root cause prevention at the design level.

After the introductory assignments, the team members begin writing technical reports related to the class assignments. At the end of the training, an overall report summarizing the results is produced. The report documents the evolving state of their performance based on measured results improvement. From this analysis the team members are charged with defining challenging yet realistic improvement goals and to identify the specific changes that they will make to achieve those goals. The final training phase will implement those changes.

By the end of the training course, team members can plan and control their personal work, define processes that best suit them, and consistently produce quality products on time and for planned costs. Obviously, translating this process to a specific project environment would require some work based on the characteristic of the planned deliverables, but conceptually this process is simply oriented toward teaching standard methods that have strong similarity to the *Project Management Body of Knowledge (PMBOK®) Guide*-type life cycle model processes. Standard templates could be used for several of these activities. General training modules and techniques would have to be designed to deal with the following activities:

1. Requirements facilitation and documentation—user group sessions designed to collect and catalog requirements.
2. Scope definition based on WBS decomposition techniques.
3. Size estimating based on local or industry standard tools and models for the application area.
4. Design reviews—this type approach is already documented in the professional literature and deals with techniques for technical peers to review designs.
5. Collecting actual performance metrics and then using them to analyze status. The host organization would have to define appropriate metrics for that class of project.
6. Root cause analysis sessions could use the Ishikawa model to teach problem analysis-type techniques for the local case.

Each of the processes outlined above could be sequenced through the same course structure as outlined for the PSP model approach.

20.3.2 Introducing Personal Process to the Team

There are several important management points to understand in introducing the PP components to a team. As indicated above, team members should be trained by a qualified PSP instructor using customized curricula. Although many of these concepts can be introduced quickly, they must also be done properly. Potential trainer resources for this could initially come from a growing number of SEI-trained PSP instructors who offer commercial training courses (see www.sei.cmu.edu). These instructors would have to understand the local model design approach as well as the PSP model and this would require support from an internal technical resource.

The second important step in PP introduction is to perform the training in coherent groups or teams who should be ready to use the methods soon. When organizations ask for volunteers for PP training, they could get a broad sprinkling of skills that will be hard to adapt to a specific training target project. If this were to occur, the productivity impact is diminished since the concepts taught would be harder to utilize. Ideally, core project teams should go through the process together. Alternatively, homogeneous skill groups could have basic material tailored for their skill segments. Selection of the participants and course materials are critical issues.

Third, effective PP introduction requires strong management support as we have pointed out frequently for other change management activities. This means that management must believe in the approach, know how to support their staff once they are trained, and regularly monitor project performance to see how the new model is working. Without proper management attention, many team members gradually slip back into their old habits. The general problem is that most technical professionals find that it is difficult to consistently follow a disciplined work process if nobody notices or cares. Team members need regular coaching and support to sustain high levels of personal performance.

The final implementation issue is to prepare the participants for moving these ideas into a team environment. The mechanics for this is the interface point between the PP and TP models.

20.4 TP Process

Humphrey's initial goal in developing TSP was to design a teachable approach to building and sustaining effective project teams. As described in this section, TP is a supportive companion concept to the higher-level CMM.

TP represents a prescriptive approach for building a productive self-directed team and it outlines how individual members should perform in their project organization. It also defines how management should guide and support their teams and how to maintain an environment that fosters high team performance. The principal benefit of TP is that it shows team members how to produce quality products for planned costs and on aggressive schedules. It does this by teaching team members how to manage their personal work in a team environment and by making each individual the owner of their plans, processes, and results.

20.5 TP Work Objects and Principles

As team members start applying their PP skills on the job, it will soon be discovered that they need a supportive team environment that recognizes and rewards sound methods. In many organizations, the projects in crisis receive all the attention. Projects and individuals who meet commitments and do not have quality problems often go unnoticed. The important point to recognize is that it is a management role to provide a supportive environment. If this is not provided, the team members soon revert to ad hoc processes.

An adaption of the five design objectives of TP are as follows (Adapted from Humphrey, *TSP Design Objectives*, 1998c.):

1. Build self-directed teams that plan and track their work, establish goals, and own their processes and plans. Team sizes should be from 3 to 20.
2. Teach PMs how to coach and motivate their teams and how to help them sustain peak performance.
3. Accelerate process improvement by installing a culture like CMM level 5-type behavior to be normal and expected.

4. Provide improvement guidance to the external organization.
5. Facilitate teaching of industrial-grade team skills through appropriate training programs.

Linked to these objectives are six underlying principles or beliefs (Davis and Mullaney, 2003):

1. Team members know the most about the job and can best define the related plans.
2. Team members who plan their own work are more committed to the plan.
3. Precise project tracking requires detailed plans and accurate data.
4. Only the people doing the work can collect precise and accurate data.
5. To minimize cycle time, the team members must balance their workload across competing activities and understand the relative priority of these activities.
6. A focus on quality will lead to maximum productivity.

Within this design structure TP has two primary components: team-building and team-working. The team-building component of the TP is called the *TP launch*, which challenges the team to follow the model development process and should produce some evidence to motivate that behavior. The management component focuses on ensuring that the process is followed through appropriate management behavior.

20.5.1 TP Launch Structure

TP mechanics provides the project organization with explicit guidance regarding operational techniques for accomplishing their objectives. For example, a WBS oriented, top-down decomposition approach is used to define the overall technical scope of the effort. From this base, estimating metrics are used to determine an overall schedule. These methods are then used to develop an aggregate schedule that is broken into manageable phases with detailed estimates done only for the current phase or segment. Each defined work unit has a named individual who is responsible for the work and for reporting status of their individual pieces. Each time a new project phase begins, whether at the start of the project or at a later transition between phases, a formal project launch is held. Figures 20.3 and 20.4 illustrate how TP guides the team through four defined phases of a project. It is assumed that projects may start or end on any phase, or they can run the complete life cycle from beginning to end. Regardless, before each phase, the team performs a complete launch or relaunch activity where they plan and organize their work for the next phase. Generally, once team members are trained in the personal work model, a three to four-day launch workshop provides sufficient guidance to complete a full project phase plan. After this, teams would hold a two-day relaunch workshop to kick off each of the second and subsequent phases. These launches are not considered training; they are part of the regular development process.

Figure 20.3 illustrates the periodic relaunching process. This approach follows an iterative and evolving development strategy; therefore, periodic relaunches are necessary so that each phase or cycle can be planned based on the knowledge gained in the previous cycle. The relaunch process also requires team members to update detailed plans, which are usually accurate for only a few months. Primary output of the TP launch is an overall aggregate plan and a detailed plan for about the next three to four months. After team members have completed all or most of the next project phase or cycle, they revise the overall plan as needed and make a new detailed plan to cover the next three to four months. This process is generally called the *rolling wave* approach to planning. This relaunch process is taught as part of team training and is illustrated schematically in Figure 20.4.

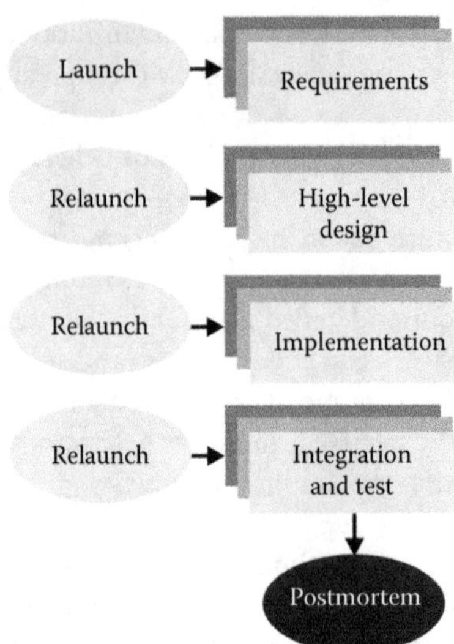

Figure 20.3 TSP launch stages. (From Humphrey, W.S., 1998c. *Crosstalk, The Journal of Defense Software Engineering*. With Permission.)

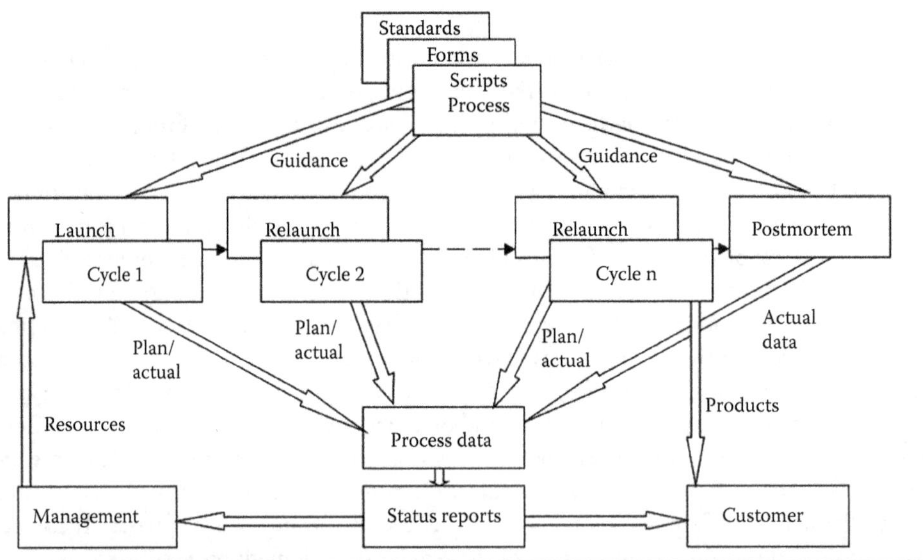

Figure 20.4 TSP process flow. (From Humphrey, W.S., 1998c. *Crosstalk, The Journal of Defense Software Engineering*. With Permission.)

20.6 TP Launch Details

The TP launch represents an important step in developing a team culture and common understanding. A team *consensus* detailed plan is a primary output from the launch process. This artifact provides the communication vehicle to help the team reach a common understanding of the work and the approach to be taken. Some formal indication that management supports this plan is also an important launch event.

The TP launch script is designed to lead the team through the required planning steps. This script is customized to the size and characteristics of the project. Humphrey outlines the following items that need to be defined and resolved as part of the launch (Humphrey, 1998c):

1. Review documented project objectives with management and agree on team goals.
2. Establish team roles.
3. Define the team's development process.
4. Produce a quality plan and set quality targets.
5. Plan the needed support facilities.
6. Produce a general plan for the entire project.
7. Develop detailed work unit plans for each for the next phase. (The TSP model says that this should be for the individual task level.)
8. Balance team workload to achieve a minimum (viable) overall schedule.
9. Verify that the individual plans will produce the team plan requirements.
10. Assess project risks and assign tracking responsibility for each key risk.

In the final launch step, the team reviews their plans and the project's key risks with management. Once the project starts, the team conducts weekly team meetings and periodically reports their status to management and to the customer.

Figure 20.5 illustrates a TP launch process composed of nine team meetings over a four-day period. The output objective for each meeting is listed in each cell.

By the end of the launch training, the team should have formed into a cohesive unit and created a plan that balances business, technical, and customer aspects. As a result of this activity, there is now an agreed upon technical solution for the effort and the whole team understands how the planned product will satisfy business and customer needs. The underlying work processes have also been

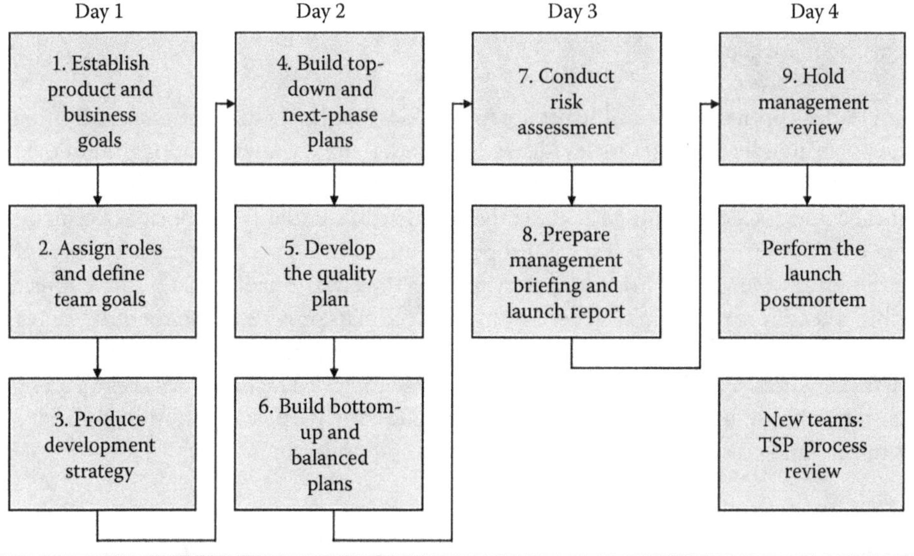

Figure 20.5 Four-day TSP launch process. (From Humphrey, W.S., 2000b. *The Team Software Process(sm), Team Software Process Institute*. Pittsburgh: Software Engineering Institute. With Permission.)

reviewed and agreed upon. These are fundamental project team decisions that should be in place for any project regardless of the methodology. Because of this activity, the team now has learned how to produce a detailed plan that they can use to guide and track the work. Less obvious in the above process is that the following items are communicated to the whole group. Specifically, team members:

- Know who is responsible for which tasks and areas.
- Understand and agree with the quality goal.
- Have a common approach for monitoring progress against the plan.
- Have explored the project risks and performed reasonable mitigation of those risks.

Once again, each of these should be team objectives regardless of the approach taken.

20.7 Teamwork Process

Once the launch process training is completed, the principal need is to ensure that all team members follow the plan through execution. This includes the following key operational activities (Humphrey, 2000b):

- Leading the team
- Process discipline
- Issue tracking
- Communication
- Management reporting
- Maintaining the plan
- Estimating project completion
- Balancing team workload
- Relaunching the project (phase)
- Quality management

The team leader's primary responsibilities are to provide high-level guidance and motivation to the team members, handle customer issues, deal with external management, and maintain the process discipline. Another important team leader responsibility is to ensure that all the issues identified are managed and tracked. Through these activities the team leader is responsible for maintaining open and effective team communication. Proper communication practices are a key part of maintaining the team's energy and drive necessary to keep the effort moving in a positive direction.

Within a team organizational structure, the project plan provides formal guidance regarding work timing and sequence. Work performance is tracked against the plan using EV and other performance metrics (Part VII of the book covers these topics). Tracking activities are designed to help team members evaluate project status and provide timely information to help various stakeholders understand current status and future completion projections.

20.8 Quality Management

All projects have variances from the plan and it is common to find product output not meeting planned standards. The TP model places principal quality emphasis on defect management.

To manage quality, teams must establish quality goals and associated measures to define the status of those goals. From this base they then establish plans to meet the goals. During the team launch training, team members are taught how to produce a quality management plan. This plan structure is based on the estimated size of the product and historical data on defect rates. Estimates are then made on defect patterns through the process. Subsequent progress tracking will monitor performance against this profile.

As defects are identified, the training program should have provided guidance regarding methods to correct or deal with these problems. In this mode, much of the quality management process is housed inside the PP or TP work activity. Quality management techniques taught as part of the TP and PP training follow the theoretical processes outlined in Chapter 16, Quality Management.

Defect management is more than just measuring results and repairing the problem. The theme of PP and TP processes is to identify ways to prevent problems before they occur. By improving individual work processes, team members typically learn how to reduce their defect rates by 40%–50%. Improved design methods can further reduce defect rates as the team members become more proficient with the method. Existence of a formal quality plan and defect tracking processes make the team members more sensitive to quality issues so that they are more careful, which reduces defects even further. As with other project management processes, the quality management focus continues through the life cycle. Defect status is reviewed at the end of each phase and the lessons learned process is used to improve downstream activities.

20.9 Experience Examples and Evaluation

Various SEI Technical Reports outline IT project case data from 13 organizations and over 20 projects. These data compare results from typical non-TSP projects with those managed using the process outlined here (Davis and Mullaney, 2003; Humphrey, 2000b). Product sizes ranged from small 600 lines of code (LOC) to 110,000 LOC projects. Corresponding team sizes ranged from 4 to 47 team members, and project duration ranged from a few months to multiple years. Application types include real-time software, embedded software, utility software, client-server applications, and financial software, among others. In these reviews, TSP teams delivered products that were more than two orders of magnitude better in quality than typical projects. Also, TSP projects completed in less than 50% of the time and resources spent in the typical project. Certainly, quantified results of this type are sufficient to get any organization's attention.

One specific set of sample data from a large Boeing avionics project team is shown in Figures 20.6 and 20.7. After Release #9 of PSP/TSP training, the number of defects detected reduced to 75%, and the system cost reduced to 94%. The final project delivered a high-quality product ahead of schedule (Humphrey, 2000b).

Two conclusions can be gained from this example. Leaving a project team alone to follow whatever path they choose is not the most productive strategy. Second, a disciplined process, once learned, can have significant positive impact on project deliverables.

20.10 TSP Qualitative Feedback Results

Besides the raw data analysis of team performance, qualitative results are equally important to review. Davis summarizes both positive and negative comments from team members in his SEI

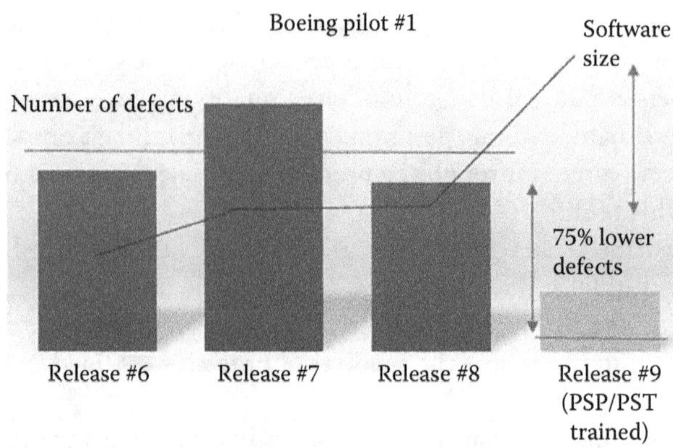

Figure 20.6 TSP test defects. (From Humphrey, W.S., 2000b. *The Team Software Process(sm), Team Software Process Institute*. Pittsburgh: Software Engineering Institute. With Permission.)

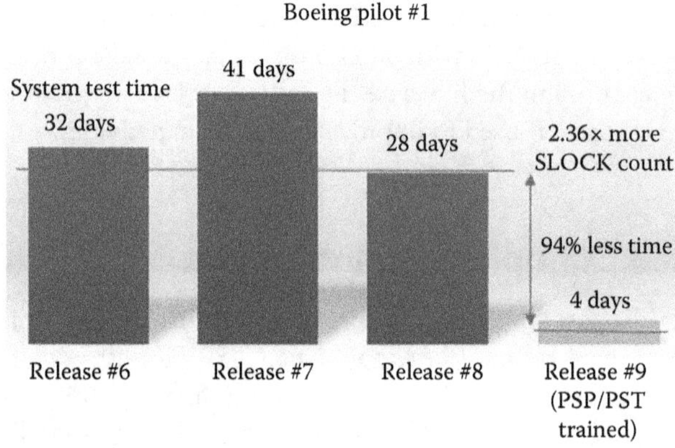

Figure 20.7 TSP Test time. (From Humphrey, W.S., 2000b. *The Team Software Process(sm), Team Software Process Institute*. Pittsburgh: Software Engineering Institute. With Permission.)

technical report. These responses form a valuable source for lessons learned. Some typical positive comments from the Davis and Mullaney survey are listed below (Davis and Mullaney, 2003):

> The best part about PSP/TSP is that collecting the metrics is for my benefit, not for someone else. I found that collecting the data proved to me that using a better process really does help my quality and productivity.
>
> Gives you incredible insight into personal performance.
>
> … [TSP is a] transparent project management paradigm—everybody has a common understanding of the plan and everyone knows what is going on in the project and where we are in the project at any time.
>
> The first TSP team I coached was surprised when unit test was completed in half a day. They said they had done a prototype of this code before the project started and it took 1.5 weeks to get it to work well enough to see any results. They have found only two defects since the code has been integrated with the rest of the software.

Some negative comments were also expressed, and these points are also valuable for the future development of the process (Davis and Mullaney, 2003):

> I am a very creative person. I liken doing software to an artist painting a picture, and so I still worry about the PSP structure taking some of the fun and creativity out of the software process. PSP tends to distill the repetitive measurable tasks out of the creative and innovative ones that occur early in the design phase. The purpose of design is to provide an early analysis that leads to products with fewer of the more costly defects later. You have to have a good design to get good code.
>
> No tool support. SEI's TSP tool is not sufficient at all.

It is important to recognize that a team development process cannot be completely distilled to a set of mechanics related only to planning and data collection. A successful project requires open human interactions that allow individuals and teams to use their intellectual skills. Also, the conflict between disciplined and creative work must be dealt with from a management perspective. Getting all humans in a team to follow a standard approach will always result in resistance, so motivation of the mechanics will be an important aspect.

20.11 Future Trends

Documentation of different TSP experiences in various organizations and projects, multidiscipline systems, and different industries shows that the TSP model approach has resulted in mostly successful outcomes. However, there are clear areas for improvement in aspects such as the process for introducing the concepts to the team, extension to large teams, and combining TSP and other traditional project management methods in a complicated project system. TSP was originally designed as a software engineering technique, so more work is needed to translate the original process model into general concepts that can be readily adopted for a broader array of project types. Techniques for customization have been outlined here but this issue will remain a challenge for specific situations.

20.12 Large, Multidisciplined Projects

A typical large project consists of multiple team skills such as engineers, IT support, business process SMEs, quality and risk management, financial, and other support personnel. This diversity and size of skill mix creates additional management issues in maintaining the type of process discipline required for a TSP model effort. Also, this diversity of background raises a few additional complexities to the implementation process.

The most obvious management issue in a large project is simply managing the flow of resources in and out of the work process with their multiple skills. Basic TSP theory suggests that work plans should be developed for each individual. This level of detail would appear onerous for the larger project and in fact may not be feasible given that the specific individual may not be identified at the planning stage. Most likely, work plans in this environment would be limited to a work package (WP) level, which would then involve a more skilled group or sub-team level focus. From this base, the day-to-day work definition would typically be managed by the owning work group manager. This means that the model process would have to be translated into a format suitable for that small sub-team size group, with an overall project management focus embedded in that view. Much of the project management theory described in this book fits that definition, but is a modification of the TSP process. Basically, this means that all project participants would have to be trained in methods that were compatible with the TSP model, but also focused and segmented into their skill groups. In other words, a business process participant would not likely need to be trained in technical design review procedures, but would need to understand the concepts of requirements definition for the type of work they were allocated and produce status reporting for that segment.

Second, the general problem of project team training is now much more complex than for a homogenous team. The variety of skills involved suggests that these training examples would have to be concocted in such a way that the audience would use the needed training in their specific segmented work environment. Examples were provided earlier showing general tools for useful for general management activities (i.e., requirements definition, WBS techniques, change management, etc.). As an example, a mixed skill group of users, engineers, operations, manufacturing, and other support groups would normally perform scope definition at the WBS level in the large team model. A skilled facilitator could guide a group of this type through the process without all members of the group being experts in the technique. What must be understood in the larger team environment is how a particular work unit interfaces with others and why it is important to produce in some particular form.

After the basic planning activities are completed, different mixtures of participants would likely perform future design reviews as lower-level technical details are debated. So, in this area, training would be more skill group oriented to deal with the specifics of that project phase. Regardless of the team size and complexity, basic literacy training is needed so that all team participants will understand the general process and the overall logic of the processes being employed. The theme of this training would be to tout the test value of the methods. Otherwise, it may well be perceived as bureaucracy without value.

Project tracking and control concepts should be basically the same for all projects and based on WP performance and a project level performance measurement methodology. Status reporting would be handled at the work group level, but individuals would need to follow a standard reporting format.

20.13 Summary

The basic management concepts described in the PSP and TSP models are not new. Their value to the management discussion is that they were developed and verified in a real project environment by a world-class organization with highly skilled researchers. Also, the results were tested across multiple organizations and publicly available. These factors add legitimacy to this approach. Clearly, the organizational reaction to any form of process standardization will be resistance so long as reasonable proof of value is not communicated. This means that the training program must be sensitive to this goal and changes should be introduced carefully and with support of top management. With each step there must be strong evidence that the techniques used will bring desired results.

The PSP and TSP team management models represent powerful techniques to facilitate project execution through tested team management processes. They provide clear methods for producing improved team skills, discipline, and commitment required for successful project execution. Research shows that in most TSP project experiences the process results in reduced cost, time, and quality defects in the project. For these basic reasons, it is important that the contemporary PM understand and utilize these basic concepts. More research is needed to broaden the understanding and implementation of the PP and TP concepts outlined here, but the fundamental ideas are sound.

References

Chick, T., 2006. Using TSP with a multi-disciplined project management system. *Crosstalk, The Journal of Defense Software Engineering,* pp 4–8. http://static1.1.sqspcdn.com/static/f/702523/9272382/1288904833337/200603-Chick.pdf (accessed May 1, 2018).

Davis, N. and J. Mullaney, 2003. *The Team Software ProcessSM (TSPSM) in Practice: A Summary of Recent Results Technical Report.* Pittsburgh, PA: Software Engineering Institute.

de Oca, C. and M. Serrano, 2002. Managing a company using TSP techniques, *Crosstalk, The Journal of Defense Software Engineering,* Vol 15 (9), pp 17–21. http://static1.1.sqspcdn.com/static/f/702523/9343070/1289330280230/200209-0-Issue.pdf (accessed May 1, 2018)

Humphrey, W.S., 1998a. Three dimensions of process improvement part I: Process maturity. *Crosstalk, The Journal of Defense Software Engineering,* Vol 11 (2), pp 14–17. http://static1.1.sqspcdn.com/static/f/702523/9167920/1288288735347/199802-0-Issue.pdf (accessed May 1, 2018).

Humphrey, W.S., 1998b. Three dimensions of process improvement part II: The personal process. *Crosstalk, The Journal of Defense Software Engineering,* Vol 11 (3), pp 13–15. tatic1.1.sqspcdn.com/static/f/702523/9167957/1288288891777/199803-0-Issue.pdf(accessed May 1, 2018).

Humphrey, W.S., 1998c. Three dimensions of process improvement part III: The team process. *Crosstalk, The Journal of Defense Software Engineering,* Vol 11 (4), pp 14–17. http://static1.1.sqspcdn.com/static/f/702523/9168048/1288289111070/199804-0-Issue.pdf (accessed May 1, 2018).

Humphrey, W.S., 2000a. *The Personal Software Process*^{SM} *(PSP*^{SM}*), Team Software Process Initiative.* Pittsburgh, PA: Software Engineering Institute.

Humphrey, W.S., 2000b. *The Team Software Process*^{SM} *(TSP*^{SM}*), Team Software Process Initiative.* Pittsburgh, PA: Software Engineering Institute.

Serrano, M. and C. de Oca, 2004. Using the team software process in an outsourcing environment. *Crosstalk, The Journal of Defense Software Engineering,* Vol 17 (3), pp 9–13. http://www.dtic.mil/dtic/tr/fulltext/u2/a574305.pdf (accessed May 1, 2018).

SUPPORT PROCESSES

This text section focuses on three model support-oriented Knowledge Areas (KAs): Procurement, Risk, and Integration. Each of these represent an important support component required to build a viable project plan and move it through execution. Upon completion of this section the following concepts should be understood as to why they are required as part of the planning process:

1. Understand the role that procurement management brings in regard to resource supply coming from external sources.
2. Understand how risk events can impact the project and management techniques that can help mitigate the impact of these events.
3. Understand the implications of integrating all KAs into a single integrated plan view that properly balances the impact of all KAs.

This section completes the final discussion of the model Knowledge Area planning processes. Each of the topics included here represent real-world issues in the project management sphere. This means that we now start recognizing that certain unplanned "issues" occur and cause plan variables to require management action. Examples of such variations are:

1. Planned resources are not supplied in either quantity and skill level.
2. Duration estimates are wrong and the plan deviates.
3. All team member motivation and skills are not as planned.
4. Internal and external conflict occurs and has to be dealt with.
5. Risk events begin to emerge and change the baseline plan.
6. Third-party vendors are not performing as planned.
7. Changing expectations of external stakeholders require changes to the approved plan.

Each of these situations require management action with various process variables in order to influence a change in direction of the project outputs.

The management components introduced here emphasize that the project plan must describe the desired projected outcomes, but more management action is required beyond this. These new focus areas, along with the soft skills outlined in the previous section, are summarized as management variables here. Collectively, each represent a major management area of concern in the project that needs to be dealt with as part of the overall planning, execution, and control activity. Recognize that the PMBOK model calls these items Knowledge Areas KAs.

In this discussion, it seems quite logical to think of some KAs as more representative of outputs (project goals) and some more oriented toward inputs (resource- or support-oriented) needed to achieve those goals. This is not a perfect separation of the 10 KAs, but represents a starting view.

In each of the management decision required situations, a change made regarding one of these areas will potentially cause a deviation in one or more of the other items, including the output deliverables. It is also important to point out that each of the KAs has some type of constraint or goal attached to it. For example, human resources are limited, cost is limited, schedule has a target goal, and so forth. Based on this multi-variable goal view, the focus of this section will be to describe more of the actions that are required to be dealt with on the input side of the plan. In other words, these are primarily actions taken on the work side that will later impact the output result (i.e., scope, time, cost, or quality). One PM described this class of actions as trying to make a large pile of mush (requirements) fit into a too small bucket. At least that gives one a metaphoric perspective of the management role.

Recall that the planning approach described in Part II focused primarily on the project output variables (i.e., project goals). Part III added to that perspective a review of the soft skills area (human resource, communications, and stakeholders). Collectively, each of the items discussed across Parts II, III, and IV represent the collection of 10 management focus areas for the project. In this section, the final three KA elements come together to deal with the following:

- Risk events deal with items that have not yet occurred and may not occur, but have a probabilistic chance of appearing to create some item not contained in the approved plan (usually negative).
- Procurement represents the processes related to dealing with third-party external supporters who deliver products and services to the project.
- Integration involves the inter-workings of the various nine other KAs as changes in one area impact one or more of the others. This is more of a macro decision view of project activities.

Another important perspective outlined in this section is to recognize that management activity related to each of the KAs described in Parts III and IV will carry over beyond the planning phase.

Chapter 21

Procurement Management

21.1 Introduction

In many cases, acquiring products and services from an external source is an economic, technical, or necessary activity. This can occur for many reasons. One obvious reason is that the buying organization is not technically capable of making the needed item. Also, they may not have the skill to produce the item and they might not wish to invest in the time and effort to create that capability. In other situations, the question is one of a trade-off between using in-house capabilities and external sources. Some of the more common reasons for using third-party suppliers are the following:

1. Internal resources are stretched to capacity and an external vendor provides temporary relief from that constraint.
2. External vendors have niche skills that are not available in-house.
3. External vendors can do it cheaper because this can be a specialty for them.
4. An external vendor may have more flexibility to meet the schedule required.
5. The buyer organization does not want to hire staff for that class of activity.

Regardless of the reasoning, all organizations deal with third-party suppliers for various goods and services. Some projects are in themselves a procurement activity for another buyer.

21.2 Procurement Management

Procurement management represents the processes involved in the acquisition of a defined set of goods and/or services from a third party for use in various project activities. Implicit in this process is the existence of a business relationship that will formally define the parameters for both parties. Some of the specific conditions of the transaction regard remuneration, delivery timing, place of delivery, payment details, failure to perform actions, and any other requirements related to the agreement. In this discussion, we observe the procurement process as a rigorous activity and not as one pursued through informal means. This means that a formal contractual document will exist to satisfy the terms of the relationship.

The first question to resolve in this process is an analysis of the types of goods and services that might be beneficial for the project to procure. The following list contains the major categories that are common for this activity:

Goods: This basically involves tangible raw materials required for execution by or for the project. Some of these items would be called commodity raw materials (metal, low-level components, food, etc.) and are sold by numerous vendors with readily definable product descriptions.

Equipment rental: This category represents various supporting items used in the execution of the project. This category is characterized by various tangible items of more or less durable nature, which are needed to ensure the success of the project activities. Examples are proprietary devices, machines, tools, and vehicles.

Finished goods: These items have been passed through a more complex manufacturing or processing method and would be considered more technically complicated to specify and procure. These items may or may not be stocked by the vendor sources. Items in this category can be viewed as boxes in the Work Breakdown Structure (WBS), meaning that some portion of the project scope has been contracted to a third part of execution.

Services: This group is usually characterized by some form of human service that is performed either in-house or outsourced to a third party external to the physical team. Because of the nature of this activity it can be the most complex of all procurement actions if the requirement cannot be clearly defined. Beyond simple service agreements for building maintenance, temporary administrative help, copying services, and the like, the procurement of technical third-party resources requires thoughtful procurement actions. Examples of these high-end services are as follows:

Consultants: Highly specialized technical resources that have knowledge needed by the project to execute the work requirements. An example would be an Enterprise Resource Planning (ERP) project that needed this level of support to ensure that they are following best of class methods.

Information/technical/engineering: Resources in this category are likely being obtained to fill capacity in the existing organization or to supply a gap skill to the project. A typical example of this group is programmers for software development services to create, modify, or support application components of the project and also the engineering services of various skill types.

Certifications: These activities involve acquiring external services to independently provide evidence to the acquirer that a product meets contractual or otherwise specified requirements.

21.3 Make or Buy Decision

The first question for the project team to decide is whether to seek an outside source for a particular activity, or whether to utilize internal resources. This is called the *make or buy* decision. This decision will be based on several factors. The first order of business is to decide exactly what work activities need to be performed and what raw input items are associated with that work. It is reasonable for a starting place to think of the WBS and its companion dictionary as offering details on this question. At this point, the project team would examine the requirements and begin to analyze how best to accomplish that work activity. Each work package (WP) has inputs and work processes required to complete the deliverable. Likewise, the work defined in the WP could be judged to be a viable candidate to procure. Each of these target issues has its own set of challenges in the procurement planning process. Questions such as:

- Will the raw materials spoil, or need special storage until needed?
- Will internal resources be available to assemble or produce finished products formed from the purchased raw material resources?
- Are semi-finished goods available to make the process easier for the project team?
- Do we have appropriate internal resources with the skills or credentials required to assemble the manufactured parts into finished or usable products?
- Would it be more cost effective to receive raw materials and assemble the product using internal resources, or seek out an external vendor to perform the entire process?
- Is there an organizational policy pro or con this activity?

Finally, it will be necessary to canvass potential vendors to see who is interested in bidding on this type of work. The effort may be low skill and easy to do, but the vendor is not interested in that type of job. Some organizations may establish a policy to procure all building cleaning and maintenance requirements since the organization does not wish to staff for that type of work. Also, many public organizations will specify that some percent of the total project must be contracted.

For project technically oriented activities, these decisions may be more subtle in both the decision and negotiating aspects. In some cases, this decision is obvious, whereas in others may be more philosophical (or political if one wanted to admit that). Consider the situation of needing an integrated computer chip as part of the project work. It would not be a long debate to decide that buying one from a competent vendor is the better choice than staffing to make the product internally.

Many times, the make or buy decision is based on whether the item required is part of the organization's defined core competency. Essentially, this is saying that the organization wants to focus on some defined skill groupings and would procure any requirements outside of this core set. An organizational core competency is defined as the collective learning and coordination skills required to produce a firm's product lines or services. Core competencies represent the true strategic strengths of a company. If the project task falls within one or more of these competencies, is it generally best to seek ways to maintain that knowledge base internally. These competencies represent the difficulty for competitors to imitate strengths and collective know-how and they contribute significantly to the end-product benefits. This does not necessarily mean that the firm owns all the resources that comprise the core competency set, but does represent their collective alliances and licensing agreements. In other words, core competencies represent the true strategic strengths of a company. If the project task falls within one or more of these competencies, is it generally best to seek ways to maintain that knowledge base internally.

The second procurement planning question is to establish whether there are experienced, capable vendors to support the defined need. If the organization has a formal procurement department, this is a good time to involve them with this question. They should either have such vendors on a preferred vendor list, or have capabilities to begin searching for such vendors. It is typically a good strategy to start a new vendor with small transactions and increase the size and scope of those as you gain experience with them. When the buyer has already established a tested relationship, this can be an influential factor when deciding to buy versus make internally. The test of a vendor involves its history of timeliness, quality, service, and flexibility in past relationships (Gray and Larson, 2008).

Through the make or buy process it is good to evaluate if the scope of a WP is adequately defined to either support a make versus buy decision, or whether a vendor would be able to understand the requirement. Project teams often forget that the WBS structure and dictionary should be kept up-to-date with changing issues and this omission can lead to a bad procurement decision. For this reason, the final test is to confirm that the required task and its output are valid and sufficiently defined. In order to do this, take the reverse view and look at the deliverable and then ask whether the underlying work process is defined.

21.4 Procurement Management Processes

In keeping with the text theme of a model-based perspective, we need to restate that Procurement Management is one of the 10 knowledge areas (KAs) in the Project Management Body of Knowledge (PMBOK). This topic covers all the processes required to purchase or acquire products, services, or results needed from outside the project team to perform the work defined in the project scope. The guide defines three processes for this KA (PMI, 2017, p. 499).

Plan procurements—determining the what, when, and how of purchases and acquisitions.

Conduct procurements—documenting products, services and result requirements, and identifying potential sellers. Obtaining information, quotations, bids, offers, and the like from the sellers. Reviewing bids, choosing among the competing sellers, and negotiating a written contract with the selected seller.

Conduct procurements—managing the contract, contract-related changes and the relationship between the buyer and seller, reviewing and documenting the seller's performance, and so on.

All procurement processes outlined here are discussed from the point of view of the buyer. Second, descriptions for the seller may also be referred to as a contractor, vendor, third party, or supplier. Third, the procurement activities have more interaction with the other KAs than any others because of the nature of the transactions.

21.5 Planning for Procurement

The results of the make or buy activity target various items for third-party procurement. To proceed beyond this point several assumptions need to be highlighted:

1. Assuming that a reasonable price can be obtained externally, the defined item is identified as best acquired external to the organization (considering resource constraints, core competency, valid sellers, etc.).
2. A similar vendor exists who is technically and financially viable for delivering the required item.
3. The internal organization does not need more control over the item than can be dealt with through a third party. This includes intellectual property (IP), core competency, status, quality, and so on.
4. Moving the defined work to a third party does not increase risk beyond the tolerance point
5. A likely third party may have a better skill capability for the defined work than exists internally.

With these assumptions, a base comparison with internal costs will be used for future procurement decisions.

21.5.1 Planning Stage Outputs

The planning stage results in the following basic documents and policies that outline the actions to be pursued going forward (PMI, 2017, p. 499):

1. Procurement Management Plan (identifying types of contracts to be used)
2. Bid document formats
3. Procurement Statement of Work (SOW)
4. Make or buy decisions (procurement targets)
5. Source selection criteria

A project Procurement Management Plan is produced from information related to the target areas defined in the make or buy analysis and is designed to provide ongoing management guidance and direction to the project team in regard to future procurement actions. In some organizations, a subsidiary document called a Contract Management Plan is used to detail the overall process in regard to vendor relationships.

One of the most important planning documents is a work or service specification for the procurement target. This is called a Procurement SOW and one of these should be developed for each target item. This specification is drawn from the WBS Dictionary description of work, but will require more breadth and detail since the target is now to be performed externally and the work involved may be more than a single WP (Heerkens, 2001, p. 68). To be successful the contract SOW should be well defined to the degree that a vendor can reasonably use it to estimate their response. Key categories included in the specification are the following:

1. Scope of work in sufficient technical detail to support a seller response.
2. Location where the work is to be performed.
3. Performance data—start dates, completion dates, and so on.
4. Deliverables schedule.
5. Acceptance process—outlines how the deliverable will be accepted.
6. Applicable standards—these can be custom defined, company standards, or industry standards.
7. Other—there are many unique items that may be relevant and should be included in the document. Examples are special test equipment required, travel, experience required, certification of the seller staff, and so on. It is also good to let the seller know what you are looking for in the way of priorities—cost, schedule, quality, expertise, and the like.

At this point the technical planning process for procurement is complete.

21.6 Conduct Procurements

The second major stage of the procurement process focuses on obtaining seller responses and awarding a contract (PMI, 2017, p. 521). This activity falls generally into the financial and legal side of the planning process, and key decisions to be dealt with at this stage are as follows:

1. Receiving seller responses from SOWs and selecting preferred vendors
2. Negotiating contracts with preferred vendors
3. Communicating status to various stakeholders and processes

Each class of procurement activity has unique characteristics and requires similar treatment in terms of methods to find and deal with the prospective sellers. Over the years, this process has become reasonably well standardized in industry. The following are the typical procurement documents:

- Requests for Information (RFI)
- Requests for Proposals (RFP)
- Requests for Quotation (RFQ)
- Invitations for Bid (IFB)
- Invitation to Negotiation (ITN)

Each of these items is worthy of note to explain their general usage in the process.

21.6.1 Requests for Information

This is a formatted seller response that is intended to allow vendors to uniformly describe how their solutions meet the functional and nonfunctional requirements. The vendor is instructed to provide their answers on the formatted worksheet, which is then combined with a response table received from other vendors to form a master worksheet. This worksheet will then be used to perform a comparative features analysis.

21.6.2 Requests for Proposals

Procurement items can be complex, nonstandard, and high in price. This class of items requires additional expertise from the seller, so the response requested is based not only on delivery of the item, but to help define the specification. The RFP method is appropriate when the buyer cannot write clear specifications for the work to be performed and when the seller's expertise is needed. In addition, this method is applied when the buyer wants the opportunity to evaluate vendors' offers that have different approaches, price, and quality. Evaluation criteria are listed in each RFP. Contract award is made to the highest rated proposal that may or may not result in the lowest price.

An RFP typically involves more than a request for the price. Other requested information may include basic corporate information and history, financial information (can the company deliver without risk of financial stability), technical capability (used on major procurements of services, where the item has not previously been made or where the requirement could be met by various technical means), product information such as stock availability and estimated completion period, and customer references that can be checked to determine a company's suitability.

21.6.3 Requests for Quotation

For those items that are standard, off-the-shelf, and relatively low in price, an RFQ is the most desirable document. For example, when planning the bulk purchase of commodity products such as PCs, printers, modems, and applications software, an RFQ should be generated. The RFQ is used when the most cost-effective solution is the overriding concern. A prepared list of qualified sellers receives the RFQ.

Creative purchasers structure the RFQ to get additional information such as value out of the price. RFQ includes specific and detailed format for basic information, such as price, delivery charges, and other charges appropriate to the quotation. The RFQ should also provide an opening for suppliers to include anything that may affect the price or the value of the goods or services being purchased. A supplier may come back with benefits of which the purchaser was unaware. Detailed RFQs also benefit the suppliers by encouraging them to quote separately. This gives the purchaser better data for determining which services are cost effective and which are not. Additional costs such as those for transportation, packaging, and supplier stocking, and additional benefits, such as extended commitment options, cash discounts, fixed term of price, and reduced lead times can be evaluated on their own merits. The purchaser can then choose which options to take and which to leave.

21.6.4 Invitations for Bid

Procurement items are standard, but high in price. All items are clearly specified by a SOW. Governments and public agencies tend to advertise their IFBs in newspapers. The IFB notifies the potential vendors about the existence of the project. It is called open competitive selection. In this case, anyone who is interested in and qualified may want to submit a bid. Private businesses rarely advertise bids except for big projects. Some private organizations may have an acceptable bid list of potential vendors who would receive the notifications. This selection process is called closed competitive selection. In this situation, the client will contact several vendors to make them aware of the project. Only those invited to bid in this manner are allowed to bid on the project.

The IFB provides a summary of the project, the bid process, and other brief pertinent procedures for the project. It informs potential bidders of the project, its scope, and ways in which they can obtain further information. The invitation also states whether a security bond is required, how much it will be, and for how long it will be held. The size or length of time for which the bond will be held may discourage some vendors from bidding.

21.6.5 Invitation to Negotiation

The purpose of this document is to create a control structure for the technical, legal, and financial negotiation areas. It aids in comparative evaluation of multiple vendor responses. A second major category of the document deal with the evaluation criteria related to each review area (Lamb and Hair, 2006, p. 59).

21.7 Bidding Process

Once the procurement targets are identified and the class of the activity is chosen, the next step is to seek out sellers. In some cases, this will come from existing preferred sellers lists that have been derived by the procurement department, whereas in other cases the requirement will necessitate a more complex vendor search process. In all cases, the goal is to obtain an acceptable response from the seller and from this obtain sufficient information to select a vendor.

21.8 Selecting Sellers

Once bids have been received from potential sellers, the process moves to selection. Earlier communication with potential vendors outlined selection criteria that would be used. These criteria are now used to evaluate the bid responses. The basic evaluation categories are technical, financial, and organizational. In some cases, the item will be a quick lead time, "in stock" commodity and the issue will be price. In other cases, the criteria will weigh the technical capability of the vendor. Finally, if the procurement cycle is reasonably long, the stability of the vendor becomes a critical evaluation. Obviously, if the vendor organization fails nothing else is relevant. From these evaluations, one or more candidates are selected for further detailed negotiations that are intended to lead to a formal contract.

In most cases, seller selection criteria are directly related to the critical success factors of the project and these include cost, previous business relationship experience with the seller, industry experience, qualification of seller employees, demonstrated understanding of the requirement, financial capacity, technical ability and alliances, industry ranking of its products, and so on. However, in some cases, a seller may be added to the candidate list in order to comply with some corporate or government regulation. For example, a government regulation might require the use of sellers with over 50% of their employees being local or minority vendors. Usually, the selection criteria is created and approved by management before the proposals are sent out. The intent of these criteria is to improve the selection process and strive toward objectivity and fairness. In some bid cases, the selection criteria are defined in the bid package and this helps the seller to know how to respond to the request.

For major procurement items, it is common to receive a preliminary proposal from the sellers and screen the larger group down to a smaller list of qualified sellers based on their data. At that stage, a full RFP is sent to each of these qualified sellers who then prepare a detailed proposal. Based on the evaluation of these proposals, a final short list of sellers is created from which the most qualified seller is selected. Proposals are often separated and evaluated as discrete technical and commercial sections in order to properly evaluate the proposals on the basis of their content.

Weighted selection criteria are one of the most commonly used methods of evaluating sellers. In this method, each selection criterion is assigned a weight (e.g., 1 for poor to 10 for excellent). Then an overall rating score (usually from 1 to 100) is produced for each seller. The seller with the highest weighted score is judged the most qualified seller. In the event that two or more sellers have the same total score, additional selection criteria may be applied to select the most qualified seller. In some cases, a vendor not rated highest could be selected, but this raises a legitimacy question regarding the evaluation process.

Other techniques that can also be used with the weighted selection criteria include a screening system in which a set of minimum requirements are established for the sellers, and those whose proposals fall short of this requirement are eliminated from further evaluation. For example, the sellers may be required to have in their proposed team some number of Project Management Professional (PMP)-certified team members. The sellers who meet these criteria will form the "qualified sellers list." It is also advisable to use independent estimates to validate the bid cost for each quotation submitted by the sellers. This will help to ensure that the score assigned to the cost criterion for each seller is based on a realistic basis. This is a very important technique to use, because in most situations, the cost criterion carries the most significant weight.

21.9 Contract Negotiation

The role of contract negotiations is to define the specific structure of the relationship from which some form of legal contractual document will be created. Many feel that procurement negotiations are purely technical and price based. Think about this philosophy for a second. If that is all the relationship needed, why write a contract at all? It is a time-consuming process and contains a lot of words that laypeople do not understand. Michael Gold offers the opinion that contracts should be written with the perspective that the relationship will not go well and it will then fall to the contract to resolve the issue (Gold, 2005). Failure to have this protection can place great stress on the relationship, so the negotiation process is the time to deal with these issues as the parties are in a more rational state of mind.

The contract negotiation process involves three functional groups—project team for technical aspects, the procurement specialist for company policy issues, and a legal representative to ensure that the proper legal protections are included. If the item is commodity-like the negotiation is simply price related and involves a standard form. This requires very little involvement of the parties after the decision is made. However, this activity can be tedious and time-consuming as the complexity of the work specification grows.

The following are the three stages of contract negotiation:

Prenegotiation: This includes gathering information about each seller and their bid proposal. Risks to the project plan are analyzed and evaluated to formulate a strategy for cost, schedule, and performance negotiation. The buyer team needs to formulate and understand the strategy and tactics to utilize in the negotiation. It also includes activities to prepare both groups for actual negotiation (meeting invitations and logistics arrangements).

Negotiation meeting: This ensures the use of proper protocol (introductions and expectations). The process will include probing, tough bargaining, compromising, closure, and final agreements (clarified and documented).

Postnegotiation analysis: Evaluate your performance in terms of the original planning goals versus the actual negotiation outcome.

Contract negotiation is an art and involves significant human interaction in the form of buyer/seller diverse opinion meetings required to reach an agreement between two parties where both are attempting to maximize their value. However, the real art is finding creative solutions where both sides can leave the process as if they got what they needed out of the deal. It should not be a win–lose game as that sets up a bad attitude for the ongoing relationship. Since contract negotiation plays a crucial role in the procurement process, some mature organizations have made a determined effort to train project team members in negotiation practices in order to ensure that their organization achieves maximum value in the process. These practices include:

1. Clear objectives: Make a list of goals before meeting the other party.
2. Be prepared: Do your research before going into the negotiation. Know relevant laws, facts, and figures. Also, have a first draft of an agreement written before meeting with the other party and use that as your goal template.
3. Have an agenda for each negotiation session: Try to keep the discussion orderly when meeting with the other party. Make a checklist of topics that should be discussed during the session.

4. Make sure that appropriate decision makers are in the meeting: This will help to ensure that final decisions can be made without undue delays.
5. Set your expectations, but be flexible: Consider what you really need to get from the other party and also decide in what areas you are willing to compromise.
6. Build trust with the other party: Trust will aid communication and agreement.
7. Listen to the other party's concerns.
8. Focus on issues, not personalities: Focusing on your goal and treating everyone as an equal will help matters become resolved quicker. By treating all fairly, you will avoid simmering grudges and ill feelings, which can become an obstacle to agreement.
9. When negotiating force majeure (Act of God) clauses, make sure that this clause applies equally to all parties, not just the seller. Also, it is helpful if the clause sets forth some specific examples of acts that will excuse performance under the clause, such as wars, natural disasters, or other major events that are clearly outside a party's control. Inclusion of examples will help to make clear the parties' intent that such clauses are not intended to apply to excuse failures to perform for reasons within the control of the parties.
10. Speak in supportive statements: Attach credibility to your statements by speaking in facts not feelings. Avoid sentences beginning with "I think," "I feel," or "In my opinion." When stating facts, be prepared to quote your sources and elaborate or deflect questions meant to deflate your position.
11. Document meeting minutes: Document all agreements reached at the meeting and obtain buy-in of all concerned by sharing the minutes of the meeting. If possible have the contract ready at the end of the meeting or as soon as possible to get a signature to what has been agreed, so you do not have to retrace old topics.
12. End negotiations on a positive note: Shake hands and smile. Also, take honest notes to yourself on your tactics and see how you can improve for next time.

Complex negotiations involve significant time on the part of the participants and they can drag on for extended periods of time. To reach a successful conclusion, both parties must be willing to compromise. Issues of risk and return will be played out in the negotiation process. Once the various terms are finally agreed to, the last step in the process is to formalize those terms into a contractual document that is legally binding on the two parties and enforceable in a court of law.

The final deliverable of the contact negotiation process is a signed contract. This document represents a mutually binding agreement that obligates the seller to provide the specified product or service and obligates the buyer to pay for it. Depending on the type of item being procured, a contract may also be called an agreement, subcontract, purchase order (PO), or memorandum of understanding (MOU). Beyond the technical and financial aspects, a contract will include legally oriented items, such as effective date, scope of agreement, quality assurance process, milestones, payment schedules, warranties and guarantees, conflict resolution process, retainage, termination and cancellation provisions, penalties and fees, force majeure, confidentiality, labor rates, IP rights, applicable law and jurisdiction, and so on. Beyond these clauses, Michael Gold recommends defining breach and specific remedies for nonperformance (Gold, 2005, p. 2). Many parties stay away from this topic because of fear that these discussions will set the wrong tone. However, thinking about nonperformance at negotiation time helps both parties to think more clearly about the responsibilities that need to be included. Both parties need to think about the arrangement in terms of their required performance.

21.10 Contracts

In this discussion, the term "contract" is implied to be a formal, singular type document; however, this is not always the case. Think of a contract more as a state of the relationship, not a particular document. In fact, a contract can exist from verbal conversation between two parties so long as that conversation can be verified. In any case, such contracts are dangerous because the specifics would be almost impossible to reproduce. Also, a contract can exist using documents known as agreements, POs, MOUs, and subcontracts. Regardless of the communication mechanism, there are seven elements in a contract:

1. Mutual understanding of the subject area
2. Legal offer
3. Legal acceptance
4. Consideration (something of value)
5. Genuine assent (understanding of the propositions involved; freely entered; no fraud, undue influence)
6. Competent parties (not minor, insane party, or intoxicated)
7. Legal object (not in violation of state, federal, or public policy)

It is not the role of this text to teach contract law. It is, however, important to understand the importance of this process. Parties that fail to understand the legal consequences of a soured relationship will spend much more than they want either defending themselves or striving to obtain penalty remedies. To counter this problem the contractual documentation should be viewed as the mechanism to structure the relationship and make it clear as to the role of both parties. Every reasonable effort should be made to define the relationship in regard to delivery of the item involved and reciprocal compensation from the buyer. As part of this effort, there are several legal terms that need to be understood and each should be considered for use in your procurement document.

1. Acceptance
2. Agent
3. Arbitration/mediation
4. Assignment
5. Authority
6. Breach/default
7. Change process
8. Force majeure
9. Indemnification
10. IP
11. Material breach
12. Mediation
13. Ownership
14. Payments (details)
15. Principal
16. Reporting
17. Site access

18. Time is of the essence
19. Warranties
20. Privity

A more detailed definition of each term is included in the appendix to this chapter.

21.11 Administer Procurement

After the contract has been formalized the administration period begins. This phase is a monitoring and control-oriented activity and is designed to ensure that the seller's performance meets the contractual obligations. This involves performance monitoring and reporting on cost, schedule, and results. It may also involve the following:

- Quality control to assure conformance to requirements
- Change control related to the project change control process
- Financial control (payments)
- Compliance with special terms for payment and warranties
- Audit activities related to a contract

Individuals performing the contract administration function should be aware of the legal stipulations in each agreement and know when to elevate deviations for management review. This phase of the procurement relationship can be one of the most troublesome if change in specifications, seller stalls, quality issues, and other variances emerge during the delivery cycle. The main focus of contract administration is to ensure that the buyer acquires everything defined in the contract in regard to quantity, quality, time, and cost constraints. Related to this activity is a stream of formal delivery and payment documentation that needs to be carefully matched.

21.12 Procurement Audits

Procurement audits involve a structured analysis to identify lessons learned and to document the successes and failures of the project (Heldman et al., 2007). In this process, the team gathers information and evaluates the projects' goals versus the outcome of the product or services including all activities and processes that were undertaken during the project. It is important to include any corrective actions taken, outcomes, unforeseen risks, mistakes that could have been avoided, and causes of variances. Whatever the outcome of the project, successful or failure, it should be documented and recorded in the formal archives of the organization. Future team projects can learn from past experiences and make improvements. The PM has to be humble and honest in order to document mistakes that occurred, even if he/she does not want to admit to them. Everybody makes mistakes and the key is to learn from them, not to be afraid of criticism, but gain knowledge and an opportunity to learn and do better next time. Of course, this can only happen when upper management encourages an environment of responsibility linked with trust and a space to make your own decisions.

Even if both parties work to achieve defined schedules, there are several external factors that influence and can affect the project time frame, such as forcing the parties to consider an extension, or even an early termination. They need to evaluate if it is more costly to continue with a new end date, or force an early termination and closing the contract at that point. The cost considerations arise from an increase in budget, penalties, and legal fees.

21.13 Contract Review and Reporting

Throughout the contract administration period both parties must evaluate if the overall performance of both parties meets the contractual obligations. Three major control functions must be evaluated: quality control, change control, and financial control. Quality control evaluates the process as producing correct items per the specification and quality assurance procedures must in place handle an overall quality review from the buyer standpoint. Philosophically, the quality process should evaluate whether the vendor has designed quality into their product, and then created that quality into the product during their execution process. One of the major administrative issues concerning quality control is making sure that the proper quality measurements are in place. A poor quality control process can lead to an ineffective product to be dealt with by the buyer. An effective quality control and quality assurance process in the vendor organization will help avoid this problem. For complex procurement, this implies that the buyer must have some access to the internal operations of the seller to confirm this process state.

The change control process must be documented in the original contract and this involves a mini process similar to the original procurement. This means that a captive seller must also agree to this aspect of the contract. Changes often create variances in overall cost and schedule for the deliverables. They also complicate the interpretation of the terms as they stream through time. Changes can relate to anything in the scope of the contract, not just legal requirements, payments, and other small elements. They can relate to the defined work environment, regulations, or business landscape. Through all of this, correct procedures must be followed to ensure that the contract is still valid from both sides. All of the process elements outlined for a legal contract must remain for each of the changes.

The following checklist should be used for each change request:

1. Is the change really necessary?
2. Does the change deliver benefit or value?
3. What is the cost of the change?
4. Has the change been approved by all relevant parties? Have all the contractual issues been reviewed by technical, legal, and procurement staff?
5. Can all the parties still meet the revised obligations with the contractual changes?

The third segment of contract administration is financial control. The purpose of this process is to establish effective cost control and to trigger the vendor payables side of the relationship. The following should be addressed: current authorized budget, expenditures to date, commitments, agreed variations, potential claims, pending change orders yet to be approved, and future changes anticipated.

21.13.1 Record Keeping and Audits

A major component of contract administration is record keeping and audits as the project moves its life cycle. In some situations, an independent auditor will be utilized to handle the review and final processing of procurement contracts. The Department of Defense (DoD) uses the Defense

Contract Audit Agency to perform all its contract records and auditing process; "These services are provided in connection with negotiation, administration, and settlement of contracts and subcontracts" (DCAA, 2008, Chapter 1). All audits begin with a statement of objectives and those objectives determine the type of review to be performed. The Contract Audit Manual states that "Audits vary in purpose and scope. Some require an opinion of the adequacy of financial representations; others an opinion on compliance with specific laws, contractual provisions, and other requirements; others require evaluations of efficiency and economy of operations; and still others require some of all of these elements." The auditors should review the legality of the contract and verify that the work was performed as specified. If no seller work was performed and only goods were delivered, the auditor should be able to physically find the delivered goods. A full audit of contract status is a good measure to ensure integrity of the procurement process since there is obvious fraud potential in this activity.

21.14 Close Procurements

Formally closing the contract is the final step in the procurement process. In this step, the buyer verifies that all tasks and requirements defined in the contract have been produced and the contract is completed. Once this process is done, the buyer provides the seller a formal written acceptance stating that the products, services, or other items that the seller was responsible for delivering were completed within the time frame agreed, with the quality desired. The buyer asks the seller to respond to this letter stating that they have received payment as specified in the agreement. Failure to produce the formal acceptance letter and corresponding payment confirmation leaves the door open for future claims, so this activity needs to be pursued to avoid that later when the project team is dispersed and the corporate memory on these events has faded. Outputs of the contract closure process are the formally closed contracts with signed formal acceptance letters from both sides and updates to the organizational asset documentation. All of the contract documents, approval letters, change records, and any other supporting documentation are then moved to an archive contract file usually maintained by the procurement department.

Keeping with the project management model of striving for continuous improvement, the lesson learned report should also be filed outlining vendor performance, process issues, and any other items that would aid future projects.

21.15 Procurement of Human Services

Up to this point, we have attempted to describe a classic model-based procurement cycle. The general implication is that some tangible goods were involved. This process is the most standardized and mature KA of project management. This does not say that procurement cannot be mishandled, but standardized practices are defined and used for it. When the item being procured is a human-oriented service, the stability statement is no longer accurate. There are many forms of human services. A typical one is to "farm out" some internal process to an external vendor. This is called outsourcing among other names. Case in point is the trend of outsourcing various information technology services to India, China, and other low-labor cost areas of the world. Most of these become complex procurement activities for many subtle reasons. First, dealing in international procurement is complex, but the most typical hidden complexity is involved with the specification issue. Second, it is difficult to write the specification for a business process that will likely change over time such as Information Technology. Even more difficult is to describe how to handle the evolution of the process over time? Many firms have been attracted to lure of cheap foreign labor and jumped into outsourcing agreements only to find that they did not understand fully what they were contracting. In spite of some notable failures in this class of procurement there continues to be a migration to global human services outsourcing in many areas—IT, engineering, manufacturing, administrative, and more recently medical. Based on these trends, the PM needs to understand the environment of global human services procurement. This understanding involves more than a comparison of internal versus external labor rates for a defined task. Communications and cultural differences can add to additional cost to the process and sometimes reduce effectiveness.

Procurement of human resources leads us to one of the modern challenges of both project and procurement management. Traditionally, these resources were internal project team members. Now, they are 8000 miles and eight-time zones away, speaking English as a second language. They are at arm's length in every sense of the word and this adds significant issues to the overall process. The relationship possibilities for this class of procurement are endless, but structuring these agreements and plans in such a way so as to make the outsourced supplier effective and manageable is a great challenge. Interestingly, this text was edited in India at arm's length to both the author and the publisher who met only through email.

Putting aside issues of managing outsourced HR, and the costs involved, leaves us with the final issue: the risks in outsourcing. In some cases, outsourcing component parts of a project may effectively reduce risk by supplying needed technical capacity and removing schedule constraints. However, the loss of control and status visibility for these tasks leaves success in the hands of the outsourcer and may well introduce a new set of risks.

One of these risks comes in the form of lost IP. Organizations that indiscriminately outsource projects with patented, sensitive, confidential, or critical IP content are courting balance sheet disaster. Nevertheless, this is happening on a routine basis today in companies around the world. If an outsourcer can learn the organization's marketable IP, what is to be done to keep that organization from becoming a competitor? Today, we can see a great deal of this from China and Japan. Several years ago, the United States sent manufacturing work to these locations because of cheap labor, only to find later that some of these organizations captured the underlying IP. Later, they became not only competitors but also owners of the market. This "bleeding" IP process needs to be considered by the buyer even more when human skills are involved. In general, using external resources to process sensitive information and technologies should be avoided, as this can risk the security of the company itself. Beyond this, quality of the result can be compromised with an improper vendor choice.

Regardless of whether the procurement target is human services or tangible products, the risk analysis for that decision is important. The ultimate goal of procurement planning should be to reduce the uncertainty in the project plan as well as to protect the organization from losing its competitive position as a result of this decision.

21.16 Ranking Vendor Proposals

Prior to sending out a vendor proposal, you need to have an agreed-upon rating/ranking system that is fair and objective. This will help remove bias or politics during the selection process. Use of a weighting worksheet similar to the sample below can help rate a vendor response. This evaluation approach helps to assess the vendor strengths and weaknesses by category. Keep in mind that the main objective is choosing a vendor that provides the best overall solution based on the criteria that is most important to your organization.

21.16.1 Worksheet Instructions

The sample worksheet shown in Table 21.1 contains 19 evaluation criteria, their assigned weight scores range from 0 to 4, and evaluation rankings are also rated 0–4. Note in the calculation column that the weighted score is computed by multiplying the weight times the rank. In the sample calculations, vendor X has the highest weighted score (135) and would be considered the best fit.

Table 21.1 Rating Vendor Proposals

Weighted Proposal Ranking Matrix—Unix Servers							
		Vendor X		*Vendor Z*		*Your Vendor*	
Category–Criteria	*Weight 0–4*[a]	*Rating 0–4*[b]	*Weighted Weight X Rating*	*Rating 0–4*[b]	*Weighted Weight X Rating*	*Rating 0–4*[b]	*Weighted Weight X Rating*
Technical							
Long-term viability	4	2	8	2	8		
Performance	4	2	8	3	12		
Robust admin tools	4	3	12	1	4		
Processor technology	3	3	9	4	12		
Clustering solution	2	3	6	2	4		
Unplanned downtime	2	2	4	2	4		
Fault tolerance and disaster recovery	1	2	2	3	3		
Weighted technical total		49		47			
Vendor Support							
Global presence	4	2	8	3	12		
On-site on-line support	3	3	9	2	6		
Ease of doing business	3	3	9	4	12		

(*Continued*)

Table 21.1 (*Continued*) Rating Vendor Proposals

Weighted Proposal Ranking Matrix—Unix Servers							
		Vendor X		*Vendor Z*		*Your Vendor*	
Category–Criteria	*Weight 0–4*[a]	*Rating 0–4*[b]	*Weighted Weight X Rating*	*Rating 0–4*[b]	*Weighted Weight X Rating*	*Rating 0–4*[b]	*Weighted Weight X Rating*
Support contract options	3	3	9	3	9		
Self-support programs	2	2	4	1	2		
Flexibility to negotiate terms	2	3	6	3	6		
Record of promised functionality	2	3	6	2	4		
Professional services	1	2	2	2	2		
Service performance reviews	1	1	1	2	2		
Weighted vendor support total		54		55			
Cost							
System	4	2	8	1	4		
Upgrade	4	3	12	2	8		
Support	4	3	12	1	4		
Weighted cost total		32		16			
Weighted proposal total		135		118			

Source: This worksheet authored by Ron Smith and Mike Sowers has been adapted from a similar version originally published in Baseline Magazine, December 2008. The authors approved this version.

[a] Key-weight: 0—intangible; 1—nice to have; 2—desirable; 3—highly desirable; 4—mandatory.

[b] Key-rating: 0—does not satisfy requirement; 2—satisfies requirement; 4—surpasses all aspects of requirement.

As with all evaluation worksheets, the weight values and criteria can be modified for a particular proposal or changed for all proposals depending on the needs. Use the last two columns to score your sample rating by criteria and then calculate your vendor score.

21.17 Summary

Executing the Procurement Management Plan ensures that the goods and services required to make the project successful are made available, on time, within budget and aligned with the project goal. It involves a series of processes that include requesting seller responses, selecting sellers, contract administration and contact closure. The project team can leverage the expertise of specialist from the functional departments within the organization, for example, procurement, contracts, and legal. These will serve as resources to the project team in developing procurement documents such as the RFP, RFQ, IFB, Contract Terms and Conditions, POs, and so on. They can also participate in some of the activities like the contract negotiation, the selection process, contract administration, and closure. This is much easier in organizations that have these departments in place and structured in a manner that enables them to work with various project teams. However, since these resources belong to the functional departments and report to their functional managers, it may pose some challenges with regard to their availability and commitment to the project team; hence, some projects add these resources to the project team at this stage of the project.

Outsourcing is an option that can be used to execute the procurement plan. It enables an organization to leverage the expertise of a contractor in procuring goods and services. It also transfers the risk of the procurement process to the contractor based on an agreement. Outsourcing helps to reduce overall cost of production for the organization and directly reducing time for the product delivery to the market. Outsourced contracts needs to be well managed to avoid delays that would impact the project delivery date, which could lead to increased overhead cost. However, some variances to the contract may occur on the part of the seller that will need to be addressed by the project team. For example, the outsourcing contractor for a services contract may not be delivering the right personnel for a project and the project team may have to work with the HR department to obtain some in-house resources to accommodate the gaps. Or the seller is not delivering goods according to the schedule, which may impact the overall project schedule. In this case, the project team will need to adjust their schedule, cost, and communication plans to accommodate the delays. Similarly, the risk that the seller may go bankrupt during a project thereby posing a threat to the supply of resources is something that may need to be put into consideration as part of the Risk Management process.

To be able to successfully execute a procurement plan we recommend following a certain number of best practices to make the plan as effective as possible. When the plan calls for outsourcing it is best to use a partner approach, provide colocation when needed, and establish long-term outsourcing relationships. These in combination with the above best practices will help your organization make the most of outsourcing. When the RFI/RFP stage comes along it is best to use the RFI to gather information and the RFP to secure the highest-quality proposals. It is highly important to give your partners strong and adequate timelines, be firm with your dates. When contracts come around it is most important to do complete due diligence from your side of the contract. Make sure all items are ironed out in the contract no matter how small they seem. Make sure that the contract has clear objectives, is prepared correctly, and is done with trust in your partner. It is also important to focus mostly on the main issues and to set expectations but be flexible. In the administration of the contract make sure that both parties are aware of all the legal implications and the contract is set up correctly for the current situation. It is extremely important to set up quality control, change control, and financial control to help manage the contract and mitigate any problems throughout the project. Adhering to these best practices will significantly increase the likelihood of executing a successful procurement plan.

Discussion Questions

1. Core competencies are the strongest skills and assets of a company. Would you think it wise to target improvements in new skills that could broaden those competencies, or should the organization outsource this class of activity assuming that it could be done with no significant risk and at least equal cost and quality?
2. Besides cost, what other sacrifices do you potentially make when you choose to outsource a human-oriented service?
3. What are the advantages and disadvantages of outsourcing?
4. What are the various types of functions and processes that can be outsourced? What distinguishes the better targets?
5. How do you differentiate when to use an RFQ or IFB?
6. What are the critical items that need to be included in an RFP?
7. Which would you utilize if you were trying to give the seller an opportunity to negotiate and work with you—RFQ, RFP, or IFB?
8. Which type of contract provides the highest risk to the buyer?
9. What is a weighted selection criterion and how is it used in the selection process?
10. What is the role of contract negotiation?
11. What are the primary functions of procurement administration?
12. What can happen if contract administration activities are not performed?
13. What is the most important activity involved in formal contract closure?
14. Why do you think it is important to document and archive all activities of the procurement process?
15. What document should be created before procurement planning begins?
16. What are the primary reasons for outsourcing HR?
17. What type of contract minimizes the risk of supplier cost overruns assumed by the purchasing organization?
18. What other costs, besides salary, should be factored into personnel outsourcing decisions?
19. What sources may be used to collect a list of vendors?
20. What are the most important parts of a contract?

Glossary of Key Procurement Terms

Contract negotiation: A procurement activity designed to produce a formal contract results from a bid that may be changed through bargaining. It involves clarification and mutual agreement on the structure and requirements of the contract prior to signing.

Cost-plus-fixed-fee (CPFF) contract: Cost may vary but fee remains firm.

Cost-plus-incentive-fee (CPIF) contract: Contractor reimbursed 100% of costs. Contractor fee varies between maximum and minimum fee and can have multiple incentives.

Cost-plus-percentage-fee (CPPF) contract: Allows flexibility as the contractor and owner work together on all costs of the project.

Fixed price (FP) contract: Contract with a fixed price or lump sum.

Fixed-price-incentive-fee (FPIF) contract: Target price = target price + target profit. Contractor pays sharing ratio of costs above target cost. Final price never exceeds ceiling price.

Force majeure: Force majeure literally means "greater force." These clauses excuse a party from liability if some unforeseen event beyond the control of that party prevents it from performing its obligations under the contract. Typically, force majeure clauses cover natural disasters or other "Acts of God," war, or the failure of third parties—such as suppliers and subcontractors—to perform their obligations to the contracting party. It is important to remember that force majeure clauses are intended to excuse a party only if the failure to perform could not be avoided by the exercise of due care by that party.

In sourcing: In sourcing is the opposite of outsourcing, that is, in sourcing can be defined as the allocation of work within a project to an internal entity that specializes in that operation. In some cases, this implies that the work is being moved back from a previous outsourcing arrangement.

IP rights: These are a bundle of exclusive rights over creations of the mind, both artistic and commercial. The former is covered by copyright laws and the latter by patents (Ward, 2000).

IFB: The IFB is one of the solicitation documents that companies use in the procurement process when the procurement items are standard, but high in price.

Milestone: An identifiable point in a project or set of activities that represents a reporting requirement or completion of a larger or more important set of activities.

Outsourcing: Outsourcing is subcontracting a process, such as product design or manufacturing, to a third-party company.

Procurement audits: These are structured analyses that identify lessons learned and are used to document the successes and failures of the project (Heldman et al., 2007).

RFI: The RFI is one of the solicitation documents that organizations use to gather information about the potential sellers.

RFP: The RFP is one of the solicitation documents that organizations use in the procurement process when the procurement items are complex, nonstandard, and high price.

RFQ: The RFQ is one of the solicitation documents that organizations use in the procurement process when the procurement items are standard, off the shelf, and relatively low price.

Retainage: In the contracting business, retainage refers to a portion of the payment that is withheld until the completion of a project. The client does not pay the contractor the retainage until all work on the project is complete. Retainage is negotiated up front and is stated as a percentage of the overall cost of the project. A common retainage amount is 10%. Retainage incentivizes the contractor to provide quality work up until the very end of the project.

Selection criteria: This is a set of criteria developed by the project team and approved by management to be used when evaluating the proposals or bids from a qualified list of sellers.

Appendix: Common Legal Terms

The following terms are commonly used in procurement contract language.

1. *Acceptance*—deals with the processes by which the deliverables are accepted by the buyer. An acceptance may be conditional, express, or implied (West's Encyclopedia of American Law).
2. *Conditional acceptance*—acceptance of an offer provided that certain conditions are met (such as specific changes in terms of an agreement).

3. *Express acceptance*—a definite and clear acceptance of an offer without added conditions (as-is).
4. *Implied acceptance*—an acceptance of an offer demonstrated through acts that indicate that the accepting party consented to the terms.
5. *Agent*—any person who is authorized to act on behalf of another party. This representation by the agent brings with it the power to bind that party into contracts, and tie them to liability by the agent's actions (The People's Law Dictionary).
6. *Arbitration*—a small version of a trial held outside of court, conducted by a person or panel who are not judges, in an attempt by the parties in dispute to resolve their issues without going to formal trial (The People's Law Dictionary).
7. *Assignment*—the transfer of rights, interests, or benefits from one benefiting party to another (The People's Law Dictionary).
8. *Authority*—permission to act, or order others to act on behalf of another party (The People's Law Dictionary).
   Apparent authority—authority given to an agent through various signs from the principal to make others believe that the agent has authority.
   Express or limited authority—authority that has certain, defined limitations.
   Implied authority—authority granted from the position the agent holds.
   General authority—"broad power to act for another."
9. *Breach*—a failure to meet agreement obligations, willingly or not (The People's Law Dictionary).
10. *Change process*—this clause defines how contract changes will be processed and names individuals who have authority to approve those changes. The implied authority in this case would be anyone on the buyer's team who holds themselves as an agent of the buyer would be accepted by the seller as a legitimate decision maker. This is not a situation that should be left undefined in the contract.
11. *Default*—a failure to respond; to make a payment when it is due; or to file an answer or other response to a summons or complaint (The People's Law Dictionary).
12. *Force majeure*—an event that is caused by forces of nature (West's Encyclopedia of American Law).
13. *Indemnification*—guarantee through compensation for losses or damages (e.g., insurance) (West's Encyclopedia of American Law).
14. *IP*—intangible products of the human mind and creativity such as patents, trade secrets, copyrights, and trademarks (West's Encyclopedia of American Law).
15. *Material breach*—a serious enough breach to destroy the value of the contract, which often leads to legal action (lawsuit) (WordNet 3.0).
16. *Mediation*—the process is designed to use a third party to help resolve disputes of either legal or contractual interpretation. The mediator works to find points of common agreement and helps to find some fair resolutions. Mediation differs from arbitration where the third party (arbitrator) acts much like a judge in an out-of-court less formal setting (The People's Law Dictionary).
17. *Ownership*—legal possession of an entity through title and legal rights (The People's Law Dictionary).
18. *Payments* (details)—deliveries of money or equivalents by indebted parties to parties to whom the deliveries have been promised (West's Encyclopedia of American Law).
19. *Principal*—the grantor of authority to a person or party to act on his or her behalf (West's Encyclopedia of American Law).

20. *Privity*—(access the fourth parties)—"A close, direct, or successive relationship; having a mutual interest or right" (West's Encyclopedia of American Law).
21. *Reporting*—"An official or formal statement of facts or proceedings. To give an account of; to relate; to tell or convey information; the written statement of such an account" (West's Encyclopedia of American Law).
22. *Site access*—permission and freedom to visit a particular location (West's Encyclopedia of American Law).
23. "*Time is of the essence*"—"A phrase in a contract that means that performance by one party at or within the period specified in the contract is necessary to enable that party to require performance by the other party" (West's Encyclopedia of American Law).
24. *Warranties*—statement, assurance, or guaranty that the quality of an item is good, or that a contractual fact is true (The People's Law Dictionary).

References

Defense Contract Audit Agency (DCAA), 2008. DCAA Contract Audit Manual.pdf. www.dcaa.mil/cam.htm (accessed January 9, 2009).

Gold, M.L., 2005. They signed what? A customer's approach to software development contracting. *Cutter IT Journal*, Volume 18 (11), pp 6–10.

Gray, C.F. and E.W. Larson, 2008. *Project Management: The Managerial Process*, 4th ed. New York: McGraw-Hill/Irwin.

Heerkens, G., 2001. *Project Management*. London: McGraw-Hill Professional.

Heldman, K., M.B. Claudia, and M. Jansen Patti, 2007. *PMP-Project Management Professional Exam—Study Guide*. Indianapolis, IN: Wiley Publishing, Inc.

Lamb, Jr., C.W. and J.F. Hair Jr., 2006. *The Distribution of Request for Proposals, Essentials of Marketing*, 5th ed. New York: McGraw-Hill.

The People's Law Dictionary. S.v. Agent. http://legal-dictionary.thefreedictionary.com/Agent (accessed December 5, 2008).

PMI, 2017. *A Guide to the Project Management Body of Knowledge (PMBOK® Guide)*, 6th ed. Newtown Square, PA: Project Management Institute.

Ward, J.L., 2000. *Project Management Terms: A Working Glossary*, 2nd ed. Arlington, TX: ESI International.

West's Encyclopedia of American Law, 2nd ed. S.v. Acceptance. http://legal-dictionary.thefreedictionary.com/ (accessed December 5, 2017).

WordNet 3.0, Farlex clipart collection. S.V. Material Breach. www.thefreedictionary.com/material%20breach (accessed December 5, 2008).

Chapter 22

Risk Management

22.1 Introduction

Risk management is the systematic process of planning for, identifying, analyzing, responding to, and monitoring project risks. This activity is the means by which uncertainty is systematically identified and managed in order to increase the likelihood of meeting project objectives. These uncertainties can be related to functionality, schedule, cost, or quality variability of the end deliverable. A more technical view of this concept is that the term "risk" can be interpreted to represent an uncertain opportunity (positive) or threat (negative).

One might argue that project risk is represented by all of the things that make the project plan inaccurate. Based on this view project management becomes risk management. If nothing ever went wrong with the plan variables, we would simply call the project manager (PM) "project checker" because that would be what the person would be doing with their time—checking off accomplishments as they occurred. When organizations consider whether to introduce a new product to the market, the decision to pursue the idea contains both opportunities and threats. Decision makers have formally struggled with the opportunity side of this subject for many years as they pursue organizational goals; however, it has only been in the past few years that techniques to formally assess the threat side have been structured into some usable and teachable forms. This is not to imply that the art of risk assessment has reached a scientific state of accuracy, but major progress has been made to reveal techniques that aid in minimizing project risks. Risk profiles are now being defined for various project types and these will help in at least better tracking of the event even if there are not so many techniques to identify them.

One of the complex management issues related to risk is that it is a *potential* event that may or may not occur. How do you manage something that is not? This means that it cannot be recognized in the project work plan if it does not exist. Beyond this dilemma there is the related issue that we do not know when it will occur or the impact—unfortunately, those are the two basic elements to accurately deal with the problem. It is little wonder that a problem with this characteristic has been less formally considered and thus avoided in the project management sphere for so long. One lesson that we have observed in previous situations is that problems that are not looked at carefully will remain unsolved. This is the case with risk. Organizations are finding that the more they look at this area of the project the better they become in identifying the general situations that can be monitored. Once the identification process improves other supplementary techniques are derived.

After this stirring description of the risk problem you may be asking "If I learn this material will I be able to avoid project risk in the future?" The answer to this question is clearly "No." But the potential impact of risk events is so important to deal with that it cannot be ignored. There is now a working model to deal with the problem and techniques to handle the mechanics will certainly evolve with experience. This is another continuous improvement theme to the management process. Being sensitive to the risk issue and monitoring risk situations is a critical activity for the project team. In order for the risk management process to be truly effective it needs to be proactive throughout the project life cycle. Recording that it happened is not the theme for this topic. This implies not only anticipating the event and trying to minimize it, but effectively dealing with the results and staying within approved boundaries. The dimensions of this problem area outlined above should be enough to motivate one to want to understand more about it.

The ultimate management goal for risk management is to understand the realm of potential problems that can occur in the project and effectively deal with them in such a way that the project can still succeed. The management steps that fit this are involve identifying, analyzing, and responding to risk events throughout the life of a project. Through this process the objective is to increase the probability and impact of positive events, and decrease the probability and impact of events adverse to the project. Given all the things that can go wrong in a project there is no anticipation that all can be either identified or resolved. On one hand, the time to do this research is not available and frankly the value in doing it is questionable. Hence, the operative goal is to find a technique to identify the major issues and work with them, while monitoring the lesser ones.

The term *risk* in the common vocabulary means potential for positive (opportunity) or negative (threat) outcomes; however, that term as used in the project world almost universally is viewed as a threat. This is the operative term that the rest of this discussion will use to imply negative outcomes. Negative risk management is similar to a form of insurance, whereas positive risk management is more like the goal of stock market investing. In the latter case both results are more recognized. Given that most of the opportunity risk assessment side occurs outside the project envelope. The main objective of project risk management can be primarily viewed as minimizing negative risks. Do recognize that the same theoretical decision processes work in either direction. A classic example of both aspects of risk can be seen in the Apple corporate decision to make a new type phone when they were a computer company with no customer recognition in that industry. That was a high risk decision with now obvious high opportunity, but even more significant negatives if it didn't work or the customer didn't buy them. Once that decision was made it was up to the project team to deliver a suitable product. Obviously, there were many technical threats in the development project that could have derailed the outcome. The outcome of this decision changed the course of Apple, but note both sides of the risk equation were at play throughout.

A technical project consists of a myriad of activities required to achieve its required goals. Due to the complex nature of these activities they often encounter problems that were not planned. This results in missed schedules, budgets, and substandard outputs. There is no known management technique that can cure all these ills; however, the risk management process described in this chapter is one that must be considered as a mandatory activity if one desires to avoid many of the potential negatives waiting in the project life cycle. Recognize that the process described is considered to be the least mature operational mechanic within the overall model. But the potential negative impact on the project from this area says that it is a mandatory consideration.

There is evidence today suggesting that even though the arithmetic aspects of risk assessment are not accurate an increased risk culture helps to mitigate the events that do occur. In other words, if the culture collectively is sensitive to this there is a higher probability that it will be recognized quicker and deal with at a lower level. As an example of risk culture, assume that employees have been trained in fire drills. Would it make sense to conclude that if a fire does occur the reaction might be more effective than the case where no prior training had occurred? This is how a risk culture would work. To carry this example further, what would happen is local fire teams were trained and equipment was installed in each area. Now, if the fire occurred would the result be less significant? This would fall into the category of risk mitigation—i.e., allocating resources to decrease the potential damage (for an event that might not happen by the way). Therefore on one hand, we can see the value of human training to help deal with risk events, even here not all events are fire related that still leaves the question of how to know what to be ready for. In our world today, there is certainly more sensitivity to negative events that might occur in daily life than existed 20 years ago. This is one kind of risk identification, but still leaves the question of how to handle this newly recognized event. This cross-translation between the outside risk world and the project environment might help to relate to the cultural idea. Unfortunately, more than cultural recognition is needed to accomplish the project management goal. The desired risk management model needs to include both identification, mitigation, and control aspects. And, as stated earlier, these events may not happen so how can they be shown on our project plan? One possible view of this is to recognize that when some risk event does emerge the likely scenario is to activate some type of reaction. That involves the need for resources not shown in the current budget and new work tasks that are now visible in the project plan. This class of problem is called *known/unknowns*. The model goal for this class of activities is to find a way to systematically identify and manage their occurrence throughout the project life cycle. This process requires a structured set of steps progressing from the initial risk event assessment, developing impact assessments, defining mitigation strategies to deal with the selected events, and then tracking status of the event.

On the threat side of the equation, risk management represents an organizational discipline for dealing with the possibility that some future event will cause harm to the enterprise or one of its projects. The ultimate concept behind risk management is to better manage potential problems that may occur in the project, and from this develop techniques to minimize their impact. In its present state, it is both an art and a science of identifying events, analyzing their impact, and then responding to those events throughout the life of a project. Identifying potential events prior to their occurrence provides time to either minimize their impact or avoid them completely. This technique is called mitigation.

There are many real-world examples where some catastrophic event destroys the success of an organization or a project. For example, approximately 50% of the businesses that occupied the World Trade Center did not survive the terrorist attack, whereas other similar organizations were able to resume operations with minimal impact. How can this be? At the foundation level, all organizations should have business contingency plans to cover loss of their facility and infrastructure—buildings, technology, equipment, and people. Each of these categories represents classes of events that would be catastrophic if something significant occurred. There was certainly no precedent for this class of event, but it was reasonable to suggest that backup systems should not have been in the same location. An active risk culture would have likely concluded that. In project situations, the risk events tend to be less dramatic and generally less severe, but in the cases where the entire organization was impacted the project would get carried along. For this reason, it is hard to completely separate enterprise level risk from project risk.

The concern domain of risk is large and uncertain. Given this, it is impossible to deal with everything that can go wrong in the project life cycle. For that reason, the domain is divided into two categories: known risks and unknown risks. A brief definition of each is as follows:

Known risks are those that fall into a class that could be logically expected to occur and for which some general probabilities and impacts can be estimated. These risks can be reasonably dealt with by effective risk management techniques and can be minimized by following those techniques.

Unknown risks are not in the domain of predictable events and are not generally anticipated. These are not generally identifiable or predictable. These occur at quite random intervals.

Classification of risks into these two categories is difficult in reality. Basically, the only difference is in the handling strategy for the event after the fact. A somewhat amusing example of this classification problem is offered (i.e., that is if you are not a big fan of owls). One of the popular certification exam questions for project management describes the situation where two endangered species spotted owls have taken up roosting in one of the exhaust towers of a nuclear power plant just as the project is being completed and ready to go into operation. An environmental group is pressuring to keep the plant shutdown for an extended period of time until the owls decide to leave. The thought question is asking what type of risk is this, a known or an unknown. The author's Texas students say that this is not a risk at all; it is dinner (easy workaround; not a problem at all, or at least not a major one). Some would answer this by knowing mating owls like this area and the event should have been known and early action taken to chase them away sooner. Others might say that knowledge of owls is not reasonable and therefore is classified as an unknown risk. Management solution to this latter interpretation is still unresolved. Although the example is unusual, it makes a good point on risk type classification issues and their corresponding event results (i.e., impact on the plant varies depending on recognition and treatment of the event). In this example, where is the boundary of concern for risk assessment? Normally, mating owls would not make the list. Regardless of your view on this it does illustrate how a risk is classified lies in the level of ability to identify known events. In order for projects to be successful, its associated risk items need to be successfully identified and then managed proactively and consistently throughout the life cycle. Even if the events are not fully defined an active monitoring process is still required. Not all risks can be taken out of the equation, but an active management process is mandatory.

As we have indicated, the biggest problem in dealing with risk is guessing which set of events is most likely to occur and at what probability level. If we could do that accurately the rest of the process is not difficult. It is important to recognize that doing a great job of risk management evaluation on the wrong set of events has essentially no value. The only way an organization is going to get better at this process is to start doing it and learn from its experience and that of others in similar efforts. In the case of enterprise level risk, is there a known potential for a facility fire? What about extended power outage? One should consider the potential for a similar common set of general environmental risk events common to all project activities.

At the project level, risk identification becomes more focused to activity internal to the project. When new technology is involved, that immediately becomes a risk target to assess. Why then do we observe the type of technical failures often observed in this class of project? In many cases, the organizations did not have a risk culture. That is, they simply did not think about the issue or were naïve to its existence. Why do older employees typically believe in risk more than younger ones? The answer probably lies in the fact that they have seen these negative events occur and are more sensitive to them.

22.2 Risk Terms

In order to begin working toward a risk model several terms and concepts need to be introduced. The start of a working vocabulary set is summarized as follows:

- *Risk event*—An identified potential negative event.
- *Probability of occurrence*—An assessment of the likelihood that the identified risk event will actually occur.
- *Impact of the event*—An assessment of the cost to deal with the identified risk event.
- *Expected value of the event*—A measure of probabilistic impact of an uncertain event.
- *Mitigation*—An action taken to decrease the impact of an event if it were to happen.
- *Contingency fund*—A supplementary reserve fund that will be used to handle risk events once they have occurred.

The mathematics of risk is quite simple. If you know what the event and its related probability, the expected loss would be calculated by multiplying the probability times the impact. Statistically speaking, if there are a large number of these events the sum of these calculations would represent a valid contingency fund to handle the problem. We know an answer! When the event triggers resources are needed to deal with it. We put the fix plan into the project plan (scope is now increased), then we dip into the magic contingency fund and add that to the project budget. Everything is back to normal. Conceptually, this is the answer but there are a couple of little problems in setting this up. They are:

1. We really don't know all of the events.
2. We really don't know how to estimate the impact.
3. We really don't know how to estimate the probability.

So, our nice model just fell apart. As a former U.S. President once said we are now going to have to introduce "fuzzy math." The concepts are still there, but the quantification accuracy is suspect for sure.

This is the way the tactical model will work until more refined data is available. The basic steps will go as follows:

1. Risk events will be defined using best judgment.
2. A qualitative impact assessment will be made.
3. Mitigation actions will be undertaken for higher risk items.
4. All items defined will be documented in a risk register data base along with risk owners to help ensure oversight.
5. A contingency reserve will be set aside and used to fund events as they occur. The size of the reserve will be based on expert judgment and historical patterns.

These five steps then are the tactical operation mechanics for the risk management activity. Now that we have the vocabulary, goals, and crude tactical view of this problem let's look at the Project Management Body of Knowledge (PMBOK®) Guide approach for comparison.

22.3 PMBOK Model

The *PMBOK® Guide* defines the following risk management processes (PMI, 2017, p. 395):

1. *Plan risk management:* This involves how to approach, plan, and execute the risk management activities for a project. The main output of this process is risk management plan.
2. *Identify risk:* This involves determining the risks that are likely to affect a project and documenting the characteristics of each. One output of this process is to document details in the risk register.
3. *Perform qualitative risk analysis:* This involves prioritizing risks for subsequent further analysis or action by assessing and combining their probability of occurrence and impact. One main update is to define the risk matrix showing criticality of the event which will be used for further examination.
4. *Perform quantitative risk analysis:* This involves numerically evaluating selected high impact risks for further examination. The main output of this process also involves updating the risk register.
5. *Plan risk responses:* This activity involves developing options and actions to mitigate selected risks and document these plans. Also, other risk responses are mad, which result in updating the risk register and project management plan as well as risk-related contractual agreements.
6. *Implement risk responses:* Decisions made result in work being added to the project plan.
7. *Monitoring and control risks:* This process involves tracking identified risks, monitoring residual risks, identifying new risks, executing risk response plans as needed, and evaluating their effectiveness throughout the project cycle. The main outputs of this process are recommended corrective and preventive actions, requested changes, updates to the risk register, and a revised project management plan.

This process structure is shown schematically in Figure 22.1.

Completion of the seven processes summarized above involves the collective efforts and skills of multiple persons or groups based on the nature and requirements of the project. These analytical

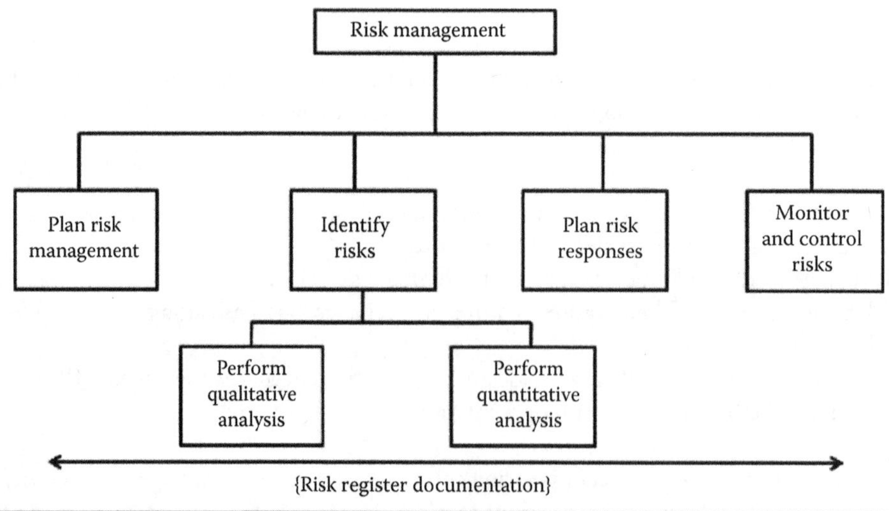

Figure 22.1 Risk management structure.

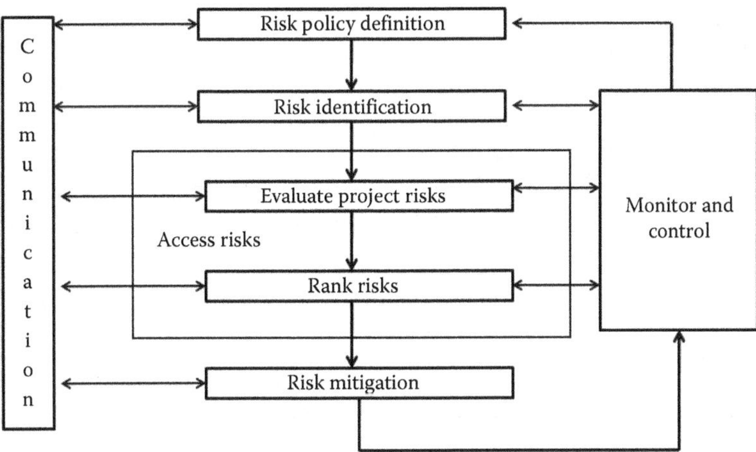

Figure 22.2 ERMA risk management process.

processes may occur once in the project or be formally repeated for each project phase, but it is important to recognize that risks can be identified at any point in the life cycle and for that reason one should think of this as an ongoing requirement. The sections below will further operationalize these steps and show their interrelationships.

The Environmental Risk Management Authority (ERMA) of New Zealand is chartered by their government to foster improved risk management and they offer a real-world operational view of this process to show how the basic processes are grouped and interrelated (AS/NZS4360-2004, 2004). Figure 22.2 melds their view of the process into a model similar to *PMBOK® Guide* view.

22.4 Risk Management Planning

The risk management model describes how this aspect of the project will be structured and performed. It is included as a subsidiary plan of the project management plan. This is the portion of the planning process where decisions are made regarding how to formulate, plan, and execute the risk management activities for a project. The process involves a systematic approach to planning the activity based on the premise that careful planning enhances the possibility of project success. The main output of this process is a risk management plan that documents the procedures to execute and manage the risk-related activities throughout the duration of the project. Careful and explicit risk planning helps guide the project team's reactions when a particular event occurs later. Developing a plan to outline how the risk management steps will be executed is essential to ensure the proper level, type, and visibility. The risk planning process is embedded in the basic project planning process activities and interrelates with those activities as decisions are made regarding handling of specific work activities. Various knowledge area plans can be impacted and modified as a result of these actions. A summary of topics addressed in the risk management planning model is as follows:

Methodology: This involves the various approaches, tools, and data sources that are to be used to perform risk management on the project.

Roles and responsibilities: Defines the event manager, support, and risk management team membership for each type of activity in the risk management plan, assigns people to these roles, and clarifies their responsibilities.

Budgeting: Assigns resources and cost estimates for inclusion in the project contingency plans.

Timing: Defines when and how often the risk management process will be performed throughout the project life cycle, and establishes risk management activities to be included in the project schedule.

Risk categories: Provides a structure that ensures a comprehensive process of systematically identifying risk to a consistent level of detail and contributes to the effectiveness and quality of Risk Identification. An organization can use a previously prepared categorization of typical risks. A Risk Breakdown Structure (RBS) is similar in look and concept to a Work Breakdown Structure (WBS). Other views can also simply list the various risk aspects of the project in named groups.

Definitions of risk probability and impact: The quality and credibility of the Qualitative Risk Analysis process requires that different levels of the risks' probabilities and impacts be defined. General definitions of probability levels and impact levels are tailored to the individual project during the Risk Management Planning process for use in the Qualitative Risk Analysis process.

Risk documentation: This segment of the plan defines the formats and processes that are going to be used to document the risk items identified.

There can be various types of risks shown in a RBS. Generally, the risk events fall into broad categories such as market risk, financial risk, technology risk, people risk, and structure/process risk.

The output of the risk planning stage is an RBS, which is a useful tool to determine potential risk categories for the project. This structure guides the project team in considering the risk categories for their respective project. In addition to this, checklists and templates are often used to review areas and stimulate thinking for risk identification.

Apart from identifying risks based on the nature of the project, it is also essential to identify potential risks according to project management knowledge areas such as scope, time, cost, and quality. Examples of various risk conditions associated with different project knowledge areas (KAs) are as follows:

Integration: Inefficient planning, improper resource allocation, poor integration management, and lack of post project preview.

Scope: Maximized scope, poor definition of scope, and poor definition of work packages.

Time: Errors in critical path calculations, early release of competitive products, errors in time estimation, errors in calculating resource availability, poor allocation, and management of float.

Cost: Errors in estimating cost, inadequate productivity, change, or contingency.

Quality: Inadequate quality assurance program, substandard design, substandard materials, and substandard workmanship.

Human resources: Poor conflict management, inadequate leadership qualities, and poor organization of responsibilities.

Communication: Insufficient communication with the key stakeholders and improper planning.

Risk: Less interest in risk management, less concern toward insurance management, and improper analysis of risk.

Procurement: Unenforceable conditions and contract clauses, and hostile relationships.

Stakeholders: Conflicting goals with multiple groups. Insistence on changes that clearly don't fit the Charter.

One key output of the Risk Planning process is the Risk Management Plan that identifies and establishes various procedures for managing risk throughout the project. A key metric for this plan is to determine at what level the potential risks are considered to be relevant. Other components outline other risk management activities and communicate the plans to appropriate stakeholders. This document outlines the *what, who,* and *why* questions and establishes an operational context for the remaining steps.

22.4.1 Developing an RBS

One major aspect of the risk plan is categorization of risk elements and one approach to outlining a macro-view is to use an RBS as illustrated in Figure 22.3.

The use of an RBS aids in categorizing potential risk groups for a project. Each project will have to modify this structure, but it does offer general guidance for a high-level view. The specific example areas listed underneath the major risk groups represent subareas that can spawn this type of risk. The basic role of the RBS is to help ensure that the project team considers important risk areas.

22.5 Risk Identification

The second and most complex step is *risk event* identification that consists of identifying and documenting potential risk events to the project. This process is performed by the PM, project team members, risk management experts, business process experts, customers, end users, other technical resources, stakeholders, and outside experts. It is an ongoing, iterative process because new risks may become known as the project progresses through its life cycle. The frequency of iteration and who participates in each cycle will vary from case to case. The project team should be involved in the process so that they can develop and maintain a sense of ownership and responsibility for the risks and associated response actions. In this phase, the context of the risk is an important consideration. Issues such as organization, political, economic, time frame, and other such trigger mechanisms will help to understand why the item is perceived to be an opportunity or threat. It is crucial to identify potential risk events as early as possible in the life cycle of the project. A risk cannot be properly managed if it is not identified—surprise events later lead to a chaotic environment. A localized checklist possibly structured into an RBS format can be developed to guide the project team even more specifically to items relevant for the local environment.

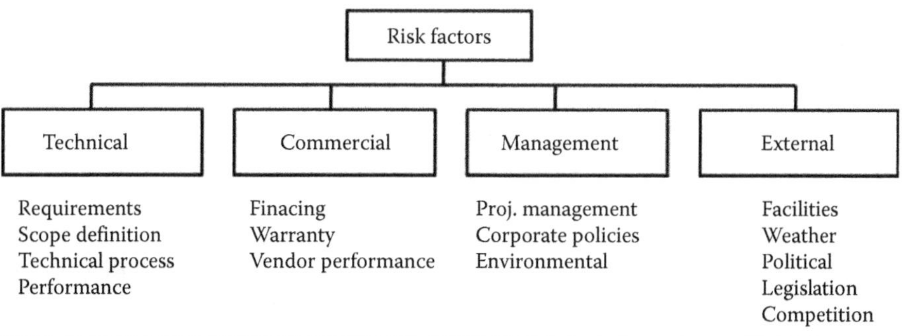

Figure 22.3 Sample RBS.

Related to the RBS view of risk identification is a checklist format. This is illustrated by a sample checklist of risk-related questions. This sample list is adapted from the software development risk methodology used at Hill Air Force Base (GSAM, 2003):

1. Is the PM dedicated to this project, and not dividing his or her time among other efforts?
2. Are you using a proven development methodology?
3. Are requirements well defined, understandable, and stable?
4. Does an effective requirement change process exist and is it being used?
5. Does your project plan call for tracking/tracing requirements through all phases of the project?
6. Are you implementing proven technology?
7. Are suppliers stable, and do you have multiple sources for hardware and equipment?
8. Are all procurement items needed for your development effort short-lead time items (no long-lead items?)
9. Are all external and internal interfaces for the system well defined?
10. Are all project positions appropriately staffed with qualified, motivated personnel?
11. Are the developers trained and experienced in their respective development disciplines (i.e., systems engineering, software engineering, language, platform, tools, etc.)?
12. Are developers experienced or familiar with the technology and the development environment?
13. Are key personnel stable and likely to remain in their positions throughout the project?
14. Is project funding stable and secure?
15. Are all costs associated with the project known?
16. Are development tools and equipment used for the project state-of-the-art, dependable, and available in sufficient quantity, and are the developers familiar with the development tools?
17. Are the schedule estimates free of unknowns?
18. Is the schedule realistic to support an acceptable level of risk?
19. Is the project free of special environmental constraints or requirements?
20. Is your testing approach feasible and appropriate for the components and the system?
21. Have acceptance criteria been established for all requirements and agreed to by all stakeholders?
22. Will there be sufficient equipment to do adequate integration and testing?
23. Has sufficient time been scheduled for system integration and testing?
24. Can software be tested without complex testing or special test equipment?
25. Is the system being developed by a single group in one location?
26. Are subcontractors reliable and proven?
27. Is all project work being performed by groups over which you have control?
28. Are development and support teams all collocated at one site?
29. Is the project team accustomed to working on an effort of this size (neither bigger nor smaller)?

The intent of such a checklist is to uncover a risk event based on that area. A review of this checklist against each WBS element would also aid the risk review process regarding specific event discussions about that area. From this type of review one or more specific risk events could emerge. As stated earlier, no predefined checklist will capture all such possibilities, but they do represent a way to get started with the process. As items are identified, they are documented in the *risk register*, which becomes the master repository source for the rest of the process. Figure 22.4 illustrates the steps that follow the identification process.

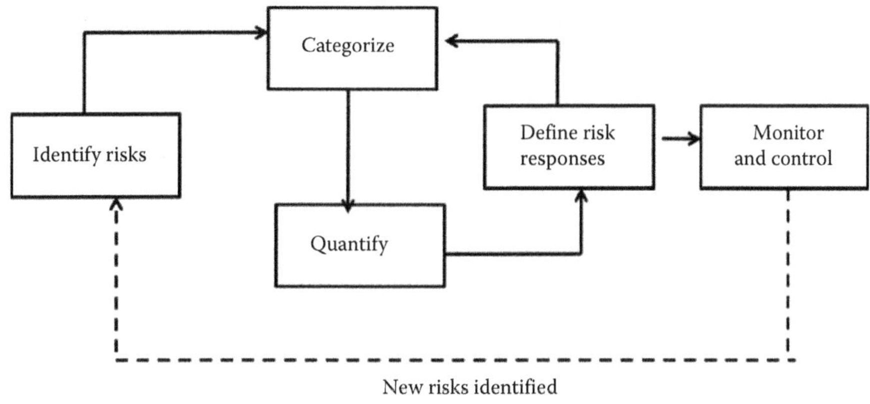

Figure 22.4 Risk response planning steps.

The first operational step in the process is to identify and document potential events that could negatively affect or enhance a particular project's ability to achieve its objectives. This activity should be ongoing during the planning stage and continue throughout the project life cycle. One of the key themes of risk management is to identify potential risks that can affect the project outcome and manage these events in an improved fashion over what would have been the case if that process had not been undertaken.

Potential risks can be identified based on a general understanding of common risk sources and by reviewing project scope documents, the WBS details, environmental factors, and other sources. Participants in risk identification activities include the PM, project team members, appropriate subject matter experts (SMEs), customers, end users, other stakeholders, and risk management technical experts. The risk identification team should consist of people with appropriate project and domain experience (Glazewski, 2005). Several tools and techniques are useful in the identification process. A sample of these is included below (DAU, n.d.):

Personal interviews sessions: Structured interviews sessions with experts help identify target areas for further analysis. This class of activity will develop high-level ideas and potential solutions. The goal of this activity is to generate ideas spontaneously and without judgment. Individual interviews are an effective way to work on more detailed issues and group interviews can help gain consensus on various aspects of the process.

WBS: The WBS serves as a checklist of work activities to review for risk. Each box in the structure represents a work effort with associated technical, resource, and other risk aspects. Think of it this way; if each of these work units were completed on schedule and within budget, the project would achieve its goal. Conversely, if that were not the case a risk event probably entered the scene. We reiterate that the WBS is the single-most important management artifact and this is just one more of its roles in the life cycle.

Documentation review: Artifacts created by previous projects can provide a wealth of information regarding risk. Specifically, lessons learned documentation from an earlier project team could provide specific insights into issues that might translate to the new initiative.

Root cause analysis: Oftentimes, a visible event is the result of some hidden relationship. For this reason, it is not adequate to just say "this bad thing might happen." What is more relevant to this process is the root cause behind those potential "bad things." This level of understanding enhances the manageability of the event and facilitates grouping risks by source. From this, effective risk responses can be developed.

Means-ends analysis: A chain of underlying lesser items can trigger many significant risk events. As an example, the threat of a catastrophic fire could be lessened by several underlying mitigation processes (fire alarms, sensors, trained staff, extinguishers, etc.). In the analysis process, this means–ends view becomes part of the required activity. By understanding the means–ends relationships we can better decide how to manage the event.

Checklist analysis: As organizations deal with a common project type they develop a clearer view of risk events. From this understanding, checklists can be developed to guide the analysis process and help ensure that potential items are not overlooked. As an example, a pilot's checklist before takeoff is designed to ensure that some critical activity is not overlooked. Similarly, a checklist can form the redundant core of risk analysis, but it will not deal with the unique characteristics of a project. Only human intelligence will deal with that.

Brainstorming: This is a free-form idea collection process in which project team members, SMEs, stakeholders, and anyone else who might have information or knowledge about this project meet to identify potential risks for consideration.

Delphi technique: This technique involves experts in a specialized area being reviewed to identify an event, or the potential for an event. Participants rank their answers and the results are reviewed by the group. After multiple iterations a consensus tends to occur and this is used as expert input on the topic.

Strengths, weaknesses, opportunities, and threats (SWOT) analysis: This is an orderly review for assessing the strengths, weaknesses, and opportunities of a particular risk event. The SWOT technique ensures examination of the project from each of the four perspectives, which increases the breadth of considered risks.

Details related to the risk events identified in the identification phase are added to the original event data originally captured in the project *risk register*. Conceptually, this is an evolving database of all identified risks and their associated status information. These data items represent information sources for the ongoing planning and control activities related to risk management. Data elements captured for each risk event would include:

1. Reference number
2. WBS impact area(s)
3. Description of risk—possibly a short and long version
4. Statement of consequence—a code reference could be used here
5. Likelihood of occurrence
6. Impact of occurrence
7. Frequency—one time, monthly, and so on
8. Other items, as the process evolves

There are two significant outputs from the Risk Identification. These are:

Triggers: Triggers are early warning signs that a risk has occurred or is about to occur. Any triggers that are identified during this process are documented and the list is updated and used as a monitoring and control aid.

Table 22.1 Sample Risk Register Format

Risk Register												
ID	*Rank*	*Name*	*Desc.*	*Cat.*	*Root Cause*	*Triggers*	*Potential Resources*	*Risk Owner*	*Probability (H, M, L)*	*Impact*	*Status*	*WBS*
R6	1											
R43	2											
R21	3											

Risk register: This repository is a formal source for capturing all project knowledge regarding risks and their status. It is a document that contains results of various risk management processes and is a tool for documenting potential risk events and related information.

In addition to the two main data items documented, each risk event identified in the register should contain an identification number, a severity ranking, a description of the risk event (probably both a short and a long one for different purposes), the category under which the risk event falls, triggers for each risk, potential responses to each risk, the risk owner or person who will own responsibilities for the risk, the probability of the risk occurring, and the impact to the project if the risk occurs. Sample risk register data elements are summarized in Table 22.1.

22.6 Qualitative and Quantitative Risk Analysis

These two related steps are designed to provide a "fuzzy math" measure of quantification to the identified risk events. This stage deals with the determination of qualitative and quantitative rating values for the identified threat or opportunity. The first pass through the risk event list will qualitatively label each item as to their likelihood of occurrence and impact. Various grading systems are utilized for this: It is common to use H, M, L, or numeric grades from 1 to 5 as the severity coding scale. The goal at this stage is to select the highest probability and impact grade items on the list, realizing that some sizing partitioning is going to be required in order to focus on the most likely and troublesome ones.

At this point, we hit a critical operational problem with the methodology. If it were possible to assign numeric values to each event in terms of probability and dollar impact, the mathematics for risk would be quite reasonable. Before moving further with the model methodology let us review our previous expected value calculation in this context. If a risk event was estimated to occur one time in the project with a probability of 10% and if it occurred the impact would be $100,000, we could model the expected impact of that event at $10,000 (i.e., 0.10×100,000). This is related to the actuarial process that an insurance company would use to calculate customer premiums. In both cases, the goal is to set aside sufficient funds to cover the probabilistic event. In this case, we would set aside a contingency fund of $10,000 to cover the expected impact of this known/unknown event. It is always confusing to those exposed to this idea for the first time as to how $10,000 can cover a $100,000 event. A short answer to this is that we have a lot of such probabilistic events and all of them will not happen. In mathematical terms, if all of the estimates have been just right and we have a sufficient number of them, the contingency fund will be exhausted at the end of the project with zero remaining. Obviously, given our rough quantitative method of defining probability and impact our math is not that accurate. Regardless, this is process used to estimate the size of the contingency along with other data.

22.7 Risk Assessment

Once the potential risk event list is developed, some additional judgment is required. The assessment progresses in two stages: qualitative review, then quantitative. The number of risks identified will be too numerous to review each in detail, so the goal of the preliminary phase is to categorize this population into more manageable groups. Basically, this often results in a high, medium, low grouping or some numerical grouping (e.g., 1–5). From this level a more detailed quantitative analysis will follow.

Qualitative risk assessment: This process essentially involves a grading of the defined events by evaluating the likelihood and consequences with the "pseudo-mathematical" scoring scheme as outlined above. This process should also assess other factors such as time frame of occurrence and risk tolerance based on project constraints of cost, schedule, scope, and quality. The techniques involved here are as follows:

Risk potential and impact assessment: This assessment explores the likelihood of each risk event occurring, whereas the impact assessment explores how such an event could affect a project objective such as time, cost, scope, or quality. This includes both negative effects for threats and positive effects for opportunities. Risk potential and impact are rated according to the definitions given in the risk management plan. In some cases, an event with obviously low ratings will not be analyzed further, but will be kept on a *watch list* for future monitoring.

Qualitative risk analysis matrix: This evaluation matrix is defined in the risk management plan and is used accordingly at this point to categorize the risk events on a relatively crude basis. This matrix provides the scoring logic for combining scores for the likelihood and consequences of a risk. A sample five-level qualitative analysis matrix is shown in Table 22.2. A risk class score for a given event is defined by the matrix intersection using the assigned likelihood and consequence descriptors.

Table 22.2 Qualitative Risk Analysis Matrix

Impact					
	1	*2*	*3*	*4*	*5*
Probability	*Insignificant*	*Minor*	*Moderate*	*Major*	*Catastrophic*
Highly likely	H	H	E	E	E
Likely	M	H	H	E	E
Possible	L	M	H	E	E
Unlikely	L	L	M	H	E
Rare	L	L	M	H	H

Note: E, extreme, formal risk assessment must be performed; H, high, formal risk assessment should be performed; M, moderate, for possible and above ratings, a formal risk assessment should be performed; L, Low, formal risk assessment at discretion of the PM.

In order to populate the risk matrix, the following three steps should be considered for organizing the risk view:

Risk categorization: Project risks can be developed by categorizing potential sources of risk using the RBS. This is basically a view of the WBS sorted into risk groupings. This type of organization can be useful for identifying risk events or developing effective risk responses.
Risk data quality assessment: Analysis of the quality of risk data is a procedure to assess the degree to which the data about risks are useful for the process. This involves examining the degree to which the risk is understood and the accuracy, quality, reliability, and integrity of the data about the risk.
Risk urgency assessment: Risks requiring imminent responses may be considered more urgent to tackle. Risks that should be addressed immediately are indicated with priorities such as time to affect a risk response, symptoms and warning signs, and the risk rating.

Upon conclusion of this process, risk events are identified, graded using the matrix codes, and results recorded in the *risk register.*

Quantitative risk assessment: Once the risk events are categorized according to the qualitative process, quantification of these is needed to help decide how to deal with the items. Some items may be sufficiently severe to necessitate some amount of mitigation effort to remove or minimize the risk. Alternatively, some will be so small that further mitigation work is not justified. In all cases, the quantification results are captured in the risk register. Risk quantification requires two analytical components: the impact of the potential loss and the probability that the loss will occur.

The Risk Matrix is a simple tool to help prioritize risks and is used to translate the qualitative risks into impact/probability groups that can be further analyzed. The normal approach would be to deal with all of the high impact events (dark gray), many of the middle tier, and probably few of the less significant ones (light gray) (Table 22.3).

One potential method of quantifying risk is to assign a numeric value to the risk matrix groups and to multiply these values times the impact estimate for the event to form a pseudo expected value. There are many operational problems with this approach as actual probabilities are seldom

Table 22.3 Quantitative Risk Analysis Matrix

	Impact				
	1	*2*	*3*	*4*	*5*
Probability	*Insignificant*	*Minor*	*Moderate*	*Major*	*Catastrophic*
Highly likely	0.15	0.15		0.30	0.35
Likely	0.10	0.15	0.15	0.20	0.30
Possible	0.07	0.10	0.15	0.20	0.20
Unlikely	0.07	0.07	0.10	0.15	0.20
Rare	0.05	0.07	0.10	0.15	0.15

known, but as one gains experience with the process it may be possible to develop forecasting contingency metrics based on the calculated values.

The Risk Matrix serves two basic purposes. First, it guides the risk assessment process by the color-coding and helps establish policies as to what level of risk needs specific treatments. In the ideal case, it is conceptually a method to develop risk probability values that would be useful for computing expected loss estimates.

To assist in the risk event grading process, there are several supporting analytical techniques used in quantitative risk assessment including data gathering, quantitative risk analysis, and simulation modeling techniques. Commonly used tools and techniques are summarized as follows (Elyse, 2007):

1. *Decision tree analysis:* Probabilistic evaluation of an event can be modeled using the decision tree diagramming technique. This method traces the various outcomes of their projected results and from this one can judge the appropriate course of action. It encompasses the cost of each available choice, the probabilities of each possible scenario, and the rewards of each alternative logical path. Solving the decision tree provides the expected monetary value (EMV) for each alternative, when all the rewards and subsequent decisions are quantified. A sample decision tree is shown in Figure 22.5.

   This example evaluates the decision whether to request arbitration or a lawsuit. The tree branches enumerate the results of the projected outcomes. In his case the two variables are impact and probability. Each of the branches of the tree outlines the collective result of the two strategies. The monetary result is shown at the end of each branch. By multiplying the probability of the event times the outcome and summing the branch values we see that the decision to pursue a lawsuit receives the greatest expected value. Also, note that it has the highest potential for loss at $250,000. However, in some decision cases the avoidance of a major loss is more desirable than achieving maximum return.
2. *Modeling and simulation:* Creation of simulation models is a sophisticated quantitative risk analysis technique. The typical method used to simulate project outcomes is to assign variable activity time and/or cost probabilities to project activities. Then, using this data the model is executed many times (say 1000 cycles) by randomly selecting values for each cycle.

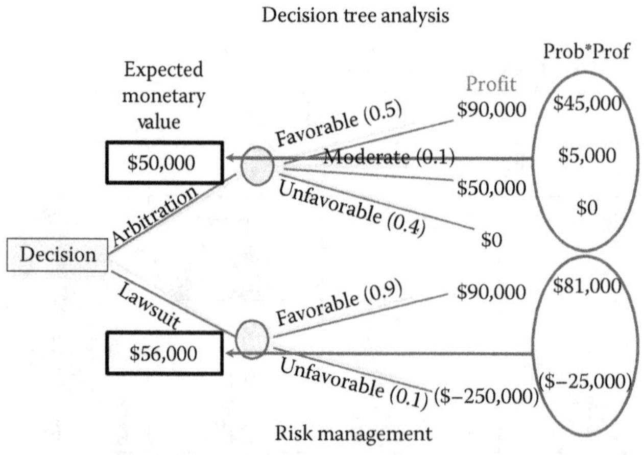

Figure 22.5 Decision tree example.

This in turn produces a probabilistic outcome distribution for the project and from this output appropriate risk-related decisions can be made.
3. *Sensitivity analysis:* Sensitivity analysis is used in determining which risks have the most potential impact on the project. One typical display of sensitivity analysis is the *tornado diagram* that ranks the project activities in order of significance for, say, critical path. From this view one can decide where to focus schedule oriented risk attention.
4. *EMV analysis:* EMV is a common calculation used in probabilistic applications to measure decision outcomes. This variable is calculated by multiplying the value of each possible outcome by its corresponding probability of occurrence and then adding the results. The EMVs for opportunities are expressed as positive values, whereas those of threats are shown as a negative.
5. *Data availability:* A common risk analysis mistake is to base risk ratings on incomplete specification data. It is always necessary to review the data used in the assessment as part of the process.
6. *Data quality:* Use of lessons learned data for comparable projects is a valid approach so long as that data are timely and relevant. Comparing a current project using data from a project 20 years ago is not normally a viable practice.
7. *Data integrity and reliability:* Qualitative Risk Analysis is imprecise and its ratings reflect subjective opinions and judgment. However, with this fact in mind, it is important to obtain the most accurate and unbiased information available. For example, if the previous project fought a war of politics among key stakeholders, it may not be appropriate to use that environment for comparison purposes.

22.8 Risk Response Planning

Envision at this stage of the process that the full slate of potential risk events has been defined, along with some measure of their probability and impact. The key question now is what to do with this list. While it is true that the risk environment across industries, organizations, and projects may have common elements, it is also true that different organizations will likely react to these similar events in varying ways. Terms such as *risk tolerance* or *risk aversion* are used to describe how one organization will go to great lengths to avoid a potential event, whereas another will judge the same type event to be tolerable and not spend funds to minimize the event. In this situation, both organizations may be making perfectly valid decisions for their particular environment. Such is the nature of this activity.

As risks are identified they are entered into the *risk register*, which is essentially a database containing all information about the status of the known/unknowns. At this point, the known data are the event itself, but the detail level grows as more data are added through the process. More specifically, it will contain data related to the following four activities:

1. Each defined risk will score characteristics including their likelihood, mitigation potential, and person in charge of dealing with the risks.
2. Rank the risks identified in order of priority using the Risk Matrix coding.
3. Calculate the impact on the project if the identified event does trigger.
4. Identify a response to each risk and in some cases define a contingency reserve for that particular event.

Risk Response planning involves developing responses to named risk events. The goal of these responses is to enhance opportunities and reduce threats to the project's objectives. The result of this activity is to define the action taken for specific risks and the associated steps that are required to carry them out. It should not be difficult to see that these actions have a high potential to add scope, time, or cost to the original project. Each mitigation strategy selected is designed to help ensure project success at minimal cost, but this is a probabilistic statement. These strategies thus represent resources spent to avoid significant bad events (Elyse, 2007). Collectively, these actions represent the risk mitigation plans for the project and these should be documented in the risk register for future access.

The decision options for the identified threat events are as follows:

Avoid: This involves changing the project plan to eliminate the events. This can be done by changing some element of the work requirement or reducing the scope of the project. Also, this can be accomplished by removing the risky item and replacing it with another more tested version. Replacing new technology with a more stable, older version is typical in this case.

Transfer: Risk transfer requires transferring or shifting the negative impact, along with responsibility for its management to a third party. The process reduces the risk only if the third party is more capable of taking steps to reduce the risk. It typically involves payment of a risk premium to the party taking on the risk.

Mitigate: Risk mitigation is a process designed to reduce the probability or impact of a potential risk to a more acceptable level. This can involve a host of options that are designed to lower the risk exposure to the project.

Accept: Some risks are so small and easily dealt with that it is not economical to spend time developing a response mitigation plan. In these cases, the event is simply put on a *watchlist* for monitoring, but nothing else is done to minimize the potential occurrence.

In some situations, there are risks that are significant, but cannot be mitigated or avoided. They are embedded in the fabric of the project itself. Obviously, in this case the event monitoring process is much more aggressive and should be kept under careful watch.

In similar fashion, the three strategies to deal with positive risks (opportunities) are as follows:

Exploit: This strategy is selected for positive risk impacts where the organization wishes to ensure that the opportunity is pursued. This strategy seeks to eliminate the uncertainty associated with a particular upside risk by making sure that the opportunity will have a higher potential to be successful.

Share: Sharing a positive risk involves allocating partial ownership to a third party who is best able to use the opportunity for benefit of the project. The examples of sharing include forming risk-sharing partnerships, mutual teams, working with elected officials, joint ventures, and joint ownership companies.

Enhance: Enhancing a positive risk involves changing or modifying the size of the opportunity by improving its probability and/or impacts, and by identifying and maximizing key drivers to positively influence these items.

Initial decisions made at this point in the process represent the culmination of the planning stage. Likewise, decisions made in the response process are used to populate the remainder of the Risk Response Plan elements. Specifically, the wrap-up activities involve the following:

Risk register (updates): Risk Register updates of the appropriate risk response.

Project management plan (updates): Project Management Plan updates occur as response actions are added after being processed through integrated change control.

Risk-related contractual agreements: Risk-related contractual agreements for insurance, partnerships, and services will generate language specifying each party's responsibilities.

22.9 Risk Contingency Budget

After decisions have been made regarding all identified risks, the final planning challenge is to set aside sufficient reserves to support handling these future events. The simple example shown in Table 22.4 illustrates some sample mechanics of this process.

In this example, precise probability and impact data is presented. However, there are still issues remaining which can invalidate sizing of the contingency fund. Experience will help with this, but recognize that there is a hidden error built into the process. Also, recognize that other risk events will occur that have not been identified. In this example, the risk contingency fund would be sized at $33,500; however, given the calculation estimate error and other unknown events, the fund should be sized higher. Tom Mochal, CEO of TenStep says "I believe the project manager should request an additional 5% of the total budget for risk contingency [just] to cover the undefined risks that you will encounter later. This is in addition to the risk contingency of the known risks that have already been identified" (Mochal, 2008). Sizing the contingency fund is clearly both a pseudo math and experience-related activity. As with all visible reserve funds management will challenge the value shown.

22.10 Risk Monitoring and Control

The risk monitoring and control process represents the ongoing management activities involved for this aspect of the project. During the course of the project some of the identified risks will likely occur (trigger) and the risk plan details will aid in working through the management of that event. In addition, new risks may arise during the life cycle and they will need to be processed as previously described for the planning phase steps.

Activities related to the risk monitoring and control process often lead to plan changes, updates, and revisions. If carried out properly, this process improves the overall effectiveness of the project outcome by providing workable reactions to negative events.

Table 22.4 Contingency Fund Calculation

Risk	*P (Risk Probability)*	*I (Cost Impact) ($)*	*Risk Contingency ($)*
A	0.80	10,000	8000
B	0.30	30,000	9000
C	0.50	8000	4000
D	0.10	40,000	4000
E	0.30	20,000	6000
F	0.25	10,000	2500
Total		118,000	33,500

22.11 Risk Events versus Issues

There is a general confusion in the project management lingo regarding the difference in a risk *Event* and an *Issue.* The *PMBOK® Guide* defines an Issue as follows:

> An issue is a "current condition that may have an impact on the project objectives."
>
> *(PMI, 2017, p. 709).*

Said another way, an Issue is an event that is causing some disruption to the project, but is anticipated to be resolved in a manageable time frame. The sticky definitional area here is that Issues look a lot like risk events. Some would argue that an Issue could evolve into a risk event if the anticipated resolution goes beyond the manageable time or cost threshold.

Regardless of one's view of this term, it does represent a real management topic. Let's illustrate some of the management approaches to handle this fringe area. During the planning phase an item of important equipment is identified as a potential risk event and maybe even has some contingency reserve added for it. Later, during the execution phase the equipment in fact does breakdown but the initial prognosis defines that the failure is minimal and the local technician believes that he can have it working in four hours. This outage does not significantly disrupt the project—i.e., this is an *issue.* The project keeps a log, called an *Issue Log,* which is used to document such items to ensure that they do not escalate into something more significant. At this point, we define this situation as an Issue and record it for tracking purposes. However, four hours later it is determined that the problem is much worse than forecast and will take a week to obtain the necessary parts to repair. This may well transfer the issue to a risk event and trigger the risk management process. In this example, an Issue became a risk as it evolved into a more significant outage deemed to significantly impact the project.

Projects have a seemingly endless list of daily minor Issue items that need to be resolved quickly. These do not represent regular work items as defined in the WBS, but are more often supporting activities—a drawing needs to be fixed, a vendor is slightly late in delivery, or a key team member is ill and a replacement is needed for one month (solution is available).

Regardless of how one views these two terms, there is likely to be confusion over how to handle those that begin to look like a risk event. This cataloging would be even worse if there was no risk event defined initially and it became major. In either case, the event (Issue or Risk) needs to be tracked and managed accordingly so the project can move on without major disruption.

22.12 Project Risk Assessment Worksheet

During the early stages of a project it is good to get a general assessment of the overall risk of the effort. One way to do this is through a high-level weighted criteria worksheet. This method provides a quantitative assessment of the aggregate risk as well as a checklist for the project team as they deal with the internal detailed risk management process. Later, during project execution these same parameters can be computed to see if there is an increased view of overall risk compared to the initial values. Another use of the worksheet data is to provide a mandatory monthly risk assessment to be used as part of the standard reporting data.

The use of this type of assessment can provide initial insights into overall project risk level and help assess areas where the risk profile is changing during the execution phase. Table 22.5 shows an example risk analysis worksheet. As with all worksheets of this type, the parameters and

Table 22.5 Risk Analysis Worksheet

Tracking Your Project Risks How Likely will this Adversely Affect your Project?	*A Project's Risk (Filled in Example)*				*Your Project*			
	Low (1)	*Med. (3)*	*High (5)*	*Risk Level*	*Low (1)*	*Med. (3)*	*High (5)*	*Risk Level*
Application complexity			5	5				
Baselines	1			1				
Contract or statement of work	1			1				
Customer expectation			5	5				
Customer involvement		3		3				
Customer acceptance	1			1				
Design level of detail		3		3				
External dependencies like deliveries	1			1				
Hardware, i.e., switching to new technology	1			1				
Software, i.e., switching to new technology	1			1				
Interfaces with other systems		3		3				
I.T. experience with system applications		3		3				
Productivity rates of I.T. team members		3		3				
Project management		3		3				
Project planning/scheduling	1			1				
Project resources		3		3				

(Continued)

Table 22.5 (*Continued*) Risk Analysis Worksheet

Tracking Your Project Risks How Likely will this Adversely Affect your Project?	*A Project's Risk (Filled in Example)*				*Your Project*			
	Low (1)	*Med. (3)*	*High (5)*	*Risk Level*	*Low (1)*	*Med. (3)*	*High (5)*	*Risk Level*
Requirements change		3		3				
Requirements definition	1			1				
Subcontractor involvement		3		3				
System performance requirements			5	5				
Telecommunications/network		3		3				
Workload estimate of I.T. team members		3		3				
Current month	8	33	15	56				
Last month	8	30	30	68				
First month	8	24	50	80				

INSTRUCTIONS: If an item is not relevant to your project, delete it and add new ones as needed. Grade each item for risk from 1 for low, 3 for medium and 5 for high.

For each item, enter your assessment grade and the same number in the risk level column.
When done, compute your monthly totals. Analyze what is happening over time; look for negative trends and take corrective action such as taking all of your high risks and creating a risk containment plan with your team.

measuring scales can be altered over time to fit the local project profiles and experiences. Relevance of a particular score will be learned over time as these numbers are compared to actual projects.

22.13 Conclusion

Before we exit the theoretical risk discussion let us leave you with this final project management point. All projects should go through a risk management assessment process as outlined here. The less maturity an organization has with this process, the less accurate the project results will likely be. However, experience with the methods outlined here can help develop that maturity level, and simply thinking about risk in a formal manner will help sensitize the organizational culture to its existence and the associated fact that mitigation strategies exist to minimize their impact. The last step in the maturation process will be developing techniques to produce a quantification process closer to a true expected value mathematical form. Nevertheless, value is gained even through just the risk assessment process.

Formalized risk management is now becoming widely recognized in both the public and private sectors as an integral facet of effective business practice as it provides management with a deeper insight and wider perspective regarding effective management of the organization activities within its dynamic environment. Also, risk management at the project level is an essential contributor to success as it focuses attention on issues that potentially affect achievement of its objectives.

The key to effective risk management is to be able to identify, measure, and minimize probabilistic events affecting project execution. A structured risk management approach involves event policy planning, risk identification, qualitative risk analysis, quantitative risk analysis, risk response planning, and risk and monitoring and control. The benefits of adopting a structured approach for managing risks are significant. Sample advantages are more successful projects, fewer surprises, less waste, improved team motivation, enhanced professionalism and reputation, increased efficiency and effectiveness, and more.

Project risks are a potential collection of uncertain events or conditions that, if they occur, create a positive or negative effect on at least one objective of the project. Experience suggests that the risk management process does not have to be complicated or time consuming to be effective. By following a simple, tested, and proven approach, the project team can prepare itself for the events that may occur. There is no tool that can avoid or fix all potential risk events; however, risk management offers a process to produce higher success in navigating through this minefield.

Discussion Questions

1. Risk Case Study—Mishap Foils Latest Attempt at a 25-Mile Skydive

   Note: Details of this case excerpted from a New York Times May 28, 2008 article written by Matt Higgins.

   Michel Fournier, a retired French Army officer who had hoped to fly a helium balloon about 25 miles above the Earth and parachute down, has failed again. As spectators watched, his 650-ft-high balloon inflated and then suddenly floated away, leaving the gondola with Fournier inside on the ground. The damaged balloon was recovered 25 miles away.

The launch team is investigating whether static electricity might have led to the setting off one of charges at the release point between the capsule and the balloon, the agency said.

Fournier had planned to climb into the pressurized gondola of the balloon and make a two-hour journey to 130,000 ft. Then he planned to step out of the capsule, wearing only a special spacesuit and a parachute, and plunge to Earth in a 15-min free fall. If successful, Fournier would fall longer, farther, and faster than anyone in history.

Fournier has spent 20 years and nearly $20 million in pursuit of the milestone. He sold his house and most of his belongings and solicited funds from sponsors to finance his project.

He has attempted the feat twice already, but technical and weather-related problems foiled the efforts before he left the ground. The most recent attempt, in 2003, failed when his balloon ruptured before takeoff.

If money was no object, outline what you would have done to bring this project in on time (note that the schedule had already been delayed by a previous problem with the balloon).

2. What could a project team have done to mitigate the known/unknown issues causing the latest balloon failure from the case study outlined above?
3. If a project is dealing with a new technology, what risk mitigation strategies should be considered?
4. When must a risk event be accepted?

References

AS/NZS 4360-2004, 2004. The Australian and New Zealand Standard on Risk Management (Tutorial Notes). www.broadleaf.com.au/pdfs/trng_tuts/tut.standard.pdf (accessed January 19, 2009).

Defense Acquisition University (DAU), n.d. Risk Management. https://acc.dau.mil/CommunityBrowser.aspx?id=17607&lang=en-US (accessed January 19, 2009).

Elyse, 2007. Risk Response Planning. www.anticlue.net/archives/000820.html (accessed April 15, 2008).

Glazewski, S., 2005. Risk Management (Is Not) for Dummies, *Crosstalk, The Journal of Defense Software Engineering*. www.stsc.hill.af.mil (accessed January 19, 2009).

GSAM, 2003. Guidelines for Successful Acquisition and Management of Software-Intensive Systems. Chapter 5. www.stsc.hill.af.mil/resources/tech_docs/gsam4.html (accessed January 19, 2009).

Mochal, T., 2008. Personal Correspondence (accessed January 23, 2009).

PMI, 2017. *A Guide to the Project Management Body of Knowledge (PMBOK® Guide)*, 6th ed. Newtown Square, PA: Project Management Institute.

Chapter 23

KA Integration and Plan Completion

23.1 Introduction

The final project plan derived from the planning stage activities is the result of a complex interaction of the 10 knowledge areas (KAs). Part II of the book covered the four output-oriented KAs that essentially describe the desired output attributes (i.e., scope, schedule, cost, and quality). Part III described the soft skills aspect of project management. We now have completed the final set of KAs, except for the concept of integration. It is now time to review this last KA and begin to see how the other KAs interact to serve the overall project goal.

The concept of integration is a very important element in the management role and in essence it illustrates much of what the project manager (PM) does in regard to tweaking the various processes to achieve the best output.

23.2 Introduction to Integration

The integration process covers the entire life cycle from Initiation to project close. Beyond the raw mechanics of integration there are seven model processes defined by the Project Management Body of Knowledge (PMBOK®) Guide. These are (PMI, 2017, p. 69):

Develop Project Charter—to authorize formal existence of project.

Develop Project Plan—steps designed to produce an integrated, viable plan that will be used to guide the execution process.

Direct and Manage Project Work—involves guiding the project through the planned steps to completion.

Manage Project Knowledge—involves the process of using existing knowledge and creating new knowledge for the betterment of the project and the organization.

Monitor and Control Project Work—involves tracking, reviewing, and reporting project status.

Perform Integrated Change Control—this process is responsible for reviewing and controlling all change requests and acting as an agent of the sponsor to ensure that the project direction does not violate Charter defined limits.

Close Project or Phase—this process involves formal activities designed to formally close either a project phase or final termination.

Up to this point, each KA grouping was discussed primarily as though it was an isolated activity. That is certainly not the case as any action on any of the KAs will have some impact on one or more of the others. The role of integration is to understand this interaction and use the knowledge in making operational decisions. As can be seen from the titles of the integration processes, the activity involves guiding the project from birth to death as dynamic events occur. Initially, this process commences in overseeing the Charter creation that formally spawned the project then guides the construction of the plan with all KAs considered. The remaining life cycle stage activities involve managing the dynamics of execution, status monitoring, and change control. Finally, the Close Project process formally terminates the effort and all related activities required in shutting down the project team and associated documentation.

The processes outlined above are reasonably straightforward as to the goal of each; however, this view would be considered the macro-level life cycle management perspective. When one looks at the concept of integration below the macro-level there is a somewhat different perspective. As the planning cycle evolves there are a host of decisions made that have to be integrated across the KA list. The final approved plan must exhibit the trait of integration. For instance, the plan cannot have a schedule that does not address required resources to support it. On the other hand, a defined shortage of resources might be covered by third party contract resources (procurement) to fill the gap. All of the above examples also affect cost and likely other KAs as well. These interworkings across KA groups is more of a micro-level view of the concept in that KA entities decisions can be traded off—cost for time, procurement for HR, quality for cost, etc. All these management actions also fall into the category of integration. The Project Management Body of Knowledge (PMBOK®) Guide defines this term as "...the processes and activities to identify, define, combine, unify, and coordinate the various processes and project management activities with the Project Management Process Groups" (PMI, 2017, p. 109). Within this sphere of activities, the PM is making decisions that touch not only the KA interactions, but:

- Resource allocations
- Conflicting requirements
- Alternative strategies
- Process decisions across the life cycle
- Team conflict management

In each of these cases, the resultant decision impact will be felt across multiple segments of the project resources and processes.

At this point, we will assume that all of the various KA decisions have been integrated into a single homogeneous plan. There is balance in the resources defined to the work defined. Likewise, the budget contains elements defined for human resources, material, procurement, and risk. In other words, there is integrated harmony across all of the KAs and process groups. The assumption at this point the project team has produced a plan that will support a successful outcome if the component parts are executed as defined. The team has collectively negotiated and resolved all required internal issues dealing with the KAs—not necessarily agreed with, but resolved sufficiently to support the version as defined. The final draft plan resulting from this activity undoubtedly involves compromise in various ways. Therefore, the last step in the planning stage is to obtain formal approval of the plan and formally close out the planning stage.

23.3 Project Plan review and Validation

Once the plan is completed, it will be used much like a road map to guide the project through the execution process in the same way that a highway road map serves to guide a planned trip. Either of thcsc map examples may not be 100% correct, but hopefully the detours will be minor, and we will always be able to track where the project currently is versus the approved baseline. To accomplish this goal the plan must have accurately captured the stated requirements, mapped a work pathway to achieve those requirements, incorporated various necessary technical items into the plan to support the output, and balanced all of these together such that all necessary components are in synchronization. To the best of the team's knowledge, this plan, if followed, will achieve the goal. Just as in any marketing effort, the plan now needs to be packaged in such a format to make it salable both internally and externally.

During the execution stage the management philosophy will be to "work the plan" as defined and report actual status into the monitoring and control process. In order to match this need, many of the final planning steps relate to setting up the project for next stage management and control activities. In the ideal case, the final plan would be so accurate that all that will be required of the execution team is to simply allocate defined resources to defined work units and record results. Since no surprises would occur in this mythical world there would be nothing else to do. However, coming out of this dream state we know that this is not the upcoming environment, but still realize that the more accurate the planning effort the less confusion later.

23.3.1 Final Plan Approval Process

Five major groups and 21 activities are defined below as being required to move the plan through the final stage. Each of the major groups is elaborated in regard to the associated decisions required.

Planning Formal Artifacts

1. Review final Work Breakdown Structure (WBS) structure and related dictionary items; match WBS work units to requirements statement
2. Review underlying planning assumptions and constraints to ensure that the plan has accommodated them
3. Review plan schedule, budget, and critical path for consistency (both technical and organizational)
4. Review defined integrated change control process and obtain formal approval
5. Review HR staffing and training plan with resource owners
6. Review risk management plan
7. Review procurement management plan
8. Review quality management plan

Financial and Control Structures

9. Define Control Account Packages (CAPs) and Control Account Managers (CAMs) who will be primary operational managers for the variance tracking process
10. Review contingency and management reserves

Documentation Plan Packaging

11. Complete subsidiary plan documentation and obtain approval from SMEs
12. Obtain sponsor signoff plan
13. Communicate final plan with key stakeholders; obtain feedback
14. Draft executive summary overview

External Communication

15. Project board briefing—explain board responsibilities
16. Communicate formal senior management approval process
17. Communicate plan to key users and external stakeholders

Planning Stage Close

18. Set plan baseline—multiple performance control items possible
19. Document planning lessons learned
20. Archive planning documents in project repository
21. Activate the execution-phase activities

23.3.2 Review Major Planning Artifacts

During the document review process, each of the KA subsidiary plans is validated for completeness and clarity. In the final version, each of these will be attached to the summary overview to supply details for those that need more explanation. From a technical viewpoint, the one issue that needs to be confirmed in this review is that all of the documented requirements are included in the WBS. Tagging the WBS to show where each requirement is produced is a good confirmation of this process and this action makes a good cross-check of requirements to planned work units. Later, a review of these artifacts with the project team will be performed and that activity is a good introductory technical communication activity. Since the project team may not yet be formed, this step might have to be repeated for them until later. Recognize that this document set will be used throughout the project life cycle, so its value should not be underestimated.

Every project plan will not include a full complement of these artifacts because of small size or other factors, but every project planning effort should have considered all KAs and have their implication discussed whether a full subsidiary document is included or not. For example, some projects would have no procurement requirement, so not much is necessary in that case. Many projects do not perform a formal risk assessment, but to leave out the discussion all together increases the probability of unforeseen events impacting the project.

The project management plan is a document used to coordinate all project components and to aid in directing activities. Because of this role the plan is an important input to the future control process. As changes are approved the project plan should be adjusted to reflect their impact. This artifact is the blueprint for all project activities; it offers insight when considering changes and deciding whether to proceed with the change. As the plan evolves, it maintains the view of both approved baseline and current plan.

One of the key attributes of the plan is its goal statement. Not only does this mean what is to be accomplished, but the corresponding resource limits that are defined. The *performance measurement baseline (PMB)* represents the approved plan baseline parameters for a project, activity, or deliverable. A working definition for this term "...Is a collection of Work Packages that define (PMI Utah Chapter):

- The deliverables that fulfill the needed business capabilities,
- Is a collection of Work Packages that define the deliverables that fulfill the needed business capabilities,
- The estimated duration and work effort for each Work Package,
- The resources needed to produce these deliverables within the needed time period, and
- Any dependencies—internal or external—needed to initiate a Work Package."

Project baselines can be established for any project attribute and these simply provide for a comparison value through the life cycle. Typical baselines relate to cost and schedule, but additionally could also be established for some technical performance goals in the plan. Metrics of this type help the PM to communicate both project and product performance status to various stakeholders.

23.3.3 Financial and Control Structures

Even though there are only two items on the summary list for this category the substance of those items is significant. First, identification of formal Work Breakdown Structure (WBS) Control Accounts (CAs) becomes the focal point for financial performance monitoring. Also, the associated CAMs are the operational agents responsible for execution of their individual elements of the overall project. Refer to Chapter 12 for a refresher regarding the role of a CA.

The enterprise accounting system is generally the official system of record for capturing actual project resource costs and the operational requirement is to establish whatever formal accounts are required in this system to supply needed actual data. The enterprise system will need to map its internal accounting structure to the WBS codes to support this process. As resources are charged against these accounts, it will be possible to link from the accounting system back to the project WBS structure. This will supply needed actual performance information. Beyond this linkage, there are also issues regarding the granularity of data related to fund types (i.e., expense versus capital), material, hours, and so on. The metaphor has been used multiple times before that the organization is like a flowerbed to the project. The better the flowerbed, the easier it is for the project. This is a perfect example of that abstraction. If the project has to invent its own tracking system, it will be costly, time-consuming and crude.

As documents emerge in the planning process, they should be stored in a formal configuration management repository so that there is no confusion as to which reports are the latest. Appendix B describes a model project document repository architecture, but recognize that every organization will be unique in their delivery systems and approaches to store and retrieve project data (another flowerbed metaphor example). In any case the PM needs to ensure the flow of plan and actual data into an appropriate repository to support various control activities links to the CA level.

It may be a surprise to learn that the complete project budget process is still not been completed as yet. Final structure of this document involves both financial and political elements. The financial components are deterministic, but the method of communicating and approving these becomes more of a political nature. The final set of activities logically consists of incorporating various

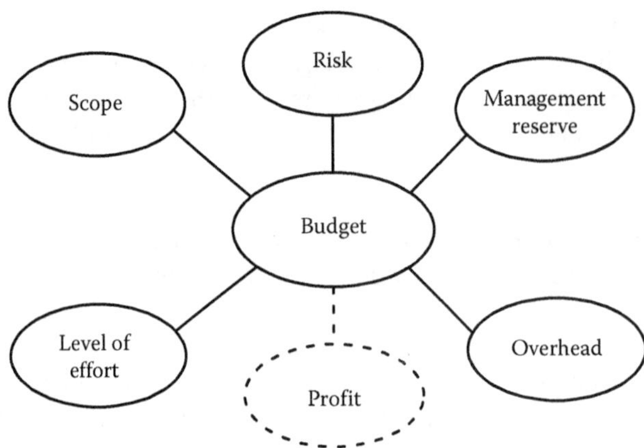

Figure 23.1 Budget components.

resource groupings, some of which are not part of the basic work units. Figure 23.1 illustrates these logical components schematically.

Five non-direct budgetary components listed below exist in every project to some degree. If the project is being performed under contract, then profit would be a sixth element. Since these elements are anticipated to consume resources the budget package needs to address and incorporate them as dictated by the local organization's financial policy and format:

1. Scope reserve
2. Contingency reserve for risk events
3. Level of effort (LOE) allocations for various support charges
4. Overhead allocations
5. Management reserve
6. Profit—if the project is done under contract

The implication of these items is to emphasize that the total project costs are derived from more than just low-level work packages (WPs). As indicated in Chapter 15, the direct project budget is produced by an aggregation of WPs Added to this level are the five supplementary groups and a profit margin may be added to this total if the project is performed under contract. Finally, it is also important to recognize that overruns in the lower direct budget levels can invade upward to consume these reserves and profit. Any time the total project budget exceeds this total envelope value it is vulnerable to be shutdown. This means that all anticipated costs for the project need to be recognized in the budget and the project management system must keep these values visible in future reporting.

Some of the most difficult items to justify in the budget are the various reserve items surrounding change, internal buffers, risk, and management reserves (in that order). These items are often viewed as padding and they are typically frowned on by management reviewers thinking that they do not represent real events. For this reason, budgets often will not show such reserves as outlined here. While it is true that scope change, triggered risk events, and management reserves are not real work; some consideration of these reserve types will be needed. Actual budget values for these items are even more difficult to estimate accurately than the project work itself, but these do represent valid potential cost elements that need to be reflected. To reject these as valid categories is ignoring the real-world phenomenon related to each. The alternative is to hide these categories in various lower-level work units and that clouds the picture from an estimating and control viewpoint.

Previous discussions have mentioned terms such as scope creep, risk reserves, and estimating variability, so there is a solid basis for understanding the role of budget reserves during the execution stage. Mature organizations will use these concepts to better deal with this class of variability.

Let us examine what happens when the reserve class of activity is hidden by duration padding in various WBS units. It is true that padding of work units has the effect of absorbing overruns, but the location of such overruns will not be clear and will certainly confuse future estimation of similar work. Later, looking at the history of the project it will not be easy to see why or where the actual overruns occurred. Not only has the organization not learned from the experience, it has confused itself. A more logical approach would be to estimate the future impact of these items and then develop a mechanism to compare what actually happens in each work unit and then compare that to the plan value. Some new components in the budget structure are needed to help with this process. Behavior of each non-direct budget group then adds additional ability to judge why the variances occurred.

Scope reserve. Some level of scope creep is normal for a project and needs to be planned for. The integrated change control process is established explicitly to manage and control the flow of such activity. However, scope work units are not explicitly part of the initial budget, hence, cannot be shown in the WBS view or the baseline direct budget line items. However, later when a scope change is approved by the project board that amount of resource should be somehow added to the budget to support the new work. Simply stated, some budget mechanism is needed to support the activity. One straightforward method to handle this would be to extract the approved change amount from the scope reserve and move that into the WBS structure as a normal work activity. It would now become part of the revised base budget. More importantly, the overall budget for the project would not have changed and the controlled flow of funds fits the management requirement. A related mechanical issue for this is the impact on the project baseline. Conceptually, all changes in scope represent changes in the approved project baseline, but in most cases this is not recognized unless the change is significant. The normal method is to keep the original baseline for comparison purposes. Movement of funds from the scope reserve pool to the base budget would be under the control of the project board and the PM. In the case of scope, the project board approves the change and this could be the management trigger authorization for the PM to move the funds.

Risk reserve. The technical name for this formally recognized fund is *contingency reserve* and it represents a level of funds estimated to cover future risk events that are evaluated during the planning risk assessment process. These events are formally defined in Chapter 18 as *known/unknowns.* Even if no formal risk assessment process is performed during planning some budget reserve should be setup for this class of event based on history, gut feel, or whatever technique the organization wishes. Movement of funds from this reserve pool should also be under the control of the project board or the PM and could then be mechanically allocated within the change control process. This mechanism is very similar to the model process described for the scope reserve.

Management reserve. This reserve category is defined to handle *unknown/unknowns* which according to our model are considered separate from the risk contingency reserve. In other words, these items were not anticipated as part of the planning exercise. Do recognize that some organizations will combine the risk and management reserves into one.

There is a certain amount of mystique surrounding this reserve type. Some organizations that do not accept the reserve concept just ignore budget overruns in this category so long as an explanation is supplied. The problem that this option brings is that such variances do occur and the budget overruns by definition. Our model management goal is to establish a planning and control environment that has the attribute that it will deliver the defined product at the cost defined by the budget. If we reject the padding option, some reserve strategy is needed to accomplish this goal.

There are several ways in which this class of project resource can be budgeted and controlled. One way is for management external to the project to hold the funds and require explanations of all variances. This is not a practical operational solution and would invoke many poor behavior traits within the project to minimize this. This overly controlled approach is also a poor use of management's time. A more practical approach is to allow some small percentage of the budget to be assigned to the PM to handle small undefined overruns (essentially a project reserve). These variances would be managed by the PM without external oversight up to the limit of the reserve fund. A second component of this could be kept at some higher level and either be known to the PM or not as the organization sees fit. This fund could be included in some external budget category and added into the overall organizational budget for the project. In any case, some formalized approach for the management reserve category is recommended.

In theory, when a WP overruns that amount should be extracted from a reserve and tracked accordingly. This process would serve to balance the budget books appropriately, but does require financial mechanics not often found in organizations. Regardless of the method used, strong consideration should be given to an unknown/unknown reserve in the neighborhood of 10% to protect the WBS work budget. The logic for this value lies in the statement that a well thought out project budget should be accurate within 10%. If that is not the case, then some other accuracy value would be appropriate.

Lack of formal recognition of this budget category places the PM in a tenuous position in that when the project budget begins to overrun because of these events the budget overruns, yet the phenomenon involved is really not unexpected. Just the exact source was not predictable. In a professional trust relationship both parties should understand these dynamics and provide the proper operational environment for the PM to do his job.

Based on this interpretation the management reserve concept becomes a split responsibility between the PM and his sponsor who has funded the effort. Both parties understand that the items in this category are not anticipated, but some of them will occur. The desired enterprise culture would be to encourage honest work unit estimates and manage the resulting potential overruns rather than to bury resource padding in all such units and ignore the problem. If we look at this issue politically rather than technically the real problem is how to show it on the visible budget, not the concept itself. For that reason, it may be necessary to keep management of the reserve group off of the visible view, but make these funds known in some format as generally described here. From an academic viewpoint the project budget should be considered an ethical contract between the PM and the sponsor. It also represents an initiative to achieve some higher-level organizational goal, so in that perspective the contractual view spans upward even further. The sponsor and the organizational management support units have shown willingness to commit some amount of their total resource pool to the project effort and in return anticipate receiving the defined benefits. In this view, the PM must be looked at as the change agent who will get that job done as specified by the plan and the cost management process should support that requirement.

LOE. Most projects will have some categories of work that fall into the definition of recurring activities that do not directly create WBS deliverables. A classic example of this is IT support of project equipment or the PM. Given the nature of these charges it would be more useful to be able to segregate them from the normal WBS activities.

LOE charges are difficult to map to regular WBS work units so it would be best to isolate them. These items can be shown as one or more defined lines in the budget (i.e., help desk, desktop support, office administration, copy center, documentation department, etc.). Control of this class of account would simply be comparing actual with plan because the concept of work completed does not fit the activity.

Budget overhead. Projects that are hosted in an organization will have various overhead values assigned to defined budget line items. These cost elements come from various sources and represent the overall cost of support from the organization. For example, the project utilizes the organization's buildings, executives, and managers, various support organizations, employee benefits, basic support infrastructure, and so on. The normal accounting approach is to attempt to show costs in proportion to their impact on the organization, so a full budget view would be required to recognize these costs. Some overhead items fit into the WBS structure and some do not. For example, team personnel have benefits beyond their salary, so rather than simply showing direct salary estimates it may be decided to show the fully "burdened" impact of an employee in the budget. This overhead amount would be embedded in the HR line items. Other items are not so easy to link to work efforts. In those cases, the budget might simply apply a factor called a burden rate to some portion of the budget to cover these expenses. These items need to be categorized on the budget structure outside of the working portion of the project because they are not controlled internal to the project.

Profit. Not all projects have profit in their budget. Some are executed internal to the organization, so this line item would not appear. However, if the project is being executed under contract there generally would be a profit line item in the budget. In some case, showing profit on a budget is avoided or visible only to certain management levels. Profit targets are often established by senior management, so this number would be derived as part of the project goal.

23.3.4 Budget Structure and Format

Organization of the formal budget line items is typically standardized within the enterprise in order to fit their accounting structure. However, from a project viewpoint, the format that would make the most sense is one based on the WBS organization. During the planning process, the majority of cost estimates were made on this basis at a WBS, WP, planning package, or summary-level activity; however, when presenting the budget to senior management it may be necessary to reformat this view into the enterprise format. This could also include dealing with various accounting issues such as types of funds (capital, expense, etc.). During the planning process these were likely not the paramount concerns, but they must be resolved before the formal approval is given.

During the planning stage, numerous notes and spreadsheets are created to support the final plan. At this point, the documentation set needs to be segmented into two basic groups—work papers and final plan elements. Work papers should be archived and stored until later. Some of these documents have no future value, but for now they should be kept. Other items become a part of source data to be included in the formal project documentation. Items to consider for inclusion in the final plan package are summarized in the following 23-item checklist:

1. Project Charter
2. High-level assumptions and constraints
3. Project Objectives
4. Scope statement

5. WBS
6. Labor and Time Estimates with background notes
7. Work units defined and their dependencies
8. Resource Allocation
9. Network Diagram (or Gantt chart)
10. Milestone Schedule
11. Staffing Plan
12. Communications Management Plan
13. Risk Management Plan
14. Procurement Management Plan
15. Quality Management Plan (quality objectives and approach)
16. Budget/Spending Plan
17. Documentation Plan
18. HR Management Plan (staffing, skills, and training issues)
19. Testing Plan (component testing, system testing, stress testing, etc.)
20. Configuration Management Plan
21. Baseline plan for all control attributes (time, cost, performance, quality, etc.)
22. Performance Analysis Plan (control process and metrics to be used)
23. Defined project document archival structure

In the pure model view, the project plan consists of a subsidiary plan for each KA and a high-level summary overview; however, local standards will define the actual format of the final plan. Depending on the underlying technology related to project goal there may need to be supplemental information collected for this aspect. Not only does the plan prescribe how the work will be performed, but a performance measurement plan should be included to outline how the project will be monitored and controlled.

A summary overview lays out the issues of greatest interest and concern to the various review groups. It is an important document in that many readers will not wade through the full set of subsidiary documents, so this becomes the face of the project for most.

23.3.5 External Communications

As the project plan phase reaches completion the need for communication to external entities increases. To motivate this behavior, realize that the primary core reason for project failure is judged to be communications related. At this stage no execution has begun, so the main goal now is to communicate the results of the planning effort and make sure that key management players understand the communication support role required.

Packaging of the project plan documentation for presentation must be sensitive to the communication value of this activity. For that reason the presentation material will have multiple versions in order to focus on the needs and interest of a particular audience. Senior management typically wants a summary version of project objectives with planned milestone dates. Cost is usually their main focus, although showing how the project will contribute to some aspect of organizational goal alignment will be of interest as well. Second, user presentations focus more on the projected deliverables functionality and related schedules. This review segment will want to see how the original requirements or vision statement was translated, particularly if some original requirement was deleted through a planning rationalization process resulting from resource, cost, or time constraints. Third, if there is a Project Management Office (PMO) in the organization they may well want to review many of the plan details (see Chapters 36 and 37 for a detailed overview of this functional group). A fourth review group will be the new project team. Once the project team is formed a kickoff session provides the opportunity to go through the work plans in detail and this is a vital communications step.

The key requirement in presentation content packaging is to communicate to the respective audiences how the planning process translated the original project vision. Significant changes could have been approved during this phase and these need to be explained to the appropriate user community. This communications cycle is the time to clear up planned deliverable gaps and level-set expectations. If requirements changes did occur, be prepared to discuss why they occurred and in some cases be prepared to go back to management and report stakeholder concerns. The user presentation process should also outline where they are needed for support to make the project successful. Activities such as design reviews, product prototype reviews, test acceptance, and training are typical user interface points requiring some defined action on their part. The presentation process has a defined audience sequence as summarized below:

1. Review the final plan package details with a broader group of formal stakeholders that either have a major involvement in providing resources to the project or will be major users of the output from the project. The goal of this step is to obtain formal approval of the final plan version and to gain commitment for their support of that version. If issues occur in this review cycle they should be resolved before going forward to the next step.
2. Package the planning document into a format suitable for management review (i.e., higher-level details with key points). The primary external audience for this formal plan approval would consist of the project sponsor, resource managers, and senior management who have authority to formally approve the project or who need to understand what the plan entails. In some high visibility projects this can include a Board of Directors level overview. Once appropriate management has approved the plan, the last step of the review process is designed to communicate the results to other key stakeholders.
3. The final review step communicates the plan details and should strive to obtain a positive buy-in from key parties. Most of these groups will have some active involvement in the execution or implementation phases and it is important to keep them involved. Accomplishment of the buy-in goal will help the effort move successfully through its remaining life cycle. Remember that failure to obtain user support is one of the top two reasons projects fail.

One of the key planning artifacts that will live through the life cycle is the communications plan that outlines the who, what, when, and where of various defined status documents. *Performance reports* are an effective method of conveying project status information to a broad audience; however, recognize that this audience may have different needs for status and the communication plan should recognize that. Typical formats for this class of reporting include histograms, Gantt charts, S-curves, schematics, colored graphical icons, and tables. More will be discussed on the topic of project status and metrics will be discussed in Chapters 30, 31, and 32.

23.4 Budget Control Roles

After all of the budget components and machinations described above are properly formatted into the plan, the final item in this category is to communicate how the various budget categories will be controlled. One important aspect of this is a need for clear communication from management as to what types of financial authority the PM has and how much baseline overrun will be considered acceptable. The budget components outlined above provide a structure for delegation of authority, but the organization needs to formally communicate roles and responsibilities for each of these as each budget group represents a potentially different control model.

As described here, the base work budget would use its associated WBS structure to compare planned (baseline) versus actual resource status. This comparative data would drive the various formal project monitoring and control processes that will be described in more depth later in the text.

Another aspect of budget management involves controlling the movement of funds across categories and the authority to make decisions that create expenditures (i.e., buy material, contract resources, hire, etc.). The PM cannot utilize the total amount of these approved resources as his open fund to spend or manipulate in any form desired. For example, the scope reserve fund has been approved to handle anticipated scope changes. Resources from this fund should only be moved into the base budget with an approved scope change indicating the amount associated with the change. This is a formal reallocation process. Likewise, a risk event occurring would be analyzed along with the associated impact amount. From this, the project board would authorize a resource allocation out of the risk reserve into the base budget.

LOE and overhead categories would be controlled depending on how these resources are shown in the budget structure. If overhead is embedded into discrete project budgets sections such as personnel, then the overhead would be automatically taken care of in the resource accounting process as time is charged to work units. Alternatively, if benefits and other items are budgeted separately, these overhead amounts would be shown in that manner. One tracking method for the LOE budget groups would be to report actual charges into their assigned budget line items. An alternate method would be to charge these items at some summary level. From an analysis viewpoint, it would be best to keep this work group separate from the basic WBS WPs, but that might not be feasible. Regardless of the way these funds are to be handled during execution, the process must be formally defined. Also, a mature organization should allow some minor overrun in the budget as being normal. Defining how much overrun is allowable is an important process question.

The final budget structure including all of the categories described here is a formal document that will live with the project through its life cycle and it basically represents the scorecard performance template for the project. Specific methods to deal with the dynamics related to scope, risk, and unanticipated overruns have been covered in this model view. At this point, the PM and the project board are committing to the organization that they will produce what has been shown in the plan and will report their performance in a manner described here. They are now asking senior management to approve the venture to move forward into execution. If that approval is received, the project plan and its major tracking details are baselined for use in future plan versus actual control comparisons.

23.5 Planning Stage Close

At this point, the plan has now been formally approved and it is time to move the project into the execution phase. These last steps fall into the category of stage closing and preliminary execution activation. Realize that up to this point changes in the plan have been lightly controlled form a management view, but from this point the plan details are frozen (baselined) and changes are under much tighter process control. There are now formally defined rules as to what change decisions can be made and by whom. In the model case, changes within the Charter boundaries should be delegated to the Project Board, but anything outside the Charter would have to be approved by the sponsor. This is an area where the PMB could be the dividing line for each of these decision points.

Moving into the execution phase usually starts the expansion of the project team size and may activate other geographical teams and vendors. Prior to this point each of these groups should have been kept in the communications loop as to timing of a probable start date. If internal resources are used to staff the team, physical facilities become an active topic. If the team is being collocated, this will involve physical space for which the requirement should already have been anticipated. All of these related transition actions are on the fence between planning and execution. These also illustrate how the project phases overlap. A good PM must always be thinking ahead and trying to anticipate what will be needed before the project has to stop and wait. To not deal with these transition issues until the end of this phase would simply delay the schedule.

Before leaving the planning closure stage it is important to document lessons learned and share these with the team and organization. Finally, various individuals have been involved with the planning process. The last step involves being a good HR manager. These individuals need to know how much you appreciated their contribution and this should be transmitted both personally and formally to their manager. Find a suitable nonwork activity to celebrate the successful completion. A nice lunch or dinner (whichever is more appropriate) is often used for this purpose. If the planning team has had to work long hours to finish the effort it is also nice to include the spouse in this celebration. In some cases a gift, bonus, or other memento is appropriate. All of these gestures are part of building a team culture now and into the future.

Discussion Questions

1. What project status and issues need to be communicated within the planning process and what media is best to the defined audience?
2. Do you agree with the level of planning detail outlined in this chapter? What issues do you see with this model theory versus your view of reality?
3. Assuming that your management instructed you to move into execution before you were comfortable with the plan what would you do?
4. How would you react to receiving significant negative response to the plan after you have received formal approval from management? Discuss your strategy and actions.
5. What is the purpose of a project baseline? Do you think that all scope changes represent new baselines? What alternatives would you propose?
6. Given that most real-world projects do not create the level of planning or budget documentation outlined in this chapter, what rationale do you attribute this to?
7. Most PMs say that they have never seen reserve pools used as outlined here. Do you agree that these reserves should be managed this way or do you see another option that would work better? Does the real-world culture impact this question?
8. How would you sell the idea of building a common project document?

References

PMI, 2017. *A Guide to the Project Management Body of Knowledge (PMBOK® Guide)*, 6th ed. Newtown Square, PA: Project Management Institute.

PMI Utah Chapter, Establishing the Performance Measurement Baseline (PMB). http://projectmanager.org/images/downloads/PDC_2012_Breakout_Tracks/performancemeasurementbaseline_glen_alleman.pdf (accessed October 9, 2017).

ADVANCED PLANNING MODELS

This section of the text describes four models useful for evaluating non-fixed duration time estimates. Each of these models differ from the traditional fixed task duration network plan structure. The motivation for inclusion is that each of these models offers an advanced method to either simulate the real-world dynamic environment, or help to manage it in a more creative way. The four techniques described are:

1. Managing variable time with the classic PERT model—Chapter 24
2. Contemporary adaptive life cycle model (agile/scrum)—Chapter 25
3. Monte Carlo simulation modeling—Chapter 26
4. Critical Chain modeling—Chapter 27

These techniques are unique and offer insight into the more advanced ways of planning and executing a project plan. Even though each of these are different in their construct and would be difficult to embrace totally, they offer collective insights into other ways of looking at the project management process. A contemporary professional PM should understand these models and use them as appropriate. Also, each of these has high potential for future evolution into greater use.

Chapter 24

Analyzing Variable Time Estimates

24.1 Introduction

One of the restrictive assumptions made in previous chapters was that estimated activity time was deterministic and accurate. Obviously, this assumption is not valid in a real-world project, yet relaxing the assumption introduces a nondeterministic answer regarding when the project will be finished. This means that management and user stakeholders are going to have to deal with a different kind of completion discussion. The proper answer will no longer be to say that the project will be finished on June 1. Instead, the answer will be couched in statistical terms such as "we have a 50% chance of finishing by June 1 and a 90% chance of completing by August 15." It is this characteristic that keeps variable time schedules from being popular. Stakeholders seem to want a single answer even if it is wrong (which it will be most of the time). Figure 24.1 shows what this result might look like with a histogram of probabilistic completion dates. This chapter will explore a classical technique to accomplish this type of analysis.

Note from the completion diagram represented in Figure 24.1 that there is a 50% chance of project completion by May 9; however, the computed project range is from April 27 to May 21, which is more than a three-week variability range. As activity uncertainty is higher, the corresponding calculated completion dates would also expand. This type of analysis is a valid way of looking at project schedules and should be pursued whenever possible. This chapter will describe the mechanics of variable time analysis and then show how the activity estimates can be translated into a meaningful view of project completion.

24.2 History of Variable Time Estimates

Variable time estimating techniques were initially formulated in the mid-1950s in high-technology military projects, most notably the Navy's Polaris project. The technique was contained in the network management model named PERT (Project Evaluation and Review Technique). Up until this point, project schedules had been created using vague scheduling tools such as the Gantt chart.

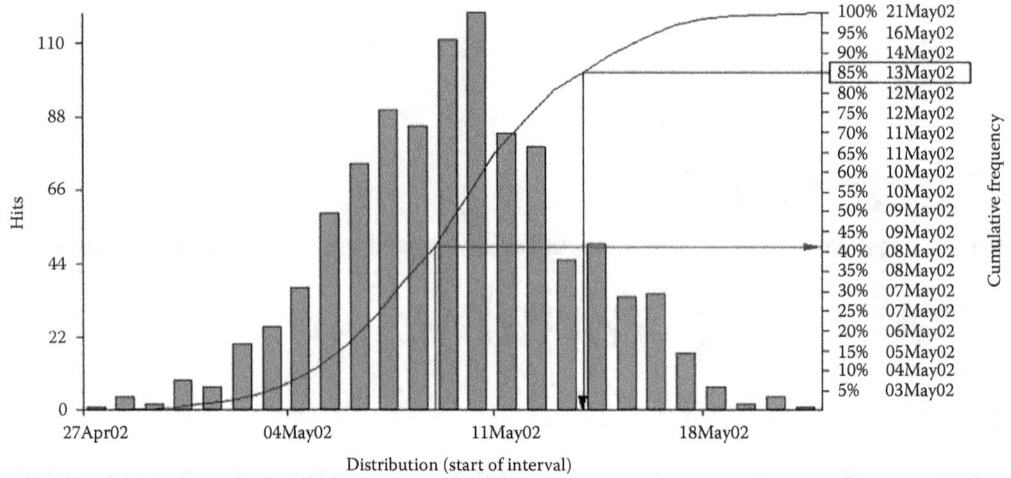

Figure 24.1 Probabilistic schedule.

The complexity of this new breed of project forced a more advanced view of the scheduling process (Verzuh, 2005). This class of project focused on time management more than cost, so the focus of the original PERT model was heavily time oriented.

Since time was a primary issue, PERT modeling used statistical techniques focused on assessing the probability of finishing the project within a given time range (Gale, 2006). The PERT model was based on an Activity on Arrow (AOA) network format with arrows depicting activities (see details of AOA in Chapter 14). Basically, the initial goal was to define project sequence and develop a quantitative technique to predict probable duration time ranges for each activity. From this, various statistical techniques were used to develop a probabilistic project completion forecast. The technical and schedule success of the Polaris project burst PERT into the project management limelight as a near magical tool.

Reiss later discussed the actual impact that PERT had on the Polaris project. He implies that it was never determined whether PERT helped, hindered, or played no significant role in the Polaris project, but that everyone seemed to think PERT had helped a great deal (Reiss, 2007). Nevertheless, publication of the Polaris project results stimulated PERT's emergence on the project management scene to amazing heights. During this period, a speaker at an American Institute of Management conference said, "Anyone not using PERT on their project ought not to be managing their projects at all" (Reiss, 1996).

As other projects began to use the PERT model, they began to recognize that it was mathematically complex and did not help with cost management. Also, computer software for manipulating this model was expensive to use at that time and available to only large organizations. Many felt that PERT did not work very well and there were some notable project failures attributed to its use (or misuse). The general attitude emerging at this point was that the Polaris project success was circumstantial and may not have had anything to do with PERT (Reiss, 1996). Russell Archibald, who was a team member on the Polaris Missile project stated:

> If you followed the developments at the time, you will remember that PERT was given a lot of favorable press, with the Navy's encouragement and grand claims were made that PERT enabled the Navy to complete the program some years earlier than it would have otherwise. I do not believe that these claims are entirely true, based on

> my experience. PERT probably did some good as far as planning and scheduling is concerned, but both the Navy and Lockheed, as the missile system integrator, failed to recognize the area of greatest payoff: integrating the schedules of many contractors.
>
> *(Archibald, 1987)*

Based on Archibald's statement, it can be deduced that there were other operational flaws with PERT during its early years. As a result of these negative factors, the use of PERT declined and it is still not used in the majority of projects today, even though much of the historical rationale mentioned is no longer valid. At approximately this same time a second network-based tool emerged. This tool was called critical path method (CPM). It utilized deterministic time estimates but dealt with cost issues better than PERT. As a result of these two basic design differences, CPM survived the early period while the PERT model began to drift back toward a single-time estimate very similar to the standard networks used today.

As a result of these evolutionary machinations during this early period, use of the terms PERT or CPM became muddled. Today, even when organizations talk about PERT, they generally use only a single activity time estimate for the activities and that essentially makes the PERT model usage equivalent to CPM. Likewise, regardless of how the project plan network is depicted it will be called by either name. In some cases, the name might be PERT/CPM, where the two are just combined. This essentially means that the plan is a network of some type and a critical path (CP) is defined. As the situation stands today, only a small minority of PMs can define the historical differences between the classical PERT and CPM assumptions (see Chapter 14 for a refresher on these two network models).

Therefore, the fundamental question here is why go back in time and resurrect something that has essentially died? The answer to that question is that the PERT model addresses a management piece of project reality that needs to be utilized as the user population and tool set matures. A fundamental value that the PERT model has is its ability to show a probabilistic estimate for project completion. The rest of this chapter will distil that idea into an easy to understand view.

24.3 Modifying PERT for Commercial Projects

PERT relies heavily on empirical mathematical averages and probabilistic distributions in order to produce its output. The two underlying empirical formulae have been translated into relatively simplistic formats, leaving only one somewhat complicated statistical relationship to deal with. For projects with a small number of activities, the formulae are manageable, straightforward, and only require a moderate amount of work; however, when a project has 1500 activities, these mechanics require more robust utilities to manipulate (Reiss, 1996). In the mid-1950s, computer software was not readily available for this type of analysis activity and project management maturity was not sufficient to see the need for using variable time estimates. One reason why PERT may have initially worked on the Polaris project was availability of adequate computing resources, which was not the case for many contractors at that time, or even over the next decade.

Most project management experts do not rank network modeling with variable time estimating as their most important activity, but it actually provides an improved insight into how the project might progress. Certainly, personal credibility is lost when a fixed date is given and the project overruns that date with little understandable explanation. The variable time concept represents reality, and with a mature management this approach can build credibility for the project manager (PM). The fact is that the model duplicates the activity variability much better than a simple deterministic estimate that does not reveal the level of uncertainty. Based on this logic PERT supports an improved level of communications. Stires and Murphy summarize the use of this tool as follows:

> There is, however, the danger that a foolish manager will use PERT not as a tool, but as a weapon, a clobbering instrument. The system has that potential; but the degradation would of course result in the utter destruction of faith in the system, a hardening of the natural resistance to change, and deprive the manager of all the benefits that PERT offers when used intelligently.
>
> *(Stires and Murphy, 1962)*

It can be deduced from this statement that their main concerns are based on an abuse of power in the assignment of activities. As with any tool used for managing groups of people, this tool is no better than the one using it. This old adage says it well—"*A fool with a tool is still a fool.*"

24.4 Defining Variable Time Estimates

If you are not reasonably certain about the time it takes to execute a work unit, how do you express this? Descriptive statistics offers a traditional technique through the use of a probability distribution. The question then arises as to what kind of distribution to use. Early definers of the PERT model found that they needed a distribution that had the ability to be skewed in either direction (task overruns or underruns). This means that we need to be able to define a task that might finish very early, but we also need a method to express the opposite situation or any combination between these two extremes. The two distributions shown in Figure 24.2, parts a and b, illustrate these two extreme situations.

The distribution on the left is positively skewed, while the one on the right is negatively skewed. Let's interpret these in an estimating format. In both figures, time is the x-axis variable and probability of occurrence is the y-axis variable. As an example, the positively skewed diagram indicates that the estimated time to perform this activity was optimistically 3, most likely 8, and pessimistically 30 time units. In other words, we are not at all confident that this particular task will be any

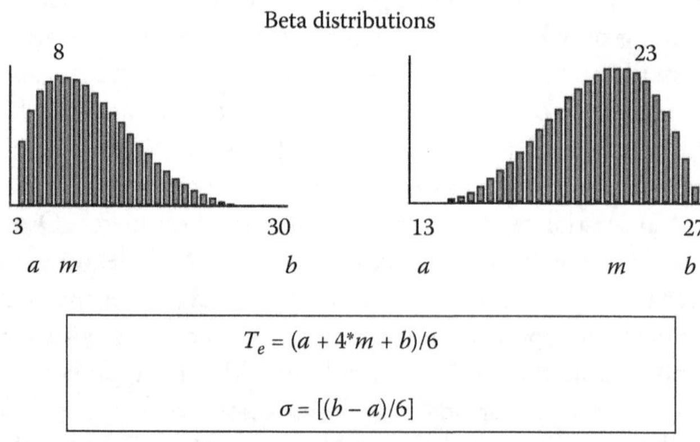

Figure 24.2 Sample beta distributions.

one particular value. Obviously, this example shows a wide degree of uncertainty regarding the estimate. In the case where the estimate had less variability, the shape of the curve would become more symmetrical. In this case, estimate range values might be more like 8, 10, and 12 to suggest a more confident time estimate. In both of these examples, we see measures of uncertainty that can then be used to project the entire project view. The right-hand beta distribution figure shows the opposite scenario. This example shows the activity estimate to complete as early as 13 time units, but more likely will require times in the 23–27 range.

Project activities actually behave in the manner as modeled above, so the probability distribution selected has to be able to fit these shape characteristics. Based on these considerations, the PERT originators decided to use a beta distribution based on its shape flexibility. It can take on the characteristics of all scenarios described above—positive skew, negative skew, and normal distribution. The next design parameter requirement involves how to specify the shape of an activity. It was decided to use the following three estimating parameters to define the distribution shape characteristics:

a—an optimistic time estimate
m—the most likely time estimate for the activity
b—a pessimistic time.

There are two statistically oriented parameters that need to be extracted from this. First, we compute a time that is equally likely to occur given the defined shape. In descriptive statistics terms, this would be called the median of the distribution. PERT mathematicians then went about developing an easy to use empirical formula for this value and the result was

$$T_e = \frac{(a + 4m + b)}{6}$$

Where T_e is the median time estimate for the activity.

A second required parameter is a measure of dispersion for the estimate. In statistical terms, this can be defined by the standard deviation. Once again, an empirical formula was developed to compute activity standard deviation, known as sigma. The formula for this is:

$$\sigma = \frac{(b - a)}{6}$$

Sigma (σ) is the common Greek symbol used to denote standard deviation.

We now enter the more confusing part of the calculation. First, the variation of the project will be determined by the variance of the CP. Variance is another statistical relationship and is in fact sigma squared as shown below

$$\text{Variance} = \sigma^2$$

A variability measure of the CP will be defined as:

$$\text{CP variability } (\sigma) = \text{SQRT } (\textstyle\sum \text{CP activity variances})$$

To calculate the CP standard deviation, calculate the variance for each individual CP tasks, sum the values for all CP activities, and then compute the square root of that total value. This yields the sigma (σ) value for the network. Now the question is "what to do with that?"

Step two in the calculation process is to calculate T_e values for activities and then use that value as a duration as typically done for the deterministic network. This will yield a standard CP value assuming 50/50 (Median) time estimates for the network. The network originally shown as Figure 14.9 in Chapter 14 is reproduced here as Figure 24.3 to illustrate this.

This network calculation defines the median time estimate for this project to be 21 time periods. Now, for the last calculation step let's see what these mechanics have delivered to the question.

Step three. Note that the CP is A–C–E–G–I. For sake of arithmetic simplicity let's say that the computed sum of the variances for these five activities was 4.0. Remember that these individual values were computed from the *a*, *m*, and *b* parameters for each activity. These calculation steps have produced two "shape parameters." The median time of 21 which is called μ and the sigma (σ) value of the network which is calculated by the square root of the CP variance, so sigma is 2.0 (SQRT of 4.0). From this we have shape parameters of $\mu = 21$ and $\sigma = 2$. For the last step we have to go into basic statistical theory as outlined in the next section.

24.5 Central Limit Theorem

The central limit theorem offers us a pathway to interpret the result, although some math purist will quibble with this theorem matching the conceptual assumptions in the network context. Most believe that these shortcomings fall within the accuracy of the data involved.

This theorem basically states that as the sample (activity) size becomes large, the sampling distribution of the mean becomes approximately normal regardless of the distribution of the various individual activities (Brown, 2002). Assuming that a sufficiently large set of activities exists (say 30 on the CP), this theorem would justify projecting the resulting project distribution to be normal or symmetrical. At that point the shape parameters can be interpreted back into more meaningful explanations.

For example, let us now suppose that the sample network is large enough. We will use the shape parameters defined above to interpret the result. From these two parameters we can describe the schedule variability of the project, since the characteristics of the normal distribution are well defined. Figure 24.4 shows the standard areas under the normal distribution curve.

Using our shape parameters here are some interpretations for schedule range calculations:

- There is a 68% probability that this project will complete in the time range of 19–23 (i.e., one standard deviation range).
- There is a 98% probability that this project will complete prior to time 23. (two standard deviation range)

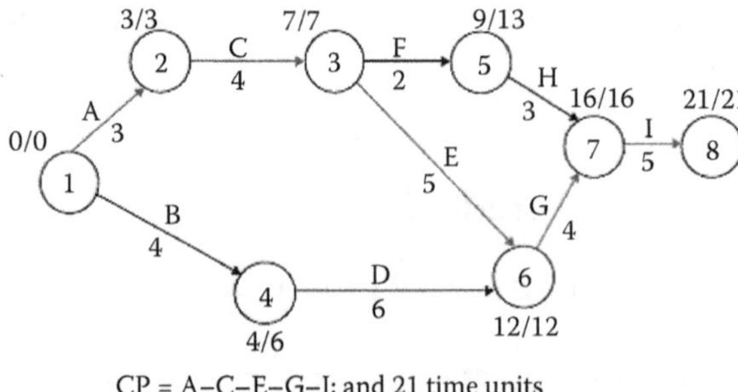

Figure 24.3 AOA network. *Note*: This figure is taken from Figure 14.9.

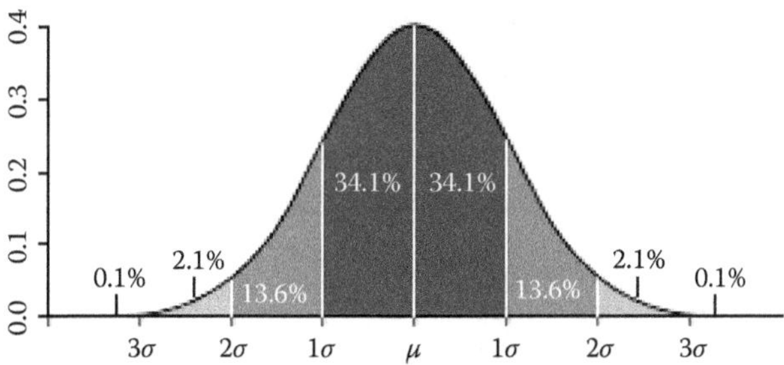

Figure 24.4 Normal distribution areas under the curve.

Review these two calculations with the standard normal curve figure and verify that you understand how to interpret the area under the curve.

Using project shape parameters in this manner we can now describe our confidence level of project completion. Figure 24.4 provides what would be called the typical view of this in terms of a distribution with its sigma values. As can be seen from the areas under the curve, values for the common unit standard deviations are

$$1\sigma = 68.2\%$$

$$2\sigma = 95.4\%$$

$$3\sigma = 99.7\%.$$

Looking at this data in a slightly different way, we could estimate the probability that this project will finish later than some percent. Let us now examine the probability that the project will finish after one standard deviation. Examining Figure 24.4, we see that the approximate area to the right of this point is approximately 34.1%. This then means that there is a 34.1% probability that this project will finish after time period 23, in spite of the fact that the original deterministic calculation said that it would complete at time period 21. This provides a good example of the power of this technique.

24.6 Triangular Distributions

One of the complicating factors that have inhibited broader PERT adoption is the general level of statistics literacy in organizations. Beta distributions and the central limit theorem offer too many Greek symbols for many to digest. One simplifying view has been to use a triangular distribution. Figure 24.5 illustrates what this distribution looks like.

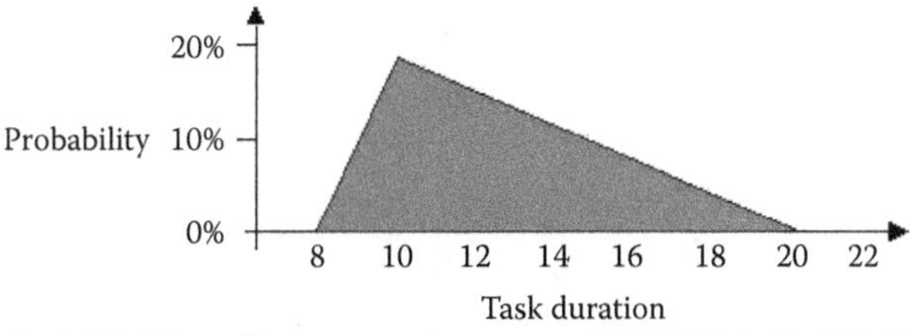

Figure 24.5 Triangular distribution.

The three shape parameters (a, m, and b) introduced for the beta distribution can also be used to describe this distribution. A triangular distribution median value (T_e) can be estimated using either the sum of the three parameters divided by three, or simply use the PERT model formula. Differences for the values in Table 24.1 averaged approximately 5% with the PERT model always estimating the lower value. These two formulae would be:

$$T_e = \frac{(a + 4m + b)}{6} \quad \text{PERT beta model.}$$

$$T_e = \frac{(a + m + b)}{3} \quad \text{Triangular model.}$$

In practice, there is some disagreement regarding how to compute the standard deviation for a triangular distribution. Many still use the PERT empirical beta distribution formula because it is supported in the literature; however, the University of Virginia has published the following more accurate but very complex formula for a triangular distribution standard deviation (σ_Δ) (University of Virginia, 2008):

$$\sigma_\Delta = \left\{ \frac{\left[(b-a)^2 - (m-a)(b-a) + (m-a)^2 \right]}{18} \right\}^{0.5}$$

Table 24.1 Comparison of Beta and Triangular Standard Deviations

Activity	*a*	*m*	*b*	*PERT σ*	*σ*	*% Error*
A	1	2	4	0.50	0.62	19.8
B	1	2	6	0.83	1.08	22.8
C	1	2	3	0.33	0.41	18.4
D	1	2	2	0.17	0.24	29.3
E	1	2	4	0.50	0.62	19.8
F	2	3	6	0.67	0.85	21.6
G	2	3	4	0.33	0.41	18.4
H	2	3	4	0.33	0.41	18.4
I	3	4	8	0.83	1.08	22.8
J	3	4	7	0.67	0.85	21.6
K	6	7	9	0.50	0.62	19.8
L	7	8	12	0.83	1.08	22.8
M	7	8	11	0.67	0.85	21.6
N	9	10	14	0.83	1.08	22.8
O	11	14	20	1.50	1.87	19.8

Normally, a formula as complex as this would be avoided because of its complexity; however, a desktop spreadsheet utility make this somewhat more reasonable. Table 24.1 shows a comparison of the results in using the Triangular sigma (σ_Δ) formula compared to the classic PERT beta (σ) version.

Note that the simplified PERT formula generates results for the sample data that average about 21% lower in comparison with the complex formula. Users will have to decide whether this error level is significant enough to warrant using the more complex version. In either case, the mechanics are the same, but clearly it must be recognized that these calculations are analytical estimates more than highly accurate numerical results. The goal of this calculation set is to derive a measure of project variability more than computation accuracy.

24.7 Calculating Probability of Completion

We have now covered the basics of variable time completion estimates. This last section is simply a way to add some flexibility to the analysis. Up to this point, the examples have used unit standard deviation interpretation (i.e., sigma values 1, 2, or 3). Once the basic shape parameters, μ and σ, have been calculated, there are other more granular questions that can be answered. For example:

1. At what point can we be 90% confident that the project will be completed?
2. If the model says that the project is expected to be completed by time period 50, what is the probability that the project will in fact be completed by time period 54?

The process to answer each of these questions involves finding non-unit value areas under the normal curve that are not at the standard unit points described earlier. One easy way to accomplish a more general computation model is to use one of two Excel® built-in functions.

Normdist: Computes the probability of finishing at a specified time.
Norminv: Computes the time for some specified confidence level.

For this calculation example, we will use μ to be 50 (expected project completion time) and σ to be 4 (computed standard deviation of the CP).

Scenario 1: What is the probability of the project finishing by time period 52, given the expected time of 50 and standard deviation of 4? This would be entered into the Excel function as Normdist (52,50,4,TRUE). The results indicate that this project would have a 69% probability of completion by that time.

Scenario 2: At what time period do we have a 90% confidence of completing this project? This would be entered as Norminv (0,90,50,4). The results returned indicate that this occurs at time period 55.

These two functions provide a great deal of analytical flexibility to answer completion probability questions. A little practice with them will help understand their dual roles. Figure 24.6 illustrates graphically the two shape factors necessary for this analysis. In this figure, $\bar{X}$ is equivalent to μ (the expected time for the project).

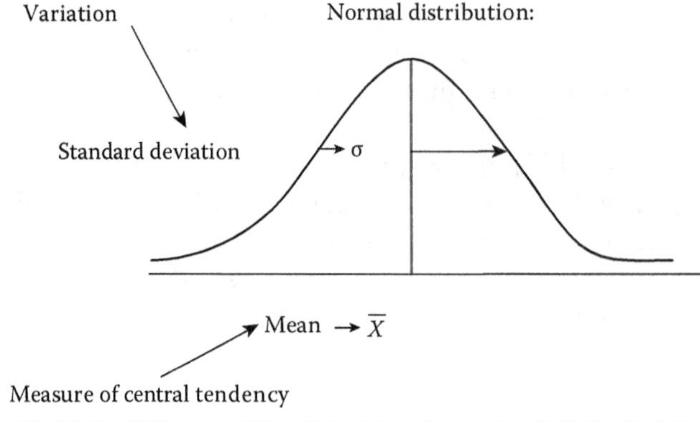

Figure 24.6 Shape factor curve.

24.8 Summary

This chapter has demonstrated sample basic mechanics for analyzing project plans for which multiple time estimates for activities are available. The list below summarizes the eight computational steps required to perform variable time analysis using the classical model:

1. Collect a, m, and b parameters for each activity (optimistic, most likely, and pessimistic).
2. Compute the project schedule using values calculated for the network.
3. Calculate the CP using deterministic rules from Chapter 14. Select the activities on the CP for probability analysis. The calculated CP duration becomes μ for future analysis.
4. Calculate standard deviations (for each CP activity using an appropriate formula.
5. Square the individual standard deviation values to produce a variance estimate for each activity on the CP.
6. Sum the computed variances for the CP activities.
7. Take the square root of the summarized variances from the step above. This will be the variability shape parameter for future analysis (refer to Figure 24.6).
8. Use μ and σ parameters to perform the desired probability analysis.

Mature organizations need to become familiar with this class of analysis since it is a more accurate representation of a future project completion than a single estimate. In some cases, a schedule overrun can doom the project. This technique offers a way to measure the probability of an overrun value. For these reasons, the ability to model a project schedule with variable activity times is a worthy addition to the PM's toolkit.

Problems

1. Calculate the project variable time plan using the activity data outlined below and then answer the following questions:
   a. What is the expected completion date for the project?
   b. Calculate the probability that this project will complete by duration 155?
   c. At what duration can we offer the management a 95% probability of being finished?

Task ID	*Predecessor*	*a*	*m*	*b*
A	...	10	15	20
B	...	14	23	50
C	B	40	60	30
D	A	40	45	50
E	D, C	30	35	42
F	A	5	10	12
G	B	3	16	26
H	E, F, G	10	15	13
I	B	7	12	13

2. Assume that the calculated shape parameters for a project are:

$$\mu = 50, \quad \sigma = 4.$$

Use an Excel function to calculation completion parameters for the following situations.

a. What is the probability of completing the project by time period 56?

b. What is the point in time for which we have a 75% confidence level in completion?

References

Archibald, R.D., 1987. Archibald associates. *Project Management Journal: Key Milestones in the Early PERT/CPM/PDM Days*, 28, 29–33.

Brown, K.L., 2002. Program Evaluation and Review Technique and Critical Path Method—Background. Reference for Business. http://www.referenceforbusiness.com/management/Pr-Sa/Program-Evaluation-and-Review-Technique-and-Critical-Path-Method.html (accessed March 17, 2008).

Gale, T., 2006. Program Evaluation and Review Technique and Critical Path Method Background. Reference for Business. http://www.referenceforbusiness.com/management/Pr-Sa/Program-Evaluation-and-Review-Technique-and-Critical-Path-Method.html (accessed November 19, 2017).

Reiss, G., 2007. *Project Management Demystified: Today's Tools and Techniques*, 3rd ed. New York: Spon Press.

Stires, D.M. and M.M. Murphy, 1962. *PERT/CPM*. Boston, MA: Materials Management Institute.

University of Virginia, 2008. A Brief Primer on Probability Distributions, UVA-QA-0517SSRN. Darden Business Publishing. http://store.darden.virginia.edu/Syllabus%20Copy/data-analysis-and-optimization.pdf (accessed November 19, 2017).

Verzuh, E., 2005. *The Fast Forward MBA in Project Management*. Hoboken, NJ: Wiley.

Chapter 25

Adaptive Life Cycle Models

25.1 Introduction

Project Management Institute (PMI) describes the project life cycle as "the series of phases that a project passes through from its start to its completion. Within a project life cycle, there are generally one or more phases that are associated with the development of the product, service, or result. These are called a development life cycle. Development life cycles can be predictive (plan-driven), adaptive (agile), iterative, incremental, or a hybrid" (PMI, 2017, p. 665).

The Project Management Body of Knowledge (PMBOK®) describes four types of life cycles, which are and shown in Table 25.1 (PMI, 2017, p. 17):

1. **Predictive life cycle.** A more traditional approach, where the bulk of planning occurring input upfront, then executing in a single pass; a sequential process.
2. **Iterative life cycle.** An approach that allows feedback for unfinished work to improve and modify that work.
3. **Incremental life cycle.** An approach that provides finished deliverables that the customer may be able to use immediately.
4. **Agile life cycle.** An approach that is both iterative and incremental to refine work items and delivery frequently.

25.2 History

The infrastructure for the early days of software development (the 1950s and 1960s) was primitive in comparison to today's environment. A programmer wrote logic using paper-based coding sheets that were then given to a key-punch operator who would produce a deck of punch cards. Then, based on a sign-up schedule, the punched card deck would be placed into a hopper of the card reader. Finally, the program runs and the output, e.g., program error messages or test output, was sent to the printer. On the user-side of production software, user involvement was similar, i.e., key-punching a data deck that would be the input for the program. Depending upon where these users were located relative to the data center (e.g., in another city), it could take hours or days or

Table 25.1 Lifecycle Characteristics

	Predictive	*Iterative*	*Incremental*	*Agile*
Goal	Manage cost	Correctness of solution	Speed	Customer value from frequent deliveries and feedback
Requirements	Defined upfront	Elaborated at periodic intervals	Elaborated at periodic intervals	Elaborated frequently during delivery
Product	Deliver final product at end of project	Can be divided into delivery subsets	Can be divided into delivery subsets	Deliver frequently with customer-valued subsets
Change	Constrained as much as possible	Incorporated at periodic intervals	Incorporated at periodic intervals	Incorporated in real-time
Stakeholders	Involved at specific milestones	Regularly involved	Regularly involved	Continuously involved
Risk and cost	Controlled by detailed planning	Controlled by progressive elaboration	Controlled by progressive elaboration	Controlled as requirements and constraints emerge

weeks before the user got his computer-generated output. Of the many adjectives that might be used to describe this environment, agile isn't one of them.

There are five major drivers that are the impetus for agile: technology platform, corporate culture, managements dissatisfaction with IT results, uncertainty work (versus definable work), and the graphical user interface.

25.2.1 Technology Platform

Beginning in the 1970s with interactive, time-shared systems and especially with the commercial success of the PC in the early 1980s, the user experience for both software developers and users changed dramatically. The programmer used an online editor to create files that would contain the logic in place of the physical card deck. The ability to view and alter the code online versus a printout and card deck was tremendous. This change alone reduced cycle time significantly.

25.2.2 Corporate Culture

During the 1980s, companies began introducing total quality management (TQM) as part of a corporate culture transformation to improve performance. TQM introduced team management into organizations that were designed with hierarchical, command-and-control structures and cultures. TQM has its starting point following World War II, when Toyota first implemented quality circles in its production process (www.kanbanchi.com). The concept was called Kaizen, which is the philosophy of continually seeking ways to improve operations. An important belief in Kaizen is that those closest to the operation are in the best position to identify changes that should be made.

25.2.3 Management's Dissatisfaction with IT Results

Beginning in the 1960s, companies were hiring programming staffs to automate business processes, such as their general ledger, payroll, credit card, and so forth. These were very large, complex undertakings for which there was no experience or previous history in doing so. The programmers themselves didn't have computer science educations as universities were just beginning to formulate curricula. Companies gave tests to prospective programmers to assess their analytical and logical abilities. Those that they deemed 'passed' were given training in writing programs, typically in COBOL. Developing these very large, complex programs would take multiple years to deliver. It was not uncommon for these projects to run several years late and overrun millions of dollars. Even worse, by the time they were delivered, they no longer met the need. The bottom line: management was not happy with IT.

25.2.4 High-Uncertainty Work (vs. Defined Work)

Aaron Shenhar and Max Wideman describe a method of classifying project types based upon two attributes: product to be created (tangible, intangible), and type of work required to create it (craft, intellect) (Shenhar and Wideman, 2002). Using their framework, a new plant, car, and infrastructure are example project results that are tangible (craft). Characteristics of these types of projects include:

- high-level of repetitive work
- learning curve effects
- resources predictable
- relatively high cost involved

Projects, however, that are high-uncertainty are intangible (intellect). They exhibit the following characteristics:

- non-repetitive, first of its kind
- creative effort
- minimal repetition
- resources unpredictable; exploratory

These types of projects produce a new piece of intellectual property, such as, a new book, poem, algorithm, theory, technology process, and software. Developing a new application, especially using the latest technology, is complex and risky. It is difficult, if not impossible, to determine the user requirements completely upfront largely because once users work with a new system they invent new ways of working which cannot be anticipated at the beginning of a project.

25.2.5 Graphical User Interface

At the 1968 Fall Joint Computer Conference in San Francisco, Douglas Engelbart gave the "Mother of all Demos." He demoed NLS (oNLine System), which grew out of his 1962 paper, *Augmenting Human Intellect: A Conceptual Framework* which he published for the U.S. Airforce Office of Scientific Research (Engelbart 1997). The technology used in NLS included a cathode ray tube (CRT), a keyboard, and a mouse, which he invented. It also incorporated live audio, video, windowed hypertext, and screen-sharing in real-time. These technology components are the basis for today's windowing systems.

With the pressure from management to improve IT performance and address the challenge of high-uncertainty projects, software practitioners began experimenting with new approaches to software development that would leverage these newer, graphical-oriented platforms and team-based cultures.

25.3 Agile

In 2001, 17 software practitioners who had been working with new, yet different, approaches to software development met at a ski lodge in Utah. The outcome of that meeting was the Manifesto for Agile Software Development shown in Figure 25.1 (Agile Manifesto Authors).

In addition, they defined 12 principles based on the manifesto: (Agile Manifesto Authors):

We follow these principles:

1. Our highest priority is to satisfy the customer through early and continuous delivery of valuable software.
2. Welcome changing requirements, even late in development. Agile processes harness change for the customer's competitive advantage.
3. Deliver working software frequently, from a couple of weeks to a couple of months, with a preference to the shorter timescale.

We are uncovering better ways of developing software by doing it and helping others do it. Through this work we have come to value:

Individuals and interactions over processes and tools
Working software over comprehensive documentation
Customer collaboration over contract negotiation
Responding to change over following a plan

That is, while there is value in the items on the right, we value the items on the left more.

Kent Beck	James Grenning	Robert C. Martin
Mike Beedle	Jim Highsmith	Steve Mellor
Arie Van Bennekum	Andrew Hunt	Ken Schwaber
Alistair Cockburn	Ron Jeffries	Jeff Sutherland
Ward Cunningham	Jon Kern	Dave Thomas
Martin Fowler	Brian Marick	

Figure 25.1 Manifesto for Agile Software Development.

4. Business people and developers must work together daily throughout the project.
5. Build projects around motivated individuals. Give them the environment and support they need, and trust them to get the job done.
6. The most efficient and effective method of conveying information to and within a development team is face-to-face conversation.
7. Working software is the primary measure of progress.
8. Agile processes promote sustainable development. The sponsors, developers, and users should be able to maintain a constant pace indefinitely.
9. Continuous attention to technical excellence and good design enhances agility.
10. Simplicity—the art of maximizing the amount of work not done—is essential.
11. The best architectures, requirements, and designs emerge from self-organizing teams.
12. At regular intervals, the team reflects on how to become more effective, then tunes and adjusts its behavior accordingly.

Using an agile approach for a project requires that the project team adopt an agile mindset. PMI suggests these questions to help in shaping how to implement agile (PMI, 2017, p. 843):

- How can the project team act in an agile manner?
- What can the team deliver quickly and obtain early feedback to benefit the next delivery cycle?
- How can the team act in a transparent manner?
- What work can be avoided in order to focus on high-priority items?
- How can a servant–leadership approach benefit the achievement of the team's goals?

There are many approaches to agile. Some of the most popular ones are: Scrum, XP, and Kanban.

25.3.1 Agile Teams

A "team" in the agile sense is a small group of people, assigned to the same project or effort, nearly all of them on a full-time basis. A small minority of team members may be part-time contributors, or may have competing responsibilities. The notion of team entails shared accountability: good or bad, the outcomes should be attributed to the entire team rather than to any individual. The team is expected to possess all the necessary competencies, whether technical (programming, designing, testing) or business (domain knowledge, decision-making ability).

Roles and responsibilities do not matter as much as results: a developer may test, perform analysis, or think about requirements; an analyst or domain expert can suggest ideas about implementation, and so on. Team size is usually 3–10 people.

Hoegl and Gemuenden propose a Teamwork Quality framework for project outcomes that consists of (Hoegl and Gemuenden, 2001, p. 437):

- Communication—frequent, informal, direct and open communication
- Coordination—individual efforts that are well structured and synchronized with the team
- Balance of member contribution—team members utilize their expertise to their full potential
- Mutual support—team members help and support each other in carrying out their tasks
- Effort—team members exert all effort to the team's tasks
- Cohesion—team members are motivated to maintain the team

There are three primary agile roles: product owner; cross-functional team member; and team facilitator (PMI, 2017, p. 40). The product owner is responsible for providing the direction of the product. He creates and ranks the work in the backlog based upon business value. The cross-functional team comprises all the skills necessary to produce the working product. In software development, for example, that typically include: designers, developers, and testers. The team facilitator may go by different names, such as scrum master, project team lead, or team leader. He is a servant leader and serves as a combination of facilitator, coach, and impediment remover.

The team develops and maintains a high-level summary of the project's key success factors, synthetic enough that it can be displayed on one wall of the team room as a flipchart-sized sheet of paper. This description includes at least the major objectives of the project, scope boundaries, and reciprocal agreements between the project's implementation team and external stakeholders.

25.3.2 Common Agile Practices

The following sections describe common agile practices: backlog preparation; backlog refinement; iteration planning; daily standups; demonstrations/reviews; task boards; and retrospectives. Figure 25.2 illustrates the flow in an agile cycle.

25.3.2.1 Backlog Preparation

A backlog is an ordered list of all work that might be needed in the product as shown in Figure 25.3, for example. It is also the single source of requirements for any changes to be made to the product. The product owner is responsible for the backlog, including its content, availability, and ordering (Scrum Guides). The work in the backlog is called a 'user story'. Each user story is expected to yield, once implemented, a contribution to the value of the overall product.

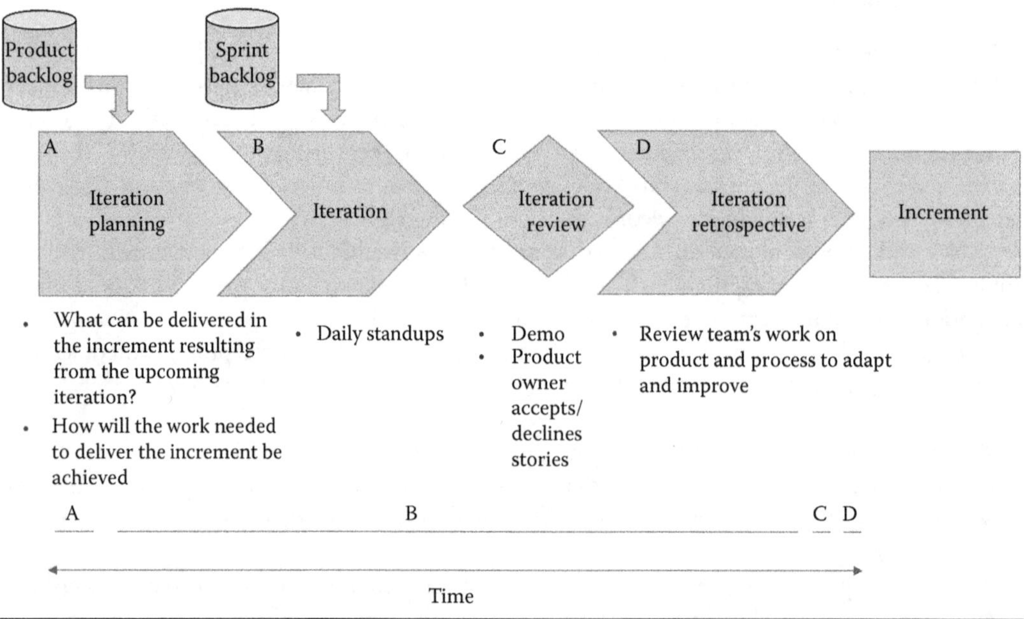

Figure 25.2 Iterative framework.

Feature Type	Feature ID	Story ID	Status	Size	Sprint	Description
						So that employees do not have access to information that they no longer are authorized to view
Development	141	141-2	Ongoing	13	11	As Division HR I want to select which employees from my division have access to reports on a per module basis So that the developers are not overwhelmed with requests
Development	233	233-3	Pending	5	11	As Division HR on the Succession Planning Homepage, I want to see "Initial Succession Required" changed to "Without Succession Plan" So that I know the number represent employees who need succession plans. See attachment in 233-0.
Development	233	233-0	Pending	3	11	As Division HR on the Succession Planning Homepage, I want to see the "Succession Planning To Do' title changed to "Succession Planning Score Card'. Remove "To Do List" and replace with "Scorecard". Replace the entire list under "Total Employees" with the following: Ready Now, Ready 6 Months, Ready 12 Months & Without Succession PlanSee attached example
Development	233	233-1	Pending	1	11	Change green text on Succession Planning Home Page. See attachment in 233-0. The Succession Planning Scorecard displays the Status of Succession Plans for employees. Click on the number in the Scorecard to display the employee details. To see all employees, click the number listed next to "Total Employees."
Development	233	233-2	Pending	13	11	As Division HR on the Succession Planning Homepage, I want to remove, "To Do", & "All To Do Items" from Succession Planning Homepage, As this does not represent a clear picture of things I have to do. See attachment in 233-0. (Note this will be a text change please work this Story with 233-0.)
Development	262	262-0	Ongoing	8	11	Add Assist DPO job family to the 2011 Senior Appraisals.
Defect	264	264-0	Ongoing	8	11	In Succession Planning the Asst DPO Job family is showing "Status Date" as a Job Change in June 2011, but in PeopleSoft, there is no "Job Change" or "Dept Change". Need to understand criteria used to determine job / dept change. See attached example
Defect	267	267-0	Ready for UAT	8	11	There is bad data in the progression table. The Sr Subsea Supervisor MUX job family is missing. Please see attached example
Development	268	268-0	Ongoing	3	11	C2 comments - Delete face to face comment for EMPLID 322235

Figure 25.3 Product backlog example.

The product backlog lists all features, functions, requirements, enhancements, and fixes that constitute the changes to be made to the product in future releases. Each item in the product backlog has the attributes of description, order, estimate, and value.

25.3.2.2 Backlog Refinement

Backlog refinement is when the product owner and some, or all, of the rest of the team review items on the backlog to ensure the backlog contains the appropriate items, that they are prioritized, and that the items at the top of the backlog are ready for delivery. This activity occurs on a regular basis and may be an officially scheduled meeting or an ongoing activity. Some of the activities that occur during this refinement of the backlog include:

- removing user stories that no longer appear relevant
- creating new user stories in response to newly discovered needs
- re-assessing the relative priority of stories
- assigning estimates to stories which have yet to receive one
- correcting estimates considering newly discovered information
- splitting user stories which are high priority but too coarse grained to fit in an upcoming iteration

It is an ongoing process involving the product owner and the development team. Higher-ordered product backlog items usually are clearer than lower-ordered items. More precise estimates are made based on the greater clarity and increased detail. Items for an upcoming iteration that are refined such they can be "done" by the development team within one iteration are considered "ready" for selection during iteration planning.

25.3.2.3 Iteration Planning

Each team's capacity is different. Each product owner's typical story size is different. Teams consider their story size, so they do not try to commit to more stories than there is a team capacity to complete within one iteration. Team capacity may change from one iteration to the next depending upon the availability to the developers (e.g., holiday, vacation, training). When teams have a reduced capacity, they will only plan for work that meets the capacity. Teams estimate what they can complete, which is a measure of capacity. Agile teams do not plan just once in a single chunk. Instead, they plan a little, deliver, learn, and then re-plan a little more in an ongoing cycle. An iteration, in the context of an agile project, is a timebox, typically one to four weeks. Figure 25.4, shows the relationship between the product roadmap, release plan and iteration plan.

The product roadmap is derived from the product vision. The product roadmap drives the release plan, which in turn drives the iteration plan. The following describes an approach to iteration planning used in Scrum called sprint planning (Scrum Guides). This is created by the collaborative work of the entire team. It answers the following:

- What can be delivered in the increment resulting from the upcoming sprint?
- How will the work needed to deliver the increment be achieved?

The team works to forecast the functionality that will be developed during the sprint. The product owner discusses the objective that the sprint should achieve and the product backlog items that, if completed in the sprint, would achieve the goal. The input to this meeting is the product backlog, the latest product increment, projected capacity of the developers during the iteration, and past performance. The number of items selected from the product backlog for the sprint is solely up to the developers. Only they can assess what it can accomplish over the upcoming sprints.

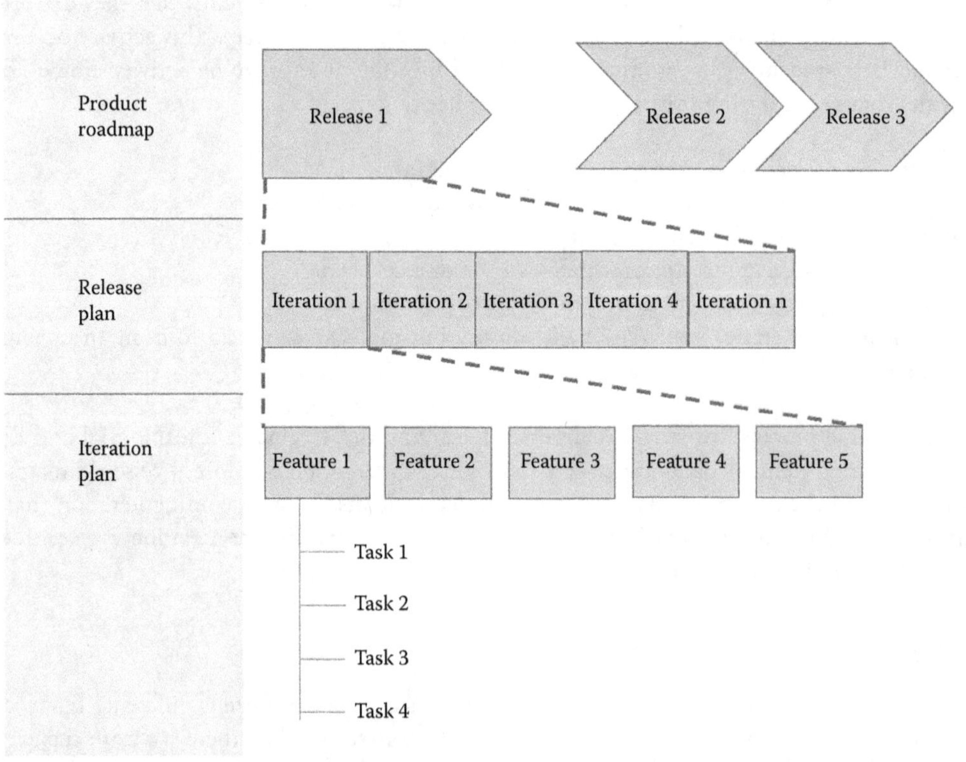

Figure 25.4 Relationship between product roadmap, release plan, and iteration plan.

After the developers forecast the product backlog items it will deliver in the sprint, the team crafts a sprint goal. The goal is an objective that will be met within the sprint through the implementation of the product backlog, and it provides guidance to the developers on why it is building the increment.

Having set the sprint goal and selected the product backlog items for the iteration, the developers decide how it will build this functionality into a "Done" product increment during the sprint. The product backlog items selected for this sprint plus the plan for delivering them is called the sprint backlog. The development team usually starts by designing the system and the work needed to convert the product backlog into a working product increment. Work may be of varying size, or estimated effort. However, enough work is planned during sprint planning for the development team to forecast what it believes it can do in the upcoming sprint. Work planned for the first days of the sprint by the development team is decomposed by the end of this meeting, often to units of one day or less. The development team self-organizes to undertake the work in the sprint backlog, both during sprint planning and as needed throughout the sprint.

The product owner can help to clarify the selected product backlog items and make trade-offs. If the development team determines it has too much or too little work, it may renegotiate the selected product backlog items with the product owner. The developers may also invite other people to attend to provide technical or domain advice.

By the end of the sprint planning, the development team should be able to explain to the product owner how they intend to work as a self-organizing team to accomplish the sprint goal and create the anticipated increment.

25.3.2.4 Iteration/Daily Standups

Each day at the same time, the team meets to bring everyone up to date on the information that is vital for coordination: each team members briefly describes any "completed" contributions and any obstacles that stand in their way. This meeting is normally no longer than 15 minutes, and it is recommended that participants stand to encourage keeping the meeting short. Any topic that starts a discussion is cut short, added to a "parking lot" list, and discussed in greater depth after the meeting, between the people affected by the issue.

These meetings typically take the form of three questions for each member in round-robin fashion:

1. What did I complete since the last standup?
2. What am I planning to complete between now and the next standup?
3. What are my impediments (or risks or problems)?

Although seldom highlighted as a full-fledged agile practice, the allocation of tasks based on self-selection rather than assignment by a third-party (whether a project manager, lead developer, or other role) appears to be an important, possibly an essential, feature of agile work.

25.3.2.5 Iteration Review/Demonstrations

As the team completes features (user stories), the team periodically demonstrates the working product. In Scrum teams, it is done at the end of a sprint, which is typically two or four weeks. The product owner sees the demonstration and accepts or declines the stories.

This review is a four-hour time-boxed meeting for one-month iterations, or less for shorter iterations. The team facilitator ensures that the event takes place and that attendants understand its purpose. The Iteration Review includes the following elements (Scrum Guides):

- Attendees include the team members and key stakeholders invited by the Product Owner;
- The Product Owner explains what Product Backlog items have been "Done" and what has not been "Done";
- The Development Team discusses what went well during the Sprint, what problems it ran into, and how those problems were solved;
- The Development Team demonstrates the work that it has "Done" and answers questions about the increment;
- The Product Owner discusses the Product Backlog as it stands. He or she projects likely completion dates based on progress to date (if needed);
- The entire group collaborates on what to do next, so that the Sprint Review provides valuable input to subsequent Sprint Planning;
- Review of how the marketplace or potential use of the product might have changed what is the most valuable thing to do next; and,
- Review of the timeline, budget, potential capabilities, and marketplace for the next anticipated release of the product.

The result of the Iteration Review is a revised Product Backlog that defines the probable Product Backlog items for the next Sprint. The Product Backlog may also be adjusted overall to meet new opportunities.

25.3.2.6 Task Boards

In its most basic form, a task board can be drawn on a whiteboard or even a section of wall. Using electrical tape or a dry erase pen, the board is divided into three columns labeled "To Do," "In Progress," and "Done." Sticky notes or index cards, one for each task the team is working on, are placed in the columns reflecting the status of the tasks.

The task board is updated frequently, most commonly during the daily standup meeting based on the team's progress since the last update. The board is commonly "reset" at the beginning of each iteration to reflect the iteration plan. The purpose of the task board is to ensure that everyone has a visual picture of the plan.

25.3.2.7 Retrospectives

A primary practice in agile is the retrospective. It is a look back that can occur at any time though often it follows a sprint. The format is a meeting where all team members, including the team facilitator, participate to review the team's work on both the product and process to adapt and improve. During the meeting, team members identify, and rank improvement needs. The team then selects a few to implement for the next sprint.

25.3.3 Testing

The team must test at all levels: system for end-to-end information; and unit for the building blocks. It is also important to understand when integration and integration testing is needed. The following are practices commonly deployed in agile teams.

Acceptance Test-driven Development (ATDD) involves a cross-functional team with members representing customers, development, and testing. This team works together to develop acceptance tests in advance of implementing the corresponding functionality. These acceptance tests are designed from the user's point of view and act as a form of requirements to describe how the system will function. They serve as a way of verifying that the system functions as intended. In some cases, the team automates the acceptance tests.

Test-driven development (TDD) refers to a style of programming that integrates coding, testing, and design. The Agile Alliance describes it in the following set of rules:

- write a "single" unit test describing an aspect of the program
- run the test, which should fail because the program lacks that feature
- write "just enough" code, the simplest possible, to make the test pass
- "refactor" the code until it conforms to the simplicity criteria
- repeat, "accumulating" unit tests over time

Behavior-driven development (or BDD) is an agile software development technique that encourages collaboration between developers, quality assurance (QA) and non-technical or business participants in a software project. It focuses on obtaining a clear understanding of desired software behavior through discussion with stakeholders. It extends TDD by writing test cases in a natural language that non-programmers can read. Behavior-driven developers use their native language in combination with the ubiquitous language of domain-driven design to describe the purpose and benefit of their code. This allows the developers to focus on why the code should be created, rather than the technical details, and minimizes translation between the technical language in which the code is written and the domain language spoken by the business, users, stakeholders, project management, and so forth (North, 2018).

25.3.4 Measurements

Agile utilizes empirical and value-based measurements instead of predictive measurements. Agile measures what the team delivers, not what the team predicts it will deliver. Agile is based on working products of demonstrable value to customers. Baselines are often an artifact of attempted prediction. In agile, the team limits its estimation to the next few weeks at most. In agile, if there is low variability in the team's work and if the team members are not multitasking, the team's capacity can become stable. This allows better prediction for the next couple of weeks.

After the team completes work in iteration or flow, they can re-plan. Agile does not create the ability to do more work. However, there is evidence that the smaller the chunk of work, the more likely people are to deliver it. Software product development, like other knowledge work, is about learning—learning while delivering value. Hardware development and mechanical development are similar in the design parts of the project. Learning takes place by experimenting, delivering small increments of value, and getting feedback on what has been accomplishes thus far. Many other product development projects incorporate learning also.

Some iteration-based projects use burndown charts to see where the project is going over time. Story Points rate the relative work, risk and complexity of a requirement or story. "Velocity," in the sense agile teams use the term, has no preferred unit of measurement, it is a dimensionless quantity. Velocity allows teams to compute the expected remaining duration of the project, as a number of iterations, each iteration delivering some number of features.

Another important reason has to do with the social and psychological aspects of estimation: using units such as story points, emphasizing relative difficulty over absolute duration, relieves some of the tensions that often arise between developers and managers around estimation: for instance, asking developers for an estimate then holding them accountable as if it had been a firm commitment.

Burndown charts show where the project is going over time. The Burndown chart in Figure 25.5 shows that the team is planning to deliver 28 story points. In reviewing it, the team is behind on Day 3.

To see work completed, teams use the Burnup chart as depicted in Figure 25.6. It uses the same data as shown in Figure 25.5, which also shows the team getting behind on Day 3.

These charts are typically displayed in the team room. They constitute an "information radiator," provided it is updated regularly. This practice results in up-to-date project status being visible to everyone involved, which encourages the team to confront any difficulties sooner and more decisively.

The Features Burnup/Burndown chart, shown in Figure 25.7 may indicate that requirements grew during the release. The total features line shows how the features changed over time. The remaining features line shows how the rate of completion changes over time. As features are added, the features remaining line changes. The features completed line shows the accumulated number of features completed over time.

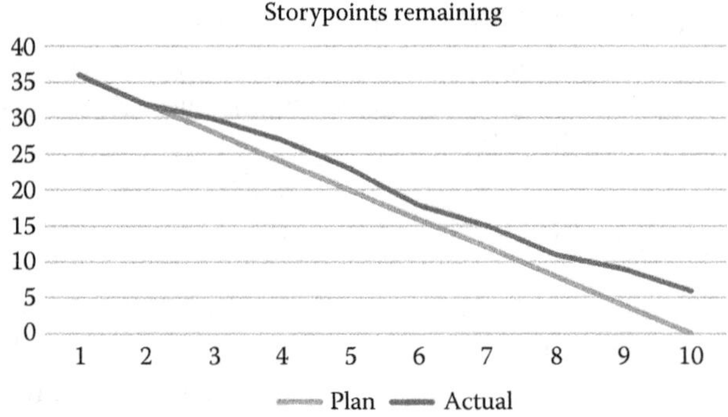

Figure 25.5 Burndown chart.

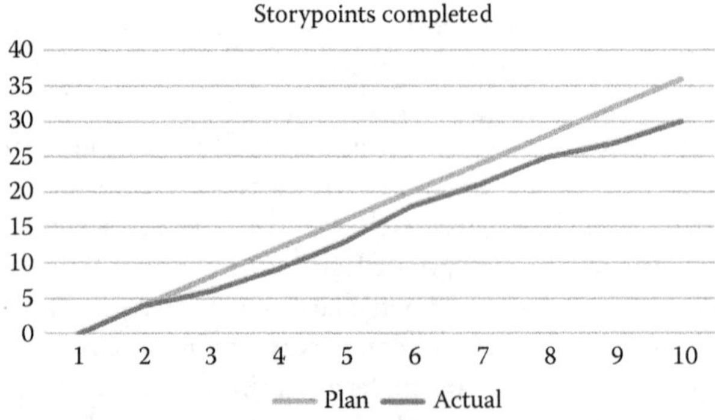

Figure 25.6 Burnup chart.

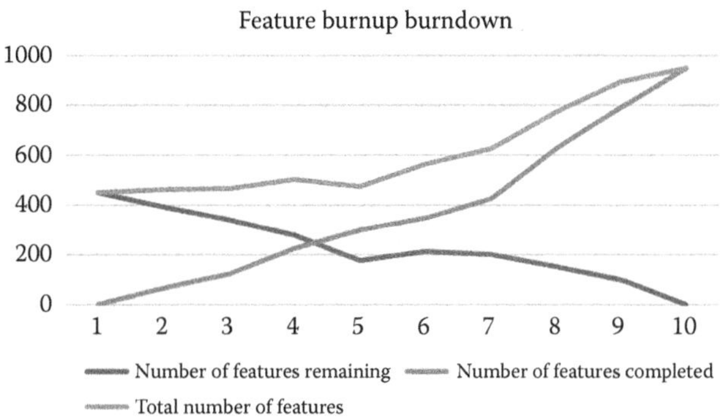

Figure 25.7 Features burnup/burndown chart.

Neither the burndown or burnup chart provides any indication of which product backlog items have been completed. This means that a team can have a burndown chart that shows continued progress, but it does not indicate whether the team is working on the correct things. For this reason, burndown and burnup charts can only provide an indication of trends rather than giving explicit indication of whether a team is delivering the right product backlog items.

Velocity, the sum of the story point sizes for the features completed in this iteration, allows the team to plan its next capacity more accurately by looking at its historical performance.

25.4 Further Reading

For the reader interested for additional materials on agile the following are useful resources:

- Agile Alliance (www.agilealliance.org)
- Scrum Guides: (www.scrumguides.org)

References

Agile Manifesto Authors, 2001. www.agilemanifesto.org. (Accessed on May 4, 2018).

Engelbart, D.C., Workstation history and the augmented knowledge workshop, *Proceedings of the ACM Conference* on the Mitchell, R.K., B.R. Agle and D.J. Wood, 1997. Toward a theory of stakeholder identification and salience: defining the principle of who and what really counts. *Academy of Management Review*, 22, 4, 853–888.

Hoegl, M. and H.G. Gemuenden, 2001. Teamwork quality and the success of innovative projects: a theoretical concept and empirical evidence. *Organization Science*, 12, 4, 435–449.

North, D., January 2018. www.dannorth.net (Accessed May 4, 2018).

PMI, 2017. *A Guide to the Project Management Body of Knowledge (PMBOK® Guide)*, 6th ed. Newtown Square, PA: Project Management Institute.

Scrum Guide. www.scrumguides.org (Accessed May 4, 2018).

Shenhar, A.J. and R.M. Wideman, April 2002. Optimizing Success by Matching Management Style to Project Type. www.maxwideman.com (Accessed May 4, 2018).

Chapter 26

Project Simulation

There are many events that can lead to project failure, but it can be argued that one of the most significant and visible outcomes of performance gone awry is variance of time estimates from plan. Regardless of the reasons for this, it is sometimes easier to estimate time variance than to guess at all of the possible reasons it might occur. Traditional network models are the most frequently used tools for time analysis, yet they suffer from many limitations in modeling real-world projects. The next section will describe some of the issues that occur in projects but are not reflected in standard network models. The previous chapter described the classic Program Evaluation and Review Technique (PERT) statistical approach to estimating variable completion times. This chapter will use the same network setup parameters, but utilizes computer simulation technology to generate a similar and more contemporary view.

26.1 Traditional Time Modeling Tools

The main questions that traditional network analysis seeks to answer are the following:

- How long is the project going to take?
- What is the critical path for the project (i.e., deterministic critical path)?
- How variable is the project duration?
- How variable is the project budget?

Four traditional network-modeling shortcomings are summarized next. In each of these cases, a simulation model offers improved analytical capabilities for dealing with the defined scenario.

26.1.1 Near Critical Path Activities

Variability of parallel activity durations can allow other near critical paths to become critical as the durations change, thereby confusing a static analysis process. The increasingly parallel nature of activities in today's complex projects makes this topic an important consideration (Williams, 2002). Envision a network with 10 essentially parallel and independent activities. Assume that all have the same duration estimate of 10 days, with each having a time probability distribution. Traditional

PERT network calculations for this situation will determine an estimated time for the task, and a project critical path will be computed from that value. However, during the project execution, other critical paths may well occur as a result of unplanned time variation. Therefore, note that failure to understand near critical paths is one key piece of analysis missing with the traditional network tool. Simulation modeling adds that capability to the analysis process.

26.1.2 Task Existence Risk Modeling

A second traditional model shortcoming occurs in the situation where the actual existence of a task is probabilistic. As an example, let us say that the project involves building a bridge. Historical data from this class of project indicates that there is a 20% chance of finding archaeological remains during the excavation process, and if that were to occur this probabilistic activity could create an additional 20 extra days due to the required extra labor and handling. There is no reasonably accurate method to model this type of zero to *X*-type task in the traditional model. Either adding the activity with some value or ignoring the event are both misleading. The ideal situation would be to evaluate the probability impact of the two events, but that is not within the traditional capability.

26.1.3 Conditional Activity Branching

A slight modification of the conditional activity is a multibranch conditional option for an activity. Traditional project networks define an activity relationship structure as fixed; however, in practice, there can be situations where one path or another is taken depending on some probabilistic conditional (Williams, 2002). Modifying the archaeological example above, we could envision three possible branches as follows:

- Archaeological remains that need expert removal are found (Probability 5%, 7 days).
- Archaeological remains that can be discarded are found (Probability 20%, 5 days).
- No archaeological remains are discovered (Probability 75%, 3 days).

In this example, the three events defined would be mutually exclusive—that is, one of them will occur but not all three.

26.1.4 Correlation between Task Durations

The third nontraditional example involves the situation where tasks are interrelated across the network in a probabilistic way, but not in a work-related manner. For example, there are two tasks in a project and it has been shown that one task that overruns will likely cause the second to also overrun. In other words, their time probabilities are not independent of each other. These would be called correlated tasks. By correlating the duration estimate of the two tasks, it assures that when one task is finished quickly the second will follow in the same manner. Correlations can be either positive or negative, that is, their relationship will follow in the same direction or opposite. These situations cannot be modeled in the traditional structure.

26.2 Simulation in Risk Management

One tool that has the capability to match these real-world project complexities is simulation modeling. In such models, the network parameters are represented by probability distributions that

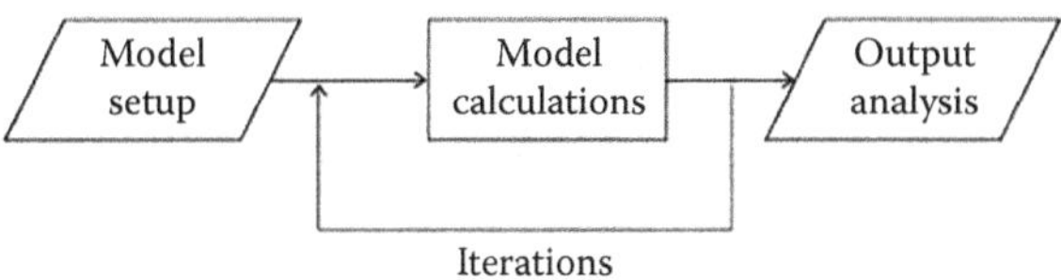

Figure 26.1 Simulation analysis process.

represent each one's behavior. From this definition, a time or cost for that event is randomly created and the model is executed with this set of values. In order to test variability, the model will be run hundreds of times and each iteration creates a unique project estimate. The simulation results are collected and these summaries are used to provide analytical insights into the performance of the project. Because of the "roulette" type randomness of the event selection, this is often called Monte Carlo simulation after the famous Monte Carlo casino. An overview of this process is represented by Figure 26.1.

The simulation model will collect computed project status after each iteration for the following:

- Project completion date
- Status of any defined milestone
- Critical path activities

Summary information from the iterations is collected and displayed in both graphs and tables.

By running hundreds or even thousands of iterations, a picture of the project's risk profile can be built up (Khan, 2007a,b). The profile can then be used to achieve a better understanding of the potential time or cost outcome of the project. From this understanding, project resources can be better used and risk consequences can be better understood.

Simulation models have the potential to provide much more flexibility in the project assessment process beyond what traditional network techniques can offer. However, two warnings come with this added capability:

- There is an added learning curve involved in setting up this model. Results obtained will only be as good as the model design.
- Analysis of the results is more complex than previous methods. New concepts are introduced and making sense of the new parameters will take time and experience.

Considering the limitations outlined for traditional analysis, simulation seems to be an obvious candidate. New generations of easy to use simulation utilities further enhance this opportunity. These new tools simply add into existing computer software network utilities such as Microsoft Project and Primavera. Several of these bring ease of use, which should help popularize the technique more.

As project managers (PMs) learn more about situations not handled by traditional networks, more pressure will be brought on the traditional models to conform. A few of these missing items were summarized in the section above; however, there are more similar to this. Simulation tools offer one possible mechanism to bridge these gaps and may in fact be the preferred strategic method.

The fact that every project is prone to variable duration times and makes a strong case for favoring simulation as a key technique. Use of probability distributions to show project completion is a much more realistic presentation than a deterministic Gantt view that is erroneous. Maturation of computer and hardware and software are also favoring proliferation of this approach. In order for this method to be successful and used more frequently, the individuals involved with project management (i.e., team, PM, users, and senior management) must be accustomed to thinking probabilistically about potential outcomes and forecasts (Raftery, 2003). This means that probabilistic estimates resulting from the planning stage would now be a probability distribution defined for each individual activity.

A summary of the rationale and potential benefits for moving to a simulation view of project analysis follows:

- Improved project understanding in regard to duration and cost
- Improved understanding of the actual critical path under different scenarios
- Better assignment of contingencies and resources on high-risk activities
- Improved chances of selecting more profitable new projects based on improved risk assessment
- Better management of project expectations

The following sections of this chapter will illustrate some of the output results from a simulation model approach. Oracle's Pertmaster utility will be used to illustrate this, but other similar utilities exist in the marketplace such as Full Monte and @Risk.

26.3 Pertmaster Modeling

The Pertmaster utility is now under the Oracle corporate umbrella (www.primavera.com). The vendor's description of the utility follows:

> *Pertmaster is a full lifecycle risk analytics solution integrating cost and schedule risk management. Pertmaster provides a comprehensive means of determining confidence levels for project success together with quick and easy techniques for determining contingency and risk response plans.*
>
> *(Pertmaster)*

The goal here is not to go through the mechanics of using this tool, but to review the types of outputs commonly generated from this class of analysis.

Figure 26.2 Defines the critical path for a traditional network reproduced from figure 14.9.

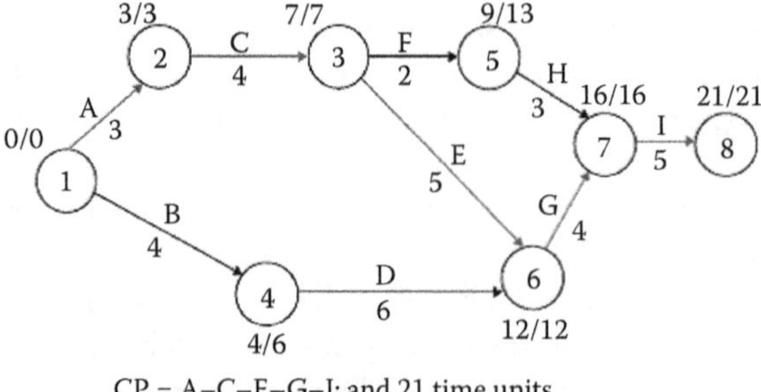

Figure 26.2 AOA network with critical path.

	Task Mode	Task Name	Duration	Predecessors
1		XYZ Project	210 days	
2		A	30 days	
3		B	40 days	
4		C	40 days	2
5		D	60 days	3
6		E	50 days	4
7		F	20 days	4
8		G	40 days	5,6
9		H	30 days	7
10		I	50 days	8,9

Figure 26.3 Gantt chart using Microsoft project.

As we have done before, we will use the same basic network that originally appeared in Chapter 14 (see Figure 14.9). In order to make the analysis more visible, each of the activity durations will be multiplied by 10, so activity A will be 30 time units instead of three as shown. That modification just spreads out the network, but does not change the calculated critical path. The interested reader can download a demo copy of this tool with sample programs, but we will just concentrate on the sample outputs generated here

The first step in the translation is to see what a traditional view of this would look like. Figure 26.3 shows how the project utility translates the network view into a Gantt bar structure. The critical path is identified. If we had supplied multiple PERT-like time estimates, this could have been handled by the utility, but the results would look the same as shown here. Also, if we wanted to do activity variance analysis as described in Chapter 14, that would have to be done manually or with a computer spreadsheet (no automated analysis). Note that the critical path is shown in dark black as path A–C–E–G–I and 210 time units (remember, we multiplied all activities by 10 to improve output visibility). The simulation results will evaluate the probability of project completion at specified time periods by showing a probability distribution indicating dates and percentages.

Pertmaster can import the definitional data directly from Microsoft Project. Figure 26.4 shows an equivalent Pertmaster diagram. This display is a little different in format from Microsoft Project, but not significantly so. Note that the critical path and activity relationships

Figure 26.4 Pertmaster view of Figure 26.2.

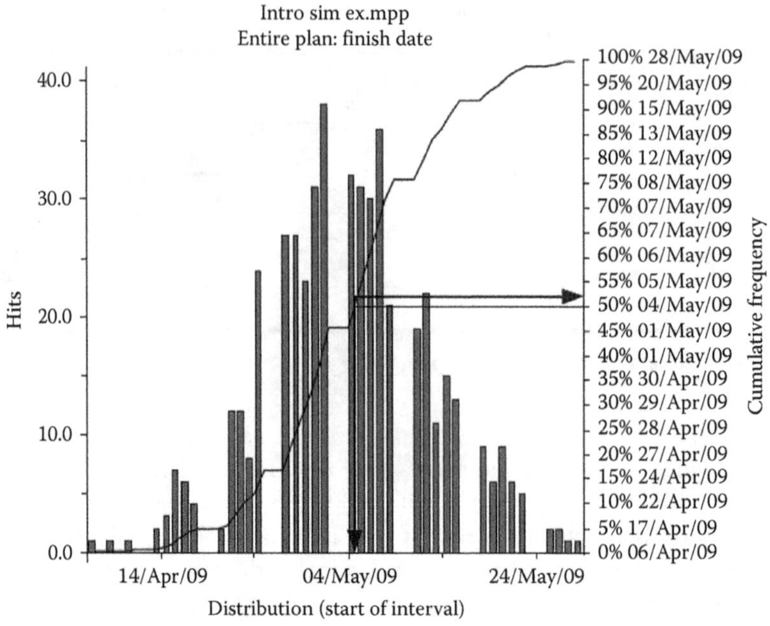

Figure 26.5 Pertmaster schedule histogram.

display is very similar to MS Project. The one major difference shown here is that Pertmaster works from "Rem (remaining) Duration," rather than (total) duration. At the beginning of the project these are the same values, but in execution the remaining duration values would decline toward zero as the activity is completed. From a simulation standpoint Pertmaster would require specification for the probability distribution for each activity, whereas project has a very limited view of this type of definition. One way to get a quick view of variability is to simply define each activity as having some percentage variability and a singular probability format (i.e., normal, triangular, beta, etc.). Obviously, this is quicker and less accurate than the more detailed by activity specification, but may suffice for the initial analysis. Recall that this method required more definitional work than traditional modeling, and this is one example of that.

A quick simulation using this example is performed by instructing the model to use a triangular distribution and let each activity time vary over the range of +/–10%. We then instruct the model to run 500 iterations and capture the results. Figure 26.5 shows the histogram of the time results recorded. One interesting conclusion is that the project completion could range from as early as April 6 to as late as May 28 just from a 10% error is estimating. If management or users wished to talk about completion dates this type presentation would show them how logically the completion date could have variability. For many, this would be a new approach to schedule definition, but one that needs to be added to the organizational culture.

A second analytical chart shows an output called the duration sensitivity and is illustrated in Figure 26.6. The duration sensitivity ranking shows the activities that are most influencing project duration. Variability in these tasks will have the most impact on project completion. The ranking of these represents key drivers causing the schedule, and this format can be produced for cost and risk as well.

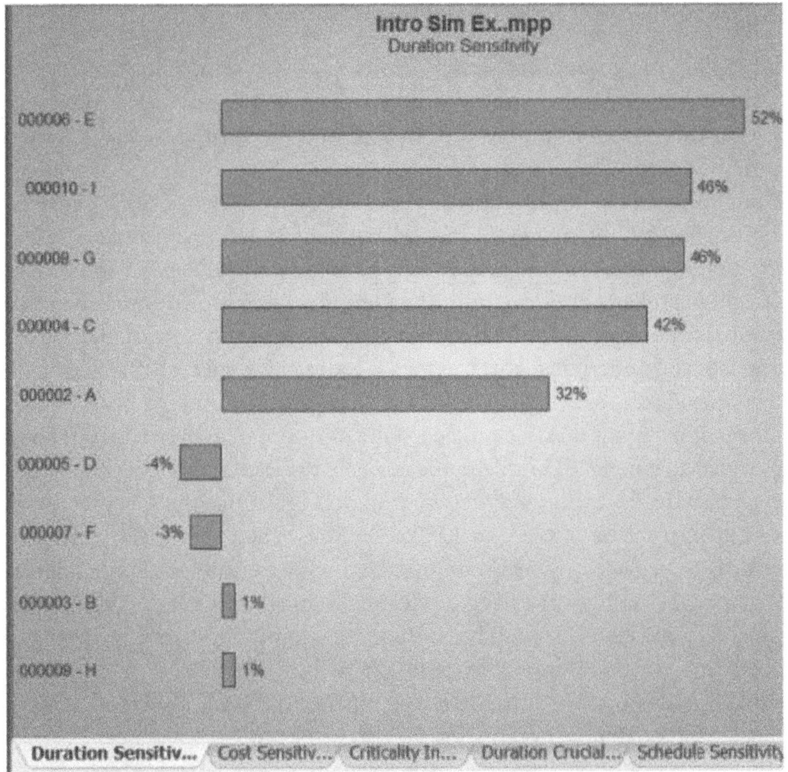

Figure 26.6 Critical path sensitivity.

26.4 Other Pertmaster Metrics

There are a host of other analytical metrics generated by Pertmaster and each of these brings insights regarding the behavior of the project beyond what is available in the traditional PERT or critical path method (CPM) models. A brief list of other table and graphic analytical options are shown below. Basically, Pertmaster can describe various project situations through the production of the following outputs:

1. Tornado chart showing activities that have the greatest impact to schedule, duration, cost, or risk
2. Near critical path analysis to warn of activities that have potential of becoming critical as time estimates vary
3. Scatter diagram showing cost versus schedule potential outcomes
4. Time-based S-curve showing potential project schedule and cost information over time and by various project stages

Hopefully, the examples used in this section are sufficient to illustrate the added value that a simulation model can bring in understand project issues. This class of analysis is the most complex of the examples described in this section of the text, but certainly one to be considered.

26.5 Summary

Simulation is a sophisticated quantitative project risk analysis methodology. Pertmaster is the tool used to describe this methodology; however, there are a growing number of vendors offering specialized models for this purpose. Availability of cheap and powerful desktop computers provides a cost-effective method for this class of analysis.

Before simulation becomes the preferred method of project analysis, a broader recognition of the underlying reasons for its emergence must occur. The most obvious of these is that quoting a deterministic project due date is patently lying to your stakeholders. If the PM is truly going to become an honest broker of information, then he must begin to educate his constituency into the variability issues of a project. In the beginning, this can simply be variability of time and cost without delving into the underlying issue too much. Later, more specifics in regard to risk management need to be introduced.

A second view of simulation in the project is one of internal analytics. All stakeholders do not necessarily need to understand all of the implications of these concepts but the project team members do. If we go back to the traditional network models introduced in Chapter 14, it is clear that those early models introduced in the mid-1950s now show their age. Clearly, deterministic views of projects need to be replaced by methods that deal with variability. Basic time variability was discussed in Chapter 24. Using the PERT model and a more sophisticated Theory of Constraints will be described in Chapter 27. Collectively, these techniques highlight key management methods to describe the way work is scheduled and executed. The PERT model first recognized the value of variability analysis, while this chapter expanded that with improved analytical capabilities. Both concepts offer valuable insights for the design of project schedules.

A simulation model is often described as a "what if" view. This means that the simulation mirrors whatever characteristics are designed in the model. It does not say that the model is accurate, nor does it say what should be done. It simply describes the scenario as defined. This has a lot of power, but the warning is that the model builder must also validate that the model represents the appropriate relationships. Said succinctly, *it describes not prescribes*. This is an important management consideration.

Simulation modeling has great potential to improve project analysis. The following advanced analytical capabilities are inherent in its process:

1. Display scheduling characteristics of projects to include time, cost, and risk variability
2. Model complex relationships between activities
3. Model complex characteristics of an activity (i.e., conditional occurrence)
4. Aid in analyzing resource allocation issues resulting from variable time results
5. Aid in identifying the real constraints of the project—activity variability, resources, and (constraint management)
6. Allow evaluation of alternative scenarios with complex assumptions
7. Show multiproject interactions

For these reasons, the use of simulation modeling needs to be pursued by the PM. This will take some time to incorporate in the organization management process, since the new views will be quite different and the learning will require time to absorb. Clearly, project analytics are a key planning and control skill set that needs to be developed.

Traditional network models portray the project as a static series of linked activities, often with padded duration times. This view is sometimes called a "train schedule," that is, it does not represent what could be done, but what we are scheduling. In the meantime, the players often sit around and wait for the "train." In order to deal with inefficient time management practices, PMs have to break this paradigm and find more effective methods of planning and analyzing project performance under more dynamic model assumptions. Simulation is one candidate for this.

References

Dibiasio, L., 2007a. Predicting risk in an uncertain world, *Primavera Magazine*, Spring, 20–21.
Dibiasio, L., 2007b. Understanding risk within the Portfolio. *Primavera Magazine*, Summer, 20–26.
Khan, S., 2007a. Dealing with risk the intelligent way. *World Pipelines*, 7, 29–30.
Khan, S., 2007b. Taking Control of Risks in Project Schedules and Portfolios. *Project Manager Today*.
Primavera, P., 2007. Pertmaster Help Manual.
Raftery, J., 2003. *Risk Analysis in Project Management*. New York: E & FN Spon Press.
Williams, T., 2002. *Modeling Complex Projects*. West Sussex: Wiley.

Chapter 27

Critical Chain Model

27.1 Introduction

This chapter examines one of the contemporary project planning models based on Critical Chain (CC) theory. This model is based on the application of Dr. Eliyahu Goldratt's *Theory of Constraints (TOC)* (Goldratt, 1997). CC's approach to project planning and execution requires project managers (PMs) to abandon traditional estimation and project control practices. Management of the CC elements is handled by the use of resource alerts and buffer management for the chain. Implementing these concepts will require a cultural change throughout the organization, beginning with a radical shift of focus from the near-term (task completion dates) to the long-term (final delivery dates). Topics described here are drawn both from published material authored by Dr. Goldratt and from other published sources by successful implementation practitioners, most notably Larry Leach and Frank Patrick.

Implementation of Critical Chain Management (CCM) looks at projects in a new light, changing the way projects are estimated, scheduled, executed, and controlled. In an ever-intensifying global competitive market, the management of projects, particularly product development efforts, is increasingly one of the factors that can produce a sustained competitive advantage. Firms that can bring products to market faster than their competitors can extract higher initial market share and margins. The underlying theme of this model is to complete prioritized projects faster and to make more efficient use of critical resources. As a prior warning, be aware that conversion to this model will require major process re-engineering and organizational culture changes. One of the significant cultural change involves a radical shift of focus from near-term task completion dates to long-term delivery dates.

Industry practitioners have labeled this CC-based model as CCM. The material described here is based on concepts from Patrick, Leach, Mannion, Ehrke, and others. Each have each published particularly notable work in this area and their collective contributions have been used extensively in this chapter. These individuals translated a theoretical approach into workable techniques that can be successfully applied in the project structure. Other translations of this concept have been implemented in operational environments such as manufacturing.

The CC method accomplishes building project network chains with restricted task duration, buffers to protect overruns, and disciplined resource management across the project. This discussion includes a general explanation outlining how CC principles are applied to project management to construct the resulting plan and underlying process. Also, the implementation complexity of the model and some of the challenges faced will be described.

27.2 CC Design Concepts

The key design focus in CC is in increasing speed of project completion, but it is clear that speed must be achieved without compromising other aspects of the project deliverables such as service, features, or flexibility. As the demand for shorter project cycle times and more deliverable flexibility grows, so does the frustration level of both PMs and their team members. Cut throat competition both at home and abroad and the need for process improvement encompass virtually every aspect of modern business. This has increased the popularity of downsizing, rightsizing, and re-engineering in hopes of achieving a competitive advantage. These trends will continue into the foreseeable future and this projection makes knowledge of the CC model worth including in our knowledge base. Any new approach must support significant leaps in performance, but it will also have to be sensitive to the current organizational culture.

The CCM model is basically a process improvement methodology resulting from a different manner of looking at tasks and their associated resources. According to the model, a project's failure to deliver as planned is tightly linked to failure to recognize and manage it as a network of dependent events with statistical fluctuations. CCM consists of a number of commonsense tools and processes that address this aspect of the project. In operation, these tools focus efforts on a few selected areas of the project plan, called "constraints," which restrict the project work flow. These constraints are the leverage points toward which successful improvement efforts are directed. According to Leach project management can be improved based on utilization of the following three model perspectives (Leach, 2005c):

1. *Project Management Body of Knowledge (PMBOK®) Guide* management model—providing general guidance on the overall methodology of planning and control.
2. Total Quality Management (TQM) and six sigma concepts (covered in Chapter 16)—represents a methodology outlining how to improve organizational processes.
3. CCM concepts—describes how to overcome typical time management issues by identifying system constraints and increasing activity throughput.

Figure 27.1 outlines how these three aggregate improvement strategies impinge on the project.

The next level concept involves analyzing the resource patterns embedded in the defined tasks. A common strategy involves finding one or more scarce (called drum) resources that are inhibiting the project from completing faster. Many times, multiple demands are being placed on these resources, which causes a capacity gap and schedule disruption. Within these tasks, there is also recognition that the task performance process exhibits natural variation and that many of the individual tasks are interrelated (Leach, 2005c). To summarize, the following operational realities are observed:

1. Scarce resources are demanded across the global task set
2. Activities exhibit unplanned time variability.

Recognizing this, the base state efficiency of the task set could be improved by identifying constraints that restrict completion and using buffers to deal with the scheduled time variation.

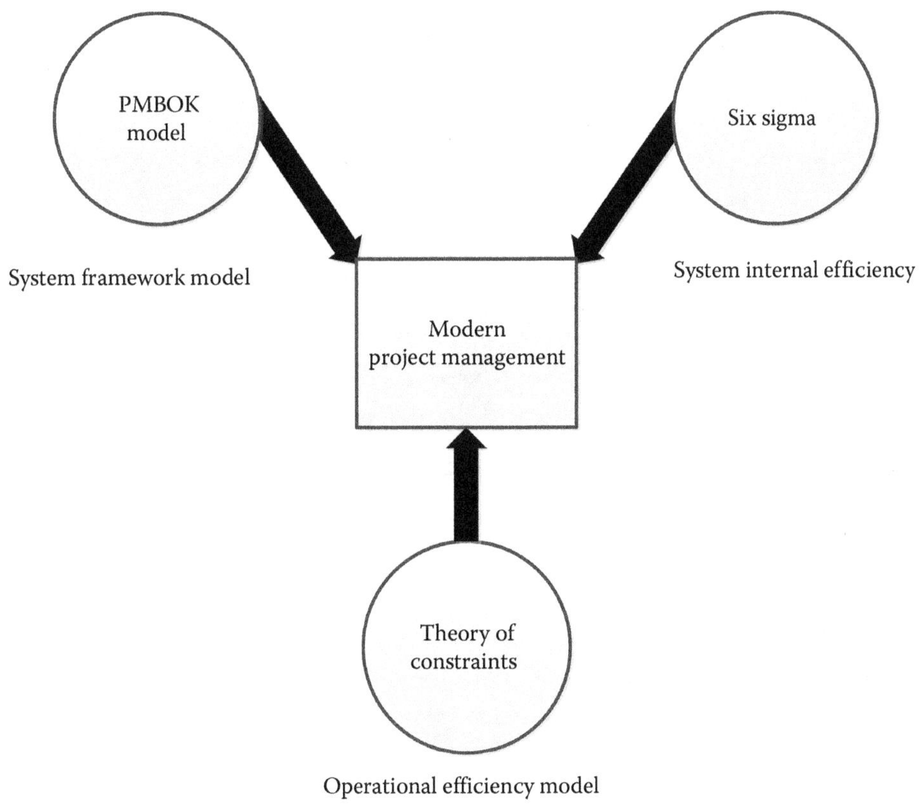

Figure 27.1 Impact models on the project.

From this base set of issues CCM strives to improve the constraint situation and manage the flow issue better. The essential idea is that system outputs are limited by its constraints and the flow of work through those constraints. The management trick in implementing CCM is to identify the constraint points and apply CC logic to them. Once the constraints are decreased, improvement in work flow can occur. Goldratt stated that (Leach, 2005c):

> *Before we can deal with the improvement of any section in a system, we must first define the system's global goal; and the measurements that will enable us to judge the impact of any subsystem and any local decision, on this global goal.*

Beyond the resource aspect, the basic concept behind CC constraint theory is best described using a physical chain analogy (thus the origin of the name). The goal of a chain is to provide strength in tension. A chain's weakest link determines its overall strength, so increasing the strength of any link other than the weakest link will have no effect on the overall strength of the chain. In similar fashion, consistently managing the weakest link in a project will improve performance of the overall project. Figure 27.2 depicts two work sequential packages chained together. The time required to execute both is then the sum of the two packages times. We'll see more how this works in the model below.

Figure 27.2 Weakest link analogy.

27.3 CC Mechanics

Leach outlines the following steps to set up and operate the CC model:

1. Identify the system's constraints.
2. Decide how to exploit the constraints.
3. Subordinate everything else to the defined constraints.
4. Buffer the system's defined constraints.
5. Is another constraint found? (If so, return to step one)
6. During operation, do not allow external events to create a constraint.

A typical starting point for CCM is to construct the baseline schedule using activity duration estimates based on a 50% completion confidence level. All activity milestones are eliminated and multitasking is avoided by allocating work on a priority basis. Herroelen et al. offers the following list of mechanics to describe the fundamental process (Herroelen, et al., 2002):

1. 50% probability activity duration estimates
2. No activity due dates
3. No fixed project milestones and no multitasking
4. Minimize work in progress (WIP)
5. Determine a precedence and resource-feasible baseline schedule
6. Identify the critical activity chain
7. Insert appropriate buffers into the defined task chain
8. Keep the baseline schedule and CC fixed during project execution
9. Determine unbuffered schedule and track completion schedules
10. Use buffer status as a proactive warning mechanism during execution

To minimize WIP, a schedule is constructed by timing activities at their latest start dates based on critical path calculations. If resource conflicts occur, they are resolved by moving activities earlier so as to not impact schedules. From this design a critical chain is then defined as, "that chain of the precedence and resource dependent activities which determines the overall duration of the project" (Herroelen et al., 2002). More detailed discussion of these mechanics is offered below, but this summary is a good overview.

In the project model view, CCM is defined as groups of dependent tasks that have potential to constrain the project schedule. In this case, the term "dependent" refers to resource timely availability and contention across tasks and projects, as well as the sequence and logical dependencies of the tasks themselves (Goldratt, 2007). This view differs from the classic critical path network definition as described in Chapter 14. In the traditional network critical path, only the fact that the task exists and is linked to other tasks is recognized, while CC recognizes how related resources are assigned to the tasks across the project. This is conceptually similar to capacity management, but with a more dynamic flavor. In the CC view, resources are managed dynamically based on current status. Thereby supporting faster project completions. By doing this, the task chain completes faster and generally decreases overall project cost as a by-product. The underlying subtlety of this statement is there is no fixed completion time and the resources are managed to be available as soon as needed. Think of this as a relay track meet with the baton representing the completion time for the next task. Everyone is poised to move as fast as the chain can be accomplished.

27.4 CCM Model in Operation

As indicated above the model focuses on improving work process flow. In a project, the entire system will degrade if any one element in a chain of tasks fails. CCM focuses on the amount of time required to complete a "chain" of tasks, whereas in a multiproject view, the model focuses on the collective tasks that most effect the cumulative cycle time of all the projects. The resources involved in these views are known as the organization's strategic or critical resources, also called the "Drum" resource. Operationally, CCM manages the Drum resource in such a manner as to optimize overall project performance. One metaphor for the Drum resource is "marching through the project to the beat of a drum."

There are basic external and internal factors that need to be dealt with in setting up the CCM resource environment. A summary of these are as follows:

External Factors

- Synchronization—task network with resources identified
- Queuing—sequencing and prioritization of tasks

Internal factors

- Student syndrome—execution procrastination avoided
- Parkinson's law—overly conservative estimating
- Multitasking—too many work tasks in play at the same time

One of the fundamental resource management tenets of CCM involves the process to deal with the way project team members are allocated throughout the project life cycle. This tenet is basically a project management discipline as applied to people and tasks. Kendall et al. (2005) offer the following summary list of concepts and mechanics used to manage the CCM process regarding people and tasks:

1. Project team members are dedicated to a single prioritized task until it is completed and they are challenged to execute this as quickly as possible with minimal disruptions from other activities. Periodic status reports are required to indicate time remaining for the task. Every effort is taken to eliminate delays and work procrastination.
2. Task estimates do not have padding. They are planned at some probabilistic completion level, such as 50% probability that the task can be completed at the defined time.
3. Multitasking is eliminated by assigning workers to tasks in priority order and completing that task before moving on to a new task. Industry experience suggests that multitasking creates inefficiencies amounting to 30%–40%.
4. Managing tasks by due date is not followed. Workers and tasks are not measured based on scheduled completions. The management approach is to pass on the task to the next activity as quickly as possible. *This is the track meet metaphor.*
5. By taking resource dependency and logical dependency into account, the longest sequence of dependent tasks can be seen more clearly. This longest task chain sequence may cross logical paths in the plan network. So, the management view is to deal with resource status across the chain and not just with critical path schedule management.
6. Buffers are a key mechanism to manage desired schedules. These will be defined to protect various aspects of the project including Drum (scarce) resource, non-critical feeding chains, and the project completion itself. Project status will be monitored through evaluating status of these buffers.
7. Task completion is viewed as passing the baton to the next task in the chain. When a task is close to reaching completion, the next task's resource is queued to get ready to go immediately after the preceding task is complete. In this manner, there is little delay in the chain and early completions can be used to speed the process. Every effort is made to create this culture in the project team.
8. Recognition of resource constraints requires a staggered introduction of multiple projects into the system and resources for these efforts will be allocated on a priority basis. This method improves completion of projects in priority order, increases the outcome predictability for each project, and increases the effectiveness of critical resources by minimizing multitasking. Shorter project cycle times improve overall delivery of the project set.

27.5 Buffer Management

Since every activity in the project is scheduled with no safety padding, it is expected that some tasks will overrun their estimated times. Project buffers are used in various places to keep the overall schedule under control and particularly the critical path protected from overrun. Location logic for the buffers will be discussed below, but for now let us look at how a buffer works. Imagine "chains" of activities in the plan. Each activity is sized at 50% of typical estimates (say the median estimate, for example). This means that 50% of the time the schedule is anticipated to overrun (and hopefully 50% underrun). The goal of a buffer in this chain is designed to protect that group of tasks from overrunning. Of course, the trick is to properly estimate how large such a buffer should be. For this discussion, a typical number will be used, but accurate estimation can be improved through experience with specific project types.

Patrick provides in Figure 27.3 a good overview of buffer logic using feeding and project buffers (Patrick, 1998, p. 6). A feeding buffer represents a set of non-critical path activities that need to be protected from impacting the critical path. A project buffer inserted at the end of the critical path is used to protect the project from schedule overrun. In this operational mode, the focus for management moves

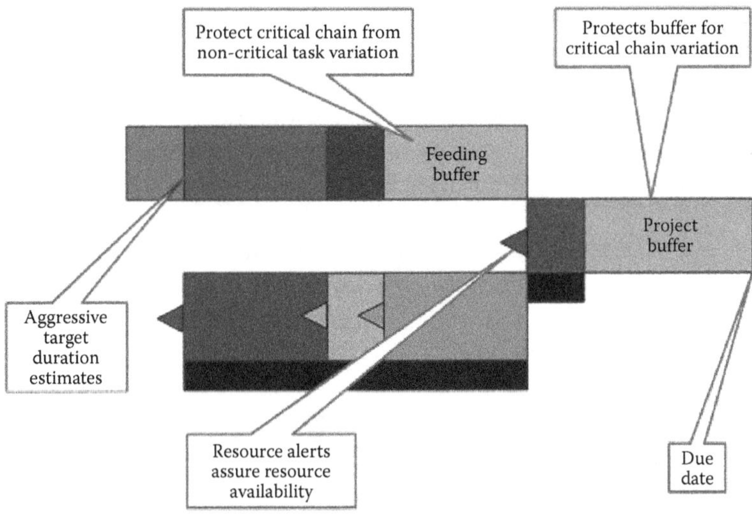

Figure 27.3 Buffer logic.

to buffer status since some tasks are now expected to overrun. There is now no management value in looking at plan versus actual task performance, which becomes one of the main cultural changes associated with this implementation. If the various chains are protected by appropriate buffers, the overall project will finish on or before planned schedule and quicker than would occur with the traditional model. Assuming this model works as advertised, the CC model would be of great interest to all organizations and there is growing evidence that it, in fact, does work when properly implemented.

One way to view buffer status is to divide them into three equally sized regions as shown in Figure 27.4. The first-third could be color-coded as the green zone, the second-third as the yellow zone, and the final-third as the red zone. As chain overruns occur, the buffers are "eaten." If the buffer penetration is in the green zone, no action is taken. If penetration enters the yellow zone, the problem should be assessed for possible corrective action. Finally, if penetration enters the red zone, careful review is required to protect the project schedule. Action plans should involve ways to finish uncompleted tasks in the chain earlier, or ways to accelerate future work in the chain to correct excessive buffer penetration rates (Retief, 2002).

Defining project and feeding buffers will be a new skill requirement for the project team to master. Published research is available on this topic, but it will be necessary to test various methods before settling on a local approach. Leach offers detailed explanations for three methods in *Critical Chain Project Management* (Leach, 2005c). Understanding buffer sizing is a key element in successful implementation. The first time this model format with multiple buffers appears in a project plan it will likely necessitate an explanation for various stakeholders, and it may even be necessary to prepare a "shadow" plan showing only key completion dates. So long as the project team meets those key dates, a lower-level view may not be required outside of the project team.

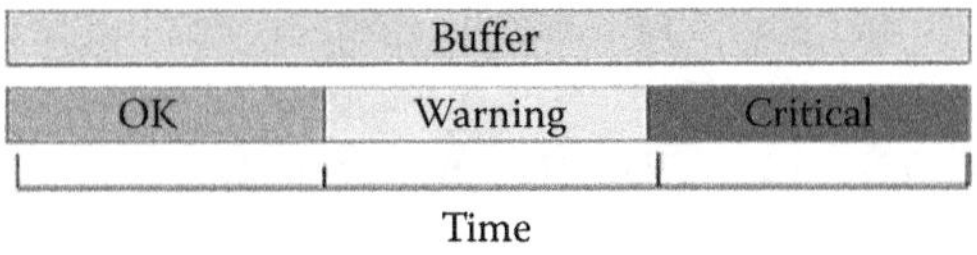

Buffer

OK | Warning | Critical

Time

Figure 27.4 Buffer penetration status scheme.

Conceptually, buffer sizing is a probability and statistics-based issue (Geekie, 2008). The basic methods follow similar logic similar to that described in the critical path variable time discussion in Chapters 24 and 25. However, as with most items in the project management domain, the underlying accuracy of data is the Achilles heel in accurate quantification. So, until there is a more tested local strategy, Leach (2005c, p. 137) recommends utilizing the "Half the Chain" method for buffer sizing. The method was initially recommended by Goldratt as follows (Leach 2005c, p. 135):

> *Size the project and feeding buffers to one half of the buffered-path task length. Use only the total task length; do not count the gaps in the chain when sizing buffers.*

Many organizations will likely reject such an approach because it seems too simple and the buffers appear to be too large. In fact, it has a mathematical basis resulting from the way the time estimates were initially formed at 50%. Remember, the role of the buffer is to protect critical points in the chain from delay and approach the process with that mindset.

27.5.1 Buffer Types

Discussion to this point has focused on the project and feeding buffer roles, but there are other buffer types defined in the model as well. Each one serves a similar role to that described earlier—that is protecting the project from delay. This section briefly summarizes the various buffer roles.

Project buffers: As illustrated in Figure 27.3, this buffer type is located at the end of the critical path to protect the project completion date from the estimate variability in the chain activities. The project is protected by this buffer because any total overrun of activities on the longest chain of dependent tasks can be protected, since the actual completion date will not overrun the planned date. As a rule of thumb for an initial strategy the project buffer is recommended to be half the size of the chain it is protecting. The net impact of this is a project schedule that should result at 75% of a "traditional" project network length (Goldratt, 2007).

Feeding buffers: These buffers are placed wherever a non-CC activity chain joins the CC. Their role is to protect the CC from interference. Sizing of the feeding buffer is typically recommended to be half the related chain duration (Goldratt, 2007).

Resource buffers: These buffers are placed whenever a non-critical resource is needed for an activity on the CC. The goal of this buffer is to ensure that the associated task does not have to wait for the resource to become available.

Drum buffers: This buffer is placed so that critical resources are available when needed. In that respect, the drum buffer is similar to a feeding buffer. They are placed in the project schedule immediately prior to the activity using the drum resource. This buffer protects the activity start date and lead time. A drum resource is considered to be a system constraint and is viewed as a potential bottleneck to the schedule. For this reason, projects are synchronized around these resource constraints, which otherwise result in schedule delays. These resources will be allocated on a priority basis and the buffer attempts to ensure that the priority project does not have to wait for that resource.

Capacity buffer: When synchronizing multiple projects around a drum resource, a capacity buffer is created between the tasks of different projects on which the drum resource is needed (Retief, 2002). Figure 27.5 shows how this buffer would be applied.

For each of the buffer types, the amount each buffer is consumed relative to project progress is the status assessment monitoring variable. Assuming that the time variation throughout a chain is uniform, the project buffer would erode at the same rate as the chain is completed. If the buffer

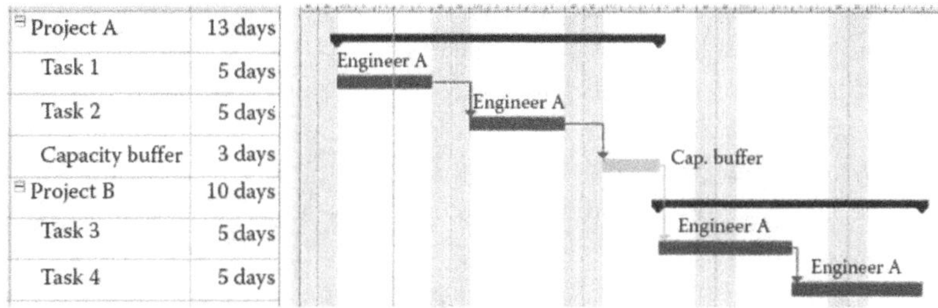

Figure 27.5 Drum buffer between two projects.

sizing is perfect, it will be fully consumed when the chain is completed. By monitoring each buffer's status, it is now up to the PMs to determine the appropriate corrective actions necessary to recover if a buffer is being consumed faster than planned.

A second aspect of status tracking is to review remaining duration for all active tasks as opposed to percentage complete in the traditional mode. Resource and completion status will be monitored for all tasks in progress based on the number of days estimated to completion. If a remaining duration value on an active task stays static, a warning is triggered to review that activity. This logic is caused by the fact that no active task should stay static given the model design. No progress means that something has gone counter to the plan.

27.6 Building the CC Schedule

In Figure 27.6, the letter in each block represents the resource type necessary to complete the given task. In this view, the assumption is that only one resource (a person or work group) is available for each given letter and the CC estimated duration of the task is 50% of the traditional network value and represented by the number in each block.

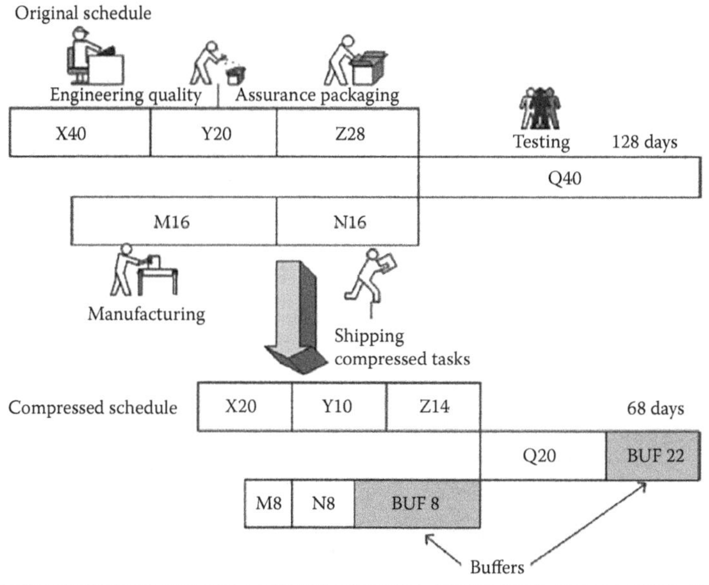

Figure 27.6 Critical chain in action.

After the CC plan structure is defined, the next step is to define the size of each buffer. This is a complex issue, but use the sizing rules outlined earlier—50% for CC buffer, but 25% used here for the feeding buffers (arbitrarily). In reality, these values would be adjusted with experience. The published project completion date is now defined by the end of the project buffer, but not the end of the task "Q" per the original network schedule. This example shows the same project structured first as a traditional network with no buffers, then each task cut to 50%. Task durations are indicated by the number after the task ID (i.e., X40 indicates that the task is 40 days). A feeding buffer is inserted after task "N" to project the CC and a project buffer is inserted at the end of the CC to protect the project. Observed from this example, a delay in the feeding buffer chain segment will not affect the project unless that buffer is overrun. Also, note that the overall project is cut essentially in half (i.e., 128 versus 68 days).

In a CC schedule, the tasks are started as late as possible, which is convergent from the way traditional network models would schedule them. This strategy reduces WIP considerably as the work is started later and worked on until it is complete. However, additional risk is incurred by not having the security of a finished item in place waiting. Obviously, this method requires that the outlined process works effectively.

In real-world CC projects, the reduction in time is found to be more often in the range of 25% less than an equivalent traditional plan with the same activities (Cook, 1998). This improvement is created from aggregating the total duration protection into buffers rather than allowing each activity to have a separate buffer.

27.7 Resource Allocation

Once the CC structure is established, the problem turns to resource allocation and resource allocation conflicts. In Figure 27.7, resource "Y" was originally scheduled to perform two tasks at the same time so there is a conflict as to which activity to perform. In order to resolve the conflict, the feeder branch is started earlier and now becomes part of the longest chain. Also, a buffer is inserted after activity "X" in order to allow time for the feeder chain to complete.

Placement of resource buffers helps the PM focus on that particular aspect of the project. These become a communication target between the project schedule and the team. As work progresses, the resources report time estimates for task completion. When a predecessor chain task resource reports having five days remaining (Goldratt recommended), the schedule process is triggered to inform the successor activity to prepare to start work on their assigned activity. In the relay race metaphor, this is analogous to getting ready to pass the baton. This mechanism represents a dynamic countdown for the successor. If the predecessor reported two days later that there was

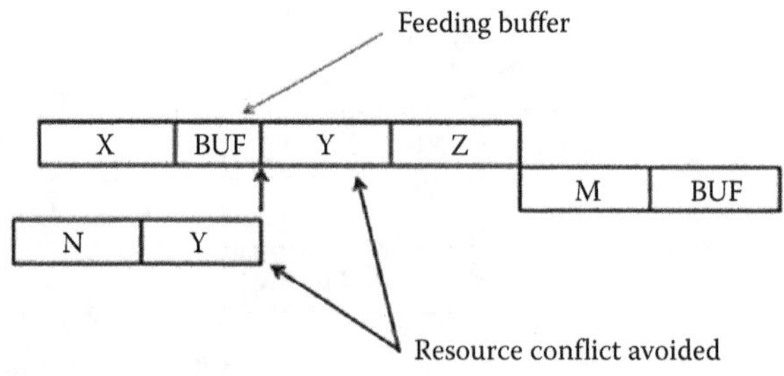

Figure 27.7 Resolving resource conflicts.

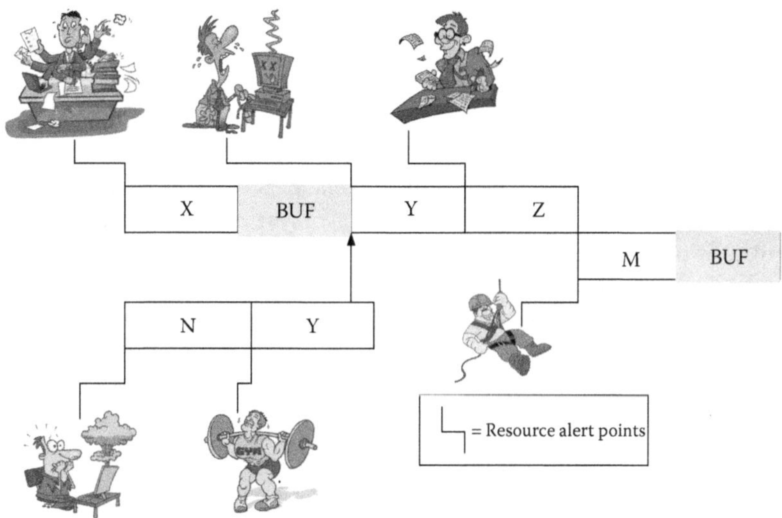

Figure 27.8 Resource readiness alerts.

still five days remaining, this information would be passed on to the successor and a review of the activity would be performed. Note in this process that the focus of all activities is in having resources ready and prepared to execute the next task and then move as quickly as they can to completion. The "elbow" lines on Figure 27.8 represent the resource alert points for the project. Five days before each task is estimated to complete, the alert would be passed to the named resource that should then start getting ready to commence work. Tactically, the focus is on being sure that resources are in place as required.

The final descriptive step of CCM involves the manner in which the schedule is managed. This is basically performed through buffer management. Earlier discussion described the green, yellow, and red zones of buffer status. Project status reports would basically focus on these. More sophistication can be added by calculating "burn rate" of the buffer so that if one is decreasing faster than task completion it would trigger to review of that chain to see what needs to be done. The buffer management process highlights potential problems much earlier than they would ordinarily be discovered using the typical project management techniques. In this manner, the status report becomes more than just showing the project due dates. It has more of a focus on run rate! Also, there is more ability to have greater insight into trends. Unfortunately, the process of computing Earned Value as a status metric is impacted by this structure and interpretation of this model will have to be assessed for interpretation: another cultural impact to consider.

27.8 Implementation Challenges

There is real-world evidence that successful implementation of the concepts outlined for the CC methodology will improve project throughput. In fact, improvement has been observed in several documented cases. However, recognize that the operational and cultural impact of these methods on the organization is significant and makes the conversion more complex than converting to the method itself. There are three major areas where complex conversion will be experienced: organizational barriers, leadership challenges, and skill requirements. The sections below will describe some of the main issues in these areas.

The first barrier involves organizational maturity in that the model requires the project team and other stakeholders be versed in the fundamentals of the method and it will require a new way of looking at the project plan and subsequent status. So, in order for the transition to work, there will need to be revisions made to existing planning methodology, which historically has been a difficult item to standardize. Once the new plan format is in place, status reporting and resource allocation methods would have to change. Some stakeholders would need to be enticed to try the method with a promise of improved completion times. Unfortunately, there are subtleties involved that will require visible changes to a formal priority process. Mature organizations with proven track records might be the easiest to convert, since much of the operational discipline would already be in place. The less disciplined an organization is in regard to overall project planning and resource allocation the more this change will be noticeable. PMs with a proven track record would likely be the best trend setters for this change. Stakeholders and team members would tend to follow creative leadership into new territory. Finally, mature supporting processes such as Integrated Change Control (ICC), risk management, issue/action management, and communication processes are also essential for CCM to succeed (Leach, 2005c, p. 206).

As indicated earlier, the concept of extensive use of buffers and the related sizing of these will often cause a negative response from traditional managers. Historically, PMs have been discouraged from visibly adding buffers into project schedules. In the traditional case, buffering is added on top of padded estimates, thereby hiding real task times. Consequently, buffers that existed in the traditional plan were more viewed as management reserve and controlled by a combination of primary stakeholders or the project sponsor, not the PM. Contingency reserves are recognized in some organizations and they are like a buffer in that they are associated with the project but not explicitly shown until a risk event actually occurred. Hence, the concept of seeing visible task variance buffers flies against the standard operating process in most organizations. When implementing CCM, managers and stakeholders will be challenged to accept not only the existence of the chain concept and its buffers but also the acceptance of task overruns. Patrick (2001) makes the following comment regarding the nature of buffer use:

> *Once developed, assessment of the full schedule, including the contribution of the buffers to project lead-time, provides a clear view into the identified potential of schedule risk for the project. In non-CC environments, when a reserve is included, it is often hidden either in management reserve or in other less visible sources. The common practice of keeping these components off the table hides their true impact and implications. The open and explicit communication of buffers allows a clear assessment of what could happen 'in the best of all possible worlds,' versus what might happen if individual concerns accumulate to affect project performance.*
>
> *(Patrick, 1998, p. 44)*

The third cultural issue lies in the approach to task status tracking. CCM tracking moves the process away from milestone or activity completion into buffer status tracking. Since task or activity estimates are at the 50% probability level (as defined here), it is necessary to expect frequent task duration overruns. Because of this modified approach to task estimating, the concept of "due date" loses its meaning. The due date now is as quick as you can finish the activity (Patrick, 1998, p. 5). Stakeholder agreement on this view is crucial to success. Also, securing stakeholder agreement on an acceptable project reporting methodology must be resolved during the project planning phase. Leach (2005c) and Patrick (2001) both recommend using a "Red–Yellow–Green"

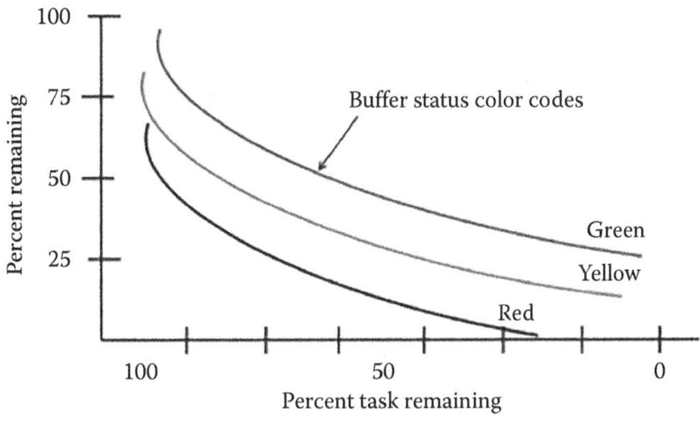

Figure 27.9 Buffer consumption reporting.

icon approach to reporting, representing percentage of buffer penetration over time. Figure 27.9 illustrates what this status reporting format could look like.

Compared to traditional project management, the philosophical changes outlined here are a shift away from focusing on "what we've done" with reporting percent of work completed to now focusing on what represents more of "when are we are going to be finished with the current task and where are the potential resource roadblocks."

27.9 Changing the Organization

Organizations with established Project Management Offices (PMOs) or standardized project management policies and procedures may not possess the flexibility required to implement CCM. For example, estimating at the 50% confidence level may be seen as an undisciplined approach by senior staff and management. Leach (2005c, p. 193) asserts that the final step in implementing CCPM is

> *... assuring that the CCPM approach permeates all policies, procedures, and measures of the organization and is formalized into training programs to ensure that new people are properly indoctrinated into the organizational process. In the end, CCPM should not be an additional thing. It should just be 'how we do business around here'.*

There is an old adage "If it ain't broke, don't fix it" and this attitude often results in a rationale for resisting change. Experienced project practitioners may argue that CCM is just "rearranging stuff." To counter that statement, try to influence the notion that the starting place for CCM is a good critical path network that has been effectively resource leveled. Using that as a base, the CCM approach enhances the ability to optimize the schedule and set the stage for improved project monitoring and control (Kendall et al., 2005, p. 3).

Suddenly faced with the challenge to estimate activities in the 50% probability range, organizations may counter with "we already use overly aggressive estimates and always work to meet or beat them" (Leach, 2005c, p. 207). That is in fact not a reality given task variances. What is a reserve in CCM is a padded task in the traditional model. Nevertheless, upper management may see CCM as locking them out of the actual status of the project since interim due dates are now harder to see.

Mature organizations often develop existing processes and project templates to aid in plan development. One such example is an estimating technique or model that has been found to be "accurate." What this might mean is that it is seldom overrun and has significant buffering built in. The same might hold with a standard project life cycle template based on a traditional network structure. In such situations, there is likely to be resistance to changing approaches for project management that are working adequately.

The issue of status tracking was mentioned previously. Organizations may either have in place a standard tracking and reporting system, or may be contractually obligated to use a traditional approach for an external customer. Also, the CCM created problem with Earned Value performance measurement calculations was mentioned earlier and the same issue could exist for other traditional reporting approaches. If milestone reporting is required for contractual reasons, Leach (2005c) recommends placing a buffer before the milestone, then treating those segments of the project as defined dates (pp. 146–147). Christ (2001, p. 2) relates the following from his own experience:

> *There was an assumption in place that since the customer required Earned Value Management (EVM), no other method of management [approach] was authorized or acceptable. When queried, the customer indicated that factory management methods were company business, but the customer wanted data in EVM report format. This response opened the door for CCPM schedules in conjunction with EVM reporting.*

More details on this approach can be found in Christ's (2001) article.

Changing an organization for any purpose is difficult and CCM-created changes will be equally tough. Classical human nature regarding change in existing work processes will clearly be a complicating factor. Low tolerance for change is often rooted in a fear that one will not be able to develop new skills and behaviors that are required (Bolognese, 2002, p. 20). Leach (2005c) states that resistance to change is a characteristic of any stable system. One might argue that CCM could be harder to sell in stable, mature organizations that were doing well and therefore not motivated to make what might be viewed as a radical change. Regardless of the particular organization there will likely be negative reaction from the various entities with these new approaches to planning and control (Leach, 2005c, p. 203).

On the counter side of this argument, Bolognese (2002, p. 26) comments that in certain instances employee resistance may play a positive and useful role in supporting organizational change. Insightful and well-intended debate, criticism, or disagreement do not necessarily equate to negative resistance but may be intended to produce better understanding as well as additional options and solutions. With proper selling, the CCM theme will certainly resonate with many organizational groups seeking faster project completion.

From a leadership perspective, PMs should respond to critics in a positive, constructive fashion. It is important to communicate how the local project links with organizational success (Wynne, 2006). The case for CCM must also be couched in these same terms. It is not a technology initiative. Rather, it is a management technique designed to deliver defined value to the stakeholders quicker than would be done otherwise.

CCM attempts to speed delivery of the project without sacrificing requirements. It is well known that faster completion of the project has value to the organization well beyond just cutting project times. For instance, the longer a project takes the greater the risk that some portion of the originally defined specifications will become obsolete. A shorter cycle time can positively impact the rate of scope change observed. Leach (2005c) states that PMs who complain about scope creep admit to having an ineffective project change control process (p. 163). Although seemingly just a process issue, project scope control is recognized as one of the most important factors for project success. By completing the project sooner the level of scope change should be less.

27.10 Summary of CCM Impact

There are a myriad of project impacts related to CCM that need to be recognized. These include processes, skills, and various organizational cultural items. This section will offer brief comments on the most obvious of these.

Creation of an effective project plan requires an iterative process and sufficient time (Leach, 2005c, p. 163). CCM will certainly not shorten that time given the need to have a well-developed critical path and resource capacity evaluation. In addition, the method requires multiproject analysis of resources and buffer design on top of the traditional model (Kendall et al., 2005, p. 11).

A well thought out Work Breakdown Structure (WBS) is important for various reasons as outlined in Chapter 12. This artifact contains vital information helping to organize, integrate, assign responsibility, and measure and control the project (Leach, 2005c, p. 106). It is also an important planning artifact to help identify work units that can be done in parallel, contracted, allocated to lower-level skills, and a host of other decisions that can help decrease the overall project time (Kendall et al., 2005, p. 9).

During schedule development the project team must be permitted to manipulate the structured work unit schedule (early versus late starts) and establish the necessary feeding and project buffers in order for the CCM model to work. This includes a disciplined process of assigning resources to all tasks, and having tight control over those resources to work on one project task at a time. Management must support the overall process for schedule development, including resource allocation, predecessor relationships, buffer allocation, and of course the CC model itself. Patrick (1998, p. 1) reminds us that the scheduling mechanisms provided by CC require the elimination of task due dates from project plans. Christ (2001, p. 25) summarizes the following schedule results obtained from the CCM process:

> *The result is a robust schedule considering resource capacity, work sequence, and task variability, with visibility provided by buffer reports. This process simplifies complex projects and provides management time to identify and address problems as they arise.*

As indicated earlier, the calculation of buffer sizes will be immature in the early stages of implementation. Regardless of the methodology used the buffers should be calculated based on the length of the related chain. Arbitrary manipulation of buffer sizing will destroy the concept and resultant confidence of the CCM methods.

When used solely as a status mechanism, a dictated "interim milestone" or "phased deliverable" defeats the purpose of using CC. Setting an arbitrary delivery date without validating the time and resource implications invalidates the plan. In some cases, an exception to this might be necessary as some external driver such as a regulatory requirement or market date may dictate such an approach. When a fixed delivery date is used, it will need to be prioritized against the existing workload to test for feasibility.

Utilizing a multiproject portfolio selection process, or some form of project prioritization and coordination at an organizational level, will help decrease the severity of resource contention in a CCM model environment. In order to minimize this issue, projects must be prioritized in terms of criticality of current commitments, value to the organization, and use of the synchronizing resource (Patrick, 2001, p. 7). As seen below, Leach's view is more direct (Leach, 2005c, p. 162):

> *If management does not adhere to a priority list, the multiproject system will not work. It is a simple choice, really. Behave to double throughput, or do not. Once they see the results, many management teams are able to do much better at this than many thought. After all, when the system makes more money, people's jobs are protected, and often they make more money too.*

The organizational methods used to select and initiate new projects can be a source of interruption or resource contention for ongoing projects. If the new project is placed at a higher priority than some of the ongoing projects, the schedule of the ongoing projects will quickly change because of the CCM dynamic resource allocation scheme. It is necessary to keep in mind that the worst possible priority decision is not to make a priority decision, but to simply encourage everyone to do his or her best and hope the problem goes away. This inevitably causes bad multitasking and poor performance on all of the projects (Leach, 2005c, p. 161).

The practice of "pulling" an already committed resource from an ongoing project is a management challenge for any project, but can be a disaster for a CCM-driven effort. Upon receiving the advance warning that their task will start, task resources must be prepared to finish up interruptible (noncritical) work and get ready to start work on the assigned critical project task. The new view has to change from "when is my task due?" to ask "when will my next prioritized task start."

The change management process must also be charged with the responsibility to protect project resources from unnecessary or significant changes in scope (Patrick, 1998, p. 4). No project can be successful when new, approved work is being added to the requirements on a daily basis. It is common for organizations to "pull" project team members away from project work in order to address some important operational issues, and sometimes this is unavoidable. Once again, failure to deliver the required resource at the right time and in the quantity needed will adversely affect the schedule. Management has the responsibility to make a priority call on resources, but the PM should attempt to quantify the impact of a resource reallocation and not just assume the schedule can be maintained.

The ability to handle multiple tasks concurrently (i.e., multitasking) is one of the "merit badges" of today's work environment. This is often cited in job descriptions and is true for PMs as well. This was once considered a productivity multiplier, but management and workers alike are beginning to recognize the overall negative limitations of multitasking (Anderson, 2001). Recent research is confirming those observations, pointing to multitasking as a productivity inhibitor. Rubinstein and his associates determined that for various types of tasks, subjects lost time when they had to switch from one task to another. There is an increased job complexity and time lost when workers have to switch between complicated tasks. Leach states as similar conclusion:

> *Practical applications of CCPM have demonstrated the greatest gains in multi-project enterprises. The reason for this is that those environments usually require everyone to multitask much of the time. Elimination of much of the bad multitasking has the greatest impact on overall enterprise project throughput.*
>
> *(Leach, 2005c, p. 163)*

When one considers the productivity degradation effect of multitasking, it should be clear that assigning resources to jump back and forth across task or project boundaries is not an efficient mechanism.

Replacement of a more systemic process to allocate resources with synchronization, combined with their management in a "relay race" behavior, will go a long way to reduce this issue and will help accelerate project completions (Patrick, 2001, p. 8). Leach (2005c, p. 197) recommends for one of his success factors that project resources be expected to work on one project task at a time. In this same vein, a more orderly task allocation process is a stress reduction technique for team members.

In the CCM mode team members must have clear task priorities communicated and managed. In the CC world, there are two kinds of resources; those that perform critical tasks and those performing noncritical tasks. The ones that have to be most carefully controlled are the critical group, since they most directly determine how long the project will take. The operational process must make sure that critical task assigned resources are available when the preceding task is done, without relying on a predetermined predecessor completion due dates. There is the underlying assumption that the work of a task will take as long as it takes, no matter what the schedule estimate says. Once allocated to a priority task the resource will work on it until there is nothing more they can do. During this time there should be minimal distraction until they are complete (Patrick, 2001, p. 6). In an ideal case this means meetings, email, or anything else that takes away focus on the assigned task. The resource view outlined to this point deals with the management process, rather than the technical skill to produce the product.

Parkinson's Law is often used to describe the work behavior of human workers and it particularly well fits the traditional estimating mindset. Parkinson's Law is:

> *Work expands to fill [and often exceeds] the time allowed.*

Goldratt (1997) based much of his original Theory of Constraints (TOC) model on the assertion that individuals will procrastinate when working toward a fixed due date. This is also known as the "student syndrome"—Remember that term paper you had to write in school and how you procrastinated about starting it until the last minute and then went through chaos and late hours to finish? The modern project environment often works a lot like this. If CCM is to be successful, breaking out of that cycle must be a priority for the organization.

The concept of variable time scheduling means that it is impossible to pick the exact execution time for a task. There are simply to many variables involved to make this a deterministic value. CCM recognizes this by requiring that task durations be built with only the median time required to do the work without any safety factor. The idea of estimating a task at the 50% likelihood level instead of a 90% level will be a significant philosophical shift for many. Work unit estimators will need to be coached and encouraged not to develop task estimates with built-in safety. Safety has to be consolidated into the various model buffers. Patrick (2001, p. 2) suggests using the following method for developing task estimates:

> *Resources are first queried for a safe estimate—one in which there is a high level of confidence and the work unit owner would be willing to consider a commitment. This value defines the upper end of the possible time estimate. Once this upper limit is initially established, a second "aggressive but achievable" estimate is solicited—one that reflects a near "best case" situation that is "in the realm of possibility" assuming things go well in the performance of the task in question.*

Figure 27.10 is a simple illustration of this concept. The traditional estimating approach is to cover time contingencies and use a padded estimate that has very little risk involved. This often results in the procrastination mode because the worker feels that they have plenty of time built into the

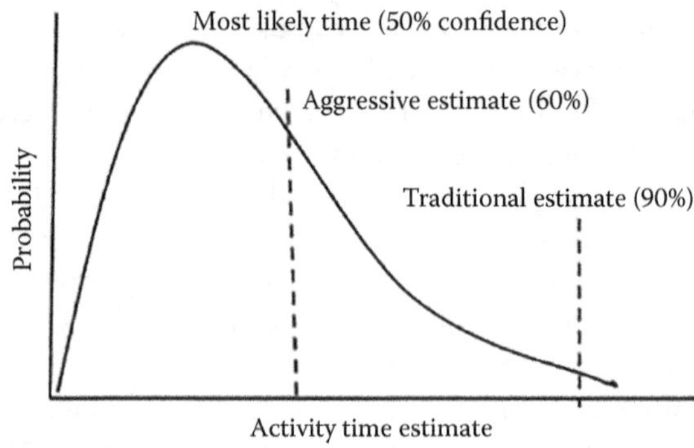

Figure 27.10 Duration estimating logic.

estimate. In the CCM method, the schedule strategy is to push toward the 50% point and use buffers to handle overflows. This has the impact of prodding the process to not procrastinate because there is no planned idle time. A 60% probability time represents a slight compromise that might be used as a beginning strategy since the 50% point represents a significant cultural change for the organization. Leach describes the tendency of organizations to overestimate tasks because they are concerned that something could go wrong to elongate the task (Leach, 2005c, p. 192). This is often the case in an organization with extensive multitasking and interruptions. Regardless of the rationale, there is a strong tendency to overprotect an estimate by adding significant padding to its expected duration. Team members and work unit owners will have similar biases left over from traditional management practices. This cultural item will be a leadership challenge by showing all that meeting a particular padded activity time estimate is no longer the criteria for success. Rather, finishing the project as quickly as feasible.

Efforts to educate the team members on the principles of CCM, and the planned estimation and implementation methodology, should ideally be led by the PM charged with the implementation. It may be necessary to bring in external expertise to teach the new estimating strategy.

Once the decision is made to move forward with this overall approach it should be tested on a relatively small project with an experienced PM who believes in the new method. Every reasonable effort should be made to gain prior commitment from the team and careful metrics should be kept to evaluate the results. Recall the experience found in the 1930s Hawthorne lighting experiment (refer to Chapter 2). There are some similarities in this implementation and some of the Hawthorne reactions could be achieved.

Task estimating will likely be the first activity stressed in the implementation and the first opportunity to either commit or resist. Newbold (1998, p. 195) recommends running the team with a "Pit Crew Mentality." Everyone must understand how their individual work contributes to a car or track race and attempt to translate this to the new process.

CCM status reporting is based on team members accurately reporting task completion status. This is done not as the traditional percent complete, but focuses on the estimated time required to finish the task. Actual completion of tasks, as well as forecast for completion must be communicated in a timely manner. The traditional once a week status reporting will not work well for this requirement. Activity reporting and resource management need to be a real-time mechanism Leach (2005c, p. 201). Status reporting and resource management become tightly linked in the CCM operational environment since status information is used to tightly control the next step in the various project chains. Patrick (1998, p. 5) details two simple steps required to accomplish this:

Step one: Ask the responsible work unit owner how much of an advance warning they need to finish up their other work (non-critical if all is going well) and shift to uninterruptible work so they can drop what they're currently doing and start work on their critical task.

Step two: There must be discipline in providing appropriate status updates for each active task. When the estimate to complete task A matches the advance warning needed by the task B resources, the resource management alert system will trigger and communicate this to that resource. They then need to plan on shutting down what they are doing and prepare for soon to be completed predecessor task.

This advanced warning process is referred to as a "resource alert" in the CCM vernacular. Team members and their managers may resist the frequency of reporting requirement, as previous project assignments may have only required weekly or even monthly reporting, however, the importance of this must be stressed. Remember, the new culture more resembles a track relay-race or race car pit crew mentality. The traditional model has been characterized as waiting at the train station for a scheduled train to come in. If that train were European in origin this might actually happen on that schedule, but that is not the typical view of traditional project task completions. One should be able to see from this dialogue that the resource alert process is used in CCM to manage a smooth workflow. It along with the frequent status reporting process are key processes in achieving CCM success.

At this point, it may not be sufficiently obvious why tasks are estimated in terms of how much longer to complete rather than percent complete as often used in the traditional process. One way of conceptualizing this logic is to see it as a just-in-time process. It would not be efficient to pick a planned completion date and have the resource standing by. The only way to maximize the efficiency is to have the resource there exactly on time, whether that is earlier than anticipated or later. To accomplish this goal, two events must be accomplished in synchronization—a timely notice of task completion is sufficient time to schedule the required resources and a dynamic resource allocation approach each that can coordinate the movement of said resources. This requires receiving daily information on each active task and the estimated work time remaining on that task. Leach (2005c, p. 201) feels that the reason for using remaining duration rather than percentage of completion estimates is that humans tend to overestimate task percentage complete. When called upon to look forward and consider the work remaining to complete a task, the estimates tend to be much more accurate. Remaining duration is also the number needed to measure downstream status. Estimating it directly avoids the other assumptions necessary to convert a percent complete estimate to a remaining duration estimate.

Using this reporting approach, task performance data can be entered into the network plan and from it status of each buffer can be computed. Note that as actual task values are reported on the plan the related buffer size will need to be adjusted to reflect the amount remaining. The red–yellow–green approach shown previously illustrated in Figure 27.4 can be used for high-level exception reporting, but more complex status can also be derived through percent of buffer used compared to percent of chain task accomplishment type metrics. This latter view would provide a more detailed insight into how the chain is progressing. Obviously, collection and reporting tools would need to be in place to support this level of sophistication. Operating the project in this form gives it a more urgent view and that is important in changing the organizational culture to recognize that completing the project is important.

The only dates in a CC schedule will be launch dates for chains of tasks and final due dates associated with related deliverables (Patrick, 2001, p. 6).

27.11 Organizational Challenges Summary

This chapter has presented a project model that has great potential, although culturally difficult to implement. CCM brings with it new processes and concepts related. Before leaving this subject, it will be good to summarize eight of the most significant challenges that organizations will find. The review summary items are the following:

1. *High-level management support:* As with all organization changes the support of senior management is paramount.
2. *Cultural change in managing teams and projects:* CCM changes the way in which project activity is pursued. The entire organization must understand and work with the new paradigm.
3. *Status reporting methods:* Traditional status reports will have to be replaced and all stakeholders will need to be educated in the new approaches. There will likely be the need to compromise some in regard to subproject completion reporting. There are many related status-oriented changes embedded in the CCM. It is important to remember that effective communications to the stakeholder community is a prime goal for the PM. CCM will not be a transparent change in this regard.
4. *Translate estimating techniques to 50% probability:* Taking away time padding will be a major cultural problem because of the stigma of time overrun in the traditional view.
5. *Task overruns are now the norm:* Traditional status reporting looked unfavorably at time overruns. In the CCM model, they are expected. Management and other stakeholders will have to understand this new phenomenon.
6. *Team evaluation:* In a relay race, the team wins and that is the way CCM must work.
7. *Resource allocation and project priorities:* Resource alert and formal project prioritizations are required to manage the work flow process. Both of these issues require more discipline than exists in the typical organization.
8. *Multitasking avoided:* This implies that once a resource is moved to a task, they will work on that task until it is completed. No jumping around to other tasks.

27.12 CC Implementation Strategies

There are two seemingly viable scenarios to introduce the CC model into an organization. The first scenario would be to present CCM as a challenge to an existing high-performance, recognized, and established team that is routinely assigned difficult or high-priority projects. In this case, the team would not likely be intimidated by the change in control approach and their ego could be a stimulus to move higher in respect. This would be similar in behavioral concept to the 1930's Hawthorne experiment in modern times (see Chapter 2). Offering this group the opportunity to utilize the new method to reduce their delivery time, and increase their effectiveness and value to the company, would provide the level of challenge such teams often thrive on. This strategy is similar to introducing a new tool or technology. Successful project delivery by this pilot team would serve to demonstrate the capability of the organization, thus paving the way for wider acceptance.

A second implementation scenario is to introduce the concept in a project with an experienced and respected PM, coupled with a technically proficient team, but not one who is steeped in traditional methodology. Many of the behaviors described in the CCM model would possibly appeal to such a group since they would recognize the logic behind the model. This second type of environment would not be so inclined to protect an existing approach and this would avoid a defensive reaction often found in a traditional team.

27.13 Conclusion

The CC model represents an exciting new option that gives organizations the ability to increase the number of projects that can be done by the same number of resources and to reduce the average duration of projects. This approach offers interesting insights into the slow project completion problems that exist. Even though the processes embedded in the CCM model seem unusual, they really are more of a logical extension of current project management practices than first appears. To focus on these differences may be academically interesting, but one should look at the concepts and see how they might be implemented first prior to taking on the formal model.

This overview of the Critical Chain model concepts examined the basic mechanics and some of the operational complexities associated with the model design. It should be clear to the reader that there are potentially excellent project management ideas embedded in this model in regard to methods for improving project throughput. Certainly, the use of buffering and restricting time estimates could be implemented in some fashion even in the traditional view of projects.

Many organizations today are searching for better ways to achieve major breakthroughs in project development cycle times in order to stay competitive. They need to complete more projects through their organization per unit of resource allocation. This goal must also often be achieved without increasing the number of people allocated to projects, or having the option of hiring additional people. Availability of skilled resources will always be a project constraint in both good and poor economic times. In healthy periods, the aggressive requirement outstrips demand and in tough economic times executives are reluctant to hire even though the demands for new projects remains.

Out of all the project management schemes proposed today, the CC logic is probably the best thought out from a conceptual point of view. The uniqueness of the CC concept is that it hits at the heart of why projects take too long to execute. The best traditional project management process known can be implemented, but so long as padded estimates and multitasking remain the norm, the excessive time results will not change significantly. CC projects in mature support organizations have verified the concepts outlined here and throughput improvement in the 25%–30% range have been demonstrated.

Many of these ideas and processes will be tested in various project environments broadly over the coming years. The logic underlying the CC model concept is so compelling that it is necessary for the modern PM to understand both the power and operational complexity of this model.

***Author note:* A representative CC schedule is available from Frank Patrick's "Critical Chain Scheduling and Buffer Management: Getting Out from between Parkinson's Rock and Murphy's Hard Place." Reference http://www.focusedperformance.com/articles/ccpm.html.

References

Anderson, P., 2001. Study: Multitasking is Counterproductive. http://www.umich.edu/~bcalab/articles/CNNArticle2001.pdf (accessed February 9, 2008).

Bolognese, A.F., 2002. Employee Resistance to Organizational Change. http://www.newfoundations.com/OrgTheory/Bolognese721.html (accessed April 8, 2008).

Christ, D.K., 2001. Theory of Constraints Project Management in Aircraft Assembly. http://www.cnaf.navy.mil/airspeed/content.asp?AttachmentID=57 (accessed April 18, 2008).

Cook, S.C., 1998. Applying Critical Chain to Improve the Management of Uncertainty in Projects. http://www.pqa.net/ProdServices/ccpm/ref/r9z00034.pdf (accessed April 16, 2008).

Geekie, A., 2008. Buffer sizing for the critical chain project management method. *South African Journal of Industrial Engineering*, 19, 1. http://findarticles.com/p/articles/mi_qa5491/is_200805/ai_n25501281 (accessed December 15, 2008).
Goldratt, E., 2007. Critical Chain. http://www.goldratt.co.uk/resources/critical_chain/index.html (accessed April 12, 2008).
Goldratt, E.M., 1997. *Critical Chain*. Great Barrington: The North River Press.
Herroelen, W., R. Leus, and E. Demeulemeester, 2002. Critical chain project scheduling—do not oversimplify. *Project Management Journal*, 33, 4, 48–60
Kendall, I., G. Pitagorsky, and D. Hulett, 2005. Integrating Critical Chain and the PMBOK® Guide. http://logmgt.nkmu.edu.tw/news/articles/criticalChain-PMBOK.pdf (accessed April 12, 2008).
Leach, L., 2005a. EMV and Critical Chain Project Management. http:/pmchallenge.gsfc.nasa.gov/Docs/Presentations2005speakers/Day%202/newideas/LarryLeach.pdf (accessed April 16, 2008).
Leach, L., 2005b. *Lean Project Management: Eight Principles for Success*. Boise: Advanced Projects, incorporated.
Leach, L.P., 2005c. *Critical Chain Project Management*, 2nd ed. Norwood, MA: Artech House. pp. 23, 53.
Newbold, R.C., 1998. *Project Management in the Fast Lane: Applying the Theory of Constraints*. Boca Raton: St. Lucie Press.
Patrick, F.S., 1998. Critical Chain Scheduling and Buffer Management: Getting Out from between Parkinson's Rock and Murphy's Hard Place. p. 6. http://www.focusedperformance.com/articles/ccpm.html (accessed February 9, 2008).
Patrick, F.S., 2001. Critical Chain and Risk Management: Protecting Project Value from Uncertainty. http://www.focusedperformance.com/articles/ccrisk.html (accessed February 9, 2008).
Retief, F., 2002. Overview of Critical Chain Project Management. http://www.hetproject.com/Francois_Retief_paper_Overview_of_Critical_Chain.pdf (accessed April 12, 2008).
Wynne, J., 2006. Running with Change. http://www.gantthead.com/content/articles/232629.cfm (accessed April 12, 2008).

PROJECT EXECUTING, MONITORING, AND CONTROL

The learning objectives for this section are summarized below and involve three major life cycle stages (Executing, Monitor and Control, and Closing). *Executing the Project*—This phase of the project consumes the most resources and is the one focused on creating the approved deliverables.

1. Understand the techniques to measure project performance.
2. Apply established policy in order to identify needs for corrective action.
3. Perform timely corrective action by addressing the problem area root cause in order to eliminate or minimize negative trends.
4. Evaluate the effectiveness of the corrective actions by measuring subsequent performance in order to determine the need for further actions.
5. Ensure compliance with the change management plan by carefully monitoring response to change initiatives in order to manage scope.
6. Manage the process of implementing approved changes to the plan.
7. Manage the allocation of project resources to formally planned work units.
8. Assess work in process to ensure that all activities and only those activities required to produce the project deliverables are performed.
9. Implement the approved project plan by authorizing the execution of project activities and tasks required to produce project deliverables.
10. Communicate project progress by producing execution work performance data needed to provide timely and accurate project status and decision support information to stakeholders.

Monitoring and Control

Monitoring and Control processes cover the entire life cycle of the project, with major focus on the execution phase. The monitoring process involves evaluating work performance data, then producing an analysis of variances to the established baseline. From this activity, required changes will be identified, plans modified, and overall external communication performed.

There are six major control-related topics discussed in this section:

- Execution and control overview
- Change control process
- Project and enterprise metrics
- Earned Value Management (EVM)
- Tracking project progress

Each of these topics introduces some important aspect of monitoring or control. The underlying logic of the chapters in this part covers the following general control concepts:

- Defining the items that are used to identify performance status (i.e., metrics—what to measure)
- Evaluating status throughout the life cycle (tracking)
- Managing the change request process to ensure that the project stays within approved constraints
- Decision-making required to influence direction (performance analysis)
- Managing the project process (final clean-up and lessons learned)

The chapters in this section represent critical control concepts. Surprisingly, many organizations do not accomplish these goals very well. As an example, failure to identify and capture meaningful metrics to evaluate project status means that the wrong performance data are reported and the receiving stakeholders are left with an ineffective understanding of project results. More importantly, the internal decision makers are not given proper information needed for their role in the control process. The philosophical idea of control is to support the project decision-making process and supply needed information to appropriate stakeholders. The following short chapter summaries will highlight the role of each in this context.

Execution and Control Overview (Chapter 28). A common mantra of control says that—*you cannot control what has not been planned.* Each of the control items mentioned in this part and throughout the book has this fundamental requirement built into its internal design mechanism. The basic premise for the execution phase is to produce the approved plan and manage the resource allocation to that goal. In concert with this, the control phase oversees that progress and attempts to influence corrections required based on observed variations from the plan. We must be sensitized to the reality that every project will experience some degree of variation, but the essence of control is to minimize the impact of these variations. The collective tools discussed in this part represent subparts of each formal KA group. The PM must clearly understand these control-oriented processes to achieve project success.

However, there is much more going on in this domain than passive monitoring. It is clear that the PMBOK model management philosophy also focuses on "*influencing*" factors that either may affect, or are affecting project performance. This implies a much more dynamic control process than simply measuring the output. In addition to this, the monitoring and control (M&C) activity list specifies that stakeholders are to be recognized and appropriate performance status reported to them, so there is an honest and open information-sharing component as well. The various operational systems described in this part are important tools in achieving project success.

Change Management (Chapter 29). Change management is a vital activity in the management control process. Failure to keep the level of change at some reasonable level almost surely dooms the project. Too often, scope creep occurs because of excessive or subtle changes have been allowed to creep into the project scope. Each such event adds incremental time and resource effort to the project, with the result being an out-of-control situation. Some change is required, but excessive change is disastrous. It would be controversial to take a hard position on which major control process is most important; however, the management of scope change has to be considered a mandatory control requirement if the goal is to stay within planned boundaries.

Project and Enterprise Metrics (Chapter 30). A metric is a defined quantitative measure used to compare and report project status. This chapter summarizes the use of these in the monitoring and control process. Management and other stakeholders also use these measures to evaluate various aspects of the project. Traditional metrics were output oriented and dealt basically with schedule- and cost-related issues, but the more contemporary approach uses a broader set to focus organizational attention on more strategic objectives. The adage "What gets measured gets done" summarizes how the use of metrics can shape the day-to-day activities of various organizational units.

Earned Value Management (EVM) (Chapter 31). EVM is one of the fastest growing control techniques in the contemporary project management scene. Interest in this concept has been slow to emerge and continues to be a difficult one to implement in many lower maturity organizations; however, there is a growing acceptance of the concept as the underlying infrastructure has improved, along with supporting tools. For the modern PM, EVM must be understood in its potential role for monitoring and control.

A classic control error is observed when status reporting involves only planned versus actual resource consumption status. The Earned Value Management (EVM) discussion will show why such comparisons do not highlight the real issue of status and by itself is misleading. EVM theory emphasizes that effective cost and schedule control requires a focus on work accomplished as well as resources consumed.

Tracking Project Progress (Chapter 32). Regardless of the techniques involved, one of the basic management requirements for every project is to communicate status. The internal project team needs to identify areas of deviation from plan. Likewise, similar elements of this are also important to external management and stakeholders. This chapter will outline the theoretical constructs to be considered in project status tracking.

Closing the Project (Chapter 33). Interest in formal project closing has now become well recognized as a worthwhile and proper activity for the learning organization. Not only is this needed to verify that the required deliverables are produced and accepted by the customer, but there are also associated activities to properly deal with the formal closing and release of project resources and evaluating lessons learned.

Chapter 28

Project Execution and Control

28.1 Introduction

Other than the impact of the real world on the project there is nothing new to be added in this chapter. Unfortunately, the mythical laws of Murphy and Parkinson often serve to create a turbulent and chaotic picture for the project in the real world. Recognizing these real-world factors can often make the project environment appear to be filled with snakes, spiders, and vampires all swirling like the plot of a cheap movie. All through the other chapters of this text, various project management model concepts have been defined with less than subtle hints that each of the related processes can go awry. We also know that the success rate of projects is not good and there must be a reason for that beyond the model descriptions (a lot of these have been previously described). If approximately 50% of the projects are judged to be unsuccessful what is going on? Our theme here is to highlight a reasonable cross-section of ways that project performance can drift away from the defined path. As a project manager (PM), the goal is to "influence" the desired output despite undesirable events that invade our nice model world.

28.1.1 Magic Twelve Success Indicators

We start this journey with a summary list of the *magic twelve* visible indications of a project going well. Each of the following indicates that the project trend is positive:

1. Planned milestones events are being met.
2. Budget is under control.
3. Quality control results are within specifications.
4. Change control process indicates reasonable level of requests for change.
5. Project resources are being supplied per schedule and skill levels are adequate.
6. Project team appears to be cohesive and morale is good.
7. Users seem satisfied with the progress of the work.
8. Top management remains visibly supportive of the project goals.
9. Third-party vendors are delivering quality items on schedule.
10. Risk events are under control and nothing unusual is appearing.

11. Project training program is progressing according to plan.
12. Relationships with support groups appear to have no identifiable issues.

It might be best to describe this list as a wish list because it likely will not be the real-world case. However, this set of attributes does provide a visible overview of desirable attributes representing project execution status. If we observe one or more of these not going so well, it would indicate some underlying management issue that needs to be dealt with. A second point that emerges from this list is that all the knowledge areas (KAs) are simultaneously in play during the execution phase and the list above contains visible components from those KAs.

The Project Management Body of Knowledge (PMBOK®) Guide has defined several model operational execution and control-oriented processes for the project. Previous KA-oriented discussions of these have somewhat described these within a single KA, but these now need to be combined into one working management overview. The model list basically contains the communication and control levers that the PM has at his disposal. If there is a problem with the project, one or more of these processes represents a control knob that needs to be tweaked to correct the deviation. In many ways, one can look at this array of knobs (processes) as the airplane dashboard designed to help a pilot navigate through rough weather. There is a visual display of data providing flight status information and a ground control system providing various status information. From these various sources the skilled pilot (manager) manipulates the knobs with the goal of successfully landing the plane (sometimes not at the planned airport by the way). This metaphor provides the right initial abstraction for the execution and control process.

Table 28.1 summarizes 19 *PMBOK® Guide* processes related to the Execution and Control life cycle domains.

Note that each of the 10 KAs shown here describe a similar goal for this segment of the life cycle. The key management theme for each KA is to keep it within approved plan control limits.

Prior to the project moving into the execution phase, the project management activities have been "soft" in the sense that plans are derived, communications are based on visionary goals, and nothing tangible has gone wrong. One could describe this early segment as a whirlwind of activity, but that does not mirror the activity in the execution and control area. The management efforts in this later segment are more linear in the sense that the issues to resolve that emerge are more defined along the lines shown in Table 28.1.

28.2 The Human Interface

We now have a summary of the execution areas required for this stage. It is now important to interject that these activities are driven by the combination of project status data interleaved with human decision makers. That is where the complexity emerges. To deal with is breadth of decision processes the PM must understand the individual human and team traits associated with these processes. It is in this intersection that the success or failure of the PM emerges.

28.2.1 Project Team Member Motivators

Chapter 17 summarized the Herzberg behavior outlining what motivates individuals and some factors that if not provided become dissatisfiers. Research indicates that individuals will leave or be less productive in their job for both reasons; however, some will stay if the dissatisfiers are met and yet not be motivated to perform. This model offers a good starting point to explore management

Table 28.1 Execution and Control Model Processes

	PMBOK ID	*KA*	*KA Process*
1	4.3	Integration	Direct and manage project work
2	4.4	Integration	Manage project knowledge
3	4.5	Integration	Manage and control project work
4	4.6	Integration	Perform integrated change control
5	5.5	Scope	Validate scope
6	5.6	Scope	Control scope
7	6.6	Schedule	Control schedule
8	7.4	Cost	Control cost
9	8.3	Quality	Control quality
10	9.3	Resource	Acquire team
11	9.4	Resource	Develop team
12	9.5	Resource	Manage team
13	9.6	Resource	Control resources
14	10.2	Communications	Manage communications
15	10.3	Communications	Monitor communications
16	11.7	Risk	Monitor risks
17	12.3	Procurement	Control procurements
18	13.3	Stakeholder	Manage stakeholder engagement
19	13.4	Stakeholder	Monitor stakeholder engagement

actions during the execution stage. Recall that the following are the top seven Herzberg motivators in general order of severity:

1. Achievement
2. Recognition
3. Work assignment
4. Responsibility
5. Advancement
6. Salary
7. Possibility of growth

The top four items on this list are viable factors for the PM to focus on. For each of these items, the goal of allocating recognition rewards should be predicated on performance. These can be looked at as motivational control knobs to improve performance.

28.2.2 Project Team Member Dissatisfiers

On the dissatisfier side of the equation, Herzberg provided an extensive set of potential negative job factors that are more dissatisfiers, but also affect job performance if not properly dealt with. The five highest dissatisfiers ranked in order of severity were:

1. Company policy and administration
2. Supervisor (the PM)
3. Relationship with the supervisor (PM)
4. Working conditions
5. Salary

It should be intuitively obvious that the PM should understand and focus on the motivational items above, but at the same time it is also necessary to deal with minimizing the dissatisfiers. If not properly dealt with, these will cause team members to disengage and even leave the organization. In the dissatisfier category, the primary role of the PM is to shield the team from these and minimize them as much as possible. Company policy and administration issues lie above the level of the project and will be difficult for the PM to change, although he should use every opportunity to shield the project team as much as possible. Items two and three on the list deal with the PM's personal supervisory actions. This involves personal interactions with the team member. The key point for the PM from this list is to be sensitive to these issues and not just focus on the motivators. Inadequate focus on the dissatisfiers can cause loss of team member productivity just as well. As an example, salary and working environment are two items on the dissatisfier list that the PM will struggle with the most. Both are primarily driven by organizational level decisions and therefore somewhat out of the PM range of control. Salary programs often have rules for amounts and the range is not sufficient to make everyone feel like they are paid properly. Personal bias is difficult to overcome here.

The term working conditions has a wide variety of interpretations. Items such as who has an office with a window would be considered a working condition perk in many organizations. Ditto an office with a wall versus an open cubicle. Employees often say that their building is old and dingy as though this is a dissatisfier. However, a refinery engineering group may seem perfectly ok with their open control room environment, while at the same time sitting in the middle of a potentially dangerous environment. To offer some insight into the complexity of this seemingly innocent term, the author once worked on a project that got moved to the back lot in an abandoned Quonset hut with scrap furniture—all seemingly negative work condition items. This facility had zero class or status; nevertheless, that project team was one of the most happy and productive teams ever experienced. We had our own world, team communications were good, and the social environment was great. More important, the team got a lot done without disruption from the main building.

28.2.3 Dealing with Both Positive and Negative Factors

A review of the various positive and negative factors outlined by Herzberg should be used to help guide some of the daily operational approaches one might use. It is up to the PM to evaluate these and see what can be done to mitigate the negatives and stimulate the positives. Something as simple as free pizza for lunch every Friday can go a long way to make working conditions better, and in some ways can even have internal motivation as well. Note that free pizza does not appear in the model list.

The most controversial item among the dissatisfier list is the role that salary plays as both a motivator and a demotivator/dissatisfier. The discussion offered here will likely not change any personal views on this topic, but may offer some insights into the subject. It is common for many companies to have a central HR-derived compensation program that is to be applied consistently to all employees. Experience suggests that the amount offered by these programs is never enough to satisfy the individual, so salary is looked at more as a potential dissatisfier than a motivator in most cases. Even if their team member gets the maximum amount allowed that will only be a positive motivator for a few days. So, how is salary viewed in organizations? HR managers often say that they cannot pay enough to really be a motivator and keep the company competitive, so the compensation plan is designed around two targets: the low target is to try to pay a competitive salary sufficient to keep the individual from being motivated not to leave the company. At the same time, raise amounts would be set to provide some small measure of positive motivation for good performers. The net effect of this is that in most cases salary will not be part of the overall motivation package that the PM can use to any great degree.

Ideally, it would be nice to have a performance bonus for project participants based on some defined set of metrics. In any case, salary issues at best will be a neutral situation in most cases and other motivational strategies will be required.

28.3 Managing the Project

Part of the management action triggers come from comparing plan versus actual measures. An essential question is to define how the status will be transmitted. There are many formal and informal methods for receiving status. Some PMs walk around and observe, while other methods are more quantitative and formality based. For example, we have seen the role of various measurement techniques to highlight schedule, cost, and quality status. Observations related to the volume of change requests, status of risk contingency funds, technical performance measures, test results, and variance analysis all help paint the overall status picture of the project. Beyond these more quantitative and mechanical values unstructured conversations with team members, sponsors, users, and senior management add an additional level of understanding to the status view (in some cases, a timelier and better one).

28.3.1 Status-Tracking Processes

Status tracking basically attempts to map how the project is moving in comparison with the approved plan. There are two important execution and control concepts that must be in place for the tracking process to work. First, a well-defined plan with quantifiable objectives is necessary to establish comparison targets. Without this base, there are no measurable targets that can be used to identify the project goals. Second, the control process involves measuring actual performance against these planning targets. These two concepts are called the *Siamese twins of management*. Another important control concept is that of a baseline. Baselines can be established for any parameter of the project (i.e., cost, schedule, speed, weight, etc.), although they typically focus on scope, schedule, cost, and quality metrics. One of the management problems with comparing ongoing status to the original baseline parameters is that approved changes by the project board can logically change the original baseline and by that action create a variance that is not produced by the actions of the project team. This means that the Integrated Change Control (ICC) process activity becomes a vital component of management and control. The point to be made here is that any changes that are approved to the baseline values need to be incorporated into the control process, but that is often not done. Let us illustrate the potential magnitude of this problem. Scope creep in technical projects is often in the range of 2% per month. So, for a one-year project this amounts to a 24% increase in project scope, which in turn would likely have a significant impact on schedule and budget. Does this mean the project team has done a poor job? Maybe the requirements definition process was done poorly, or maybe the environment changed. At any rate, simple comparisons with the original baseline may not be measuring the correct status view. Keeping the original baseline and adjusting it for approved changes would seem to give a more balanced set of data for evaluation. Alternatively, keep the original for historical comparison and the updated on for performance analysis. The original baseline comparison would show the project variance compared to the approved version and the current baseline would help to show performance compared to the formally approved scope of work.

As a PM, one of the most important aspects of control is to get formal sign-off of the requirements. Given this, the changes that occur after that should be relatively low in volume. This adds more credibility to the notion that the current baseline should be the primary measurement metric.

During execution, work units are completed in various Work Breakdown Structure (WBS) segments. Given the Performance Measurement Baseline (PMB) described in Chapter 15, this information can be translated into overall status. Using this comparative data, the listing below summarizes various formal project control-oriented activities that collectively deal with project status data and analytics. These collectively are the PM's information source that will be used to support any needed corrective action. They are as follows:

1. *Scope control:* This involves various factors that influence project scope changes and corrective actions associated with that activity. The change control system is an integral part of this process.
2. *Scope verification:* This process deals with formal customer acceptance of the completed project deliverables.
3. *Schedule control:* This involves the use of various tools and techniques to evaluate and influence the status of the project schedule and related variances. Work performance data is used to help evaluate project status.
4. *Cost control:* This involves the use of various tools and techniques to evaluate and influence the status of the project baseline budget and related variances. It is also a portion of the ICC system. The goal of this activity is to keep the project within budget limits.
5. *Quality control:* This "involves the monitoring project results to determine whether they comply with relevant quality standards and identifying ways to eliminate causes of unsatisfactory results." Another major supporting activity is to influence process quality improvements.
6. *Project team performance:* This involves several quantitative and qualitative processes to track team and individual performance and provide feedback.
7. *Status meetings*: Status meetings provide an unstructured communication forum for team members to share their experiences and inform other team members of their plans.
8. *Risk monitoring and control:* This involves monitoring the risk register and other sources for the emergence of both identified and unidentified risks. Once previously identified or new risk items emerge, there is a management activity required to properly handle each category.

9. *Third-party deliverable status:* Monitoring of third-party activities is essentially done through the contract administration process. Key metrics here are deliverables, funds flow, and status reports.
10. *Risk audits:* This examines and documents the effectiveness of risk responses in dealing with identified risks and their root causes, as well as the effectiveness of the overall risk management process.
11. *Reserve analysis:* This compares the status of contingency and management reserves for the project to ascertain whether the remaining reserves are sufficient.
12. *Variance and trend analysis:* This process is used to translate the raw data into meaningful decision format. Both the degree of the variance and the trends are important metrics for the PM. These also lead to corrective actions and completion estimates for various project parameters.
13. *Technical performance measurement (TPM):* This represents a set of techniques to identify deficiencies in meeting system requirements, and provides early warning of technical problems and related technical risks. This process attempts to compare the ongoing project with specified performance goals to estimate the degree of success in achieving the project's scope.
14. *Performance data:* This involves collecting data from various sources regarding project performance and then comparing these values to established baselines. Summary regarding scope, schedule, budget, quality, risk, procurement, and team resources is used to evaluate overall status. Collectively, these parameters aid the PM and team and are used to define status to appropriate stakeholders.
15. *Managing stakeholder expectations*: This activity involves keeping appropriate stakeholders involved in the overall project.

The status data and analytic-oriented processes outlined above are internally focused on project results versus the baseline plan. In addition to these sources, additional insight into the project status is obtained from a less formal set of external sources. These relate to the project sponsor, senior management, future users, and possibly outside regulatory-oriented sources. Each of these perspectives can have a bearing on the project future and need to be assessed by the PM, even though that data may be difficult to obtain and less formal in format.

One of the most likely external control issues that can affect the project relates to the original vision. In some cases, the organization objectives change before the project is completed and/or the external market for the product changes because of some economic or technology event. In any case, this means that the existing specifications may be wrong, and it is up to the PM to air these issues with appropriate management. In this situation, a PM must be willing to shut the project down or significantly change directions if that is in the best interests of the company. The paramount consideration is that the project is to maintain alignment to organizational goals and stay aligned with that notion. One of the dangers of a project is that it will finish successfully according to the plan only to find that the reason it was chartered is no longer valid. This situation is difficult for the PM to deal with, but he needs to be sensitive to the point (i.e., landing his plane successfully at the wrong airport). With this dual set of success criteria, the execution management goal portion is to complete the project according to an approved plan that aligns with *current* organizational goals.

28.3.2 Turning the Management Control Knobs

Through all the defined communications paths we have defined a collective status delivery perspective. As some aspects of the project begin to show a troublesome variance management actions are needed. We liken this to turning a specific control knob with the intention of influencing the status back to the planned value. Just to complete this thought, the control panel will light up with such events and they do not come one at a time for handling. KA-related variations often come in waves, so a second management issue is to decide which items to deal with first and will fixing one create an even worse situation elsewhere. In other words, the knobs are not independent and changing one variable in the process can cause other situations to change as well. The level of variance chaos to expect is correlated with how accurate the original plan was. If the plan was well thought out and the support organization is mature, then one might expect the work to flow somewhat according to that plan with a reasonable level of issues to deal with. Otherwise, a poorly created plan can leave the PM fighting all KA status issues at one time.

Since our management control knobs are metaphorical we must translate this into the physical management reality of the knob-turning process. When some execution event needs to be corrected, the management process most often deals with a decision involving human elements either internal or external to the team. The trigger for action is often a defined variance in plan versus actual for a defined work unit. When that happens, the project schedule, budget, or other output status is in jeopardy. If the target work unit is on the critical path it might be necessary to add resources to bring the project back in line. However, if budget status is more critical than time it might be better to let the project schedule slip.

As a second example, when human resource conflicts emerge they need to be dealt with in a timely manner. The style of resolution can have wide-ranging positive or adverse impacts on the project situation (review the events above to evaluate how conflicts impact each area). In many cases, human conflicts are hard to match to a work unit, but from more random sources. Once again, the management issue is which control knob to turn. The option in this case is the management knob that has the PM's authority and influence attached (there are some authority-related knobs that are not available to the PM). Our two examples have shown that control mechanics can be a tangible decision (money or human reallocation) or a communications decision that is designed to influence behavior. In all such control scenarios, the goal is to influence the project variables to a more desirable state—schedule, cost, scope, quality, morale, and so on.

One of the control concepts that is often difficult to understand initially is the interaction across the impact areas. As an example, the late delivery of an item by a third-party contractor can impact several different internal areas (i.e., schedule, budget, resources, activities, etc.). Having a team member do a customer a "quick favor" by making an unauthorized and unapproved change can result in schedule, budget, quality, and risk issues. So, the last step before turning a control (change) knob is to attempt to evaluate the consequences of that action.

Hopefully, the use of the physical airplane analogy for the information dashboard and control knobs has not been too abstract. A much more idealistic metaphor is the orchestra maestro who waves his baton and the orchestra members follow the "plan." If the musical "plan" is well designed the outcome can be beautiful based on the skills of the members. This metaphor is correct up to a point, but falls apart when we must admit that some of the players are not in synch. In that case, waving the baton will not correct the problem. This view does not show the control aspect of the orchestra leader very well when the organizational and staffing environment is in place. However, both examples are still interesting enough to keep in mind as a management perspective. We would like to develop the team to the point where we can be more of a maestro and less of a control knob-turning-oriented manager.

One of the common reasons why projects get into stress during execution is the negative impact that changes have on the plan and the project team. As the volume of these grows, there is increased coordination resulting from the related resource allocation changes required and the interaction of the change across the overall project becomes unwieldy to manage. Ideally, the PM would like to edict that no changes will be made in the project, but that is seldom a viable option. The best compromise is to establish a formal and rigorous integrated change control process. The model acronym name for such a process is ICC and it deals with the following activities (PMI, 2017, p. 152):

- Manage the process for analyzing, reviewing, executing, and implementing a project change.
- Decide resolution to all change requests.
- Manage the overall project baselines and management constraints.
- Ensure that appropriate documentation and configuration control are followed.
- Act as an agent for the sponsor to manage project changes in concert with the Charter and approved baseline values.

The ICC process operates under the oversight of a project board that represents the organizational management and project sponsor. It is their responsibility to protect the project from excessive changes and to help keep the project on track from an overall perspective. This process represents more than just the scope change control activity. It is also the focal point for recommended internal project process changes that can improve operational productivity and quality. A third area of activity for the ICC is configuration management control. During a project's life cycle, a great deal of documentation is produced. Lack of version control for these artifacts can be just as damaging as lack of scope control.

The PM reacts to the ICC process primarily by analyzing proposed changes and managing approved requests. PM's basic role involves providing technical assistance to the decision process of the project board, re-planning the project based on approved changes, and managing work execution through implementation. A second thread of activity occurs in the improvement side of the ICC role. These actions could originate from lessons learned sources, or other inputs from the team which are then converted into change requests. Handled properly, the ICC process brings a measure of project operational stability that would not otherwise be possible.

28.4 Human Relations and Communications Issues

Beyond the general control-oriented activities outlined earlier, a great deal of the PM's time is spent with the daily decision-making and influencing activities involving various human resources internal or external to the project. Winters says that poor communication, vaguely understood project goals and objectives, and poor leadership pave the way to project failure (Winters, 2003). From these and other studies we can conclude that communications failures are at the heart of many control-related issues. It has been previously stated that 90% of a PM's time should be spent in various forms of communication. For this discussion, we will focus on the communications issues around the major human-related management processes dealing with team acquisition, development, and general management.

28.4.1 Team Acquisition

The basics of the team acquisition process were outlined in Chapter 17 and the major item to add here is that the initial acquisition decision may not be permanent. This second phase occurs when a team member does not deliver planned results, leaves the project early, or the functional department planned staff commitment does not occur. Also, it is important to recognize that failure to properly staff the work activities is the most direct way to lose control of the project output. If the original staffing estimates were accurate, but the actual staffing rate was slow, it is reasonable to predict that the project schedule will drift. This same result can occur if the functional managers do not live up to their skill level commitment for staffing. Given the direct impact that staffing has on the project, staffing status is a vitally important metric needed by the PM. That is, tracking and managing the allocation of skilled team members to work units. Of all the mechanical management tasks, this one is the most vital.

28.4.2 Team Development

Project team development relates to the processes involved in improving productivity of the team and its members. This is both a short-term and long-term management activity. Short-term actions can improve the process for the current project, but long-term-oriented actions have the potential to transform the resource skills along a path of continuous career improvement that impacts future project performance.

28.4.3 General Management Perspectives

As project teams are initially formed, there is typically some level of internal confusion as to roles and responsibilities. Later, with proper management, the team begins to form into a more cohesive unit and productivity grows. Tuckerman defines a four-stage model for team development: forming, norming, storming, and performing (Wong, 2007). In the forming stage, each member of the team focuses on the leader, accepting his guidance and authority, and maintaining a polite but distant relationship with the other team members. In the storming stage, team members are often more concerned with the impression they are making than the project in hand. They want to be respected and often battle feelings of inadequacy, wondering who will support or undermine them, and above all, proving their value to the team. The third (norming) stage moves the group into the resulting work group (good or bad) in which group feelings and cohesiveness develops, performance standards evolve, and new roles are adopted. At this stage, personal opinions are being expressed more freely (Tuckman, 2001). During the fourth stage, known as performing, a less structured environment is needed because the team members understand their roles and group energy is channeled into the task. At this point, structural and relationship issues have been resolved, and the resulting structure now generates the required performance (Smith, 2005). Not every project completely goes through this evolution, but in any case, management of the project team requires PM involvement as team members find their individual identities and roles. These are not necessarily well-defined management roles for the PM, but often more of a behavioral relationship approach to dealing with the team. Examples of management actions often used during the team-building stage are:

1. Training programs to improve team and individual skills
2. Interpersonal activities to build morale and improve performance
3. Using recognition and reward to motivate positive performance
4. Developing an effective team communication environment
5. Creating a climate conducive to high productivity
6. Providing appropriate leadership
7. Resolving conflicts that occur
8. Providing timely team and individual performance feedback

Note that most of the items outlined above are more of a behavioral relationship in nature and these occur throughout the full life cycle. Also, many of these can occur in parallel along with some other management action. As an example, process training can occur when monitoring the process of dealing with an unrealistic change request, or an internal team conflict over a controversial technology-oriented disagreement. Collectively, the method by which the PM manages the work environment of the project team will dictate many other aspects of the project outcome, both for the project deliverables, team culture, and future skills of the participants.

28.4.4 Managing Team Performance

Evaluation of overall team performance can lead to various strategies for improving outcomes. This evaluation can determine such things as tasks being frequently delivered late, not delivering what has been requested, making poor use of the tools and resources, or not integrating work efforts well. Each of these represents visible signs of a need to improve some aspect of the team. The Father of Quality, Edwards Deming, stated that the cause for poor performance was mostly related to poor processes, inadequate training, or poor management. So, based on this classical observation, much of the team development potential comes from improving project processes and team skills. This means that the PM must focus attention on the work processes being used and an individual assessment improving worker's skills. If this evaluation is not viewed by the individual as punitive, it can be a positive motivational event. The fact is, every person has some developmental need and they should be introspective enough to know what that is. The same can be said of every process, so constant attention is needed to both skill and process improvement areas. Skill changes can be dealt with through formal training or mentoring activities, while process issues would fall into more fundamental corrective arena.

28.4.5 Team Training

Once the basic team analysis is done, a training program should be defined in concert with the team members. This activity needs to be viewed as a positive exercise for career development and not punishment for being sent to school. Training can be provided in many forms, and in some cases, on-the-job training with a good mentor is even more effective than going to a class (Munby, 2008, p. 37). The operational reality of training is that it takes the individual away from "productive" project work and it consumes resources that are not actively focused on the defined deliverables. Organizations are fortunate if they have adequate budgetary funds to execute these types of improvement programs as they also contribute to improved motivation levels and help build a stronger resource pool over the longer period. Companies that shun training tend to lock their methods and skill base with the long-term result to become less competitive. Good PMs contribute to their organizations future by improving their team member skills so that when the individual moves to the next project they are better skilled than before. In this view, the "team development" goal is both designed to improve the current project and the future career of the individual.

Formal efforts to improve team and individual performance are not just a set of mechanics. Technically focused PMs often ignore improvement of soft skills. Other valuable skills involve topics such as effective listening, conversational skills, communication dynamics, presentation skills, and working with diverse cultures, among others. For team members to grow in the organization capabilities, mentoring and coaching are valuable techniques to consider for training efforts. These are not only good training topics for the junior team member, they build the confidence and knowledge levels for the senior member as well (Ivancevich et al., 2008, pp. 411–433). Each of these formal development strategies contributes to the overall skill development of the project team and represents a key management activity item for the PM.

One final point on team development. The younger generation does not have the same view of organizations, management, training, and a host of other attitudes that are common in middle-age PMs. So, in order to be effective with skill development it will be necessary to evaluate how best to plan the training programs. The new generation worker is very bright, technology savvy, and they may be more comfortable approaching the learning process in a different manner. Recent research indicates that dealing with younger employees has forced some employers to also rethink how they evaluate employee performance (Hite, 2008).

28.4.6 Team Training

When evaluating the solutions and action plans to develop the team, a similar approach to the one described for individual development can be used. If done properly, the development and contributions of individual employees should align with the team goals. Identifying the right set of skills for the team is a key for improvement in overall team performance. However, the one required team training feature is to focus on the interaction processes between team members versus simply dealing with an individual's current skill level.

One of the harsh realities of team development is to recognize that this activity is constrained by time and cost. Beyond the resource limit issue, the training approach should strive to develop the team by blending their innate skills and talents to achieve far more than would be accomplished by ignoring that aspect (McCabe, 2006, pp. 116–121). This concept should be the training mantra in team development activity.

Table 28.1 has illustrated the wide variety of execution and control management processes, including task integration, quality assurance, risk, communications, budgets, schedules, and procurement. Improper management in any of these areas can lead to adverse results in the overall project status. This point is just one more warning sign that successful project management is a very complex undertaking and requires a broad focus across the KAs.

28.4.7 Team Motivation and Morale

Team motivation and morale is certainly an issue that PMs must deal with throughout the execution phase of any project. Classical motivation theory attempts to explain how the work environment affects motivation and productivity (Bjørnebekk, 2008, pp. 153–170). Also, Myers research shows that there are first- and second-level factors affecting motivation (Myers, 1964). And previous discussion regarding the Hertzberg motivation and maintenance factors show specific areas of management that must be dealt with to preserve a positive outlook. Regardless of the strategy followed, only when employees have their own intrinsic needs reasonably satisfied, can real motivation exist (Herzberg, 2003, pp. 87–96)? Human needs are difficult to fully meet, so the key word here is "reasonable." One way to determine an employee's job motivation level is to by monitor their performance. The opportunity, capacity, and willingness to perform yield insights into appropriate management actions. Team performance is ultimately linked to individual's task-related skills, abilities, knowledge, and experiences (Ivancevich et al., 2008). It is up to the PM to ensure that the employee knows what needs to be done, plus how and when something needs to be done. High performance levels are not possible without this foundation. Once again, we see management's important role in the productivity equation beyond just building member level skills.

Another aspect of an individual's productivity is related to their personality profile. Some are motivation seekers, whereas others are maintenance seekers. For motivation seekers, "the greatest satisfaction and strongest motivation is derived from achievement, responsibility, growth, advancement, work itself, and earned recognition" (Myers, 1964, pp. 73–88). Maintenance seekers are motivated by the nature of their environment and tend to be less interested in motivation variables. "This group is chronically preoccupied and dissatisfied with maintenance factors such as pay, benefits, supervision, working conditions, status, job security, company policy and administration, and fellow employees" (Myers, 1964, pp. 73–88). These specific attributes can be seen in the Herzberg research results described in Chapter 17. In either situation, the PM is trying to maximize the motivation items and minimize the maintenance factors.

There are three components that make up individual motivation: direction, intensity, and persistence (Kidman and Hanrahan, 2004). Direction indicates if the person is motivated toward or away from a situational experience (Di Rodio, 2002). For example, if the employee is asked to work on a project with another group or individual and there are issues between them, the employee may opt to make a legitimate effort, or disengage and work alone. If the employee does agree, their primary motivation comes from the desire to comply with management directions. Conversely, if the employee chooses the second alternative of doing the job alone, there is still motivation but in this case, it does not show a desire to comply with management directions. The intensity of motivation may be the total amount of effort a person will make to satisfy a motive over time (Brehm and Self, 1989, pp. 109–131). Each employee's motivational response is different, and it may be observed quickly or later. As an example, imagine what happens to motivation when a team member identifies an issue, communicates it to the PM, and the PM fails to act quickly to resolve it? In this case, the employee concludes that the manager does not care what they think, thus, their motivation intensity will decrease over time.

Persistence is another component of motivation. This is defined as the ability to maintain action, regardless of the individual's feelings. Some employees will press on even when they feel like quitting (Pavlina, 2005). Still, this is not a good long-term situation and needs to be addressed. Managers who can identify and understand the presence of these individual motivational differences will be more effective at determining proper ways to correct such issues. For example, a reward and recognition program that links performance and behaviors can increase both the level of intensity and persistence.

28.4.8 Formal Meetings

A major management strategy for communication is to hold group meetings. This is a method to both communicate and collect status information. Traditional meetings involve bringing all or part of the team together for a face-to-face information sharing. These events can either be the richest form of team culture building, or the biggest waste of team productivity. Both results are in the hands of the PM. There are several forms of group meetings and these sessions can be also used for both technical and social purposes. Technically oriented meetings are used to disseminate information to the group that requires common understanding, technical problem solving, or status communication. It should be recognized that group socialization is a required process and a valuable part of the team-building process. The role of these sessions is to improve the interpersonal relationships of the group and rigorous information focus is not the main agenda.

A second form of meeting is group dissemination of key information. In this case, the topic is judged to be significant and complex enough to warrant holding the session. This can involve new company policy, a major initiative, reorganization, or other such events that has mutual interest to the group.

A third form of meeting involves the need to work out details related to work-oriented issues, such as methods to execute planned work. This format tends to be more of a longer time work session than an informational meeting.

The fourth form of meeting is the one most often misused. That is, a group meeting in which individuals get together to discuss some problem that could be handled by sending out a written version. This class of meeting often has no agenda and the participants have limited interest in the data being discussed. Even worse, such meeting can go well beyond the one-hour limit where attention spans begin to fade.

Regardless of the meeting type, the group should know in advance what the goal of the meeting is as evidenced by a defined agenda and the appropriate attendees. The meeting should start and finish on schedule. At the end of the session, decisions made are delegated to assigned parties for execution, formal minutes published, and future follow-up pursued. During the course of the meeting, formal rules of interchange are obeyed, and appropriate input is sought. When these basic meeting rules are not followed the value of the session is compromised.

Regardless of the meeting format or goal there are some fundament rules of procedure to follow. The issues of defined agenda and time-block remain important for all meetings. There are three fundamental meeting rules that apply to all meeting models. These are:

- Punctuality
- Rules of order
- Appropriate subject matter

Punctuality: A meeting can be mechanically destroyed by not starting and finishing on schedule. If the meeting is worth having, it is worth being on time. If participants have other activities to plan, it must be ended on scheduled time. A radical approach to this could be to lock the door at scheduled time to make this point—a little radical, but could establish the culture. One thought on meeting culture is to make the point to all that it is impolite to the group to hold up the session waiting for late arrivals. As a side note, the author observes that academic meetings are a classic example of poor punctuality and time overrun. Trying to explain that behavior is beyond our scope here.

Rules of order: Some organizations use formal rules of order for voting and other communication aspects of the meeting. Normally, such rigor is not required; however, disciple and good behavior are mandatory traits. Having multiple concurrent speakers are a mandatory no-no and it is up to the meeting chair to limit side conversations. If the goal is to share information, trying to listen to multiple conversations at one time is impossible. Establishing a team culture that all meetings have a business-like and polite behavior among the participants is a required culture.

Subject matter: As suggested above, having a circle of individuals verbalize their status for last month is seldom a worthwhile exercise for the team. So, what is worthwhile? One rule of thumb is that if it has already happened, we cannot change it. However, it may be worthwhile to perform a *lessons learned* exercise from past actions to improve future performance. One interesting strategy is to challenge the group to outline issues that could occur (risk oriented) over a coming period (next two weeks to a month ahead). Also, troublesome operational issues that are now known could be viable topics.

The key often-ignored issue with meetings is lack of recognition that they are expensive and seldom produce the value compared to the cost. When they do occur, the goal must be to have a clear focus and minimum time. One of the popular software development methodologies (see Chapter 25) requires a daily meeting to discuss key items for that day. It lasts for less than

30 minutes and everyone stands-up for the duration. Normally, this frequency is not justified, but the standing-up rule might be interesting to try. Food and comfortable seating can certainly contribute to elongating the meeting time.

As an example of what can go wrong with a meeting let's look at the often-observed situation of a status meeting. For this, it is common to bring groups together to discuss status of their individual components and this becomes the *dangerous meeting*. One reason why it is dangerous is because it wastes valuable time with essentially no return value. This format offers the forum for various players to talk about past status events that have no relevance to the future of the overall team. One must be wary of this model meeting as individuals often are trying to advertise their accomplishments more than communicating valuable information. The PM needs to think about for this type situation and all meetings in general to assess whether the session is worth the cumulative cost and time of the individuals involved and is the subject matter worthy of a meeting. In many cases, the answer to this question would be a clear negative. Team members often indicate that they get more out of free small group conversation that occurs before and after the meeting than in the meeting itself.

28.4.9 Management Style

Another factor affecting execution is the degree and style of management involvement. While management may be highly involved during the planning phase, this often declines as the project moves into the more technical aspects of the work. In many cases, the lack of management visibility begins to be interpreted as a lack of commitment toward the project, whereas the manager might be thinking that the project was moving along so well that he is not needed and would be in the way. The visibility and style of management involvement is important for various reasons. One of the key roles is that of protecting unnecessary changes to the project. A second role may well be even more important. Recall the Hawthorne experiment revealed that workers felt important with leadership attention. Simply stated, a key management role is to help the project team overcome roadblocks to success.

Regarding this coordinative role there are multiple management issues, ranging from simple to complex, that team members alone do not have the breadth of authoritative view to resolve some issues. For example, two engineers may differ regarding the way a design decision should be made. One engineer may be thinking from the design elegance point of view, whereas the other may think from a manufacturing point of view. For the most part, managers should serve as mediators and help provide proper and timely support to ensure that the facts are properly interpreted. Conflict management is clearly one of these roles and occupies approximately 20% of the typical PM's time. Proper involvement in the conflict resolution process is necessary, but it can be a team demotivator if not handled properly. Being a trusted and fair participant in the problem solution can stimulate and motivate the team. It can also serve as a mentoring opportunity in the hope that team members will get better at internal problem resolution. In general, active PM involvement will improve the overall image of the project in the team member's eyes and will serve as a style example to follow.

Failure to deal with situations of this type can breed resentment among the team members and this is visible in several ways. Based on Tuckman's four-stage development model described earlier, the needs and roles of management change through the stages (McCabe, 2006). In the early project stages, management involvement is needed to handle the role and relationship gaps that have yet to form. By the time the fourth stage emerges, the role of manager becomes more of helper than manager. Obviously, it is important to be able to recognize what the team needs and wants regarding management oversight. In some cases, the PM gets accustomed to being the knowledge base for the team, when at some later point the team has built their knowledge base beyond the PM. Many senior executives seem to believe that because they have been promoted to a high level in the organization, they now have God-given knowledge on all subjects, when in fact they have become so isolated that they know very little about their internal organization or what is the best way to proceed. To a degree, this is what happens as the project reaches the fourth, performing, stage of development.

One interesting characteristic of fourth-stage teams is their high internal cohesiveness and tendency to operate within their own established guidelines and resist cooperation with management. This situation can be very disturbing to some PMs who are not treated as royalty any longer, but in fact this behavior may be a sign of a very productive team. It takes a very secure management professional to deal with a mature team at this stage. At this point, the team is aware that they know more about the mechanics of how to get the job done than the PM does, so his suggestions will not be greeted with open arms. The problem-solving process becomes more internal to the team and less involved with the manager. PMs who cannot change their style from the more hierarchical model will be frustrated by this event. However, the same resistance can result in a team that is not highly productive and when that occurs a more aggressive management style must take over to change the result. So, the PM must understand the team capabilities and recognize which form of management is best. If the negative situation occurs, textbook behavioral theory is not so relevant and more drastic authoritative action is required. Once other positive motivational avenues have been explored, it may be necessary to transfer one or more team members out and in extreme cases dismiss them from the organization (Mind Tools, 2008). Regardless of the proper strategy needed, a good manager must be able to handle a wide range of behavioral situations.

28.5 Conclusion

The execution phase brings to bear all the KA issues at one time. Failure to have in place a viable plan can raise all the control issues outlined here, thereby creating chaos for the PM. However, if we assume a reasonable project plan, then management of the execution process becomes much more coherent. Some management actions are monitoring and analysis oriented, whereas others deal more with influencing behavior of individuals or the whole team. In almost all the management situations outlined in this chapter the PM skill required involves a good understanding of the softer side of human interactions.

Project teams will be developed through various types of training and process development. In addition to this, the PM needs to be aware of various motivation and dissatisfier variables that can impact the team's performance in either a positive or a negative manner. It is important to provide the team members with the required training and tools, but those alone are not sufficient. Capacity, lack of trust, and compensation are other issues that may also affect the team behavior and consequently their performance. If not addressed properly and in a timely manner, those issues may result in lack of motivation, development of negative group cohesiveness (groupthink), and resentment toward management within others. Understanding differences in opinions and behaviors within team members is a key factor when dealing with such situations. Each individual has a unique way of thinking and processing the information. Consequently, what will work for some individuals will not work for all. Similarly, managing all teams the same way will not provide the same results.

Execution issues require a root cause analysis to identify the problem, as well as the reasons behind the situation or behavior. Only then will a manager be able to act and provide a feasible solution to the problem. When working on those decisions, managers should consider that one minor mistake might cause major issues with the team; hence, the importance of developing team-building exercises, having defined and consistent communications guidelines, and ensuring management involvement.

Discussion Questions

1. How do you assess the general status of a project?
2. Describe two of the *control knobs* that a PM might use to correct a project's direction.
3. Can scope creep be controlled? Define some measures for this.
4. What is the role of ICC in the control process?
5. Is salary a motivator? Offer some ideas as to how the PM can provide compensation within the central organizational guidelines.
6. Are meetings an effective collaboration process?

References

Bjørnebekk, G., 2008. Positive affect and negative affect as modulators of cognition and motivation: the rediscovery of affect in achievement goal theory. *Scandinavian Journal of Educational Research* 52(2):153–170

Brehm, J.W. and E.A. Self, 1989. The intensity of motivation. *Annual Review of Psychology*. Vol. 40:109–13

Di Rodio, W., 2002. An exploration of the concept 'motivation' as a tool for psychotherapeutic assessment. Practical philosophy. *The Journal of the Society for Philosophy in Practice*. 5(2): 52–58.

Herzberg, F., 2003. One more time: how do you motivate employees? *Harvard Business Review*, January, 87–99.

Hite, B., 2008. Employers rethink how they give feedback. *The Wall Street Journal*, October 13. https://www.wsj.com/articles/SB122385967800027549 (accessed November 20, 2017).

Ivancevich, J., R. Konopaske, and M. Matteson, 2008. *Leadership in Organizational Behavior and Management*, 8th ed. New York: McGraw-Hill/Irwin.

Kidman, L. and S. Hanrahan, 2004. *Creating a Positive Environment, the Coaching Process: A Practical Guide to Improving Your Effectiveness*. Wellington: Dunmore Press.

McCabe, M., 2006. Accelerating teamwork: a personal reflection. *Musculoskeletal Care*.

Mind Tools Ltd, 2008. Coaching for team performance: improving productivity by improving relationships. *Mind Tools Ltd*. http://www.mindtools.com/pages/article/newTMM_66.htm (accessed November 20, 2017).

Munby, S., 2008. Learning on the job makes good leaders. *Times Educational Supplement*.

Myers, M.S., 1964. Who are your motivated workers? *Harvard Business Review*, 42, 73–88.

Pavlina, S., 2005. Self-discipline: persistence. http://www.stevepavlina.com/blog/2005/06/self-discipline-persistence (accessed May 4, 2018).

PMI, 2017. *A Guide to the Project Management Body of Knowledge (PMBOK® Guide)*, 6th ed. Newtown Square, PA: Project Management Institute.

Smith, M.K., 2005. Bruce W. Tuckman—forming, storming, norming and performing in groups, the encyclopedia of informal education. http://www.infed.org/thinkers/tuckman.htm (accessed November 20, 2017).

Tuckman, B.W., 2001. Developmental sequence in small groups. *Group Facilitation: A Research and Applications Journal*.

Winters, F., 2003. The Top Ten Reasons Projects Fail (Part 7), August. https://www.projectmanagement.com/articles/187449/The-Top-Ten-Reasons-Projects-Fail—Part-7- (accessed May 4, 2018).

Wong, Z., 2007. *Key Stages of Technical Development, Human Factors in Project Management: Concepts, Tools, and Techniques for Inspiring Teamwork and Motivation*. San Francisco, CA: Wiley.

Chapter 29

Change Management

29.1 Introduction

Effective change management is a vital and key ingredient to the success of projects and project management. Successful integration of change management into all aspects of a project life cycle is one of the most critical processes related to a successful outcome. In highly technical projects, where cutting-edge technology and requirements seem to constantly change, project managers (PMs) must be highly regimented in their approach to dealing with the related dynamics. As part of this process it is important to track, understand, and quantify the impact of each change to the approved project plan baseline. This suggests that the defined change management process must be formal and rigorously followed by all participants. Leadership, team focus, and effective communication are very important aspects associated with an effective change control process. Improper change procedures will result in confused expectations from various stakeholders as the initial project goals change. A key ingredient of the change process is to not only control the changes being proposed to the project, but to also communicate the status of those proposed to appropriate organizational elements.

29.2 Integrated Change Control

The Integrated Change Control (ICC) process involves identifying, evaluating, and managing changes throughout the project life cycle (Schwalbe, 2006, p. 151). One major operational objective of ICC is to ensure that the changes that are made after the plan is approved are supportive of the current organizational needs. A key question is to determine whether the value of the change is greater than the additional resources required and the disruption that it brings. "The original defined project scope and the integrated performance baseline must be maintained by continuously managing changes to the baseline, either by rejecting new changes or by approving changes and incorporating them into a revised configuration baseline" (Love, 2004).

The PM must be vigilant to the various change activities that occur on a daily basis. Each change represents a miniproject in its own right in that each has a life cycle from proposal to implementation. No change should be made to the original requirements unless it is deemed worthwhile, taking into consideration the downside of interrupting the existing plan. *Scope creep* is a term used to describe the expansion of project requirements over time. Without an effective change control system this class of events can crater the projects chance for success. Even the use of an effective change control system can suffer if the initial requirements were poorly done. Also, there are situations where the project target environment undergoes a radical change and this can cause levels of scope creep that challenge the manageability of the project.

Uncontrolled changes have subtle effects on the underlying project variables, which over time may negatively reflect the customer's view of the project. Generally speaking, requirement changes have high potential to create additional work for the project team, which then can impact schedule, project costs, resource plans, and additional risks. The following is a sample list of possible implications from a single change. It may cause:

- An expansion or reduction of project scope
- An expansion or reduction of product features
- An expansion or reduction in performance requirements
- An expansion or reduction in quality requirements
- A significant change in the target milestone or completion dates
- A shift in the implementation or deployment strategy
- An increase in resource costs
- An expansion or reduction in the project budget
- A change in any of the project objectives
- A change in any of the final acceptance criteria, including ROI forecasts
- A change in any of the project assumptions, constraints, or dependencies, especially regarding resources and work effort estimates
- A shift in project roles or responsibilities, especially on projects with contractual arrangements
- A decision to reset the performance baselines due to an unrecoverable performance variance

One metaphor for the change process is that it is like dropping a large rock in a pond. The waves reach across the entire surface and disrupt the project boat. Even small changes can have a similar impact.

Rapid and constant evolution of cutting-edge technology will make technology projects some of the most difficult to accomplish successfully. In this environment PMs are dealing with a constant state of change since stakeholders, users, and engineers are frequently at odds over requirements and technology direction to achieve those objectives. Recognition of this dilemma was one of the major drivers in the life cycle management movement that is partially reflected in this text. One of the results of this is a stronger push to better define requirements prior to execution and a corresponding focus on change management through the project.

Based on research by various organizations, there is a consistency in factors leading to project failure. Common among these are unclear goals and objectives, estimation mistakes, and high levels of scope changes requested during the project. The following list reviews some other frequently observed factors previously discussed in the book:

- Poor planning
- Unrealistic time or resource estimates
- Inadequate executive support and user involvement

- Poor project team management
- Inappropriate team skills

The FBI's Virtual Case File project makes a graphic example for showing what poor change control can do to the subsequent deliverables. In hindsight, FBI management admitted that the underlying design technology had failed to meet the operational requirements and as a result five years of development and $170 million was lost (Neimat, 2005). In a 2004 post audit, the National Research Council saw no evidence that a technology contingency plan had been formalized for this project. The development vendor claimed that they delivered the first phase of the project ahead of schedule and under budget, but the requirements for the software had changed significantly after the September 11, 2001 terrorist attacks. Subsequent research revealed that major requirement changes had also been ongoing since the start of the project. In addition, there was a high turnover of top management during this period. The final audit conclusion revealed that the requirements were never satisfactorily defined or stabile and this created many of the downstream issues. The factors outlined in this situation are not uncommon, but their results are often more clouded than in this example. When a project either does not know what the goal should be or does not properly define what the user needs, the result will be similar to the one outlined here. This example also shows that much of these difficulties are often related more to the people process than the technology itself, even though technology may also contribute to poor results (Neimat, 2005).

PMs often have the feeling that their project will never settle down and stabilize. Change requests seem endless. When this happens, it is likely a result of some dynamics either in the original specifications, or in some changing environmental variable (management, technology, marketplace, economics, organization, etc.). To sit back and simply try to incorporate the changes may not be the best strategy. In some cases, it may be necessary to halt the project and do an assessment of its initial scope compared to the current view. If the organization is not sensitive to these dynamics, they could well be assisting in creating a failed effort. The Virtual Case File system obviously followed this path with both uncontrolled and unmanaged scope and feature creep.

Scope creep refers to previously unplanned and unexpected changes in user expectations and requirements as a project progress, whereas feature creep refers to similar requested additions of features to a system. In both cases, changes of this type may appear minor, but often bring with them unseen consequences resulting from underlying technology failure or inability to manage the changing work requirements. PMs who are not sensitive to these subtle interactions inside the system will approve what appears to be isolated changes, only to find out later that there were other related implications that further increased project work (i.e., interactions with other areas, risk, quality, etc.) (Neimat, 2005).

29.3 Change Control System

Implementing an effective change control system is vital and necessary for a PM who understands the negative impact of this aspect of his project. Failure to define an effective change control process could well be the single biggest management mistake one can make. This process should be identified as part of the Scope Management Plan and agreed with by all management participants at the outset of the project. This process needs to be formal, documented, and inviolate. It specifies how changes will be requested and the associated processes for evaluation, approval, and implementation during the execution phase. A *Change Control Board* (CCB) will be specified as the approval authority and this group should be external to the project team. Also, the process will include a formal configuration management system to maintain status for all requests.

The CCB Charter should include the authority to approve changes of some specified level and to manage allocated funds set aside to handle this class of activity. Within the board structure, roles and responsibilities will be defined including chair and permanent members. Typical members include the PM, sponsor, senior users, and support manager. As new changes are requested, the project team reviews the request in regard to resources and work impact, as well as other related impacts regarding risks, quality, and rewards related to the proposed change. "Change and project management must be considered as integrated Transitional activities. The success of the one largely depends on the success of the other" (BCS, 2012). CCB decisions will then be made based on this analysis.

In all cases, the change control policy should provide guiding principles that provide the basic approach for ensuring that appropriate issues have been fully coordinated prior to being submitted to the board for review. In addition to the basic decision processes outlined above there should also be a higher-level appeals process for rejected changes (Love, 2004).

Below are some sample guidelines for the change approval process and the list details how to best apply change management:

OK to say "No": If the project team has done a good job of collecting initial requirements and managing the life cycle, many features have already been reviewed and prioritized before execution begins. If a newly proposed requirement is not worth the time to analyze it, then it is not worth the time to implement it. Therefore, it should be rejected immediately. Normally, a good CCB will say "No" more times than it says "Yes" in order to promote a more stable work environment and ensure that only critical changes are implemented.

Changes should be bundled: A large number of small changes, when done independently, can greatly affect the project timeline because each one affects many areas of the system such as testing, user documentation, support, and so on. To gain economies of scale and effective use of personnel, it is normally more efficient to bundle a set of changes into one change package and include them in a single approved change. When handled in this manner, a master umbrella change number would be created to control implementation. In this manner, it may be possible to include some minor changes at near zero cost once a major change is approved. In any case, this needs to be done to help the project team better manage their time with this activity.

Eliminate bureaucracy: Some CCBs are made ineffective by individuals who just like to say "No" because they do not want to be bothered by the change. Even though change is a negative event to the team, it may well be a required event for the success of the project. Excessive rejection creates ill will to the project when it seems as if the board is not making decisions that are in the best interest of the user community. To eliminate this problem, it is important to educate all members of the CCB regarding their roles and constraints. Ensure they understand that there will be frivolous changes that will be submitted as well as legitimate ones necessary for the product to be marketable and to meet the needs of the business. So as each new change is suggested, it is important to produce a risk/rewards discussion that analyzes the impact to the project and documents the business reasons for the change. An important part of the change process is to document and publish the findings and rationale for each change request, whether it is approved or rejected. This post-review is important to create buy-in from stakeholders that requested the change. Rejection of a change request is particularly sensitive since it by definition represents a conflict of opinions as to its value.

Change process documentation: Each change request should be identified by a unique tracking number. This scheme is important to ensure that all requests are dealt with and it helps to monitor the flow of the request through the process. Mechanics for managing the flow of these documents are important as well. One approach is to have the PM or his delegated team member initially screen the requests. In some cases, a change represents a misunderstanding and the requirement is already being dealt with. In this manner, it may be possible to delete those without further handling simply by explaining the situation to the requestor. There are other possibilities that also may be able to be screened without detailed analysis. For example, a large change request might be routed to the board to see if they would defer it outright as a change in Charter (assuming that they have the authority for such actions). All of the requests that are not filtered out by this preliminary review would need some level of detail to produce the analysis of risk/rewards for the change. One approach for the second review would be to do a quick assessment to see if the request is viable technically or within constraints. If not, a discussion could be held with the person submitting the request to show them why this needs to be deferred. If successful, that request would be simply left in the system as a deferred item that would be reviewed after the project is completed. This could be a discussion topic for a follow-up project phase. The third review level would be a full analysis of the request as described. The results of this step would be documented and reviewed by the PM prior to formal submittal to the project board. Ideally, all these review options would be supported by an online system to allow oversight into status.

29.4 Configuration Management

The configuration management process is designed to address the control of project-related documentation throughout its life cycle. Collectively, the goal of this process is to ensure that project change requests are properly defined and tracked as changes occur. There are four general activities involved in the change control process.

1. Identifying and documenting an item or system's present functional characteristics, physical characteristics, or a combination of both, which represents the configuration baseline
2. Controlling changes to the functional and physical characteristics of an item
3. Monitoring and reporting status of changes to the system
4. Supporting an audit function to verify conformance to requirements. This involves a physical inspection of the product to ensure that it meets the required standards, and to ensure consistency of the released product

Communication of change requests is also an important factor in change control because it affects the work definition for the internal team and sets expectations for the users. It also can have significant impact on project deliverables. Also, at the upper extreme, a major change can impact the planned project schedule and budget. As we have seen in this discussion, it is necessary to use both written and oral communication to identify and manage the project change process; however, status tracking of this must be done formally. Within the communication framework, the goal is to manage the overall change process and communicate this to appropriate parties. As we have emphasized, the underlying goal of the change management process is to keep the project as stable as possible in regard to teamwork assignments and to protect the project's baseline parameters as much as possible.

One of the basic management process questions involves the media and methods to communicate changes throughout the project environment. A process based on moving paper through the organization is fraught with error and using traditional email has operational limitations as well. Mature organizations develop some form of online system to manage change configuration-related issues, including not only the initial change request submittal process but also the overall tracking of the status as it moves through the system. Typical status would indicate state of the request, who has it now, and any comments that are relevant. The goal should be to not let these lay dormant and a service level response time should be stated in the system design. The three major service level issues would be initial response, analysis cycle time, and time for the board to act. Hopefully, this discussion of actions needed to manage the change process has highlighted the level of work that goes with this activity. A medium-sized project can consume a full-time person in this role if the initial requirements are not reasonably well done and that level of overhead is noticeable in the overall budget level. Appendix C offers some additional insights into a theoretical approach to structuring a project repository.

Multiple statements have been made previously that creation of an effective change control process is fundamental to project success. In many cases, this process is defined as a paper form with loosely followed procedures; however, the more modern systems would use automation for capturing, string, and distributing the data. The key is to be sure that all requests are properly handled and all approved requests are properly tracked and implemented.

29.5 Change Management Workflow

A change requirement can be stimulated by many events and various organizational sources, including the internal project team itself. The one cardinal rule of change management is that no ad hoc (undocumented) change is made to the planned deliverable. All changes will be approved at some defined management level, which could be the PM, CCB, or even some higher-level management entity if the change is of significant magnitude to invalidate the project baseline control level. If anyone asked for "one little change" the stock answer is to have them submit a formal change request.

The change management process needs to be approved at project inception. Failure to do this leaves the project team vulnerable to an uncontrolled environment. If you believe that this is one of the major sources of failure, does it not make sense to take a hard stand on keeping it under control? Remember, the original plan was approved by management. It is important to not let future changes violate that approval.

As indicated above, the change requirement could come from almost any source, *Step one* in the process is to collect the proposed details on the change. This would typically be done using a paper from or an automated system. If the project stakeholders are geographically distributed, the latter option is preferred and all mature organizations should support a robust formal change control system. The arrival of a change request requires a quick response (say 24–48 hours). These would be initially reviewed by the PM or his delegate. At this filter point the request will be assessed as to size, criticality, timing, and so on. The submitter will be informed that the team is looking at the request. If it is clear that this will not be approved, a political negotiation with the submitter should be undertaken. One reason for this could be that the requirement is already in the work plan, or it may be that the cost of doing what is proposed is clearly out of balance.

Step two involves a technical and economic assessment of the impact. This should include all aspects of the change and not just time and cost, but risk, quality, skill requirement, and the like. The ideal technical system to handle this would be an automated workflow from the initial filter person to the individuals assigned to analyze the request. This process may be handled by one or more individuals. As the change complexity grows it may be necessary to hold a technical review meeting to resolve the response. This result is passed back to the PM or his delegate for communication back to the submitter.

Step three involves a discussion of the findings with the submitter. This is very similar to taking your car to the garage, then having a technician examine it and from this create a Statement of Work (SOW). You may or may not want to get that part of your car fixed at that price and the same can occur with a project change request. If the price or impact is too high the submitter may agree to withdraw the change (forever or until a later time). If it is desired to continue, the process moves on to the next step.

Step four involves a management assessment primarily related to the cost factor. If there are adequate funds in the current budget the PM may be delegated authority to approve small changes. In other cases, the project board would handle the approval and funds allocation. Technically, an approved change should also allocate more resources to handle any new work involved, but in many cases this is not done (a mistake in the author's opinion). A rejected request would be communicated back to the requestor with the logic for rejection. Otherwise, the project team now has an approved change to execute.

Step five requires insertion of the newly approved work into the project plan and Work Breakdown Structure (WBS). Details of the change will need to be communicated to appropriate team members. Conceptually, the change is now embedded into the work process just as though it had been planned that way from the beginning.

In looking back over the flow of work required to handle a single request it should be very obvious how this class of work could sabotage productivity of the team. It essentially bleeds the resources away from the approved plan to deal with the new component. Also, band-aiding new work into the approved work is often complex and in some case portions of the original work will have to be undone.

29.6 External Communication Issues

Given the analytical complexity of change requests it will often be necessary to hold face-to-face meetings to iron out issues and negotiate a settlement strategy. In some cases, group meetings are also used for this activity, but they are often misused and are ineffective as problem-solving strategy. Regardless of the negotiation method, it is important to recognize that the flow of information through the change cycle stresses typical communication channels. This is caused by the wide organizational scope of this activity and the underlying complexity of the related issues.

Poor communications between departments and the project team are a major source of project frustrations and failure according to a report released by Unilog, an independent pan-European consultancy and service company (CRM Today June 11, 2003). This study also documented that only 10% of PMs had a formal business sponsor identified at the outset of a project and 100% had experience with a project that had failed to meet all its objectives. Although PMs work hard at avoiding many common implementation pitfalls related to failure, they are often made scapegoats for failed projects that have had inadequate input from the business side or excessive changes from that source. In order to mitigate this result the wise PM would be on the lookout for the following *Seven Deadly Sins* (CRM Today June 11, 2003):

1. Poor project scoping and undefined project objectives, roles, and responsibilities—leading to the setting of unrealistic expectations

2. Lack of communication between the project team and the business—resulting in a mismatch of requirements and expectations
3. No senior business sponsor
4. Technology put before people—ineffective involvement of key users during the scoping phase and lack of regular communication with them throughout the project
5. No project success metrics defined
6. No risk assessment or contingency plan created
7. Lack of regular checks to ensure that the project is on track per the user's perspective

This list is essentially quite similar to other surveys discussed previously in the text, but the logic of repeating it is to emphasize that these same symptoms appear in various survey forms as causal effects leading to change requests and potentially failures. A proactive PM should focus on these aspects of the project early to establish a more stable execution environment later.

More than one quarter (28%) of PMs polled cited the lack of communication between the project and the business as the primary reason for the failure of their most recent project, a figure that rose to almost a third (32%) for companies with a revenue of $350 million or more. Expectations not properly set (or communicated) and inadequate project scoping were given as joint secondary reasons for project failure, with each being identified by 20% of the respondents (CRM Today June 11, 2003). Once again, each of these factors points to poor planning at the outset of the project.

The traditional view of change management is essentially one of a reactive process. That is, managing the stream of change requests that come floating through the system to be dealt with in some fashion. This reactive mode is not conducive to either efficiency or success. The earlier rationale for going back through some statistics on project failure factors is to restate one of the cardinal philosophies of project management. That is, the PM should take proactive positions to influence desired outcomes, not sit back and reactively try to manage the flow of documents through the project. Proper requirements definition in the beginning and effective "influencing" the external user community during execution can help stabilize the project work. If users are aware that a change can elongate a time critical project, they are often willing to wait and consider the change later. By avoiding the underlying factors that contribute to project failure the change management process becomes less controversial. This means that more verification of requirements needs to be undertaken early in the life cycle and more user communication related to those requirements exercised.

The balancing act that is involved in the change process is one of attempting to complete the project as defined, while at the same time trying to hit a reasonable portion of a moving target. Successfully completing a project that no longer reflects business value is just as bad as not completing it at all. This is a fundamental mindset that goes with this topic. In order to wrestle with this two-headed equation, business managers must be involved from the outset and must be in partnership with the decision process. Project failure rates and high change volume will remain issues so long as an ineffective communications gap exists between the two (CRM Today June 11, 2003).

29.7 Change Request Checklist

The following is a detailed checklist of tasks required to process a requested change through the project organization. A review of these steps shows why changes are disruptive to the overall work flow of the project and should be avoided wherever possible. It is understood that some change requests must be dealt with, but the total impact on the team must also be considered. Table 29.1 defines the steps and responsibilities that should be followed for each change request.

Table 29.1 Change Management Process Checklist

No.	*Action*	*Owner*
1	Clarify change details with clients	PM
2	Validate business value of change with appropriate management	PM
3	Involve appropriate team with initial request review	PM
4	Document preliminary impact assessment	PM
Formal Assessment		
5	Identify deliverables and acceptance criteria, either added or deleted	Core team
6	Identify remaining deliverables impacted	Core team
7	Identify risks related to change	Core team
8	Document risk contingency issues	Core team
9	Identify team work-related issues	PM
10	Assess financial impact on project	PM
11	Assess possible reuse of existing work	Core team
12	Ensure solution's technical feasibility	Core team
13	If not feasible, assess redesign impact	Core team
14	Assess resource reallocation	PM
15	Assess impact on project schedule	PM
16	Initiate draft SOW for proposed change	PM
Project Board Approval		
17	Present change request to project board	PM
18	If approved, move forward	PM
19	If rejected, archive	Admin
Internal Change Management Activities		
20	Communicate results to customer	PM
21	Obtain appropriate signoffs	PM
22	If necessary, reallocate project resources	PM
23	If necessary, manage additional resource allocation	Team leader(s)
24	Update project plan	PM
25	Update project schedule: tasks, resource allocation, optimize, redefine critical path, rebaseline schedule	PM
26	Communicate results to core and extended stakeholders	PM

Project team members must also be restricted from executing any change other than those approved through the formal process. This process should be formally defined and approved with the Scope Management Plan during the planning phase.

29.8 Summary

The change management process has been described as covering the entire life cycle from requirements definition through implementation. Successful change management integration depends on identifying, evaluating, and managing change events in a project and eventually later in the production environment. Classic change management essentially deals with understanding and quantifying the requested change impact on the approved project plan. This involves complex impact analysis, management oversight, and effective communication to be successful.

High technology and complex projects are particularly prone to high change request rates since error-free requirements definition is difficult to do successfully in the planning phase. The incidence of project failure is particularly notable when new or cutting-edge technology is involved. Since the requirements definition process is never perfect some degree of change is inevitable; however, the specifics of acceptable change must be managed carefully with a formally defined process that weighs the benefits, risks, and costs. The basic change management system components are controlled by a project board decision, supported by a formal workflow process and appropriate communications.

It is essential that the project board and the PM maintain focus on this aspect of the project as the change dynamics emerge. Changes create instability ripples that can lead to overruns or failure if not properly controlled.

References

BCS (The Chartered Institute for IT), 2012. *Change Management within Project Management: An Integrated Structural Business Process Approach*, February 23, 2012 https://www.bcs.org/upload/pdf/hapostolopoulos-230212.pdf (accessed October 16, 2017).

Love, B., 2004, Operational Change Control Best Practices (July), *the Project Perfect White Paper Collection.* http://www.projectperfect.com.au/downloads/Info/info_occ.pdf (accessed October 16, 2017).

Neimat, T., 2005, Why IT Projects Fail (November), *Project Perfect.* http://www.projectperfect.com.au/info_it_projects_fail.php (accessed October 16, 2017).

Schwalbe, K., 2006. *Information Technology Project Management.* Canada: Thomson Learning Inc.

Chapter 30

Project and Enterprise Metrics

30.1 Introduction

A *metric* is defined as a quantitative property of a process or product whose possible values are numbers or grade values; a *measure* is a specific value of a metric (Parth and Guma, 2003). A measure is often called a Key Performance Indicator (KPI), which is a status value designed to help monitor project performance and guide decision-making.Conceptually, a metric is designed to translate vision and strategy into tangible targets and focus work activity on formal critical success factors (CSFs). KPIs help guide project results toward organizational alignment by establishing visible goals and supporting decision-making. The adage "What gets measured, gets done" summarizes how the use of metrics can shape the day-to-day activities of various organizational units.

The concepts, mechanics, and best practices presented here are intended to provide a framework for designing a custom project metrics program. Realized benefits of such programs will vary depending on the validity of selected KPIs, the organization's maturity level, and the management reaction to the data presented. Realize that a KPI does not cause action, but only points to status areas from which an action can be derived. From this monitoring and control activity more effective decision-making is potentially enabled.

An enterprise typically measures and compares its overall project performance by quantification through the use of defined metrics. Much of this activity is carried out under the auspices of the overall monitoring and control processes. In some cases, the collection of performance variables is used to compare one organization or project entity versus another. This activity is called *benchmarking*. Regardless of the use area a defined metric's role is used to identify gaps in the project or organization versus planned values for that variable. Reaction to gaps between actual and planned (or desired) performance is the focus element that management uses to establish future corrective actions. In the case of project monitoring, this process must be very dynamic, timely and tightly linked to the control process.

30.2 Fundamentals

Given the potential influence metrics has on project activity, they should be relevant, straightforward, and quantifiable. Identifying the wrong status goal and then measuring it can cause the project to make poor decisions on correct actions.

30.2.1 Alignment with Organization Goals

Every project has tangible outputs that are measurable. Albert Einstein summed up this by saying "Not everything that can be counted counts ..." Focus should be given to those factors that are key to the organization's success, which is in turn are defined as the realization of a specific goal. To this end, Reh (2008) maintains that project KPIs should be defined and limited to factors essential to the organization reaching its long-term goals. He reasons that defined KPIs serve as the basis for a metrics program and tend to stay somewhat constant over time. However, specific KPI targets may change as the organization gets closer to achieving a particular goal, or as the organization's goals change.

Reh advises that a limited number of standard KPIs should be selected so that everyone is focused on achieving the same primary goals. To accomplish this, he recommends that a metrics program in total should consist of only 3 or 4 well-thought out KPIs. Each project can support this view by defining 3–5 specific KPIs that mesh with the organization's overall KPIs. Projects that impact multiple business units will have to incorporate appropriate consolidation metrics. As an example, the organizational KPI of "Increase Sales" would translate downward to lower-level units into one or more KPIs that contribute to that higher-level goal. For instance, a customer relationship management (CRM) program could contribute to increased sales by improving the linkage between the sales force and the customer. A CRM development project metric could also fit a departmental goal. The following is an illustrative example showing how a high-level organizational goal might be translated and represented across multiple business units as follows:

- Product Department KPI—"New Product Time to Market"
- Sales Department KPI—"Number of New Customers"
- Marketing Department KPI—"Number of Telemarketing Calls Completed"
- IT Department KPI—"Online Website Up-Time"

It is generally recognized that properly translated departmental KPIs help these organizations focus on supporting an overall organizational scorecard KPI.

It is beneficial to study the metrics best practices of successful organizations. One public example of this comes from the Canadian Transportation Agency (CTA) who uses a well-developed process for ensuring that the activities they undertake are linked to strategic outcomes (CTA, 2008). In a recent request for government appropriations, the CTA developed a "basic results chain" to demonstrate how resources, activities, and outputs all link to strategic outcomes and ultimate results (see Table 30.1).

Note that the chain starts with a "Why" and then moves through the layers of:

- What output is expected?
- When and where is it to occur?
- How will the outputs be created?
- What activities are needed to be undertaken?
- What inputs are needed to support the venture?

The results chain concept is used throughout a multiyear campaign to show progress toward achieving higher-level goals. Additionally, a results chain is created for each key initiative with the

Table 30.1 Constructing a Basic Results Chain

Ultimate results	Why?	Why do we carry out this program or initiative? What is it we ultimately expect to achieve, recognizing that it may take years, or even decades to achieve this ultimate result(s)?
Strategic outcomes	What?	What do we expect to see or hear as a result of our outputs and activities?
	Who and where?	Who do we need to engage and reach and where? The strategic outcomes are often referred to as the behavioral changes that arise as a result of our work.
Outputs	How?	Outputs, activities, and inputs are effectively the operational elements required to achieve the strategic outcomes. What outputs (i.e., decisions and orders, codes of practice, etc.) are required to achieve the expected strategic outcomes?
Activities		What key activities do we need to undertake to effectively contribute to the strategic outcomes?
Inputs		What inputs (financial and human) do we have to carry out key activities?

Source: Canadian Transportation Agency (CTA), (2008). Performance measurement framework for the Canadian Transportation Agency, http://www.cta-otc.gcxa/about-nous/excellence/performance/index_e.html (accessed March 20, 2008). With permission.

overall goal of providing a map that outlines the linkage between resources and outcomes across various initiatives (CTA, 2008). To implement this concept, the CTA uses a standard template for a basic results chain. The template helps develop the local KPIs for linking an ultimate result goal downward through the defined lower-level outputs.

The Department of Energy (DOE, 2002) uses a more pragmatic approach to identify the types and categories of metrics. Tables 30.2 and 30.3.

Table 30.2 Types of Performance Measures

Process metrics	Increase capability level (i.e., Software Engineering Institute (SEI) maturity levels) Do more with less (shorter schedule, less resources), improve quality (less defects, less rework)
Project metrics	Track project progress Assess project status award contract fees
Product metrics	Determine product quality Identify defect rates Ensure product performance

Source: Department of Energy (DOE), (2002). Basic performance measures for Information Technology Projects (January 15), pp. 4, 7.

Table 30.3 Typical Metrics Categories

Schedule	Actual versus planned • Schedule and progress
Budget	Actual versus planned • Resources and cost
Functionality	Delivered versus planned • Product characteristics • Technology effectiveness • Process performance • Customer satisfaction

Source: Department of Energy (DOE), (2002). Basic performance measures for Information Technology Projects (January 15), pp. 4, 7.

In both of these examples, we see the goal of high level organizational goals being supported at the project level with defined KPIs.

30.3 Alignment with Organizational Maturity

Parth and Gumz (2003) comment that the following are examples of basic project status measurements:

- Completions of milestones for project activities compared to a baseline plan
- Planned effort and duration data compared to the plan, work completed, effort expended, and funds expended in the project.

KPIs and other metrics should also be aligned with organizational maturity improvement objectives. For example, metrics should be designed to track relatively new or immature processes and procedures. Conversely, the use of basic metrics within a mature process may cloud some of the management needs of the more mature process and restrict the organization from further improvements. Use of metrics can drive the organization in either good or bad directions; hence, it is important to understand how to formulate the metric to focus on the desired outcome. Therefore, in considering appropriate metrics for an advanced environment, it might be more appropriate to include the following areas (Parth and Guma, 2003):

- Project management effort compared to plan
- Frequency and magnitude of replanning efforts, given requirement changes (i.e., change level compared to projection)
- Realized risks compared to estimated loss (i.e., contingency reserve status)
- Frequency, number, and size of unanticipated impacts to the project (i.e., management reserve status)

The point of using a basic versus advanced view is that the latter will focus on more breadth than the former, therefore, use of basic KPIs may not be worthwhile in that environment. In the list above, the risk-associated metric would be looking at contingency reserve status. A lower maturity process would not have dealt with the topic. Ditto for the other reserves.

30.4 Performance and Change Drivers

Defined correctly, a KPI succinctly communicates what management deems most critical. Employees will likely take action and adjust their activities according to the KPIs and established targets based on their understanding of the metric. Expanding on this principle, Eckerson (2006) describes metrics as levers that executives can pull to move the organization in new and different directions. He states, "as powerful agents of change, metrics can drive unparalleled improvements or plunge the organization into chaos and confusion" (Eckerson, 2006). This underscores the importance of establishing well-thought out KPIs that are directly tied to what the organization is trying to accomplish on a strategic level and linking these to specific KPIs (Parth and Guma, 2003).

30.5 KPI Categories

Leading or lagging indicators. KPIs are those represented by activities that have an effect on future performance. A lagging indicator reflects output of past activity (i.e., most financial metrics fit this), whereas a leading indicator would signal future trends (i.e., the number of customer contacts scheduled for next two weeks). From a management point of view, leading indicators help the most with decision-making and should be designed in the KPI suite. Metrics based on future state items are valuable and powerful as they provide an opportunity to have an insight into what may occur (Eckerson, 2006).

Simple or composite indicators are metrics can be expressed as counts, percentages, ratings, numbers, or trends. Simple metrics commonly denote items completed, such as lines of code, number of widgets produced, or tests performed. Composite metrics combine one or more factors and are usually expressed as ratios. Examples are the number of change requests received per work unit or the number of defects found per work unit.

Quantitative or qualitative indicators are generally measured using quantitative or qualitative valuations. Qualitative measures would be less auditable and often based on raw judgment. The various numeric and statistical metric examples cited above fall into the quantitative category.

The major concern with any metric is whether it means anything or not. In some cases they can actually be misleading. The classic example of this is the metric of planned versus actual resource consumption. Does spending less than planned mean that all is going well? At some future status meeting someone will show a chart or metric that says that the actual budget for the project is below plan, therefore, this project is doing quite well. Taken by itself that metric may send the wrong message. This project could be hopelessly behind and doing nothing, therefore, no expenditure of resources. Be careful with metrics that have this potential. On the positive side, a measurement showing that a milestone date has been met has an obvious value and recording hours for work performed on a particular Work Breakdown Structure (WBS) ID may have value, but this also falls into the gray area described above. As a general rule, a simple quantitative metric by itself will only tell part of the story.

Qualitative metrics are judgment or perception measures and they may also be translated into some form that appears to be quantification. Samples of such measures could deal with topics such as customer satisfaction or team morale. Upon completion of the requirements definition process the room could be polled for a measure of satisfaction on a scale of 1 to 10. Effectiveness could be presented as the number or percentage of respondents who felt the process was successful or not. A typical method of translating perception-based measures is the classic five-stage Likert scale (i.e., very good, good, neutral, not good, and poor). In most cases, quantitative metrics based on objective measurements are inherently more objective and useful; however, in some situations use of qualitative metrics is necessary to provide a general status in an area difficult to quantify (i.e., team morale, customer satisfaction, etc.). Hence, the total metrics suite will likely contain some of each type.

In a more specific categorization, White (2001) categorizes project management metrics by project stage (See Tables 30.4 and 30.8). A sample of the planning and execution metrics is

Table 30.4 Planning Phase Metrics

Planning Phase	
Schedule estimate	
Meaning	Estimated amount of elapsed time required to complete the project
Measure	Number of planned work days based on work effort and required resources
Benefit	Establishes a baseline to support comparison during later project phases
Cost/hours estimate	
Meaning	Amount of resources (dollars, people, and equipment) it will take to produce the project
Measure	Number of planned work hours and estimated costs based on work effort and required resources
Benefit	Establishes a baseline to support comparison during later project phases
Defect rate	
Meaning	Anticipated amount of rework (numbers, average time to repair)
Measure	Based on past experience, number of defects to be incurred based on size of product
Benefit	Establishes a baseline to support comparison during later project phases
Component size	
Meaning	Anticipated size of products to be delivered
Measure	Based on past experience, number of functional modules, and documentation pages to be developed
Benefit	Establishes a baseline to support comparison during later project phases
Quality	
Meaning	The metric that will be used to determine acceptability of the end products
Measure	Varies from project to project—could be expressed as a factor of defects, defined Number of defects measured at various test points
Benefit	Removes ambiguity about product acceptance

Source: White, K.R.J., (2001). Measuring and managing success: *PM Solutions*, pp. 4–8. http://www.jamesheiresconsidting.com/IT_Project_Metrics.pdf (accessed February 22, 2008). With permission.

Table 30.5 Execution Phase Metrics

Execution Phase	
Actual hours	
Meaning	Actual labor hours spent to date on project activities
Measure	All labor hours, including those of support personnel and contractors
Benefit	Provides comparison to budget and business case and supports schedule analysis
Actual schedule	
Meaning	Schedule performance to date
Measure	Number of days behind or ahead of schedule
Bene tit	Supports early determination of potential late delivery
Actual cost	
Meaning	Actual costs associated spent to date on project activities
Measure	True total costs spent to date, including all labor, software, and hardware costs
Benefit	Provides comparison to budget and business case
Defects per peer review	
Meaning	Quality of work produced to date, prior to testing phase
Measure	Number of defects per peer review
Benefit	Early measure of quality of product; indication of a training, or specification problem
Staff productivity	
Meaning	Average staff productivity
Measure	Number of function points per staff hour
Benefit	Determine rate of work to be anticipated in the remaining software-build activities

Source: White, K.R.J., (2001). Measuring and managing success: *PM Solutions*, pp. 4–8. http://www.jamesheiresconsultiiig.com/IT_Project_Metrics.pdf (accessed February 22, 2008). With permission.

shown next. Note that different KPIs are identified for each phase indicating a change of management focus. This is an important idea in that KPIs need to reflect the goal in the appropriate project phase.

The process of correlating metrics across project phases is performed by establishing a metric baseline value and comparing progress against those baselines as a means of monitoring and predicting the final outcome.

Phase level metrics: The tables in this section (Tables 30.4–30.8) illustrate examples of metrics by project phase. Each of these examples offers a set of general options by project phase that might help to decide what parameters to use, or even if they are worth collecting. This set of tables is offered here not only to help illustrate the types of variables that are common to each major phase, but also to recognize that others also may be defined.

Note that the planning phase KPIs are focused on raw data collection, simply showing consumption of time and resources with no tangible deliverable to compare it with. After the planning stage, most metrics would be formulated based on requirements or desired future levels. The basic role of the metrics defined here would be to help track progress through the subsequent project phases. Execution phase metrics help to determine how the project is proceeding compared to

Table 30.6 Testing Phase Metrics

Testing Phase	
Schedule estimate	
Meaning	Schedule performance to date
Measure	Number of days ahead of or behind schedule, and amount of float
Benefit	Ability to predict actual completion date, and approximate risk
Cost/hours estimate	
Meaning	Amount of resources (dollars, people, and equipment) it will take to produce the project
Measure	Resources/cost spent to date
Benefit	Predict total cost of the project
Defect rate	
Meaning	Determines the quality of the work produced to date
Measure	Number of defects per some predetermined value (functional modules)
Benefit	Determine rate of future rework
Response time	
Meaning	Ability of the application to handle volume in a timely manner
Measure	Response time in seconds per hundreds of users
Benefit	Advance notice of performance problems
Average time to repair	
Meaning	Amount of duplicate work due to errors
Measure	Number of hours and dollars spent for correcting the problem
Benefit	Reduce unnecessary costs and increase work efficiency

Source: White, K.R.J., (2001), Measuring and managing success: *PM Solutions*, pp. 4–8. http://www.jamesheiresconsultmg.com/IT_Project_Metrics.pdf (accessed February 22, 2008). With permission.

Table 30.7 Deployment Phase Metrics

Deployment Phase	
Defect rate	
Meaning	Determines the quality of the work produced to date
Measure	Number of defects per some predetermined value (functional modules)
Benefit	Determine rate of future rework
Response time	
Meaning	Ability of the application to handle volume in a timely manner
Measure	Response time in seconds per hundreds of users
Benefit	Advance notice of performance problems
Quality	
Meaning	The metric that determines acceptability of the end products
Measure	Varies from project to project—could be expressed as a factor of defects, response time, and the number of users supported
Benefit	Removes ambiguity about product acceptance
Average time to repair	
Meaning	Amount of duplicate work due to errors
Measure	Number of hours and dollars spent for correcting the problem
Benefit	Reduce unnecessary costs and increase work efficiency

Source: White, K.R.J., (2001). Measuring and managing success: *PM Solutions*, pp. 4–8. http://www.jamesheiresconsulting.com/IT_Project_Metrics.pdf (accessed February 22, 2008). With permission.

Table 30.8 Sample Linked Metrics

Category	*Focus*	*Purpose*	*Measure of Success*
Schedule performance	Tasks completed versus tasks planned at a point in time	Assess project progress Apply project resources	100% completion of tasks on critical path; 90% of all others
	Major milestones met versus planned	Measure time efficiency	90% of major milestones met
	Revisions to approved plan	Understand and control project "churn"	All revisions reviewed and approved
	Changes to customer requirements	Understand and manage scope and schedule	All changes managed through an approved change process
	Project completion date	Award/penalize (depending on contract type)	Project completed on schedule (as per the approved plan)

Source: Department of Energy (DOE), (2002). Basic performance measures for Information Technology Projects (January 15), pp. 4, 7.

baseline or current plan, or to aid in evaluating where some corrective action is needed (White, 2001). Also note that there is some emphasis here on leading indicators.

White identifies cross-linked phase metrics by showing how the testing phase metrics for a software development activity are linked to its planning activity targets. In similar fashion, implementation metrics indicate the readiness of the product for production release and may represent good predictors of future customer satisfaction.

Table 30.8 summarizes the approach defined by the DOE methodology for creation of performance measures that link from focus and project purpose into a defined measurement variable. Also, note that a measurable target level is specified for each metric.

30.6 Evaluation Criteria

Although there is no right or wrong method for selecting appropriate metrics for status tracking, the following criteria should be reviewed when selecting a metrics candidate:

1. *Validity:* Is the granularity of the value adequate for interpreting results?
2. *Relevance:* Does the metric actually relate to the area of concern?
3. *Reliability:* Is it a consistent measure over time?
4. *Simplicity:* Is information available to capture a value?
5. *Affordability:* Is it cost-effective to collect and analyze the data?

Selecting project metrics should not be a once-and-done activity. Procedures should be put in place to continually assess whether the current metrics are sufficient or excessive. Also, are they useful in managing the business or driving the project toward organizational strategic goals (National Public Review, 1997)? Beyond this assessment, modifications may be necessary to respond to changing market conditions or regulatory requirements. From this review process some metrics may be discarded, or replaced over time. If a metric is not focusing the project on meaningful targets, it should be considered for retirement.

30.7 Setting Targets

One other approach to establishing a KPI is to set a benchmark value based on a competitor's product or process. This may be set in various ways, but should be a formally recognized event. In some cases, the value for the target could be initially identified in the Charter, or it might be derived as part of the planning process. Other metrics can be set from past practices, externally in accordance with industry standards, or a stretch goal for a new product. In some cases, a stretch goal is set to entice performance improvements. Comparing internal metrics with industry equivalents will not only add motivation to improve, but will validate that those goal levels are attainable. For example, a 100% customer satisfaction goal sounds admirable, but when the industry standard is 80% there may be factors in play that are not easy to overcome. Logic would suggest a more realistic target since setting unrealistic and possibly unachievable levels can be demotivating.

Figure 30.1 illustrates a company's benchmarking approach for their internal field performance.

Comparisons of this type are often used to evaluate needed areas of competitive improvement. Also, this same presentation format could be decomposed into geographical units for a lower-level

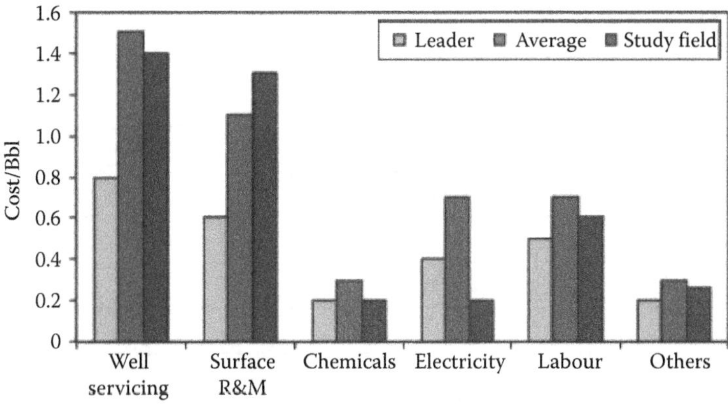

Figure 30.1 Oil field productivity benchmarking.

comparison. The automobile industry uses benchmarking values for creating their design specifications regarding time to produce a unit, miles per gallon, performance measures, defect measures, and so on.

30.8 Beware of the Pitfalls

The 6th Sense Analytics identifies the following five reasons why metrics fail to promote strategic results (6th Sense, 2006):

1. *Use of inappropriate metrics or measures:* Measuring the wrong things and creating an artificial incentive system (i.e., measuring lines of code produced that leads to a greater number of short lines of code or verbose code that is optimized for size rather than function or quality).
2. *Garbage in, garbage out:* The metric that has no meaning.
3. *Poor support processes:* The process of tracking some activities is inefficient and distracts from productivity and progress (i.e., excessive overhead in the collection process).
4. *Information is not timely:* Metrics are not produced or evaluated in a timely manner and out-of-date results lead to bad decisions (i.e., accounting data that is six weeks old).
5. *Inadequate follow through:* No actionable results or specific decisions are identified based on the metric.

Overriding all the combined mechanics of metrics creation, collection, and use is the human element surrounding this process. According to a National Public Review survey, employees in best-of-class organizations focus on achieving organizational goals by using performance measures to gauge goal achievement, but they do not focus on the measures *per se* (National Public Review, 1997). Performance measurement overall is seen as a means, not an end. Establishing metrics that motivate employees in a particular direction and establishing a sense of camaraderie around meeting performance targets may be the most important tactic related to a successful metrics program.

30.9 Mechanics

Table 30.9 illustrates how a target set of metrics can be translated into a scorecard format. Note that this scorecard contains quantitative and qualitative evaluations of schedule, cost, technical

Table 30.9 Project Scorecard

WBS	*SPI*	*CPI*	*Tech. Perf.*	*Quality*
A	1.10	1.10	5	4
B	1.25	0.79	3	3
C	1.30	0.65	4	3
D	0.90	1.10	5	4
E	0.75	0.65	2	5
F	0.75	1.10	5	4
G	0.75	0.65	2	5
H	0.75	1.10	4	4
I	0.75	0.60	4	4

WBS, a work breakdown structure unit; SPI, a quantitative measure of schedule performance computed by EV (see Chapter 27); CPI, a quantitative measure of cost performance computed by EV (see Chapter 27); Tech. Perf., a qualitative measure of technical performance based on a scale of 1 = poor to 5 = exceeds requirement; Quality, a qualitative measure of estimated current status quality based on a scale of 1 = poor to 5 = exceeds requirement.

performance, and quality measures for selected WBS units. From this basic set of metrics, it is also possible to produce a WBS-weighted assessment for a project; however, such computations have to be evaluated carefully

A scorecard-type model terms must have understandable audience meaning. For this example, the two Earned Value (EV) columns would need some interpretation. More background detail regarding EV will be explored in Chapter 31. In this example, the use of qualitative scores might be easier to understand, but are these values auditable? Who defined the value and what was it based on? These are two classic interpretation issues for metrics usage. A custom reporting scorecard as shown in Table 30.9 might fit well in one project and create confusion in another if the vocabulary used was foreign. This typically means that common metrics need to be defined and used by all projects both for comparability and understanding.

30.9.1 Miscellaneous Issues

Metrics should be reported in such a way as to help the receiver comprehend his project status at the appropriate level of detail. If these data are to be used internal to the project team, a low level of detail might be required; however, giving the same data to a senior manager would not be appropriate. Therefore, a fundamental design issue is level of *granularity*. For instance, should the detail shown be the first level of a WBS, or something deeper into the structure?

In addition to this consideration, there are subtleties related to phase tracking. As an example, tracking of quality and technical performance in the design phase is difficult if not meaningless; likewise, cost and schedule can be better tracked in execution than in planning.

Should quality, technical performance, and weighting metrics be omitted during the early phase and then picked at some later point in the life cycle when the values can be more accurately determined? The answers to type issue are based on the way in which the project life cycle is defined. In the case of software development some status variables would be hard to capture before the execution phase and, even then, would probably be based on subsystem-level results. This class of concerns is more complex to resolve than it appears given the goal is to produce a system that can be used by all projects and not custom built for each.

One final point before we leave this example. As metric reporting moves out of the project level and becomes more standardized the focus moves to higher levels and in some cases narrower perspectives. One example of this is to translate a quantitative scorecard table into colored balls for each of the major parameters. The color will be based on some threshold definition. For instance, if the overall project score for schedule were less than 0.80 the ball would be red; between 0.80 and 0.90 yellow; greater than 0.90 green. Each parameter could be specified in this manner so that the senior manager can quickly look at status by color rather than numbers. Also, there might be a capability in the reporting system to drill into any red area for more detail. This dual approach provides the best combination of ease of evaluation and on demand low-level granularity as needed.

When all the KPI specification process is dealt with, the issue of appropriate stakeholder reporting format remains. Should the status metrics be sent to all stakeholders or is there a graphical format that would be best for the masses? Dealing with issues of this type highlights an additional view of the complex nature of a metrics program.

The following three chapters outline essentially a composite of project monitoring and control approaches that are commonly used—these are EV (Chapter 31) and basic tracking using KPIs (Chapter 32). In addition to these techniques, traditional financial measures are often used to show either planned status or current projections of the project effort.

Technology in various formats is now embedded in almost every business process and projects are the common mechanism to transform these processes. One common tactic is to measure the incremental value of technology-enabled business processes (Symons et al., 2006, p. 4).

In regard to IT projects, Symons et al. (2006) states that standard methodologies help organizations more accurately predict returns from their investments and overcome many of the weaknesses in using simple financial metrics. Other industries follow similar patterns with common WBS structures, life cycle standardization, common metrics, and the like. Two weakness areas related to these strategies are questionable risk handling and assessing tangential opportunities. Forrester compared the following four different custom business methodologies to illustrate how various organizations handle more complex evaluations.

- Business Value Index (BVI)—Intel
- Total Economic Impact (TEI)—Forrester
- Val IT—IT Governance Institute
- Applied Information Economics (AIE)—U.S. Government methodology

A brief summary of these approaches is included below.

Intel's BVI methodology was developed in 2001 with the goal of incorporating common business value measures, efficiency, and financial attractiveness of the initiative (Nisman, 2002). Business value is measured by factors such as customer need, business and technical risks, strategic fit, revenue potential, level of required investment, innovation, and learning generated. Efficiency is established by how well the project complies with standards, architecture, and core competencies. Also, projects are scored using weighted criteria from each of the three vectors and depicted on a three-dimensional Business Value Chart. In order to enable all projects to be compared with one another, the final evaluation grid maps business value versus IT efficiency was used. This technique was considered the most traditional and simplest of the four compared. This supports the goal of a common evaluation scheme.

Forrester's methodology, called TEI, is similar to BVI in that it includes use of a business case, valuing intangibles, and calculating financial returns (Forrester, 2013). More specifically, TEI evaluates three economic areas: flexibility, business value, and technology cost. This data is then matched against risk factors to produce a total organizational impact. Cost impacts are quantified by the incremental change in costs associated with the effort versus maintaining the status quo. Business benefits are quantified by their impact on various business units and this reflects the impact of the initiative on the overall user organization. Overall, this metric indicates the level of effort required to absorb a new system across the organization. Flexibility is based on the value of the option to take subsequent future actions. The specific future option does not have to be defined; rather a value is associated with the ability to take action in the future. Risk analysis provides "risk-adjusted" costs and benefits that are then used to compute a risk-adjusted Return On Investment (ROI). Projects are scored across each of the categories by weighted criteria. The weighted scores are summed to represent a single quantitative number, which is the TEI for that proposal.

The third methodology, called VAL IT, is a complement to the governance framework (see www.Itgi.org). The goal of this technique is to provide a means to optimize the realization of business value from the organization's portfolio investments in information technology. This approach consists of practices related to the project life cycle, project selection, and investment management. There are 11 key management practices, 15 portfolio management practices, and 15 investment management practices. Through these combined 41 practices, ITGI claims that the value of IT investments, overall portfolio, and individual IT investment programs can be measured and optimized (Symons et al., 2006, pp. 10–11). This type of methodology is an example of layered metrics and would require a very mature organization to manage the approach. Forrester judges this as a work in process; however, given the broadly recognized sponsor level of ITGI it could well be accepted as it matures given their corresponding role in Sarbanes-Oxley and COBIT.

The fourth comparative methodology reviewed is AIE. This is used in governmental organizations and contains the most quantification of the review group. Its design goal is to "clarify, measure, and optimize" investment alternatives even when there are "intangibles" (Symons et al., 2006, p. 12). AIE removes definitional ambiguity by focusing on variables that can be expressed as units of measure. One key differentiator of this method is use of a risk/return metric to compare a proposal across all investment categories. Many technology-based strategies and their related metrics are very difficult to forecast compared to evaluating a new building, purchased equipment, and the like. The techniques embedded into AIE are similar to those used by financial and insurance organizations for portfolio selection. The Environmental Protection Agency (EPA) used this method to calculate a global equipment replacement strategy, but vague results were available to assess the technique further. It is the most complex of the four examined and requires analysis expertise.

To summarize, the four custom methodologies reviewed differ most notably in their emphasis on breadth of topic coverage and use of quantitative or qualitative assessments. The general assessment is as follows:

- BVI is the simplest to implement.
- TEI values flexibility as well as traditional metrics.
- Val IT takes a layered governance approach.
- AIE offers the greatest rigor and deals with risk and cross-functional-type initiatives.

The point made in looking at a cross-section of valuation methodologies is that essentially all organizations are looking for techniques to accomplish this type of analysis. None are known to have found the optimum method and all seem to be focusing on slightly different goals in their selection process. Once again, we see that metrics are designed to guide direction and organizations have different views on that direction.

30.10 Industry Standard Metrics

The EV methodology is defined as an ANSI-EIA 748 standard that is created to define sophisticated project status analysis guidelines that aid in evaluating the classes of metric area to review. One of the primary metrics in this standard is EV. It is useful for evaluating status and forecasting completion costs and schedule (see Chapter 31 for more details). Interpretation of these results is standardized across broad industries and offers a somewhat universal analysis tool.

EV parameters do not cover all required aspects of project performance, but certainly should form the core of a metrics program in regard to cost and schedule performance. These parameters enable supply early warning if trends regarding project performance. Likewise, EV metrics can assist in evaluating future budgets status, or can help the project team evaluate areas within the WBS where progress is lacking.

30.11 Conclusion

Defining key project performance indicators, collecting data, and producing status metrics throughout the project life cycle are only valuable to the extent that the resulting information is used by the organization in a manner which drives the project toward appropriate objectives. Use of a formal metrics program influences behavior in the defined directions. For this reason, the selection of collected values needs to be considered carefully. Examples shown in this chapter have demonstrated some of the key issues related to definition and use of this strategy.

Best-of-class organizations include metrics as part of individual and departmental performance review and reward systems. In order to successfully implement a formal metrics program, careful time and attention must be paid to the formulation of the parameter, data collection techniques, and training of the organization to utilize the results.

References

6th Sense, 2006. The 5 essentials of effective software development metrics. *6th Sense Analytics White paper.* http://osalt.tradepub.com/free/w_aaaa1479/ (accessed October 18, 2017).

Canadian Transportation Agency (CTA), 2008. Performance measurement framework for the Canadian Transportation Agency. http://www.cta-otc.gc.ca/about-nous/excellence/performance/index_e.html (accessed March 20, 2008).

Department of Energy (DOE), 2002. Basic Performance Measures for Information Technology Projects (January 15), pp. 4, 7.

Eckerson, W., 2006. Making Sense of Metrics. http://www.b-eye-network.com/blogs/mt/mt-search.cgi?search=Making+Sense+of+metrics&IncludeBlogs=62&limit=20 (accessed October 18, 2017).

Forrester, 2013. Total Economic Impact (TEI). https://www.forrester.com/staticassets/marketing/consulting-pdfs/Consulting_TEI.pdf (accessed October 18, 2017).

National Public Review, 1997. Benchmarking Study Report. http://govinfo.library.unt.edu/npr/library/papers/benchmrk/nprbook.html (accessed March 22, 2008).
Nisman, M., 2002. IT Business Value Index, https://link.springer.com/content/pdf/10.1007%2F1-4020-8000-X_13.pdf (accessed October 19, 2017)
Parth, F. and J. Guma, 2003. How Project Metrics Can Keep You from Flying Blind. http://www.projectauditors.com/Papers/Whiteepprs/ProjectMetrics.pdf (accessed March 22, 2008).
Reh, J., 2008. Key Performance Indicators. http://management.about.com/cs/generalmanagement/a/keyperfindic.htm (accessed February 15, 2008).
Symons, C., L.M., Orlov, and Sessions, L., 2006. Measuring the Business Value of IT, Forrester. http://www.virtualization.co.kr/reference/157.Measuring-The-Business-Value-of-IT.pdf (accessed November 20, 2017).
White, K.R.J., 2001. Measuring and Managing Success, *PM Solutions*, pp. 4–8. http://www.jamesheiresconsulting.com/IT_Project_Metrics.pdf (accessed February 22, 2008).

Chapter 31

Earned Value Management

31.1 Introduction

Earned Value Management (EVM) is a project management technique that has gained increasing industry acceptance over the past few years. This acceptance process has taken over 50 years of scrutiny and prodding, mostly by the Department of Defense (DoD) and Federal agencies with their contractors. Evidence now shows that Earned Value (EV) provides one of the most effective and meaningful status analysis tools available today to measure and report project cost, schedule, and performance. The technique has the unique ability to combine cost, time, and scope completion measurements within a single integrated status parameter set.

EVM was originally developed within the DoD to support their control processes with large defense acquisition programs. In 1965, the U.S. Air Force defined 35 management criteria for their acquisition projects. Two years later, the DoD adopted these same criteria as their Cost/Schedule Controls Systems Criteria (C/SCSC) as part of Department of Defense Instruction (DODI) 5000.1 and these guidelines were used to evaluate vendor performance in various large projects over the next three decades. In 1996, private industry formally recognized the EVM process by rewriting and publishing the revised C/SCSC regulation under the title of ANSI/EIA-748 (Fleming and Koppelman, 2006). Even with this level of formal support the commercial project world continues to be slow in adopting this methodology. The goal of this chapter is to show that the mechanics for EV are not complex if one follows the model tenants previously outlined in this text. However, the process does require discipline in the development of the project plan and subsequent monitoring.

Experience indicates that application of the EV model cannot be accomplished without a reasonable degree of operational maturity. Initially, EV was viewed as excessive project overhead and some contractors were able to negotiate it out of this requirement set through this claim. Like many government regulations EVM was initially over-defined without proof of value. Lack of industry ownership, inadequate training, and awkward technical jargon further contributed to its early lower acceptance problems. Even though EVM was intended to serve both cost and schedule needs, it came to be seen as a purely financial exercise due to the fact that financial personnel managed the process (Christensen, 1998, p. 5). During the 1990s, governmental procurement groups streamlined their acquisition regulations and EVM not only survived the reform movement, but also became strongly associated with the reform implementation itself (Haugan, 2003, p. 70).

After 20 years of prodding inside DoD contractor organizations the concepts of EV were eventually adopted by the National Aeronautics and Space Administration (NASA), the U.S. Department of Energy (DOE), the U.S. Office of Management and Budget (OMB), the construction industry, and several foreign countries. In 1987, the Project Management Institute (PMI) included an overview of EVM in their *Project Management Body of Knowledge (PMBOK®) Guide* and expanded that support in subsequent editions. Efforts to simplify and generalize EVM gained further momentum in the early 2000s and to date experts in the field continue to validate it as an effective tool for management of projects of any size and risk (Christensen, 1998, p. 13). In the hands of a trained technician EVM is currently the most robust project management tool available for evaluating project status and forecasting completion cost and schedule.

Computation of EVM parameters requires an integrated project plan, one that packages defined work, schedule, and resources into a single view. This view is consistent with the theory outlined in Chapters 12–15. From this base-level definition, it is possible to compare project plans versus actual status in a more meaningful way than the traditional planned versus actual resource presentation. Variances between the actual cost (AC) of the work and the current progress provide a timely warning of performance problems at both the project level and lower levels of granularity.

31.2 Basic Principles

Based on its underlying conceptual model, EVM principles incorporate multiple project management areas including scope definition, resource allocation, scheduling and budgeting, accounting, analysis, reporting, and change control. EVM's specific mechanics include the use of the formal work packages (WPs), Performance Measurement Baseline (PMB) curves ("S" curves), and a defined set of work unit metrics. Before delving further into the computational methodology, it is important to review one underlying concept critical to EVM implementation—that is, the Work Breakdown Structure (WBS) and its associated dictionary.

As we have described in earlier chapters, a WBS is used here as the fundamental technique for defining and organizing the total project scope into a hierarchical tree structure. The WBS defines a set of project deliverables and related work units that collectively represent 100% of the project scope. At each subsequent level, the children of a parent node represent 100% of the scope of their parent. The lowest level of decomposition for each parent node is called a WP and represents the lowest level of control in the structure. Figure 31.1 shows a skeleton representation of the WBS. In this type of structure, each of the WPs is work estimated, resources allocated, time scheduled, and linked into the next higher-level WBS element.

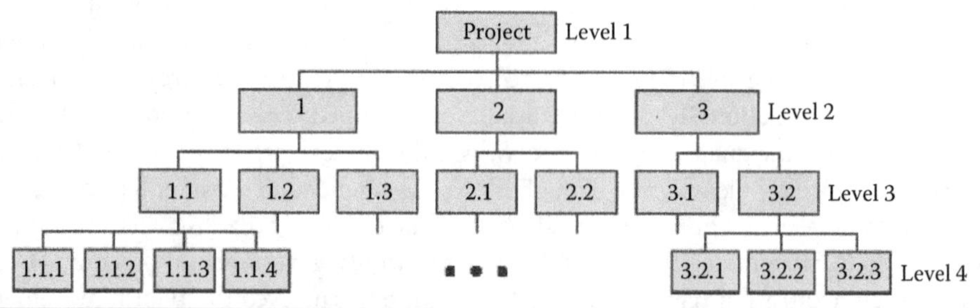

Figure 31.1 Work breakdown structure.

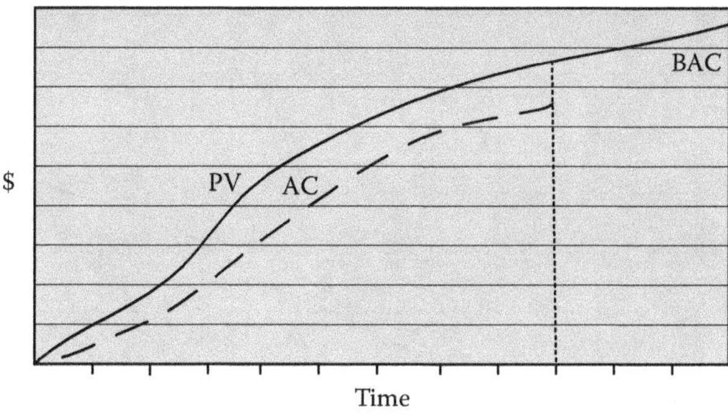

Figure 31.2 Traditional project status chart.

In this fashion, the project schedule and budget are integrated, defined and once approved will become the baseline against which the project performance will be measured. In EVM terminology, the WBS boxes represent the Planned Value (PV) for that work unit and this value will be used for actual performance comparative purposes.

In the baseline schedule, WBS work units become discrete measures for assessing periodic progress. As the project progresses, work unit planned performance through time is measured against actual work accomplished to yield a metric called EV. AC for the work unit is then compared to provide both cost and schedule measures for the project at that status point.

To illustrate the concepts of EVM, it is useful to review a more traditional method for tracking project performance. If the project has been planned in detail, a graph as shown in Figure 31.2 can be used to represent the planned cash flow for the defined work units.

A visual of this type is a traditional method to show project status. Note in this example, the planned versus actual curves indicate that ACs are below plan. Some would feel that this project is doing just fine. Right? Well, maybe not! The missing ingredient in this view is a coherent measure of work accomplished at some status point. If the level of planned work was completed by the status date (July), then the project would in fact be underbudget and ahead of schedule. Conversely, if the project was only 70% complete by the sixth month, but only 50% complete for the planned activities, it would be significantly behind schedule. If we assign a planned measure credit for each work unit that has been completed, then compare that value to the planned work units up to that point and actual resources consumed the earlier status chart might look as shown in Figure 31.3.

Inclusion of the EV curve in the status view supports an improved evaluation of the current project cost and schedule in a quantitative and objective fashion. As an example of an improved status analysis, let's review the sample project status for July (see Figure 31.3):

PV = \$10 million
AC = \$8.2 million
EV = \$6.2 million

This status view better quantifies how the project is actually doing. Note that the data indicates work status is around 62% of plan (6.2/8.2) and the budget status is 75% of plan (i.e., EV/AC). Stated another way, the project is running about 25% higher than planned budget for the work produced. From the schedule view, it is running at about 62% (6.2/10) of planned "speed." Or the project is approximately 38% behind schedule. We will see more on calculation mechanics for

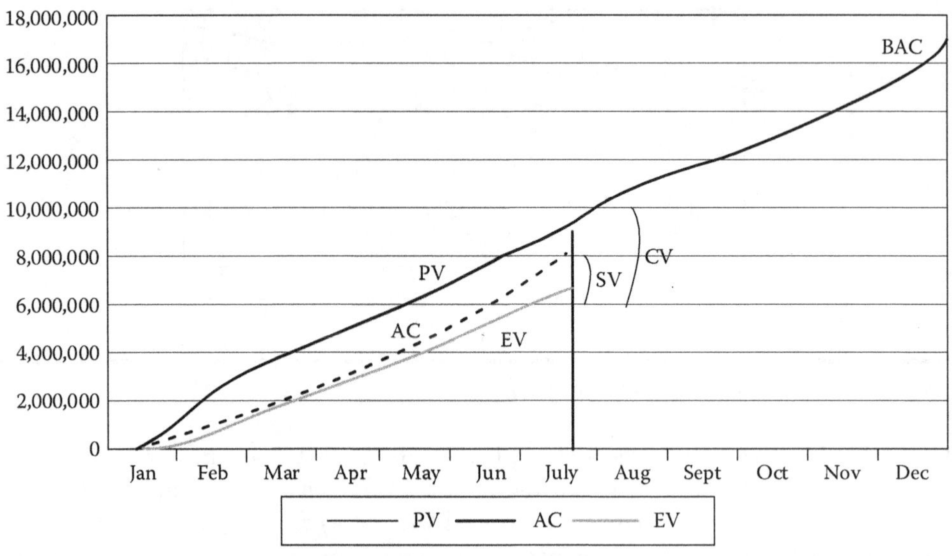

Figure 31.3 Earned value metrics tracking.

these metrics and their interpretation in the next section, but recognize that this is a significant performance management capability.

31.3 EV Parameter Mechanics

Three status variables form the basis of EV metrics. They are the AC, EV, and PV. As a memory device remember these in alphabetical order (A, E, and P). We will show how this leads to the calculation formulae shortly. At the project status point (July) it is necessary to calculate the three parameters as shown above. The following is a definitional view for each:

AC. The AC incurred for the planned WPs up to the status point.
EV. A measure of completed WPs and partially completed portions of WPs up to the status point. For example, a 50% complete WP would receive 50% of the PV as earned.
PV. The sum of planned baseline cost for all WPs scheduled to be accomplished up to the status point.

Using these three parameters various performance metrics can be computed for cost and schedule performance. The four core EVM status metrics are:

- Schedule Variance (SV)
- Schedule Performance Index (SPI)
- Cost Variance (CV)
- Cost Performance Index (CPI)

As a second formulae memory device, remember the performance variables in alphabetical order (C for cost and S for schedule). The formulae set now consists of five parameters—AEP and CS.

Table 31.1 EV Memory Table

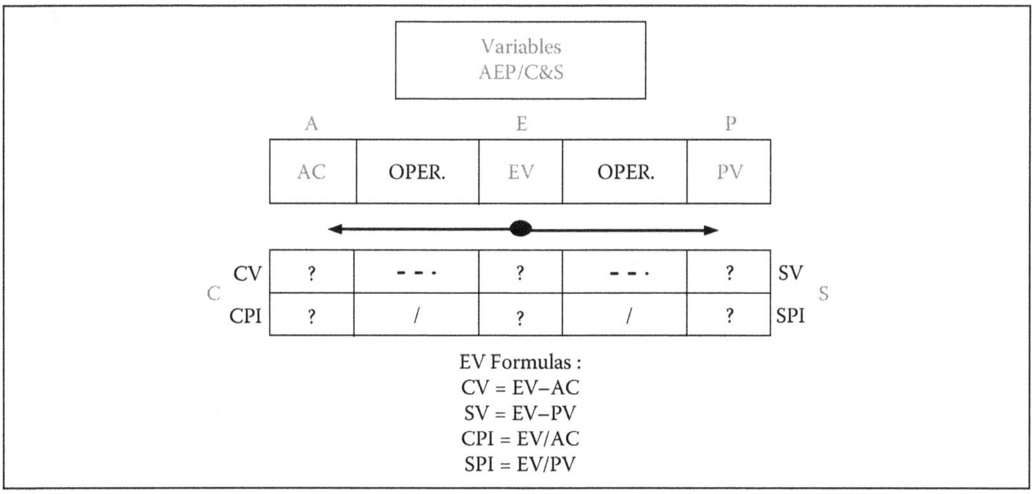

Variables
AEP/C&S

		A		E		P		
		AC	OPER.	EV	OPER.	PV		
C	CV	?	- - -	?	- - -	?	SV	S
	CPI	?	/	?	/	?	SPI	

EV Formulas :
CV = EV−AC
SV = EV−PV
CPI = EV/AC
SPI = EV/PV

This structure provides a memory the key to calculating the four core parameter values. The "memory table" shown in Table 31.1 simplifies how the formulas are structured.

From the table view, we see the AEP values as column headings, with C to the left and S to the right. Once the raw data has been placed into this structure the calculations are easy. The memory table can generate EV Schedule and Cost formulae by starting from the middle of the table (with EV) and move outward toward either the Cost (left) or Schedule (right). So, CV would be EV−AC. The proper operator is a minus for variance formulae and a divisor for an index formula. All formulae either have EV as the first variable or the numerator. Examine the index and variance formulae shown below the table and compare that to the memory table and the associated memory tricks described. Experience suggests that having a method to organize the raw data will save having to memorize formulae. Once you have mastered these basic mechanics the next challenge is to learn how to interpret the quantitative results. This is the challenge for the section below.

31.4 Interpreting EV Parameters

Working definitions for core EV performance parameters are defined below:

SV. Is the difference in dollar value between the amount of work that should have been completed in a given time period and the work actually completed.

CV. Is the dollar value by which the project is either overrunning or underrunning its estimated cost.

CPI. The ratio of cost of work performed (EV) to AC. CPI of 1.0 implies that the AC matches to the estimated cost. A CPI <1.0 indicates that work is accomplished for less cost than what was planned or budgeted. CPI >1.0 indicates that the project is running over the planned cost.

SPI. The ratio of work accomplished (EV) versus work planned (PV), for a specific time period. SPI indicates the time rate at which the project is progressing. Index values have the same interpretation as those for cost.

Budget at Completion (BAC). BAC is the total WP budget for the project. Be aware that a project budget may contain other components such as reserves, overhead, profit, and the like. Those components will have to be analyzed as part of the total project cost, but they should be removed from the status analysis part since they are not "productive" in the sense of the WPs. If material costs are a significant part of the project budget, these should also be removed for the same reason.

Estimate at Completion (EAC). Represents a forecast of the total WP portion of the project costs based on values of CPI and SPI parameters, plus other assessments of past and future conditions. Four alternatives rationale for forecasting EAC are described below. The first formula (EAC1) is used when the prediction is the future project will progress the same as previous history. The estimation formula for this would be:

$$\text{(Standard forecast) EAC1} = \frac{\text{BAC}}{\text{CPI}}$$

However, there are situations where past performance is not forecast to be relevant to current performance. This can be caused by some significant change in the project environment that would indicate a different assumption would need to be used to estimate future results. For the second example assume that the startup has been rocky, but the current view suggests that the project will progress according to plan for the rest of the life cycle. In this view, the appropriate formula would be EAC2:

$$\text{(Poor start-up) EAC2} = \text{AC} + \text{(Remaining WP budget)}$$

This approach is most often used when current actual cost variances are seen as atypical and the project management team expectations are that similar variances will not occur in the future.

The third forecasting option is typically used when the project is going notably bad in both schedule (SPI) and cost (CPI) parameters. This formula would generate a pessimistic forecast EAC3 as follows:

$$\text{(Pessimistic estimate) EAC3} = \frac{\text{BAC}}{\text{(CPI * SPI)}}$$

When CPI and SPI values vary significantly from 1.0, this indicates a likely significant deviation from the baseline plan. Even if one variable is below 1.0 and the other is above 1.0, there is reason to question the plan structure. More typically, both indices will be less than 1.0, which means that both cost and schedule are below the plan. If there is no identifiable reason for these trends to change, a pessimistic EAC can be generated from the EAC3 formula.

Selecting the proper EAC formula to use is based on an assumption related to the future environment. If there is no reason to believe a change will occur, the EAC1 formula or the pessimistic EAC3 formula should be used. Otherwise, EAC2 may be most appropriate. In some cases, calculating all three EAC optional values can provide insights into the potential range of future outcomes.

From this mechanical introduction it is now time to bring up an important point regarding EVM calculations in general. One has to look at these parameters as methods to quantify assumptions. Each of the calculations uses the baseline plan as a comparative target. None of the calculations have "written in stone" interpretations. Think of them as *sophisticated quantification* of assumptions that in turn leads to status or forecasting statements.

Once the core parameters are defined they can be used for further status calculations. Three more vocabulary terms are used in project analysis and forecasting. These are:

PMB. The sum of all PV WPs aggregated by time period for the total duration of the program. The PMB forms the time-phased approved time phased budget plan against which project performance is measured. The PV curve in Figure 31.3 is a considered the project's PMB.

Estimate To Complete (ETC). This parameter is an estimate for the project remaining cost from the status point. It is calculated as the difference between EAC and AC. Senior management and financial groups are the ones most concerned about this number.

Variance at Completion (VAC). This is the difference between BAC and EAC. VAC represents the amount forecast for the project to be over or under budget.

PMB. The sum of all PV WPs aggregated by time period for the total duration of the program. The PMB forms the time-phased approved budget plan against which project performance is measured. The PV curve in Figure 31.2 is a PMB display.

For large projects Christensen found that CPI values tended to stabilize to within ±10% by the 20th percentile point into the project execution cycle (Christensen, 1998, p. 10). This means that once the project reaches this point, CPI is a reasonable predictive forecasting parameter. This is the base logic for the EAC1 formula.

Use of EV parameter values provides great insight into cost and schedule performance for the project. For instance, if the CPI was reported at 0.8 this would imply that the project was using resources at approximately 20% above plan (i.e., running at 80% of plan efficiency). In similar fashion, the SPI metric describes schedule performance. So, an SPI value of 1.2 would suggest that the project was running ahead of schedule by about 20%. General interpretation of the index values is as follows:

- Index values >1.0 is good (better than plan performance)
- Index values <1.0 is bad (below plan performance)
- Negative variance values are bad (below plan efficiency)
- Positive variance values are good (better than plan efficiency)

31.5 EVM Criteria

In the late 1960s, the original DoD definition of EVM was very complex for the contractor community to deal with. Looking back, we would say that these organizations had a fairly low operational maturity; however, we also need to recognize that computer technology was still in an early evolutionary phase and its use was restricted to formal operational systems that did not extend to project management. Plans could be stored, and the accounting system could deliver some measure of ACs, but in general neither the operational infrastructure nor the associated project management processes were capable of collecting the required data. In addition, the original specification contained 35 management criteria (eventually reduced to 32) and very few contractors could satisfy the full set of these support level process requirements. The reader can explore the modern view of these guidelines through various web sites (see www.ndia.org/-/media/sites/ndia/divisions/ipmd/2017-09-meeting/t-ipmd-eia-748-refresh-9-2017-update.ashx?la=en).

Owing to the initial guideline complexity, the vendor community had strong resistance to many of the underlying requirements. These simply did not fit the management mindset of that early period. Over time, there was slow acceptance of a subset of this requirement and eventually a lesser level of implementation was defined. The first simplification is characterized as "simplified" for small projects and a second expanded one appropriate for the typical commercial project of moderate size. This early translation is described below.

31.6 EVM Simplified model

Since there are many more small and simple projects than there are large and complex ones, a simplified version of EVM is desirable for many commercial projects and it still offers the basic EV status overview benefits. The simple criteria are contained in three steps as outlined below (Christensen, 1995, p. 156):

1. Scope definition. Advocates of formal project management techniques would typically do this using a WBS for requirements definition; however, the work may also be defined just through a simple list of tasks. In either case, the work definition needs to be comprehensive and decomposed into reasonably sized WPs that are mutually exclusive.
2. The second step is to assign a PV or budget for each WP. This budget could be in terms of units of currency (e.g., dollars), in hours, or both. For very simple projects, each WP may simply be assigned a weighed "point value" instead of a budget number, so progress is measured in terms of points rather than planned cost values.
3. The third step is to define the earning rules for each WP. One simple method is to apply just one earning rule, such as the 0/100 rule, in which no credit is earned until the WP is complete. Other rule variations may be more applicable to WPs that have greater time duration, such as the 50/50 rule, where 50% credit is earned as soon as the WP is started and the remaining 50% is earned upon completion. These can be further modified to 25/75, 20/80, or any other work credit rules desired.

Typically, these modified earning rules serve to allocate performance credit to WP completion, yet still gives motivation for the project team to get a WP started. Use of earning rules help focus the team's attention on work completion. Nonlinear earning rules tend to work well in situations where WPs are short in duration (e.g., an average of two to four weeks duration). One final rule option is to estimate percent completion for each WP. The challenge here is to get honest status evaluations. From a pure mathematical view, this would provide the most accurate status measure if one can assume an accurate completion assessment. Regardless of the method selected, the process requires a calculation of an "EV" for each work unit. Everything else in the process fits the calculation mechanics described earlier.

Using the steps above, each WP would yield a cost and schedule performance EV metric. It is important to recognize that even crudely calculated metrics, such as those described here, has management benefit because they provide both a measure of current status and a projection model for forward visibility. Overall, this process helps to provide a performance scorecard for the project team.

31.7 EVM for Commercial Applications

Fleming and Koppelman (2006) studied control requirements contained in the ANSI/EIA-748 Standard, and from this review distilled 10 basic management steps necessary to implement a reasonable form of EVM that will satisfy control requirements for most moderate to small projects in any industry. These management process steps are summarized below:

Step 1. Define the scope of the project. One of the most useful tools available to the project manager (PM) is the WBS and it is critical to the EV calculation method.

Step 2. Work definition. Determine who will perform the defined work, and identify all related procurement. The PM must evaluate and assign internal or external HR by balancing constraints such as experience, cost, and whether or not the desired expertise resides in-house. These choices are called the make or buy decisions, and selecting those items that must be bought for the project is an essential extension of the scope definition process. If the work is outsourced, proper care must be given to legal arrangements to adequately protect the project. Whether the staffing is internal or external, the measurement and reporting mechanisms must be defined. The project must be able to continuously measure the EV of a work unit versus the AC of the work being performed.

Step 3. Plan and schedule defined work. EV methods represent little more than a good scheduling system, with authorized resources (budgets) embedded into the schedule (we call this an integrated plan). The schedule must reflect the authorized scope and time frame. From this base, earnings are calculated as work is accomplished. A formal work scheduling system is thus necessary because it is the vehicle that translates the project scope into a time sequence that is necessary for the status calculations.

Step 4. Estimate the required resources and formally authorize the budget. Once the project scope has been fully defined and subsequently planned and scheduled, the next step is to estimate the resource requirements (budgets) for all the defined work units. Each defined WBS element must have a resource value estimated for the specified work. Management will then assess the requested resources and approve this in the form of an authorized project budget. Individual WBS budgets will not contain contingencies or management reserves in the EV analysis portion. They are held separately.

Step 5. Determine the metrics to convert PV into EV. The challenge for this step is to identify viable methods to quantify the authorized work units and then measure the completion of the authorized work. There are various methods of measuring project performance; the most respected ones use some type of discrete measurement. Specific completion milestones representing points in time can be assigned values, which are earned when fully completed. Also, tasks are assigned values, which can be measured as they are partially completed and assigned some EV for the reporting period.

Step 6. Define a PMB and determine the points of management control. EV requires the use of an integrated project baseline containing the defined work, baseline schedule, and authorized budget. Parameter calculation takes place within each of the defined WBS elements. Management control then occurs at focal points placed at selected WBS elements and are referred to as Control Account Packages (CAPs)—See Chapter 15 for a review of the CAP concept. A CAP can be best described as an arbitrary point in the WBS where AC data are collected. On some projects, the total baseline cost may sometimes include such things as indirect costs and even profits or fees to match the total authorized project commitment. The cost baseline must include whatever executive management has authorized for the project, but realize that EV analysis only applies to the direct work portion and not so much for items such as level of effort tasks and material.

Step 7. Record all direct costs consistent with the authorized baseline and in accordance with the organization's general accounting structure. This criterion requires the PMs to have access to the current level of expenditures at the level of detail required. It is essential that direct costs be tracked to a work unit or CAP. In order to employ EV metrics on any project, the ACs must be aligned with the baseline budget. For instance, EV must be relatable to AC by work units in order to determine the CPI, which is the single most important EV performance metric.

Step 8. Continuously monitor EV parameters to determine cost and schedule departures from the base plan (i.e., determine EV variances). Projects employing EV must monitor their cost and schedule results against the authorized baseline throughout the duration of the project. Management should focus their primary attention on exceptions to the baseline plan, particularly those work units that exceed previously defined acceptable tolerances. In this role, EV is a management by exception concept. As previously indicated, the single most important aspect of employing EV is its ability to monitor ongoing cost and schedule status of the project at WP levels of detail.

Step 9. Forecast the final project status. One of the more beneficial aspects of EVM is that it provides the capability to forecast cost and schedule of the project based on current performance. The use of CPI values is particularly valuable in the cost analysis and forecast aspect. However, there is a subtlety in using the SPI metric and one must be more careful using it. Recall that the SPI formula is EV/PV and the rules of EV dictate that the EV of a work unit is its PV at completion. Therefore, unfortunately as a project moves passed the 60th percentile point, this formula begins to lose its predictive value and by definition starts to approach 1.0 at the end of the project. This means that SPI is not a good schedule predictor past this point. We will see another option, called ES, to deal with this later.

Step 10. Manage authorized scope by approving or rejecting all changes, and incorporating the approved changes into the project baseline in a timely fashion. The project PMB set at the project start is only valid as a benchmark value so long as no changes occur. Once a change is approved, the PMB becomes only a historical comparison point. Since changes complicate the status interpretation process they must be handled carefully and effectively. For this reason, a formal change control process is a mandatory operational requirement. Even with this process in place, the EV calculation process becomes more complex as new work units are added to the WBS during the course of the project.

Utilizing the 10 process steps outlined above will provide the typical PM with a reasonable mechanism to satisfy most basic monitoring and control needs. Once an organization becomes comfortable with these steps they can begin to move on to the full standard with 32 defined processes. As we explored in the quality chapter, Chapter 16, a learning organization seeks continuous improvement and that theme is valid here as well.

31.8 Emerging Applications of EVM

This section will describe two variations of the EV system that address peculiarities or shortcomings inherent in the traditional EV metrics. These are presented as an extension of the base theory and are considered complementary to the analysis potential provided by EVM.

31.8.1 Earned Schedule

Historically, the EV measure for cost performance has been based on work unit completion compared to the resource budget plan (i.e., EV compared to AC). This approach works well for cost performance, but as mentioned above poses limitations in the analysis of the project schedule since the value for EV approaches PV at the end of the life cycle. So, calculations of SV and SPI after the 70th percentile begin to generate values that have lost analytical integrity. SV and SPI are measures of work accomplished, versus the time planned for that work. With the benefit of hindsight, these measures might better be called an "Accomplishment Variance." To correct this computational issue Walt Lipke conceptualized an alternative approach to evaluating schedule performance (Lipke, 2003). Following this introduction, Lipke and Henderson have been key proponents for maturing the concept under the banner of *Earned Schedule* (*ES*) (Lipke and Henderson, 2006). ES is an extension of EVM and is designed as a time-based measure. ES is analogous to SV and SPI, except that it is formulated from a duration basis instead of a cost-based measure.

The ES concept is conceptually simple and is illustrated graphically in Figure 31.4. Basically, the SV(t) represents the time variance from the baseline plan (7–5) in the example. This is a measure of how far ahead or behind the planning of the project is at the status point. The advantage of this geometry is that it holds valid through the entire life cycle rather than collapsing as the traditional schedule parameters do.

Figure 31.4 shows the current EV at the status point (value 7) and the ES value is found by moving horizontally from that EV point to the PV curve (value 5). This shows that the actual accomplishment is equal to only time period 5, therefore, the project is two time periods behind the plan. This description may seem a little confusing at first, but becomes very simple by tracing the geometry on Figure 31.4. Based on this view, the time-based metric values translate to a similar interpretation as the traditional EV metrics (Lipke and Henderson, 2006):

$$SV(t) = ES - AT,$$

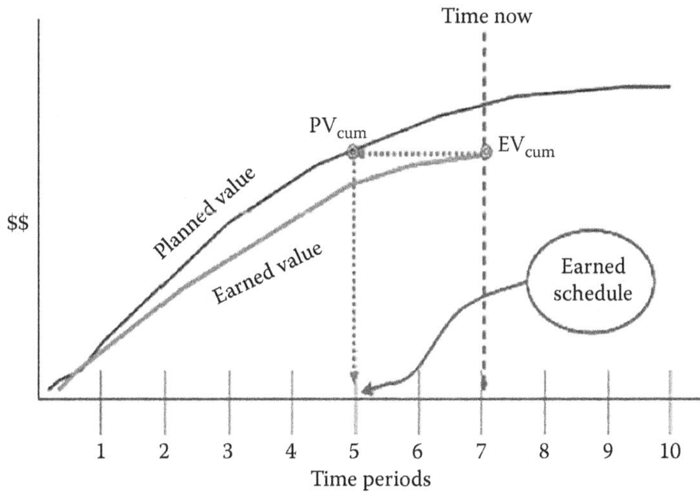

Figure 31.4 Graphical view of ES. (From Lipke, W., 2006. Earned Schedule—An Extension to Earned Value Management. www.earnedschedule.com (accessed May 25, 2018). With permission.)

Where ES is the calculated ES value and AT is the current time; for example, SV(*t*) = 5 − 7 in the example figure.

$$\text{SPI}(t) = \frac{\text{ES}}{\text{AT}},$$

The estimate to completion can now be calculated using this formula:

$$\text{EAC(time)} = \text{actual time} + (\text{planned duration} - \text{ES}) * \text{CF},$$

Where CF is a confidence factor used to forecast how future performance will progress compared to plan. If no change in project efficiency is anticipated the value of SPI(*t*) could be used for this value.

Values generated from these formulae are quite similar in interpretation to the original EV formulae, except that this view is created more from a time perspective that does not suffer from formula degradation as the project goes beyond the 70th percentile point. Translating this view from the graphical view into a more formal quantitative notation is beyond our scope. The interested reader can find more details on this method in the references from Lipke and Henderson.

31.9 ES Mathematical Formulation*

ES as defined by Lipke is: "*The basic idea behind ES is to determine the time at which the EV accrued should have occurred.*" Figure 31.4 shows this by the horizontal line between the EV curve and the PV curve at the status point. Now, let's review the numerical details shown in Figure 31.5 to further explain what the words above attempted to say.

Assume the status point is time period 7. If you trace a line horizontally across to the PV curve you will see that it intersects at time period 5. The interpretation of this says that the project should have been at this point two time periods back. The ES parameter is a number indicating the value of project time. The example shown in Figure 31.5 illustrates that ES is a whole number; however, this is normally not the case. More typically, the dotted line B would fall between two time periods. When this occurs, ES is determined by first counting the number of PV periods completed and then adding the earned fraction of the incomplete period. The amount earned in the partially completed period is determined by linearly interpolating from the known costs (EV and PV) as shown in Figure 31.6

From the schematic in Figure 31.6 and some trigonometry relationships, we see that interim period values can be calculated, even though the math is a little more complicated than the basic EV parameters. More on these mechanics can be found at www.earnedschedule.com/Papers.shtml. Note that the ES indicators are set apart from the traditional EVM schedule indicators by appending a (*t*) to each. When the (*t*) is seen, you know that the indicator comes from ES mechanics rather than the traditional formula approach.

* This section is written by Mr. Walter Lipke who is generally recognized as the inventor of the ES concept and continues to be a strong proponent. More of his material on this topic can be obtained through www.earnedschedule.com/Papers.shtml.

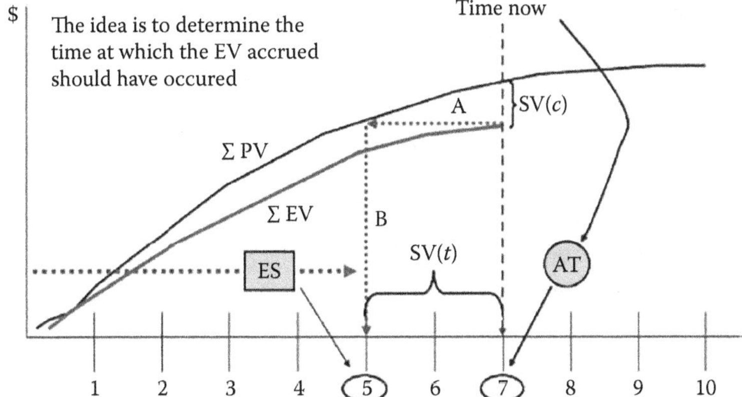

Figure 31.5 ES arithmetic calculations.

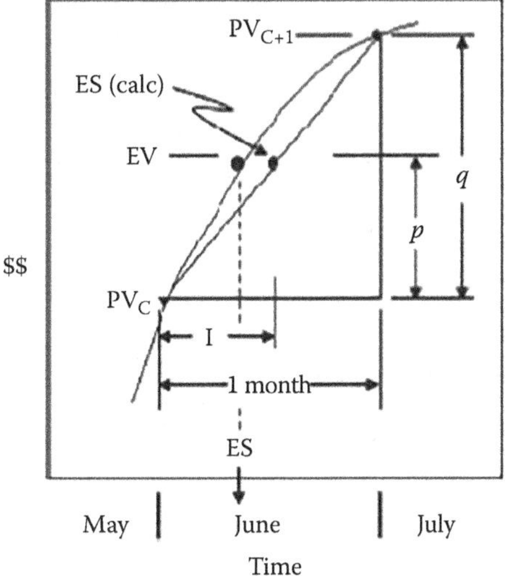

Figure 31.6 ES interpolation.

This section has briefly illustrated how ES parameters can be produced both graphically and mathematically. The interested reader should review further writings from Lipke and Henderson at www.earnedschedule.com.

31.10 TCPI

TCPI stands for To Complete Performance Index and is termed the third type of EVM forecasting tool. This relatively new parameter is designed to help organizations evaluate the potential that a project can complete on budget given current EV parameter values. The basic formula for this term is:

$$\text{TCPI} = \frac{\text{Remaining work}}{\text{Remaining funds}}$$

The definition of remaining work is BAC−EV, which is a straightforward concept given the definition of EV, since EV represents the amount of planned work actually completed. However, the definition of remaining funds can be one of two options. These are:

Option 1. Using planned budget value

$$\text{Remaining funds} = \text{BAC} - \text{AC}$$

Option 2. Assuming an overrun budget value

$$\text{Remaining funds} = \text{EAC} - \text{AC}$$

As can be seen from the basic formula if there is more work remaining than funds remaining the project is going to have to perform better than plan to finish on budget. So, if the value of TCPI is 1.2 the project would have to operate 20% better than plan the rest of the way to finish at BAC, or the same interpretation if EAC is used. Every project manager feels that they can accelerate a plan, but the question is how much is reasonable? That interpretation is where the value of TCPI emerges.

At this stage of evolution this parameter needs more research, but there is growing evidence that projects do not recover budgets easily. Lipke has evaluated this process somewhat and concluded that project TCPI values greater than 1.1 would have a poor chance of budget recovery (Lipke, 2009). When one looks at this parameter in this way we see a check on the project beyond what the EAC forecast provides. As more research is performed, the Lipke conclusion may be refined slightly, but there is some evidence now that the 1.1 value is close to the recovery limit.

31.11 EVM Pros and Cons

While there is general consensus that EVM concepts are useful and meaningful tools for project monitoring and control, it is also acknowledged that their implementation, as defined by the original C/SCSC criteria, or the newer ANSI/EIA-748 Standard, are likely too complex and costly for many commercial organizations. DoD project studies also seem somewhat polarized on this topic. One supportive study contends that the full implementation of the C/SCSC criteria is significant and represents requirement ranked third among the top 10 cost improvement drivers in projects (Fleming, 2006, p. 16). Another study supports this view in finding that stronger implementation of the EVM principles results in greater levels of project success (Goodpasture, 2004, p. 178). A third study concludes that, ultimately, the measure of whether the benefits provided by EVM systems exceed their cost is not quantifiable, but rather subjective in nature. The same study also states that the most compelling evidence that the benefits of EVMS exceed the cost is the major increase of EV usage outside of DoD by other agencies, commercial companies, and other countries (Henderson, 2003).

Fleming and Koppelman outline a list of EVM benefits derived from three decades of government contracts and assert that the application of the criteria is essential for large projects by providing a single management control system providing reliable data. Their research showed that EVM had benefit in the following nine areas (Corovic, 2006):

1. Integrates work, schedule, and cost using the WBS.
2. Supports a performance database of completed projects useful for comparative analysis.
3. The cumulative CPI is an effective early warning signal.
4. The SPI as an early warning signal (with limitations).
5. The CPI as a predictor for the final cost of the project.
6. An index-based method to forecast the final cost of the project.
7. The TCPI to evaluate the forecast final cost.
8. Using the periodic (e.g., weekly or monthly) CPI as a benchmark.
9. Supporting the management by exception principle to reduce information overload.

The list above does not separate the benefits of EV metrics from the general benefits derived from other supporting management processes. One might infer that the application of mature management practices also contributes to these benefits. Issues in producing valid EV parameters can be reasonably summarized by the following eight items:

1. Planning packages can distort results.
2. Level of effort (LOE) and material can distort interpretation.
3. Contracted work packages can distort interpretation.
4. Scope creep can distort the baseline role and distort interpretation.
5. Use of computer-generated parameters may not compute the way you think.
6. SPI formula begins to fail around the 70th percentile through the life cycle.
7. Measurement rules can distort results.
8. Actual cost collection can generate errors by timing or collection accuracy.

This list implies that the operational process requires discipline to achieve valid parameters and the analyst must understand how to properly understand the results.

31.12 Conclusions

EV methodology offers an integrated system for tracking project cost, schedule, and scope and is effective in influencing project performance. There is consensus that the EVM criteria defined by the ANSI/EIA-748 as standard, while suitable for large, cost-reimbursable projects, are considered overkill for small- to moderate-sized initiatives. Given that most projects fall into this lower category, the key to broad-scale successful integration of EVM in commercial practice is to define a subset of management support processes that are simplified, yet effective in providing accurate and reliable performance data necessary for the proper utilization of EV metrics. In this sense, the "lighter" implementations of EVM described here may offer a more feasible solution for most projects. Fleming and Koppelman's 10-step simplified approach outlines the rudiments of a fundamental and sound project management process, which should be practical for most organizations. Use of this would move the basic theory into a broader operational mode and help derive improved monitoring and control metrics.

31.13 Technical Appendix

This section contains three miscellaneous background mechanical items related to this topic. These are:

- Notes on earning rules
- DoD notation translation
- How to use a spreadsheet for crude EV calculations

31.13.1 Notes on Earning Rules

One of the basic tracking issues for work units is to define what portion of the work has actually been completed. EVM methodology requires that some formal consideration be given to this issue and it should be applied consistently across all projects. Summarized below are a few operational rules to consider when making this selection:

WPs. The general rule of thumb for a WP size is 2/80, meaning that it will be sized in the general range of two-week duration and 80 hours of work effort. Other values can be used as guidelines, but effort should be made to keep these as short as possible since large WPs can hide overruns.

LOE. This class of WP can cloud the project status analysis since these charges are independent of accomplishment. Productivity studies should be done without including these WPs in the mix.

Material costs. As with level of effort, material cost variances are caused by factors other than productivity. If material costs represent a significant percentage of the total budget, these should be extracted from the analysis.

Work accomplishment rules. There are several options for recording WP earning. The list below summarizes the implications of the most used approaches.

a. 50/50. This rule gives a 50% credit once the WP is started and the last 50% is withheld until the unit is completed.
b. 0/100. This rule penalizes WIP since no credit is given until the unit is completed.
c. Percentage. This is the most accurate mathematical calculation of accomplishment if one can assume that this can be done and will be done honestly.
d. LOE. This class of resource charge is normally allocated to the WP as defined in the support agreements or as billed to the project based on actual charges.

31.13.2 DoD Notation Translation

Over the last 50 years, the DoD has pioneered the use of EV and through this process has created extensive documentation. Table 31.2 shows a translation from the simplified modern symbols to the classic DoD literature symbols.

The key differences between the contemporary EV symbols and the classic view sponsored by the DoD is found in the definition of AC, EV, and PV equivalents. There is no difference in definition of the respective terms, just notation. It is also important to note that most modern computer systems that deal with EV use the DoD notation since that historically has been the largest audience. The translation shown in Figure 31.2 should be sufficient to allow one to read the governmental documents or computer-generated output without too much confusion.

Table 31.2 DoD Symbol Translation Table

New Terminology	*DoD Terminology*	*Symbols*
Plan value (PV)	Budgeted cost for work scheduled	PV/BCWS
Earned value	Budgeted cost for work performance	EV/BCWP
Actual cost	Actual cost of work performed	AC/ACWP
Authorized work	Budget at completion	BAC
Forecasted cost	Estimate at completion	EAC
Schedule variance	Schedule variance	SV
Cost variance	Cost variance	CV
Completion variance	Variance at completion	VAC

31.13.3 EV Calculations Using a Spreadsheet

The spreadsheet shown below (Figure 31.7) illustrates how a summary level project plan can be used to produce aggregate EV parameters. Reviewing the sample calculations would be a good way to test your knowledge of the basic EV concepts.

Note in this example that the work units are major project phases. Beyond that, all the mechanics described in the chapter are the same. This level of analysis represents an easy starting place for working with the EV model. One disadvantage of this approach is the high level of granularity does not support detailed analysis of lower-level problems.

Problems

1. Basic Gantt Plan

   The simple Gantt chart below contains three activities. PVs for each activity are shown in bold font on each bar. Total completion estimates are shown as a percentage. Time period 2 is the status point. The accounting system has collected ACs for the three activities as 6, 12, and 6, respectively. Compute the EV parameters for this model. What is your prediction for cost and time completion of this project?

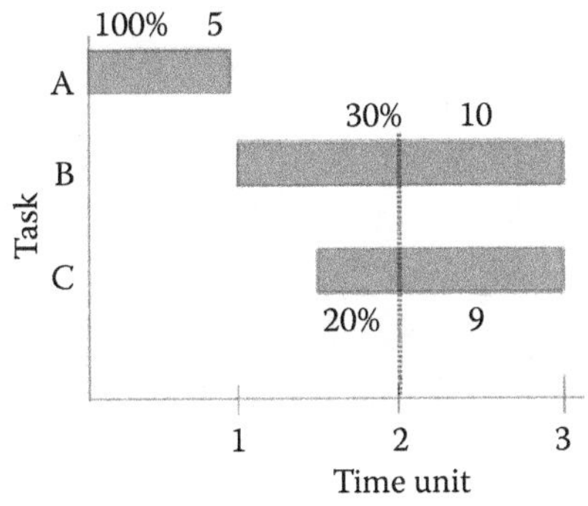

Earned Value Calculation Spreadsheet														
Activity	Jan	Feb	Mar	Apr	May	Jun	Jul	Aug	Sep	Oct	Nov	Dec	PV	% Complete
Soil Work	24,123												24,123	100
Engineering		954,544	1,189,225										2,143,769	100
Equipment and Fabrication				1,851,278	2,328,825	1,708,280							5,888,384	70
Construction							1,730,460	1,766,129	900,042				4,396,631	25
Instrument and Electrical										797,011	786,970		1,583,981	0
Completion Work												1,580,061	1,580,061	0
Planned Value (PV)	24,123	954,544	1,189,225	1,851,278	2,328,825	1,708,280	1,730,460	1,766,129	900,042	797,011	786,970	1,580,061	12,452,907	
**Cumulative Planned Value (PV)	24,123	978,667	2,167,892	4,019,170	6,347,995	8,056,276	9,786,736	11,552,865	12,452,907	13,249,918	14,036,888	15,616,949		
Monthly Actual Cost(AC)	45,000	1,500,000	1,250,000	1,500,000	2,000,000	1,100,000	1,200,000							
Actual Cost (AC)	45,000	1,545,000	2,795,000	4,295,000	6,295,000	7,395,000	8,595,000	8,595,000	8,595,000	8,595,000	8,595,000	8,595,000		
Monthly Earned Value (EV)	24,123	954,544	1,189,225	1,295,895	1,630,178	1,195,796	432,615							
Cumulative Earned Value (EV)	24,123	978,667	2,167,892	3,463,787	5,093,964	6,289,761	6,722,376							
Project EV as of July 31	6,722,376													
Project PV as of July 31	9,786,736													
Project AV as of July 31	$ 8,595,000													
CV=EV–AC	$ (1,872,624)													
SV=EV–PV	$ (3,064,360)													
CPI=EV/AC	78%													
SPI=EV/PV	69%													
EAC cost = BAC/CPI	$ 19,967,298	(original plan divided by CPI)												
EAC time = BAC/SPI	17.47	(original plan divided by SPI)												

Figure 31.7

2. EV Dog Pen Exercise

   Assume that you are the PM for the Dog Pen project. The goal is to build a four-sided dog pen. Each side is budgeted to cost $100 to complete and require one day of your time. As the project progresses the following results are recorded:

   Day 1. Side A completed; spent $100
   Day 2. Side B completed; spent $120
   Day 3. Side C 50% completed; spent $60
   Day 4. Side D not started; spent $0

   a. By inspection and without resorting to EV formulae what is the general status of this project? What is cost at completion? What is schedule completion estimate?
   b. Calculate the following EV parameters

      PV =
      EV =
      AC =
      BAC =
      CV =
      SV =
      EAC =
      ETC =

   c. Using your knowledge of EV interpret the status of this project.

3. Microsoft Project Presentation

   Microsoft Project is a popular project planning utility. The table below shows a sample output from that utility.

	Task Name	Duration	Cost	Baseline Cost	% Complete	CPI	Actual Cost	EV/BCWP	PV/BCWS	SPI	EAC
1	EV Proj	25 days	$5,000	$4,000	45%	0.67	$2,250	$1,500	$3,000	0.5	$6,000
2	A	15 days	$3,000	$2,000	75%	0.67	$2,250	$1,500	$2,000	0.75	$3,000
3	B	10 days	$2,000	$2,000	0%	0	$0	$0	$1,000	0	$2,000

   Use the data shown in the MS Project output to answer the following questions:

   a. What is the current cost status?
   b. What is the current schedule status?
   c. Why is EV value zero?
   d. Given these parameters, how much overrun would you expect for cost and schedule?

4. EV Spreadsheet Template

   One of the more common methods to compute EV parameters is through the use of a spreadsheet. The sample below contains a summary level project plan for a selected level of the WBS.

   Percentage completion estimates for each activity are recorded in column "O." The status point for EV evaluation is May as indicated by the vertical bar. AC data are recorded in rows 15 and 16. Answer the following questions using your knowledge of EV.

   a. Translate these data to produce the project EV status.
   b. What is the condition of the project based on these parameter values?
   c. What is the estimated cost and schedule at completion?

5. Use the schematic below to answer these EV questions. Assume the status point is time 15. Calculate the following EV parameters based on this schematic.

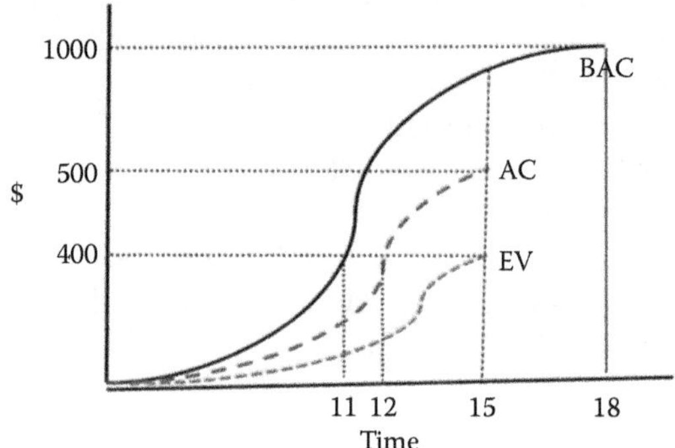

A. SPI = ______________________________
B. CPI = ______________________________
C. EAC = ______________________________
D. ETC = ______________________________
E. Using the theory of Earned Schedule calculate the schedule status for the project shown above. Show your calculations and explain the result.
ES is ______________________________

6. Use your knowledge of EV to evaluate the following data and answer the status questions that follow.

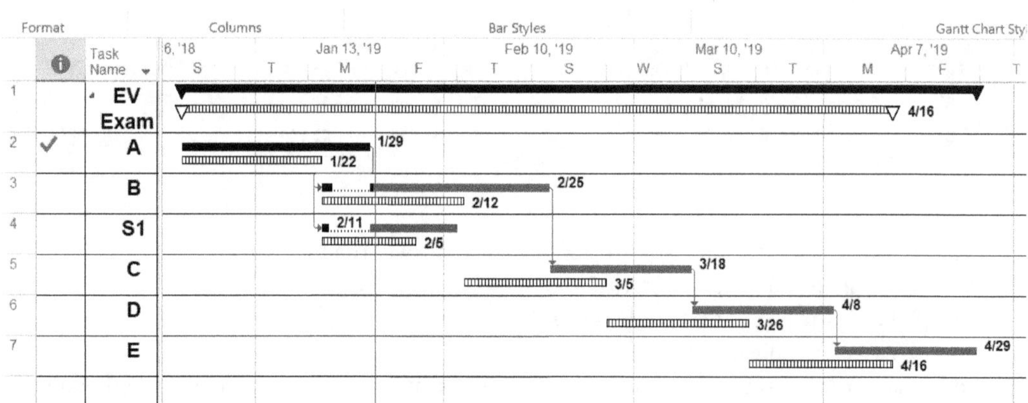

Task Name	Duration	Base;ome Duration	Cost	Actual Cost	% Complete	Baseline Cost	CPI	ACWP	EV/BCWP	PV/BCWS	SPI	EAC	TCPI
EV Exam	83.5 days	75 days	$32,000	$8,000	24%	$28,000		$8,000	$5,800	$8,800			1.11
A	20 days	15 days	$7,000	$7,000	100%	$5,000		$7,000	$5,000	$5,000		$7,000	0
B	20 days	15 days	$6,000	$600	10%	$5,000		$600	$500	$2,000		$6,000	1.02
S1	10 days	10 days	$4,000	$400	10%	$3,000		$400	$300	$1,800		$4,000	1.04
C	15 days	15 days	$5,000	$0	0%	$5,000		$0	$0	$0		$5,000	1
D	15 days	15 days	$5,000	$0	0%	$5,000		$0	$0	$0		$5,000	1
E	15 days	15 days	$5,000	$0	0%	$5,000		$0	$0	$0		$5,000	1

Table View

a. What is the length of this project as approved? _______
b. What is the budget for this project as approved? _______
c. How much of this project has been completed? _________
d. How much has task A changed since the project started? _________
e. What is the value of CPI for task S1? ________
f. What is the formula calculation for EAC for the total project?
   a. (Show only formula and numbers to calculate) _________
g. What is the value of SPI for the project? __________
   a. (Show only numbers for calculations only, not result)
h. If this project had a CPI value of 0.70, what would be the project cost overrun? ______
i. Do you think this project can recover its budget by completion time? Explain your answer. ____

Gantt Bar View

j. How much is the project now scheduled to overrun? ________
k. Discuss your logic for the answer used for question #10_
l. Why is the bar for task S1 split at 1/29? _________________
m. What is the name of the long solid black bar at the top of the view? _______ ______________
n. What do you think the hashed bars represent in this view? ________________
o. What does the value "4/16" in the Gantt bar section represent for task E?

References

Christensen, D.S., 1998. The cost and benefits of the earned value management process. *Acquisition Review Quarterly.* http://citeseerx.ist.psu.edu/viewdoc/download?doi=10.1.1.216.7640&rep=rep1&type=pdf (accessed January 8, 2018).

Christian, D.S. and V.F. Daniel, 1995. Using earned value for performance measurement on software development projects, *Acquisition Review Quarterly*, 156.

Corovic, R., 2006. Why EVM is not good for schedule performance analyses, *The Measurable News*, Project Management Institute.

Goodpasture, J.C. 2004. *Quantitative Methods in Project Management.* Boca Raton, FL: J. Ross Publishing.

Fleming, Q.W. and J.M. Koppelman, 2006. Start with 'Simple' earned value on all your projects, *Crosstalk.* www.crosstalkonline.org/back-issues/ (accessed May 7, 2018)

Haugan, G.T., 2003. *The Work Breakdown Structure in Government Contracting*, Management Concepts.

Henderson, K., 2003. Earned schedule: A breakthrough extension to earned value theory? A retrospective analysis of real project data, Summer, *The Measurable News*, Project Management Institute.

Lipke, W., 2003. Schedule is different, *The Measurable News*, Project Management Institute.

Lipke, W., 2009. The complete performance index … an expanded view, *The Measurable News*, Issue 2. www.earnedschedule.com/Docs/TheToCompletePerformanceIndex.pdf.

Lipke, W. and K. Henderson, 2006. Earned schedule: An emerging enhancement to EVM, November, *STSC Crosstalk.* www.crosstalkonline.org/back-issues/.

Chapter 32

Tracking Project Progress

32.1 Introduction

This chapter will describe a model-based status tracking framework that is focused on monitoring of common project problems and general progress tracking. Basic examples for each of these areas will be offered. The intent here is to build a foundation on to which a new or existing project manager (PM) can develop strategy for managing project execution, tracking, and control in an effective manner. Since each industry and organization has its own nuances, no one source or approach can claim that it has the silver bullet or magic formula of Key Performance Indicators (KPIs) that will fit every tracking and control requirement. The concepts and examples described here are intended to provide reasonable insight into general project control functions. In addition to this, examples of control parameters are discussed along with formal methods for dealing with each.

32.2 Status Tracking

There are six project model status measurement categories: team efficiency, process efficiency, project efficiency, output quality, value, and execution effectiveness. Each of these groups will be compared to the baselined project plan and will be measured using both quantitative and qualitative techniques. The essence of control is measurement, comparison, and corrective action. A key management component of this is tracking ongoing performance against the project baseline.

Previous chapters have described the selection of specific metrics to track status. The focus of this chapter is the use of these parameters in the control process. Specifically, measurement of defined project metrics is the base mechanic for monitoring and control. As the execution process unfolds, project tasks will typically deviate from planned values. The four basic control steps are: define actual task status during execution, measure variances against baseline targets, report performance results, and take appropriate management action to bring the project back into alignment with the plan.

Selecting an appropriate tracking method for a project depends on several factors including the following:

Size of the project: If the project is very small, the PM may track task progress manually. Alternatively, if the project has more than 50 tasks the use of a more automated tracking tool would be desirable.

Communication tool availability: Email systems and other organizational communication tools are often used to distribute progress tracking status. Each of these tools provides a level of capability in providing methods to collect and disseminate task status. The features offered by each tool add incremental value to the overall monitoring and control process.

Tracking granularity: Typically, the needs of the project determine the level of detail at which the progress needs to be tracked. For example, if the project plan has specific resources formally assigned to tasks, a tight budget, or critical deadline the required approach may dictate detailed tracking of the work and costs associated with that task. However, if this level of detail is not needed the PM may choose to track status at higher levels in the WBS (such as summary tasks). Realize that the higher level being tracked leaves an absence of detail at levels below this and that represents the fundamental management decision.

Each organization offers a unique set of tools and project culture. From a project management standpoint, the monitoring and control process requires the following six basic elements:

1. An approved and baselined project plan.
2. A Work Breakdown Structure (WBS) that reflects the level of control appropriate for a particular project. The model rule of thumb is that this means to control work packages (WPs) of approximate 80 hours size. Control Accounts (CAs) represent the chosen cost level of control in this structure, which is often guided by the accounting system capability.
3. A defined method for recording work performed using some form of an Earned Value model (see Chapter 31). Work accomplished for each WP will be monitored according to the defined measurement technique. This process requires measurement of deviations in schedule, work effort, cost expended, risk event, and HR issues. In many cases, the presentation of these items would be presented in a planned (baseline) versus actual manner format, often in graphical views.
4. Estimation of work remaining on each active WP provides a cross-estimate for the work left to be performed.
5. One strategy to deal with variances is to assign follow-up through the Issues log. This action would help ensure formal follow-up and timely action. These items should outline what needs to be resolved to improve future performance. A prioritized list of these issues then becomes a work list for the project team to follow in removing roadblocks.
6. A project communications plan needs to be established during the planning stage to formalize how status data is to be distributed. Mature organizations will have this structure in place, but in some organizations, this will have to be cobbled together by the project team. This plan requirement involves defining formats for stakeholder status reporting along with the timing, media, and mechanism to deliver that status to specific stakeholders.

Figure 32.1 describes a schematic model overview of the basic project monitoring process.

This process is driven by a set of defined control parameters that are the focus of the control process. Physical delivery of control metrics is reflected by the "information distribution" process,

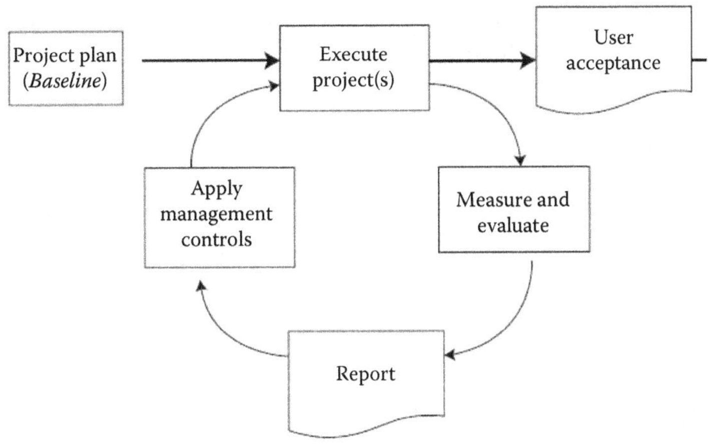

Figure 32.1 Project monitoring and control cycle.

which can be based on a wide variety of technologies. The classic format of status distribution is a printed standard template manually delivered to the recipient; however, the more modern approach for information delivery is to use Internet-based technologies to produce on demand status in flexible formats.

32.3 Tracking Metrics

As described in earlier sections, the project schedule consists of a detailed layout of WPs to be performed and the expected completion time for each. The aggregation of scheduled WPs then represents the tracking schedule targets for control and reporting. Next, some determination must be made for the execution cycle to evaluate schedule, budget, work effort, and accomplishment. Planned hours of work and labor expenditures are measured against actual hours worked. For instance, the project may be showing labor budget variances because of either lower or higher labor rates. In addition, actual hours accrued can be greater than planned because team members may be working additional time in order to meet a project deadline (whether the team resources are being paid for this or not). Deviations from planned resource expenditures from the original schedule will lead to corresponding changes in the cost of the project. In order to collect actual project status, it is often necessary to consolidate inputs from various operational systems such as the organizational accounting system, procurement, and others.

The measurement of project status includes, but is not limited to, project team members, supporting team members, external HR contractual resources, materials, facilities, training, defects, risk events, and team monetary expenditures (i.e., travel). From this array of sources the challenge is to distill the important items that will most dictate future direction. The ongoing question is whether the project will be completed within the originally budgeted cost, schedule, and scope. Analysis of each status parameter can provide an overall mosaic of the project. Various stakeholder groups have unique views regarding what status KPI set is most important to them and this broad perspective requires customization of status presentation to allow the stakeholder to judge the project from their point of view.

The PM must sort through this myriad of status items to decide how to proceed and what items in his tool kit apply to which problem. There is an old adage about how the PM often feels like a one-armed paperhanger and that would seem to apply to this situation. That is, many things popping at once can be a real management challenge to resolve. One final point about the tracking problem is that the data received must occur in a time frame appropriate to effectively use that data. Oftentimes, formal enterprise accounting data are six weeks old when available and it may only be good for historical comparisons. Hence, keep in mind, having accurate data too late is worse than not having data at all. The key is to have usable data in a timely fashion.

32.4 Information Distribution

Distributing project status to appropriate stakeholders is an integral part of the monitoring and control phase. The goal for this activity is to focus on effectively relaying status metrics to team members and stakeholders. Formal status reports should be a regular means of communication throughout the life cycle of the project. These communications should contain appropriate information summarizing activity status, accomplishments, upcoming activities, nontechnical and technical project issues, defined actions to mitigate critical issues, resource usage, and risk status. PMs not only have an obligation to effectively manage a project, they must also be an honest broker of status information, whether that information is what the stakeholders want to see or not.

32.5 Control Model

As described above there are several aspects of a project that must be measured, guided, and maintained. Consequently, effective tracking of project status is a key management step to its success. Control of the project is exercised through formal and informal processes exercised by the PM, project team, and stakeholders. Also, the process of conducting reviews and monitoring reports is a common strategy to exert a degree of control over the project.

The basic project control model components were summarized earlier. Let's now look a little deeper into what support processes are needed for this activity. Specifically, the core components that are required to support the project control process are the project plan, the Issue Management process, the Configuration Management (CM) processes, and the Integrated Change Control (ICC) process. A brief explanation of the role each of these plays is described below.

32.5.1 Project Plan

Project planning is the process of using detailed analysis to chart the step-by-step approach to solve a variance problem, take advantage of an opportunity, or meet a competitive challenge. The project plan establishes the target goal, sets the project schedule, work requirements, and resources needed to complete the project. This plan is then used to guide the execution of WPs; it also establishes procedures for dealing with quality, risk, communication, and change management. The ongoing planning process must be flexible and open to modification as communications within the team provides new insights. The more that planning is based on good analysis, the better the chances of ultimate success. The full life cycle plan considers everything in an organization and its long-term achievement of a desired objective. In this view, planning may consist of an orchestrated collection of sub-plans for specific short-term projects.

32.5.2 Issue Management Process

Issues represent relatively short unplanned events that need to be resolved to keep the project moving forward. These are typically supporting items such as a copy machine down, key employee out sick, or other such events that are thought to be fixable with proper monitoring. PMs cannot predict what or when a specific issue will occur, but all agree that such events will occur during the life cycle. In many ways, these are like small risk events that can be resolved reasonably quick. Issues occur from many sources: natural events, technological glitches, supporting resources, and economic fluctuations. Within this unplanned domain an Issue Management process provides a mechanism for organizing, maintaining, and tracking the resolution of these ad hoc items that might not be resolved in the normal course of activity, or in a timely manner.

The Issue Management process entails establishing appropriate identification and control mechanisms and defined processes to aid the project team in identifying, addressing, and prioritizing ongoing problems and issues. In order for this process to be effective, documentation and communication is key. Detailed understanding regarding the issue needing resolution triggers the process. From this base point, the PM makes sure that the item has appropriate documentation and priority for resolution and a named person responsible for tracking that resolution. Without a system of this type various daily issues get lost in the maze of work and can lay unresolved until they become major roadblocks. Proper management of this class of activity is a critical success factor for the PM.

32.5.3 Configuration Management

Configuration Management (CM) a key process used to manage and control change in documents and products throughout the life of the project. Various work activities result in continual modification for most product and management documents and these changes are a normal part of every project. Failure to monitor this activity and provide appropriate management oversight is considered by many to be the number one operational control requirement.

The CM process involves ensuring that both the process and product artifacts are properly managed. For example, in a durable manufacturing project this process would ensure that a drawing for a part was the latest version. A common problem source in product-oriented projects is having two individuals work on a document at the same time, but only the last person saving the document would have their changes reflected. In the project management domain, the control process would ensure that all management documentation is the latest version. Most CM solutions require a formal controlled repository for managing the flow of these project artifacts. Some organizations call this activity *Version Control.* In the contemporary environment, automated document management software is often used to manage the flow of documents. Prior to this, manual processes struggled to ensure changes to descriptive documentation created in the project were tracked effectively.

32.5.4 Integrated Change Control

Integrated Change Control (ICC) and CM are brothers in the control process. One way to separate these two processes is to view CM as the static control mechanism and ICC as the workflow and decision-making component. The ICC process allows the PM, sponsor, and stakeholders to be aware of and manage changes made to the project during its life cycle. Many projects have scope increases in the range of 2% a month, or more, and with this rate of change it is easy to see how the control process can get out of hand. Change control is the process that is designed to manage changes requests and ensure that any changes made are appropriate to the goals of the project. Approval for these changes should occur externally to the project team and a project board representing management usually handles the decision-making part of the approval process. Without this type of control, a project can become a runaway effort. In addition, this activity adds the required higher-level management oversight to the project. The project board in theory keeps the project within the boundaries established by the Charter, or approved baseline. Within this boundary they attempt to balance user needs and the approved milestone values of the plan.

32.6 Knowledge Area Controls

Basic status tracking processes exist for each of the four output knowledge areas (KAs)—scope, schedule, cost, and quality. A brief summary of tracking issues related to each of these is provided below.

32.6.1 Scope Control

Scope changes can be stimulated by either external requests, or from activities within the project team. In either case the scope control process is designed to manage approval of any changes, manage the actual changes as they occur, and to ensure that the change is properly integrated into the overall project deliverables. Execution of this process requires a formal change procedure (ICC) to document the request and then map the process through which such requests flow. This includes project board approval, tasking to the team for execution, checking results to ensure proper results, and monitoring of the activity through its life cycle. The term for changes in a project is "scope creep." Certainly, one of the major goals of scope control is to minimize this activity based on its potential adverse impact on project success.

32.6.2 Schedule Control

This is managed at the project level by the PM and should be proactive in nature as is the case with all control strategies. When variations from the planned schedule are measured they must be evaluated as to root cause, then appropriate action must be taken to solve the issue with the least negative impact on the project.

32.6.3 Cost Control

The *Project Management Body of Knowledge (PMBOK®) Guide* defines cost control as "monitoring the status of the project to update costs and manage changes to the baseline" (PMI, 2017, p. 257). An additional aspect of this process is to ensure that the changes are beneficial, determining that the project budget estimates have changed, and managing the actual changes when as they occur (Commonwealth of Virginia, 2006). Effective project cost control includes the following activities (PMI, 2017, p. 258):

- Influencing the factors that create changes to the authorized cost baseline;
- Ensuring that all change requests are acted on in a timely manner;
- Managing the actual changes when and as they occur;

- Ensuring that cost expenditures do not exceed the authorized funding by period, by WBS component, by activity, and in total for the project;
- Monitoring cost performance to isolate and understand variances from the approved cost baseline;
- Monitoring work performance against funds expended;
- Preventing unapproved changes from being included in the reported cost or resource usage;
- Informing appropriate stakeholders of all approved changes and associated cost; and
- Managing expected cost overruns within acceptable limits.

Budget issues should be considered strategically, not just taking into account cost but the department's responsibilities concerning payment and the details thereof.

32.6.4 Quality Control

Emphasis on quality management is a process performed throughout all the project life stages. From a project management model standpoint a quality management plan will be defined during the planning phase in order to define the process for measuring the attributes of work performed at each stage, as well as to provide control specifications and guidelines for team members to ensure the quality of work required for the deliverable and overall workflow of the project.

There are differing schools of thought regarding the proper control metrics and processes for a project. However, the control examples outlined above should be considered a requirement for keeping the project on task. Do recognize that every approach to standardization brings with it a potential negative if misunderstood or mismanaged. Some feel that the style of control outlined by the model described here is very inefficient and causes more harm than good. For example, Koskeia and Howell state that "control as described in the *PMBOK® Guide* causes problems" (Koskeia and Howell, 2000). They cite the following five counterproductive issues that arise from a standardized control model:

- A standard guide control process is focused on explanations rather than corrections. In other words, more time is spent explaining why there is a problem, instead of resolving the problem. In this mode, team members can be distracted from current real project-related tasks in order to create historical accounts of the previous day's work. Unless this activity is related to finding root-cause solutions, such actions fall under the banner of sunk costs that are not productive to pursue.
- Koskeia and Howell suggest that managers will find ways to manipulate tasks and schedules to give the illusion of good performance. "In order to make cost variance positive, managers try to show a decrease in the actual cost of work performed as much as possible" (Koskeia and Howell, 2000). This can have the effect of making the metrics appear normal, but in fact there will be underlying negative implications in the actual output. Manipulating output measurements for the simple goal of improving status appearance is obviously against the goal of good project management.
- A tight control strategy can limit the ability to manage the team's resources by taking away flexibility of the PM. Low-level external monitoring can lead to increased pressure to stay within planned parameters at a low level. This, in turn, hinders project performance because resources cannot be moved from one activity to the next throughout the project as dictated

by the skill of the PM. In this situation, there is the implied suggestion that project schedules force WP managers to focus only on their portion of the project and show no concern for the overall project. Therefore, managers may hoard idle resources that could be actively used to complete other aspects of the project.

- "Control may give the wrong interpretation of performance" (Koskeia and Howell, 2000). Continuous measurement and comparison of each activity does not yield control of a project. Large projects cannot be effectively measured using such yardsticks.
- Control does not always succeed in revising the plan after variances have been detected. Regardless of how a plan or schedule has been laid out for a project, sticking to that plan without analysis of current issues or planned deviation may result in poor judgment calls because management may be overly focused on staying within the bounds of an already failed plan.

Implementation of any control process must include the awareness regarding how over-specification can impact success as much as under-specification.

We have seen many examples to illustrate how projects are complex undertakings. The management theme regarding control communications says that we must remain true to all of the stakeholders in regard to honest status reporting. We have also seen that proper selection of status metrics as important in this activity. So long as the project is moving along with minimal plan versus actual variances, the control process tends to be orderly. However, when these variances start to become larger and the goal becomes one of moving the project back into some baseline structure the corrective actions become more radical. At that point, the need for a more enlightened management approach becomes critical and the PM needs to have more flexibility in how to approach the problem and make "appropriate" trade-off decisions. In this situation, the future outcome will likely be some major deviation from the baseline plan. For a PM hamstrung with minimal decision authority, this situation becomes untenable.

32.7 Project Status Tracking Case Study

A good example of project control comes from the F/A-18 Advanced Weapons Lab (AWL) software upgrade. Bowers writes the following description of that effort which consisted of an extraordinary number of project requirements representing new technology in the specified capability, aircraft systems, and configuration parameters (Bowers, 2002):

> "The biggest challenge, by far, was providing for efficient use of critical mission computer resources to allow for successful implementation of all the requirements," says Brestal. "An MC resource team was formed to devise and implement risk mitigation plans for each affected resource."
>
> Capers Jones, a Top 5 judge agrees that this project was large and complex. "The combination of low rates of delivered defects and high levels of customer satisfaction indicates this project was very well planned and managed." Jones cites the control processes used as a key to their success. "The project was produced by a SEI CMM Level 4 organization, and demonstrates the value of the higher CMM levels."

To achieve this quality goal, the AWL team achieved the following:

- Improved organizational maturity levels to achieve repeatability.
- Used a formal maturity measurement process to assess organizational maturity and process area capability. Established priorities for improvement and methods to implement these improvements.
- Published, updated, and distributed a strategic plan that defines basic core beliefs, visions, and mission.
- Tested jointly with the Operational T&E Squadron throughout the verification phase of 15C. This gave them an early look at the product and gave the AWL earlier insight into operational problems in the product.
- Published an F/A-18 Management and Systems Engineering Process Manual to systematically identify and apply leverage to areas of weakness and expand on what they do right.
- Maintained and improved its system-configuration review board process to obtain a very solid, well-thought-out, and adequately funded set of requirements.
- Improved on and used a comprehensive set of metrics.

Embedded in this case is a clear indication that success was achieved by formulating formal control processes linked to tracking and control. Also, note that even a mature organization such as Boeing designed custom activities for this project. These processes and metrics were used to monitor the outcome and there is evidence of a well-developed project plan.

Lessons learned from previous projects offer the best design guidance for new projects within the organizational culture. Companies such as Raytheon and NASA report how the analysis of past less than desirable results provided them the guidance for project tailoring. Raytheon went through several iterations before they finally developed a standardized process that was in line with the company's culture. NASA learned from eight previous failed projects by identifying common issues in their project failures and using this knowledge to foster a culture of project success.

Although it is somewhat difficult to map these specific examples across other project types, the underlying thought processes illustrated here are consistent with the model described in this chapter. This general approach has been used successfully by other projects and there are case studies of failed projects that have not followed this model. Collectively, knowledge gained from experiences across many organizations have led to the conclusion that in order to have successful project execution a project should have a detailed and flexible plan of attack. Progress tracking and control should be primary components of day-to-day management activities, but the mechanics regarding how to handle these measured results is the key to success. Regardless of how structured the organization can make the project management process, they ultimately conclude that humans defy complete structure. One should not view any model control structure as a cookie cutter exercise with no changes.

32.8 Conclusion

Successful execution control of any project is complex because of the wide variety of causal factors. For this reason, tracking progress and control-related activities are key elements to success. The methods discussed here represent a cross-section of core monitor and control concepts used in the project management arena. Beyond the raw mechanics of this activity, it is important to recognize that the collection of a planned versus actual status metrics neither hinders nor enhances project success. These simply passively describe what is occurring, or what did occur. It is up to the management process to take this data and use it properly in influencing an improved outcome. Also, this discussion has highlighted that the design of the tactical control process must be reviewed for each project to decide which combination of methods and degree of granularity will work best in that set of project characteristics.

The concept of management control flexibility is an important ingredient to effective control and one that many organizations do not always adhere to. In these situations, the goal of control standardization is so strong that management flexibility is removed out of the process. For average skilled PMs and less technical projects this may be a suitable strategy, but for complex projects being managed by a highly skilled manager, this overly structured approach can result in a less effective outcome. It is important to not tie the hands of the PM to the point where he has no degrees of freedom left in tracking and resolving the deviant issues.

References

Bowers, P. 2002. The F/A-18 Advanced weapons lab successfully delivers a $120-million software block upgrade. *Crosstalk*. www.stsc.hill.af.mil/crosstalk (accessed November 25, 2017).

Commonwealth of Virginia, 2006. Project Management Guideline, Section 4 Project Execution and Control Phase, ITRM Guideline CPM 110-01. www.vita.virginia.gov/uploadedFiles/Library/cpmg-appendix-c.pdf (accessed November 25, 2017).

Koskeia, L. and G. Howell, 2000. Reforming Project Management: The Role of Planning, Executing, and Control http://usir.salford.ac.uk/9384/ (accessed May 4, 2018).

PMI, 2017. *A Guide to the Project Management Body of Knowledge (PMBOK® Guide)*, 6th ed. Newtown Square, PA: Project Management Institute.

Chapter 33

The Closing Process

The *Project Management Body of Knowledge (PMBOK®) Guide* defines the Close Project the process "as finalizing all activities for the project phase and contract…" (PMI, 2017, p. 634). For multiphase projects, the Close Project process closes out that portion of the project scope and associated activities applicable to the phase. The closing process should address activities related to all knowledge areas. This process also establishes procedures to investigate and document the reasons for actions taken if a project is terminated before completion (PMI, 2017, p. 633). Collectively, these activities include actions related to project administrative and contractual issues.

Administrative closure procedure: This procedure finalizes all activities for the project, phase, or contract. This includes defined work completed, organizational resources, and releasing resources back to the enterprise for re-assignment (PMI, 2017, p. 160).

Seningen describes the closing process as (Seningen, 2008):

> Sharing knowledge in a systematic format, documenting lessons-learned, and ensuring frequent communication will maximize project success factors.

Whether managing one project or multiple projects, the value of lessons learned sharing and communication should not be undervalued. It can be the difference between total project success and missing key issues. When managing a team of PMs who work on similar and ongoing projects, the value of lessons learned documentation and communication should be evident, although polls would probably show that this discipline is limited in practice (Seningen, 2008).

33.1 Project Implementation Review

When conducting a Project Implementation Review (PIR), updating the lessons learned documentation, as well as holding lessons learned review meeting is critical for at least the following:

1. Supply knowledge that will help to not repeat the same mistakes.
2. Improve the probability of balancing the triple constraint so as to not have cost or schedule overruns on future projects.

An example of the mistakes and problem areas that typically occur and that could be reviewed as part of lessons learned documentation is as follows:

1. Vendor management
2. Equipment issues
3. Project approval process
4. Budget approval process
5. Communication issues (lateral and vertical)
6. Testing
7. Technical support
8. Training

All projects commence with an optimistic forecast for their completion. Unfortunately, experience suggests that the actual outcome is often quite different. In fact, these variances can have implications for future project outcome. Some may say that a project team just does the best they can under uncertain conditions, so why worry about documenting these results after the project is completed. In fact, there are multiple reasons why a formal closing process is not only prudent, but a required activity. The sections below will explore this point in greater detail.

Cleland and Ireland (2002, p. 435) describe that all projects end, even though it may not be because the planned deliverables have been achieved. Whatever may be the final state of a project, the outcome should be closed in a formal fashion as outlined in this chapter. Cleland (2004, p. 503) describes two kinds of a project termination:

> "Positive termination occurs when the project comes to closure with a positive outcome and an upbeat relationship with the customer and stakeholders." Negative termination occurs when the project is terminated but with less-than-positive sentiments between the project and client organizations.

Meredith and Mantel (2003, pp. 644–648) offer a broader view of reasons for project termination and an adaptation of that list follows:

- The project is terminated when the required deliverables have been completed. Planned schedule and budget may or may not be as planned.
- Termination by extinction—original reason for the project has changed.
- Project is terminated because the time, cost, and functionality balance is no longer deemed worthy of continuation. As an example, although a new product is developed, it does not show any remarkable result.
- Merge or affiliation between two companies or organizational groups makes the project redundant. One of the projects would be terminated as a result.

Cleland (2004) describes five specific objectives for a formal closing process:

1. When the project is over, what do you expect to see changed in the organization?
2. What documentation and physical materials do you expect to have at your disposal after the project is disbanded?
3. What form do you expect these preferred changes to take?

4. What communication media will be used for sharing lessons learned data (e-mail, telephone, instant messaging, etc.)?
5. What specific protocol is to be followed to communicate closure results to the organization?

33.1.1 Normal Project Termination

In the normal termination situation, the project produces a successful outcome, and a new product or process is now installed and working. For this case the lessons learned format and protocol should follow a standard set of activities. One of the basic management activities required is to formally transfer the project dedicated property, equipment, human resources, and material to appropriate organizational entities. The deliverables from the project now are operational entities in the organization, and so a new support infrastructure is required. Meredith and Mantel (2003,p. 647) provide a scenario example for this situation:

> The project team that installed a new piece of software, instructed the client in its operation and maintenance, and then departed, probably leaving only minor problems behind it. This is a scenario familiar to experienced managers. However, if the installation was an entire flexible manufacturing system, or a major software system complete with multiple terminals and many different pieces of software, then the complexities of user integration are apt to be much more severe.

As a general rule, the more mature global organizational processes are more likely to handle project closing activities in a consistent manner. Organizations that do not formally recognize this activity would be categorized as process immature.

33.2 Abnormal Termination

When projects are terminated for reasons other than successful completion, the closing process will tend to be more customized in nature. Contractual relationships will need to be carefully negotiated and clauses related to early termination will have to be reviewed. This will involve more than just checking payment and delivery status for a completed contract. If termination occurred because of a management action, those conditions will have to be addressed. In these early termination situations, the skill levels required may be higher than simply closing out accounts.

33.3 Termination Model

Figure 33.1 outlines a Work Breakdown Structure structure of activities structured around project, scope, contract, and site-related activities required to close the project (Taylor, 2001).

When a project is finished or terminated, some organizations employ specially trained managers and technicians to close the project. One of the key activities for this team is to review the status of work packages by budget, schedule, and technical performance parameter. Cleland and Ireland (2002, pp. 443–444) summarize their view of these activities as follows:

1. Ensure that all project deliverable end products are properly transferred to the new asset owners, along with appropriate standard records.

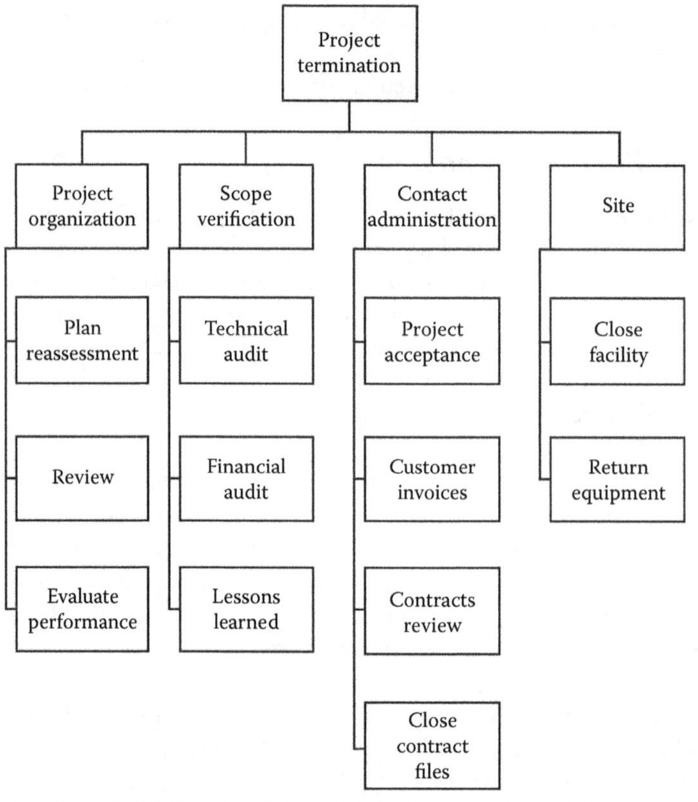

Figure 33.1 WBS for project termination.

2. Review that all contractual requirements have been met and properly record any variations along with their resolution conditions.
3. Define the list of stakeholders related to new environment (i.e., product or process support)
4. Help the project team members find other project assignments.
5. Prepare "lessons learned" to assist future project teams in assessing similar situations.
6. Analyze the weakness and strengths of the project, and explain how the project team dealt with the problems and what is necessary for future project teams to avoid negative situations and utilize the positive items identified.

33.4 Project Termination Checklist

One of the typical organizational approaches to implementing a formal closing process is to produce a checklist that the project team must execute for official project ending. Horine (2005, pp. 282–284) outlines the following 13 important topic areas to be covered in the project checklist:

1. *Obtain client acceptance:* This stage has to be accomplished before the team attempts to close the project. In this activity, the most important result is that the client formally verifies and accepts the project deliverable and this event is formally documented.

2. *Transition deliverables to owner:* In this activity, the team formally hands off the project deliverables to the new owner. This includes not only possession of the item, but also ability to support the item long term.
3. *Close out contract obligations:* The project team will coordinate with procurement personnel to document status of all contractual relationships. This should include not only the status, but resolution plans for all variances to the agreements. Items such as warranty process and bonus clauses need to be documented as well.
4. *Capture lessons learned:* Documenting the project team's experience-related activity enables future projects to avoid some mistakes and challenges faced by the existing team. Horine explains that "lessons learned should be documented throughout the project lifecycle and include both positive and negative aspects of the project."
5. *Update organization's central information repository:* This activity involves documenting project records and deliverables as a formal archive for the organization. Horine states that "it is a powerful way to reduce learning curves and gain efficiency on future projects."
6. *Document final project financials:* This activity involves documenting the final project financial reports such as a budget status summary and variance analysis.
7. *Close various accounts and charge codes:* This activity involves the process of closing team member accounts and codes related to financials, infrastructure, and security.
8. *Update resource schedules:* Work to ensure that team members have appropriate job opportunities following the closure.
9. *Conduct performance evaluations:* The PM needs to ensure that appropriate performance feedback is performed and documented for all team members.
10. *Update team resumes:* The team members should update their resumes to reflect the new project activity.
11. *Market project accomplishments:* Formally recognize team member accomplishments and overall project positive experiences.
12. *Review project performance with clients:* Horine says that "the best testament to evaluate client satisfaction is to see whether the sponsoring or [user] individuals (organization) will officially endorse team's work." This is a process to know whether the team really achieves the desired goal.
13. *Celebrate:* From at least a morale standpoint, it is important to find something to celebrate at the conclusion of a project. Almost all projects have had some good experience, and reminiscing about these is a good way to leave the project team feeling positive about their experience. These experiences have long-lasting motivational value to the individuals involved and help build a positive culture.

The steps above have value not only for the termination phase but can also be of intelligence value as each life cycle stage is completed.

33.5 Project Team and Client Relationship

Basically, the closing role of the project team is to gain client acceptance for the items delivered. In many cases, this will not be exactly what the original plan defined. Wysocki (2007, p. 358) states that "... acceptance can be very informal and ceremonial, or it can be very formal, involving extensive acceptance testing against the client's performance specifications."

Ceremonial acceptance represents the opposite of formal acceptance, and two situations fall under this heading. The ceremonial form might be orchestrated as a scheduled demonstration of the product capabilities. This is usually a management level session that occurs after the technical acceptance has been completed. Wysocki describes formal acceptance as a predefined process through which the project team proves conformity to planned results that the client wanted. In this case, a checklist has important meaning, and "… is used and requires a feature-by-feature sign-off based on performance tests. These tests are conducted jointly and administered by the client and appropriate members of the project team." Both forms of acceptance are important client relationship processes.

33.6 Creating Lessons Learned Documentation

Creating lessons learned documentation is a key evaluation methodology for the project. Two of the key guiding philosophies of project management are planning and measurement. The lessons learned documentation serves the role of describing the project environment beyond what has previously been communicated in formal reporting documentation variables. This exercise gives the team an open format opportunity to analyze all aspects of a project phase or the entire project, both positive and negative. Organizations should have a goal of continuous improvement and this is one of the key processes that can support this goal. Morris and Pinto (2007, p. 253) comment that an effective internal evaluation is necessary for at least three reasons:

1. Evaluation defines what the unfinished project needs to accomplish and helps in classifying future project objectives.
2. Evaluation provides formal feedback to the project team and their peers in regard to measurable accomplishments.
3. Evaluations are a core element of organizational learning and should be carried out with a view of providing guidance on future ventures.

Baca (2007, p. 447) states that the lessons learned process helps in evaluating processes, tools, and techniques that worked either well or poorly on the project. The lessons learned process can be produced either by the project team or by an external audit model. Regardless of the data collection process used, the following ground rules should be followed:

- No topic area is off-limits.
- Speak in terms of process, not people problems.
- When successful events are documented, it is appropriate to credit specific individuals.

33.7 Lessons Learned Report

Wysocki (2007, p. 363) describes the final lessons learned report as a formal representation of the project's memory and history. This document serves as a valuable source for others to learn and research situations faced by the project team. During the project life cycle the project team can use this document for their internal analytical and review purposes; however, the more likely value will be for future project efforts. This means that the document should be readily accessible for other teams to use as a reference document. Use of computerized document management tools is useful for opening up access to this class of data. In the operational mode, this archive should be a shared, searchable online database. One issue that may be encountered when implementing shared knowledge comes from the behavioral trait that some people tend to be territorial about the knowledge they have gained.

An example data set for the lessons learned document follows:

Overall success of the project: The project team should summarize the areas they feel the project succeeded in.

Organization of the project: The life cycle used by the project team is an important item for others to see and this can be an important factor in how the project progressed. Issues such as major stages, milestones, project authority details, project board organization, and the like are key items.

Techniques used to get results: The document should record a list of major problems faced and the solution strategies used to resolve them.

Project strengths and weaknesses: Each project is unique with their strengths and weaknesses. These should be expressed in terms of features, practices, and processes utilized by the team. The goal would be to avoid less successful items and take advantage of the more successful ones. Weaknesses that lead to individuals should be avoided, but positive attributes linked to an individual are appropriate for the document.

Project team recommendations: The project team should translate the project-related items outlined above into an organizational improvement recommendation format. Peer recommendations are one of the strongest support sources for subsequent teams. These recommendations are not formulated by remote staff, but by individuals who have fought through the real problems.

33.8 Project Team Celebration

Regardless of the reason for a project's termination, the project team should celebrate prior to disbanding. Essentially all projects have both high and low events and the celebration process helps to build a positive morale boost for the time spent together. Rationale for this is that it is easy to just walk away with the feeling that the entire effort was a failure and thankless. One goal at this point is to give the team a lasting positive experience. There is always something positive in the project experience and the team members need to have this reinforced for both professional and morale reasons. For projects that have successfully delivered a complex product or process the celebrations are easy and long lasting. However, in cases where the project produces less than planned results, it may be necessary to be more creative in finding a celebration theme, but in either case the effort is a necessary management activity.

Team performance bonuses are a nice way to make the celebration process easier to execute for sure. The low end of a celebration can be just a team meeting to discuss the experience and thank the individuals for their hard work. At the high end of the spectrum, a catered party for the families with a live band certainly makes a positive impression. The final advice for this activity is to be sure that lessons learned are documented and the appropriate celebration is orchestrated. Do not underestimate the positive value of this activity.

33.9 Conclusion

One of the major closure activities for the project team is to produce lessons learned documentation and transfer their acquired knowledge to others. Project termination is one of the most mishandled tasks in the life cycle of a project. It means the end of the relationship between the project team and their client. At this point, final resolution of the effort is no longer in doubt. Hopefully, the effort has been successful and the team morale is high. Regardless, this is the time to dissolve the team and help them move on to another job location with a positive feeling.

References

Baca, C.M., 2007. *Project Management for Mere Mortals: The Tools, Techniques, Teaching, and Politics of Project Management.* Boston, MA: Pearson Education Inc.

Cleland, D.I., 2004. *Field to Project Management,* 6th ed. Hoboken, NJ: Wiley.

Cleland, D.I. and L.R. Ireland, 2002. *Project Management: Strategic Design and Implementation,* 4th ed. New York: McGraw-Hill.

Horine, G.M., 2005. *Absolute Beginner's Guide to Project Management.* Boston, MA: Que Publishing.

Meredith, J.R. and S.J. Mantel, 2003. *Project Management: A Managerial Approach,* 5th ed. Hoboken, NJ: Wiley.

Morris, P.W.G. and J.K. Pinto, 2007. *The Wiley Guide to the Management of Projects.* Hoboken, NJ: Wiley.

PMI, 2017. *A Guide to the Project Management Body of Knowledge (PMBOK® Guide),* 6th ed. Newtown Square, PA: Project Management Institute.

Seningen, S., 2008. Learn the value of lessons-learned. www.projectperfect.com.au (accessed April 1, 2008).

Taylor, J., 2001. *The Project Management Workshop,* Amacom.

Wysocki, R.K., 2007. *Effective Project Management: Traditional, Adaptive, Extreme,* 4th ed. Hoboken, NJ: Wiley.

PROJECT ENVIRONMENTAL SUPPORT

This final section of the text offers a collection of various organizational concepts that collectively impinge on the internal project world. Many project managers are so focused on their internal management issues that they do not stop and think about this more abstract collection of organizational level items. Upon completion of this part the reader should understand the role of these selected topics in the overall project infrastructure. Specifically, the section learning goals are to:

1. Expand the reader's view of the traditional standalone project environment with an introduction to selected organizational level topics.
2. Understand the concept of organizational maturity and its impact on the project environment.
3. Understand the operational issues of portfolio management (PPM).
4. Understand the theory, value, and challenges related to the Project Management Office (PMO) structure.
5. Describe the role of organizational governance on the project.
6. Describe the role that ethical practice has on the project decision-making role.
7. Introduce the PMI code of ethics and professional responsibility.

The concepts discussed in this section of the text are devoted to a selective set of topics that essentially reside above the project operational level, yet collectively represent important support concepts for the project manager to understand. The sections below provide a short definition and rationalization for each topic.

Organizational maturity (Chapter 34). Projects exist inside their support host organizations and those with higher maturity levels tend to produce more successful project outcomes. One of the key items in a mature organization is that it will tend to have various support functions that help the project function more efficiently. Otherwise, the project will have to invent these functions, which is both time-consuming and costly.

Portfolio Management (PPM) (Chapter 35). In the past few years, there has been a growing recognition that many projects are underway in an organization at any one time, each consuming critical resource. A proper decision-making approach for this situation is to deal with the overall project selection and management in much the same fashion as one would invest in a diverse set of financial stocks. The basic goal of PPM is to maximize the return on resources invested in project ventures. This chapter will provide an overview of this strategic view of project management.

Enterprise Project Management Office (EPMO) (Chapter 36). As a companion activity to portfolio management, the EPMO concept represents a strategy to centralize various project process and decision-making at the enterprise level. This concept is extracted from the traditional departmental PMO model, but is extended in this discussion to all enterprise projects. There is not a single standard definition for roles and responsibilities of a PMO-like structure and the multiple design options each have potential advantages and disadvantages. One simple way of looking at an EPMO organization is to see it as providing some form of leadership role in the selection, development, and implementation of a variety of project management processes. This chapter will outline the structure for such an organization and show various roles that it can have.

Project Governance (Chapter 37). Every project needs a well-defined decision-making structure, both inside and external to the project. Surprisingly, this is not always the case and its absence results in confusion and inefficiency for the project. Roles of the project manager, sponsor, stakeholders, team members, and senior management are often vague or misunderstood. Thus, when specific decisions are required the resolution process is slow and cumbersome. Project governance is the aggregate set of decision-making processes needed by the project so that the results will properly align with business needs. Hence, it can be viewed as the decision coupling of the project's activities with business vision, strategy, and objectives. In a large organization this can be a very complex linkage mechanism, especially if the organization is not mature. This chapter will provide a general theoretical overview of governance.

Ethical Practices (Chapter 38). Outlines fundamental philosophical practices that the professional PM must understand in the course of executing their job responsibilities. Daily news articles reinforce the negative impacts on both the employee and the organization when an improper decision is made. This occurs whether the individual is an elected public official, Hollywood mogul, CEO, PM, or a member of the project team. Individuals without these traits will eventually create some negative result for either themselves or the organization. Surprisingly, the act of being ethical and honest is not as easy as one might think as this chapter will attempt to illustrate. The PM must understand the basic tenets of the topic and, from an operational view, must be able to translate these into workable job traits.

It is difficult to draft a set of text that offers a checklist of clear guidelines regarding how to be ethical. So, anticipate that each of the topics discussed in this section are somewhat theoretical and variable from what might occur in a particular situation or context. Regardless, it is important for the project manager to stay current with these ideas. A professional project manager must exhibit these traits to maintain proficiency and frankly remain employed. Dedicating time for continuing education in areas such as these are high potential targets for that activity.

Chapter 34

Organizational Maturity

34.1 Introduction

The goal of this chapter is to review the concept of enterprise level maturity and the underlying attributes of this concept. A sample of five well-known maturity-oriented organizational specifications will be discussed in this chapter. The selected examples are:

- CMM (Capability Maturity Matrix) from Carnegie Mellon University (CMU), Software Engineering Institute (SEI)
- CMMI (Capability Maturity Model Integrated)—a follow-on extension from SEI
- Project Management Institute (PMI)'s Organizational Project Maturity Management (OPM3) model
- ANSI-EIA 748 Earned Value Management System Guidelines
- P3M3 Project, Programme and Portfolio management model (UK)

Traditional thinking regarding project management has focused on the internals of executing the project life cycle efficiently. As understanding of the more global issues has grown, this perspective has broadened in two key ways. First, there is now recognition that projects inherit much of their operational and resource support from the host enterprise. Second, organizations pursue a wide array of projects at any one time, all of which are competing for the same enterprise resource pool. Both of these situations impact management actions necessary to produce successful outcomes. One implication of this view is that a project can be more effective if the host organizational processes support its needs. If not, the project will be negatively impacted as it must use internal resources and time to deal with these and other similar issues. *We translate this supporting organizational cocoon concept as "organizational maturity."* The basic theory underlying this idea is that the higher the maturity level, the better support for the project environment and statistically higher outcome success rates.

Current industry literature is filled with many factors related to project success, but many of these sources often tout a singular solution as the *magic bullet* for success. What often escapes these writings is a clear broad focus offering an understandable prescriptive set of guidelines for moving in the right direction. In addition, the solution should also provide a clear understanding of the key success-oriented items that need to be focused on.

Translating the level of maturity into a working operational view says that the host organization has many processes that can either help or hinder successful project execution. If these various support processes are not in place and working well, the project will suffer and never blossom to its full potential. In the absence of an appropriate enterprise support structure, it will be up to each project to build its own support processes and this extra effort fragments the project resources, adds expense, and consumes additional time. Each such remedial effort is subtle, but collectively each gap has a negative influence on the final results.

Cooke-Davis defines maturity as "the extent to which an organization has explicitly and consistently deployed processes that are documented, managed, measured, controlled, and continually improved" (Cooke-Davies, 2009). Maturity measures are compiled from attributes such as efficiency, consistency, and continuous improvement in operational processes. Paulk et al. (1993a) describe maturity as the "potential for growth in capability" and continuous improvement "through focused and sustained effort towards building processes and management practices." Figure 34.1 illustrates a visual metaphoric picture of the maturity concept. This indicates that the ability of an organization to have a stable platform, represented by the stool legs (i.e., technology, processes, and people), must be in place and balanced.

Table 34.1 adds substance to this idea as described by Paulk in offering a brief summary of characteristics of mature and immature organizations.

Assessing the maturity of any organization is a very complex undertaking and can only be done empirically by observing various discrete components within the organization. The capabilities of these components are measured using some form of performance indicator. Each of the sample maturity standards discussed here will provide a composite overview of this concept. Each of the models described are different, but one should be able to see a common thread running through each one of the models.

34.2 Capability Maturity Model

The Capability Maturity Model (CMM) definition of maturity is considered the classic model. It summarizes by quantitative level the general value of having certain defined processes that collectively represent a layering from low through high maturity. This model also describes an evolutionary process-oriented improvement path from ad hoc, immature processes to disciplined, mature ones with associated improved quality and effectiveness (CMMI Product Team, 2002).

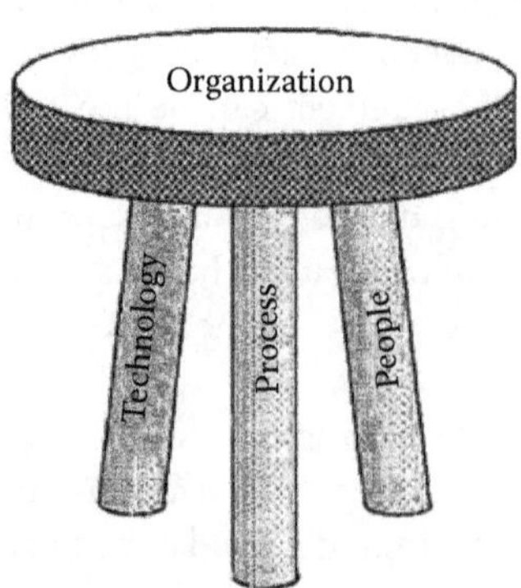

Figure 34.1 Balanced organizational elements.

Table 34.1 Characteristic Differences Between Mature and Immature Organizations

A Mature Organization	*An Immature Organization*
• Ensures organizational processes are accurately communicated to all members	• Lacks proper communication between levels and departments in the organization
• Ensures that all activities are carried out according to the developed processes	• Is reactionary, and managers are usually focused on solving immediate crises
• Established processes are continually reviewed, updated, and tested as required	• Have no defined process for ensuring high and consistent product quality
• Ensures that the established processes complement the organizations area of competence and business model	• Will tend to overlook failing processes to meet deadlines
• Establishes clear and defined roles and responsibilities for all members	• Lacks clear and defined roles for its members
• Ensures that product quality and customer satisfaction are priority	

Source: Paulk, M.C. et al., 1993a. *Capability Maturity Model for Software, Version 1.1,* Technical Report: CMU/SEI-93-TR-024 ESC-TR-93-177:I–5. With permission.

34.2.1 CMM Structure

Although the original CMM developed by SEI focused on software-oriented projects, its concepts have since been applied across many other industries and project types. Paulk et al. (1993b) describe the CMM objectives as containing the following attributes (Ref. SEI-93-TR-025 ESC-TR-93-178):

- Based on actual practices
- Measured values reflect the state of the practice
- Matches the needs of individuals performing the process
- Improves capability to efficiently produce output
- Technically documented
- Publicly available

The CMM high-level grading structure as shown in Figure 34.2 shows that each maturity level is made up of various lower level process capabilities and Key Process Areas (KPAs), with the exception of the first level that simply indicates no defined structure. Each KPA achieves some defined operational goal in that it supports a specific improvement in management and control of the project.

CMM maturity levels are defined as a numeric measure of organizational capability. The CMM high-level grading structure and related key processes are shown in Figure 34.2. Each maturity level is made up of various lower level process capabilities and KPAs. Lower maturity values indicate minimal management capability, while the higher levels indicate a higher functioning entity about specific capability improvement in management and control (Paulk et al., 1993b).

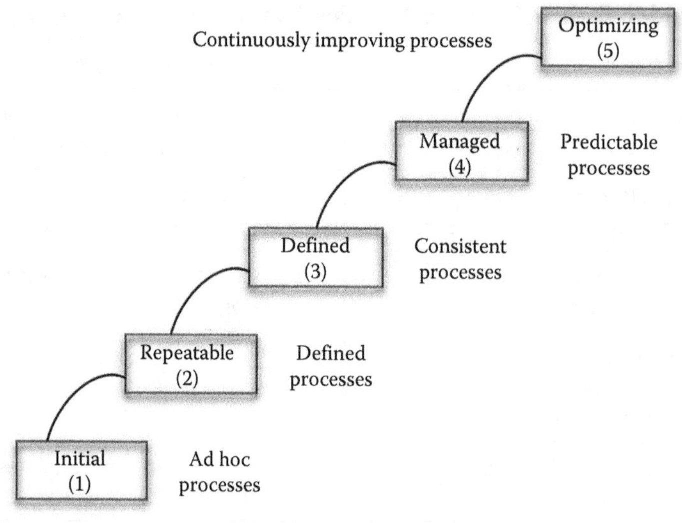

Figure 34.2 CMM architectural components.

34.2.2 CMM Maturity Levels

Each CMM level represents the "degree of process improvement across a predefined set of process areas" (CMMI Product Team, 2002). Process capabilities are measured to develop the maturity level grade for the organization. The four key elements are:

KPAs: Identify a cluster of related activities that, when performed collectively, achieve a set of goals considered important for improved goal achievement (Paulk et al., 1993b).

Goals: These represent controls that identify "scope, boundaries and intent of the KPA."

Common features: Address the implementation and/or institutionalization of KPAs. There are five common features of each KPA are: Commitment to perform, ability to perform, activities performed, measurement and analysis, and verifying implementation.

Key practices: Describe the elements of infrastructure and practice that contribute most effectively to the implementation and institutionalization of the KPAs.

34.2.3 CMM Maturity Level Descriptions

Table 34.2 offers a high-level view of the key process areas focused on within each maturity level. Five defined levels of maturity and a basic name descriptor for each level is shown.

34.2.3.1 Initial Level (Level 1)

This level is termed the chaos stage since organizations operating within this maturity realm lack proper procedures or defined roles for its members. Also, its departments are typically disconnected from a goal alignment view. Operating at the initial level of maturity means that the organization would heavily depend on an undefined competency of its employees, rather than on defined and tested processes (Paulk et al., 1993a). A survey conducted from 1996 to 2000 by SEI involving 1012 organizations indicated that a significant number (34.2%) of organizations operate within this initial level (SEI, 2003, p. 10). Data from other surveys indicates that this number

Table 34.2 CMM Key Process Areas and Goals

Level	*Title*	*Focus*	*Key Process Areas*
5	Optimizing	Continuous improvement	Innovative management
4	Quantitative	Measurement	Quantifying status
3	Basic management	Process standardization	Training programs Risk management Contract management Performance management Procurement management User requirements Process management
2	Basic management	Initial attempt to formalize processes	Portfolio planning Requirements management
1	Ad hoc	No formal structure	

Source: Adapted from data in Cooper, J and M. Fisher, March 2001, Software Acquisition Capability Maturity Model (SA-CMM), Version 1.03, CMU/SEI-2002-TR-010, Software Engineering Institute, Pittsburg, PA.

has declined over subsequent time periods, but still many organizations have not embraced the maturity concept in a formal manner.

34.2.3.2 Repeatability Level (Level 2)

As the name implies, organizations operating in the repeatability level have developed some processes that can be applied to multiple projects within the organization. While these processes are not always enforced, they exist within the defined processes of the organization. Projects operating at this level have operational data to help track cost, schedule, and apply best practices. Also, these organizations are somewhat similar to those at level 1 in that they are still prone to overrun project cost and schedules. This maturity level could be characterized as an organization trying to move toward reasonable maturity, but not yet achieving that level.

34.2.3.3 Defined Level (Level 3)

Level 3 organizations use developed and tested processes. Roles of members are defined and tailored toward proven organizational processes, which are in turn enforced throughout the organization as standards. Operational processes are frequently reviewed and appropriate revisions are issued when required. This maturity level organization tends to have formal training programs to continually improve understanding of processes within the organization (Paulk et al., 1993b, pp. O9–16). Level 3 maturity fits the description of many organizations.

34.2.3.4 Managed Level (Level 4)

One of the key differential characteristics of operating at level 4 is the ability to measure and possibly quantify organizational progress and status within a project. This distinction also involves the predictability of process performance. Level 4 organizations use competitive benchmarking best practices to assess all aspects of their processes. Organizational processes are followed systematically to execute all projects, and changes are enacted through planned procedures. These organizations also have an enhanced ability to *predict* outcomes for future projects. This level of maturity is above the operational norm for most organizations.

34.2.3.5 Optimizing Level (Level 5)

Operating at level 5 signifies that the organization is fully matured according to the model definition. There are only a few organizations that can effectively claim to operate at this level. Consistently repeatable results, effective customer-oriented quality assurance (QA), and continual improvement of the organizations processes, and products become the cultural norms at this point.

A SEI survey in 2003 indicated that 43% of the population was level 2 maturity and 27% was level 3. Only 17% were graded higher than level 3 (SEI 2003, p. 6). Another interesting statistic from this survey indicated that non-U.S. organizations had higher percentages of level 4 and 5 than comparative U.S. A similar survey taken in 2015 indicated that the level 3 group had increased to 67% and the levels 4 and 5 had increased to 27% (CMMI 2015, p. 14). Most of the maturity growth over the last decade has occurred in the level 3 category, which suggests that organizations are focusing on defining their project management processes.

Research evidence shows positive incremental improvements produced by achieving each of the higher levels. However, it must be recognized that the time for an organization to move from one level to the next is typically in the two-year range and requires significant support by senior management. Recognize that in some cases there is a diminishing value return at level 5 compared to the cost of obtaining it and for this reason all organizations should evaluate the cost versus value for achieving each of these levels.

34.3 Capability Maturity Model Integration (CMMI)

CMMI is an evolutionary expansion of the original CMM experience and was created by SEI in association with the Office of the Secretary of Defense (OSD) and the National Defense Industrial Association (NDIA). The CMMI Product Team describes this model as a means of improving an "organization's processes for development, acquisition, and maintenance of products or services" (CMMI Product Team, 2002). Like the architecture of CMM, CMMI is made up of components including maturity levels, process areas, common features, and key practices. Figure 34.3 illustrates the CMMI component structure.

CMM and CMMI are well thought-out concepts and are excellent models to describe the operational role of our project flowerbed metaphor concept (i.e., the project is like a seed in the enterprise flowerbed). These models provide an enhanced understanding regarding the processes required to effectively produce project results. Thousands of organizations have and are continuing to pursue these capabilities. The interested reader should review the SEI website for a broad array of technical documentation for these two models (Ref. www.sei.cmu.edu).

34.4 OPM3

OPM3 is an evolutionary step in model description. Although somewhat like the CMM model, it was explicitly defined to fit all organizational types. Starting around 1998, various members

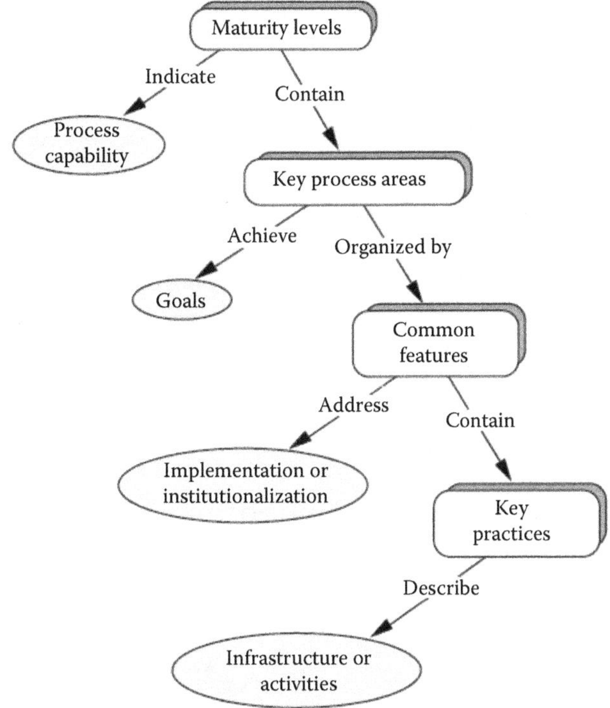

Figure 34.3 CMMI component structure.

of PMI became sensitive to the fact that the *Project Management Body of Knowledge (PMBOK®) Guide* was focused heavily on a single project view and basically ignored the overall organizational impact on the project environment (Schlichter et al., 2003). Perspective gained from the CMM experience suggested that they should consider a way of integrating organizational maturity into the PMI project model structure and that became the initial stimulus for the development of OPM3. PMI defines OPM3 as a model that "...identifies and organizes generally accepted and proven organizational project management practices. The *OPM3* framework provides processes to assess an organization's practices against *OPM3* Best Practices." (PMI, 2013, p.14).

The design concept behind OPM3 is that all state change initiatives of an organization can be grouped into three sectors—projects, portfolios, and programs. The OPM3 model mechanics are based on industry best practices that are used to assess the organization or subcomponent maturity level (PMI, 2013, p.17). The OPM3 model is structured into the following three main elements (PMI, 2013, p. 37):

Knowledge: The main body of the model that explains organizational maturity with respect to Best Practices.

Assessment: Describes the evaluation methods compared to Best Practices and Capabilities.

Improvement: Describes the practices required for implementing changes.

The interrelationship between these three items first involves a comparison of the current organization against OPM3 Best Practices. From this data, an assessment of the defined gaps is analyzed to create an "improvement model." This prioritizes which practices need to be addressed. Finally, the defined changes are implemented and evaluated. Conceptually, these steps follow the basic project model driven by the requirements.

34.4.1 Overview of OPM3 Architecture

During the early model development project phases, the PMI design team struggled to find the best way to define specifics regarding what elements comprised maturity. Eventually, this process resulted in the identification of 10 individual elements required to provide needed support to the project. The following 10 process areas were defined (Schlichter et al., 2003):

1. Standardization and Integration of Processes
2. Performance Metrics
3. Commitment to the Project Management Process
4. Alignment and Prioritization of Projects
5. Continuous Improvement
6. Using Success Criteria to Cull or Continue Projects
7. People and Competence
8. Allocation of Resources to Projects
9. Organizational Fit
10. Teamwork

Embedded in each of these groups are defined lower level sub-processes, called *design cells*, which were then elaborated and transformed into a directory of 600 operational Best Practices.

OPM3 is defined as "the application of knowledge, skills, tools, and techniques to organizational and project activities to achieve the aims of an organization through projects" (PMI, 2013p. 5). The design concept of OPM3 was to apply the general structural guidelines established by the *PMBOK® Guide* to organizational processes that impacted the project. The model describes the management structure of an organization in terms of project, programs, and portfolio and then links the organizational capabilities to these three groups. Evaluating the degree to which an organization practices the defined levels of maturity provides a grading mechanism for improvement (Paulk et al., 1993b). Figure 34.4 shows schematically the relationship of organizational strategy to projects through OPM3.

During the early model definition stage, there were many design disagreements among the PMI volunteer-driven teams. Because of this the design and implementation efforts basically floundered through the first two rounds of development. Finally, in 2003 during the third design iteration a beta version was finally moved into production (thus OPM3) (Schlichter et al., 2003).

34.4.2 OPM3 Analysis Steps

Attempting to implement OPM3 standards in any organization requires a firm understanding of the underlying model knowledge base. The first step in the implementation cycle is to assess the current degree of maturity of the organization with respect to existing processes compared to the defined Best Practices. This step is carried out in two stages; maturity assessment with respect to defined Best Practices and formal assessment of specific capabilities. In this stage, the organization would use the Self-Assessment procedure provided by *OPM3 Knowledge Foundation* to determine maturity levels of specific processes with respect to Best Practices. From this assessment, process

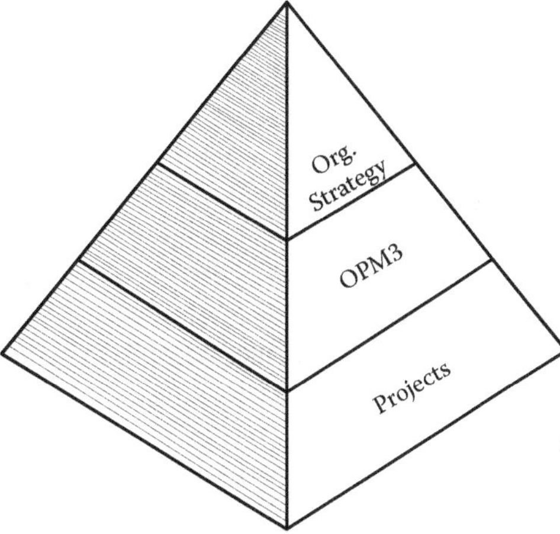

Figure 34.4 OPM3 strategy layer.

capability gaps are identified. Once an organization has determined its capability gap areas, an improvement strategy is developed in the following four steps (PMI, 2013, p.36):

Acquire the knowledge. At this stage, the organization must review their current capabilities in relation to benefits that would occur at the higher maturity level with improved processes. This must be evaluated in regard to both cost, and productivity impact to the organization. Also, the issue of change management complexity for the new capability is a consideration to ensure a smooth and easy transition between capability levels.

Perform the assessment. After the completion of organizational gap analysis, the next step involves deciding which items to pursue. In many ways, this is similar to a business case in the standard project environment. An organization must keep in mind that these implementations could affect factors such as culture, structure, or goal strategy.

Manage the improvement. This step involves the design and execution steps to move the organization to the desired process level. As with all organization change activities, a post-assessment is required to evaluate results. Deviations from the planned result must be evaluated and lessons learned captured.

Repeat the process. This final step implies that the model requires a continuous improvement activity. Quality management theory says that the organization must understand that no state is optimum forever.

34.4.3 OPM3 Best Practices

Best Practice is a term indicating the currently recognized best method to achieve a stated goal or objective. The OPM3 directory defines the model's library of Best Practices; it essentially qualitatively defines the associated maturity level, and provides a brief explanation of the defined practice. Collectively, this set of processes provides the organization with a standards checklist to review for defining their custom operational portfolio.

From this gap perspective, a strategic planning goal model is constructed. Based on the internal evaluation cycle, the organization derives action plans ranging from the project level and upwards to full organizational levels. All the defined action plans are linked to ensure proper integration.

34.4.4 OPM3 Benefits

OPM3 formalizes the study, understanding, and application of organizational maturity models for a broad range of organizations. It provides working definitions of key processes from not only the project management perspective but also from program and portfolio management aspects. Through its definition of best practices, OPM3 offers organizations an opportunity to link their maturity improvement strategies to corresponding operational performance, thereby helping to guide a path toward continuous improvement of those processes. Improving portfolio, project, and program management outcomes plays an important role in achieving strategic objectives.

OPM3 implementation documentation outlines three key benefits to the organization as follows:

- It helps the organization identify and decrease the gap between best practice and current maturity level.
- It provides a process for organizations to analyze their maturity gaps and from this guide the development of focused action plans for continuous improvement.
- It defines a library of model best practices that identifies the characteristics of specific process targets. This will help organizations implement improvements without requiring extensive requirements analysis time.

From OPM3's formalized process definitions and review process an organization can evolve their adoption of predefined Best Practices. "The OPM3 methodology offers companies a rare opportunity to introspectively look at the link between their goal strategies and how well they are able to systematically *translate* those goals into tactical reality." OPM3 provides an added advantage to organizations by allowing them to bridge gaps between an organization's strategic plans and its ability to achieve those plans through the execution of projects (Schlichter et al, 2003).

34.5 ANSI-EIA 748

ANSI-EIA 748 (called 748 after this), was published in the latter 1990s to outline a high-level best practices process model (GSA, p.3). Included in this model is a formal body of synthesized and tested best practices that have proven to provide benefits in project planning and control. These guidelines were originally published in the late-1960s and have evolved through observing actual project results. The current version has survived the test of time with minimal change in basic design. It is important to recognize that this broad set of guidelines was too complex for use in 1960s organizational maturity, but are quite manageable in the current technology and management domain.

As currently defined, 748 is defined as a set of management guidelines that offer a reasonably clear set of descriptions regarding key management and control processes. Included in this model is a formal body of 32 synthesized and tested best practices, grouped into five broad areas of the life cycle. Collectively, this guideline specification list should now be strongly considered as part of every organization's maturity level evaluation. One major difference exists in this approach over the traditional CMM five level grading system; that is, in this case the evaluation would look more at granular gaps across the full 32 areas, rather than five levels. One can view the 748 guideline list as a strategic global target, with shorter-term defined tactical action areas to pursue in a continuous improvement cycle. So, the maturity concept would be more of an analysis of status across the full range, rather than a single digit maturity score. This is more akin to OPM3 approach than CMM.

One can look at the scope of 748 as establishing an appropriate management and control structure within which "adequate integration of a cost/schedule/performance management system will fit" (GAC, p.3). The five defined major guideline groups are:

1. Organization—organization support elements,
2. Planning and budgeting—integrated plan compliance,
3. Accounting—obtaining valid actual data,
4. Managerial analysis and reporting—tracking project status,
5. Baseline management—managing the approved target.

The various guidelines within each of these groups define certain vocabulary and related management roles that are important to project success. What should be somewhat obvious here is that the scope of this document is broad in its organizational impact on the project management process. For that reason alone, no organization can just say "let's implement this." The operational approach should be to look at the guideline list as the template and then design specific high impact "chunks" for tactical implementation. Clearly, the scope of the model is too much for the average organization to absorb short term.

Organizations often have a difficult time selling project management rigor into existing cultures, so the fundamental question here is how to do this same type of selling at the organizational level and minimize resistance to change. One way to sell such a goal is to view it as moving toward a level 2 or 3 equivalent organizational maturity (level five being the optimum long-term view), where level 3 is often considered to be the beginning of a formal management structure. In this manner 748 may be used in parallel with other maturity models and provide more specific process targets than the other models offer. In many ways, this model is more prescriptive in approach than any of the others.

34.5.1 ANSI 748 Model Guidelines

One important point has not been made yet. That is, the 748 guidelines are more of a general goal statement (called guideline) and these do not specify tool formats or exactly how to achieve that goal. It would be instructive for the reader to download the full model guide for further review to see more detailed examples. In addition, there are other support documents available to help further define specifics for each guideline. A summary of the full guideline list will offer more definition as to the intent and scope of these guidelines. One should be able to see a great deal of similarity to many of the management items and previous chapter material introduced in this text. Note that the guidelines are organized into five sub-groupings as shown in Table 34.3, which offers a more detailed listing of the 32 guidelines.

Recognize that all the 32 guidelines are worthy management goals, but not all of them have the same operational value in every situation. It is important to note that these specifications represent what would be called strategic and tested best practice processes. For large, complex projects, all the guidelines would be required; however, for smaller projects some of the items would have lesser importance. While in the process of attempting to move an organization toward a best practice implementation goal it is important to avoid jumping at the latest contemporary management idea until more proven processes as described here have been dealt with. The scope of this section does not provide for a more detailed discussion of this model, but it is an important introduction

Table 34.3 ANSI\EIA 748-C Project Management Guidelines

Organization
1. Define work scope (WBS)
2. Define project organization (OBS)
3. Integrate processes
4. Identify overhead management
5. Integrate WBS/OBS to create control accounts
Planning, Scheduling, and Budgeting
6. Schedule with network logic
7. Set measurement indicators
8. Establish budgets for authorized work
9. Budget by cost elements
10. Create work packages, planning packages
11. Sum detail budgets to control account
12. LOE planning and control
13. Establish overhead budgets
14. Identify management reserve and undistributed budget
15. Reconcile to target cost goal
Accounting Considerations
16. Record direct costs
17. Summarize direct costs by WBS elements
18. Summarize direct costs by OBS elements
19. Record/allocate indirect costs
20. Identify unit and lot costs
21. Track and report material cost and quantities
Analysis and Management Reports
22. Calculate schedule variance and cost variance
23. Identify significant variances for analysis
24. Analyze indirect cost variances
25. Summarize information for management
26. Implement corrective actions
27. Revise estimate at completion
Revisions and Data Maintenance
28. Incorporate changes in a timely manner
29. Reconcile current to prior budgets
30. Control retroactive changes
31. Prevent unauthorized revisions
32. Document project management baseline changes

Source: Earned Value Management Systems ANSI/EIA-748-C Intent Guide, April 29, 2014, National Defense Industrial Association.

to our topic or organizational maturity and does reveal primary target areas. Public documentation can add more detail to this model.

34.6 P3M3®

Since 2006, The UK Office of Government Commerce (OGC) has been guiding the development of this international organizational maturity model. The official title is *Portfolio, Programme and Project Management Maturity Model*, but known in the industry as P3M3®. Although more familiar to a UK audience this model has established itself as a flagship management tool in helping to achieve its mission of defining standards and capability in both public and private sector portfolio, project, and program management. This effort has brought improvement measured in both performance and output quality.

P3M3 originated as an enhancement to OGC's earlier *Project Management Maturity Model*, which in turn was based on the process maturity framework that evolved from SEI's CMMI in the United States (P3M3, p.6). P3M3 has now become a key standard amongst international maturity models, and it provides a framework with which an organization can assess their current performance and put in place improvement plans with measurable outcomes based on industry best practice (P3M3).

34.6.1 P3M3 Design

P3M3's design approach offers a holistic view of an organization's performance, using a broad spread of attributes across seven processes areas and three views of business endeavor. Its design focus addresses the following key sources of project failures (P3M3, p.12):

1. Design and definition
2. Decision-making
3. Discipline failures (i.e., risk and change management)
4. Supplier management
5. People failure

As in several other maturity models, P3M3 uses a five-level scale with the following maturity level definitions (P3M3, p.7):

1. Awareness of process (not documented)
2. Repeatable processes (defined)
3. Defined process (documented, standardized and integrated)
4. Managed process (quantified measures)
5. Optimized process (a learning organization)

This model is touted as improving outcome capabilities in the following ways (P3M3, p.5):

- Higher rate of return on investment
- Greater production efficiency
- Lower production costs
- Better quality outcomes

- Improved customer satisfaction
- Enhanced employee morale

Using the seven model process areas, organizations can be graded as to their maturity level:

- Management control
- Benefits management
- Financial management
- Stakeholder engagement
- Risk management
- Organizational governance
- Resource management

Regarding a maturity grading strategy, P3M3 offers a 35-cell matrix of maturity descriptions for each of the seven focus areas and five maturity levels. Using these descriptions for each level and process, one can grade the maturity for each of the seven processes and use this to decide on gaps that need to be addressed. In addition to this, the grading can be further segmented by project, program, or portfolio organizational groupings. This type of grading segmentation allows a quantitative maturity scoring to be interpreted in a much more granular way than found in other models. One other very significant attribute in favor of this model is its high-level independent governmental sponsor, OSG.

34.7 Impact of Organizational Maturity

Intuitively, it seems logical that improved processes should lead to better productivity and there is industry evidence that this is indeed the case. Dr. William Ibbs, University of California at Berkley, has developed a custom project management maturity model and associated grading structure like CMM (Ibbs, 2007). One of the hanging questions in the maturity discussion is "how much maturity do you need?" Ibbs research results help answer that question for both schedule and cost performance. The computed relationship between organizational maturity and project schedule performance (SPI) is shown in Figure 34.5.

The correlation shown here for project schedule performance improvement versus organizational maturity is a strong motivator to embrace the maturity concept. Note in this figure that as organizations approach level 4 maturity, they can meet scheduled completion dates, whereas a lower maturity level 2 correlates to overrun in the range of 200% of plan (i.e., SPI of 0.5). Also, note that maturity levels approaching level 5 correlate with even better schedule performance.

A similar maturity result is shown in Figure 34.6 for cost performance.

In this example, cost performance versus maturity level is somewhat more varied, but the main trend is still quite similar. That is, maturity levels 2 correlate to cost overruns of double budget, whereas the cost performance follows similar improvement trends to that shown for schedule graph. In both displays, the important message is to note the improvement correlation trends for both schedule and cost as maturity levels increase. Chapter 9 previously summarized industry performance statistics for cost and schedule performance as an industry comparison to this data.

In addition to the cost and schedule maturity correlations shown here, this research also indicates that higher maturity organizations spend more time planning projects and formally

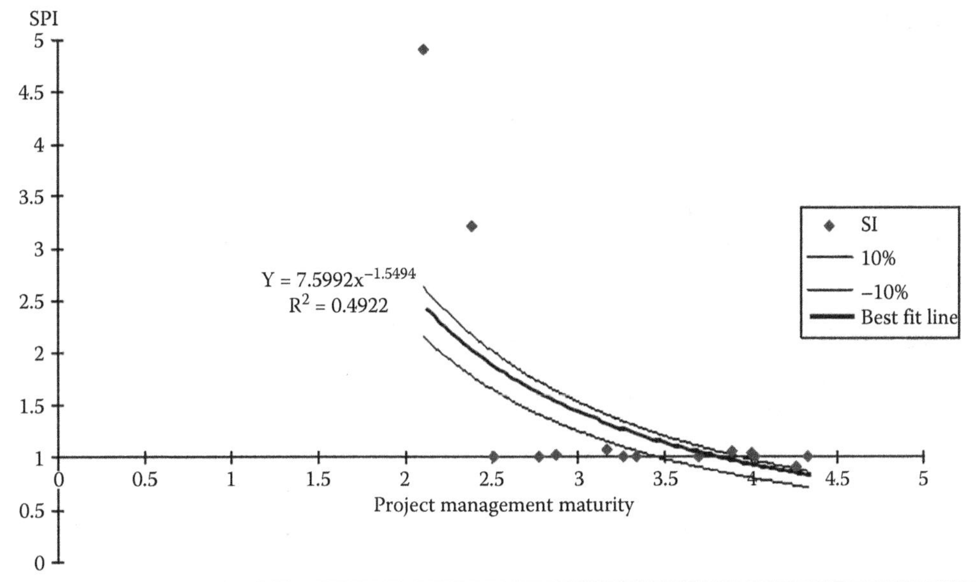

Figure 34.5 Project schedule performance versus maturity. (Courtesy of Dr. William Ibbs, private communication, 2007. With Permission.)

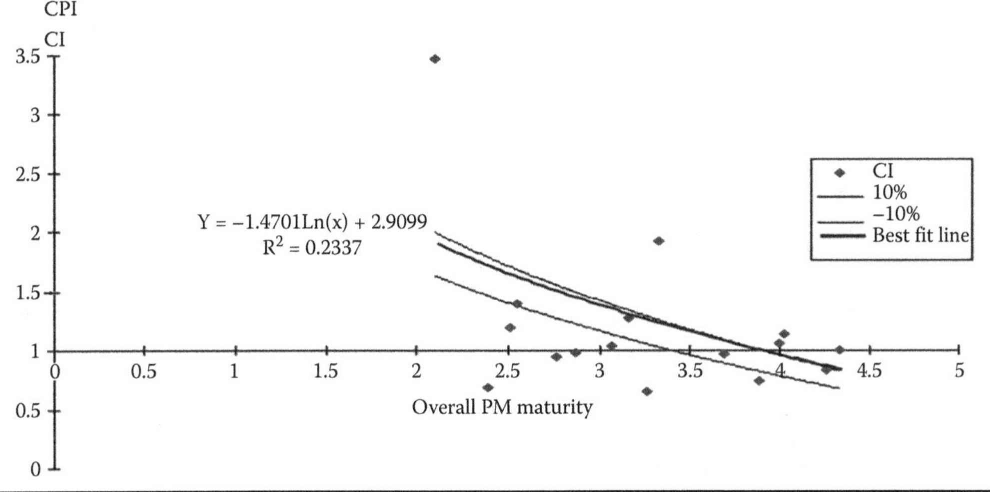

Figure 34.6 Cost performance versus maturity level. (Courtesy of Dr. William Ibbs, private communication, 2007. With Permission.)

closing them. They also spend more time communicating than the lower maturity levels do. One of the classic arguments against formal project management is the belief that planning is not worth the time spent given all the vagaries associated with projects. This research data would support an argument that improved processes, developing better requirements, and more project postmortem evaluation all add value to the outcome. If all organizations shared this belief, the job of implementing formal management methods would certainly be easier.

34.8 Conclusion

Formal model-driven evaluation of organizational processes is a relatively unused industry concept, but one that fits a needed role for project improvement. In order for this type of high-level analysis to be accepted widely, it will take more tangible evidence of its resultant value. However, there is little doubt as to the logical approach embedded in the basic concepts of published maturity models such as CMM, CMMI, OPM3, ANSI 748, and P3M3. Organizations that understand the idea of process maturity, formal internal process evaluation, and continuous improvement are on the right trail to overall organizational productivity improvement and project success. One of the key operational questions regarding maturity assessment involves how to continually maintain a Best Practices structure and then evaluate whether a specific externally defined formal model will best serve the role of standards guidance.

It is important to recognize that many organizations have not accepted the notion that improved maturity as defined by a model does in fact lead to improved operational performance. Hence, before this concept moves forward the following two issues will have to be dealt with:

- What evidence will be compelling enough for an organization to formally pursue the concept of maturity and what model or definition will guide such an effort?
- What mechanics will be used for validating the assessment and gap analysis process?

Only time will predict the measured results that come from organizations that follow this general direction. The Ibbs performance results have offered quantitative evidence, but a broader sample is needed to substantiate this and to verify a specific measurement. Regardless of how an organization pursues this strategy, the modern project manager must understand how his project is impacted positively or negatively by the maturity level of his host organizational environment. Insight into some of the key support processes described in the models discussed here can be gained through an understanding of these models. Therefore, even this summary level of description should provide some motivation to pursue this area more formally.

References

Cooke-Davies, T.J., L.H. Crawford, and T.G. Lechler, 2009. Project management systems: Moving project management from an operational to a strategic discipline. *Project Management Journal*, 40, 1, 110–123. DOI: 10.1002/pmj.20106.

(CMMI) CMMI Product Team, 2002. *Capability Maturity Model Integration (CMMI) Version 1.1.* Pittsburgh: Carnegie Mellon Software Engineering Institute.

(CMMI) CMMI Institute, 2015. *Maturity Profile.* Pittsburgh: Carnegie Mellon Software Engineering Institute. http://cmmiinstitute.com/sites/default/files/resource_asset/Maturity%20Profile%20Ending%20June%2030%202015%20Quality%2020150818.pdf (accessed December 6, 2017).

(GSA) General Services Administration, 2008. *Earned Value Management System (EVMS) Compliance Review Guide.* Washington DC.

Ibbs, W., 2007. Ibbs Consulting Group, private communication with Dr. William Ibbs.

Paulk, M.C., B. Curtis, M.B. Chrissis, and C.V. Weber, 1993a. Capability Maturity Model for Software, Version 1.1, Technical Report: CMU/SEI-93-TR-024 ESC-TR-93–177: pp. 1–5.

Paulk, M.C., C.V. Weber, S.M. Garcia, M.B. Chrissis, and M. Bush, 1993b. Key Practices of the Capability Maturity Model, Version 1.1, Technical Report: CMU/SEI-93-TR-025 ESC-TR-93–178: pp. O–9–16.

(P3M3). Portfolio, Programme, and Project Management Maturity Model, Introduction and Guide to P\3M3, Version 2.1. UK: Office of Government and Commerce (OGC). www.ogc.gov.uk (accessed November 5, 2017).

PMI, 2013. *OPM3 Knowledge Foundation*, 3rd ed. Newtown Square, PA: Project Management Institute.

Schlichter, J., R. Friedrich, and B. Haeck, 2003. *The History of OPM3*. The Netherlands: PMI's Global Congress.

(SEI) Software Engineering Institute, 2003. Process Maturity Profile Software CMM 2003 Year End Update. https://www.sei.cmu.edu/sema/profile_about.html (accessed December 6, 2017).

Chapter 35

Project Portfolio Management

35.1 Introduction

Companies today are awash with projects, either underway or proposed. Typical examples of these initiatives are to create and launch new products, implement new processes, integrate new acquisitions, or upgrade existing products or technologies. Organizations spend billions of dollars and untold numbers of work hours on countless thousands of projects. Each organization has some method of selecting and managing multiple projects, but not all are geared to selecting a slate of projects that optimize organizational goal alignment, which should be the appropriate strategy. The desired portfolio goal is to ensure that the right projects are being selected at the right time. Also, companion decision processes are needed to ensure that there is appropriate comparison made between competing proposals. The goal is not just to select a good project; it is to select the best one from all competitors.

Project Portfolio Management (PPM) represents a centralized management process for project related activity and it is a companion activity to a Project Management Office (PMO) in many cases. The primary goals for this function are to identify, prioritize, authorize, manage, and control projects, programs, and other related work. Actual selection decision processes for this type of function vary widely. Included in this process is a single, organized view of all proposed and active projects and programs, including data regarding objectives, costs, timelines, status, resources, risks, and other critical factors.

Just as any investor must select the right balance of investments to meet their "return" goals, each company desires to select the right mix of projects to meet its goals. PPM is a formalized view of this valuation process and it attempts to find the optimum mix of projects in pursuit of formal valuation objectives. Recognize that the wrong project that is well executed is still the wrong project. Organizations have countless choices of targets to spend their time, capital, and human resources. This means that making these decisions in a highly competitive environment is a critically important business activity. In contrasting the goal of PPM versus project management, the former is the strategic arm of organizational continuous improvement actions, whereas project management is the tactical arm focused on ensuring that individual projects are completed according to plan. These two processes must be linked together to achieve the proper outcome.

35.2 Role of PPM

The logic of looking at organizational project activity as a collected whole represents the basic theory of portfolio management, but the question remains as to its specific defined role in the organization? Is this just another gimmick management technique with little substance that will die away when the next one comes along? The answer to these basic questions is based on how one views the material in this chapter. It is important to point out that this topic is still maturing and that is the rationale for placing it among the contemporary topics rather than as a core management process. Likewise, its organizational framework is evolving and in many organizations, this is closely associated with their Project Management Organization (PMO) initiatives that will be discussed in the next chapter. In fact, there are three evolving roles intertwined—project management, PPM, and PMO. In this chapter, we will focus on the portfolio aspects and then add to that with the PMO role in Chapter 36.

One of the major values for having a portfolio level view of projects is to get away from the more isolated departmental (stovepipe) view can result in suboptimal funding of these initiatives. The portfolio approach places all projects on the same evaluation plane and allocates resources centrally to those selected. The vocabulary term for the array of value ranked projects is the *efficient frontier*, meaning essentially to choose the highest value option first, then second best, and so on. Thus, the output goal of portfolio management is to define that prioritization of options.

We have now reached an important conceptual cross-road. Up to this point, the theme of this book has been focused on improving the execution of an approved project. We are now at a higher level asking which project to approve. For the sake of discussion let's say that good project management can improve execution efficiency by 25% and selection of the right project can improve the overall organizational project investment return by a similar amount. That suggests that these two initiatives have a collective significant value to the organization. Chapter 9 presented data to show how better management affected project outcomes and there is every anticipation that better project selection also has similar value. The merits of the PPM concept have been hinted at in several other sections of the book.

Pennypacker and Cabinis report industry examples where project lead times to market have been reduced by better overall management and selection by as much as 60%, development costs significantly declined, quality improved, and forecasting accuracy increased (Pennypacker and Cabanis, 2003). Positive reports of this type are causing organizations to look carefully at this organizational strategy. Table 9.5 previously showed that PPM was the sixth most popular management process strategy in 2012, but what is not so obvious from this statistic is that it is both popular and frequently cancelled. Some organizations do well with the strategy and others seem to give up the idea after two or three years. In concert with this popularity, there is a growing vendor market for support tools, consulting, and implementation assistance. One might anticipate this improving support base to also improve the organizational success rate. Conceptually, one cannot argue with the logic for this type of organization, so the failures would seem to come from more the decision culture of the host organization.

As stated previously, *doing the wrong project well does not make it the right project*! Selecting proper targets is the piece of the original selection puzzle that we are tackling here. By making better decisions regarding which projects are funded, how they are governed, and which projects are allowed to continue to completion supports the organizational goal of being better able to deliver competitive value to the marketplace.

35.3 Improving Project Selection Decisions

PPM processes and tools help to provide real-time information to help the organization make better decisions about their overall project environment. To support the PPM process, each initiative (existing and planned) must have timely valuation and status metrics collected and analyzed. These data are then continually matched against organizational goals to help define which initiatives best align the entire portfolio with the organization's business strategies and objectives, thereby maximizing the competitive value.

35.4 Improving Visibility of Project Performance

Improved visibility provided by PPM processes and software tools gives an unprecedented view into the overall "health" of the organizational projects. This process produces project portfolio status in the form of graphical summaries, project scorecards, bubble charts, and communication portals utilized by a wide range of technicians and managers. Individual project health can be evaluated and analyzed using predefined metrics related to cost, schedule, scope, quality, risk, market value, and customer satisfaction. Because of this improved overall visibility, the project decision-making process can also be improved.

35.5 Better Understanding of Project Value

Thomas and Mullaly documented the complexity of assessing project value (Thomas and Mullaly, 2008). As we now understand it, this concept involves more than simple, measurable financial metrics. Using multivariable analysis complicates all project assessment techniques and that process remains an immature component for PPM. However, the current PPM processes and tools have expanded the ability to handle both heuristics (rules of thumb) and financial data manipulation to evaluate a portfolio. Also, the ability to group and score in "what if" mode yields an improved insight into the overall picture. For example, projects can be easily re-grouped into categories such as new products, maintenance, or process upgrades. Scoring methodologies based on ratings such as competitive value, improvement rating, risk assessment, and financial calculations can also be specified to better understand the return on investment from each project within or across the different types of projects. These capabilities support improved project selection and oversight.

35.6 Conducting "What If" Analysis

Just as in financial stock situations, business trends change continuously. A primary tool in managing dynamic and uncertain situations of this type is simulation, or conducting "what if?" type analysis. Analyzing probabilistic characteristics through simulation modeling can enable a better understanding of how uncertainty impacts the outcome of a project. This knowledge can be used to evaluate the outcome sensitivity to various assumptions in the project. More use of this same type of decision logic is relevant at the portfolio level. Simulation modeling is a critical tool for situations that have more variables and complexity than can be reduced to deterministic mathematical equations. This form of evaluation allows a much richer assessment than would be possible with traditional metrics.

35.7 Project Investment Management

The traditional view of project success has been defined by the delivery of planned requirements on time and on budget. The PPM view of project success is more focused on delivering an optimum set of projects that contribute the most collective value relative to their cost. If all projects are aligned with the organizational goals, then proper execution of them will deliver the greatest overall returns to the organization.

Fundamentally, PPM is a process discipline used to ensure that a correct mix of investment activity is initiated, grouped, funded, and managed. In order to execute this activity, the following five components must be in place:

- Process to manage the overall process
- Prioritization techniques based on organizational value metrics
- Evaluation process that includes senior management
- Decision insight and support—understanding the organization goals
- Balancing current needs and future requirements—tactical versus strategic perspectives.

35.8 Who Needs a PPM?

Given the theoretical logic presented thus far, one might conclude that every organization needs a PPM. If that were true all would have been installed and working, but that is not the case. Summarized below are visible indicators that the existing internal de facto project selection process is not working effectively (Greer, 2008):

- Frequent difficulties in having enough qualified human resources for selected projects
- Excessive project overruns from "not enough resources"
- High personnel turnover due to "burn out" of key project contributors because they are working on too many projects and spending too many overtime hours
- Frequent changes in project status (i.e., moving from "active" to "on hold" to "top priority" and back)
- Completion of projects that do not meet organizational goals—too much tactical and not enough strategic in the mix
- Intense competition among departments rather than cooperation.
- Department level projects are favored over global projects

At the minimum, a properly functioning PPM process aids in the following ways:

- Improving fiscal management
- Improving communication between the project team and business management
- Quantifying the benefits of a project
- Deciding how best to assign resources
- Setting priorities
- Identifying and managing risks
- Assessing the impact of adverse events
- Selling a project vision concept
- Obtaining funds for a project

Effective portfolio management ensures that projects continue to support the organizational mission as defined by formal goals.

As organizations develop a strategy for achieving their mission, executives have to consider the following business drivers as they make their investment decisions:

- How do we ensure that we are working on the right initiatives to support business objectives?
- Do we have a consistent method to measure the key performance indicators on active initiatives?
- Can the organization define standards that improve the consistency of business initiative outcomes?
- Do we have enough people and dollars to deliver our commitments?
- Can the organization respond adequately to changing business conditions and realign the initiatives required to respond to the identified changes?

There is often a close linkage between a project or a group of projects to an organizational goal initiative. Once an organizational level initiative is established, one or more projects may be envisioned to move the organization in that direction. From that view, portfolio data would follow ongoing status to quantify the value of that initiative. At the beginning point the portfolio entry represents a conceptual project. As the project specifics are further identified, various resource and performance metrics are added. This includes data related to cost, human resources, and time requirements for the initiative. Also, a corresponding valuation score is updated based on the new information. Other decision considerations might be added to indicate items such as a timing constraint. As these decision elements are combined, a more accurate assessment becomes possible to evaluate how the individual project fits into the overall portfolio scheme.

35.9 PPM Goal Structure

At the highest level we have now described the conceptual goal of PPM as matching projects to organizational goals and through this make related decisions to improve organizational competitiveness. Associated with this high-level goal are more definable sub-goals that support this. They are described briefly below.

35.9.1 Sub-goal 1: Goal Alignment

The first aspect of this is "What is the value of strategically aligned projects?" Basically, a project should exist to achieve a company goal, or a set of goals. Projects are initiated to improve an existing state for a product, service, produce a desired result, or some variation of these three scenarios. A project should not normally exist if it does not support organizational objectives. The solution to this requirement does not "just happen." Many times, the selection process is disjointed and fragmented throughout the organization. The PPM process helps to ensure alignment and contribution to company goals. One area that a PPM helps to deal with is departmental bias as a selection criterion regarding which project to fund (i.e., no "pet" projects unless they specifically bring appropriate goal value to the organization). Regardless of all other considerations, the final portfolio of projects should truly reflect the business' strategy (Cooper et al, 2001). Additionally, aligning the portfolio selection to the business strategy helps companies to adapt quickly to meet new business challenges as well as leverage current investments, and make better investment decisions (Spizzuco, 2005).

35.9.2 Sub-goal 2: Resource Investment Focus

Why is a resource investment focus important? Resources are the fundamental execution units that will produce the outcome and they are essentially always constrained. Consequently, resources must be allocated to targets wisely in order to deliver maximum return where expended. An effective PPM process brings an investment focus to the analysis of projects and allocates resources to obtain maximum gain. Without this type of dual focus the organization can easily undertake projects that essentially have inadequate resources available and therefore deliver less value. Without this analysis perspective it is common practice to projects approved, but insufficient resource support. These are labeled non-viable decisions. In some cases, this occurs when the organization does not have a valid information source that accurately matches the project allocations to the available resource pool. In other situations, the planners are just not concerned about the supply side issues. When either of these situations occur, the result is project gridlock (Cooper et al., 2001). To be successful with the resource allocation issue, it is vital that some meaningful measure of resources for all projects be used as part of the project selection process.

35.9.3 Sub-goal 3: Better Project Control/Governance

Projects are dynamic entities that can quickly spiral out of control on multiple fronts. The organizational governance process affects many related decision domains including setting business priorities, budgeting, project selection, resource allocation, application portfolio strategy, and performance measurement (Gruia, 2005). To support these requirements, an effective control and governance process is required to ensure that the portfolio remains within the organization's defined performance framework. However, an appropriate balance must be struck between too much control (nothing significant gets done) and too little control (observed outputs are of lesser value). PPM processes and status data can provide much of the informational framework required for this activity. The organizational question involved here involves how to energize that data into an effective management and control environment. To accomplish this, it is necessary to define an effective governance framework for both the project and portfolio levels. Putting portfolio management in place can uncover the need to strengthen governance structures (Datz, 2003).

The PPM structure serves as a driver of greater engagement and visibility in project activity by senior management through the selection process. PPM governance involves providing oversight, control, and decision-making for all ongoing initiatives (Hanford, 2005). Improved project governance also leads to improved cost control, which is often a weakness for many projects. As a part of continuously managing the portfolio, project costs are also carefully analyzed. Areas where costs can be reduced across the portfolio or within particular projects are more visible given the enhanced data environment. In addition, the increased level of attention to overall status helps to answer the key question of whether the project is still viable given its current status. If the answer to this question is "no," then there is an opportunity to restructure the portfolio and save resources. If this type of ongoing analysis is also not done, poor value initiatives can continue to completion, even though the result is not viable on a cost–benefit basis.

35.9.4 Sub-goal 4: Efficiency

Closely tied to better governance and cost control is the concept of efficiency. The overall concept of PPM deals with how to achieve efficiency. That means a focus on desired results and resource control. This root of this process begins at project selection by ensuring that the best project option is selected for funding and continues through the project life cycle with dynamic monitoring and control. Also, the efficiency concept involves providing continuous oversight of the portfolio and to seek out areas which can be corrected, cancelled, and/or improved. PPM also helps to achieve efficiency through its process of measuring efficiency and performance as projects are tracked through their life cycles.

Some of the issues that the PPM process can surface include the following:

- Projects not having clear critical success criteria
- Project management processes and tools that are not working well
- Project managers (PMs) not having clear mandates, sufficient competence, or capacity to achieve satisfactory project outcomes

By surfacing these issues and ensuring that they are dealt with, portfolio management methods help create greater efficiency in project completion (Wideman, 2005).

35.9.5 Sub-goal 5: Balance

Modern organizations increasingly have multiple and changing goals that they desire to attain over varying time periods. Consequently, it is necessary to have an appropriate mix of projects synched to those goals to achieve these diverse objectives. A balanced portfolio considers the timing factor, as well as the goal structure. Having a large number of projects in one goal area while neglecting other goals will violate the concept of balance. Effective balancing through the PPM evaluation process helps to achieve a desired portfolio balance in terms of a number of parameters. For example, the right balance in terms of long-term projects versus short ones; or high-risk projects versus lower-risk projects; and across various markets, technologies, product categories, and project types (Cooper et al., 2001). Obviously, the driver for the balancing process is a set of articulated organizational goals and strategies that can be translated into specific portfolio initiatives. From this base, PPM will help match viable projects across the various goals.

35.9.6 Sub-goal 6: Value Optimization

Projects are initially envisioned and designed to bring value to the organization. While there are many that can be funded and bring value, not all can be pursued because of various constraints. So, a critical sub-goal of PPM is to maximize the value produced from the selected projects given the constraint set.

Having all the projects overseen "under one roof" and with a standardized set of evaluation criteria are a design prerequisite for the PPM process. In reality, not all projects will subsequently bring value despite the best attempts and good intentions of the decision makers. However, this reality should not deter the PPM process, but should stimulate interest in improving the evaluation process over time. Recognition that an optimum solution was not being achieved is a strong motivator for improvement.

A final point on value optimization is to recognize that better project visibility obtained at the executive level through PPM methods enables a quicker termination of projects that turn out to be "nonvalue added," thus saving resources for the organization over time. From a pragmatic viewpoint, this is one of the quickest value paybacks for a PPM process.

35.10 Models of PPM

There are many tools and techniques utilized in project evaluation. Two sample techniques to structure the portfolio are described below:

Financial portfolio analysis: Portfolio balance and risk mitigation are achieved by spreading investments over many different initiatives. In this fashion, projects are balanced across several categories that can include strategic or tactical business objectives, compliance, required maintenance, operational efficiency, and research and development. Depending on the organization's objectives these factors would be used in the selection process to achieve the best match regarding overall goals and market dynamics.

Top-down/bottom-up approach: There are two basic methods to develop the portfolio—either by looking at top-level goals and decomposing downward to projects that will develop those goals, or by sorting through individual project proposals and lower-level business unit objectives to aggregate a draft portfolio. Both approaches are popular with immature project organizations (Pennypacker and Cabanis, 2003). If the portfolio design process is conducted separately with either option, it will produce a disconnected view of the interrelationships of projects to the linked organization goals. A combined top-down/bottom-up approach is the desired solution to link the two layers and that is essentially what the PPM mechanics are designed to do.

35.11 Implementation Models

There are two traditional organizational models for implementing a PPM system (INNOTAS, 2007, p. 1):

- *The engagement profitability model*
- *The budget alignment model*

In the *engagement profitability* model, "projects" and "programs" are vehicles for managing revenue-generating engagements with customers that produce profit margins. Decisions and behavior are driven by the profitability of customer engagements. Examples of this model include IT services firms and professional services departments within product companies. The focus at each level includes project, resource, and customer performance evaluation.

As Figure 35.1 implies, the PPM initial focus is typically on project and resource performance. However, as processes mature over time, automation and expertise also evolves, management focus often turns more toward the higher-order benefits of improved performance based on increasing focus toward customers, products, and new lines of business emerge.

The *budget alignment* model corresponds with an operational environment in which the value of a project is harder to assess (and these project types typically do not generate revenue directly), and project costs are considered overhead. In this type of environment, decisions are more driven by the need to squeeze value out of the available budget. Examples of the budget alignment business model include IT and product development organizations.

Once the project portfolio is identified and managed as a coordinated portfolio of investments, the management challenge becomes one of prioritization among the viable options. At this stage, the key issues involve an assessment of existing projects and dealing with the resource allocation activities needed to support those initiatives. A final parallel concern is the ongoing maturation of

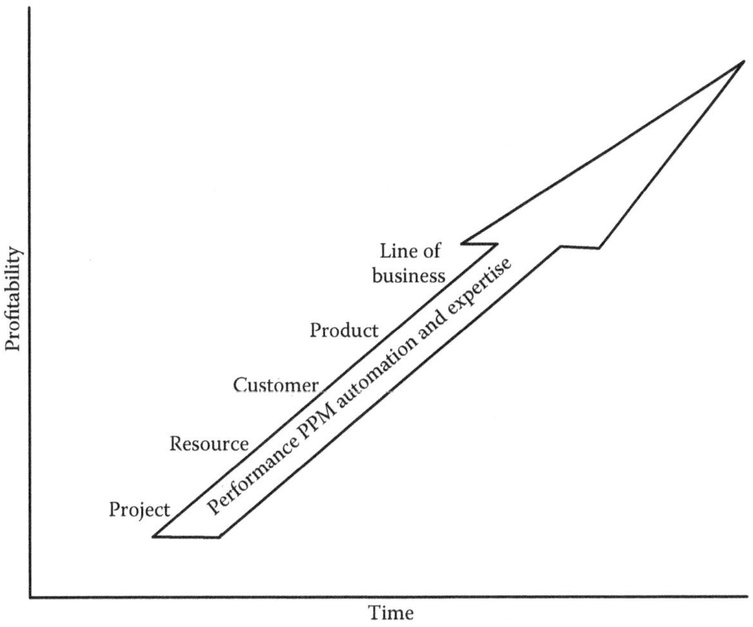

Figure 35.1 PPM profitability ladder.

standardized processes and metrics development. If we look at this evolutionary process in stages, the sequence focuses first on demand related to identification and valuation of the target portfolio. Stage two involves methodologies for planning and scheduling the portfolio, which in turn deals with matching resources and constraints to the target portfolio. This results in an identification of the efficient frontier and scheduling considerations. Finally, at stage three the concerns migrate toward executing the plan, monitoring status, and implementing the solutions.

In both models described, achieving *customer satisfaction* is a critical driver, but the customers are different in each case. In the engagement profitability model, the customer is the target market being served, whereas in the budget alignment model, the customer is usually internal.

35.12 The Hybrid Model

Some environments structure a combination of the two basic models described above, extracting the best benefits from both. An example of this would be to produce a development organization that uses an in-house professional services organization to implement their products. To drive development decisions and deliver new products, the product development team will use the supply–demand delivery framework, while the professional services team will use the performance process for their segment.

35.13 Efficient Frontier

The efficient frontier maps specific projects against their value in rank order. So, the highest value items would start at the origin. Each succeeding project would have a lesser value and the shape of the curve would be as shown in Figure 35.2.

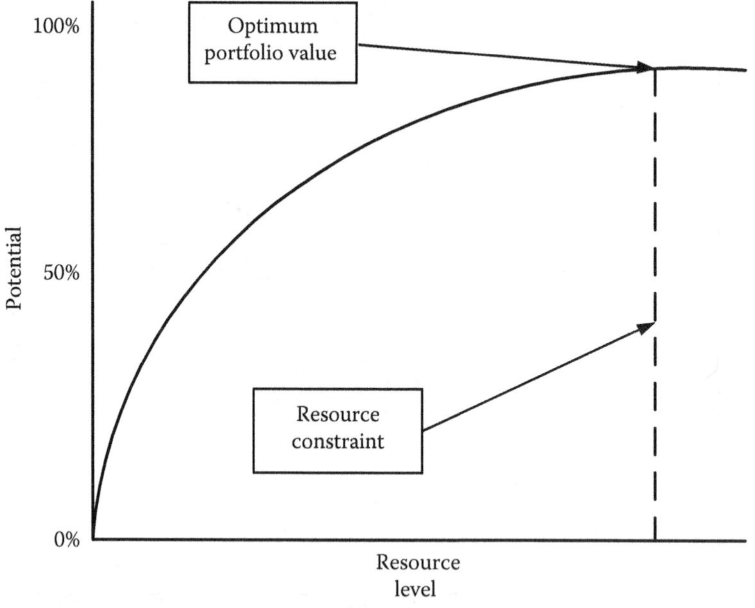

Figure 35.2 Efficient frontier.

This curve defines the maximum value that can be achieved from the optimum portfolio given some defined financial constraint as shown by the dotted vertical line. In the operational mode, it will be necessary to allocate some projects that are not on the efficient frontier. For example, regulatory requirements are a typical reason to change a priority against internal value. When these decisions are included in the portfolio the overall value is decreased. In concept, this curve represents the target portfolio and is used to assess the penalty taken by choosing lesser alternatives. Also, it helps to assess the penalty taken by a resource constraint being at some particular point. Various vendors have PPM tools that can produce these figures and manipulate a decision impact for alternative portfolio options.

35.13.1 Communicating Status

As the PPM database is populated with various data regarding project proposals and status the question arises how to display meaningful information for decision-making. There are various types of reports that can be created to show status grouped in a wide variety of output forms. The efficient frontier is one new assessment format and a second one is called the *bubble chart.* This is a visual representation of projects based on risk versus value. Figure 35.3 provides a hypothetical sample view of this format.

In this example, the highest value and lowest-risk projects would be reflected by bubbles in the top-right quadrant, whereas lowest value and highest-risk initiatives would be closer to the origin. Also, the size of the bubble is a visual measure of the size of the project. Each bubble would have a reference number that would link back to the portfolio data base for further details. A display of this type is useful for envisioning the overall portfolio. In association

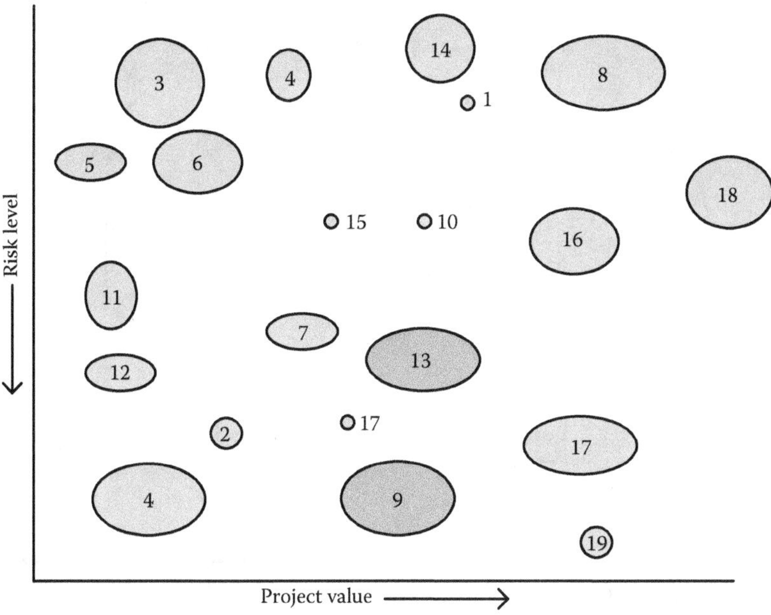

Figure 35.3 Bubble chart.

with this, the portfolio database supports different views and options with graphics and other decision analytics.

Information capabilities as briefly summarized here help facilitate an enhanced dialogue between the technical analysts and management executives, allowing a better balance between project demand and the optimum use of available resources (capital and HR). These new informational capabilities represent just one of the ways in which PPM processes provide a new perspective for an organization to achieve more with less.

35.14 Keys to Implementing PPM

Portfolio management does not just consist of selecting the right project investments; it also means ensuring proper execution and regularly measuring effective performance, notably in the delivery of the anticipated benefits and the correct usage of the invested budgets. Figure 35.4 summarizes the basic components of the overall PPM structure. This diagram is considered a summary of the basic implementation roadmap.

One of the difficulties in PPM implementation is the need to dynamically review ongoing status and add that perspective to the overall process. This concept does not show well in the schematic above, but failure to recognize it would mean that the process just continued to approve new projects into the pool and not consider status of the ongoing items. Business changes, variation in ongoing project performance, triggered risk events, and a host of other factors can well mean that an optimal decision six months ago may now result in zero value to the organization. The status system results must be frequently evaluated to ensure that previous decisions are still valid in relation to other projects.

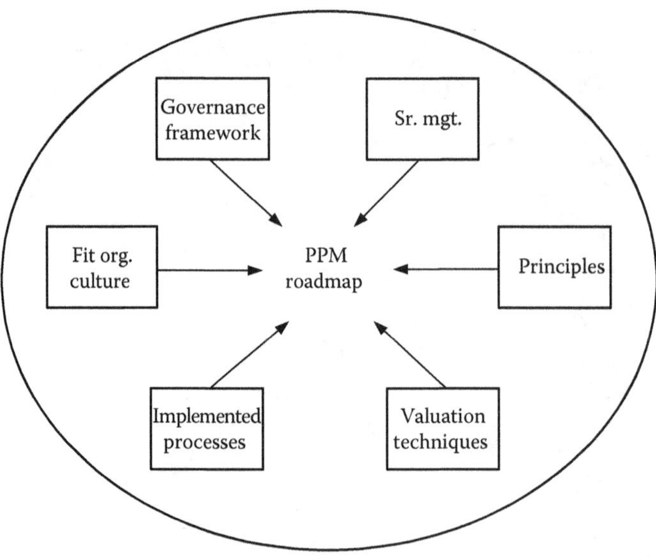

Figure 35.4 Implementing PPM.

35.15 PPM Principles

PPM is not just another project management process. It really is also a management philosophy—one that is quite like stock market financial portfolio management. Getting the most from PPM requires that an organization to fully embrace the following principles:

- Projects will be managed as a portfolio of resource investments.
- Projects will be identified based on their match to organizational goals and related value.
- Resource availability and risk will be considered in the decision process.
- Projects will be defined and selected to include the full scope of activities necessary to generate value.
- Value delivery practices will recognize that there are different types of projects that will be evaluated and managed differently.
- The delivery process will be managed throughout the life cycle to ensure that the value equation is intact.
- All relevant stakeholders will be engaged in the process and assigned appropriate accountability for the delivery of capabilities and the realization of value.
- Projects that fall out of the optimum mix will be terminated in place.

35.16 Finding the Approach that Fits

Just as in the rest of project management theory, PPM is not a "one-approach fits all" solution. Despite the general applicability of common principles, there is not a single roadmap approach for implementation or organizational structure. Various alternative approaches reflect different views regarding how best to accomplish these goals considering the individual culture, maturity, and other realities. Different approaches reflect different assumptions, methodologies, models, structures, roles and responsibilities, reporting lines, resource demands, and levels of authority. The implementation challenge involves designing an approach that will work well within a specific organizational culture.

The first design step is to define the PPM processes that will initially best support the business need and from this obtain buy-in and general consensus for that approach. Without this basic rationale and consensus, the subsequent steps will fail. Once the appropriate initial approach has been designed, use the desired output requirements of that approach as a checklist for choosing the right follow-on operational support processes.

35.17 Executive Support

According to surveys, the biggest challenge for implementing PPM is lack of adequate executive support (this is just another form of a project, so same factors apply). Introducing PPM into an organization requires a significant investment of time and money. It requires learning new concepts and skills, instituting new processes, and achieving a significant cultural change. Realistically, deployment within the organization will not be popular with everyone. Support from the top is needed to lend credibility and authority and to guide the right behavior in the organization.

35.18 Governance Framework

Effective governance also starts with executive leadership, commitment, and support; however, this by itself is not sufficient to achieve the final result. An overall hierarchical governance framework must be defined with roles and responsibilities for all participants. A sample summary of roles and responsibilities for various stakeholder groups is outlined in Table 35.1.

Merkhofer described a model organization to illustrate roles and responsibilities for the PPM function (Merkhofer, 2007). A similar sample organizational structure is shown in Figure 35.5, although there are obviously other structural options as well. Note that the grouping of program

Table 35.1 PPM Roles and Responsibilities

Role	*Responsibilities*
Executive team	This group establishes portfolio funding constraint levels, approves project recommendations, and provides policy guidance.
Portfolio management team	The organizational unit is delegated responsibility for carrying out PPM duties such as making project acceptance recommendations and working with the Executive Team.
Portfolio administration	Responsibility for collecting project information, applying tools, and coordinating the day-to-day portfolio management process.
Business managers	Responsibility for managing project deliverables to the business environment.

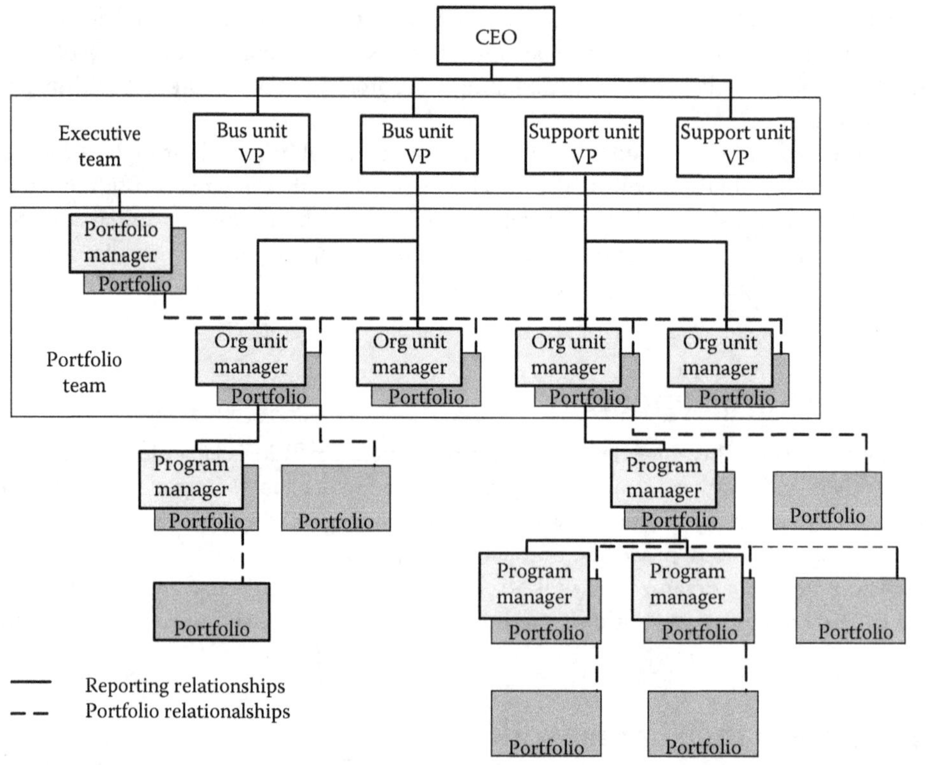

Figure 35.5 Model PPM organization structure.

managers in an organizational structure implies their control of associated lower levels of this structure. In many cases, this might be viewed as a departmental grouping more than a program grouping, but the responsibilities would be similar for both roles.

35.19 Value-Measurement Framework

A value-measurement framework defines how the organization will create a value expression for a particular initiative. There are various methods used for this process; however, different organizations create project value in different ways. This means that the models for measuring project value are necessarily somewhat unique by organization. Among other things, creating a value-measurement framework requires that the organization decide for whom value is to be created (i.e., shareholders, external customers, internal customers, etc.), and how to measure the different kinds of value that are being created (i.e., financial, customer satisfaction, quality level, speed of service, etc.). A value framework will need to help answer the following questions:

- What is the value of conducting this project (probably needs to have some numeric score format)?
- What are the sources of value (e.g., reduced costs, increased revenue, increased customer satisfaction, new learning, process capability, etc.)?
- What are the risks compared to the organization's risk tolerance and what is the risk-adjusted value of the project?

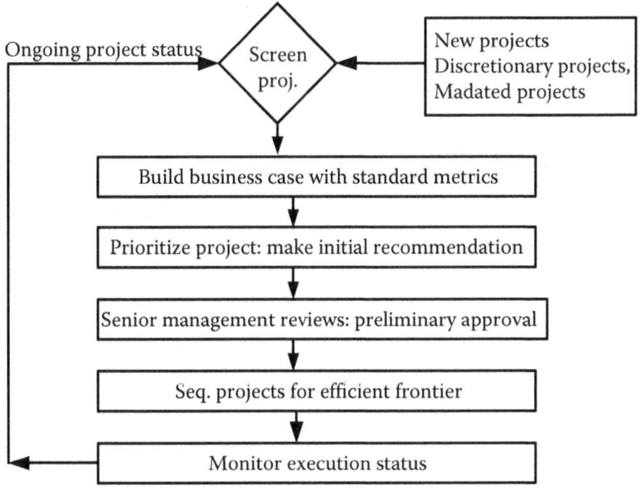

Figure 35.6 PPM process steps.

35.20 Institute Effective Processes

An organizational PPM process must be established as a formal, documented, and repeatable activity. By definition, these process steps cannot be *ad hoc*. The rigor by which the process is executed will drive the results. Excellence can only be achieved when standardized procedures, tools, training, and support functions are established, implemented, and continuously improved upon. In sum, PPM should be looked at as an ongoing improvement process. Each step along the implementation trail will uncover a weakness that will need to be resolved. The basic process steps for PPM are summarized in Figure 35.6.

35.21 PPM Implementation Roadmap

The basic process components of the PPM approach have now been described. The key at this stage is how to stage the defined components into the organization successfully. Each implementation step should be built off the previous one. This requires a formal assessment of each step, then package the next step design from that foundation. The following nine steps should be considered as a basic implementation process (INNOTAS, 2007, p. 3):

1. Assess the current organizational status as to management gaps in project selection and execution.
2. Review the gap analysis with key stakeholders.
3. Develop a formal vision for the future PPM process.
4. Create a project charter for the first stage process; senior management approval is required for this.
5. Design stage one PPM tools and processes.
6. Test stage one concepts in pilot organization.
7. Design production version tools and processes from pilot lessons learned. Production scale tools required for next stage. Plan roll out program.

8. Execute enterprise roll out.
9. Monitor ongoing status and evolve process.

35.22 External Expertise

The PPM process involves specialized expertise that will likely be in short supply within an organization. Oftentimes, a consulting organization provides the fastest access to best practices and brings an outsider's perspective. Consultants also generally can gain better access to senior executives and from that perspective help serve as catalysts for change. There are many training and mentoring activities that can also be supported by a specialized consulting firm.

35.23 Implementation Goals

PPM can be a significant enabler for enhanced efficiency, effectiveness, and productivity in the project domain, while reducing exposure to risks related to project failures. However, it would be a mistake to think that this is a cookie-cutter solution that is easy to implement, or that there is one defined solution. Any new idea that involves large segments of the organization brings with it a complex change management process. For this reason, choosing the right scope and approach can dramatically improve the initial success. Choosing the wrong approach can harm the organization by increasing costs, wasting valuable time, and generating useless and inaccurate information. For this reason, it is important to first invest the effort it takes to identify and understand alternatives and to make the right choices for the specific organization.

35.24 Key PPM Interfaces

There are five key organizational interface components to PPM. These are

1. Strategic planning
2. Business stakeholders
3. Executive management
4. Project management
5. Project management office

A summary for each of these component areas is included below:

Strategic planning. Strategic planning is a high-level function charged with guiding the organizations focus on long range, critical business areas. One of the key goals of this function is to define, assess, and adjust the organization's direction in response to a changing environment. Executives use this information in their management role in deciding how to lead the organization toward strategic objectives and the strategic planning function is a major support element for this activity. Decisions made in the strategic planning process are a guiding prerequisite for PPM. Without a clear strategy, there will be no defined criteria for choosing among the many competing project requests.

Business stakeholders. Stakeholders are individuals or groups interested in or affected by the projects in the portfolio. These individuals are not only affected by the projects' performance, but often will also be the future users of the product or process being developed. By making project performance more visible, PPM allows not only executives more insight and better decision-making, but also stakeholders benefit from increased information. This group needs to be actively involved in the process as subject matter experts and they offer key knowledge regarding how to use the initiatives effectively. Failure to involve key stakeholders is a major source of project failure. By facilitating project communication with stakeholders early and often, PPM ensures that stakeholders know what is going on and fully understands the project benefits. This means that stakeholders can provide better feedback and actively support the development process. The PPM communication mechanism also means that executives get improved feedback and better know when to kill a project that stakeholders have indicated will not work as envisioned.

Executive commitment. A critical prerequisite to executing PPM methods and tools is the commitment of senior executives. Just as with any other major initiative, the organizational implementation of PPM is a megaproject that requires commitment, focus, and dedication from senior leadership, otherwise it is lost in the sea of departmental level disagreements. The entire executive team must be committed to the principles described here and an appropriate senior executive should serve as the project sponsor. Implementation of PPM processes will require changing how functional managers, PMs, project workers, and stakeholders deal with the project culture. Creating this cultural change will require strong, consistent, focused leadership from the highest level, otherwise the project will be doomed to be another "band aid" or "management fad" that will be announced with great fanfare, practiced half-heartedly for a year or so, forgotten as soon as the next crisis surfaces, and then the organization returns to previous business as normal.

Project management. As indicated earlier, it is the role of the project teams to execute and deliver the defined initiatives. PPM processes drive the high-level project requirements and project management then supplies status back to the PPM for overall assessment activities.

PMO. A formal PMO provides a central organizational focal point for managing the portfolio. As such, it is the companion process to PPM (or vice versa) and may in fact be the organization entity that runs the PPM process. The PMO is often formally delegated to oversee strategic PPM processes and tools as well as individual project management practices, plus selecting and utilizing tools and methods that help stakeholders understand the status and progress of projects. Chapter 36 will dwell into this organizational function further.

35.25 PPM Implementation Challenges

Typically, projects are driven and defined by customers who set project and goal milestones, schedules, and other requirements. This approach leads to difficulty in defining what a project should be from a goal value point of view. Quite likely, the major challenge in implementing a PPM process is the change it will require in the organizational project selection process and the associated resource allocation process. PPM processes clearly have the flavor of centralization and that characteristic has long been correlated with implementation complexity and resistance by lower levels of the organization. As with all centralization strategies, lower-level decision freedoms will be reduced by this process. There is a popular axiom in organizations that says "we are from headquarters and are here to help." The PPM has a lot of that flavor and the implementation strategy must recognize this trait if it is to be successful. As a specific example, the PPM analysis process makes it difficult to hide someone's favorite project that should not be pursued, and lower levels will not appreciate this type of negative recognition.

35.26 Advantages of Implementing PPM

In many cases, one can judge the merit of an idea by how many organizations are moving in that direction. The 2017 PMI Pulse of the Profession edition indicates that 71% of the organizations surveyed had a PPM/PMO organization (PMI, 2017). This number rises to above 80% for the best performers in the survey. Other surveys indicate that half of these initiatives fail within five years, so once again the warning that organizational change is difficult.

It is easy to see that having a comprehensive and shared view of all ongoing or planned projects and initiatives and associated key indicators has value from a management perspective. One can also argue that this should lead to better organizational project decision-making. The basic principle of selecting the best global project slate is obviously logical as is the notion of matching resources to projects. These concepts are nothing more than basic management best practices. It would also be difficult to say that ideas such as the efficient frontier did not make sense. Ditto for communicating overall status was a bad idea. How can one argue that matching projects against organizational goals, assessing risk, and continuous monitoring of status is a bad strategy? For these reasons the rationale for recommending PPM-type processes is essentially irrefutable. So, it is not the logic of the idea that makes these initiatives fail. One must look deeper into the culture and maturity of the host organization for the root cause.

35.27 Summary

PPM initiatives are now one of the most popular project management concepts; its obvious logical reason to exist has created a supporting tool and consulting industry. Some organizations have found the concepts to be highly effective if managed properly, whereas others have failed in their attempts to change their existing culture. Implementing a PPM structure to support project selection is an essential element in achieving organizational goal alignment, investment focus, governance, cost control, and valuation assessment. Regardless of the structure selected for an organization, it needs to be carefully thought out, as there is no one single best choice for this process.

PPM implementation success will be fueled by embracing the following key principles:

- Selecting an approach that fits the organization
- Securing executive support
- Establishing an appropriate governance structure
- Developing a value measurement framework
- Instituting effective processes
- Following a well-planned incremental roadmap for implementation

All large organizational process changes have challenges and so does the implementation of PPM. Once in place, project variances become public and this makes it difficult to hide mistakes. For that and many other reasons the project culture is typically slow in accepting PPM. As a matter of fact, the real value of PPM may be more high level than low level if one just looks at the day-to-day work. Despite the inherent challenges, PPM has a variety of advantages. It provides the advantage of having a comprehensive and shared view of all ongoing or planned projects and initiatives and associated key value and cost indicators. It also offers various information distribution features that help the stakeholder community understand what is going on.

PPM and project management together represent two of the most significant strategies that an organization can follow to produce more goal achievement with less resources. Accomplishment of both represents a major undertaking for the organization and requires significant involvement of senior management. Chapter 36 will follow this discussion with more details regarding the PMO model, which is also a popular management strategy dealing with this same topic area.

References

Cooper, R.G., S.J. Edgett, and E.J. Kleinschmidt, 2001. *Portfolio Management: Fundamental for New Product Success*, 2nd ed. New York City, NY: Perseuas Publishing.

Datz, T., 2003. Portfolio Management Done Right. www.cio.com/article/31864/Portfolio_Management_Done_Right?page=1 (accessed October 24, 2008).

Greer, M., 2008. What's Portfolio Management (PPM) and Why Should Project Managers Care about It?. www.michaelgreer.com (accessed November 25, 2017).

Gruia, M., 2005. Measure What Matters: New Perspectives on IT Portfolio Selection. www.umt.com (accessed October 24, 2008).

Hanford, M., 2005. Portfolio Management: An Introduction. A white paper published by IBM. www.ibm.com/developerworks/rational/library/oct05/hanford/index.html (accessed January 11, 2009).

INNOTAS, 2007. The Two Models for Implementing Project Portfolio Management. http://hosteddocs.ittoolbox.com/Innotas102406b.pdf

Merkhofer, L., 2007. Seven Keys to Implementing Project Portfolio Management. www.prioritysystem.com/PDF/implementingppmcomplete.pdf (access November 15, 2017).

Pennypacker, J. and J. Cabanis-Brewin, 2003. Why Corporate Leaders Should Make Project Portfolio Management a Priority. www.primavera-aus.com/pdf/npd/PPM.pdf (accessed June 23, 2008).

PMI, 2017. *Pulse of the Profession*. Newtown Square, PA: Project Management Institute.

Spizzuco, T., 2005. Optimize Your Vision: Aligning Your IT Portfolio & Business Strategy. http://hosteddocs.ittoolbox.com/TS072407.pdf (accessed November 15, 2017).

Thomas, J. and M. Mullaly, 2008. *Researching the Value of Project Management*. Newtown Square, PA: Project Management Institute.

Wideman, R.M., 2005. Project Portfolio Governance Guidelines (But are they complete?) www.maxwideman.com/papers/governance/governance.pdf (accessed November 17, 2017).

Chapter 36

Enterprise Project Management Office

36.1 Introduction

As an expansion activity to the traditional IT functional portfolio management organization, the Enterprise Project Management Office (EPMO) concept represents a strategy to centralize various project-related decision-making processes at the enterprise level. This concept is adapted from the classic Project Management Office (PMO) model, but extended in scope here to deal with all enterprise projects.

> Definition: A project management office (PMO) is "a management structure that standardizes the project-related governance processes and facilitates the sharing of resources, methodologies, tools, and techniques"
>
> *(PMI, 2017, p. 216)*

The formal responsibility scope of this function can vary from simple project coordination to full ownership of the project portfolio and related execution resources. Other potential roles can involve defining and maintaining the project process standards, documentation, and metrics related to the operational activities. In its normal organizational role, a PMO is an aligned management companion to the portfolio management analysis process. As discussed here the scope is enterprise-wide; therefore, the acronym EPMO is used.

36.2 PMO Functions

There is not a singular standard functional description for a PMO and working versions of this type of organization unit are quite varied. The scope and depth of a particular PMO will be based on the organizational philosophy of the host. Notably, implementations of this organizational concept have had both high praise and failure. Mature organizations often have higher success with an EPMO. Less mature organizations that are still struggling with formalizing project management will likely struggle more to achieve the same level of success with centralizing the portfolio decision functions. There is a broad range of potential responsibilities that can be grouped under this title and they are closely linked to a particular organizational management philosophy. These functional responsibilities will have a strong influence on operational project management processes. The following is the list of operational functions that might be assigned to the PMO (Richardson and Butler, 2006, p. 407):

- Standardized processes and methods for project development
- A formal archiving system to capture lessons learned
- Administrative support for project teams
- Assistance or management activities in staffing projects
- Training programs for project teams
- Consulting and mentoring of project teams
- Evaluating and managing the resource capacity issues related to overall project requirements
- Centralized tracking and communication of project status to appropriate stakeholders
- Aiding or managing the alignment of project activity to business goals
- Performing project quality reviews and audits
- Performing post-implementation reviews
- Managing technical resource capacity for project efforts
- Assessing status of current project work in progress (WIP)

The schematic shown in Figure 36.1 provides an overview of the EPMO processes. Note that there are essentially three tiers of management illustrated here—project, portfolio, and enterprise. The decision role of the EPMO process is to allocate appropriate resources to each decision class and manage the execution (build) process through the entire life cycle.

One can see that the full scope of this model would not be a simple implementation, but the logic of such a goal is irrefutable. It is also easy to see the organizational boundaries that these processes cross and that is just one of the implementation complexities to deal with.

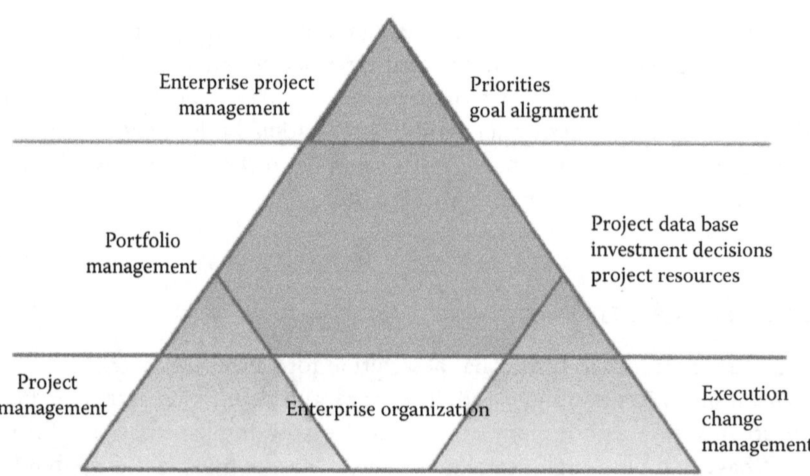

Figure 36.1 EPMO decision processes.

36.3 EPMO

The organizational label PMO is most typically linked to information technology (IT) project selection within the enterprise; however, the basic principles are valid for the entire organizational level project portfolio. Because of this view the term EPMO is used here to denote that it is organization-wide in scope. In concert with its companion Project Portfolio Management (PPM) process, the basic operational goal is to align the selection of projects with organizational goals and recognize the associated needs to integrate internal processes, technology, organizational structure, and HR. This would also include a contemporary project management approach that deals with the challenges of organizing, managing, and tracking projects throughout the organization. Figure 36.2 contains a schematic overview of this concept and clearly shows the related layers of management and key processes.

Note that there are multiple management groups in the EPMO structure that collectively form the links between lower-level processes and organizational strategy. At the lowest level, project management focuses on the efficient execution of selected projects. A second grouping of portfolio management (PPM) coordinates project selection and resource allocation. EPMO serves the general role of connecting the strategic vision of the enterprise to the selection of specific projects and programs that support this vision. In order for these layers to work together, sophisticated collaborative technology is required among the players. A physical organizational structure for EPMO has the same potential variability as that for a traditional PMO, meaning it can be focused on strategic planning, or fragmented and buried in various functional departments. Ideally, the EPMO and PPM functions would be centralized and housed together to facilitate coordination between them.

One issue that is visible from Figure 36.2 is the organizational grouping issue involved in creating a decision-oriented management level above the project layer. Project managers (PMs) and

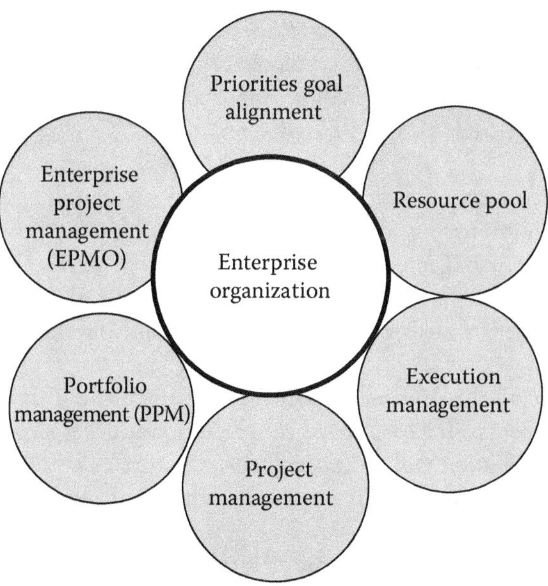

Figure 36.2 Enterprise project management model.

organizational departments tend to be an independent lot and many will feel that they do not need this level of higher-level "help." Often, a centralized group with this type role is viewed as bureaucracy that adds no value. This is the sticky human side of the PMO or EPMO-type organizations that makes implementation tricky.

36.4 Communication

The EPMO function must have an effective communication system between the project teams, key stakeholders, and senior management in order to carry out its required functions. The core information flows involve the following:

- Project selection activities
- Metrics collection for ongoing projects
- Information distribution
- Project status assessment

Delegated level of authority attached to these activities is the undefined variable. An EPMO organization can alternatively be an information collector, observer, transfer agent, or it can have significant authority over the entire grouping shown in Figure 36.2. Regardless of the balance between these options, an active communication system is required if this concept is to be successful.

36.5 Performance Metrics

The EPMO decision environment area is rich in its use of various metrics. Some of the early metrics relate to the valuation of the project proposal, whereas the later metrics become more ongoing status oriented. In all these roles, it is important to identify the success criteria that will be used for decision-making. Also, some aggregate level metrics are needed to evaluate the EPMO function itself. This activity is overhead when one looks simply at the work being accomplished and therefore the internal evaluation activity will be important to maintain the organization. Some of the key evaluation questions related to an EPMO are:

- Is project cycle time better than it was?
- Is the organization improving competitively as a result of better project selection?
- Are resources being managed better than they were previously?
- Is overall organizational maturity improving as a result of EPMO functions?
- Are negative attitudes from lower-level groups compromising the EPMO organization?

Specific metrics to evaluate this level of assessment are complex, but formal assessment must be part of the operational process. If a value perspective cannot be developed and sold to senior management, the natural inclination will be to scrap the structure as not adding value. Department level functions will be happy to see this go away as they will regain more freedom in project selection.

When the EPMO structure is created and its formal charter is set, its operational role within the organization is also defined. Based on these defined roles (which are highly dependent on the level of authority allocated), the range of performance metrics for the function would also be defined. Metrics should be chosen such that they motivate the desired behavior in project teams. Use of status baseline metrics is one of the primary ways an organization can communicate its values and expectations to project teams. It is up to senior management to validate the Key Performance Indicators (KPIs) they want to use for this.

As a result of implementation complexity, the initial metrics collection process will be somewhat crude, but is a required component for the startup. Initial data requirements at this stage are oriented toward obtaining valid project status information that will be used to make GO/NO GO decisions for ongoing projects. Another important startup data activity is to identify all projects and evaluate resources being used.

One of the major organizational values for the EPMO is to curtail projects that either no longer fit the organizational goal structure, or those whose value has declined because of poor performance compared to approved plan. In both cases, status metrics will play a major role in this assessment process. We point out once again that this type role for the EPMO is not going to be popular with the project teams if their project is cancelled. It is probably best to initially keep this decision away from the EPMO and place it in the hands of a senior steering group who would be supplied metrics by the EPMO.

For all of the reasons outlined here, the role and scope of metrics will increase in an EPMO environment and this requires a mature operational framework to support the defined decision structure. EPMOs can fail because of either poor goal definition from the top, or poor metrics reporting from the supporting groups. One of the major roles of the EPMO is to collect and analyze status of the portfolio and make coherent sense out of this broad collection of data. In this role, it helps the management team make informed decisions regarding the allocation of resources to various projects.

36.6 Status Reporting

As the volume of raw data grows the EPMO organization has a significant communications system design problem to resolve. Basically, it has to opt for either a "pull" or "push" delivery model. Design of this infrastructure will be driven by the maturity level of the data users and the overall scope of the data to be delivered. In a "pull" model, the target user has the ability and infrastructure maturity to actively request status information and progress in a wide variety of formats. One major benefit of this approach is that it gives the user freedom to choose which data items to extract and concentrate on. In order for this approach to be successful, the data must be clearly defined as to meaning and the user has to be analytically oriented.

The alternative design choice, push, is to give the user a defined or "canned" view of metrics that they are interested in and do not wish to browse the data. In this case, the "push" model is more appropriate. Here, the process is to push out a formatted view of the data on a preset schedule.

In the contemporary environment the pull strategy is becoming more popular as the user community information literacy level increases and delivery techniques become more intuitive to use. At the top of the EPMO information structure, a flexible process will be needed by the analyst in order to mine the data in multiple formats and define trends and issues. This suggests a sophisticated pull model. The information distribution characteristics outlined above signal a need for a much more sophisticated communication system than exists in many organizations. This includes both the structure of the data and the delivery technology. A notable design requirement is to standardize the project status-reporting format so that all data can be combined into a single comparative view. This involves much more than a schedule and budget report, especially if we add the analytic analysis capability to the equation.

Creation of the formal information distribution infrastructure to deliver this class of information is yet another example of the overhead required to support an EPMO organization. New development of processes and tools can be a schedule constraint for the implementation process. Personal observation suggests that many organizations will struggle to collect appropriate portfolio information. Until that is successfully accomplished, the portfolio selection decision-making framework is hampered. Also, if an organization does not know what projects are being currently pursued and what resources are being allocated to those projects, then the EPMO level decision functionality is hamstrung. The breadth of this problem suggests that the implementation of the communication system will be a phased process and likely require significant time and resources to mature. Many organizations of this type operate with heavy use of spreadsheets, but that data manipulation technology will limit the analytical capability.

The EPMO charter should describe the standard metrics and forms of status communications that the project teams are to deliver. One of the implementation tasks will be to define the data collection process and report formats for at least the initial operational stage. One goal of the reporting process is to make it as transparent as possible, meaning that the data collection is not intrusive to normal work activities. This is just one of the strategies to minimize conflicts between the project teams and the EPMO.

Standardized status reporting has a twofold benefit in reducing the amount of work required to compile the higher-level view for analysis. When status reporting is standardized, the inputs and the content of the report are well defined. Getting organizational level buy-in on this item will be a challenge, but an important one to accomplish.

36.7 EPMO Communication Linkages

Formal communication channels between the various project teams and the EPMO strategic layer are needed to drive the standard data collection process. After a project is selected and moved into formal development, subsequent analysis may show that it is no longer a viable effort and should be cancelled. In the case where the EPMO organization has a high level of formal authority over the project teams there is the additional responsibility for more direct communication with the PMs. In this structure option, the EPMO organization is chartered to influence timely changes to recover the overall project goals. In any case, the EPMO function would analyze status of ongoing projects and develop conclusions related to the health of the project. Their delegated level of authority would dictate specific actions beyond that point.

36.8 EPMO Organizational Models

The organization models presented in this section are derived from PMO organization experiences and extrapolated here to show enterprise level versions. They collectively provide a vision regarding how the EPMO organization might be structured based on the underlying design philosophy and assumed maturity level. These models also help to understand how the design philosophy would lead to a physical organization.

As indicated earlier, there are many different ways of packaging EPMO functions into an organizational structure. Some of the structures focus on a key role for the function, while others simply describe the authority structure, or concentrate solely on the operational roles, and so on. Fundamentally, an organizational structure should reflect the goals that the host has for the function.

Mark Mullaly describes four alternative organizational role categories for a PMO and each of these would also fit an EPMO structure (Mullaly, 2008). The four standard models and their key roles are:

Scorekeeper

- Monitor and report progress of project portfolio
- Program and project information conduit
- Clearing house for consolidated status updates

Facilitator

- Enable improvement efforts
- Source of best practices

Quarterback

- Focus on project delivery
- PMs report to the PMO
- Central point of accountability

Perfectionist

- Control focused improvement
- PMO is the "center of excellence"
- Agent for change regarding how the organization does projects

In addition to these four, Billows names three other common groupings as described in more detail below (Billows, 2017).

36.8.1 Weather Station Model Overview

36.8.1.1 Organization Driver

When senior management gets nervous about all the money being spent on projects and do not have a good feeling about the value derived, they are looking for information. The current status is a collection of different reporting formats coming from various projects with different varieties of metrics, jargon, and formats. To end this confusion one option is to set up a "Weather Station" organization to standardize reporting, but essentially leave the project management process alone. In this mode, the EPMO organization becomes a central clearing house for project information. More robust versions of this may perform the following roles:

- Maintaining a database of action items, project archives, and lessons learned
- Developing a formal enterprise reporting system for executives and key stakeholders
- Defining advanced standard metrics for reporting such as EV
- Track post-project actual results and communicate this status to management

Table 36.1 Advantages and Pitfalls of the Weather Station Model

Advantages	*Pitfalls*
Easy start-up	Low authority to enforce
Less conflict	Participation may be low
Improves process	May be viewed as bureaucracy
Starts standardization	Actual change questionable

36.8.1.2 Formal Authority

Although the Weather Station's functions sound minor, almost clerical, they require that the projects obey the frequency, format, method of delivery, and associated tools for reporting and planning. Table 36.1 lists the key advantages and pitfalls for this model. This is probably the best choice when frequent project failures are noted and there is insufficient data to ascertain corrective strategy. It also is the easiest to implement without internal conflict and negative political reaction. This type of organization does not have formal authority to propose fixes for the project situation and is only an information conduit.

If the Weather Station model is not given enough authority to ensure cooperation with the project teams, it will have to resort to "nag authority." This approach has potential for inefficiencies, embittered relationships, and being disliked by the project teams. If a PMO-type organization is to be successful, it must be given both accountability and commensurate authority for its assigned roles. It is easy to see the potential value of a central project decision authority; however, it is not so easy to see why it is filled with such internal conflict and takes so long to install successfully. Regardless of the model tenants, this strategy has to be viewed as a tactical decision given that it does not accomplish the higher-level goals outlined in the theory. Billows offers this conclusion for the weather station model—"The Weather Station PMO is a good solution for organizations at the chaos stage in managing their projects" (Billows, 2017).

36.8.2 Control Tower Model Overview

36.8.2.1 Organization Driver

This organization form is derived from a term coined by project management consultant Jan Renerts. Basically, a control tower collects status data and directs traffic. In this model, the underlying management function is recognized as a valuable process in creating new strategic value for the organization; however, management believes that the current portfolio management function is not working as well as it could. A few visible observations supporting this model are:

- Project team training is haphazardly done or not at all.
- Multiple expensive and voluminous "methodologies" have been purchased, but are essentially unused. Projects seem to follow whatever ad hoc structure the team decides.
- Business stakeholders do not know how to support their respective projects and conflict results between them and the project team over roles and relationships.

- Lessons learned on one project are not applied to other projects. The same issues seem to recur across projects.
- Management rewards heroic efforts in project teams rather than projects that are well run. The culture seems to be nurturing the heroic model.

36.8.2.2 Formal Authority

The basic design goal of the control tower is to treat projects like business processes that need to be protected and nurtured—putting an envelope around them if you will. This view follows Edwards Deming's classic quality dictate to reduce variability. In practice, this model has four general functions:

- Establishing standards for managing projects
- Consulting project teams regarding how to follow those standards
- Enforcing the use of those standards
- Improving the standards through experience

Hence, this organization format would be somewhat viewed as an in-house consulting organization with some degree of conformance clout. Note that the focus is still only downward to the project and there is no visible role in project selection or portfolio management. Table 36.2 highlights the major pros and cons of this type of structure.

Effective control tower-oriented organizations are rare. They belong only in organizations that have solved the authority problems of cross-functional projects and developed a cadre of skilled PMs who apply a consistent protocol of planning, budgeting, and tracking their projects (Casey, 2001).

One of the other potential pitfalls of this model is that updating formal standards writing can be a never-ending process. There has to be a review of standards imposed and not just published versions without coordination. If project teams are required to meet a set of standards, then they need to understand those standards and the reason for which they exist. Also, training programs are needed to translate the standard. In this model, internal consultants become the key to success in that they can carry the message as experts and gain firsthand experience in their value. An intrinsic authority level would come from this level of expertise. This type of relationship would benefit the project team and the control tower organization would share be viewed as a positive contribution to the process. This has the elements of a loose partnership, if done well. Without this element of perceived value, the whole EPMO organization will be treated as a bureaucratic nuisance—or worse, a joke.

One of the pitfalls of all standards-oriented organizations is the philosophy of "build it and they will come" often does not work as well as the movies might suggest. One might think

Table 36.2 Advantages and Pitfalls of the Control Tower Model

Advantages	*Pitfalls*
Improved standards	Over control of project
Projects prioritized	Workload issues
PM role recognized	External audit

that PMs would naturally seek out standard, proven processes, and that they would embrace the internal consultant who aims to help them install those standards. That is very often not true! Intrusion of a staff function into the project is almost always viewed as meddling. PMO structures in general add some additional level of formal authority and responsibility and this is where the organizational design becomes difficult. Quite possibly, the "trick" to getting this form of organization working is to first educate the PMs on factors and processes to produce successful outcomes. Assuming some level of this can be achieved, the next step would be to test the resulting standards on a project with a good PM. Let the success be advertised at the grass roots level, then move the successful PM to either the consulting role or the EPMO manager role. At this point, the respectability of the organization is established, standards have been shown to work, and migration toward overall use is initiated. This migration path is no small task, but these steps seem appropriate from experience. Once organizational standards have been embedded in the culture to some reasonable degree, it then becomes possible to start incrementally improving those standards. This type of organizational change management scenario provides a glimpse of the complexity related to implementing a macro-level process such as an EPMO.

36.8.3 Resource Pool Model Overview

Often, the organizational function that hires, assigns, and manages PMs knows less about the internal project management issues than the PM does. In this situation project management talent tends not to be managed as an asset, but more as a body count. This then contributes to other related negative issues in the long term.

36.8.3.1 Organizational Driver

The organizational driver for this model is an explicit increased recognition that something needs to be done to improve functioning of the project management talent within the organization.

36.8.3.2 Formal Authority

The perceived organizational solution in this case is to create a centralized "resource pool" allocation process for all project resources. Project teams would then "hire" a PM from this repository of expertise. This role would make logical sense to combine with other EPMO-like functions, but given its negative behavioral reaction is probably not the first management issue to be dealt with, so this is not considered to be a normal startup structure.

With a resource pool properly in place, the EPMO functions would be involved with the following.

- Hiring and preparing the resource pool for allocation
- Developing high-quality skills in the resource pool
- Managing career paths for the resource pool members

In this model, the resource pool resource is a highly skilled "hired hand" brought in to deliver the stated requirements much like an outside contractor, except in this case the individual would be

Table 36.3 Advantages and Pitfalls of the Resource Pool Model

Advantages	*Pitfalls*
Improves project performance	Project selection process
Creates skilled PM's	Who gets to decide?
Provides authority	How to capture results?
Tools provided	

very knowledgeable regarding standard methods. The basic function of the resource pool member is to ensure that projects are done correctly, but not that the correct projects are done. There is some hanging question as to what would happen if the sponsoring organization would choose to not accept this person and go it alone with their preferred approach using other resources. In that case it may be necessary to have some type of high-level audit function performed by the EPMO organization that is then delivered to management for their action. Once again, we see potential conflicts in this situation.

The major advantage of this model is that it helps to protect and improve the skill level of each PM in the resource pool, which in turn improves and ensures the quality of the project's deliverables. Table 36.3 lists some of the major advantages and pitfalls of the resource pool model.

This model is another example of a structure in which "build it and they will come" does not apply. Executive leadership must agree on some basic authority regarding how this process would work in regard to the project process. Described below are two authority-based options for this process.

The first option is to give the resource pool manager formal and exclusive authority to supply PMs to approved projects. There would need to be some form of negotiation process used for this because each project would be after the PM with the best reputation.

A second option would be to give the pool manager formal authority only over the resource pool, but not so much over the actual allocation of the resources to projects. Project sponsors might be able to select whomever they wish to run their project. In this case the pool manager would handle the following:

- Hiring members from the pool
- Supervising pool members' performance
- Coaching pool members to help them upgrade their effectiveness
- Managing various career development actions such as professional certification
- Disciplining pool members who do not perform to their capabilities

On an informal basis, the pool manager should also help remove organizational barriers to the practice of good project management by working to persuade and educate executives and on the overall value of this process.

When comparing the Weather Station, Control Tower, and Resource Pool models the common pitfall seems to be lack of agreement regarding selection of correct projects being chosen based on priorities. Instead, the focus of each model is more on the growth and skills of each individual PM and less attention in developing or improving the EPMO methodology.

36.9 Which Model Is the Right One?

In the discussion above, seven different models were summarized for organizing this function. Admittedly, there is overlap between the various views. Each option represents a somewhat different goal and authority approach for the function. From this, we are still left with the basic question "what's the right choice?" This is a good question and one might guess that a proper response is "It depends." Even though this would not be satisfying, it is the real answer. Organizations should be constructed in a manner to focus best on solving their problems and not just selecting a standard model.

One of the keys to selection of the right EPMO strategy is the general maturity level of the host organization and the goals that management wishes to focus on. In some cases, the organization itself is not capable of supporting the concepts underlying the breadth of an EPMO. So, the organizational choice model requires matching the capability and culture to the corresponding model that fits. In the section below, we will take a look at how EPMO maturity might be matched with a corresponding organizational level maturity.

36.9.1 EPMO Maturation Stages

EPMO maturity should evolve in logical steps and this process can involve significant organizational process redesign. If an organization recognized the merit of the full EPMO functional scope and decided to implement that as described, it would require a significant time period. This time scale is measured in years more than months. The normal implementation strategy for a macro initiative of this type is to pick out the most pressing needs for the organization and initially focus on that target as Phase one. As each stage is proven, more functions are added in priority order. Over time, the organizational EPMO maturity would evolve to the point where adding more functionality does not deliver equivalent value, so the organization may choose to stop further expansion. At that point the EPMO-related processes would stabilize.

As we have seen in previous discussions, typical maturity grading scales are based on five levels as originally defined by the Capability Maturity Matrix research (as described in Chapter 34). Following that general approach, a five-stage EPMO maturity development process is shown in Figure 36.3.

There are other functional packaging options that could also be shown, but the option outlined here fits a general functional evolutionary approach. Regardless of the defined stages, the key concept of EPMO maturity is that the lower levels should focus on identified critical startup project problems, whereas the higher organizational levels work would focus on processes to move the

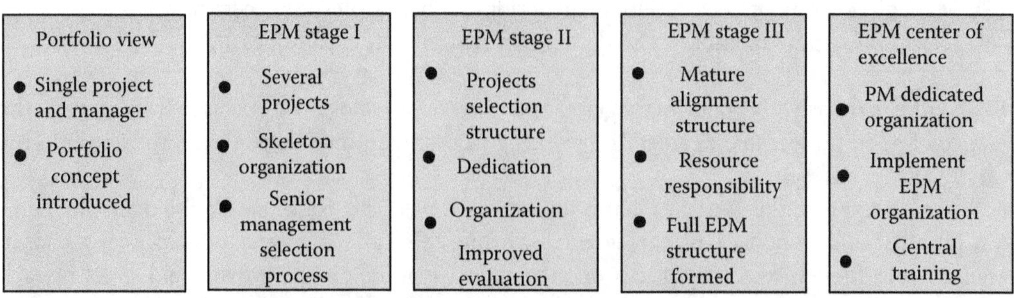

Figure 36.3 EPMO maturity stage model.

organization toward achieving the broader-valued aspect of the concept. At the top maturity level, the organization would be fully integrated in its EPMO, project management, and PPM processes. Project portfolios would be mapped to the business goals in such a manner as to optimize their value to the enterprise and project teams would be developing their deliverables in a standardized manner. The EPMO organization would be the focal point for orchestrating these various processes and would be accountable for their outcomes. Significant incremental value would be anticipated from each of these maturity levels. Moving through these stages should not be anticipated as an overnight journey, but more like a three- to five-year effort with good management sponsorship, dedicated resources, and overall support. The major difficulty during the evolution period will be the insertion of a new and powerful layer into the existing organizational culture. Project teams will have to understand that they are truly global organizational team players and not just a project team focused on a local goal.

36.10 EPMO Tools and Technology

Information is a critical asset in today's business world. PMs must be able to gather, store, and analyze large amounts of data to properly manage project processes. As a result of this, sophisticated tools and technology are needed to support any of the EPMO models pursued. Addition of an EPMO organization certainly increases the information collection and distribution requirement. Multiple projects must be tracked at the same time and the selection process will be more complex than the traditional standalone project analysis today. In order to deal with the data collection, analysis, and information distribution processes, an appropriate set of tools is needed. However, before attempting to buy a particular tool, the first consideration must be to have a workable process and then attempt to match the tool to the process. Not vice versa.

In most cases, suitable EPMO tools will not initially exist in the organization, or at least not fully. This means that the tool issue will be one of reviewing what is available both internally and commercially. Hill (2008) summarizes an approach to dealing with the tool question in Figure 36.4.

The first phase of the selection process is to define the sequential high-level steps that will be taken, which are very similar to all projects—that is, requirements, execution, and implementation. Once these tools have been decided upon, the proper deliver technology can be pursued. The software chosen can then be used to develop the final delivery functionality. The second phase of the model outlines steps for tool implementation. This includes the need for user training.

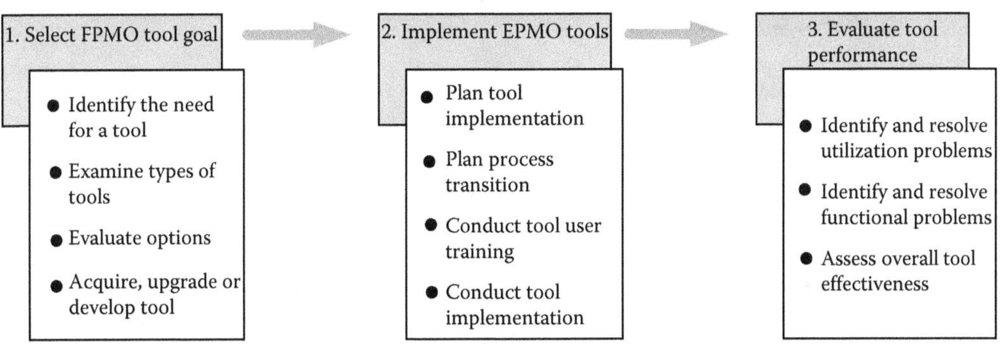

Figure 36.4 EPMO tool selection steps.

Once the implementation of the tool package is complete, the process moves into the third phase to evaluate the chosen tools. This model follows the basic idea of quality management in that it can be repeated as often as necessary to ensure continuous improvement.

Hill states there are three important keys in the evaluation of support tools. First, an organization must analyze the existing environment. In this example, the target EPMO process should have been defined by this point and from this the starting point for tools is to evaluate availability with the goal being to buy rather than build internally. Technicians have a bias toward custom building and then find out that they now have to maintain the custom tool. The general rule of thumb is that the organization is not in business to build tools. Commercial vendors are and, if selected properly, will do it better and cheaper. In some cases, an existing tool might make a good starting place and that would be first choice in the selection. Included below is a brief sequence of steps needed for this process:

Step one. Once the model assessment is done and internal tool gaps are defined, the next step is to evaluate whether to acquire, upgrade, or custom develop the required tool.

Step two. The normal implementation cycle for a new process or tool is to first pilot test it in an appropriate role. Very seldom should a "big bang," (all at once) new tool be introduced, so the pilot option is recommended. Training is an important element is getting the new user comfortable with the tool. Done properly, this should be a motivational process. At this stage, there should be a back-out plan in case the pilot is not successful. After the pilot, it will be very hard to change directions.

Step three. All along the implementation process, a formal post-installation review should be undertaken. Wherever possible, react to the reported negative lessons learned situations.

As the EPMO organization evolves, more standardized tools will be required. Some examples of common support tool requirements are:

- Project proposal and analysis
- A life cycle stage-gate project management process
- Common templates for the various stages of projects (charter, requirements document, project plans, deployment plans, support plans, etc.)
- Financial analysis models
- Risk analysis templates
- Project planning templates
- Status report formats
- Project closing procedures and audits

Beyond these base level tools, there is a requirement for other tools related to information distribution and archiving. These would fall into the category of infrastructure, but are important to the overall delivery process. At least a crude version of these would have to be defined in the early organizational stages. It is important to recognize that excessive use of email is not a suitable method to accomplish this class of communication management.

Until recently, there has been a lack of comprehensive software packages with the ability to support this class of activity; however, in recent years several products have been introduced that focus on the portfolio aspects of management. Eric Verzuh states that an EPMO process package needs to have broad capabilities with the software being capable of tracking numerous individual projects while integrating the status of those projects into a coherent set of metrics that can judge overall status and adherence to organizational goals (Verzuh, 2008). The following broad capabilities are needed for the enterprise level information views:

- Individual project status data
- General project team communications and collaboration
- Visibility of project interdependencies
- Visibility of resource use across all projects
- Project portfolio status summary
- Project status reporting
- Cost information (current and projected)
- Interfaces to other support areas (i.e., HR, accounting)

The tool selection process and EPMO adoption both should be managed just like a project. The process necessary to make the right decision in choosing the future path of an organization is vitally important. This process can consume large amounts of time and capital, so it should be planned, executed, and managed properly. Future users should be involved in the selection process and not just forced on them by a consulting organization.

36.11 Summary

This chapter and Chapter 35 have introduced the concept of an advanced organizational concept to provide an integrated approach to project selection, portfolio management, and project management processes. The functions of an EPMO organization were described and illustrated based on models that have surfaced from traditional PMOs. The rationale for managing projects globally is easy the theorize, but not so easy to implement.

Whether one looks at this concept as simply a departmental PMO structure, or an enterprise level EPMO initiative, the discussion should fit equally well. In the case of PMO-type installations, the early history reveals that they are frequent failures (around 50%), yet the theory of pursuing them seems ironclad. Much of the difficulty in implementing this class of process comes in the cultural change required by the organization and realignment of responsibility and authority to the new organization. One causal factor arises from the fact that a PMO, or an EPMO type organization, represents a centralization image and lower-level units often resist such initiatives. Keep in mind, then, that the real implementation issue is not in deciding what appears to be a very logical solution to a universal problem, but more one of how to obtain buy-in from affected decision groups. A senior manager once described his personal view of delegation and centralization this way—"you can call it whatever you want so long as I get to make the decision." The implication here as related to an EPMO type organization is to recognize that it tends to take away local flexibility and therefore would be resisted.

References

Billows, D., 2017. PMO—Project Management Office Types and Strategies, Enterprise Projects. https://4pm.com/2017/09/08/3-kinds-project-management-office/ (accessed January 11, 2018).

Casey, W. and W. Peck, 2001. Choosing the right PMO setup. *PM Network*, 15, 2, 40–47.

Hill, G., 2008. *The Complete Project Management Office Handbook*, 2nd ed. New York: Auerbach Publications.

http://mediaproducts.gartner.com/reprints/ca/157924.html (accessed January 13, 2009).
Mullaly, M., 2008. Four Archetypes of the PMO. www.gantthead.com (accessed November 15, 2008).
PMI, 2017. *A Guide to the Project Management Body of Knowledge* (*PMBOK*® Guide), 6th ed. Newtown Square, PA: Project Management Institute.
Richardson, G. and C. Butler, 2006. *Readings in Information Technology Project Management*. Boston, MA: Course Technology.
Verzuh, E., 2008. *The Fast Forward MBA in Project Management*. Hoboken, NJ: Wiley.

Chapter 37

Project Governance

37.1 Introduction

Merriam-Webster dictionary defines governance as "the organization, machinery, or agency through which a political unit exercises authority and performs functions and which is usually classified according to the distribution of power within it." This definition can be applied to both the total organizational structure and project management. In this context, governance is more defined as a set of management and control relationships. At the project level this involves the principles and decision-making processes-related actions to ensure successful completion of the venture.

Project governance is the decision environment by which a project is managed within an enterprise. Hence, it can be viewed as the management coupling of project activities with business vision, strategy, and objectives. This process has always been complex given the many different stakeholder expectations related to the project. Conceptually, governance provides a decision framework that can help achieve the objectives of a project. It relates to accountabilities and responsibilities for the overall management decision structure and culture.

Figure 37.1 shows a schematic illustrating the nature of governance. Here it is symbolized as an envelope wrapped around the project structure to help ensure that all the underlying processes are effectively managed.

37.2 Need for Project Governance

Project governance extends the general principle of enterprise governance downward into individual projects. Many organizations today have recognized their shortcomings in this aspect of project management methodology and are developing formal project level governance structures. This level structure differs from an organizational equivalent structure in that the project view is more fragmented, virtual, and transient in nature. In both cases, the basic intent is to clarify how decisions are made and accountability established. This discussion focuses on that role in project decision-making. More specifically, the governance activity is particularly focused on processes such as change management and strategic (project) decision-making that lie outside of the project manager (PM)'s normal decision domain.

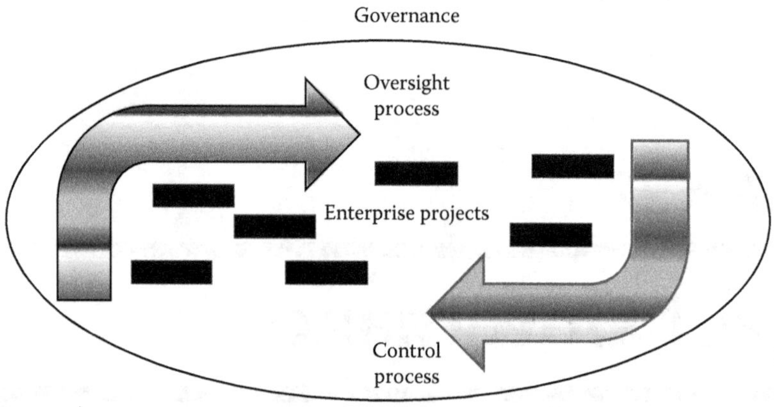

Figure 37.1 Project governance life cycle model

In recent years, corporate level governance has placed additional responsibilities on their board of directors to monitor enterprise performance and this requirement has caused a cascading impact downward to lower levels of the organization and into the project environment. Board members are now held responsible for low-level issues; therefore, they want better visibility into those levels. The higher-level management requirement encompasses the need for control and to assure the following:

- Projects are being managed well and in accordance with the requirements of defined governance procedures.
- Organizational project portfolios are being optimized regarding the return from corporate resources and are maintaining alignment with strategic objectives.
- Strategic projects are being properly managed.

37.3 Project Governance Definition

As used here, the term *project governance* implies external controls linked to enterprise management regarding project activities, and they are designed to ensure that the project serves its intended goals. Lack of senior management commitment is a consistent cause of project failure, and the governance processes are meant to better deal with this aspect of a project's management. The need for increased project governance is at least partially stimulated by this recognition. Today, adequate governance processes are not in place in many organizations and even less well executed overall. Formal project management methodologies provide various templates and processes that support the notion of external management requirements, but these alone do not accomplish the required decision support requirements needed to make a project successful. When implemented properly governance forms an integrated decision cycle that yields a closed-loop feedback system between strategic planning, budgeting linked to execution, and delivery controls (Jennings, 2005). The basic requirements for a project governance system consist of the following 11 key roles:

1. Formally identify *opportunities*? (Competitive analysis, track and assess employee suggestions, customer feedback, etc.)
2. Select/authorize/fund the *formal approval* for projects? (e.g., only a formal strategic executive group has the authority to update or reprioritize the enterprise project portfolio!)

3. Establish the basic *approval* and measurement processes, including defining roles, accountabilities, policies, standards, and associated processes.
4. *Evaluate* project proposals using a defined methodology to select those that represent the best enterprise investment of funds and scarce resources and those that are within the firm's capability and capacity to deliver.
5. *Enable* staffing of projects through the allocation of internal and external resources, along with business support.
6. *Define* the desired business outcomes (end states), benefits, and value for approved projects, along with business measures of success and an overall value proposition.
7. *Control* the scope, contingency funds, overall project value, and other business attributes of approved projects.
8. *Monitor* approved project's progress, stakeholder's commitment, results achieved, and leading status indicators.
9. *Measure* the outputs, outcomes, benefits, and value of project performance against both the plan and ongoing expectations.
10. *Management* will be actively involved in steering the project into goal alignment with the organization, removing obstacles, managing critical success factors, and providing guidance on benefit-realization shortfalls.
11. *Develop* the organization's process maturity delivery capability by continually building and enhancing its ability to deliver more complex and challenging projects in less time and for less cost while generating maximum value.

37.4 Enterprise Level Project Governance Principles

To support the project level governance processes, the following governance capabilities must be defined at the enterprise level. Ultimately, senior management up to the board of directors needs to recognize their project governance responsibilities in the following four areas:

1. Portfolio selection and effectiveness
2. Project sponsorship effectiveness and efficiency
3. Project management effectiveness and efficiency
4. Disclosure compliance

To satisfy these requirements, all senior management should take an active interest in the following project-related areas and activities:

1. Recognize that they have ultimate responsibility for governance of projects.
2. Be actively involved in defining the roles, responsibilities, and performance criteria for the governance of projects.
3. Ensure that disciplined governance arrangements, supported by appropriate methods and controls, are in place within the organization and are being properly applied throughout the project life cycle.
4. Maintain a coherent and supportive relationship between the overall business strategy and the activities related to project selection. This is a responsibility that a Project Management Office (PMO) or Enterprise Project Management Office (EPMO) organization might be utilized for (see Chapters 35 and 36 for more details).

5. Ensure that all projects have an approved plan containing management milestone authorization points at which point the status is formally reviewed and approved. Decisions made at authorization points are formally recorded and communicated.
6. Ensure that the project resource allocation process is guided by a formally delegated authorization body that has sufficient representation, competence, authority, and resources to enable them to make appropriate decisions.
7. Oversee project selection processes using business case data supported by relevant and realistic information that provides a reliable basis for making authorization decisions.
8. Ensure that appropriate independent scrutiny of projects and project management systems is performed and properly communicated to relevant management groups.
9. Ensure that clearly defined criteria for reporting project status, including risks and major issues, is being performed for all projects.
10. Support a positive organizational continuous improvement culture and frank internal disclosure of project information.
11. Support processes to ensure that project stakeholders are engaged at a level that is commensurate with their importance to the organization and, in a manner that fosters successful completion of the requirements.

In reviewing the responsibility list above, one would quickly conclude that most senior management groups are more removed from the tactical project working level than this implies, and this is one motivation for including an overview of this topic. Government regulations such as Sarbanes–Oxley are heightening recognition and consequences of these high-level responsibilities. Given this somewhat theoretical view of governance, the PM needs to understand the logic inherent in these requirements and must take a supportive responsibility in supporting these management principles.

37.5 Tactical Level Project Governance

The starting point for the establishment of an appropriate project level governance process is to define what elements need to be managed and those that will make a positive contribution to the project outcome. The trade-offs in this selection are better management on one side and excessive bureaucracy overhead on the negative side. Governance must be geared toward helping the project be successful and not slowing it down just for control sake. One example of this help would be to assist in resolving internal conflict over whether a large change request should be approved or not. In this mode, the governance process serves a Supreme Court role when the lower-level processes are unable to resolve the issue, or the issue is larger than their delegated authority levels. This same type of role would be appropriate for issues related to resources, budgets, and cross-departmental issues. Beyond the aforementioned examples, there are many other situations that are in the domain of ineffective project governance created by poor enterprise level processes. The list below represents governance-related events or processes that need to be delegated to either the PM, project board, or other organizational entity. Failure to successfully assign formal responsibility and authority for any one of these, either initially or during the project, represents a governance gap that will then have to be resolved ad hoc with no clear answer. Gaps like this are disruptive to the smooth flow of a project's decision environment. A basic project-oriented checklist of these key process items includes the following:

1. Existence of a documented business case stating the objectives of the project and specifying the in-scope and out-of-scope items

2. An acceptance mechanism to assess the compliance of the completed project to its required objectives
3. Formal identification of a project's stakeholders who are identified as having an interest in the project
4. A defined method of information distribution to each defined stakeholder
5. A defined set of project requirements that are developed with adequate involvement of defined stakeholders
6. A management-approved scope specification outlining the project work to be performed and associated deliverables
7. Formal appointment of a PM (before or soon after the project charter is approved).
8. Clear assignment of project roles and responsibilities
9. A current, published project plan that spans the full life cycle from project initiation to operational status
10. A formal status and progress reporting process that includes work status, schedules, budget, resource, and risk status.
11. A formal central document repository for project archives
12. A centrally held glossary of project terms
13. A defined process for conflict and problem resolution
14. A defined and formal process for managing change requests
15. A process for the identifying, recording, communicating, and tracking project risks

A review of this summary list raises the point that these are all basic project management processes, so why go through this? The answer is that one or more of these processes will not be defined from within the project, which in turn creates gaps in the overall process. Mature project management environments will have each of these items formally defined. This is essentially part of an overall management methodology, but with a more high-level view.

37.6 Operational Governance Model

There is yet a middle tier to the concept of governance. This tier involves the method used by the organization to map project requirements to business needs. Chapters 35 and 36 discussed the roles for project portfolio management (PPM) and EPMO. For this layer of management to be effective, a high-level of involvement from senior management is required.

Capgemini defines four key component layers involved in their governance process. These include both the project and normal operational environments (Capgemini, 2006). A fifth layer, "innovation," also exists as an overriding driver to guide the overall adoption of technical and business capabilities that emerge with new technology options. Experience has shown that high levels of innovation will be disruptive to existing activities and cannot, therefore, be expected to fit neatly into one of the other four categories without some additional imaginative thought as to its application. A summary of the five layers follows (Capgemini, 2006, p. 13):

1. *Innovation*. Understanding new technologies, products, and practices to build proposals regarding how to improve a technology or business area. The organization needs the ability to make decisions regarding the best time to adopt a technology and to ensure a persistent rate of improvement.

2. *Information.* This area involves the form, content, and context of data management processes to actively support and record business decisions. Current information related to key business processes is increasingly important with faster moving markets and the demands for compliance.
3. *Integration.* The definition relates to all standards, naming conventions, practices, and architecture reference models required to support cost-effective integration technology aspects.
4. *Infrastructure.* This covers the technical architecture capability to support common project elements; networks, processors, directories, security, and storage.
5. *Industrialization.* The awareness of the methods, best practices, and suppliers that can be used to improve operational effectiveness support of a market competitive position.

Accomplishment of these attributes aids in overall goal alignment between the organization and the project. The matrix shown in Figure 37.2 structures this view for a combined business and project perspective. Capgemini refers to this as the "5i & 3c" (5 rows and 3 columns) matrix and it forms the high-level structural first step in identifying the necessary goals for governance by delineating technology in terms of what it provides to the overall enterprise, as opposed to a single-point evaluation view (Capgemini, 2006, p. 14). Grading the adequacy of governance in each cell of this matrix would be done by assessing the status of each element for a project with its specified technology.

The 15 cells shown in Figure 37.2 represent an assessment categorization model for evaluating future technology roles in the organization with a governance focus. In this example, the governance process is tightly linked to the project selection activity. The major difference in this case is more governance focused, than just looking for improved processes. Also, this view forces enterprise level examination. Goal visions identified by this process would then lead to more goal-oriented proposals that in turn would be structured into specific project targets through the normal project selection processes. The tactical governance process would then guide and support further definition into a deliverable product specification. Level of detail required for this overall

		Business targets		
		Compliance	Cost Mgt.	Competitive
Technology units	Innovation			
	Information			
	Integration			
	Infrastructure			
	Industrialization			

Figure 37.2 Capgemini's 5 × 3 technology governance matrix.

process is variable based on individual enterprise needs, but the framework shown is still useful for establishing high-level targets and responsibility assignments at the matrix cell or row level. In addition, the matrix can help guide resource allocations and other aspects such as constraints, issues to consider, and the like. During a technical assessment review, it is also possible to target specific technology vendors' products by using the cells to partition how a product supports that goal segment. One should view the Capgemini matrix as an enterprise level guide to governance-oriented project formulation. In this perspective, we see a completely different view than that which would be visible from a typical departmental organization (stovepipe) approach.

Even though the focus here is on the project role, the same activities could be mapped to other organizational tiers without altering the process described. Any organization looking at its environment in this manner should not be looking at low-level processes to repair, rather how to pursue high-level organizational goals. It also seems reasonable to suggest that the column headings for the matrix shown in Figure 37.2 could also be expanded to include other specific goals.

37.7 Governance versus Portfolio Management

One point that is not intuitively obvious from general description is the distinction between governance versus portfolio management. Basically, governance is more of a principle-based view, whereas the project selection process is more nuts and bolts mechanics based on data collection and analysis. Desired results from a well-defined governance culture will come from the intelligent application of its principles combined with clear delegation of responsibility and managerial monitoring of internal control systems (Reid and Bourn, 2004).

The decision-making element of governance—i.e., who makes what decision, when and based on what information—is not easy to implement based on the many decision scenarios that are involved. Operationally, some organization entity needs to be clearly charged with each of the decision areas. The procedures outlined in this section can be applied to all projects and the corresponding governance management principles outlined here should be reviewed to ensure that appropriate decision environment exists. Gaps in governance processes will create nagging problems and delays for the project as gaps in the defined levels of authority surface. It is important to note that in most cases the PM cannot easily fix a governance gap, but realizing in advance that the gap exists can help in mitigating its impact. Also, recognize that governance issues cover the entire organization and there needs to be continuity regarding how the layers of the enterprise decisions interact from a decision-making view.

The decision areas outlined in Figure 37.3 are adequate as a starting point. This would clarify the basic "who" processes, although in most cases there would need to be more detail regarding naming specific individuals or titles to the roles. The design challenge is to define what types of decisions should be made by whom and who should be responsible for preparing the information to support the decision-making process. The MIT Sloan Business School collected data from 100 top-performing organizations to categorize how they made governance decisions. Figure 37.3 categorizes the related roles and responsibility domains for the organization. The one striking thing about this view is the implementation variability. One might conclude that many different approaches will work so long as the design is well defined.

Figure 37.4 illustrates a custom governance matrix based on the various organizational governance options described here. Each organization will have to design its own unique specifications and further clarify the roles. Even if the first version of this effort is just a working draft, it would provide the basis for further clarifying general decision categories.

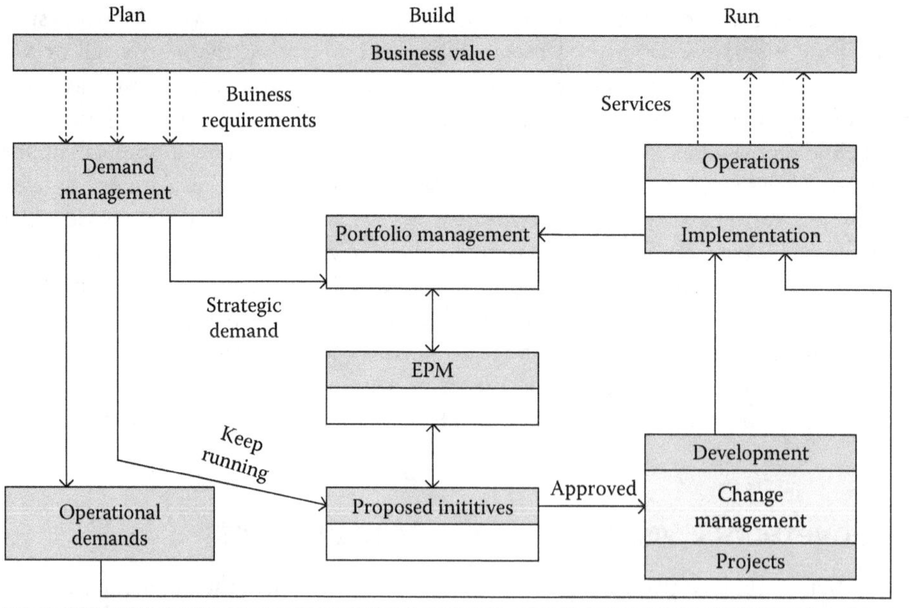

Figure 37.3 Governance decision areas.

Decisions / Community	Appointment of governance board		Cost/budget		Compliance		● ● ● ● ●	Information	
	Input	Decision	Input	Decision	Input	Decision		Input	Decision
Business monarchy									
Project monarchy									
Feudal or department							Populate from 5i by 3c matrix		
Federal or cooperative									
Duopoly or project + business									
Anarchy or individuals							● ● ● ● ●		

● Populate with roles or people
● To suit the specific enterprise

Figure 37.4 Roles and responsibilities matrix (Capgemini).

37.8 Populating the Project Governance Framework

To populate the Capgemini framework, defined core values need to be established for each decision area. In this view, we see a slightly different perspective. That is, we now recognize that there is a wide variety of goals to examine. Surprisingly, in some cases the goal for a decision area is not always to improve. There are situations where the goal is to simply describe a current view. As can be seen in the four-cell matrix shown in Figure 37.4, three of the cells are more static. Only one fits the highly competitive view initially described.

There are several reasons why it might be best to select one of the static modes for some areas of the organization. Examples to illustrate this point are as follows:

1. That area is not a core objective and by holding cost down in that area more resources can be applied to another higher priority area
2. There is no great operational value added by improving this area beyond the current state
3. The target area is being considered for spin-off and sale.

Many more examples are available to show how this type of logic can be applied to various organizational units, but the key thought is that continuous improvement is not always the singular operative goal. It is important to note that one of the fundamental reasons for an effective governance structure is to be able to properly prioritize and orchestrate this type decision environment. All organizations attempt to accomplish decision-making through their planning processes, so the point here is to recognize that a governance process helps the organization focus on more than just a singular global improvement view. By selecting the right growth targets at the expense of others a more efficient allocation of resources can occur. It is also possible for governance processes to vary by project given the diversity of goals as described above. Experience has shown that if an individual project initiative cannot be defined into one of the four quadrants, the governance requirement overlaps across two or more quadrants that clouds the criteria for its related decisions.

The model framework outlined for governance formalization can be also used for determining whether there is a benefit in moving individual new project objectives, or existing systems and services, from one quadrant to another to better evaluate their value. Realize that there is a significant management decision style difference in moving from the top right "Innovation/Lead" quadrant counter clockwise to the bottom right "Reduce Exposure" quadrant. The variations in approach indicated through the cells of Figure 37.5 also represent variability in governance strategies and likely any related array of project types related to those cells.

There are other uses for assigning projects into one of the four quadrants. For instance, the business planners should question each target area as to its desired quadrant position in Figure 37.5. This would lead to a decision for an excellent proposal in a "Cost Manage" category of rejecting since the goal is to not invest. In another case, if moving a process from "Maintain Position" to an "Innovate/Lead" would add value, that proposal would be accepted. Similarly, a "Cost Manage" situation might be improved in value by some selected technology initiative. Capgemini describes the boldest strategy with the biggest payoff as one which links the top right to bottom right in a transformational outsourcing to view the area as a commodity rather than a valued leadership position (Capgemini, 2006, p. 20). This strategy can free resources and money for reallocation to other initiatives, but represents a major organizational change decision. The desire to pursue a new wave of technologies may be the driver for this level of change, but the recognition of degree of change helps with the decision process.

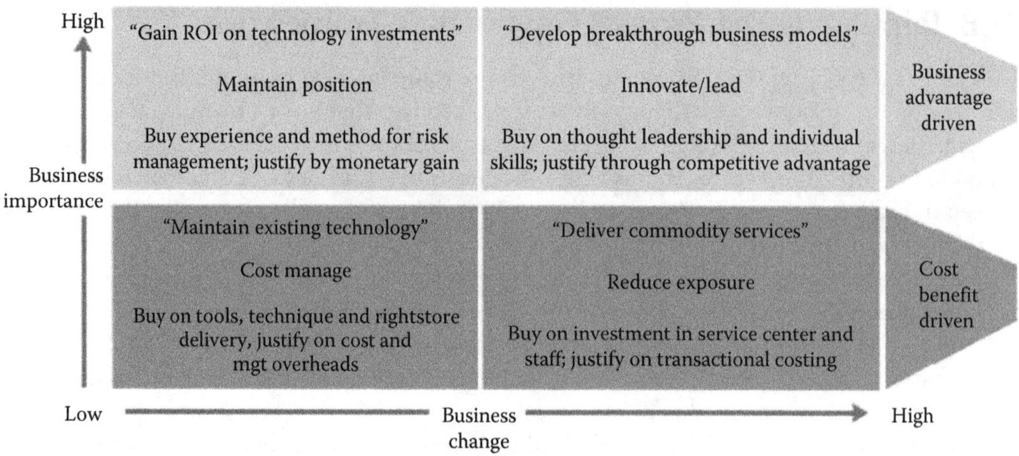

Figure 37.5 Business importance versus business change.

Figure 37.6 illustrates the complexity of technology evolution at the enterprise level. This also shows some sample attributes of organizational governance when done well. These technology stages show a typical sample of evolving maturity levels for information technology organizations as they moved through a series of steps involving technology, process integration, rationalization, industrialization, and innovation. Although this specific example may

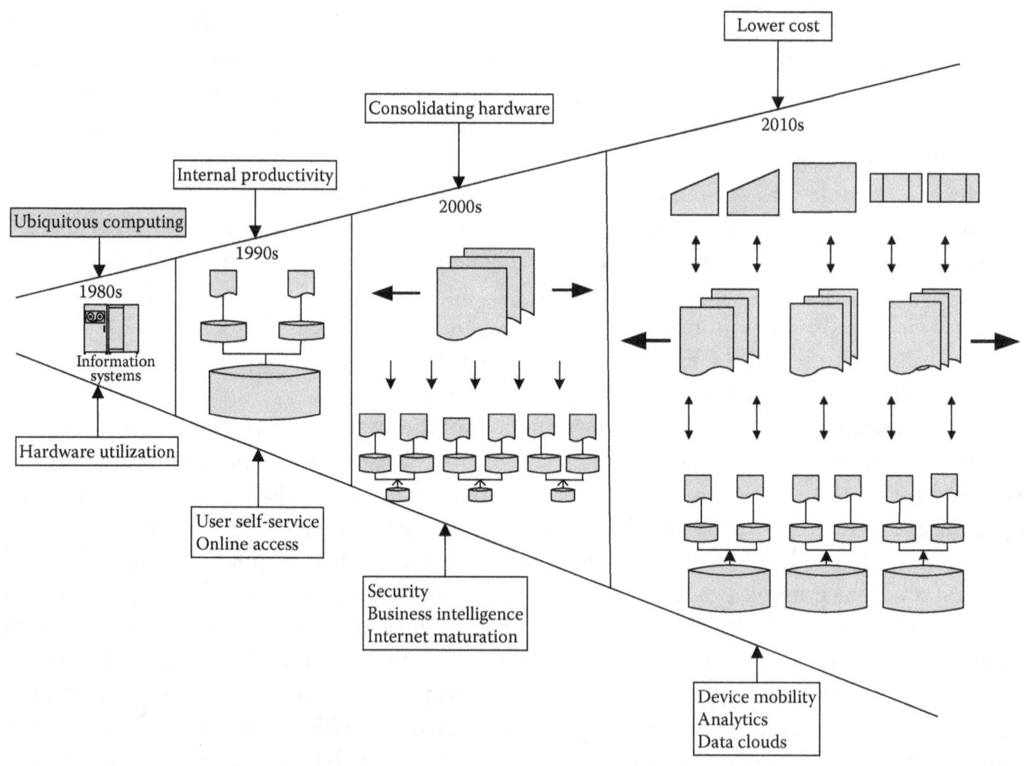

Figure 37.6 Managing technology evolution.

be hard to extrapolate to specific environments, it is a good example of what a high-level governance process needs to deal with at the enterprise level. In this example, the result of each evolutionary stage resulted in lower unit cost and increased capability through what could be mapped as strategic governance. This process would not occur easily with traditional planning techniques that looked only at lower-level items for improvement. If one examines the key steps that drove this result, it would reveal a combination of knowledge sharing, technology selection, high-level process redesign, and process integration (implementation). This would not occur smoothly without a governance process that helped focus the decision goals at the right level and this macro-level capability is one of the key value drivers for a strategic governance model.

37.9 Governance Life Cycle Maturity Model

Figure 37.6 shows a real-world example to illustrate some of the dimensions of the linkage between maturity and governance. These two concepts are truly management cousins with common organizational improvement goals. In this figure there are four maturity levels defined. The capability labels on each stage describe the general characteristics of each level. A translation of this maturity scale into a more general governance statement view is summarized below:

Level-1: This level is characterized by *ad hoc* processes, with minimal formal governance.
Level-2: This level represents a basic governance structure with regular reviews and implemented standards, trust between business and the project begin to occur.
Level-3: This intermediate level is characterized by portfolio prioritization and increased respect between the business and project layers.
Level-4: This maturity level is graded "advanced," which indicates above average capabilities in portfolio selection and governance. An enterprise level view of projects is recognized with common project management methods that deal with change management. Included here are programs and PPM-reporting mechanisms that provide senior management with metrics and overall project status visibility at an appropriate level.
Level-5: This level is characterized by "best practice" processes and an organization that is dedicated to continuous improvement and root cause analysis. The organization can achieve desired goals consistently.

37.10 Governance Value Process

Measurement of governance value is complex, multifaceted, context-specific, and dynamic. Actual value received occurs from successful execution of well-chosen and focused organizational initiatives. Successful achievement of approved targets is the fundamental goal of the governance process. The key concept here is focus. No single strategy or approach will accomplish everything, every time. One underlying cause of the difficulty in realizing business value lies in the complexity of the environment and in the changing sources of value creation. Organizations today now recognize value from intangible assets, such as brands, intellectual property, information systems technology, e-business, improved processes, organizational structures, human talent, and the enveloping management represented by enterprise governance.

One level of governance implementation strategy challenge lies in understanding and managing a project-oriented value-creation process that is dynamic, complex, and characterized by a myriad of interconnected parts. This process must be anchored to an explicit, clear, and focused business strategy. Without a clearly articulated and understood strategy, it is difficult to align resource investment decisions with strategic direction to select the right things to do and equally important to decide what you will not do.

If organizations are to be successful in tackling the question of value, they must recognize that the basic challenge is managing change and a dynamic refocusing of organizational initiatives in the proper direction. This must include focus beyond improving what exists now and look outward at forecast future states. This action involves the following:

- Defining comprehensive programs of business change—programs that include all aspects of the business, processes, people, technology, and the subsequent change efforts
- Developing complete and comparable business cases to aid in proper target selection
- Selecting investments based on the overall value to an enterprise, not to just a functional or geographic unit
- Recognizing that the decision to select and proceed with an investment is only the beginning of an ongoing governance relationship

Most organizations have some strategic governance capability in place; however, project failure rates indicate that something in the management governance domain is still lacking. Clearly, best performer organizations have recognized this issue and have higher levels of maturity in the governance domain. Rarely do all the governance model components that have been described in this chapter exist in an organization. This would require at least a level 4 or 5 maturity. Regardless of the actual scope of governance implementation, the driving theme is to have sufficient implementation to provide value to the business through alignment of organizational objectives and priorities with project and other initiatives.

One of the key management questions involves where to start maturing the organizational governance processes. The schematic model outlined in Figure 37.7 shows how the governance process is the central component that drives a series of linked high-level processes related to planning, running, and building the organization decision process environment. A key role of the maturity process is to support organizational decision-making regarding pursuit of issues related to running the business, growing the business, and transforming the business.

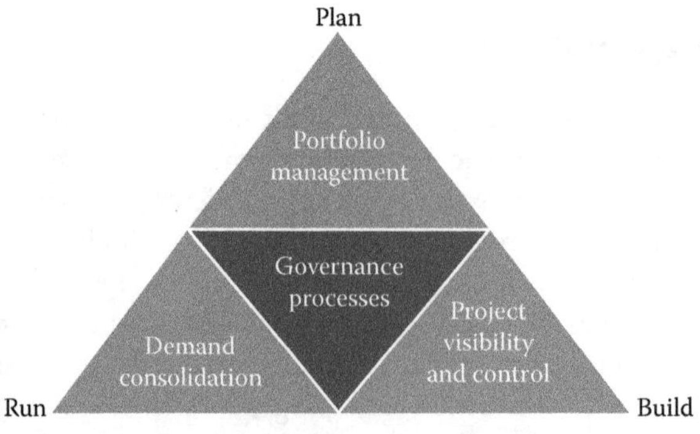

Figure 37.7 Governance triangle.

37.11 Corporate Governance and Project Teamwork

To close this discussion of organizational maturity we will offer a humorous metaphor to make a critical point regarding the role of governance. The web site www.maxwideman.com contains a wealth of project management information and sometimes humor. An allegory authored by Peter Halas was originally published on the website as a somewhat abstract metaphor for corporate governance. It is re-published here with the permission of Max Wideman (Halas, 2008).

Organizations work in much the same way that the human body does. This allegory clearly illustrates how confrontation across "elements" can quickly cause a situation to get out of control. Underlying the story line, however, is a clear message for PMs and project practitioners in general.

37.11.1 Scenario: Final Report from the Body Management Governance Team

In January, the Liver said to the Lungs, "Justify yourself. I do not see your value." The Lungs were so shocked at this "power play" that they started hyper ventilating. By February, the Brain had to issue a general alert (bio email) saying that lack of oxygen is starting to affect the entire body, and started orchestrating a coordinated release of hormones, adrenalin, blood supply constriction activators, and so on.

In March, the Brain proceeded to monitor the levels of hundreds of actions to see, in real time, that they are again doing the job—and issued reports to the Heart, Kidneys, and Skin, advising them to make adjustments as needed. During April and May, the entire Body had benefitted from this response. Flows of work orders were being processed efficiently by all stakeholders, even traditionally less than cooperative areas such as the Thyroid, Pancreas, and Adrenalin Glands were now if not happy, at least not throwing stones.

By June the crisis was over; but in July, the Liver that had been relatively unaffected by all this, and had not really seen (nor fully understood) what had just unfolded, issued a message to the Brain. Evidently, the Liver had determined that too large a percentage of the Body's blood supply was residing in the head. But not only that, the blood was too rich. It knew that other species can live without so many red blood cells and white blood cells, so it recommended the Brain cut back its blood supply. Further, it recommended "thinning out the blood" itself by 14%. (This was a magical number it had learned at a Gartner Executive briefing on "Offshoring, and Cutback Best Practices.")

By August, the Brain, having made these adjustments, was then just in subliminal mode and the Autonomic Nervous System was by then the one really running the Body. The Brain was no longer functioning as before, but was just handling the vital "needs of the business."

From September onward, some of the results of the thinning out of the Blood (i.e., outsourcing, and resource cutbacks) and the fact that there was now less blood in the cranium began to show (i.e., Willy-nilly project initiatives, no clear "alignment," no tools to assist in "governance" structures).

The effects were as follows:

- The Eyes did not see as well and as far down the road as they used to, so any truck coming in the opposite direction could "blind side the Body" at any time.
- The Hands did not work as fast and as nimbly, so many items picked up slipped out of them, were dropped and broken.
- When the Body consumed alcohol or smoked, it was so overwhelmed that it practically shut down. Similarly, it could hardly withstand any competition at all.

Since many other cells did not like the climate that the Liver had unintentionally caused, they started leaving inconspicuously through skin pores, by being exhaled through the Lungs, and yes, whenever the opportunity arose, through the gastro and urinary tracts. Since metrics were no longer kept of this turnover rate, no one noticed.

By October, the Stomach was no longer working efficiently because of the new restrictive (cost-cutting) measures; bile that was spewing out the liver and was starting to accumulate. As a result, the bilirubin, biliverdin, and haematopinid metrics were off the charts, and no one seemed to know what to do about it anymore.

In November, the Liver started fighting with the Stomach, not realizing that the Brain was the real reason for the way things being as they were. The fact is that whether one likes it or not, one cannot ignore the Brain, for it orchestrates the entire health of the organization and its ability to cope with its environment. Finally, the whole system collapsed and Body died (went into liquidation) in December.

The Cast:
Brain Played by PM
Heart Played by HR (Human Resources)
Liver Played by Finance
Lungs Played by Sales/Marketing
Hands, Stomach Played by Manufacturing and Inventory Logistics

37.12 Commentary

Does the Halas medical scenario look familiar? Does it sound like infighting among the various stakeholders, both internal to the project team and external? This type of interaction is mainly a result of how the various players can negatively perceive and impact each other. For example, there can be significant differences between two prevailing viewpoints, such as:

"PM" as a "commodity provider—just let me manage the project"
"PM" as a "strategic partner—help me make my business better."

This is *not* an "either/or" comparison. The project team and its leader need to be respected as a value-added provider, and for the most part, are looked at as falling somewhere on a continuum between these two perspectives.

When it comes to projects and their management, we can gather from this Halas story the sort of interactive complexity involved. The key is to distinguish the difference between managing the organizational goal segment and managing the project. The organization needs specialists in each bodily area (i.e., technology) to maintain the health of each (i.e., tactical management). Then you also need a wellness campaign (i.e., strategic project management) to ensure that the whole collection runs smoothly. A "wellness campaign" (i.e., project management) can be as intensive or casual as you wish (i.e., level of project management ceremony), but without it, things will quickly unravel. One thing is clear: the long-term effect is quite a different exercise from the day-to-day control of the body (technology) as a whole. In project work, project management and technology management cannot be divorced, but they do need to be understood as different disciplines and, where necessary, managed separately often by different people working together.

37.13 Conclusion

This chapter has offered a look at the breadth and structure of the governance process from the enterprise level down to the project level. The final section left us with a little abstract humor on this topic. As this discussion outlined, if all the components are not working together the organism will eventually fail. A governance process represents the driver for that enterprise level integration.

Organizations that recognize and start the governance process with a portfolio management initiative are those that are sensitive to controlling their "front door"—that is, the projects being pursued, but they may then feel that their biggest management gap is the project approval process and not having "apples to apples" data that allows meaningful comparisons. The result from this environment is often a disorganized collection of funding that does not deliver optimum value to the business.

Second, organizations that have tactical project management problems staying on schedule, on budget, and using resources efficiently tend to focus their initial governance initiatives on improving project visibility and control.

Third, organizations determined to minimize how much they spend in the day-to-day "keeping the lights on" activities will focus their initial governance on better demand management, better prioritization, and operational efficiency—all aspects of running the organization. This will lead to various initiatives for demand consolidation efficiency.

Regardless of which side of the governance triangle (Figure 37.7) is viewed as the appropriate initial starting point, once value from this activity is demonstrated, there will be a tendency to expand into the other sides of the triangle on a priority basis. Typically, this evolution happens gradually, folding in more processes and bringing more value into the organization. The key to starting is in finding where the organization will get the biggest initial gain. Typical strategies for this include eliminating/combining projects, defining resource allocation processes, reviewing decision-making processes for project approval, focus on make versus buy decisions, and so on.

Governance of project management activities involves those areas that are specifically related to project activities. Effective governance of project management ensures that an organization's project portfolio is dynamically aligned to its goals and objectives, is delivered efficiently, and is sustainable. This activity also supports how senior management and other major strategic project stakeholders are provided with timely, relevant, and reliable information (i.e., visibility into the tactical realms). An associated project governance role is to balance the risk of the organization's investment against the opportunities and benefits that those outcomes will provide the business. It addresses the risks to ensure that the value to the organization is received in balance with properly mitigated risks.

Current organizational governance processes tend to be inadequate in managing what is, in most cases, an uncertain project journey to a fuzzy destination. To support such an environment there needs to be an evolutionary process directed toward a full project investment life cycle from goal setting to fruition; one that senses and responds to changes in the internal and external environment and improves internal understanding regarding what is working and not working as expected. Without such a process, the risk of ending up in the wrong place, with the associated undesirable business consequences, is significantly increased.

To be effective in delivering value, the governance process must ensure that organizations understand their desired business outcomes, understand their sources of value, and develop value-focused strategies. From this view, they can then take a structured approach to developing comprehensive, value-based business change programs to execute those desired business strategies, and manage the realization of value.

References

Capgemini, 2006. Governance—Improving Governance between Business and IT Services. www.capgemini.com. pp. 14, 16, 20, 21 (accessed October 12, 2008).

Halas, P., 2008. Final Report from the Body Management Governance Team. www.maxwideman.com/musings/governance.htm (accessed November 8, 2017), Used with permission.

Jennings, T., 2005. Planning for Value: Artemis Solutions for IT Management. www.konsultex.com.br/artemis/arquivos-e-imagens/artemis-butler-report.pdf (accessed on November 8, 2017).

Reid, B. and J. Bourn, 2004. Directing Change: A Guide to Governance of Project Management. www.totalmetrics.com/process-improvement/Project-Governance-Guide.pdf (accessed November 8, 2017).

Chapter 38

Projects Responsibility and Ethical Practices

38.1 Ethical Code of Conduct

This final chapter describes basic concepts regarding a project management code of professional ethics and social responsibility as outlined by Project Management Institute (PMI). The code specifies that a professional project manager (PM) should exhibit the following characteristics and skills (PMI):

1. Ensure individual integrity and professionalism by adhering to legal requirements and ethical standards in order to protect the community and all stakeholders
2. Contribute to the project management knowledge base by sharing lessons learned, best practices, research, and other information within appropriate communities in order to improve the quality of project management services, build the capabilities of colleagues, and advance the profession
3. Enhance individual competence by increasing and applying professional knowledge to improve services
4. Balance stakeholders' interests by recommending approaches that strive for fair resolution in order to satisfy competing needs and objectives
5. Interact with team and stakeholders in a professional and cooperative manner by respecting personal, ethnic, and cultural differences in order to ensure a collaborative project management environment.

A more detailed preamble to the PMI code can be extracted from the Code of Ethics for Project Managers (Leland). This source also includes the process for ethical inquiry and appeals. O'Brochta offers the following research evidence:

> *A recent study conducted by Vrije University Amsterdam found that the more a leader acts in a way that followers feel is appropriate and ethical, the more that leader will be trusted*
>
> *(O'Brochta).*

To add to this quote, the attribute of trust is a primary reason that subordinates will follow, so lack of that attribute will certainly affect project performance.

38.2 Introduction

The professional PM must understand this aspect of his role. It is no longer sufficient to just focus on getting the job done. Daily news articles reinforce the negatives that can occur when a manager or organization decides to short cut either ethical or legal limits for which they are responsible. Improper actions by middle and upper management can destroy promising careers and even the organizations these individuals work for. In all such cases, a poor decision choice lays at the root of the failure. We categorize these under the category of professional responsibility and ethics. This occurs whether the individual is president of the United States, CEO of a large organization, or PM. The positive value of ethical behavior has been increasingly recognized in recent years. Surprisingly, the act of being ethical and honest is not as easy as one might think as this chapter will attempt to illustrate. From a PMI perspective, the PM must understand the basic tenets of the topic and from an operational view one must be able to translate these into workable daily job traits.

In support of this recognition, PMI has developed a formal Code of Ethics and Personal Conduct. The basic structure of this code deals with the following attributers (PMI CODE2):

- Responsibility to uphold standards of behavior
- Respect
- Fairness
- Honesty

Although each of these terms is reasonably familiar to most, implementation of the underlying concepts in the work environment is not necessarily easy. Figure 38.1 provides a good overview of the basic actions related to each of the key structure components.

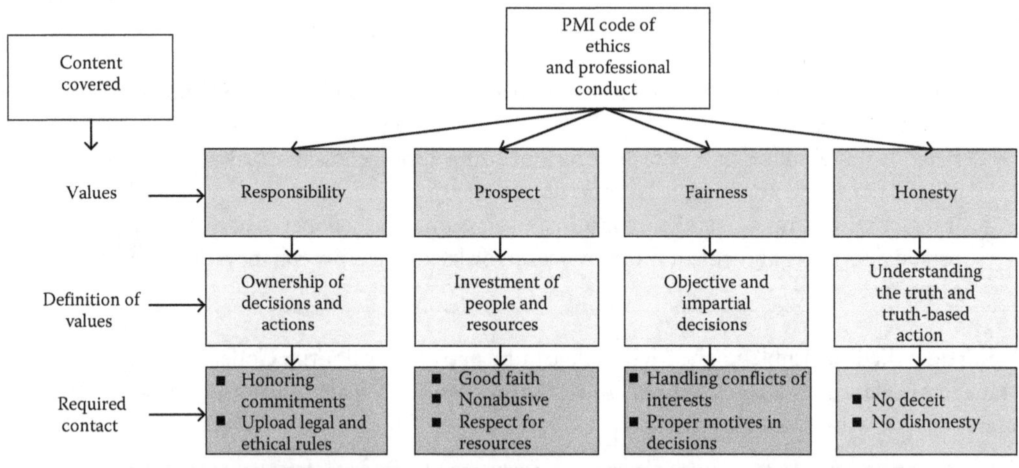

Figure 38.1 PMI code of ethics and professional responsibility.

Source: Adapted from the 2006 version of PMI's Code of Ethics and Professional Conduct, www.pmi.org/About-Us/Ethics/Code-of-Ethics.aspx.

It is essential that PMs not only be good employees for the organization that they work for, but they also must behave as a broader representative of the project stakeholder population that may consist of external parties outside of their organization. Given this broad scope of stakeholder involvement, normal behavioral rule interpretation can become complex in the real world. The external influences come from the various needs and interest groups with various diverse stakes to project. The key theme of this code is that the PM must follow a prescribed set of professional responsibility and ethical principles. These principles include the following areas:

- Ensuring individual integrity
- Contributing to the base of project management knowledge
- Enhancing individual performance
- Balancing stakeholders' interests
- Interaction with the project team and stakeholders in a professional and cooperative manner

Ensuring one's individual integrity requires taking ethically based responses into a number of common project scenarios. Generally speaking, the PM must do what is right, but that term is difficult to define in every case. Specifically, written and oral communications with project stakeholders and governmental authorities must be truthful. The PM must also adhere to the approved processes for project management activities. Lastly, any known violations of applicable laws and ethical standards must be immediately reported to the appropriate authorities.

To contribute to the project management knowledge base, a PM must do a number of things. First, any lessons learned from their personal project experiences must be shared with others who would profit from that knowledge. Following this principle also requires that the PM contributes to the education of and mentoring to less experienced PMs. In addition, he needs to engage in research to determine how to improve the profession and its processes, and then the findings of this research. Finally, he should strive to find techniques for improved measurement of project performance and work to continuously improve those outcomes.

In order to improve individual competence, the PM must take a number of steps. Initially, it is important to appraise and understand his own personal strengths and weaknesses. Next, the PM needs to take advantage of learning opportunities to address these weaknesses. Furthermore, he should prepare and execute a personal development plan in much the same manner as he pursues a project objective. Finally, the individual must continue to stay updated on knowledge related to relevant professional topics. This entails seeking out new information about project management and the industry.

Balancing project stakeholders' interests requires that a PM consider the interests of all internal and external stakeholders. Initially, the PM needs to examine the interests and needs of these individuals and groups, then seek to understand ways in which these diverse interests can be best met. Following this, he must also work to resolve conflict with the understanding that the customer's needs be given careful and primary consideration.

Interacting with the project team and stakeholders in a professional and cooperative manner requires a number of actions. Cultural differences can impact the smooth functioning of a project team. The PM needs to understand these potential conflict areas and take them into account in his dealings. In addition, he must deal with differences in communication preferences, work ethics, and work practices among these groups. All future stakeholder dealings should recognize and respect these differences. Cultural and language differences across country boundaries are particularly prone to critical concerns. When projects contain multinational stakeholders, the PM needs to follow local practices and customs so long as doing so does not violate laws or his ethical boundaries.

Significant differences in interests can also occur within a single country environment. These include customers, government agencies, other business functions involved in the project, sponsors providing financial resources for the project, the internal project team, parties from inside or outside the organization, end users of the project's product, members of society who will be affected by the project, and others. Clearly, this diversity of interest requires that PMs to give adequate attention to numerous potential problem areas during the course of a project. These dealings almost assuredly will have some ethical concern in regard to information handling or project decision-making. It is only by being sensitive to this topic that the PM can ensure that his ethical responsibilities to these stakeholders will be effectively and properly discharged. The list below summarizes five basic rules of thumb to guide PMs in their behavior regarding honesty and ethics. Following these rules do not guarantee appropriate behavior, but the following list should help guide managers in conducting themselves in an ethical and professionally responsible manner:

1. Not misuse access to, or control over financial resources that stakeholders have given them for legitimate use in the project, for example, engage in illegal manipulation of organizational resources
2. Not mislead stakeholders in regard to the status of the project by providing them with inaccurate information or failing to provide them with timely information relevant to the project
3. Inform the proper authorities regarding legal or professional violations by other stakeholders taking place in the context of the project
4. Not reveal trade secrets provided to in confidence, unless holding such information in confidence would violate a law, contractual provisions, or professional responsibility/ethical rules
5. Not use information obtained in the context of the project for the purpose of gaining an unfair advantage over the stakeholder, or that would be harmful to the stakeholder if revealed.

Each of the items outlined above seem straightforward and easy to follow; however, situations will occur in the project environment that will challenge individual interpretation of a specific action.

PMs are frequently faced with opportunities to obtain additional rewards for themselves or their organizations if they are willing to take a professionally or ethically marginal or inappropriate action, such as conducting one less audit or inspection than they know they should, or looking the other way when faced with clear evidence of others' wrong doing, and so on. Unfortunately, such actions can have far-reaching negative impacts, as well as having the potential to ruin the manager's career if the acts are discovered. Even the simple acts of accepting a meal or a football ticket are judged unethical in some organizations. This means the definition of ethics is not a national or international standard. For all of these reasons it is important to know what each organization defines as its ethics and behave according to those rules. Avoiding such situations can be a veritable minefield if a PM does not clearly understand which actions constitute inappropriate professional or ethically irresponsible behavior.

38.3 PMI's Code of Professional Conduct

Given recent experiences in American industry regarding misplaced ethics among senior executives, PMI has supported the formal publication of a professional ethics code for the PM. Basically, the PMI code deals with the following (PMI, 1988):

1. Organizational rule and policy compliance
2. Personal ethics in terms of reporting qualifications and representations
3. Respect and honesty toward the profession
4. Honesty in reporting facts to stakeholders
5. Maintaining proper confidentiality of data and other information
6. Care in avoiding conflict of interest
7. Care in avoiding receipt of payment from outside sources for questionable reasons.

The PM must think of themselves as *honest brokers of process and information*. The PMI code document referenced here is a good overview for appropriate project behavior. It is important to remember that shortcuts in this area can have significant negative impact on one's career.

38.4 Sample Ethical Scenarios

Although the idea of honesty and ethics would seem like a simple issue, the real world often presents some tough interpretations for the PM. Twenty sample questions are shown in this section to provide an opportunity to review the theoretical material in simulated real-world settings and give you practice in thinking about the appropriate way to react. Also, discussing these questions with your peers and changing the scenarios slightly will offer good discussion material.

1. You are working for a U.S. organization and have just finished a very large and successful project in a foreign country. It is common in this culture to reward people for good work. The sponsor is extremely happy with the outcome of the project and wants to hold a formal ceremony and give expensive presents to you and key team members to show his appreciation. He has told others that it will hurt his feelings if you do not take these gifts. What do you do?
2. You are a member of a Project Management Professional (PMP) certification study group. One of the members says that he has a friend who is wired into the exam question authors and can get significant input on key topics being addressed this round. What do you do? Do you report this situation to the certifying organization?
3. Success of your foreign project depends on receiving materials in a timely manner; however, the goods are being held up in local customs for long periods of time. A nephew of the local *Grand Po Bar* says that he can provide an expediting service for you and get the goods moved through customs quickly. In checking around, you find that this seems to be in fact true and also seems to be the only way that the goods get moved. What do you do? Who would you coordinate this decision with?
4. You are told by your boss to cut your project budget estimate by 20% in order to get your project plan approved by senior management. All other cost "cutting" strategies have been exhausted and you now feel that the current estimate is accurate for the work defined. What do you do? What if your boss says, "just cut the budget and get the project done with the cut specified?"
5. Your boss asks you to write an invited article for a national industry publication for him. You do this and the boss does not include your name on the article. What do you do?
6. While working on an external (contracted) project that has extra budget funds your customer asks you to perform some additional tasks that are not included in the formal contract. You should

A. Honor the customer's request as a sign of cooperation to ensure future business
B. Refuse the request and report the customer to your sponsor
C. Acknowledge the request and advise the customer to submit a formal change request
D. Convene a meeting of the project team and rewrite the scope statement.

7. You are managing an internal project. The initial product test results are very poor and do not meet the minimum customer requirements. If these results are made available to your customer you are afraid that they might cancel the project and this could reflect poorly upon you. Rerunning the product test can be done quickly and inexpensively. Based on this set of circumstances you should
   A. Be the first to recommend canceling the project
   B. Inform your external sponsor about the results and wait for a response
   C. Inform your management immediately and recommend retesting for verification
   D. Withhold the information from management until you perform additional tests to verify the initial results.
8. Your project is running out of budget allocation and significant work remains. You are directed by senior management to instruct your team to charge their work time to another project's account. Given these instructions you should
   A. Follow instructions
   B. Inform the corporate auditors
   C. Understand the background of management's instructions before taking any action
   D. Shutdown the project, if possible.
9. You are working in a country where it is customary to exchange gifts between contractor and customer. Your company code of conduct clearly states that you cannot accept any gifts from a client. Failure to accept the gift from this client may result in termination of the contract. The action to take in this case would be
   A. Provide the customer with a copy of your company code of conduct and refuse the gifts
   B. Exchange gifts with the customer and keep the exchange confidential
   C. Contact your project sponsor and/or your legal or public relations group for assistance
   D. Ask the project sponsor or project executive to handle the gift exchange question with the client.
10. You are a PM working on a time and material contract. The target price for the project is $2,000,000 and the project schedule is 12 months. The most recent completion estimate indicates that the project will finish two months early and if this happens your company will lose about $250,000 in billings. What should you do?
   A. Bill for the entire planned amount since this was the approved budget
   B. Bill for the target amount by adding nice to have features to the design at the end of the project so that the schedule and budget are met
   C. Report the project status and completion date to the customer
   D. Report the project status and completion date to the customer and ask if they would like to add any additional features to account for the monies not spent.
11. In order to balance the needs of the many stakeholders involved in your project, the most desirable method to achieve resolution of conflicts would be
   A. Compromise
   B. Forcing
   C. Controlling
   D. Confrontation

12. You receive a contract to perform testing for an external client. After contract award, the customer provides you with the test plan to use for the acceptance process. The vice president for Quality Assurance (QA) says that the customer's test plan is flawed and he will correct the plan that will be used and it will be more in line with the organizational quality program. The contract says that the customer will supply the acceptance test plan. In this case you should
    A. Use the customer's test plan
    B. Use the QA manager's revised test plan without telling the customer
    C. Use the QA manager's revised test plan and inform the customer
    D. Tell your sponsor that you want to set up a meeting with the customer to resolve the issue
13. You have just been assigned as the PM for an ongoing project and discovered that your project team is routinely violating OSHA, EPA, and affirmative action regulations. You should
    A. Do nothing; it is not your problem.
    B. Start by asking management if they are aware that regulations are being violated.
    C. Talk to the corporate legal department.
    D. Inform the appropriate government agencies about the violations.
14. One of your employees has an opportunity for promotion in another area. If this promotion is granted, the employee will be reassigned elsewhere causing a resource problem for the project. You have the authority to delay the promotion until your project is completed. You should
    A. Support the promotion but work with the employee and the employee's new management to develop a good transition plan
    B. Ask the employee to refuse the promotion until your project is completed
    C. Arrange to delay the promotion until the project is completed
    D. Tell the employee that it is his responsibility to find a suitable replacement so that the project will not suffer
15. In accordance with the compensation agreement for your project you have been given a $70,000 bonus to be distributed to your seven-person team as you see fit. One of the team members has not performed particularly well and another of the team is in your car pool. Based on this situation you should
    A. Allocate an equal share to each team member to avoid the image of favoritism
    B. Provide everyone a share based on your personal assessment of their performance
    C. Give the decision to the team and follow their advice
    D. Ask the sponsor to make the decision
16. You are the PM and your customer has requested that you inflate your planned cost estimates by 25%. His logic is that management always reduces the cost of project estimates by about this amount so this strategy would balance out the required budget. Which of the following is the best response to this situation?
    A. Do as the customer asked to ensure that the project requirements can be met by adding the increase as a contingency reserve
    B. Do as the customer asked to ensure that the project requirements can be met by adding the increase across each task
    C. Do as the customer asked by creating an estimate for the customer's management and another for the actual project implementation
    D. Complete an accurate estimate of the project. In addition, create a risk assessment showing why the decreased project budget would be inadequate

17. You are the PM working in a foreign country. Your local support person from the client organization presents you with a list of local team candidates for you to hire and you find that several of these are related to him. What is your reaction?
    A. Reject the team leader's recommendations and assemble your own project team
    B. Review the resume and qualifications of the proposed project team before approving the team.
    C. Determine if the country's traditions include hiring from the immediate family before deciding on how to address the family member situation.
    D. Replace the project leader with an impartial project leader.
18. You discover that one of your project team members has sold pieces of equipment that were allocated to the project. Upon further investigation you find that his rationale was a need for cash to pay for his son's college tuition. He says that he considers this remuneration for overtime hours worked without pay and he asks for your support in this view. You also find that his claim of unclaimed and unpaid overtime is true and that he has been a hard worker on project. What should you do?
    A. Fire the project team member
    B. Report the team member to his manager
    C. Suggest that the team member report his actions to the HR department
    D. Tell the team member that you are disappointed in what he did, and advise him that you will consider this a fair trade for the unpaid overtime. You also inform him that this will be grounds for dismissal if it occurs again.
19. You are a PM working within your functional organization and you do not get along well with the departmental manager. There is a serious disagreement regarding how the project should be conducted. This disagreement involves schedules, sequence of tasks, quality objectives, and other aspects of the project. While this disagreement is still unresolved the department manager tells you to start work on what he considers critical activities. Which of the following choices is the best for you?
    A. Go to higher-level senior management and voice your concerns
    B. Complete the activities as requested
    C. Ask to be taken off of the project
    D. Refuse to begin activities on the project until the conflict issues are resolved.
20. PMI has contacted you regarding a PMP candidate's experience claim. The individual involved is a friend and he says that he worked as a PM in your organization. He did work there, but not in the capacity individuated. This is a violation of which of the following?
    A. The PMP code to cooperate on ethics violations investigations
    B. The PMP code to report accurate information
    C. The PMP code to report any PMP violations
    D. Law concerning ethical practices.

References

O'Brochta, M. 2016. Why project ethics matter: Leadership is built on trust. If the foundation is cracked, a project's future is in doubt. *PM Network,* 30, 1, 29. www.pmi.org/learning/library/why-project-ethics-matter-9838.

PMI, Code of ethics for the project management profession. https://www.pmi.org/-/media/pmi/documents/public/pdf/ethics/pmi-code-of-ethics.pdf (accessed May 4, 2018)

Appendix A: Financial Metrics

Financial metrics represent one of the core techniques used to evaluate the business value of a project proposal. Organizations use various forms of these metrics and three are illustrated here. The role of financial measures is to evaluate a life cycle view of benefits and costs related to a particular project proposal. In this view, the goal is to assess the relative measure of benefits versus the associated costs over some expected useful life.

The three classic financial measures demonstrated here are payback (PB), net present value (NPV), and internal rate of return (IRR). Each of these has inherent advantages and disadvantages in their constructs and these should be understood before making decisions based on any one of them.

Step one in the financial measurement process is to estimate the net benefits and costs of the project proposal over some useful life cycle. In many cases, this is done for five years given the inaccuracy of estimates longer than this. As an example, Table A.1 shows the estimated cost-benefit values for the five-year life cycle:

An interpretation of the forecast data shown indicates that the initial project would cost $50,000 and would be installed one year later at which point positive returns would occur over the next four years. During its expected lifetime (years 1–4), the project would generate net business benefits (benefits minus cost) as shown. Summing the total list of values shows that the project would generate $55,000 in net benefits over the period. A basic financial question related to this set of data is "Is this considered a good financial project?" The answer to this depends on how we look at the data using the basic financial measures. Let us explain the three classic measures before going further.

PB method is the simplest and often used financial measure. This calculation simply looks at the cash flow estimates and defines the time required to recoup the initial investment. The goal in using this measure would be to favor projects that pay back their investment the quickest.

NPV is the calculated present value of the benefit stream. This measure is sensitive to the time value of money, and the analysis is based on some *hurdle rate*, that is, it has to be measured positive compared to a required value of 15%. This would favor any projects that returned values greater than this amount.

IRR represents the rate of return calculated for the estimated benefit stream. This is analogous to investing money and getting some measured percentage return from that investment. This is the most difficult financial calculation, but the one that has the best comparative value across the project portfolio.

Table A.1 Cost-Benefit Estimate

0	–$50,000
1	$15,000
2	$30,000
3	$10,000
4	$50,000
Total	$55,000

A.1 Calculation Interpretation

PB—This represents the time required to pay back the initial investment. In this example case, we can visually examine the data and see that it would take slightly over two years to recoup the initial investment.

NPV—this value is calculated by the formula $(1 + i)^n$, where i is the interest (hurdle) rate and n is the number of years in the future. In the NPV calculation, each year value would be translated back to the current time using the formula above, and then all values are added together for the NPV value.

IRR—this uses the same concept as the NPV, except that the value of i is unknown; therefore, it is necessary to repeat the calculation until a value of NPV is zero. Hence, IRR is the value of i where the NPV is zero.

A.1.1 Timing Issues Related to Estimates

In the use of these measures there is some timing issue to consider. That is, do we assume in the estimate that all of the costs are incurred at the beginning of the year, middle of the year, or spread equally through the year? For these examples, we will follow the end-of-period Excel assumptions, but for a particular analysis, the timing question should be reviewed to make sure that the calculated values properly reflect the estimates used.

A.2 Sample Calculations

The ABC company is considering investing in three projects. The projects are expected to cost the company $500,000 and the future cash inflows for the three projects being considered. Table A.2 shows the cost-benefit estimates.

Note that all three projects have the same total benefit stream; however, timing of these benefits is different for each. We will see the impact this has on the calculated financial measures that each produce.

One more important item regarding Excel's NPV function is that if we include the initial project cost or the initial investment into the Excel NPV function, we get incorrect results that are indicated in the worksheet below as *NPV (Incorrect)*. This is an idiosyncrasy of the Excel's NPV function that must be understood.

Table A.2 Portfolio Cost-Benefit Estimates

Project X		*Project Y*		*Project Z*	
1	$50,000	1	$325,000	1	$130,000
2	$150,000	2	$175,000	2	$130,000
3	$300,000	3	$75,000	3	$130,000
4	$100,000	4	$50,000	4	$130,000
5	$50,000	5	$25,000	5	$130,000
Total	$650,000	Total	$650,000	Total	$650,000

A.2.1 Manipulating the Data

For this calculation assume the company wants to not undertake projects that return less than 10%. Each of the projects will show estimated net benefit flows for five years. The worksheets below illustrate the calculations with Excel and a flow diagram. Follow the arrows from the Excel Table A.3 to the various calculation sections.

Figure A.1 Illustrates the process of moving the future values back to time zero using the NPV formula. Note how the $5,836.66 value is derived in the Excel calculations shown in Table A.3.

Calculations for Projects Y (Table A.4) and Project Z (Table A.5) are similar to those shown for Project X in Table A.3.

A.3 Project Summary Comparison

From the various financial options calculated in the previous tables, we can compare the financial parameter values for the three projects.

Note that project Y is the best financial option in all three parameters. The PB method is very simple to calculate but often favors short projects with quick returns and penalizes excellent longer-term projects where large benefits do not start until years 3 and beyond. However, in this case it leads to the same result. In this example, all three methods favor project Y. This would not be the case if the flows were changed to show benefits later in the stream (Table A.6).

There are many different reasons for a company to select a project that has benefits other than financial and therefore would not be reflected in the measurement techniques discussed

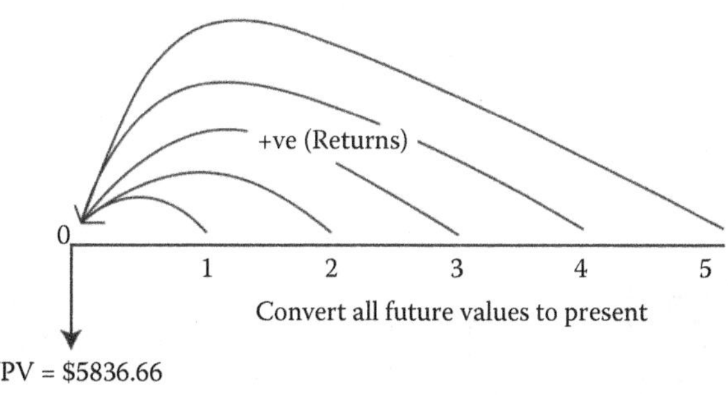

Figure A.1 Arrow flow diagram.

Table A.3 Project X Financial Calculations

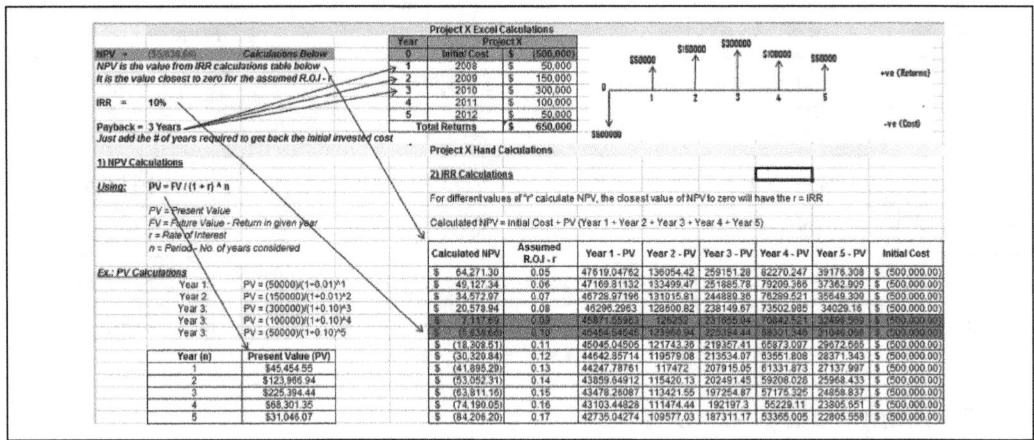

Project X Excel Calculations

NPV = ($5,836.66) Calculations Below
NPV is the value from IRR calculations table below
It is the value closest to zero for the assumed R.O.I - r

IRR = 10%

Payback = 3 Years
Just add the # of years required to get back the initial invested cost

Year	Project X		
0	Initial Cost	$	(500,000)
1	2008	$	50,000
2	2009	$	150,000
3	2010	$	300,000
4	2011	$	100,000
5	2012	$	50,000
	Total Returns	$	650,000

1) NPV Calculations

Using: PV = FV / (1 + r) ^ n

PV = Present Value
FV = Future Value - Return in given year
r = Rate of Interest
n = Period - No. of years considered

Ex.: PV Calculations

Year 1: PV = (50000)/(1+0.01)^1
Year 2: PV = (150000)/(1+0.01)^2
Year 3: PV = (300000)/(1+0.10)^3
Year 3: PV = (100000)/(1+0.10)^4
Year 3: PV = (50000)/(1+0.10)^5

Year (n)	Present Value (PV)
1	$45,454.55
2	$123,966.94
3	$225,394.44
4	$68,301.35
5	$31,046.07

Project X Hand Calculations

2) IRR Calculations

For different values of "r" calculate NPV, the closest value of NPV to zero will have the r = IRR

Calculated NPV = Initial Cost + PV (Year 1 + Year 2 + Year 3 + Year 4 + Year 5)

Calculated NPV	Assumed R.O.I - r	Year 1 - PV	Year 2 - PV	Year 3 - PV	Year 4 - PV	Year 5 - PV	Initial Cost
$ 64,271.30	0.05	47619.04762	136054.42	259151.28	82270.247	39176.308	$ (500,000.00)
$ 49,127.34	0.06	47169.81132	133499.47	251885.78	79209.366	37362.909	$ (500,000.00)
$ 34,572.97	0.07	46728.97196	131015.81	244889.36	76289.521	35649.309	$ (500,000.00)
$ 20,578.94	0.08	46296.2963	128600.82	238149.67	73502.985	34029.16	$ (500,000.00)
$ 7,117.69	0.09	45871.55963	126252	231655.04	70842.521	32496.569	$ (500,000.00)
$ (5,836.66)	0.10	45454.54545	123966.94	225394.44	68301.346	31046.066	$ (500,000.00)
$ (18,308.51)	0.11	45045.04505	121743.36	219357.41	65873.097	29672.566	$ (500,000.00)
$ (30,320.84)	0.12	44642.85714	119579.08	213534.07	63551.808	28371.343	$ (500,000.00)
$ (41,895.29)	0.13	44247.78761	117472	207915.05	61331.873	27137.997	$ (500,000.00)
$ (53,052.31)	0.14	43859.64912	115420.13	202491.45	59208.028	25968.433	$ (500,000.00)
$ (63,811.16)	0.15	43478.26087	113421.55	197254.87	57175.325	24858.837	$ (500,000.00)
$ (74,190.05)	0.16	43103.44828	111474.44	192197.3	55229.11	23805.651	$ (500,000.00)
$ (84,206.20)	0.17	42735.04274	109577.03	187311.17	53365.005	22805.558	$ (500,000.00)

Table A.4 Project Y Financial Calculations

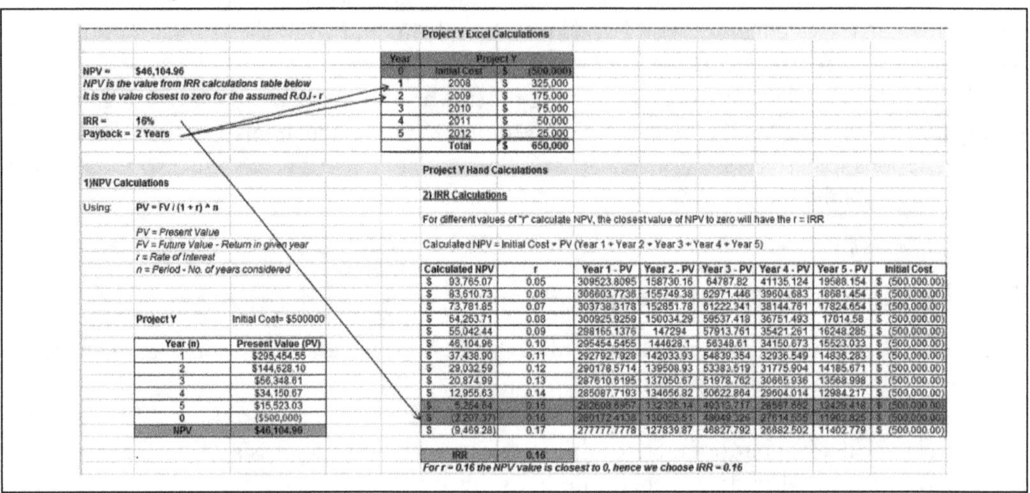

Project Y Excel Calculations

NPV = $46,104.96
NPV is the value from IRR calculations table below
It is the value closest to zero for the assumed R.O.I - r

IRR = 16%
Payback = 2 Years

Year	Project Y		
0	Initial Cost	$	(500,000)
1	2008	$	325,000
2	2009	$	175,000
3	2010	$	75,000
4	2011	$	50,000
5	2012	$	25,000
	Total	$	650,000

1)NPV Calculations

Using: PV = FV / (1 + r) ^ n

PV = Present Value
FV = Future Value - Return in given year
r = Rate of Interest
n = Period - No. of years considered

Project Y Initial Cost= $500000

Year (n)	Present Value (PV)
1	$295,454.55
2	$144,628.10
3	$56,348.61
4	$34,150.67
5	$15,523.03
0	($500,000)
NPV	$46,104.96

Project Y Hand Calculations

2) IRR Calculations

For different values of "r" calculate NPV, the closest value of NPV to zero will have the r = IRR

Calculated NPV = Initial Cost + PV (Year 1 + Year 2 + Year 3 + Year 4 + Year 5)

Calculated NPV	r	Year 1 - PV	Year 2 - PV	Year 3 - PV	Year 4 - PV	Year 5 - PV	Initial Cost
$ 93,765.07	0.05	309523.8095	158730.16	64787.82	41135.124	19588.154	$ (500,000.00)
$ 83,610.73	0.06	306603.7736	155749.38	62971.446	39604.683	18681.454	$ (500,000.00)
$ 73,781.85	0.07	303738.3178	152851.78	61222.341	38144.761	17824.654	$ (500,000.00)
$ 64,263.71	0.08	300925.9259	150034.29	59537.418	36751.493	17014.58	$ (500,000.00)
$ 55,042.44	0.09	298165.1376	147294	57913.761	35421.261	16248.285	$ (500,000.00)
$ 46,104.96	0.10	295454.5455	144628.1	56348.61	34150.673	15523.033	$ (500,000.00)
$ 37,438.90	0.11	292792.7928	142033.93	54839.354	32936.549	14836.283	$ (500,000.00)
$ 29,032.59	0.12	290178.5714	139508.93	53383.519	31775.904	14185.671	$ (500,000.00)
$ 20,874.99	0.13	287610.6195	137050.67	51978.762	30665.936	13568.998	$ (500,000.00)
$ 12,955.63	0.14	285087.7193	134656.82	50622.864	29604.014	12984.217	$ (500,000.00)
$ 5,254.64	0.15	282608.6957	132325.14	49315.717	28587.662	12429.418	$ (500,000.00)
$ (2,207.37)	0.16	280172.4138	130053.51	48049.326	27614.555	11902.825	$ (500,000.00)
$ (9,469.28)	0.17	277777.7778	127839.87	46827.792	26682.502	11402.779	$ (500,000.00)

IRR	0.16

For r = 0.16 the NPV value is closest to 0, hence we choose IRR = 0.16

Table A.5 Project Z Financial Calculations

Project Z Excel Calculations

NPV = ($7,197.72)

IRR = 9%
Payback = 4 Years

Year	Project Z	
0	Cost	$ (500,000.00)
1	2008	$ 130,000.00
2	2009	$ 130,000.00
3	2010	$ 130,000.00
4	2011	$ 130,000.00
5	2012	$ 130,000.00
	Total	$ 650,000.00

Using: 1) NPV Calculations

PV = FV / (1 + r) ^ n

PV = Present Value
FV = Future Value - Return in given year
r = Rate of Interest
n = Period - No. of years considered

Project Z Initial Cost= $500000

Year (n)	Present Value (PV)
1	$118,181.82
2	$107,438.02
3	$97,670.92
4	$88,791.75
5	$80,719.77
0	($500,000)
NPV	$7,197.72

Project Z Hand Calculations

2) IRR Calculations

For different values of "r" calculate NPV, the closest value of NPV to zero will have the r = IRR

Calculated NPV = Initial Cost + PV (Year 1 + Year 2 + Year 3 + Year 4 + Year 5)

Calculated NPV	r	Year 1 - PV	Year 2 - PV	Year 3 - PV	Year 4 - PV	Year 5 - PV	Initial Cost
$ 62,831.87	0.05	123809.5238	117913.83	112298.89	106951.32	101858.4	$ (500,000.00)
$ 47,607.29	0.06	122641.5094	115699.54	109150.51	102972.18	97143.562	$ (500,000.00)
$ 33,025.67	0.07	121495.3271	113547.03	106118.72	99176.378	92688.203	$ (500,000.00)
$ 19,052.30	0.08	120370.3704	111454.05	103198.19	95553.881	88475.816	$ (500,000.00)
$ 5,654.66	0.09	119266.055	109418.4	100383.85	92095.277	84491.08	$ (500,000.00)
$ (7,197.72)	0.10	118181.8182	107438.02	97670.924	88791.749	80719.772	$ (500,000.00)
$ (19,533.39)	0.11	117117.1171	105510.92	95054.88	85635.027	77148.673	$ (500,000.00)
$ (31,379.09)	0.12	116071.4286	103635.2	92531.432	82617.35	73765.491	$ (500,000.00)
$ (42,759.94)	0.13	115044.2478	101809.07	90096.521	79731.435	70558.792	$ (500,000.00)
$ (53,699.47)	0.14	114035.0877	100030.78	87746.297	76970.436	67517.926	$ (500,000.00)
$ (64,219.84)	0.15	113043.4783	98298.677	85477.11	74327.922	64632.976	$ (500,000.00)
$ (74,341.83)	0.16	112068.9655	96611.177	83285.498	71797.843	61894.692	$ (500,000.00)
$ (84,085.00)	0.17	111111.1111	94966.762	81168.172	69374.506	59294.45	$ (500,000.00)

IRR	0.09

Table A.6 Project Summary Comparison

Project	*NPV*	*IRR*	*PB*
X	–$5,836.66	0.10	3
Y	$46,104.96	0.16	2
Z	–$7,197.72	0.10	4

above. Let's assume that the following additional criteria need to be assessed along with the basic financial measures:

- Strategic fit
- Availability of resources
- Likelihood of success
- Increases revenue
- Process efficiency impact.

This example adds some additional assessment criteria to the evaluation and assigns weights to each of these. Note in Table A.7 that some of the evaluation attributes shown are more pure

Table A.7 Multi-Criteria Project Assessment

		Project X		*Project Y*		*Project Z*	
		Criteria Rating		*Criteria Rating*		*Criteria Rating*	
Criteria	*Weight (%)*	*1 = Low, 5 = High*	*Weighted*	*1 = Low, 5 = High*	*Weighted*	*1 = Low, 5 = High*	*Weighted*
Strategic fit	20	4	0.8	3	0.6	5	1
Availability of resources	10	3	0.3	4	0.4	4	0.4
Probability of success	5	4	0.2	3	0.15	5	0.25
Revenue impact	10	2	0.2	4	0.4	2	0.2
Operation cost impact	10	4	0.4	2	0.2	4	0.4
IRR	40	1	0.3	4	0.8	1	0.2
PB	5	3	0.15	4	0.2	2	0.1
	Score		2.65		3.55		2.75
	Ranking		3		1		l2

financial, while others are qualitative assessments translated into an integer score. Let us see what summary values emerge from this type analysis.

As we can see from the weighted average shown above, Project Y is still rated the best option based on the highest weighted score of 3.55. The weights assigned for each category are somewhat arbitrary, and it is often wise to perform this type analysis using other weightings to see if the answer is sensitive to some particular weight value.

Discussion Questions

1. What other evaluation criteria might be added to Table A.7?
2. What might be the value in selecting one of the other projects?
3. Do you see any flaws in the manner in which weights are assigned to the various criteria?
4. Is there a situation where PB might be the best financial metric?

Appendix B: Templates

One of the operational irritants of project management is the creation of formalized documents. As a result of this many projects shun the documentation process and produce only the bare minimum. For those external stakeholders dealing with such projects the lack of professional looking documentation can make the management process appear amateurish, whether that is a valid assessment or not. Use of templates can be a great asset in making the overall project look more professional and save a significant amount of time in the process. Throughout the book, various project management artifacts have been described as to their role, but not so much in detail as to what they might look like in format. If one were to undertake developing a format for all of the required documents, there would be significant wasted time spent in that activity.

A more efficient approach to document production is to have ready access to standard samples that can be extracted and edited quickly (see Appendix C for more on this). A search of the Internet will yield a wide array of online sources where tested template formats can be found. Some of these have moderate costs and some are free. This appendix will summarize a few such sites that are worthy of reviewing.

A sample listing of documentation template types would include the following:

- Project plan
- Change request
- Scope management plan
- Scope change register
- Work Breakdown Structure (WBS)
- Change tracking
- Requirements definition
- Estimating worksheet
- Standard development network plan
- Life cycle development activity list
- Issue register
- Project status reporting
- Project standards

The locations listed here are well-known sources for various project management information, including methodologies, articles, training, and templates.

B.1 Web Sources

TenStep is a free site offering technical source material in project management. One of the unique aspects of this site is its partnership with *Cordin8*, which is a repository and distribution utility. These two sources offers an inexpensive approach to implementing a tested methodology along with the Cordin8 tool for information sharing and collaboration. Both of these options offer a good potential for improving project selection, delivery, and collaboration processes. Their URLs are www.tenstep.com and www.cordin8.com.

Method123 is an online reference for project management. This site sponsors an excellent methodology and templates for various project management functions. Their URL is www.method123.com.

Gantthead.com is a good online source for various project management articles, training, webinars, and tools related to current project management. Their URL is www.gantthead.com.

IAPPM. The International Association of Project and Program Management (IAPPM), formed in 2003 through volunteers, is established as a global organization providing knowledge and useful content to PMs and program managers. This UK organization provides links to various project management topics. IAPPM is dedicated to helping individuals achieving success in the global project community.

Matt H. Evans. This site contains an extensive listing of spreadsheets that collectively have potential value in various aspects of project management. The URL for this list is: http://www.exinfm.com/free_spreadsheets.html.

There are several interesting items referenced here, but one in particular should be looked at. The title of this is "Project management templates." This offers a suite of tools that at least trigger ideas on various areas of the life cycle.

In addition to these named sites there are various other Internet sources offering both free and for sale templates.

B.2 Governmental WebSites

The State of Texas Department of Information Resources sponsors a large set of templates. Further details can be found at www.dir.state.tx.us.

The State of Michigan hosts a very mature website dedicated to project management (www.michigan.gov/dit). Use the search option to browse through their library of methodology and templates.

The Government of Tasmania sponsors a mature project management website dedicated to various aspects of project management. This site includes a knowledge base, various resources including templates, and services. Further details can be found at http://www.egovernment.tas.gov.au/themes/project_management.

B.3 Texts

Several commercial texts publish project management templates. One notable example can be found at:

Garton, C. and E. McCulloch, 2007. *Fundamentals of Project Management.* Lewisville, TX: MC Press.

In addition, an Internet search will uncover many more.

Appendix C: Project Data Repository

C.1 Repository Design

This appendix describes a conceptual project document architecture that is envisioned to be a central information repository template for the project team and other stakeholders. The value of such a repository comes from having easy access to technical and status documentation regarding the project and its work products. These data groups have broad communication value to the various stakeholder groups involved. They also have value for management activities related to team collaboration, decision-making, and information sharing. Organizations that successfully accomplish appropriate levels of information sharing report significant improvements in operational efficiency and improved decision-making. In addition to this, the cross-communications value produced through the lessons learned process is greatly enhanced by having ready access to previous project's archival data.

An appropriate enterprise project documentation repository strategy consists of the following basic content parts:

1. Technical artifacts produced by the project (physical design and related items dealing with the technical work of the project).
2. Operational status metrics (raw performance data collected for the project).
3. Stakeholder communications.
4. Project formal status reports (complete history).
5. KA miscellaneous artifacts (filed by KA).
6. Product/process validation artifacts (test plans, testing results, etc.).
7. Project initiation repository (original vision, project Charter, business case, etc.).
8. Operational documentation (User-related documentation).
9. Configuration management libraries (formal product repository filed by WBS with version control references—this would be drawings, computer source code, or other formal deliverables).
10. Communication repository (meeting minutes, team communications, and external communications).
11. Lessons learned repository.
12. Reusable standard project management templates.
13. Scope Control (Integrated Change Control repository).

14. Risk Management (including Risk Register—this may be an isolated data base).
15. Issues log—daily problem tracking.

    Note: Items 9–15 may be separated and managed with centralized enterprise level data repositories.

Each of these repository subsets has value in executing and managing the overall work flow of the project. Note that several of these repository groups contain data that might need to be shared with external stakeholders. If the various data structures were standardized this could be an automated link. For example, data related to enterprise PPM, central accounting, human relations, corporate policies, and others would be managed by their respective custodians, but shared with external entities as needed. Appropriate access security is required to handle that type access.

Some of the repository data shown here is so focused on one aspect of the project that it would be more effective to isolate it into its own domain. For example, change control processing or the issues log both would seem unique in their role and might have custom access software that works well. There would be no need in the short term at least to redo mature subsets of this data. The key idea to focus on with regard to a project repository is to make access to the data both easy and secure. The design goal is to view this as "The one place to look for the truth": daily status, latest information, current drawing, etc. Whatever item of information desired, this would be the structure to look at for that.

Ideally, all of the data groupings described above would need to be logically interrelated; however, practically speaking, that level of integration is probably not a reasonable tactical goal for most organizations. The core discussion here is to describe a subset of those items that are most critical to serve basic project information needs. In modern terms, this repository should be viewed as automated. If that is not practical, a similar manual filing structure should be organized as indicated. Migration from manual files to automation should proceed in a priority order based on value to the team. Step one of that approach should be to develop an overall repository design structure and work toward full automation. Modern document management software is making this process much more feasible than in the past when more customization was required.

In operation, value of a structured repository will be recognized through information sharing and improved decision-making. Additional value will be recognized in supporting audit requirements and other requests for project data. One of the common complaints of project team members is the time wasted looking for various project documentation. One other aspect often not recognized is using an out-of-date document or artifact. The project repository is intended to be the one place to retrieve data and one could view this as a "Google-type" database for all project artifacts. In order to achieve these goals, both the storage and the retrieval technical aspects of the repository need to be considered in the design. The view shown here is more logical and less technical. Access to the data store will require appropriate security access control through a common portal or collaboration tool that simplifies the access process.

Computer-based storage and retrieval of text and graphics documents has been one of the most recent advances in automation, but relatively recent technology developments in document management software has made this topic one that can be effectively dealt with. Basically, large volumes of documents can now be stored cost effectively, and retrieval speed for such documents is impressive. Based on this current state of technology the structure described here represents nothing more than an internal project to improve the overall working of projects. A manager once described this environment as a *project digital workbook*. Rather than having to pass physical documents around, they can be retrieved electronically with more accuracy and timeliness than previous paper approaches.

C.2 Data Contents

A brief comment about each of the defined document subgroups is included below.

1. *Technical artifacts.* This segment of the repository contains many of the technical objects needed by team members to execute their daily work. For example, items related to the WBS and WBS Dictionary would be cataloged here. In addition, any logical or physical design notes would be stored under their respective WBS codes.
2. *Operational metrics.* This subgroup is designed to store all project performance metrics, both planned and actual. Data required to report project status externally would be extracted from this source for both internal and external status information; however, other operational KPIs used for internal analysis of performance would also be stored in this area.
3. *Stakeholder communications.* This subgroup would contain a repository of various stakeholder data organized by stakeholder. For example, the stakeholder communications plan and analysis would fit this category.
4. *Project formal status reports.* This repository would contain all formal status reports issued.
5. *KA artifacts* (filed by KA). Each of the project KAs produces various documents related to that area. For example, the management plans for each KA would fit this classification. Later, more detailed documents will be created. These groupings would contain operational items for these areas. *Note*: QC and QA documentation might be separated from this group given the testing and process audit characteristics of these documents (see below).
6. *Product/process validation artifacts.* This section would contain various operational quality artifacts such as test plans, testing results, user acceptance reports, quality audits, and so on.
7. *Project initiation.* Many historical artifacts are created during the early initiation phase of the project. Items such as the original business case, vision statements, preliminary scope statement, and the official Charter authorizing the project should be saved here for future reference and possibly reuse on another project.
8. *Operational documentation.* In many cases, there is the need for documentation regarding operational instructions for the deliverables. For example, future maintenance support personnel will need this information related to their work. All documents in this category should be kept under version control and available to authorized personnel.
9. *Configuration management.* Many projects require that certain items fall into a category where their version of the item has to be controlled. Design drawings (CAD) and computer code are well-known examples of this.
10. *Communications repository.* This repository is used for general communications documents not in the formal periodic status category.
11. *Lessons learned.* The value found in this process has been recognized in recent times and all projects should be tasked with completing their lessons learned for each phase. This should be an enterprise level system, but is first created as a project level effort and then evolves outward.
12. *Reusable standard project management templates.* The concept of reuse has been recognized for quite some time in various industries and project types. Over the past few years one of the strategies to make the project management process more time efficient is to use templates for various required items (i.e., project plans, status reports, WBSs, etc.). This also should be an enterprise level effort and shared by all projects.
13. *Scope Control.* This repository will focus on the change control process. This process could be either viewed as internal to the project structure or managed at a central level. The data

organizational option for change control will answer how this process would be designed and how the physical repository would be created. However, the formal capture, tracking, and management of scope change requests represent the most important formal configuration management and tracking goals for the project and the organization. Failure to properly manage this aspect of the process can create severe cost and schedule problems.

14. *Risk Management.* This management area represents the least mature management process for most organizations. Assuming that the process is recognized as being part of formal project management, there is a need to identify and track risk elements in the same basic manner that scope is handled. That is, to identify risk elements, decide how to handle that element, and then monitor the process. A more detailed discussion on risk management processes is included in Chapter 22 and will supply further thoughts on this data group. Much of this operational data would reside in a formal Risk Register database.
15. *Issue log.* Project issues are essentially unplanned items that arise daily in the course of the life cycle. These items need to be tracked and resolved in a timely manner, which means that the role of this repository is to ensure that the item does in fact get resolved and not elevate into some higher-level problem. As an example, an item of hardware needed by the project team breaks and needs to be fixed. It is anticipated that this is a normal maintenance activity, but someone must monitor its status. As an alternative example, a decision is needed on a particular question. The issues log would identify the issue, criticality, and person responsible.

Each of repository subgroups outlined above represents important data artifacts for the project. Mature organizations seeking to improve their project environment will support the evolution of this concept, but tactically the PM should follow these guidelines in implementing whatever physical form is available—manual files, crude project file systems, enterprise formal systems, and the like.

C.3 Implementation Strategy

A data repository architecture with the breadth and complexity outlined here typically evolves over time through several steps. The initial development phase often is triggered by the recognition that a defined data group has value. From that starting point data are collected and stored, usually in a crude form such as a spreadsheet file, or a manual paper file. Similar repository groups often migrate in fragmented fashion horizontally across the organization. Finally, at some critical decision point high-level recognition and support will surface for formalizing and centralizing the data store in order to improve the overall operational value of the data.

Each of the repository groups outlined here often follows such an evolutionary path, but ideally this subject should be looked at in total and a formal solution sponsored by higher organizational levels. It is important to recognize the value of these repositories as part of the standard project work process and to identify an official owner charged with evolution and implementation of each data group. Leaving this to the project often means that it is not a high enough work priority given the goal of the project. This is yet another example where high-level management support can add value to the project. This is a project in its own right! As these data groups become operational, there needs to be a mechanism for the overall implementation to be recognized and dealt with. Standardization of issues such as master data schema and date element definitions is needed for all subgroups. One development hazard is to allow stovepipe, isolated developments, that later do not fit together. Likewise, data element ownership needs formal recognition (e.g., where does the data come from, who owns it, and who can access it). Philosophically, a standard design is needed before implementation occurs.

Step two in the evolution is the organizational push to embed the data into the operational culture. This is typically accomplished by using these data items for formal status reporting and operational management actions. Storage and publication of approved metrics fits into this theme as well. The major support facility for this is a retrieval strategy that opens up the data store to users with little pre-training requirement—in other words, an intuitive usage approach.

Step three in the evolution involves using the data store for analytical purposes to improve understanding of the project activities—that is, source of errors, productivity variables, resource issues, resource management across the organization, and the like. Data mining utilities and search capabilities represent two types of tools to aid in ad hoc exploration through the data. These capabilities support efforts to improve performance and understand the processes better than traditional tools or ad hoc judgment provide.

Step four represents data reusability across projects. The management templates will support quick methods of producing high-quality documents efficiently. Much of the project management process requires formatting and boilerplate wording. All of this can be supplied from the template library and other structures defined in the repository. Once the entire structure matures, the repository will provide the opportunity to bring significant changes to the traditional documentation and associated development paradigms.

As with all procedural changes to the organizational culture this process requires high-level management support and an understanding of the value of stored data. Historically, this has not been the case and project documentation methods have been characterized as being similar to the cobbler's children with no shoes. Process improvement can only come through a strategic focus on the topic.

Index

D

Q

T

Z

Printed in Canada